Understanding
TERRORISM
Challenges, Perspectives, and Issues

Gus Martin
California State University, Dominguez Hills

SAGE Publications
International Educational and Professional Publisher
Thousand Oaks ▪ London ▪ New Delhi

Excerpts from the following are reprinted by permission: Bruce Hoffman, *Inside Terrorism* (New York: Columbia University Press, 1998); William Laqueur, *The New Terrorism: Fanaticism and the Arms of Mass Destruction* (New York: Oxford University Press, 1999); and Paul R. Pillar, *Terrorism and U.S. Foreign Policy* (Washington, DC: Brookings Institution Press, 2001).

For information:

Sage Publications, Inc.
2455 Teller Road
Thousand Oaks, California 91320
E-mail: order@sagepub.com

Sage Publications Ltd.
6 Bonhill Street
London EC2A 4PU
United Kingdom

Sage Publications India Pvt. Ltd.
B-42 Panchsheel Enclave
Post Box 4109
New Delhi 110 017 India

Printed in the United States of America

Library of Congress Cataloging-in-Publication Data

Martin, Gus.
Understanding terrorism: Challenges, perspectives, and issues / by Gus Martin.
    p. cm.
Includes bibliographical references and index.
ISBN 0-7619-2615-1 (cloth) — ISBN 0-7619-2616-X (pbk.)
    1. Terrorism. I. Title.
HV6431.M367 2003
303.6´25—dc21

2002155355

03 04 10 9 8 7 6 5 4 3 2 1

Acquiring Editor:	Jerry Westby
Editorial Assistant:	Vonessa Vondera
Production Editor:	Diana E. Axelsen
Copy Editors:	Rachel Hile Bassett/Linda Gray
Typesetter:	C&M Digitals (P) Ltd.
Indexer:	Mary Mortensen
Cover Designer:	Michelle Lee

BRIEF CONTENTS

DETAILED CONTENTS

ABOUT THE AUTHOR

Gus Martin is Assistant Professor of Public Administration at California State University—Dominguez Hills, where he is coordinator of the Criminal Justice Administration program. He has also served on the faculty of the Graduate School of Public and International Affairs at the University of Pittsburgh, where he was an Administration of Justice professor. He taught a popular course on terrorism at the University of Pittsburgh for several years that was offered every semester, and he has designed and taught a similar course at California State University. His research and professional interests are in the areas of administration of justice, terrorism and extremism, juvenile justice, and fair housing. He has served as a panelist for university and community symposia and interviews on the subjects of terrorism, administration of justice, and fair housing. He has also been a consultant to government and private agencies. Prior to joining academia, he was a legislative assistant to Congressman Charles B. Rangel of New York and Special Counsel to the Attorney General of the U.S. Virgin Islands. In addition, he served as managing attorney for the Fair Housing Partnership of Greater Pittsburgh, where he was also director of a program created under a federal consent decree to desegregate public and assisted housing.

ACKNOWLEDGMENTS

I am grateful to many fine people for their support, encouragement, and professionalism in bringing this project to fruition. Without them, the final product would not have incorporated the richness and scope that was its central goal from the beginning.

Thanks are extended to colleagues who shared their expert advice and suggestions for crafting this volume. I wish to acknowledge the profound contribution from my former colleagues of the Graduate School of Public and International Affairs at the University of Pittsburgh, who first kindled my desire to teach and write about terrorism. I also thank my colleagues at California State University, Dominguez Hills for their support and understanding about the demands of the writing process. Deep appreciation is especially extended to the panel of peer reviewers assembled by the able staff of Sage Publications during several rounds of review. Their insightful, constructive comments and critical analysis was truly invaluable. Special appreciation is also extended to the very professional and expert attention given to this project by the editorial group at Sage; they are indeed an exceptional shop.

And of course, I thank my wife Jane for her patience and encouragement throughout the development of this venture, as well as our two fine children (and budding young scholar-athletes), Sarah and Jonathan.

INTRODUCTION AND RATIONALE

Welcome to *Understanding Terrorism: Challenges, Perspectives, and Issues*. This is a textbook for those who wish to explore the phenomenon of modern terrorist violence. Students and instructors who fully engage themselves in the recommended course of instruction offered in the pages that follow will acquire a solid foundation for understanding the nature of terrorism. Readers will also discover that their facility for critically assessing terrorism in general—and terrorist incidents in particular—will be greatly improved.

At the outset it is important to understand that the study of terrorism is, first and foremost, a study in human behavior. It is an investigation of highly volatile human interaction. Courses that investigate terrorism must therefore review the events, ideas, motivations, theories, and histories that result in terrorist violence. None of these factors can be discussed in isolation from one another if the reader wishes to develop a facility for critically evaluating the nature of terrorism. Thus, the study of terrorism is one of the most *multidisciplinary* subjects in the social sciences. It is also one of the most dynamic subjects.

This textbook is designed to be a primary textbook for students enrolled in a single-semester course. The content of *Understanding Terrorism: Challenges, Perspectives, and Issues* is directed to courses of instruction whose subject areas include terrorism, political conflict, armed conflict, international security, social justice, social movements, and law enforcement. It can be incorporated into classes covering political science, administration of justice, sociology, history, and other disciplines in the social sciences. The intended level of instruction is upper-level undergraduates and master's-level graduate students. The writing style is therefore directed to juniors, seniors, and master's students, although many freshmen and sophomores have successfully completed this course.

No prerequisites are specifically recommended, but an introductory grounding within one of the following disciplines would be helpful: political science, administration of justice, sociology, history, or philosophy. Students need not be majors in these disciplines, because teaching experience has shown that a large number of students enroll in this type of course out of sheer intellectual interest.

COURSE OVERVIEW AND PEDAGOGY

Understanding Terrorism: Challenges, Perspectives, and Issues introduces readers to terrorism in the contemporary era, focusing on the post-Second World War period as its primary emphasis. It is a review of nations, movements, and individuals who have engaged in what many people would define as terrorist violence. It is also a review of the many typologies (different kinds) of terrorism that have existed in the postwar era. Very importantly, a serious exploration will be made of the underlying causes of terrorism—for example, extremist ideologies, religious intolerance, and traumatic episodes in the lives of nations and people.

The pedagogical approach of *Understanding Terrorism: Challenges, Perspectives, and Issues* is designed to stimulate critical thinking by students. Students and instructors will find that each chapter follows a sequence of instruction that builds upon previous chapters, and thus incrementally enhances the reader's knowledge of each topic. Chapters incorporate the following features:

- **Chapter Introduction.** Each chapter is introduced by an overview of the subject under investigation. The Chapter Introduction provides perspective for the incorporation of each chapter's topic into the broader themes of the textbook.
- **Chapter Perspectives.** Chapters incorporate focused presentations of perspectives that explore people, events, organizations, and movements that are relevant to the subject matter of each chapter.
- **Cases in Point.** At the end of each chapter, a concluding Case in Point is presented to highlight—and provide a "reality check" for—important theoretical concepts discussed in the chapter.
- **Chapter Summary.** A concluding discussion recapitulates the main themes of each chapter and introduce the subject matter of the following chapter.
- **Discussion Boxes.** Following the Chapter Summary, Discussion Boxes present provocative information and pose challenging questions to stimulate critical thinking and further debate.
- **Key Terms and Concepts.** Important terms and ideas introduced in each chapter are listed for review and discussion. These Key Terms and Concepts are further explored and defined in the book's Glossary.
- **Recommended Readings.** Suggested readings are listed at the end of each chapter for further information or research on each topic.
- **Web Exercises.** Internet exercises at the ends of chapters have been designed for students and instructors to explore and discuss information found on the Internet.

CHAPTER GUIDE

This volume is organized into four thematic units, each consisting of several chapters. A Glossary and Appendixes are included after the substantive chapters.

Part I ("Terrorism: A Conceptual Review") defines and discusses the causes of terrorism. Within Part I, *Chapter 1* ("An Introduction to Terrorism") presents an overview of basic concepts that are developed in later chapters. The discussion explores historical perspectives, definitional issues, and the morality of terrorist violence. An investigation is made of terrorism and criminal skill, as well as the symbolism of the Oklahoma City and September 11, 2001, attacks. *Chapter 2* ("The Nature of the Beast: Defining Terrorism") investigates the underlying reasons why certain groups, movements, and individuals are labeled as terrorists or freedom fighters. This chapter first compares and contrasts radical and reactionary ideological tendencies, and then defines and investigates extremism and its characteristics. Terrorism is discussed at length by sampling official definitions, reviewing the American context, and summarizing several types of terrorism. Chapter 2 then looks into several perspectives of terrorism that pose problems for definitional issues. *Chapter 3* ("Beginnings: The Causes of Terrorism") investigates significant factors in the personal and group histories of individuals and groups that become associated with terrorism. The motives of extremists and several explanations of terrorism are explored, including acts of political will, sociological explanations, and psychological explanations.

Part II ("The Terrorists") probes several terrorist typologies. Within this part, *Chapter 4* ("Terror From Above: State Terrorism") investigates state-initiated repression and terror. A state terrorism paradigm is offered to explain state sponsorship of terrorism. A detailed discussion then explores terrorism as foreign policy and terrorism as domestic policy. *Chapter 5* ("Terror From Below: Dissident Terrorism") evaluates terrorism emanating from dissident movements. A dissident terrorism paradigm is offered to explore the different typologies of dissident terrorism, and the morality of the New Terrorism is investigated. Finally, a detailed discussion explores antistate dissident terrorism and communal terrorism. *Chapter 6* ("Class Struggle and National Liberation: The Terrorist Left") probes the nature of left-wing political violence. Leftist ideologies and activism are discussed, as are regional examples of leftist terrorism. *Chapter 7* ("Race and Order: The Terrorist Right") probes right-wing political violence. Rightist ideologies and activism are discussed, along with regional examples of rightist terrorism. *Chapter 8* ("For the Faith and Profit: Religious and Criminal Terrorism") discusses two terrorist typologies that have become quite prominent in the modern era. The first half of the chapter investigates the nature of religious terrorism and uses regional case studies to probe the different manifestations of religious violence. The second half of the chapter investigates the nature of criminal terrorism. It distinguishes political violence conducted by traditional criminal enterprises from that of violent criminal-political enterprises and then discusses regional case studies of criminal terrorism. *Chapter 9* ("Terrorist Spillovers: International Terrorism") first defines what is meant by *international terrorism* and then explores the reasons for terrorist spillovers. The phenomenon of international terrorist networks is discussed, as is the concept of "stateless revolutionaries."

Part III ("The Terrorist Trade") discusses the "nuts and bolts" of the terrorist trade and the role of the mass media. Within Part III, *Chapter 10* ("Tools of the Trade: Tactics and Targets of Terrorists") investigates the methodology of terrorism. Terrorist objectives, methods, and targets are analyzed at length, as is the question of whether terrorism is "effective." *Chapter 11* ("The Role of the Media") evaluates the centrality of the media and mass communications in the modern era of political violence. The chapter first discusses the nature of mass communications and reporting within the context of terrorist environments. An investigation is then made of the war of manipulation for favorable media coverage. A discussion is also presented of the efficacy of regulating the media.

Part IV ("Final Analysis") first presents a study of the United States and then explores solutions to terrorism and discusses projections for political violence. Within Part IV, *Chapter 12* ("Terrorism in the United States") presents an overview of terrorism in postwar America. It probes the background to political violence from the left and right and then presents a detailed discussion of leftist and rightist terrorism in the United States. The chapter then evaluates international terrorism and the new millennium. *Chapter 13* ("Responding to Terror: The Options") explores counterterrorist options and security measures. Several typologies are presented: the use of force, repressive operations other than war, conciliatory operations other than war, and legalistic responses. *Chapter 14* ("What Next? The Future of Terrorism") investigates trends and other factors that can be used to project the near future of terrorism.

A glossary and several appendixes follow the substantive chapters. The glossary briefly summarizes each of the key terms and concepts explored in the book. It is intended to be a reference section for students as they progress through their course of instruction; it is also a useful pedagogical tool for instructors. The appendixes include world maps, a chronological compilation of historical examples of terrorism, Web sites with information about terrorism, and a list of interesting documentaries and films that investigate or dramatize the book's subject matter.

Part I

TERRORISM:
A CONCEPTUAL REVIEW

Bloody Sunday (January 30, 1972): A British soldier runs down an Irish Catholic demonstrator during protests and rioting in the city of Londonderry in Northern Ireland. The confrontations resulted in elite paratroopers firing on Catholic civilians. The incident was a seminal event that rallied many Catholics to support the Provisional Irish Republican Army.

Source: Hulton Archive/Getty Images; used by permission.

Chapter 1

TERRORISM: FIRST IMPRESSIONS

Terrorism has been a dark feature of human behavior since the dawn of recorded history. Great leaders have been assassinated, groups and individuals have committed acts of incredible violence, and entire cities and nations have been put to the sword—all in the name of defending a greater good. Terrorism, however defined, has always challenged the stability of societies and the peace of mind of everyday people. In the modern era, the *impact* of terrorism—that is, its ability to terrorize—is not limited to the specific locales or regions where the terrorists strike. In the age of television, the Internet, satellite communications, and global news coverage, graphic images of terrorist incidents are broadcast instantaneously into the homes of hundreds of millions of people. Terrorist groups understand the power of these images, and they manipulate them to their advantage as much as they possibly can. Terrorist states also fully appreciate the power of instantaneous information, and so they try to control the "spin" on reports of their behavior.

Some acts of political violence are clearly acts of terrorism. Most people would agree that politically motivated planting of bombs in marketplaces, massacres of "enemy" civilians, and the routine use of torture by governments are terrorist acts. However, as we begin our study of terrorism it is important to appreciate that we will encounter many definitional "gray areas." Depending on which side of the ideological, racial, religious, or national fence one sits, political violence can be interpreted either as acts of unmitigated terrorist barbarity or as freedom fighting and national liberation. These gray areas will be explored in the chapters that follow.

The Dawn of a New Era. The September 11, 2001, terrorist attacks on the U.S. homeland were seen by many as a turning point in the history of political violence. In the aftermath of these attacks, journalists, scholars, and national leaders repeatedly described the emergence of a new international terrorist environment. It was argued that within this new environment, terrorists were now quite capable of using—and very willing to use—weapons of mass destruction to inflict unprecedented casualties and destruction on enemy targets. These attacks seemed to confirm warnings from experts during the 1990s that a New Terrorism,[1] using "asymmetrical" methods, would characterize the terrorist environment in the new millennium.

Several questions about this newly emerging environment have arisen:

- How has the New Terrorism environment affected traditional terrorist profiles?
- How has traditional terrorism been affected by the collapse of revolutionary Marxism?
- What is the likely impact of "stateless" international terrorism?

Students will notice that these questions focus on terrorist *groups* and *movements*. However, it is very important to understand that terrorist *states* were responsible for untold millions of deaths during the 20th century. In addition, genocidal fighting between *communal groups* claimed the lives of many millions more. Our exploration of terrorism therefore requires us to consider every facet of political violence, from low-intensity campaigns by terrorist gangs to high-intensity campaigns by terrorist governments and genocidal paramilitaries.

Terrorism at First Glance. This chapter is a general introduction to the subject of terrorism. During this first glance, it will become clear that the history of terrorist behavior extends into antiquity and that common themes and concepts span the ages. State terrorism, dissident terrorism, and other types of political violence are found in all periods of human civilization. It will also become clear to students that there are many common *justifications*—rooted in basic beliefs—that have been used to rationalize terrorist violence throughout history. For example, the following concepts hold true regardless of the contexts of history, culture, or region:

- Those who practice revolutionary violence and state repression always claim to champion noble causes and values.
- Policies that advocate extreme violence always cite righteous goals to justify their behavior—such as the need to defend a religious faith or defend the human rights of a people.
- The perpetrators of violent acts uniformly maintain that they are freedom fighters (in the case of revolutionaries) or the champions of law and order (in the case of governments).

This chapter is an overview—a first glance—of basic concepts that will be developed in later discussions. The following themes are introduced here and will be explored in much greater detail in subsequent chapters:

- Historical Perspectives on Terrorism
- Exploring Definitions, Sources, and Ideologies
- The Morality of Terrorist Violence: Four Quotations
- Terrorism and Criminal Skill: Three Cases in Point
- The Symbolism of Oklahoma City and September 11, 2001

HISTORICAL PERSPECTIVES ON TERRORISM

It is perhaps natural for each generation to view history narrowly, from within its own political context. Contemporary commentators and laypersons tend to interpret modern events as though they have no historical precedent. However, terrorism is by no means a modern phenomenon, and it certainly does not arise from a political vacuum. Chapter 3 will explore the causes of terrorism in detail. For now, let us consider a brief summary of several historical periods to illustrate the global and timeless sweep of terrorist behavior.

Antiquity

In the ancient world, cases and stories of political violence were common. For example, there are references in the Bible not only to assassinations and conquest, but also to the complete annihilation of enemy nations in the name of the faith, as described in the story of Joshua's conquest of Canaan (see Chapter Perspective 1.1). Other passages are arguably examples of religious communal violence and terrorism, such as the following story from the book of Numbers:

> While Israel was staying at Shittim, the people began to have sexual relations with the women of Moab. . . . Just then one of the Israelites came and brought a Midianite woman into his family. . . . When Phineas . . . saw it, he got up and left the Congregation. Taking a spear in his hand, he went after the Israelite man into the temple, and pierced the two of them, the Israelite and the woman, through the belly.[2]

Chapter Perspective 1.1   **The Conquest of Canaan**

When King Jabin of Hazor heard of this, he sent to [other kings in the region for assistance to defeat the Hebrews]. . . . They came out, with all their troops, a great army, in number like the sand on the seashore, with very many horses and chariots. All these kings joined their forces, and came and camped together at the waters of Merom, to fight with Israel.

And the Lord said to Joshua, "Do not be afraid of them, for tomorrow at this time I will hand over all of them, slain, to Israel. . . ." So Joshua came suddenly upon them with all his fighting force, by the waters of Merom, and fell upon them. And the Lord handed them over to Israel. . . . They struck them down, until they had left no one remaining.

Joshua turned back at that time, and took Hazor, and struck its king down with the sword. . . . And they put to the sword all who were in it, utterly destroying them; there was no one left who breathed, and he burned Hazor with fire. And all the towns of those kings, and all their kings, Joshua took, and struck them with the edge of the sword, utterly destroying them. . . . All the spoil of these towns, and the livestock, the Israelites took for their booty; but all the people they struck down with the edge of the sword, until they had destroyed them, and they did not leave any who breathed.

Joshua 11:1, 4-8, 10-14, in *The Holy Bible, New Revised Standard Version.*

The Roman Age

During the time of the Roman Empire, the political world was rife with many cases of state terrorism. These include the brutal suppression of Spartacus's followers after the Servile War of 73-71 B.C. and the elimination and enslavement of the Dacian nation in A.D. 106. In conquered territories, Roman authority could be wielded without mercy. Conquest was often accompanied by a demonstration of terror.

Regicide (the killing of kings) was also fairly common during the Roman age. Perhaps the best-known political incident in ancient Rome was the assassination of Julius Caesar in 44 B.C. by rivals in the Senate. Other Roman emperors also met violent fates: Caligula and Galba were killed by the Praetorian Guard in A.D. 41 and 68, respectively; Domitian was stabbed to death in A.D. 96; a paid gladiator murdered Commodus in A.D. 193; and Caracalla, Elagabalus, and other emperors either were assassinated or died suspiciously.[3]

The Ancient and Medieval Middle East

Cases exist of movements in the ancient and medieval Middle East that used what modern analysts would consider to be terrorist tactics. The story of the Assassins is discussed as this chapter's Case in Point. For example, in *History of the Jewish War*—a seven-volume account of the first Jewish rebellion against Roman occupation (A.D. 66-73)—the historian Flavius Josephus describes how one faction of the rebels, the *sicarii* (named after their preferred use of *sica*, or short, curved daggers), attacked both Romans and members of the Jewish establishment.[4] They were masters of guerrilla warfare and the destruction of symbolic property and belonged to a group known as the **Zealots** (from the Greek *zelos*, meaning ardor or strong spirit), who opposed the Roman occupation of Palestine. The modern term *zealot*, used to describe uncompromising devotion to radical change, is derived from the name of this group. Assassination was a commonly used tactic. Some *sicarii* zealots were present at the siege of Masada, a hilltop fortress that held out against the Romans for three years before the defenders committed suicide in A.D. 74 rather than surrender.

The French Revolution

During the French Revolution, the word *terrorism* was coined in its modern context by British statesman and philosopher **Edmund Burke**. He used the word to describe the *régime de la terreur*, commonly known in English as the **Reign of Terror** (June 1793 to July 1794).[5] The Reign of Terror, led by the radical Jacobin-dominated government, is a good example of state terrorism carried out to further the goals of a revolutionary ideology.[6] During the Terror, thousands of opponents to the Jacobin dictatorship—and others merely *perceived* to be enemies of the new revolutionary Republic—were arrested and put on trial before a **Revolutionary Tribunal**. Those found to be enemies of the Republic were beheaded by a new instrument of execution—the guillotine. The guillotine had the capability to execute victims one after the other in assembly-line fashion and was regarded by Jacobins and other revolutionaries at the time as an enlightened and civilized tool of revolutionary justice.[7]

The Revolutionary Tribunal is a symbol of revolutionary justice and state terrorism that has its modern counterparts in 20th-century social upheavals. Recent examples include the **"struggle meetings"** in revolutionary China (public criticism sessions, involving public humiliation and confession) and revolutionary Iran's *komitehs* (ad hoc "people's committees").[8]

The Modern Era

Terrorism is deeply rooted in the human experience. As we enter the 21st century, states and targeted populations will be challenged by the New Terrorism, which will be explored at length in later chapters. The New Terrorism is characterized by:

- Loose cell-based networks
- Potential acquisition of weapons of mass destruction
- Politically vague, religious, or mystical motivations
- "Asymmetrical" methods

The New Terrorism may be contrasted with "traditional" terrorism, which is characterized by:

- Clearly identifiable organizations or movements
- Use of conventional weapons, usually small arms and explosives

- Explicit grievances championing specific classes or ethno-national groups
- Relatively "surgical" selection of targets

In addition, new technologies and the Internet create unprecedented opportunities for both state and dissident terrorists. All of these threats offer new challenges for policymakers about how to respond to the behavior of terrorist states, groups, and individuals.

EXPLORING DEFINITIONS, SOURCES, AND IDEOLOGIES

At the outset, students should develop a basic understanding of a few of the issues underlying the study of terrorism. These issues have been the subjects of research and debate among scholars, governments, the media, and activists. We will take a first look at these issues here and then explore them in greater detail in later chapters. The discussion here profiles:

- First Definitions: Extremism and Terrorism
- Sources of Terrorism
- Ideologies: The Classical Ideological Continuum

First Definitions: Extremism and Terrorism

Extremism is a quality that is "radical in opinion, especially in political matters."[9] It is characterized by intolerance toward opposing interests and divergent opinions, and it is the primary catalyst and motivation for terrorist behavior. Extremists who cross the line to become terrorists always develop noble arguments to rationalize and justify acts of violence directed against enemy nations, people, religions, or other interests.

It is important to understand that extremism is a radical expression of one's political values. Both the *content* of one's beliefs and the *style* in which one expresses those beliefs are basic elements for defining extremism. Laird Wilcox summed up this quality as follows:

> Extremism is more an issue of style than of content. . . . Most people can hold radical or unorthodox views and still entertain them in a more or less reasonable, rational, and nondogmatic manner. On the other hand, I have met people whose views are fairly close to the political mainstream but were presented in a shrill, uncompromising, bullying, and distinctly authoritarian manner.[10]

Thus, a fundamental definitional issue for extremism is *how* one expresses an idea, in addition to the question of *which* belief one acts upon. Both elements—style and content—are important for our investigation of fringe beliefs and terrorist behavior. We will build on these themes when the extremist foundations of terrorism are explored further in Chapter 2.

Terrorism would not, from a layperson's point of view, seem to be a difficult concept to define. Most people likely hold an instinctive understanding that terrorism is

- politically motivated violence . . .
- usually directed against "**soft targets**" (i.e., civilian and administrative government targets) . . .
- with an intention to affect (terrorize) a target audience.

This instinctive understanding would also hold that terrorism is a criminal, unfair, or otherwise illegitimate use of force. Laypersons might argue that this is an easily understood concept. However, defining terrorism is *not* such a simple process. Experts have for some time grappled with designing (and agreeing upon) clear definitions of terrorism; the issue has, in fact, been at the center of an ongoing debate. The result of this debate has been a remarkable variety of approaches and definitions. Walter Laqueur has noted that "more than a hundred definitions have been offered," including several of his own.[11] Even within the U.S. government, different agencies apply several definitions. These definitional problems will be explored further in the next chapter.

Sources of Terrorism

The underlying causes of terrorism have also been the subject of extensive discussion, debate, and research. This is perhaps because the study of the sources of terrorism spans many disciplines—including sociology, psychology, criminology, and political science. The causes of terrorism will be explored in detail in Chapter 3. For now, a general model will serve as a starting point for developing our understanding of which factors lead to terrorist violence. To begin, we must understand that

political violence, including terrorism, has systemic origins that can be ameliorated. Social and economic pressures, frustrated political aspirations, and in a more proximate sense, the personal experiences of terrorists and their relations, all contribute to the terrorist reservoir.[12]

Nehemia Friedland designed "a convenient framework for the analysis of the antecedents of political terrorism,"[13] outlined as follows:

First, terrorism is a group phenomenon . . . perpetrated by organized groups whose members have a clear group identity—national, religious or ideological. . . . *Second,* political terrorism has its roots in intergroup conflict. . . . *Third,* "insurgent terrorism," unlike "state terrorism,". . . is a "strategy of the weak." (p. 82, italics added)

Students should appreciate that these issues continue to be a source of intensive debate. Nevertheless, working definitions have been adopted as a matter of logical necessity. Let us presume for now that terrorist acts are grounded in extremist beliefs that arise from group identity, intergroup conflict, and a chosen strategy.

Ideologies: The Classical Ideological Continuum

Ideologies are *systems of belief.* They are derived from theories that explain human social and political conditions. There are literally scores of belief systems that have led to acts of terrorist violence. Because there are so many belief systems, it is difficult to classify them with precision. Nevertheless, a **classical ideological continuum** rooted in the politics of the French Revolution has endured to the present time.[14] It is instructive for our discussion of politically motivated violence, because the concepts embodied in the continuum will continue to be relevant through the beginning of the new millennium.

At the beginning of the French Revolution in 1789, a parliament-like assembly was convened to represent the interests of the French social classes. Although its name changed during the Revolution—from Estates-General, to National Constituent Assembly, to Legislative Assembly—the basic ideological divisions were symbolically demonstrated by where representatives sat during assembly sessions. On the left side of the assembly

Table 1.1   The Classical Ideological Continuum: The Case of the French Revolution

After the dissolution of the monarchy, the victorious revolutionaries began a complete restructuring of French society. Perhaps the most important priority was to create a new elective constituent assembly to represent the interests of the people. The configuration of this new assembly changed repeatedly as the revolution progressed from one phase to the next.

	Political Orientation		
Legislative Body	*Left*	*Center*	*Right*
National Constituent Assembly 1789-1791	Patriots (republicans)	Moderates (constitutional monarchists)	Blacks (reactionaries)
Legislative Assembly 1791-1792	Mountain (republicans)	Plain (near-republicans)	Constitutionalists (constitutional monarchists)
National Convention 1792	Mountain (radicals)	Marsh (uncommitted bourgeois)	Girondins (bourgeois republicans)

sat those who favored radical change, some advocating a complete reordering of French society and culture. On the right side of the assembly sat those who favored either the old order or slow and deliberate change. In the center of the assembly sat those who favored either moderate change or simply could not make up their minds to commit to either the left or right. These symbolic designations—*left, center,* and *right*—have become part of our modern political culture.

Table 1.1 illustrates the classical ideological continuum. Again, these designations are classical in the sense that they have become standard and traditionally accepted as ideological descriptors.

It is readily apparent from the case of the French Revolution that the quality of the classical continuum is very much dependent on the political environment of each society. For example, within American ideological culture, mainstream values include free enterprise, freedom of speech, and limited government.[15] Depending on where one falls on the classical continuum, the interpretation of these mainstream values can be very different. In the American example:

- Free enterprise might be viewed with suspicion by the far left but might be considered sacrosanct (untouchable) by the far right.
- Freedom of speech would seem to be a noncontroversial issue, but the right and left also disagree about what kinds of speech should be protected or regulated.
- The role of government is a debate that has its origins from the time of the American Revolution. The right and left disagree about the degree to which government should have a role in regulating private life.

Mainstream American values of past generations—such as Manifest Destiny and racial segregation—were rejected by later generations as unacceptable extremist ideologies. Thus, the concepts of left, center, and right shift during changes in political culture. These concepts will be further developed in Chapter 2 and applied to discussions in later chapters.

THE MORALITY OF TERRORIST VIOLENCE: FOUR QUOTATIONS

The term *terrorism* has acquired a decidedly pejorative (negative) meaning in the modern era, so that few if any states or groups who espouse political violence ever refer to themselves as terrorists. Nevertheless, these same states and groups can be unabashedly extremist in their beliefs or violent in their behavior. They often invoke—and manipulate—images of a malevolent threat or unjust conditions to justify their actions. The question is whether these justifications are satisfactory or whether terrorism is inherently wrong.

Questions of Morality

It is helpful to review two concepts that are used in the study of criminal justice. In criminal law, the terms *mala prohibita* and *mala in se*[16] are applied to behaviors that society defines as deviant acts. They represent concepts that are very useful for the study of terrorism.

- *Mala prohibita* acts are "crimes that are made illegal by legislation."[17] These acts are illegal because society has declared them to be wrong; they are not *inherently* wicked or evil. Examples include laws prohibiting gambling and prostitution, which are considered to be moral prohibitions rather than prohibitions of fundamental evils.
- *Mala in se* acts are crimes "that are immoral or wrong in themselves."[18] These acts cannot be justified in civilized society, and have no acceptable qualities. For example, premeditated murder and forcible rape are *mala in se* crimes. They will never be legalized.

Are terrorist methods inherently evil? Perhaps so, because terrorism commonly evokes images of maximum violence carried out in the name of a higher cause. However, is terrorist violence always such a bad thing? Are not some causes worth fighting for? Killing for? Dying for? Is not terrorism simply a matter of one's point of view? Most would agree that basic values such as freedom are indeed worth fighting for. If so, perhaps "where you stand depends on where you sit." Thus, if the bombs are falling on your head, is it not an act of terrorism? If the bombs are falling on an enemy's head in the name of your freedom, how can it possibly be terrorism?

The following quotations help to address these difficult moral questions:

- "One person's terrorist is another person's freedom fighter."
- "One man willing to throw away his life is enough to terrorize a thousand."
- "Extremism in defense of liberty is no vice."
- "It became necessary to destroy the town to save it."[19]

"One Person's Terrorist Is Another Person's Freedom Fighter"

The authorship of this statement is unknown; it most likely originated in one form or another in the remote historical past. The concept embodied in this quotation is, very simply, perspective. It is a concept that will be applied throughout our examination of terrorist groups, movements, and individuals.

As will become abundantly clear, terrorists never consider themselves to be the "bad guys" in their struggle for what they would define as freedom. They might admit that they have been *forced* by a powerful and ruthless opponent to adopt terrorist methods, but they see themselves as freedom fighters. Benefactors of terrorists always live with clean hands, because they present their clients as plucky freedom fighters. Likewise, nations that use the technology of war to attack known civilian targets justify their sacrifice as incidental to the greater good of the cause.

"One Man Willing to Throw Away His Life Is Enough to Terrorize a Thousand"

This quotation was written by the Chinese military philosopher **Wu Ch'i**, who wrote,

> Now suppose there is a desperate bandit lurking in the fields and one thousand men set out in pursuit of him. The reason all look for him as they would a wolf is that each one fears that he will arise and harm him. This is the reason one man willing to throw away his life is enough to terrorize a thousand.[20]

This quotation is the likely source for the better-known statement **"kill one, terrorize a thousand."** The authorship of the latter is undetermined but has been attributed to the leader of the Chinese Revolution, **Mao Zedong**, and to the Chinese military philosopher **Sun Tzu**. Both Wu Ch'i and Sun Tzu are often discussed in conjunction with each other, but Sun Tzu may be a mythical figure. Sun Tzu's book *The Art of War* has become a classic study of conflict. Regardless of who originated these phrases, their simplicity explains the value of a committed individual who is willing to sacrifice him- or herself when committing an act of violence. They suggest that a selfless application of lethal force—in combination with correct timing, surgical precision, and an unambiguous purpose—is an invaluable weapon of war. It is also an obvious tactic for small, motivated groups that are vastly outnumbered and outgunned by a more powerful adversary.

"Extremism in Defense of Liberty Is No Vice"

Senator Barry M. Goldwater of Arizona made this statement during his bid for the presidency in 1964. His campaign theme was very conservative and anti-Communist. However, because of the nation's rivalry with the Soviet Union during this period in American political history, every major candidate was overtly anti-Communist. Thus, Goldwater tried to outdo incumbent President Lyndon Johnson, his main rival, on this issue.[21]

This quotation represents an uncompromising belief in the absolute righteousness of a cause. It defines a clear belief in good versus evil and a belief that the end justifies the means. If one simply substitutes *any cause* for the word *liberty* in the quotation, one can fully understand how it lends itself to the legitimization of uncompromising devotion to the cause. Terrorists use this reasoning to justify their belief that they are defending their championed interest (be it ideological, racial, religious, or national) against all perceived enemies—who are, of course, evil. Hence, the practice of ethnic cleansing was begun by Serb militias during the war in Bosnia in 1991-1995 to forcibly remove Muslims and Croats from villages and towns. This was done in the name of Bosnian Serb security and historical claims to land occupied by others.[22] Bosnian and Croat paramilitaries later practiced ethnic cleansing to create their own ethnically "pure" enclaves.

"It Became Necessary to Destroy the Town to Save It"

This quotation has been attributed to a statement made by an American officer during the war in Vietnam. When asked why a village thought to be occupied by the enemy had been destroyed, he allegedly replied that American soldiers had destroyed the village to save it.[23] The symbolic logic behind this statement is very seductive: If the worst thing that can happen to a village is for it to be occupied by an enemy, then destroying it is a good thing. The village has been denied to the enemy, and it has been saved from the horrors of enemy occupation. The symbolism of the village can be replaced by any number of symbolic values.

Terrorists use this kind of reasoning to justify hardships that they impose not only on a perceived enemy, but also on their own championed group. For example, in Chapter 5 students will be introduced to nihilist dissident terrorists, who are content to wage "revolution for revolution's sake." They have no concrete plan for what kind of society will be built upon the rubble of the old one—their goal is simply to destroy an inherently evil system. To them, *anything* is better than the existing order. A historical example of this reasoning on an enormous scale is found in the great war between two totalitarian and terrorist states—Germany and the Soviet Union—from July 1941 to May 1945. Both sides used scorched-earth tactics as a matter of policy when their armies retreated, destroying towns, crops, roadways, bridges, factories, and other infrastructure as a way to deny resources to the enemy.

TERRORISM AND CRIMINAL SKILL: THREE CASES IN POINT

Terrorism is condemned internationally as an illegal use of force and an illegitimate expression of political will. Applying this concept of *illegality,* one can argue that terrorists are criminals and that terrorist attacks require some degree of criminal skill. For example, the radical Islamic terrorist network **Al Qaeda** set up an elaborate financial system to sustain its activities. This financial system included secret bank accounts, front companies, offshore bank accounts, and charities.[24] Al Qaeda is an example of a stateless movement that became a self-sustaining revolutionary network. It is also an example of a sophisticated transnational criminal enterprise.

Terrorist attacks involve different degrees of criminal skill. The following cases are examples of the wide range of sophistication found in incidents of political violence. All three cases are short illustrations of the criminal skill of individual extremists. These individuals are:

- **Richard Baumhammers,** an American neo-Nazi who went on a killing spree near Pittsburgh, Pennsylvania, in April 2000
- **Ted Kaczynski,** also known as the Unabomber, who was famous for sending mail bombs to his victims and who eluded capture for 18 years, from 1978 to 1996
- **Ramzi Yousef,** an international terrorist who was the mastermind behind the first World Trade Center bombing in February 1993

Case 1: Richard Baumhammers

Many terrorist incidents are the acts of individual gunmen who simply embark on killing sprees, using a *low degree* of criminal sophistication. For example, the "lone wolf" attacks in the United States have usually been racially motivated killing sprees committed by individual neo-Nazis or other racial supremacists.[25] One of these attacks occurred on April 28, 2000, near Pittsburgh, Pennsylvania, when a racial supremacist murdered five people and wounded one more.

Richard Baumhammers, a racist immigration attorney influenced by neo-Nazi ideology, methodically shot his victims during a 20-mile trek. His victims were a Jewish woman, two Indian men, two Asian men, and an African American man.[26] The sequence of Baumhammers's assault occurred as follows:

- Baumhammers went to his Jewish neighbor's house and fatally shot her. He then set a fire inside her home.
- Baumhammers shot two Indian men at an Indian grocery store. One man was killed, and the other was paralyzed by a .357 slug that hit his upper spine.
- Baumhammers shot at a synagogue, painted two swastikas on the building, and wrote the word *Jew* on one of the front doors.
- He then drove to a second synagogue, where he fired shots at it.
- Baumhammers shot two young Asian men at a Chinese restaurant, killing them both.
- Finally, Baumhammers went to a karate school, pointed his revolver at a white man inside the school, and then shot to death an African American man who was a student at the school.

The Baumhammers case illustrates how the lone wolf scenario involves an individual who believes in a certain ideology but who is not acting on behalf of an organized group. These individuals tend to exhibit *minimal* criminal skill and use minimal technology while carrying out their assault. Richard Baumhammers was convicted in May 2001 and received the death penalty.

Case 2: Theodore "Ted" Kaczynski

Using a *medium degree* of criminal sophistication, many terrorists have been able to remain active for long periods of time without being captured by security agents. Some entered into "retirement" during this time, whereas others remained at least sporadically active. An example of the latter profile is Ted Kaczynski, popularly known as the **Unabomber**. The term *Unabomber* was derived from the FBI's designation of his case as **UNABOM** during their investigation of his activities.

In May 1978, Kaczynski began constructing and detonating a series of bombs directed against corporations and universities. His usual practice was to send the devices through the mail disguised as business parcels. Examples of his attacks include the following:

- A bomb caught fire inside a mail bag aboard a Boeing 727. It had been rigged with a barometric trigger to explode at a certain altitude (these triggers are discussed further in Chapter 10).
- A package bomb exploded inside the home of the president of United Airlines, injuring him.
- A letter bomb exploded at Vanderbilt University, injuring a secretary. It had been addressed to the chair of the computer science department.
- A University of California, Berkeley, professor was severely injured when a pipe bomb he found in the faculty room exploded.
- Two University of Michigan scholars were injured when a package bomb exploded at a professor's home. The bomb had been designed to look like a manuscript for a book.
- An antipersonnel bomb store exploded in the parking lot behind a computer rental store, killing the store's owner.

During a 18-year period, Ted Kaczynski was responsible for the detonation of more than 15 bombs around the country, killing 3 people and injuring 22 more (some very seriously). He was arrested in his Montana cabin in April 1996. Kaczynski was sentenced in April 1998 to four consecutive life terms plus 30 years.

Case 3: Ramzi Yousef

Ramzi Yousef, terrorist and mastermind of the first bombing of the World Trade Center in New York City in 1993.

Source: U.S. Federal Bureau of Investigation.

Involving a *high degree* of criminal sophistication, some terrorist attacks are the work of individuals who can be described as masters of their criminal enterprise. The following case illustrates this concept.

On February 26, 1993, Ramzi Yousef detonated a bomb in a parking garage beneath Tower One of the World Trade Center in New York City. The bomb was a mobile truck bomb that Yousef and an associate had constructed in New Jersey from a converted Ford Econoline van. It was of a fairly simple design but extremely powerful. The detonation occurred as follows:

The critical moment came at 12.17 and 37 seconds. One of the fuses burnt to its end and ignited the gunpowder in an Atlas Rockmaster blasting cap. In a split second the cap exploded with a pressure of around 15,000 lbs per square inch, igniting in turn the first nitro-glycerin container of the bomb, which erupted with a pressure of about 150,000 lbs per square inch—the equivalent of about 10,000 atmospheres. In turn, the nitro-glycerin ignited cardboard boxes containing a witches' brew of urea pellets and sulphuric acid.[27]

According to investigators and other officials, Yousef's objective was to topple Tower One onto Tower Two "like a pair of dominoes,"[28] thus achieving a very high death toll.

Ramzi Yousef, apparently born in Kuwait and reared in Pakistan, was an activist educated in the United Kingdom. His education was interrupted during the Soviet war in Afghanistan, when he apparently "spent several months in Peshawar [Pakistan] in training camps funded by Osama bin Laden learning bomb-making skills."[29] After the war, Yousef returned to school in the United Kingdom and received a Higher National Diploma in computer-aided electrical engineering.

In the summer of 1991, Ramzi Yousef returned to the training camps in Peshawar for additional training in electronics and explosives. He arrived in New York City in September 1992 and shortly thereafter began planning to carry out a significant attack, having selected the World Trade Center as his target. Yousef established contacts with former associates already in the New York area and eventually became close to Mohammed Salameh, who assisted in the construction of the bomb. They purchased chemicals and other bomb-making components, stored them in a rented locker, and assembled the bomb in an apartment in Jersey City. They apparently tested considerably scaled-down versions of the bomb several times. After the attack, Yousef boarded a flight at JFK Airport and flew to Pakistan.

This case is a good example of the technical skill and criminal sophistication of some terrorists. Ramzi Yousef had connections with well-funded terrorists, was a sophisticated bomb maker, knew how to obtain the necessary components in a foreign county, was very adept at evasion, and obviously planned his actions in meticulous detail. As a postscript, Ramzi Yousef remained very active among bin Laden's associates, and his travels within the movement took him far afield, including trips to Thailand and the Philippines. In an example of international law enforcement cooperation, he was eventually captured in Pakistan in February 1995 and sent to the United States to stand trial for the bombing. He was tried, convicted, and sentenced to serve at least 240 years in prison.

TERRORIST SYMBOLISM: OKLAHOMA CITY AND SEPTEMBER 11, 2001

A comparison of the sketched witness description of Timothy McVeigh to his mug shot. An excellent example of the value of cooperation between witnesses and law enforcement officials.

Source: U.S. Federal Bureau of Investigation.

Symbolism is a central feature of terrorism. Most terrorist targets at some level symbolize the righteousness of the terrorists' cause and the evil of the opponent they are fighting. Symbolism can be used to rationalize acts of extreme violence and can be manipulated to fit any number of targets into the category of an enemy interest. As will be discussed in Chapter 11, terrorists are very mindful of their image and skillfully use public relations and propaganda to "package" themselves.

Symbolism can create abstract ideological linkages between terrorists and their victims, as seen during the wave of kidnappings by Latin American leftists during the 1970s; terrorists seized civilian businessmen and diplomats, whom the kidnappers said symbolized capitalism and exploitation. Symbolic targets can also represent enemy social or political establishments, as in the assassination of Lord Mountbatten by the Irish Republican Army and the killings by right-wing death squads in El Salvador. Or entire groups of people can be symbolically labeled and slaughtered, as happened during the Nazi Holocaust and in the killing fields of Cambodia and Rwanda.

Two examples of deadly domestic terrorism in the United States demonstrate the important role of symbolism in the worldview of terrorists. The first example is an act of terrorism perpetrated by an American terrorist in Oklahoma City. The second example is the series of attacks on September 11, 2001, by international terrorists in New York City, Washington, D.C., and in the skies over rural Pennsylvania.

The Oklahoma City Bombing

On April 19, 1995, **Timothy McVeigh** drove a rented Ryder truck to the Alfred P. Murrah Federal Building in Oklahoma City. He deliberately chose April 19 as a symbolic date for the attack—it was the 220th anniversary of the battles of Lexington and Concord and the second anniversary of the law enforcement disaster in Waco, Texas.

McVeigh was a hard-core devotee of the Patriot movement and a believer in New World Order conspiracy theories. He was almost certainly a racial supremacist, having tried to solicit advice from the neo-Nazi National Alliance and the racial separatist Elohim City group about going underground after the bombing. McVeigh had also visited the Branch Davidian site at Waco, Texas,[30] where about 75 members of the Branch Davidian cult died in a fire that was ignited during a paramilitary raid by federal law enforcement officers.

McVeigh had converted the Ryder truck into a powerful mobile **ammonium nitrate and fuel oil (ANFO)**-based bomb. He used "more than 5,000 pounds of ammonium nitrate fertilizer mixed with about 1,200 pounds of liquid nitromethane, [and] 350 pounds of Tovex."[31] When he detonated the truck bomb at 9:02 a.m., it destroyed most of the Federal Building and killed 168 people, including 19 children.

McVeigh's attack was in large part a symbolic act of war against the federal government, and he had given careful consideration to achieving a high casualty rate, just as "American bombing raids were designed to take lives, not just destroy buildings."[32] The deaths of the 19 children were justified in his mind as the unfortunate **"collateral damage"** common to modern warfare.[33]

September 11, 2001

The worst incident of modern international terrorism occurred in the United States on the morning of September 11, 2001. It was carried out by 19 Al Qaeda terrorists who were on a suicidal "martyrdom mission." They committed the attack to strike at symbols of American (and Western) interests in response to what they perceived to be a continuing process of domination and exploitation of Muslim countries. They were religious terrorists fighting in the name of a holy cause against perceived evil emanating from the West. Their sentiments were born in the religious, political, and ethno-national ferment that has characterized the politics of the Middle East for much of the modern era.

Nearly 3,000 people were killed in the attack. The sequence of events occurred as follows:

The United States' Most Wanted Terrorist poster for Osama bin Laden, founder of the Al Qaeda terrorist organization. The poster was issued jointly by the U.S. Department of Justice, Department of State, and Federal Bureau of Investigation.

Source: U.S. Federal Bureau of Investigation.

- **7:59 a.m.** American Airlines Flight 11, carrying 92 people, leaves Boston's Logan International Airport for Los Angeles.
- **8:01 a.m.** United Airlines Flight 93, carrying 45 people, leaves Newark, N.J., International Airport for San Francisco.
- **8:10 a.m.** American Airlines Flight 77, carrying 64 people, takes off from Washington's Dulles Airport for Los Angeles.
- **8:14 a.m.** United Airlines Flight 175, carrying 65 people, leaves Boston for Los Angeles.
- **8:48 a.m.** American Flight 11 crashes into the north tower of the World Trade Center.

Case in Point **The Assassins[a]**

The **Order of Assassins** (sometimes referred to as the Brotherhood of Assassins) was founded by **Hasan ibn al-Sabbah** (d. 1124) in 11th-century Persia. Al-Sabbah was a Caliph (religious head) of the Ismaili sect of Islam. He espoused a radical version of Ismaili Islam and founded the Order of Assassins to defend this interpretation of the faith. Beginning in 1090, he and his followers seized a string of fortresses in the mountains of northern Persia, the first of which was the strong fortress of Alamut near Qazvin. Because of these origins, al-Sabbah was called "The Old Man of the Mountain."

The word *assassin* was allegedly derived from the drug hashish, which some commentators believe al-Sabbah's followers ate prior to committing acts of violence in the name of the faith.[b] They referred to themselves as hashashins or hashishis, reputedly meaning "hashish eaters." During the early years of the movement, Assassin followers spread out of the mountains to the cities of Persia, modern Iraq, Syria, and the Christian Crusader–occupied areas of Palestine. The Assassins killed many people, including fellow Muslims who were Sunnis, and Christian leaders.

- **9:03 a.m.** United Flight 175 crashes into the south tower of the World Trade Center.
- **9:43 a.m.** American Flight 77 crashes into the Pentagon. Trading on Wall Street is called off.
- **9:50 a.m.** Two World Trade Center—the south tower—collapses.
- **10:10 a.m.** United Flight 93 crashes 80 miles southeast of Pittsburgh, Pennsylvania.
- **10:29 a.m.** One World Trade Center—the north tower—collapses.[34]

The United States had previously been the target of international terrorism at home and abroad, but the American homeland had never suffered a terrorist strike on this scale. The most analogous historical event was the Japanese attack on the naval base at Pearl Harbor, Hawaii, on December 7, 1941. The last time so many people had died from an act of war committed on American soil was during the Civil War in the mid-19th century.

After the Al Qaeda assault and the subsequent anthrax crisis, ordinary American culture shifted away from complete openness to a period of high security. The adaptation of the American people and political establishment to this new environment was a new experience for the nation. The symbolism of the attack, combined with its sheer scale, drove the United States to war and dramatically changed the American security environment. Counterterrorism in the United States shifted from a predominantly law enforcement mode to a security mode. Security measures included unprecedented airport and seaport security, border searches, visa scrutiny, and immigration procedures. Hundreds of people were administratively detained and questioned during a sweep of persons fitting the terrorist profile of the 19 attackers. These detentions set off a debate about the constitutionality of these methods and the fear by many that civil liberties were in jeopardy.

The symbolism of a damaging attack on homeland targets was significant because it showed that the American superpower was vulnerable to attack by small groups of determined revolutionaries. The Twin Towers had dominated the New York skyline since the completion of Two World Trade Center in 1972. They were a symbol of global trade and prosperity and the pride of the largest city in the United States. The Pentagon, of course, is a unique building that symbolizes American military power, and its location across the river from the nation's capital showed the vulnerability of the seat of government to attack.

On May 30, 2002, a 30-foot long steel beam was ceremoniously removed from the "ground zero" site in New York City. It was the final piece of debris to be removed from the September 11 homeland attack.

Suicide missions were common. Some Crusader leaders went so far as to pay tribute to the Assassins so that the Assassins would leave them alone.

The Assassins were very adept at disguise, stealth, and surprise killings, and thus the word *assassination* was coined to describe this tactic. A key component of the Assassins' beliefs was the absolute righteousness of their cause and methodology. To kill or be killed was a good thing, because it was done in the name of the faith and ensured a place in paradise after death. This belief in complete justification and ultimate reward is practiced by many modern-day terrorists.

Although their political impact was negligible and the Assassin organization was eliminated in 1256, they left a profound psychological mark on their era, and in many ways on the modern era.

NOTES

a. For a history of the Assassin movement, *see* Lewis, Bernard. *The Assassins: A Radical Sect in Islam.* New York: Oxford University Press, 1987.

b. Bernard Lewis discounts the assertion that the Assassins drugged themselves. He argues that "in all probability it was the name that gave rise to the story, rather than the reverse." *The Assassins*, p. 12.

CHAPTER SUMMARY

This chapter introduced students to some of the historical and modern attributes of terrorism, with a central theme that terrorism is deeply rooted in the human experience. The impact of extremist ideas on human behavior should not be underestimated, because there are historical examples of political violence that in some ways parallel modern terrorism. For example, we noted that religious scripture gives examples of violence—done in the name of the faith—directed against enemy peoples and nations. We also noted that state terrorism and antistate dissident movements have existed since ancient times.

The relationship between extremist ideas and terrorist events was discussed as a nexus, whereby terrorism is the violent manifestation of extremist beliefs. Ideologies are the belief systems at the root of political violence. The case of Ramzi Yousef represents not only this nexus but also the high degree of criminal skill that is often associated with terrorist attacks.

Whether terrorist acts are *mala in se* or *mala prohibita* is often a relative question. Depending on one's perspective, there are gray areas that challenge us to be objective about the true nature of political violence. Most, if not all, nations promote an ideological doctrine to legitimize the power of the state and to convince the people that their systems of belief are worthy of loyalty, sacrifice, and (when necessary) violent defense. Conversely, when a group of people perceives that an alternative ideology or condition should be promoted, revolutionary violence may occur against the defenders of the established rival order. In neither case would those who commit acts of political violence consider themselves to be unjustified in their actions, and they certainly would not label themselves as terrorists.

In Chapter 2, students will be challenged to probe the nature of terrorism more deeply. The discussion will center on the importance of ideology, perspective, and the question of how to define terrorism.

KEY TERMS AND CONCEPTS

The following topics were discussed in this chapter and can be found in the Glossary:

Al Qaeda
al-Sabbah, Hasan ibn
Ammonium nitrate and fuel oil (ANFO)
  explosives
Baumhammers, Richard
Burke, Edmund
Classical ideological continuum
Collateral damage
Extremism
Extremism in defense of liberty is
  no vice.
Ideology
It became necessary to destroy the town to
  save it.
Kaczynski, Theodore "Ted"
Kill one, terrorize a thousand.
Komiteh
Left, center, right
Mala in se
Mala prohibita
Mao Zedong

McVeigh, Timothy
One man willing to throw away his life is
  enough to terrorize a thousand.
One person's terrorist is another person's
  freedom fighter.
Order of Assassins
Regicide
Reign of Terror (*régime de la terreur*)
Revolutionary Tribunal
Sicarii
Soft targets
Struggle Meetings
Sun Tzu
Symbolism, Role of
Terrorism
Total War
UNABOM
Unabomber
Wu Ch'i
Yousef, Ramzi
Zealots

RECOMMENDED WEB SITES

The following Web sites provide general information about terrorism:

Anti-Defamation League: www.adl.org
RAND: www.rand.org
Southern Poverty Law Center: www.splcenter.org
Terrorism Research Center: www.terrorism.com
U.S. Department of State: www.state.gov/s/ct/

WEB EXERCISE

Using this chapter's recommended Internet sites, conduct an online investigation of organizations that monitor extremist sentiment and terrorist behavior. Compare and contrast these organizations.

- What are the primary agendas of these organizations?
- How would you describe the differences between research, government, and social activist organizations?
- In your opinion, are any of these organizations more comprehensive than other organizations? Less comprehensive?

For an online search of research and monitoring organizations, students should activate the search engine on their Web browser and enter the following keywords:

"Terrorism Research"
"Human Rights Organizations"

RECOMMENDED READINGS

The following publications provide an introduction to terrorism.

Combs, Cindy C. *Terrorism in the Twenty-First Century*, 3d ed. Englewood Cliffs, NJ: Prentice Hall, 2003.
Hoffman, Bruce. *Inside Terrorism*. New York: Columbia University Press, 1998.

Discussion Box   **Total War**

This chapter's Discussion Box is intended to stimulate critical debate about the legitimacy of using extreme force against civilian populations.

Total war is "warfare that uses all possible means of attack, military, scientific, and psychological, against both enemy troops and civilians."[a] It was the prevailing military doctrine applied by combatant nations during the Second World War.

Allied and Axis military planners specifically targeted civilian populations. In the cases of German and Japanese strategists, the war was fought as much against indigenous populations as against opposing armies. The massacres and genocide directed against civilian populations at Auschwitz, Dachau, Warsaw, Lidice, and Nanking and countless other atrocities are a dark legacy of the 20th century.

The estimated number of civilians killed during the war is staggering:[b]

Belgium	90,000
Britain	70,000
China	20,000,000
Czechoslovakia	319,000
France	391,000
Germany	2,000,000
Greece	391,000
Japan	953,000
Poland	6,000,000
Soviet Union	7,700,000
Yugoslavia	1,400,000

An important doctrine of the air war on all sides was to bomb civilian populations, so that the cities of Rotterdam, Coventry, London, Berlin, Dresden, and Tokyo were deliberately attacked. It is estimated that the atomic bombs dropped on Hiroshima and Nagasaki killed, respectively, 70,000 and 35,000 people.[c]

Discussion Questions

- Are deliberate attacks against civilians legitimate acts of war?
- Were deliberate attacks on civilians during the Second World War acts of terrorism?
- If these attacks were acts of terrorism, were some attacks *justifiable* acts of terrorism?
- Is there such a thing as justifiable terrorism? Is terrorism *malum in se* or *malum prohibitum*?
- Is the practice of total war by individuals or small and poorly armed groups different from its practice by nations and standing armies? How so or how not?

NOTES

a. *Webster's New Twentieth-Century Dictionary of the English Language, Unabridged*, 2d ed. New York: Publishers Guild, 1966.

b. Mercer, Derrik, ed. *Chronicle of the Second World War*. Essex, UK: Longman Group, 1990, p. 668.

c. Jablonski, Edward. *Flying Fortress*. New York: Doubleday, 1965, p. 285.

Schechterman, Bernard, and Martin Slann, eds. *Violence and Terrorism.* Guilford, CT: Dushkin/McGraw-Hill, 1999.

Simonsen, Clifford E., and Jeremy R. Spindlove. *Terrorism Today: The Past, the Players, the Future.* Englewood Cliffs, NJ: Prentice Hall, 2000.

White, Jonathan R. *Terrorism: An Introduction*, 3d ed. Belmont, CA: Wadsworth, 2002.

NOTES

[1] See Laqueur, Walter. *The New Terrorism: Fanaticism and the Arms of Mass Destruction.* New York: Oxford University Press, 1999.

[2] Numbers 25:1, 6-8, in *The Holy Bible, New Revised Standard Version.*

[3] An extraordinary and classic history of the Roman Empire is found in Edward Gibbon's great work of literature, *The History of the Decline and Fall of the Roman Empire.* New York: AMS Press, 1974, reprinted from Bury, J. B., ed. London: Methuen, 1909.

[4] For a discussion of the Roman occupation of Judea and the First Jewish Revolt within the broader context of Roman politics, see Grant, Michael. *The Twelve Caesars.* New York: Scribner's, 1975.

[5] Burke, a Whig Member of Parliament, was a progressive in his time. He opposed absolutism, poor treatment of the American colonists, and the slave trade. He expressed his opposition to Jacobin extremism in a series of writings, including *Reflections on the French Revolution* and *Letters on a Regicide Peace.*

[6] For a classic account of the Terror, see Loomis, Stanley. *Paris in the Terror: June 1793–July 1794.* Philadelphia: J. B. Lippincott, 1964.

[7] A French physician, Joseph Ignace Guillotin, invented the guillotine. He was loyal to the revolution and a deputy to the States-General. Guillotin encouraged the use of the beheading machine as a painless, humane, and symbolically revolutionary method of execution.

[8] For a good discussion about the consolidation of the Chinese revolution and the Great Proletarian Cultural Revolution that occurred later, see Fairbank, John King. *The Great Chinese Revolution: 1800–1985.* New York: Harper & Row, 1987. For an analysis of the ideology of the Ayatollah Khomeini and the Iranian revolution, see Martin, Vanessa. *Creating an Islamic State: Khomeini and the Making of a New Iran.* London: I. B. Tauris, 2000.

[9] *Webster's New Twentieth-Century Dictionary of the English Language, Unabridged*, 2d ed. New York: Publishers Guild, 1966.

[10] Wilcox, Laird. "What Is Extremism? Style and Tactics Matter More Than Goals." In George, John, and Laird Wilcox. *American Extremists: Militias, Supremacists, Klansmen, Communists, & Others.* Amherst, NY: Prometheus Books, 1996, p. 54.

[11] Laqueur (note 1 above), p. 5.

[12] Lesser, Ian O. "Countering the New Terrorism: Implications for Strategy." In Lesser, Ian O., Bruce Hoffman, John Arquilla, David Ronfeldt, and Michele Zanini. *Countering the New Terrorism.* Santa Monica, CA: RAND, 1999, p. 127.

[13] Friedland, Nehemia. "Becoming a Terrorist: Social and Individual Antecedents." In Howard, Lawrence, ed. *Terrorism: Roots, Impact, Responses.* New York: Praeger, 1992, p. 82.

[14] The politics of the French Revolution are evaluated in Skocpol, Theda. *States and Social Revolutions: A Comparative Analysis of France, Russia, and China.* Cambridge, UK: Cambridge University Press, 1990, pp. 174-205.

[15] For a comparative discussion of ideological conflict in revolutionary environments, see Skocpol (note 14 above). For seminal discussions that formed the ideological foundation for the U.S. Constitution and Bill of Rights, see Hamilton, Alexander, John Jay, and James Madison. *The Federalist: A Commentary on the Constitution of the United States, Being a Collection of Essays Written in Support of the Constitution Agreed upon September 17, 1787.* New York: Modern Library, 2000.

[16] "Prohibited wrongs." Singular: *malum prohibitum.* Black, Henry Campbell. Black's *Law Dictionary*, 4th ed., revised. St. Paul, MN: West, 1968, pp. 1108, 1112.

[17] Rush, George E. *The Dictionary of Criminal Justice*, 5th ed. Guilford, CT: Dushkin/McGraw-Hill, 2002, p. 205.

[18] Rush (see note 17), p. 204.

[19] The quote has been more widely reported since the Vietnam War as "we had to destroy the village to save it." See Oberdorfer, Don. *Tet!* Garden City, NY: Doubleday, 1971, pp. 184-85, 332.

See *also* Sheehan, Neil. *A Bright Shining Lie: John Paul Vann and America in Vietnam*. New York: Random House, 1988, p. 719.

[20] In Chinese literature and propaganda, "bandit" is often a synonym for "rebel." Sun Tzu. *The Art of War*. New York: Oxford University Press, 1963, p. 168.

[21] Within the context of the campaign, Lyndon Johnson's anti-Communist "credentials" were decisively validated during the Gulf of Tonkin crisis in August 1964. The destroyer U.S.S. *Maddox* was reported to have been attacked by North Vietnamese torpedo boats off the coast of North Vietnam. American air strikes were launched in reprisal, and Congress unanimously passed the Gulf of Tonkin Resolution, which supported President Johnson's use of "necessary measures" to protect U.S. interests in Vietnam and elsewhere. For a discussion of the incident within the context of the politics at the time, see Kearns, Doris. *Lyndon Johnson and the American Dream*. New York: Harper & Row, 1976, pp. 195 ff. For an insiders' discussion, see Miller, Merle. Lyndon: *An Oral Biography*. New York: Ballantine Books, 1980, pp. 465-77.

[22] For a discussion of this subject from the cultural perspectives of Bosnian Muslims and Serbs, see Weine, Steven M. *When History Is a Nightmare: Lives and Memories of Ethnic Cleansing in Bosnia-Herzegovina*. New Brunswick, NJ: Rutgers University Press, 1999.

[23] Associated Press reporter Peter Arnett attributed the source of the quotation to a U.S. soldier at the city of Ben Tre in South Vietnam during the Tet offensive in 1968. As reported, it was the statement of an officer higher up in the chain of command—a U.S. army major. Although widely repeated at the time and since the war, only Arnett said he heard the statement at the site, and only Arnett filed the quotation from the Ben Tre visit. The U.S. officer was not identified and has not been identified since the war. See Oberdorfer (note 19 above) and Sheehan (note 19 above). The U.S. Department of Defense launched an investigation to find the source of the quote. No officer or enlisted man was identified. See Oberdorfer (note 19 above).

[24] Katz, Lee Michael. "Financial Records Lifting Veil on bin Laden Network." *USA Today*. October 1, 1998.

[25] Exceptions to this general profile have occurred in the United States. For example, an Egyptian-born resident of the United States committed a lone wolf attack at Los Angeles International Airport on July 4, 2002. He shot and stabbed several people at the El Al (Israeli airline) counter before being killed by El Al security officers. The assailant killed two people and injured several others.

[26] Simonich, Milan. "Victims Left in Wake of Rampage." *Pittsburgh Post-Gazette*. April 29, 2000.

[27] Reeve, Simon. *The New Jackals: Ramzi Yousef, Osama bin Laden and the Future of Terrorism*. Boston: Northeastern University Press, 1999, p. 10.

[28] Comment by Judge Kevin Duffy. *United States of America v. Mohammed A. Salameh et al.*, S593CR.180 (KTD).

[29] Reeve (see note 27 above), p. 120.

[30] For a discussion of McVeigh's immersion in the fringe right—from the perspective of McVeigh himself—see Michel, Lou, and Dan Herbeck. *American Terrorist: Timothy McVeigh & the Oklahoma City Bombing*. New York: HarperCollins, 2001.

[31] Ibid., p. 164.

[32] Ibid., p. 224.

[33] Ibid., p. 234.

[34] From "A Timeline." *Christian Science Monitor*. September 17, 2001.

Chapter 2

THE NATURE OF THE BEAST: DEFINING TERRORISM

This chapter investigates definitional issues in the study of terrorism. Students will probe the nuances of these issues and will learn that the truism "one person's terrorist is another person's freedom fighter" is a significant factor in the definitional discussion. It must be remembered that this debate occurs within a practical and "real-life" framework—the nontheoretical reality that some political, religious, or ethnonationalist beliefs and behaviors are so reprehensible that they cannot be considered to be mere differences in opinion. Some violent incidents are *malum in se* acts of terrorist violence. For example, the New Terrorism is characterized by the threat of weapons of mass destruction, indiscriminate targeting, and potentially high casualty rates—as was the case in the attacks of September 11, 2001. The use of these weapons and tactics against civilians is indefensible, no matter what cause is championed by those who use them.

This debate is evident in both state-sponsored and dissident terrorist environments:

State-Sponsored Terrorist Environments. As noted in Chapter 1, the *régime de la terreur* during the French Revolution was an instrument of revolutionary justice, so that terrorism was considered a positive medium used by the defenders of order and liberty. From their perspective, state-sponsored domestic terrorism was both acceptable and necessary to consolidate power and protect liberties won during the Revolution. Modern examples of state terrorism such as Nazi Germany and Stalinist Russia also sought to consolidate an ideological vision through internal political violence—a racial new order in Germany and an egalitarian worker's state in the Soviet Union. The methods they used to build the ideological vision resulted in the deaths of millions of noncombatant civilians, and both the Nazi and Stalinist regimes are now considered to be terrorist states. State terrorism is explored further in Chapter 4.

Dissident Terrorist Environments. The definitional debate is also evident in dissident terrorist environments. The anticolonial and nationalist wars after the Second World War often pitted indigenous rebels against European colonial powers or ruling local elites. Many of these wars involved the use of terrorism as an instrument of war by both state and dissident forces. During these wars, as well as in subsequent domestic rebellions, the rebels were referred to as freedom fighters by those who favored their cause.[1] The counterpoints to these freedom fighters were the European (and American) "colonial oppressors." Thus, for example, indiscriminate attacks against civilians by rebels in French

Indochina and French Algeria were rationalized by many of their supporters as acceptable tactics during wars of liberation by freedom fighters against a colonial oppressor.

The discussion in this chapter will review:

- Reactionaries and Radicals: Revisiting the Classical Ideological Continuum
- Understanding Extremism—The Foundation of Terrorism
- Defining Terrorism
- A Definitional Problem: Perspectives on Terrorism
- The Political Violence Matrix

REACTIONARIES AND RADICALS: REVISITING THE CLASSICAL IDEOLOGICAL CONTINUUM

The classical ideological continuum summarizes the conventional political environment of the modern era. First introduced in Chapter 1, it is a useful tool for understanding:

- The beliefs and behaviors of violent movements, authoritarian states, and terrorist groups
- The ideological justifications for terrorist violence

It is not difficult to draw a conceptual distinction between right-wing and left-wing ideologies. To begin, one must be aware that the term **reactionary** has been affixed to far- and fringe-rightist ideologies, and **radical** has been affixed to far- and fringe-leftist ideologies. These terms are, of course, exercises in semantics. As such, they can be at best imprecise and, at worst, confusing. Rather than enter into an academic debate about the meaning of these terms, it is instructive for students to understand the following two concepts:

Right-wing extremism is generally a reaction against a perceived threat to a group's value system, its presumption of superiority, or its sense of specialness. Rightists often try to preserve their value system and special status by aggressively asserting this status. They frequently desire to return to a time of past glory, which in their belief system has been lost or usurped by an enemy group or culture. In this sense, rightist extremism is *nostalgic*.

Left-wing extremism is future oriented, seeking to reform or destroy an existing system prior to building a new and just society. To the extent that leftists champion a special group, it is usually one that is perceived to be oppressed unjustly by a corrupt system or government. This group is commonly a class or ethno-national category that, in their belief system, must receive the justice and equality that has been denied them. In doing so, leftists believe that reform of the system, or revolution, is needed to build a just society. In this sense, leftist extremism is *idealistic*.

In the modern era, many nationalist or religious terrorists do not fit easily into the classical continuum. For example,

To argue that the Algerian terrorists, the Palestinian groups, or the Tamil Tigers are "left" or "right" means affixing a label that simply does not fit. . . . The Third World groups . . . have subscribed to different ideological tenets at different periods.[2]

A case in point is the National Union for the Total Independence of Angola (UNITA) guerrilla movement in Angola during the 1970s and thereafter. UNITA was nominally leftist when it fought alongside the Marxist Movement for the Liberation of Angola

(MPLA) against the Portuguese colonialists, but it became strongly anti-Communist when it was supported by the United States and South Africa in its civil war against the MPLA after the Portuguese withdrawal.

Nevertheless, the classical continuum is still very useful for categorizing terrorist behaviors and extremist beliefs. Table 2.1 compares the championed groups, methodologies, and desired outcomes of typical political environments on the continuum.

An Ideological Analysis:
From the Left Fringe to the Right Fringe

Fringe left ideology is usually an extreme interpretation of Marxist ideology, using theories of class warfare or ethno-national liberation to justify political violence. At the leftist fringe, violence is seen as a perfectly legitimate option, because the fringe group considers itself to be at war with an oppressive system, class, or government. The key justification is that the fringe group pictures itself as a righteous champion of the poor and downtrodden.

This type of ideological movement frequently concerns itself only with destroying an existing order in the name of the championed class or national group, not with building the new society in the aftermath of the revolution. For example, **Gudrun Ensslin,** a leader of the terrorist Red Army Faction in West Germany, stated: "As for the state of the future, the time after victory, that is not our concern. . . . We build the revolution, not the socialist model."[3] Leftist terrorism will be discussed further in Chapter 6.

Far left ideology frequently applies Marxist theory to promote class or ethno-national rights. It is best characterized as a radical worldview, because political declarations often direct public attention against perceived forces of exploitation or repression. Far left groups do not necessarily engage in political violence and often fully participate in democratic processes. In Western Europe, for example, Communist parties and their affiliated Communist labor unions have overtly agitated for reform through democratic processes.[4] The French Communist Party has regularly had its members elected at the national level,[5] as has the Italian Communist Party.[6] In March 1977, the Spanish, Italian, and French Communist Parties embarked on an independent, yet undefined, course setting them apart from the orthodox Moscow-inspired path. The new path was called EuroCommunism.[7]

It is important to note that this environment of relatively peaceful coexistence occurs only in societies where dissent is tolerated. In countries with weaker democratic traditions, far left dissent has erupted in violence and been met by extreme repression. Latin America has many examples of this kind of environment, some of which are discussed in Chapters 4 and 5.

Liberalism is a term that has been defined differently depending on the historical or national contexts in which it has been used. In its original context, European liberalism arose as a philosophical challenge to the absolutism practiced by monarchies. It advocated the rights of the individual vis-à-vis the monarch and the state. Liberty in political expression and equality under the law were the ideals of liberalism, although as practiced, these ideals were not enjoyed by every person in society. For example, the French and American revolutions embodied liberal principles, but the French state fell into civil war and Napoleonic imperialism, and American constitutional rights were not afforded to women or African Americans until the 20th century. Thus, 19th-century liberalism was highly contextualized and even conservative by modern standards.

In the modern era, and particularly in the American context, liberalism "expects to use government in a positive and expansive role . . . motivated by the highest sentiments," and "it sees as both necessary and good that the policy agenda and the public interest be defined in terms of the organized interests in society."[8] From this perspective, the various

Table 2.1   The Classical Ideological Continuum: Modern Political Environments

Activism on the left, right, and center can be distinguished by a number of characteristics. A comparison of these attributes is instructive. The representation here compares their championed groups, methodologies, and desired outcomes.

	Left Fringe	Far Left	Liberalism	Moderate Center	Conservatism	Far Right	Fringe Right
Championed groups	Class/ nationality	Class/ nationality	Selected groups in society	General society	General society	Race, ethnicity, nationality, religion	Race, ethnicity, nationality, religion
Methodology/ process	Liberation movement	Political agitation	Partisan democratic processes	Consensus	Partisan democratic processes	Political agitation	"Order" movement
Desired outcome	Radical change	Radical change	Incremental reform	Status quo slow change	Traditional values	Reactionary change	Reactionary change

people's rights movements—such as the human, civil, women's, and gay rights movements—
are usually considered to be liberal in nature.

The **moderate center** is best described as the stable balancing segment of the political
environment. Political expression is conducted within accepted traditional institutions
and rarely exhibits sustained group-centered activism or agitation. In a democracy, the
moderate center is ideally the largest segment in the political environment, drawing
support from both liberal and conservative ranks that need its political support. Consensus,
not adversarial confrontation, is the hallmark of the moderate center.

Conservatism, like liberalism, is a concept that evolved over time and within the
context of political and social conflict. The French Revolution and subsequent upheavals
in Europe caused a backlash that sought to reestablish order and the rule of law. Edmund
Burke, who criticized the excesses of the French Revolution, is considered to be the father
of modern conservatism. Conservatives of the 19th century argued that, rather than rejecting the past in favor of an idealized vision of how humans *ought* to live, one should
preserve (conserve) the good features of the existing order. Conservatives held that
change, especially radical change, ought to be questioned. In the modern era, and particularly in the American context, "conservatism is committed to a discriminating defense of
social order against change and reform."[9] It questions government intervention in the
private sector, especially regulation of the market. In essence, conservatism wishes to
preserve traditional values and beliefs.

Far right ideology is characterized by strong adherence to social order and traditional values. There is sometimes a religious or mystical dimension to the worldview of the far right—
especially in the United States—as well as an undercurrent of racial or ethnic chauvinism. As
with the case of the far left, far right groups do not necessarily engage in political violence and
have fully participated in democratic processes. Organized political expression is often overt.
For example, rightist political parties in many European countries are a common feature of
national politics. Their success has been mixed. In Spain, Greece, and Great Britain, these
parties have little popular support.[10] However, the far right parties in Austria, Belgium,
France, and Italy have enjoyed significant popular support in the recent past.

Not all far right political movements are the same. A comparison of the American and
European contexts is instructive. In Europe, some of these parties are nostalgic neofascist parties, such as the German People's Union. Others are more populist, such as the National Front
in France.[11] They all tend to favor an open market, "articulate a low-tax, anti-welfare-state ideology . . . may support 'law and order' and a vigorous military . . . [and] condemn bureaucracy
[and] excessive state control."[12] In the United States, the far right is characterized by activism
among local grassroots organizations and has no viable political party. Some American groups
have a religious orientation, others are racial, and others embody a politically paranoid survivalist lifestyle. The American far right will be discussed further in Chapter 12.

Fringe right ideology is usually rooted in an uncompromising belief in ethno-national
or religious superiority, and terrorist violence is justified as a protection of the purity of
the group. Terrorists on the fringe right picture themselves as champions of an ideal order
that has been usurped, or attacked, by inferior interests or unwanted religious values.
Violence is an acceptable option against those who are not members of the group or
religion, because they are considered to be obstacles to the natural assumption of power
by the favored group or belief. Like terrorists on the fringe left, right-wing terrorists
often have only a vague notion of the characteristics of the new order after the revolution.
They are concerned only with asserting their value system and, if necessary, destroying
the existing order. Significantly, rightist terrorists have been more likely to engage in
indiscriminate bombings and other attacks that produce higher numbers of victims.
Right-wing terrorism will be discussed further in Chapter 7.

Table 2.2 applies this discussion to the American context.

Table 2.2 The Classical Ideological Continuum: The Case of the United States

The United States is a good case in point for the application of the classical ideological continuum. Its political environment has produced organizations that represent the ideologies included in the continuum. The representation here compares organizations that have economic, group rights, faith, and legal agendas.

Left Fringe	Far Left	Liberalism	Moderate Center	Conservatism	Far Right	Fringe Right
Economic/class agenda						
United Freedom Front	Communist Party, USA	American Federation of State, County and Municipal Employees	American Federation of Labor and Congress of Industrial Organizations	Teamsters Union	Lyndon Larouche groups	Posse Comitatus
Activist/group rights agenda						
Black Liberation Army	Black Panther Party	National Association for the Advancement of Colored People	National Bar Association	Heritage Foundation	National Association for the Advancement of White People	Aryan Republican Army
Religious/faith agenda						
Liberation theology	Catholic Worker movement	American Friends Service Committee	National Conference of Christians and Jews	Southern Baptist Convention	Moral Majority	Army of God
Legal/constitutional agenda						
Individual lawyers	National Lawyers Guild	American Civil Liberties Union	American Bar Association	Thomas More Law Center	American Center for Law and Justice	Freemen

The "New Terrorism"

Referring to the classical ideological continuum is useful for developing a good understanding of modern terrorist behavior. It is also important to understand, however, that the growing threat of the New Terrorism adds a unique dimension to the emerging terrorist environment of the 21st century. This is because "the new terrorism is different in character, aiming not at clearly defined political demands but at the destruction of society and the elimination of large sections of the population."[13]

The new breed of terrorists "would feel no compunction over killing hundreds of thousands if they had the means to do so."[14] In addition, the emerging terrorist environment is characterized by a "horizontal" organizational arrangement wherein independent cells operate autonomously without reporting to a hierarchical ("vertical") command structure. Many of these new terrorists are motivated by religious or nationalist precepts that may not fit easily into the classical continuum. The September 11, 2001, attacks on the United States are an example of this emerging environment.

UNDERSTANDING EXTREMISM: THE FOUNDATION OF TERRORISM

An important step toward defining terrorism is to develop an understanding of the *sources* of terrorism. In order to identify these sources, one must first understand the important role of **extremism** as a primary feature underlying all terrorist behavior.

Behind each incident of terrorist violence is some type of deeply held *belief system* that has motivated the perpetrators. These belief systems are, at their core, extremist systems characterized by intolerance. One must keep in mind, however, that although terrorism is a violent expression of these beliefs, it is by no means the *only* possible manifestation of extremism. On a scale of activist behavior, extremists can engage in such benign expressions of their beliefs as sponsoring debates or publishing newspapers. Or they might engage in vandalism and other disruptions of the normal routines of their enemies. Our focus in this chapter and subsequent chapters will be on violent extremist behavior that many people would define as acts of terrorism. But first, we must briefly investigate the general characteristics of the extremist foundations of terrorism.

Defining Extremism

Recall from Chapter 1 that extremism is broadly defined as "radical in opinion, especially in political matters; ultra; advanced."[15] More specifically, *political* extremism refers to

> taking a political idea to its limits, regardless of unfortunate repercussions, impracticalities, arguments, and feelings to the contrary, and with the intention not only to confront, but to eliminate opposition. . . . Intolerance toward all views other than one's own.[16]

Extremism is a precursor to terrorism—it is an overarching belief system that is used by terrorists to justify their violent behavior. Extremism is characterized by *what* a person's beliefs are as well as *how* a person expresses his or her beliefs. Thus, no matter how offensive or reprehensible one's thoughts or words are, they are not by themselves acts of terrorism. Only persons who *violently* act out their extremist beliefs are labeled as terrorists.

Two examples illustrate this point:

First, an example of extremist behavior. **Daniel and Philip Berrigan** were well-known members of the Roman Catholic pacifist left and were leaders in the antiwar and antinuclear movements in the United States during the 1960s and 1970s. *What* they believed in was an uncompromising commitment to pacifism. *How* they expressed their beliefs was by committing a series of symbolic, and often illegal, protest actions. During one such action on May 17, 1968, they and seven other Catholic men and women entered the Baltimore Selective Service Board, stole Selective Service classification forms, took them outside to a parking lot, and burned several hundred of the documents with a homemade napalm-like gelled mixture of gasoline and soap flakes. This was certainly extremist behavior, but it falls short of terrorism.[17]

Second, an example of extremist speech. The **American Knights of the Ku Klux Klan** (AK-KKK) were an activist faction of the KKK that operated mostly in the Midwest and East during the 1990s. *What* they believed in was racial supremacy. *How* they expressed their beliefs was by holding a series of rallies at government sites, often county court-houses. They were known for their vitriolic rhetoric. The following remarks were report-edly taken from a speech delivered by the Imperial Wizard of the AK-KKK in March 1998 at rally held at the county courthouse in Butler, Pennsylvania, near Pittsburgh:

> Take a stand. . . . Join the Klan, stick up for your rights. . . . Only God has the right to create a race—not no black and white, not no nigger, not no Jew. . . . Yes, I will use the word *nigger*, because it is not illegal. . . . We are sick and tired of the government taking your money, and giving food and jobs to the niggers when the white race has to go without! Wake up America.[18]

This language is intentionally racist, hateful, and inflammatory, and yet it falls short of advocating violence or revolution. A sympathetic listener might certainly act out against one of the enemy groups identified in the speech, but it reads more like a racist diatribe than a revolutionary manifesto.

Common Characteristics of Violent Extremists

Scholars and other experts have identified common characteristics exhibited by violent extremists. These characteristics are expressed in different ways, depending on a move-ment's particular belief system. The following commonalities are summaries of traits iden-tified by these experts and are by no means an exhaustive inventory. [19]

Intolerance. Intolerance is the hallmark of extremist belief systems and terrorist behavior. The cause is considered to be absolutely just and good, and those who disagree with the cause (or some aspect of the cause) are cast into the category of the opposition. Terrorists affix their opponents with certain negative or derisive labels to set them apart from the extremists' movement. These characterizations are often highly personalized, so that spe-cific individuals are identified who symbolize the opposing belief system or cause. Thus, during the Cold War, the American president was labeled by the pro-United States camp as the "leader of the free world" and by Latin American Marxists as the embodiment of "Yankee imperialism."[20]

Moral Absolutes. Moral absolutes are adopted by terrorists, so that the distinction between good and evil is very clearly drawn, as are the lines between the terrorists and their opponents. The terrorists' belief or cause is a morally correct vision of the world and is used to establish moral superiority over others. Violent extremists thus become morally and ethically pure elites who lead the oppressed masses to freedom. For example, religious terrorists often believe that their "one true faith" is superior to all others and that any behavior committed in defense of the faith is perfectly justifiable.

Broad Conclusions. Extremist conclusions are made to simplify the goals of the cause and the nature of the extremist's opponents. These generalizations are not debatable and allow for no exceptions. Evidence for these conclusions is rooted in one's belief system rather than based on objective data. Terrorists often believe these generalizations because in their minds they simply *must* be true. For example, ethno-nationalists frequently categorize all members of their opponent group as having certain broadly negative traits.

New Language and Conspiratorial Beliefs. Language and conspiracies are created to demonize the enemy and set the terrorists apart from those who are not part of their belief system. Extremists thus become a special elite who have discovered a hidden agenda and who have become targets of that agenda. For example, some American far right conspiracy proponents express their anti-Semitic beliefs by using coded references to "international bankers" or the Zionist Occupied Government (ZOG). Neo-Nazi rightists degrade members of non-European races by referring to them as "mud people."

The World of the Extremist

Extremists have a very different—and at times, fantastic—worldview compared to nonextremists. They set themselves apart as protectors of some truth or as the true heirs of some legacy. For example, racial extremists within the American Patriot movement have argued that minorities are "Fourteenth Amendment citizens" and that only

> whites are sovereign citizens whose rights are delineated, not by the government, but rather by a cobbled assortment of historical writings whose meaning is often subject to their fanciful interpretation.[21]

Likewise, extremists frequently believe that secret and quasi-mystical forces are arrayed against them and that these forces are the cause of worldwide calamities. For example, some bigoted conspiracy believers argue that the Illuminati or international Judaism mysteriously control world banking or run the governments of France or the United States. One conspiracy theory that was widely believed among Islamic extremists in the aftermath of the September 11, 2001, attacks was that Israeli agents were behind the attacks; that 4,000 Jews received telephone calls to evacuate the World Trade Center in New York; and thus, that no Jews were among the victims of the attack.

When terrorists adopt a religious belief system, their worldview becomes one of a struggle between supernatural forces of good and evil. They view themselves as living a righteous life in a manner that fits with their interpretation of God's will. According to religious extremists, those who do not conform to their belief system are opposed to the one true faith. Those who live according to the accepted belief system are a chosen people, and those who do not are not chosen. These interpretations of how one should behave include elements of the social or political environment that underlies the belief system. For example, Bob Jones University in Greenville, South Carolina, is a fundamentalist Christian university founded in 1927. It once justified its prohibition against interracial dating and marriage as an application of truths found in holy scripture. Similarly, one student at a Pakistani religious school stated,

> Osama [bin Laden] wants to keep Islam pure from the pollution of the infidels. . . . He believes Islam is the way for all the world. He wants to bring Islam to all the world.[22]

Extremists have a very clear sense of mission, purpose, and righteousness. They create a worldview that sets them apart from the rest of society. Thus, extremist beliefs and terrorist behaviors are very logical from the perspective of those who accept the extremists' belief system, but illogical from the point of view of those who reject the system.

DEFINING TERRORISM

There is some consensus among experts—but no unanimity—on what kind of violence constitutes an act of terrorism. Governments have developed definitions of terrorism, individual agencies within governments have adopted definitions, private agencies have designed their own definitions, and academic experts have proposed and analyzed dozens of definitional constructs. This lack of unanimity, which exists throughout the public and private sectors, is an accepted reality in the study of political violence.

A significant amount of intellectual energy has been devoted to identifying formal elements of terrorism, as illustrated by Alex Smid's surveys, which identified more than 100 definitions.[23] Establishing formal definitions can, of course, be complicated by the perspectives of the participants in a terrorist incident, who instinctively differentiate freedom fighters from terrorists, regardless of formal definitions. Another complication is that most definitions focus on political violence perpetrated by dissident groups, even though many governments have practiced terrorism as both domestic and foreign policy.

Guerrilla Warfare. One important observation must be kept in mind and understood at the outset: *Terrorism is not synonymous with guerrilla warfare.* The term *guerrilla* ("little war") was developed during the early 19th century when Napoleon's army fought a long, brutal, and ultimately unsuccessful war in Spain. Unlike the Napoleonic campaigns elsewhere in Europe, which involved conventional armies fighting set-piece battles, the war in Spain was a classic unconventional conflict. The Spanish *people,* as opposed to the Spanish *army,* rose in rebellion and resisted the invading French. They liberated large areas of the Spanish countryside. After years of costly fighting—in which atrocities were common on both sides—the French were driven out. Thus, in contrast to terrorists, the term *guerrilla fighters* refers to

> a numerically larger group of armed individuals, who operate as a military unit, attack enemy military forces, and seize and hold territory (even if only ephemerally during the daylight hours), while also exercising some form of sovereignty or control over a defined geographical area and its population.[24]

Dozens, if not scores, of examples of guerrilla warfare exist in the modern era. They exhibit the classic strategy of hit-and-run warfare. Many examples also exist of successful guerrilla campaigns against numerically and technologically superior adversaries.

Thus, the effort to formally define terrorism is a critical one, because government antiterrorist policy calculations must be based on criteria that determine whether or not a violent incident is an act of terrorism. Governments and policymakers must piece together the elements of terrorist behavior and demarcate the factors that distinguish terrorism from other forms of conflict.

A Sampling of Formal Definitions

In Europe, countries that endured terrorist campaigns have written official definitions of terrorism. The British have defined terrorism as "the use or threat, for the purpose of advancing a political, religious or ideological cause, of action which involves serious violence against any person or property."[25] In Germany, terrorism has been described as an "enduringly conducted struggle for political goals, which are intended to be achieved by means of assaults on the life and property of other persons, especially by means of severe crimes."[26] And the European Interior Ministers note that "terrorism is . . . the use, or the threatened use, by a cohesive group of persons of violence (short of warfare) to effect political aims."[27]

Scholars have also tried their hand at defining terrorism. For example, terrorism has been described by Gurr as "the use of unexpected violence to intimidate or coerce people in the pursuit of political or social objectives."[28] It was described by Gibbs as "illegal violence or threatened violence against human or nonhuman objects," so long as that violence meets additional criteria such as secretive features and unconventional warfare.[29] Bruce Hoffman wrote:

> We come to appreciate that terrorism is ineluctably political in aims and motives; violent—or, equally important, threatens violence; designed to have far-reaching psychological repercussions beyond the immediate victim or target; conducted by an organization with an identifiable chain of command or conspiratorial structure (whose members wear no uniform or identifying insignia); and perpetrated by a subnational group or non-state entity.
>
> We may therefore now attempt to define terrorism as the deliberate creation and exploitation of fear through violence or the threat of violence in the pursuit of change.[30]

To further illustrate the range of definitions, Whittaker lists the following descriptions of terrorism by terrorism experts: [31]

> Contributes the illegitimate use of force to achieve a political objective when innocent people are targeted (Walter Laqueur).
>
> A strategy of violence designed to promote desired outcomes by instilling fear in the public at large (Walter Reich).
>
> The use or threatened use of force designed to bring about political change (Brian Jenkins).

From this discussion, we can identify the common features of most formal definitions. These include:

- The use of illegal force
- Subnational actors
- Unconventional methods
- Political motives
- Attacks against "soft" civilian and passive military targets
- Acts aimed at purposefully affecting an audience

The emphasis, then, is on the adoption by terrorists of specific types of motives, methods, and targets. One fact that is readily apparent from these formal definitions is that they are very focused on terrorist *groups* rather than terrorist *states*. As will be made abundantly clear in Chapter 4, state terrorism has been responsible for many more deaths and much more suffering than terrorism originating from small groups of terrorists.

THE AMERICAN CONTEXT: DEFINING TERRORISM IN THE UNITED STATES

The United States has not adopted a single definition of terrorism as a matter of government policy, instead relying on definitions that are developed from time to time by government agencies. These definitions reflect the United States' traditional law enforcement approach to distinguishing terrorism from more common criminal behavior.

The following definitions are a sample of the official U.S. approach toward defining terrorist behavior:

The Department of Defense defines terrorism as "the unlawful use of, or threatened use, of force or violence against individuals or property to coerce and intimidate governments or societies, often to achieve political, religious, or ideological objectives."[32] The U.S. Code defines terrorism as illegal violence that attempts to "intimidate or coerce a civilian population; . . . influence the policy of a government by intimidation or coercion; or . . . affect the conduct of a government by assassination or kidnapping."[33] The Federal Bureau of Investigation has defined terrorism as "the unlawful use of force or violence against persons or property to intimidate or coerce a Government, the civilian population, or any segment thereof, in furtherance of political or social objectives."[34] By the State Department, terrorism is defined as "premeditated, politically motivated violence perpetrated against noncombatant targets by subnational groups or clandestine agents, usually intended to influence an audience."[35]

Using these definitions, the following common elements can be used to construct a composite American definitional model:

Terrorism is a premeditated and unlawful act in which groups or agents of some principal engage in a threatened or actual use of force or violence against human or property targets. These groups or agents engage in this behavior intending the purposeful intimidation of governments or people to affect policy or behavior with an underlying political objective.

These common elements indicate that the United States has adopted a fairly narrow and legalistic approach to defining terrorism.

Types of Terrorism

The basic elements of terrorist typologies are uncomplicated. Experts and commentators generally agree on the forms of terrorism found in the modern political environment. Although different labels are sometimes affixed, the same typologies are repeatedly found in academic and policy analyses, and this subject is rather uncontroversial among experts. For example, the following typologies have been described by academic experts:

- Barkan and Snowden describe vigilante, insurgent, transnational, and state terrorism.[36]
- Hoffman discusses ethno-nationalist/separatist, international, religious, and state-sponsored terrorism.[37]
- While undertaking the task of defining the New Terrorism, Laqueur contextualizes far rightist, religious, state, "exotic," and criminal terrorism.[38]
- Other experts evaluate narco-terrorism, toxic terrorism, and netwar.[39]

We will explore all of these typologies in later chapters within the following contexts:

State Terrorism. Terrorism "from above" committed by governments against perceived enemies. State terrorism can be directed externally against adversaries in the international domain or internally against domestic enemies.

Dissident Terrorism. Terrorism "from below" committed by nonstate movements and groups against governments, ethno-national groups, religious groups, and other perceived enemies.

Religious Terrorism. Terrorism motivated by an absolute belief that an otherworldly power has sanctioned—and commanded—the application of terrorist violence for the greater glory of the faith.

Criminal Terrorism. Terrorism motivated by sheer profit. Traditional organized criminal enterprises (such as the Mafia) accumulate profits from criminal activity for personal aggrandizement. Criminal-political enterprises (such as Sri Lanka's Tamil Tigers) accumulate profits to sustain their movement.

International Terrorism. Terrorism that spills over onto the world's stage. Targets are selected because of their value as symbols of international interests.

A DEFINITIONAL PROBLEM: PERSPECTIVES ON TERRORISM

It should now be clear that defining terrorism can be an exercise in semantics and context, driven by one's perspective and worldview. Absent definitional guidelines, these perspectives would be merely the subject of personal opinion and academic debate.

Perspective is a central consideration in defining terrorism. Those who oppose an extremist group's violent behavior—and who might be the targets of the group—would naturally consider them to be terrorists. On the other hand, those who are being championed by the group—and on whose behalf the terrorist war is being fought—often view them as liberation fighters; this can occur even when the championed people do not agree with the *methods* of the group. "The problem is that there exists no precise or widely accepted definition of terrorism."[40] We will consider four perspectives that illustrate this problem. These perspectives are the following:

1. *Participants in a Terrorist Environment.* People who participate in, or are affected by, terrorist incidents are prone to have very different interpretations of the incident.

2. *Terrorism or Freedom Fighting?* Whether the classification of a group or movement as terrorists or freedom fighters is simply a question of one's perspective.

3. *Extremism or "Mainstreamism"?* Whether extremist behavior can move from the ideological fringes into a nation's or people's mainstream.

4. *Ideologies and Ideals.* Whether ideologies that promise a better future can justify terrorist behavior in the present.

Perspective 1: Participants in a Terrorist Environment

Motives, methods, and targets of violent extremists are interpreted differently by the **participants in a terrorist environment.** These participants can, and often do, draw their own subjective conclusions about violent political incidents regardless of the accepted formal definitions that have been crafted by officials or experts. Typically, the participants in a terrorist environment include the following actors, each of whom may advance different interpretations of an incident:[41]

The Terrorist. Terrorists are the perpetrators of a politically violent incident. The perspective of the terrorist is that the violent incident is a justifiable act of war against an oppressive opponent. "Insofar as terrorists seek to attract attention, they target the enemy public or uncommitted bystanders."[42] This is a legitimate tactic in their minds. They are never terrorists from their point of view.

The Supporter. Supporters of terrorists are patrons, in essence persons who provide a supportive environment or apparatus. Supporters will generally refer to the terrorist participants as freedom fighters. Even if supporters disagree with the use of force or with the application of force in a specific incident, they will often rationalize its use as the unfortunate consequence of a just war.

The Victim. Victims of political violence, and of warfare, will rarely sympathize with the perpetrators of that violence, regardless of the underlying motive. From their perspective, the perpetrators are little better than terrorists.

The Target. Targets are usually symbolic. They represent some feature of the enemy and can be either property targets or human targets. As is the case with the victim, human targets will rarely sympathize with the perpetrators.

The Onlooker. Onlookers are the broad audience to the terrorist incident. They can be directly affected by the incident at the scene of an attack or indirectly affected via modern mass media. The onlooker may either sympathize with the perpetrators, revile them, or remain neutral. Depending on the worldview of the onlooker, he or she might actually applaud a specific incident or a general dissident environment. Television is a particularly effective medium for broadening the scope of who is an onlooker. This was evident during the live broadcasts of the attacks on the World Trade Center on September 11, 2001.

The Analyst. The analyst is an interpreter of the terrorist incident. Analysts are important participants because they create perspectives, interpret incidents, and label the other participants. Analysts can include political leaders, media experts, and academic experts. Very often, the analyst will simply define for the other participants who is—or is not— a terrorist.

Many factors shape the perspectives of terrorists, supporters, victims, targets, onlookers, and analysts. These factors include culture, collective history, individual experiences, and group identity. The same terrorist event can be interpreted in a number of different ways by participants, thus causing them to adopt biased spins on events. The following factors illustrate this problem:

- *Political associations* of participants can create a sense of identification with either the target group or the defended group. This identification can be either favorable or unfavorable, depending on the political association.
- *Emotional responses* of participants after a terrorist incident can range from horror to joy. This response can shape a participant's opinion of the incident or the extremists' cause.
- *Labeling* of participants can create either a positive or negative impression of an incident or cause. Labeling can range from creating very positive symbolism on behalf of the terrorists to the dehumanization of enemy participants (including civilians).
- *Symbolism* plays an important role in the terrorists' selection of targets. The targets can be inanimate objects that symbolize a government's power or human victims who symbolize an enemy people. Other participants sometimes make value judgments on the incident based on the symbolism of the target, thus asking whether the selected target was legitimate or illegitimate.

Perspective 2: Terrorism or Freedom Fighting?

The second perspective for understanding terrorism is the question of whether the use of political violence is terrorism or freedom fighting. Members of politically violent organizations will rarely label themselves as terrorists. Instead, they adopt the language of liberation, national identity, and even democracy. Ethno-nationalist and religious organizations such as **Hamas (Islamic Resistance Movement)** in Israel, **Liberation Tigers of Tamil Eelam (LTTE)** in Sri Lanka, and the **Provisional Irish Republican Army (Provos)** in the United Kingdom all declare that they are armies fighting on behalf of an oppressed people, and they are viewed by their supporters as **freedom fighters**. Conversely, many Israelis, Sinhalese, and British would label members of these groups as terrorists.

The declarations published by these and other organizations are in the language of liberation and freedom. For example, the Palestinian Information Center explained that

Hamas is an acronym that stands for the Islamic Resistance Movement, a popular national resistance movement which is working to create conditions conducive to emancipating the Palestinian people, delivering them from tyranny, liberating their land from the occupying usurper, and to stand up to the Zionist scheme which is supported by neo-colonist forces. . . . Hamas . . . is part of the Islamic awakening movement and upholds that this awakening is the road which will lead to the liberation of Palestine from the river to the sea. It is also a popular movement in the sense that it is a practical manifestation of a wide popular current that is deeply rooted in the ranks of the Palestinian people and the Islamic nation.[43]

Likewise, the leader of the LTTE delivered the following remarks on November 27, 2001, the LTTE's Heroes' Day:

The Tamil people want to maintain their national identity and to live in their own lands, in their historically given homeland with peace and dignity. They want to determine their own political and economic life; they want to be on their own. These are the basic political aspirations of the Tamil people. It is neither separatism nor terrorism.[44]

Despite the seemingly noble aspirations embodied in the Hamas and LTTE statements, both conflicts have been markedly violent and have included many assassinations and terrorist bombings, as well as thousands of deaths. However, as ruthless as the LTTE and Hamas organizations have been, their opponents—the Sri Lankan and Israeli governments—have regularly applied repressive measures against them, including physically coercive interrogations and assassinations. This repression has fueled fresh support for the rebellions.

Sinn Féin, the aboveground Irish republican political party that champions the unification of Northern Ireland with the Republic of Ireland, remarked in a statement titled "The Conditions for Peace in Ireland,"

The root cause of the conflict in Ireland is the denial of democracy, the refusal by the British government to allow the Irish people to exercise their right to national self-determination. The solution to the conflict in Ireland lies in the democratic exercise of that right in the form of national reunification, national independence and sovereignty.[45]

Although Sinn Féin participated in the successful brokering of a peace agreement between the Provos and their opponents, it has historically championed many of the Provos' "martyrs" and their common goal of unification.

These cases exemplify the important role of perspective in defining one's champions or opponents, and how the absence of a definitional model relegates the debate of terrorism or freedom fighting to one of opposing values and opinions.

Perspective 3: Extremism or "Mainstreamism"?

The third perspective for understanding terrorism is the question of whether political violence always lies at the political fringes of society, or whether it is in fact a rational choice of some mainstream. Members of organizations such as Hamas, the LTTE, and the Provos (prior to the peace accord) readily acknowledge that their methods are extreme but justify them as being proportional to the force used by the agents of their oppressors. In Colombia, the **Revolutionary Armed Forces of Colombia (FARC)** argued that the Colombian government's response to FARC peace initiatives

> was to strengthen the quasi-official death squads, the most despicable form of extermination. In this way, they cold-bloodedly annihilated the opposition political parties, union leaders, defenders of human rights, priests, peasant leaders and democratic personalities, among others. . . . From the moment a new agreement was made with President Andres Pastrana to establish the talks at San Vicente del Caguan on Jan. 7, 1999, the savagery grew. No week passed without a massacre, a murder or a forced evacuation, all done in the name of the paramilitaries but planned in the military bases. It is the realization of the imperialist doctrine of internal security.[46]

Governments have also adopted authoritarian measures to counter domestic threats from perceived subversives. They likewise rationalize their behavior as a proportional response to an immediate threat. Both the Chilean and Argentine armed forces seized power during the 1970s and engaged in widespread violent repression of dissidents. An estimated 30,000 people disappeared in Argentina during the so-called **Dirty War** waged by its military government from 1976 to 1983. The Chilean and Argentine cases are explored further in Chapter 7.

Thus, from the perspective of many violent groups and governments, extremist beliefs and terrorist methods are logical and necessary. These beliefs and methods become mainstreamed within the context of their worldview and political environment, which in their minds offer no alternative to using violence to acquire freedom or to maintain order. Conversely, those who oppose the practitioners of political violence reject their justifications of terrorist methods and disavow the opinion that these methods are morally proportional to the perceived political environment.

Perspective 4: Ideologies and Ideals

The fourth perspective for understanding terrorism involves the underlying ideologies and ideals that justify acts of political violence. It is not uncommon for members of ethno-nationalist and other organizations to justify their beliefs and behaviors by adopting an ideological ideal that promises a better and more just future.

Ideologies are *systems of belief*; they are derived from theories that explain human social and political conditions. Lowi describes one element of ideology as "a source of principles and a means of justifying behavior."[47] Some ideologies are very intricate, intellectual, and dynamic, such as Marxism. Other ideologies are rather uncomplicated and straightforward, such as nationalism in East Africa,[48] the Balkans,[49] and elsewhere. And some ideologies are nothing more than paranoid conspiracy theories, such as the one-world-government and New World Order conspiracies underlying the Patriot movement in the United States.[50]

Ideologies can constitute political, social, or economic programs. They can also constitute religious, racial, or ethnic systems of belief. The common attribute of all ideologies is that they guide the worldview and manner of living for individuals, groups, and nations.

Chapter Perspective 2.1 **We the Klan Believe**

We believe in the eternal separation of the church and state:

Roman Catholicism teaches the union of church and state with the church controlling the state. . . .

Every Roman Catholic holds allegiance to the Pope of Rome, and Catholicism teaches that this allegiance is superior to his allegiance to his country. . . .

We believe in white supremacy:

The Klan believes that America is a white man's country, and should be governed by whitemen. Yet the Klan is not anti-Negro, it is the Negro's friend. The Klan is eternally opposed to the mixing of the white and colored races. Our creed: Let the white man remain white, the black man black, the yellow man yellow, the brown man brown, and the red man red. God drew the color line. . . .

The Klan believes in England for Englishmen, France for Frenchman, Italy for Italians, and America for Americans. . . . The Klan is not anti-Catholic, anti-Jew, anti-Negro, anti-foreign, the Klan is pro-Protestant and pro-American. . . .

We the Klan will never allow out [sic] blood bought liberties to be crucified on a Roman cross: and we will not yield to the integration of white and Negro races in our schools or any where else. . . .

Source: Excerpts from "The Principle [sic] of the United Klans of America." Tuscaloosa, AL: Office of the Imperial Wizard, 1974. In Sargent, Lyman Tower, ed. *Extremism in America: A Reader.* New York: New York University Press, 1995, p. 139. Reprinted by permission.

In their most extreme application, ideologies permit no deviation from their perceived truth and are completely intolerant of any criticism. Chapter Perspective 2.1 illustrates the rigid intolerance of one belief system.

Several ideologies are discussed in the following sections: **Anarchism**, **Marxism**, **Fascism**, and the **Just War Doctrine**. The underlying themes of these ideologies will be referenced in later chapters.

Anarchism

Anarchism is a leftist philosophy that was an ideological by-product of the social upheavals of mid-19th-century Europe, when civil unrest and class conflict swept the continent, culminating in the revolutions of 1848. Anarchists were among the first antiestablishment radicals who championed what they considered to be the downtrodden peasant and working classes. They abhorred central government control and private property. Frenchman **Pierre-Joseph Proudhon**, who published a number of articles and books on the virtues of anarchism, coined an enduring slogan among anarchists—**"Property is theft!"** In his 1840 publication *What is Property? An Inquiry Into the Principle of Right and of Government*, Proudhon wrote:

> If I had to answer the following question, "What is slavery?" and if I should respond in one word, "It is murder," my meaning would be understood at once. I should not need a long explanation to show that the power to deprive a man of his thought, his will, and his personality is the power of life and death. So why to this other question, "What is property?" should I not answer in the same way, "It is theft," without fearing to be misunderstood.[51]

Thus, the radical undercurrent for anarchist thought began with the proposition that *property is theft*. **Mikhail Bakunin** and his philosophical associates **Sergei Nechayev** and **Petr Kropotkin**, all Russians, were the fathers of modern anarchism. They supported destruction of the state, radical decentralization of power, atheism, and individualism.

They opposed capitalism and Karl Marx's revolutionary doctrine of building a socialist state. Bakunin's theories had a particularly international influence.

Anarchists never offered a concrete plan for replacing centralized state authority. They were not concerned about building a clearly defined vision of postrevolutionary society. Instead, they considered the destruction of the state alone to be their contribution to the future. In the ***Revolutionary Catechism***, Nechayev wrote:

> The revolutionary . . . must have a single thought, a single goal—implacable destruction. Pursuing this goal coldly and relentlessly, he must be prepared to perish himself and to cause to perish, with his own hands, all those who would prevent him from achieving his goal.[52]

A portrait of Pierre-Joseph Proudhon, the ideological father of anarchism. His slogan "Property is theft!" became a rallying cry for anarchists during the 19th and 20th centuries.

Source: Hulton Archive/Getty Images; used by permission.

Bakunin, Nechayev, and Kropotkin believed that revolutionary violence was needed to destroy capitalism and state socialism. Bakunin rejected publication of the cause through traditional media such as newspapers or leafleting. Instead, he advocated achieving propaganda victories by violently pursuing the revolution, which became known as **propaganda by the deed**. Terrorism was advocated as a principal means to destroy state authority. Interestingly, they argued that terrorists should organize themselves into small groups, or cells, a tactic that has been adopted by modern terrorists. Anarchists actively practiced propaganda by the deed. In Russia, **People's Will (Narodnaya Volya)** operated from 1878 to 1881, and other anarchist terrorist cells existed in Western Europe. Around the turn of the century, anarchists assassinated the Russian Czar Alexander II, Austro-Hungarian Empress Elizabeth, Italian King Umberto I, and French President Carnot. An alleged anarchist, Leon Czolgosz, assassinated the American President William McKinley.

These themes have been applied by modern left-wing terrorists and will be explored further in Chapter 5's review of nihilist dissident terrorism.

Marxism

Radical socialism, like anarchism, is a leftist ideology that began in the turmoil of mid-19th-century Europe and the uprisings of 1848. Socialists championed the emerging industrial working class and argued that the wealth produced by these workers should be more equitably distributed, rather than concentrated in the hands of the wealthy elite.

Architects of Communism: Russian revolutionary leader Vladimir Ilich Lenin (left) with Leon Trotsky, head of the Red Army and future ideological rival of Joseph Stalin.

Source: Hulton Archive/Getty Images; used by permission.

Karl Marx is regarded as the founder of modern socialism. He and his associate **Friedrich Engels**, both Germans, argued that their approach to socialism was grounded in the scientific "discovery" that human progress and social evolution is the result of a series of historical conflicts and revolutions. Each era was based on the working group's unequal relationship to the means of production (e.g., slaves, feudal farmers, and industrial workers) vis-à-vis the ruling group's enjoyment of the fruits of the working group's labor. In each era, a ruling *thesis* group maintained the status quo and a laboring *antithesis* group challenged the status quo (through agitation and revolution), resulting in a socioeconomic *synthesis* that created new relationships with the means of production. Thus, human society evolved into the next era. According to Marx, the most advanced era of social evolution would be the synthesis Communist era, which Marx argued would be built after the antithesis industrial working class overthrows the thesis capitalist system. Marx theorized that the working class would establish the **Dictatorship of the Proletariat** in the Communist society and build a just and egalitarian social order.

Marx and Engels collaborated on the ***Manifesto of the Communist Party***, a short work completed in 1847 and published in 1848. It became one of the most widely read documents of the 20th century. In it, Marx and Engels explained the revolutionary environment of the industrial era and how this era was an immediate precursor to the Communist era. They wrote,

> The Communists disdain to conceal their views and aims. They openly declare that their ends can be attained only by the forcible overthrow of all existing social conditions. Let the ruling classes tremble at a Communist revolution. The proletarians have nothing to lose but their chains. They have a world to win. Workingmen of all countries, unite!

Marxist socialism was pragmatic and revolutionary. It was action oriented and was adopted by many revolutionary leaders and movements throughout the 20th century. For example, **Vladimir Ilich Lenin** in Russia, **Mao Zedong** in China, **Ho Chi Minh** in Vietnam, and **Fidel Castro** in Cuba all based their revolutionary doctrines on Marx's precepts. Terrorism, both state and dissident, was used during these revolutions and during the consolidations of power after victory. It is interesting to note that none of the Marxist revolutions of the last century was led by the industrial working class; all occurred in preindustrial developing nations, often within the context of anticolonial warfare waged by peasants and farmers.

Marxism and class struggle will be explored further in Chapter 6's discussion of leftist ideologies.

Fascism

Fascism was a rightist ideological counterpoint to Marxism and anarchism that peaked prior to the Second World War. Its name is derived from the Latin word *fasces*, which was a bundle of wooden rods bound together with an axe protruding from the center; it was the Roman imperial symbol of strength and power and was carried before processions of Roman officials.

Like Marxism and anarchism, fascism's popular appeal grew out of social turmoil in Europe, this time as a reaction to the 1917 Bolshevik Revolution in Russia, the subsequent Bolshevik-inspired political agitation elsewhere in Europe, and the widespread unrest during the Great Depression of the 1930s. It was rooted in a brand of extreme nationalism that championed the alleged superiority of a particular national heritage or ethno-racial group. Fascism was anti-Communist, anti-monarchist, anti-democratic, and anti-intellectual (although there were some fascist writers). It demanded extreme obedience to law, order, and the state. Fascism also required cultural conservatism—often looking backward in history to link the ancient past to the modern state—and it created its own conceptualizations of traditional values such as military duty, the Christian church, and motherhood. Strong antidemocratic leadership was centralized in the state, usually under the guidance of a single charismatic leader who symbolically embodied the virtues of the state, the people, and the underlying fascist ideology.

Italian dictator **Benito Mussolini** was the first to consolidate power and create a fascist state. Beginning with his March on Rome in 1922, he gradually eliminated all opposition and democratic institutions. He was a mentor for **Adolf Hitler**, who led the fascist National Socialist German Worker's (Nazi) Party to power in Germany in 1933. Both the German and Italian fascist regimes sent troops to fight on the side of right-wing Spanish rebels led by **Francisco Franco** during the Spanish Civil War.[53] These regimes represent three strains of fascism that reflect their own cultural and national idiosyncrasies:

1. *Italian Fascism* was nationalistic and expansionistic. It hearkened back to Italy's ancient past, seeking to symbolize the rise of a new Roman Empire. Mussolini sent his fascist legions on wars of conquest in Abyssinia, North Africa, the Balkans, and Greece.

2. *German Fascism* was also nationalistic and expansionistic. Unlike Italian fascism, the Nazis also practiced an ideology of racial supremacy. Nazism looked back to the

Architects of fascism: German *Führer* Adolf Hitler (front left) stands beside Italian *Duce* Benito Mussolini. Behind them are ranking members of the Nazi and Fascist regimes.

Source: Hulton Archive/Getty Images; used by permission.

Germanic peoples' ancient past, seeking to symbolize a time of Teutonic tribal and racial glory.

3. *Spanish Fascism* was also nationalistic but strongly rejected an expansionist ideology. The Franco regime successfully resisted intimidation from Adolf Hitler to enter the Second World War on the side of Germany and Italy. Spanish rightists looked to Spanish institutions and history to consolidate power domestically. They had a strong ideological influence in Latin America that lasted throughout the latter half of the 20th century.

The power of all three regimes was rooted in a strong political party, a leader, the military, and an organized elite. Fascist regimes during this period also took root in Hungary (1930s), Bulgaria (1934), and Romania (1938). Only Franco's regime survived the Second World War, lasting until his death in 1975.

Although the first fascist movement largely collapsed in 1945, right-wing groups and political parties have continued to promote neofascist ideals. Some terrorist groups in Europe and the United States have been overtly fascist and racist. Also, dictatorships have arisen since the Second World War that adopted many features of pre-War fascism. For example, Latin American regimes arose in Chile, Argentina, Uruguay, and El Salvador—to name a few—that fit the fascist pattern.

Chapter Perspective 2.2 discusses the Spanish Falange, which long served as a model for repressive right-wing regimes and movements in Latin America.

Rightist ideologies and neofascism will be explored further in Chapter 4's discussion of domestic state terrorism and in Chapter 7's discussion of rightist ideology.

| Chapter Perspective 2.2 | The Spanish Falange: A Model for Fascism |

The **Falange** party (pronounced "fä län′ kë" in Castilian Spanish) was born from the turmoil of 1930s Spain. A liberal democratic republic had been established when King Alfonso XIII abdicated in 1931. The republic was leftist in orientation, and strong agitation from the far left and the fringe left—anarcho-syndicalists,[a] communists, and radical socialists—spread disorder in the capital city of Madrid and elsewhere. Fear grew that a Russian-style Bolshevik state might be established; this fear was especially strong among the upper classes, the military, the Catholic Church, and the middle class. In 1936, a rebellion among elite right-wing Spanish native troops and Foreign Legionnaires in Morocco sparked the Spanish Civil War, which lasted until 1939. This was a classic case of the depiction of the military as "national savior." The war ended with the victory of the rightists.

The Spanish military was commanded by a Spanish traditionalist right-wing officer corps, many of whom had served in the recent—and bloody—colonial war in Spanish Morocco against the Moorish leader Abd el Krim.[b] At the beginning of the rebellion, the Falange party was a small, traditionalist, and right-wing party. It was not overtly fascist in its orientation, but it championed the values of nationalism, the Catholic Church, order, motherhood, antiliberalism, antimonarchism, and antileftism. Francisco Franco, the most prominent rebel general, was eventually accepted as *caudillo*, or leader, of the rebellion. He successfully revamped the Falange to become his strongest base of support within his broader **Movomiento Nacional**.[c] Falangist fascism was unique, because much of the rebels' propaganda with its appeals to a heroic past, its stress on leadership, and insistence on a Spain untouched by "internationalism" such as Jewry or liberalism or freemasonry was Fascist in tone, but it scarcely went deeper than a justification for the persecution of freemasons and liberals.[d]

Spanish Falangists were strong nationalists, and during the Second World War some even promoted the fantastic vision of reoccupying Latin America and the Philippines. Falangists formed the core of Francisco Franco's political support apparatus. They were independent nationalists and kept their distance from the German Nazis and Italian Fascists during the Second World War, never entering the conflict other than to send one volunteer division—**the Blue Division**—to the Russian Front. This infuriated Adolf Hitler.

Hard-core Falangists could be fanatical, having adopted the slogan "**Long live death!**" during the rebellion against the Spanish Republic in the 1930s. Falangist ideology became popular among elites in Latin America and influenced the political behavior of these elites. Right-wing dictatorships in Argentina, Chile, and elsewhere were influenced by the Falangist example, and the militaries in these societies often adopted the mantle of national savior.

a. Anarcho-syndicalists were radical prolabor anarchists. They championed the working class and organized labor into anarchist "syndicate" groups. They believed that these syndicates would be the central means of organized cooperation after the revolution. Government would simply be a representative body of the syndicates.

b. Abd el Krim is a remarkable figure of the 20th century. His war against the Spanish colony in Morocco caused the deaths of thousands of Spanish troops, including 10,000 at Anual in June 1921. After defeating the Spaniards, he then turned against the French in their Moroccan possessions and essentially fought them to a stalemate. He was eventually defeated by combined French and Spanish forces in 1926. Abd el Krim was exiled under honorable terms to the French island of Réunion. He died in 1963.

c. *Movomiento Nacional* was a coalition of "monarchists, conservatives, business, and the more energetically radical social fascists of the Falange." Campbell, Christopher. "Franco's Spain." In Cross, R. W., ed. *20th Century*. London: Purnell Reference Books, 1979, p. 2349.

d. Thomas, Hugh. "The Spanish Civil War." In Cross, R. W., ed. *20th Century*. London: Purnell Reference Books, 1979, p. 1602.

The Just War Doctrine

The just war doctrine is an ideal and a moralistic philosophy rather than an ideology. The concept has been used by ideological and religious extremists to justify acts of extreme violence. Throughout history, nations and individuals have gone to war with the belief that their cause was just and their opponents' cause unjust. Similarly, attempts have been made for millennia to write fair and just laws of war and rules of engagement. For example, in the late 19th and early 20th centuries, the **Hague Conventions** produced at least 21 international agreements on the rules of war.[54]

This is a moral and ethical issue that raises the questions of whether one can ethically attack an opponent, how one can justifiably defend oneself, and what types of force are morally acceptable in either context. The just war debate also asks who can morally be defined as an enemy and what kinds of targets it is morally acceptable to attack. In this regard,

> There are two separate components to the concept of just war (which philosophers call the just war tradition): the rationale for initiating the war (war's ends) and the method of warfare (war's means). Criteria for whether a war is just are divided into *jus ad bellum* (justice of war) and *jus in bello* (justice in war) criteria.[55]

Thus, *jus in bello* is correct behavior while waging war, and *jus ad bellum* are correct conditions for waging war in the first place. These concepts have been debated by philosophers and theologians for centuries. The early Christian philosopher **Augustine** concluded in the 5th century that war is justified to punish injuries inflicted by a nation that has refused to correct wrongs committed by its citizens. The Christian religious tradition, especially the Roman Catholic Church, has devoted a great deal of intellectual effort to clarifying Augustine's concept. Augustine was, of course, referring to warfare between nations and cities, and Church doctrine long held that an attack against state authority was an offense against God.[56] Likewise, the Hague Conventions dealt only with rules of conflict between nations and afforded no legal rights to spies or antistate rebels. Neither system referred to rules of engagement for nonstate or antistate conflicts.

In the modern era, both dissidents and states have adapted the just war tradition to their political environments. Antistate conflict and reprisals by states are commonplace. Dissidents always consider their cause just and their methods proportional to the force used by the agents of their oppressors. They are, in their own minds, freedom fighters waging a just war. As one Hamas fighter said, "Before I start shooting, I start to concentrate on reading verses of the Koran because the Koran gives me the courage to fight the Israelis."[57]

Antiterrorist reprisals launched by states are also justified as appropriate and proportional applications of force—in this case as a means to root out bands of terrorists. For example, after three suicide bombers killed or wounded scores of people in Jerusalem and Haifa in December 2001, Israeli Prime Minister Ariel Sharon justified Israeli reprisals by saying,

> A war of terrorism was forced on us [by the terrorists]. . . . If you ask what the aim of this war is, I will tell you. It is the aim of the terrorists . . . to exile us from here. . . . This will not happen.[58]

From the perspective of terrorism and counterterrorism, both dissident and state applications of force are legitimate subjects of just war scrutiny, especially because dissidents usually attack soft civilian targets and state reprisals are usually not directed against standing armies. The following "moral checklist" was published in the American newspaper *The Christian Science Monitor* during the first phase of the antiterrorism war begun after the September 11, 2001, terrorist attacks:

- Is it justified to attack states and overturn regimes to get at terrorists?
- Can the U.S. legitimately target political figures like Taliban leader Mullah Mohammad Omar?
- What are U.S. obligations in terms of minimizing civilian casualties?
- What type of force should be used?

Table 2.3   A Comparison of Ideologies

Social conflict in the 20th century was deeply rooted in the application of ideals and ideologies to practice. The adoption of these social and philosophical systems frequently inspired individuals and motivated movements to engage in armed conflict with perceived enemies. The following table matches proponents, outcomes, and case studies of four ideals and ideologies.

	Ideological Orientation			
	Anarchism	*Marxism*	*Fascism*	*Just War*
Proponents	Proudhon/Bakunin	Marx/Engels	Mussolini/Hitler	Augustine
Desired Social Outcome	Stateless society	Dictatorship of the Proletariat	New order	Legitimized conflict
Applications	People's Will (Narodnaya Volya)	Russian Revolution	WWII-era Italy and Germany	State and dissident violence

- When should U.S. forces take prisoners, rather than killing Afghan troops?
- Is there a plan for peace?[59]

These questions are generically applicable to all state antiterrorist campaigns, as well as to antistate dissident violence. It is important to remember that rules of war and the just war tradition are the result of many motivations. Some rules and justifications are self-serving, others are pragmatic, and others are grounded in ethno-nationalist or religious traditions. Hence, the just war concept can be easily adapted to justify ethnic, racial, national, and religious extremism in the modern era.

Table 2.3 summarizes the ideals and ideologies discussed here.

THE POLITICAL VIOLENCE MATRIX

Experts have identified and analyzed many typologies of terrorism. As students will learn in the chapters that follow, these typologies include dissident, state, international, criminal, religious, ideological, and ethno-nationalist terrorism. One distinguishing feature within each typology is the relationship between the *quality of force* used by the terrorists and the *characteristics of the victim* of the attack. Figure 2.1 depicts how this relationship (quality of force and victim characteristics) often defines the type of conflict involving the terrorist and victim.[60]

A Definitional Dilemma: Combatants, Noncombatants, and the Use of Force

Definitional and ethical issues are not always clearly drawn when one uses terms such as *combatant*, *noncombatant*, *discriminate force*, or *indiscriminate force*.

Combatants and Noncombatants

The term *combatants* certainly refers to conventional or unconventional adversaries who engage in armed conflict as members of regular military or irregular guerrilla fighting units. The term *noncombatants* obviously includes civilians who have no connection

When force (whether conventional or unconventional) is used against combatants, it occurs in a warfare environment. When force is used against *noncombatants* or *passive military* targets, it often characterizes a terrorist environment. Violent environments can be broadly classified as follows:

- **Total War:** Force is indiscriminately applied to destroy the military targets of an enemy combatant to absolutely destroy them.
- **Total War/Unrestricted Terrorism:** Indiscriminate force is applied against noncombatants without restraint, either by a government or by dissidents.
- **Limited War:** Discriminating force is used against a combatant, either to defeat the enemy or to achieve a more limited political goal.
- **State Repression/Restricted Terrorism:** Discriminating force is directed against noncombatants either as a matter of domestic policy or as the selective use of terrorism by dissidents.

The following figure summarizes factors to be considered when evaluating the application of different scales of force against certain types of targets.

Indiscriminate force, Combatant	Total war (WWII Eastern Front)	Limited war (Korean War)	Discriminate force, Combatant
Indiscriminate force, Noncombatant	Total war (WWII bombing of cities) Unrestricted terrorism (Rwandan genocide)	State repression (Argentine "Dirty War") Restricted terrorism (Italian Red Brigades)	Discriminate force, Noncombatant

Figure 2.1   The Political Violence Matrix

to military or other security forces. There are, however, circumstances in which these definitional lines become blurred. For example, in times of social unrest, civilians can become combatants. This has occurred repeatedly in societies where communal violence (e.g., civil war) breaks out between members of ethno-national, ideological, or religious groups. Similarly, noncombatants can include off-duty members of the military in nonwarfare environments.[61] They become targets because of their symbolic status.

Indiscriminate and Discriminate Force

Indiscriminate force is the application of force against a target without attempting to limit the level of force or the degree of destruction of the target. *Discriminate force* is a more surgical use of limited force. Indiscriminate force is considered to be acceptable when used against combatants in a warfare environment. However, it is regularly condemned when used in *any* nonwarfare environment regardless of the characteristics of the victim.[62] There are, however, many circumstances when adversaries define "warfare environment" differently. When weaker adversaries resort to unconventional methods (including terrorism), they justify these methods by defining them as being necessary during a self-defined state of war. Discriminate force is considered to be a moral use of force when it is applied against specific targets with the intention to limit so-called collateral damage, or unintended destruction and casualties (this concept is explored further in Chapter 9).

Case in Point   **Are "Hate Crimes" Acts of Terrorism?**

Hate crime is a legalistic concept that is given a variety of labels and definitions. They are sometimes considered to be crimes but at other times seem to fit the definition of acts of terrorism. Hate crimes laws in the United States and elsewhere are a criminological approach to a specific kind of deviant behavior. These laws focus on a certain type of motive for criminal behavior—behavior that is directed against protected classes of people (as defined in the laws) *because of* their membership in these protected classes. Thus, hate crimes are officially considered to be a law enforcement issue to be dealt with by law enforcement agencies.

The definitional debate about what is or is not "terrorism" has resulted in a large number of official and unofficial definitions. A similar definitional debate has arisen about how to define hate crimes, because "it is difficult to construct an exhaustive definition of the term. . . . Crime—hate crime included—is relative."[a] In fact, there is no agreement on what label to use for behaviors that many people commonly refer to as "hate crimes"; for example,

> In the United States, attacks by white neo-Nazi youth against African-Americans, gays, and religious institutions have been referred to with such diverse terms as *hate crime, hate-motivated crime, bias crime, bias-motivated crime* and *ethno-violence.*[b]

Are hate crimes acts of terrorism? Terrorism requires an underlying political agenda for the violent act. In this regard, *not all acts of terrorism are hate crimes,* and *not all hate crimes are acts of terrorism.* For example, dissident terrorists frequently target a state or system with little or no animus against a particular race, religion, or other group. Likewise, state terrorism is often motivated by a perceived need to preserve or reestablish the state's defined vision of social order without targeting a race, religion, or other group. On the other hand, criminal behavior fitting federal or state definitions of hate crimes in the United States can have little or no identifiable political agenda, other than animus toward a protected class of people.

It is when political violence is directed against a particular group—such as a race, nationality, religion, or generalized "undesirable"—that these acts possibly fit the definitions of both hate crimes and terrorism. Terrorists often launch attacks against people who generally symbolize the cause that they oppose. In the United States and elsewhere, many individuals and groups act out violently to promote an agenda that seeks to "purify" society. These crimes are committed by groups or individuals who are "dealing in the artificial currency of . . . 'imagined communities'—utopian pipe dreams and idealizations of ethnically cleansed communities."[c] For example, after German reunification, "street renegades [demanded] a new *Lebensraum* of a purified Germany whose national essence and coherence will not be weakened and 'contaminated' by ethnic and racial minorities."[d] Their targeted enemies were Turkish, Slavic, and southern European foreigners and "guest workers."

The separation between hate crimes and terrorism is not always clear. "Hate groups at times in their life cycles might resemble gangs and at other times paramilitary organizations or terrorist groups."[e] Thus, "hate groups are another example of small, intense groups that sometimes resort to violence to achieve their goals by committing . . . *vigilante terrorism.*"[f] This kind of perspective raises interesting questions about our perceptions of political violence. For example, are the following incidents acts of terrorism or hate crimes?

- "Lone wolf" attacks by racially motivated individuals
- Massacres of "enemy" civilians by paramilitaries
- Communal violence between religions or ethno-nationalist groups
- Genocidal campaigns by governments or ethno-nationalist groups

NOTES

a. Perry, Barbara. *In the Name of Hate: Understanding Hate Crimes.* New York: Routledge, 2001, p. 8.

b. Hamm, Mark S. "Conceptualizing Hate Crime in a Global Context." In Hamm, Mark S., ed. *Hate Crime: International Perspectives on Causes and Control.* Highland Heights, KY: Academy of Criminal Justice Sciences and Cincinnati, OH: Anderson, 1994, p. 174.

c. Kelly, Robert J., and Jess Maghan. *Hate Crime: The Global Politics of Polarization.* Carbondale: Southern Illinois University Press, 1998, p. 6. Citing Anderson, Benedict. *Imagined Communities: Reflections on the Origin and Spread of Nationalism.* London: New Left, 1983.

d. Kelly and Maghan (see note c), p. 5.

e. Barkan, Steven E., and Lynne L. Snowden. *Collective Violence.* Boston: Allyn & Bacon, 2001, p. 105.

f. Barkan and Snowden (see note e), p. 106.

CHAPTER SUMMARY

This chapter presented students with an understanding of the nature of terrorism and probed the definitional debates about the elements of these behaviors. Several fundamental concepts were identified that continue to influence the motives and behaviors of those who support or engage in political violence. For example, the classical ideological continuum is still a useful model for understanding the political behavior of many individuals, groups, and movements. It is also useful for contextualizing the justifications used by the actors for their behavior.

It is important to understand the elements that help define terrorism. Common characteristics of the extremist beliefs that underlie terrorist behavior include intolerance, moral absolutes, broad conclusions, and a new language that supports a particular belief system. Literally scores of definitions of terrorism have been offered by laypersons, academics, and policy professionals to describe the elements of terrorist violence. Many of these definitions are value laden and can depend on one's perspective as an actor in a terrorist environment.

The role of perspective is significant in the definitional debate. Terrorists always declare that they are fighters who represent the interests of an oppressed group. They consider themselves to be freedom fighters and justify their violence as a proportional response to the object of their oppression. Their supporters will often "mainstream" the motives of those who violently champion their cause. In addition, the underlying principles of long-standing ideologies and philosophies—we discussed anarchism, Marxism, fascism, and the "just war"—continue to provide justifications for the support and use of political violence.

In the United States, official definitions have been adopted as a matter of policy. No single definition has been applied across all government agencies, but there is some commonality among their approaches. Commonalities include premeditation, unlawfulness, groups or agents, force or violence, human or property targets, intimidation, and a political objective.

In Chapter 3, students will investigate the causes of terrorism. The discussion will focus on the motivations of terrorists, explanations of terrorist behavior, and cases in point that illustrate causal factors in the making of a terrorist.

KEY TERMS AND CONCEPTS

The following topics were discussed in this chapter and are found in the Glossary:

American Knights of the Ku Klux Klan
Anarchism
Augustine
Bakunin, Mikhail
Berrigan, Daniel and Philip
Blue Division, The
Castro, Fidel
Caudillo
Conservatism
Dictatorship of the Proletariat
Dirty War
Engels, Friedrich
Ensslin, Gudrun
Extremism
Falange
Far left
Far right
Fasces

Fascism
Franco, Francisco
Freedom fighter
Fringe left
Fringe right
Guevara, Ernesto "Che"
Hague Conventions
Hamas (Islamic Resistance Movement)
Hate Crimes
Hitler, Adolf
Ho Chi Minh
Jus ad bellum
Jus in bello
Just war doctrine
Kropotkin, Petr
Lenin, Vladimir Ilich
Liberalism
Liberation Tigers of Tamil Eelam (LTTE)

Long live death!
Manifesto of the Communist Party
Mao Zedong
Marx, Karl
Marxism
Moderate center
Movomiento Nacional
Mussolini, Benito
People's Will (Narodnaya Volya)
Nechayev, Sergei
New Terrorism
Participants in a Terrorist Environment

Propaganda by the deed
Property is theft
Proudhon, Pierre-Joseph
Provisional Irish Republican Army (Provos)
Radical
Reactionary
Revolutionary Armed Forces of Colombia
  (FARC)
Revolutionary Catechism
Sinn Féin
Terrorism
Terrorist

RECOMMENDED WEB SITES

The following Web sites illustrate the classical ideological continuum and the nature of extremism.

British National Party: www.bnp.org.uk/links.html
Council of Conservative Citizens: www.cofcc.org
Earth First! Radical Environmental Journal: www.earthfirstjournal.org
Front National (France): www.frontnational.com
Socialist Party USA: www.sp-usa.org

WEB EXERCISE

Using this chapter's recommended Internet sites, conduct an online investigation of the fundamental characteristics of extremism.

- What commonalities can you find in the statements of these groups?
- Is there anything that strikes you as being particularly extremist?
- Why or why not?

For an online search of different approaches to defining extremism and terrorism, students should activate the search engine on their Web browser and enter the following keywords:

"Definitions of Terrorism"
"Extremism"

RECOMMENDED READINGS

The following publications provide discussions for defining terrorism and terrorism's underlying extremist motivations.

Hamm, Mark S., ed. *Hate Crime: International Perspectives on Causes and Control.* Highland Heights, KY: Academy of Criminal Justice Sciences and Cincinnati, OH: Anderson, 1994.
Howard, Lawrence, ed. *Terrorism: Roots, Impact, Responses.* New York: Praeger, 1992.
Laqueur, Walter. *The New Terrorism: Fanaticism and the Arms of Mass Destruction.* New York: Oxford University Press, 1999.
Lawrence, Frederick M. *Punishing Hate: Bias Crimes Under American Law.* Cambridge, MA: Harvard University Press, 1999.
Sederberg, Peter C. *Terrorist Myths: Illusion, Rhetoric, and Reality.* Englewood Cliffs, NJ: Prentice Hall, 1989.

This chapter's Discussion Box is intended to stimulate critical debate about the role of perspective in labeling those who practice extremist behavior as "freedom fighters" or "terrorists."

The Cold War between the United States and the Soviet Union lasted from the late 1940s until the fall of the Berlin Wall in 1989. During the roughly 40 years of rivalry, the two superpowers never entered into direct military conflict—at least conventionally. Rather, they supported insurgent and government allies in the developing world (commonly referred to as the "Third World"),[a] who often entered into armed conflict. These conflicts could be ideological or communal in nature. Conflicts were often "proxy wars," wherein the Soviets or Americans sponsored rival insurgent groups (such as in Angola), or "wars of national liberation," which were nationalistic in nature (such as in Vietnam).

The following examples illustrate how Cuba became an important "front" in the Cold War between the United States and the Soviet Union.

The Cuban Revolution

The American influence in Cuba had been very strong since it granted the country independence in 1902 after defeating the Spanish in the Spanish-American War of 1898. The United States supported a succession of corrupt and repressive governments, the last of which was that of Fulgencio Batista. Batista's government was overthrown in 1959 by a guerrilla army led by Fidel Castro and **Ernesto "Che" Guevara,** an Argentine trained as a physician. Castro's insurgency had begun rather unremarkably, with significant defeats at the Moncada barracks in 1953 and a landing on the southeast coast of Cuba from Mexico in 1956 (when only 15 rebels survived to seek refuge in the Sierra Maestra mountains).

It was Batista's brutal reprisals against urban civilians that eventually drove many Cubans to support Castro's movement. When Batista's army was defeated and demoralized in a rural offensive against the rebels, Castro, his brother Raul, Guevara, and Camilo Cienfuegos launched a multifront campaign that ended in victory when their units converged in the capital of Havana in January 1959. The revolution had not been a Communist revolution, and the new Cuban government was not initially a Communist government. But by early 1960, Cuba began to receive strong economic and military support from the Soviet Union. Castro and his followers soon declared the revolution to be a Communist one, and the Soviet-American Cold War opened a new and volatile front. American attempts to subvert Castro's regime included the Bay of Pigs invasion in April 1961 and several assassination attempts against Castro.[b] The Soviets and Americans came close to war during the Cuban Missile Crisis in October 1962.

Cubans in Africa

In the post-War era, dozens of anticolonial and communal insurgencies occurred in Africa. During the 1970s, Africa became a central focus of the rivalry between Soviet- and Western-supported groups and governments. Thousands of Cuban soldiers were sent to several African countries on a mission that Fidel Castro justified as their "internationalist duty." For example, in the 1970s Cuba sent 20,000 soldiers to Angola, 17,000 to Ethiopia, 500 to Mozambique, 250 to Guinea-Bissau, 250 to Equatorial Guinea, and 125 to Libya.[c]

Angola

Portugal was the colonial ruler of this southern Africa country for more than 500 years. Beginning in 1961, guerillas began conducting raids in northern Angola, committing brutal atrocities that few can argue were not acts of terrorism. Three guerrilla movements eventually drove the Portuguese from Angola and declared independence in November 1975. These were the Front for the Liberation of Angola (FNLA), the National Union for the Total Independence of Angola (UNITA), and the Movement for the Liberation of Angola (MPLA).

In the civil war that broke out after the Portuguese withdrawal, the United States and China supported the FNLA, the Soviets and Cubans supported the MPLA, and the United States and South Africa supported UNITA. The MPLA became the de facto government of Angola. Cuban soldiers were sent to support the MPLA government, the United States and South Africa sent aid to UNITA, and South African and British mercenaries fought with UNITA. The FNLA never achieved much success in the field. Direct foreign support was withdrawn as the Cold War and South African apartheid ended, although the conflict continued through the 1990s. The MPLA finally forced UNITA to end its insurgency when UNITA leader Jonas Savimbi was killed in February 2002.

Nicaragua

U.S. influence and intervention in Nicaragua were common during most of the 20th century. Its governments had been supported by the United States, and its National Guard (the "Guardia") had been trained by the United States. These pro-American Nicaraguan governments had a long history of corruption and violent repression. Cuban-oriented Marxist guerrillas, the Sandinista National Liberation Front, overthrew the government of Anistasio Samoza in 1979 with Cuban and Soviet assistance.

During much of the next decade, the United States armed, trained, and supported anti-Sandinista guerrillas known as the Contras ("counterrevolutionaries"). This support included clandestine military shipments managed by the U.S. Central Intelligence Agency (CIA), the mining of Managua harbor, and an illegal arms-shipment program managed by Marine Lieutenant Colonel Oliver North.

Discussion Questions

- Che Guevara is revered by many on the left as a "principled" revolutionary. He believed that a revolutionary "spark" was needed to create revolution throughout Latin America. Guevara was killed in Bolivia trying to prove his theory. Was Che Guevara an internationalist freedom fighter?
- The United States used sabotage to destabilize Cuba's economy and government and plotted to assassinate Fidel Castro. Did the United States engage in state-sponsored terrorism? Compare this to Soviet support of *their* allies. Is there a difference?
- The Soviet Union sponsored the Cuban troop presence in Africa during the 1970s. The wars in Angola, Ethiopia/Somalia, and Mozambique were particularly bloody. Did the Soviet Union engage in state-sponsored terrorism? Compare this to the United States' support of *their* allies. Is there a difference?
- During the Soviet–United States rivalry in Angola, Jonas Savimbi commanded the pro-Western UNITA army. He was labeled as a freedom fighter by his U.S. patrons. Savimbi never overthrew the MPLA government. Promising efforts to share power after an election in 1992 ended in the resumption of the war when Savimbi refused to acknowledge his electoral defeat, and a 1994 cease-fire collapsed. From the U.S. perspective, has Jonas Savimbi's status as a freedom fighter changed? If so, when and how?
- The Sandinistas overthrew a violent and corrupt government. The Contras were presented by the Reagan administration as an army of freedom fighters fighting against a totalitarian Communist government. Contra atrocities against civilians were documented. Were the Contras freedom fighters? How do their documented atrocities affect your opinion?

NOTES

a. At the time, the First World was defined as the developed Western democracies, the Second World was the Soviet bloc, and the Third World was the developing world, composed of newly emerging postcolonial nations.

b. At least one plot allegedly proposed using an exploding cigar.

c. *See* Cross, R. W., ed. *20th Century*, London: Purnell Reference Books, 1979, p. 2365, and "The OAU and the New Scramble for Africa," pp. 2372-2373.

NOTES

[1] Hoffman, Bruce. *Inside Terrorism*. New York: Columbia University Press, 1998, pp. 25-26.

[2] Laqueur, Walter. *The New Terrorism: Fanaticism and the Arms of Mass Destruction*. New York: Oxford University Press, 1999, p. 230.

[3] Kellen, Konrad. "Ideology and Rebellion: Terrorism in West Germany." In Reich, Walter, ed. *Origins of Terrorism: Psychologies, Ideologies, Theologies, States of Mind*. Washington, DC: Woodrow Wilson Center Press, 1998, p. 57.

[4] *See* Ellis, Harry B. *Ideals and Ideologies: Communism, Socialism, and Capitalism*. New York: World, 1972.

[5] *See* Cobban, Alfred. *A History of Modern France*. New York: Penguin Books, 1965.

[6] Pryce, Roy. "Italy, the New Republic." In Cross, R. W., ed. *20th Century*. London: Purnell Reference Books, 1979, p. 2109 ff.

[7] Murphy, Brian. "Achieving a United Europe." In Cross, R. W., ed. *20th Century*. London: Purnell Reference Books, 1979, p. 2344.

[8] Lowi, Theodore J. *The End of Liberalism: Ideology, Policy, and the Crisis of Public Authority*. New York: Norton, 1969, p. 71.

[9] Clinton, Rossiter. *Conservatism in America*. New York: Alfred A. Knopf, 1955. p. 12. Quoted in Lowi (note 8 above), p. 56.

[10] Weinberg, Leonard. "An Overview of Right-Wing Extremism in the Western World: A Study of Convergence, Linkage, and Identity." In Kaplan, Jeffrey, and Tore Bjørgo, eds. *Nation and Race: The Developing Euro-American Racist Subculture*. Boston: Northeastern University Press, 1998, p. 8 ff.

[11] Ibid., p. 10.

[12] Ibid., p. 11.

[13] Laqueur (note 2 above), p. 81.

[14] Laqueur (note 2 above), p. 82.

[15] *Webster's New Twentieth-Century Dictionary of the English Language, Unabridged*, 2d ed. New York: Publishers Guild, 1966.

[16] Scruton, Roger. *A Dictionary of Political Thought*. New York: Hill & Wang, 1982, p. 164.

[17] For a good biography of the Berrigan brothers, see Polner, Murray, and Jim O'Grady. *Disarmed and Dangerous: The Radical Life and Times of Daniel and Philip Berrigan, Brothers in Religious Faith and Civil Disobedience*. Boulder, CO: Westview Press, 1998.

[18] Remarks of Jeff Berry, Imperial Wizard of the American Knights of the Ku Klux Klan, Butler, Pennsylvania, March 1998. Quoted in Weller, Worth H., and Brad Thompson. *Under the Hood: Unmasking the Modern Ku Klux Klan*. North Manchester, IN: DeWitt Books, 1998, pp. 40-41.

[19] For an excellent list of traits of extremists, see Wilcox, Laird. "What Is Extremism? Style and Tactics Matter More Than Goals." In George, John, and Laird Wilcox. *Nazis, Communists, Klansmen, and Others on the Fringe*. Buffalo, NY: Prometheus Books, 1992, pp. 54 ff.

[20] For references to the Cuban perspective, see Kenner, Martin, and James Petras. *Fidel Castro Speaks*. New York: Grove Press, 1969.

[21] Kushner, Harvey W., ed. *The Future of Terrorism: Violence in the New Millennium*. Thousand Oaks, CA: Sage, 1998, pp. 125, 126.

[22] Goldberg, Jeffrey. "Inside Jihad U.: The Education of a Holy Warrior." *New York Times Magazine*. June 25, 2000, p. 35.

[23] *See* Schmid, Alex P., and Albert J. Jongman. *Political Terrorism*. Amsterdam: North Holland, 1988. The book reports the results of a survey of 100 experts asked for their definitions of terrorism.

[24] Whittaker, David J., ed. *The Terrorism Reader*. New York: Routledge, 2001, p. 8.

[25] Whittaker (note 24 above), p. 1.

[26] Office for the Protection of the Constitution, ibid.

[27] Ibid.

[28] Gurr, Ted Robert. "Political Terrorism: Historical Antecedents and Contemporary Trends." In Gurr, Ted Robert, ed. *Violence in America: Protest, Rebellion, Reform*, vol. 2. Newbury Park, CA: Sage, 1989.

[29] Gibbs, J. P. "Conceptualization of Terrorism." *American Sociological Review 54* (1989): 329. Quoted in Hamm, Mark S., ed. *Hate Crime: International Perspectives on Causes and Control.* Highland Heights, KY: Academy of Criminal Justice Sciences and Cincinnati, OH: Anderson, 1994, p. 111.

[30] Hoffman (note 1 above), p. 43.

[31] Whittaker (note 24 above), p. 8.

[32] U.S. Departments of the Army and the Air Force. *Military Operations in Low Intensity Conflict.* Field Manual 100-20/Air Force Pamphlet 3-20. Washington, DC: Headquarters, Departments of the Army and the Air Force, 1990, p. 3-1.

[33] 18 U.S.C. 3077.

[34] Terrorist Research and Analytical Center, National Security Division, Federal Bureau of Investigation. *Terrorism in the United States 1995.* Washington, DC: U.S. Department of Justice, 1996, p. ii.

[35] Office of the Coordinator for Counterterrorism. *Patterns of Global Terrorism 1996.* U.S. Department of State Publication 10433. Washington, DC: State Department, 1997, p. vi.

[36] Barkan, Steven E., and Lynne L. Snowden. *Collective Violence.* Boston: Allyn & Bacon, 2001.

[37] Hoffman (note 1 above).

[38] Laqueur (note 2 above).

[39] Ehrenfeld, Rachel. *Narco Terrorism.* Basic Books, 1990; Tucker, Jonathan B., ed. *Toxic Terror: Assessing Terrorist Use of Chemical and Biological Weapons.* Cambridge: MIT Press, 2000; Tucker, Jonathan B., ed. *Toxic Terror: Assessing Terrorist Use of Chemical and Biological Weapons.* Cambridge: MIT Press, 2000.

[40] Riley, Kevin Jack, and Bruce Hoffman. *Domestic Terrorism: A National Assessment of State and Local Preparedness.* Santa Monica, CA: RAND, 1995, p. 2.

[41] Weimann and Winn mention the following societal participants in media events: the direct victims, the terrorists, the broadcasting audience, journalists, and governments. Weimann, Gabriel, and Conrad Winn. *The Theater of Terror: Mass Media and International Terrorism.* New York: Longman, 1994, p. 104.

[42] Paletz, David L., and Alex P. Schmid. *Terrorism and the Media.* Newbury Park, CA: Sage, 1992, p. 179.

[43] Palestinian Information Center. Hamas Web site, www.palestine-info.com (date accessed: November 30, 2001).

[44] Velupillai Pirapaharan. Tamil Eelam Web site: www.eelam.com (date accessed: November 28, 2001).

[45] Sinn Féin. "Freedom: A Sinn Féin Education Publication." Sinn Féin Online: http://sinnfein.ie (date accessed: November 30, 2001).

[46] Fuerzas Armados Revolucionarias de Colombia. Resistencia page on the FARC Web site: www.contrast.org/mirrors/farc (date accessed: October 11, 2002).

[47] Lowi, Theodore J. *The End of Liberalism: Ideology, Policy, and the Crisis of Public Authority.* New York: Norton, 1969, p. 3.

[48] Communal violence between Hutus and Tutsis in Rwanda and Burundi has claimed hundreds of thousands of lives in the post-War era. The International Committee of the Red Cross estimates in its *Annual Report 1996* that hundreds of thousands were killed or injured in 1996 in Burundi alone.

[49] Since the breakup of Yugoslavia, wars have been fought in Slovenia, Croatia, Bosnia, Macedonia, and the Kosovo region of Serbia.

[50] *See* Stern, Kenneth S. *A Force upon the Plain: The American Militia Movement and the Politics of Hate.* New York: Simon & Schuster, 1996.

[51] Kelley, Donald R., and Bonnie G. Smith, eds. *Proudhon: What Is Property?* Cambridge, UK: Cambridge University Press, 1994, p. 13.

[52] Quoted in Ferracuti, Franco. "Ideology and Repentance: Terrorism in Italy." In Reich, Walter, ed. *Origins of Terrorism: Psychologies, Ideologies, Theologies, States of Mind.* Washington, DC: Woodrow Wilson Center Press, 1998, p. 60.

[53] For a good journalistic chronology of the Spanish Civil War, see Haigh, R. H., D. S. Morris, and A. R. Peters. *The Guardian Book of the Spanish Civil War.* Aldershot, Hants, UK: Wildwood House, 1987.

[54] Janis, Mark W. *An Introduction to International Law*, 3d ed. New York: Aspen Law & Business, 1999, p. 171.

[55] Stern, Jessica. *The Ultimate Terrorists*. Cambridge, MA: Harvard University Press, 1999, p. 18.

[56] *See* Hurwood, Bernhardt J. *Society and the Assassin: A Background Book on Political Murder*. New York: Parents' Magazine Press, 1970, p. 17 ff.

[57] Jaffar. Interview with Jamil Hamad. "First Person: I Shot an Israeli." *Time*, October 23, 2000.

[58] Sharon, Ariel. "Sharon Vows to Defeat 'War of Terrorism.'" *New York Times*, December 3, 2001.

[59] Tyson, Ann Scott. "Weighing War in Afghanistan on a Moral Scale." *Christian Science Monitor*, October 19, 2001.

[60] This table has been adapted from Sederberg, Peter C. *Terrorist Myths: Illusion, Rhetoric, and Reality*. Englewood Cliffs, NJ: Prentice Hall, 1989, p. 34.

[61] For a discussion of the ambiguities about defining combatants and noncombatants, see Sederberg (note 61 above), pp. 37-39.

[62] For a discussion of the ambiguities about defining indiscriminate force, see Sederberg (note 61 above), pp. 39-40.

Chapter 3

BEGINNINGS: THE CAUSES OF TERRORISM

This chapter discusses the causes of terrorism. Students will identify factors that explain why individuals and groups choose to engage in terrorist violence. Students will also investigate the roots of ideological belief systems and activism and the reasons why such activism sometimes results in terrorist violence. This search for causes requires the examination of many possible reasons. For example, is the terrorist option somehow forced on people who have no other alternative? Is terrorism simply one choice from a menu of options? Or is politically motivated violence a pathological manifestation of personal or group dysfunction?

Experts have struggled to identify the central causes of terrorist violence. Terrorism originates from many sources. The final decision by an individual or group to accept a fringe belief or to engage in terrorist behavior can be a complex process. For example, the decision to engage in violence may be the result of:

- Logical choice and political strategy
- Collective rationality
- Lack of opportunity for political participation
- Disaffection within an elite[1]

It is useful in the beginning of our discussion to identify broad causes of terrorism at the individual and group levels.

At the *individual level,* some experts have distinguished rational, psychological, and cultural origins of terrorism:

> *Rational* terrorists think through their goals and options, making a cost-benefit analysis. . . . *Psychological* motivation for resorting to terrorism derives from the terrorist's personal dissatisfaction with his/her life and accomplishments. . . . A major *cultural* determinant of terrorism is the perception of "outsiders" and anticipation of their threat to ethnic group survival. (italics added)[2]

These factors are only a few of many theoretical sources, but they illustrate the different types of motivations that shape the individual behavior of terrorists.

At the *group level,* terrorism can grow out of an environment of political activism, when a group's goal is to redirect a government's or society's attention toward the grievances of an activist social movement. It can also grow out of dramatic events in the experience of a people or a nation. Although these two sources—social movements and dramatic events—are generalized concepts, it is instructive to briefly review their importance:

Social Movements. Social movements are campaigns that try either to promote change or to preserve something that is perceived to be threatened. Movements involve mass action on behalf of a cause; they are not simply the actions of single individuals who promote their personal political beliefs. Examples of movements include the Catholic civil rights movement of the 1960s in Northern Ireland and the African American civil rights movement in the American South during the same decade. Proponents of this type of movement seek the "moral high ground" as a way to rally sympathy and support for their cause and to bring pressure on their opponents. In both of these cases, radicalized sentiment grew out of frustration with the slow pace of change and the violent reaction of some of their opponents. The modern era has witnessed many movements that advocate violent resistance. Social movements are explored in greater detail in Chapters 5, 6, 7, and 12.

Dramatic Events. A synonym for this source of terrorism is *traumatic* events. They occur when an individual, a nation, or an ethno-national group suffers from an event that has a significant and lasting effect. At the personal level, children of victims of political violence may grow up to violently oppose their perceived oppressor. This is likely to occur in regions of extended conflict, such as the Palestinian ***intifadeh,*** or uprising.[3]

Nations may be victims of traumatic events, such as invasions, that shape their behavior and culture for an extended period of time. The Soviet invasion of Afghanistan destabilized the country dramatically, leading to a breakdown in central authority, civil war, and then the rule of the Taliban regime. In the histories of ethno-national groups, massacres, forced migrations, or extended repression can affect them for generations. The Kurds of Iraq, Turkey, Syria, and Iran have suffered from all of these traumas, including being gassed by the Iraqis in the aftermath of the Gulf War.

Regardless of the specific precipitating cause of a particular terrorist's behavior, the fact that so many individuals, groups, and nations resort to terrorist violence so frequently suggests that common motives and explanations can be found. The discussion in this chapter will review:

- Motives of Terrorists
- Explanations of Terrorism

MOTIVES OF TERRORISTS

Although not all extremists become terrorists, some do cross the line to engage in terrorist violence. For them, terrorism is a calculated strategy. It is a specifically selected method that is used to further their cause. Significantly,

The terrorist act is different in that the violence employed is not only in pursuit of some long-range *political* goal but is designed to have far-reaching psychological repercussions on a particular target audience.[4]

Affecting a target audience is an important reason for political violence. Dissident terrorists—as compared with state terrorists—are small bands of violent subversives who could never defeat a professional army or strong government, so they resort to high-profile acts of violence that have an effect on a large audience. It is necessary to review the basic motives of those who commit acts of terrorist violence. The following discussion reviews four motives of terrorists:

1. Moral convictions of terrorists
2. Simplified definitions of good and evil
3. Seeking utopia
4. Codes of self-sacrifice

Moral Convictions of Terrorists

Moral conviction refers to terrorists' unambiguous certainty of the righteousness of their cause; to them, there are no gray areas. The goals and objectives of their movement are considered to be principled beyond reproach and their methods absolutely justifiable. This conviction can arise in several environments, including the following two settings:

In the first setting, a group of people can conclude that they have been morally wronged and that a powerful, immoral, and evil enemy is arrayed against them. This enemy is considered to be adept at betrayal, exploitation, violence, and repression against the championed group. These conclusions can have some legitimacy, especially when a history of exploitation has been documented. This historical evidence is identified and interpreted as being the source of the group's modern problems. For example, many leftist insurgents in Latin America characterized the United States as an imperialist enemy because of its long history of military intervention, economic penetration, and support for repressive regimes in the region.[5] In fact, U.S. intervention in Central America and the Caribbean was unlike European imperialism elsewhere, because

> [U.S. military] officers shared several convictions about America's tropical empire. They believed the racist canards of their generation that professed the inferiority of Caribbean peoples, and they acknowledged, though occasionally grudgingly, America's obligation to police what their countrymen called "turbulent little republics." Their role was to inculcate respect for rule in what they saw as unruly societies.[6]

In later generations, native populations who shared this kind of history, and who interpreted it to be part of an ongoing pattern in contemporary times, developed strong resentment against their perceived oppressor—in this case, the United States and the governments it supported. To them, there was no need to question the morality of their cause; it was quite clear.

A second setting in which moral conviction may arise is when a group or a people concludes that it possesses an inherent moral superiority to its enemy. This can be derived from ideological convictions, ethno-national values, or religious beliefs. From this perspective, the cause is virtually holy; in the case of religious beliefs, it *is* holy. A sense of moral "purity" becomes the foundation for the simplification of good and evil. In this setting, extremists decide that no compromise is possible and that terrorism is a legitimate option.

For example, a major crisis began in the Yugoslavian territory of **Kosovo** in 1998 when heavy fighting broke out between Serb security forces, the **Kosovo Liberation Army**, and the Serb and Albanian communities. The conflict ended when the North Atlantic Treaty Organization (NATO) and Russian troops occupied Kosovo and the Serb security units were withdrawn. The strong Serb bond with Kosovo originated in 1389 when the Serb hero, Prince Lazar, was defeated by the Ottoman Turks in Kosovo. Kosovo had been the center of the medieval Serb empire, and this defeat ended the Serb nation. Over the next 500 years, as the Turks ruled the province, Albanian Muslims migrated into Kosovo and gradually displaced Serb Christians. Nevertheless, Serbs have always had strong ethno-national ties to Kosovo, considering it to be a kind of spiritual homeland. It is at the center of their national identity. Thus, despite the fact that 90% of Kosovo's population was Albanian in 1998, Serbs considered their claim to the territory to be paramount to anyone else's claim. From their perspective, the morality of their position was clear.

The Kosovo case exemplifies how quasi-spiritual bonds to a territory, religion, or history can create strong moral self-righteousness. When this occurs, extremists often conclude that their claim or identity is *naturally* superior to that of opponents and that terrorist violence is perfectly justifiable.

Chapter Perspective 3.1 illustrates the application of selective and "moral" terrorism. It is a quotation from a document captured during the war in Vietnam from the Viet Cong

---

Chapter Perspective 3.1 — A Viet Cong Directive Ordering Selective Terrorism

The **Viet Cong** were southern Vietnamese communists who fought alongside the North Vietnamese Army against American forces and the Republic of South Vietnam. The communist forces considered this war to be one phase in an ongoing effort to unify the North and South into a single nation.

During the American phase of their long war, Vietnamese communists in South Vietnam routinely used terrorism to eliminate enemies. Assassinations and kidnappings were common, and targets regularly included civilians. Thousands fell victim to this policy.

The following quotation is from a passage concerning the suppression of counterrevolutionaries in areas under American or South Vietnamese control. It is interesting because it orders Viet Cong operatives to be very selective in choosing their targets.[a]

DIRECTIVE

Concerning a number of problems that require thorough understanding in Z's task of repressing counterrevolutionary elements . . .

2. In areas temporarily under enemy control:

(1) We are to exterminate dangerous and cruel elements such as security agents, policemen, and other cruel elements in espionage organizations, professional secret agents in organizations to counter the Revolution, henchmen with many blood debts . . . in village administrative machines, in the puppet system, in enemy military and paramilitary organizations, and in [South Vietnamese political parties].

(2) We are to establish files immediately and prepare the ground for later suppression of dangerous henchmen whom we need not eliminate yet or whose elimination is not yet politically advantageous. . . .

While applying the above-mentioned regulations, we must observe the following:

– Distinguish . . . the elimination of tyrants and local administrative personnel while fighting from the continuous task of repressing counterrevolutionaries in the liberated areas.
– Distinguish the ringleaders, the commissioned officers, from the henchmen.
– Distinguish exploiting elements from the basic elements and distinguish persons determined to oppose the Revolution from those who are forced to do so or those who are brought over and have no political understanding.
– Distinguish between persons with much political and religious influence and those who have no influence or very little influence.
– Distinguish between historical problems and present-day problems.
– Distinguish major crimes with many bad effects from minor crimes or innocence.
– Distinguish determined and stubborn antirevolutionary attitudes from attitudes of submission to the Revolution and true repentance, and willingness to redeem by contribution to the Revolution.
– Distinguish counterrevolutionary elements from backward and dissatisfied persons among the masses.

a. Quoted in Mallin, Jay. *Terror and Urban Guerrillas: A Study of Tactics and Documents.* Coral Gables, FL: University of Miami Press, 1971, pp. 33, 39-40.

by American soldiers of the First Cavalry Division. It is a directive explaining procedures for the suppression of "counterrevolutionary elements."[7] The directive is remarkable because of its instructions for how to correctly conduct the suppression campaign.

Simplified Definitions of Good and Evil

Revolutionaries universally conclude that their cause is honorable, their methods are justifiable, and their opponents are representations of implacable evil. They arrive at this conclusion in innumerable ways, often—as in the case of Marxists—after devoting considerable intellectual energy to political analysis. Nevertheless, their final analysis is uncomplicated: *Our cause is just, and the enemy's is unjust.* Once this line has been clearly drawn between good and evil, the methods used in the course of the struggle are justified by the ennobled goals and objectives of the cause.

A good example of the application in practice of simplified delineations of good and evil is found in Brazilian revolutionary **Carlos Marighella's**[8] influential ***Mini-Manual of the Urban Guerrilla***. In this document, Marighella clearly argues that the use of terrorism is necessary against a ruthless enemy. The *Mini-Manual* was read, and its strategy implemented, by leftist revolutionaries throughout Latin America and Europe. Marighella advocated terrorism as a correct response to the oppression of the Brazilian dictatorship. He wrote:

> The accusation of assault or terrorism no longer has the pejorative meaning it used to have. . . . Today to be an assailant or a terrorist is a quality that ennobles any honorable man because it is an act worthy of a revolutionary engaged in armed struggle against the shameful military dictatorship and its monstrosities.[9]

As articulated by Marighella, terrorism is an "ennobling" option if it is applied by a selfless revolutionary against a ruthless dictatorship. This concept is at the heart of modern *urban guerrilla warfare,* which in practice has involved the application of terrorist violence. From this perspective, the use of terrorism is perfectly acceptable because of the nature of the enemy. Dissident terrorism will be explored further in Chapter 5, and the strategy of urban guerrilla warfare will be explored further in Chapter 6.

One fact is clear: There is a moment of decision among those who choose to rise in rebellion against a perceived oppressor. This moment of decision is a turning point in the lives of individuals, people, and nations.

Seeking Utopia

The book *Utopia* was written by the English writer **Sir Thomas More** in the 16th century. It was a fictional work that described an imaginary island with a society having an ideal political and social system. Countless philosophers, including political and religious writers, have since created their own visions of the perfect society.[10] Terrorists likewise envision some form of **utopia,** although for many terrorists this can simply mean the destruction of the existing order. For these **nihilist dissidents**, any system is preferable to the existing one, and its destruction alone is a justifiable goal. **Nihilist dissident terrorism** will be explored further in Chapter 5.

The question is: What kind of utopia do terrorists seek? This depends on their belief system. For example, religious terrorists seek to create a God-inspired society on earth that reflects the commandments, morality, and values of their religious faith. Political terrorists similarly define their ideal society according to their ideological perspective. A comparison of left-wing and right-wing goals on this point is instructive. Students will recall from Chapter 2 that *radical leftists* are future oriented and idealistic, while *reactionary*

A ritualistic Ku Klux Klan induction ceremony in the United States. The KKK is a long-standing racist movement that lives according to a code of racial supremacy. Its ceremonies invoke mystical symbols such as hooded gowns and the burning cross, as well as the adoption of bizarre titles such as Imperial Wizard and Exalted Cyclops. Klansmen adhere to an ethos of moral superiority that champions white Protestant Christian racial supremacy.

Source: Hulton Archive/Getty Images; used by permission.

rightists are nostalgic. Radical leftists seek to reform or destroy an existing system prior to building a new and just society. The existing system is perceived to be unjust, corrupt, and oppressive toward a championed group. In comparison, reactionaries on the right seek to return to a time of past glory, which in their belief system has been lost or usurped by an enemy group or culture. Reactionaries perceive that there is an immediate threat to their value system and special status; their sense of utopia is to consolidate (or recapture) this status.

Regardless of which belief system is adopted by terrorists, they uniformly accept the proposition that the promised good (a utopia) outweighs their present actions, no matter how violent those actions are. The revolution will bring utopia after a period of trial and tribulation, so that **the end justifies the means**. This type of reasoning is particularly common among religious, ethno-nationalist, and ideological terrorists.

Codes of Self-Sacrifice

Terrorists invariably believe that they are justified in their actions. They have faith in the justness of their cause and live their lives accordingly. Many terrorists consequently adopt "**codes of self-sacrifice**" that are at the root of their everyday lives. These codes are believed (by them) to be superior codes of living, such that those who follow the code are superior to those who do not. The code accepts a basic truth and applies it to everyday life. This truth usually has a religious, ethno-national, or ideological foundation. Any actions taken within the accepted parameters of these codes—even terrorist actions—are justified, because the code "cleanses" the true believer.

A good case in point of ideological codes of self-sacrifice is found on the fringe left among the first anarchists. Many anarchists did not simply believe in revolution, they *lived* the revolution. They crafted a lifestyle that was completely consumed by the cause. Among some anarchists, an affinity for death became part of the revolutionary lifestyle. The Russian anarchist Sergei Nechayev wrote in *Revolutionary Catechism:*

> The revolutionary is a man committed. He has neither personal interests nor sentiments, attachments, property, nor even a name. Everything in him is subordinated to a single exclusive interest, a single thought, a single passion: the revolution.[11]

A review of several recent codes of self-sacrifice is instructive. They are excellent reference points for understanding contemporary terrorism. The following discussion explores several modern quasi-mystical and militaristic codes of self-sacrifice. They exemplify how some modern movements inculcate a sense of superiority—and a belief in a higher calling—among their members. These examples are:

- The German Waffen SS
- Japan's Code of Bushido
- Islam's Mujahideen

German Waffen SS

The **Waffen SS** were the "armed SS" of the German military establishment during the Second World War. They are to be distinguished from the original SS, who were organized in 1923 as Adolf Hitler's bodyguard unit. The acronym "SS" is derived from *Schutzstaffel*, or "protection squad."

From the late 1920s, membership in the SS was determined by one's racial purity. Members were to be of pure Aryan stock and imbued with unquestioning ideological loyalty to Hitler, Germany, and the race. Height, weight, and physical fitness requirements were established. Their image was eventually honed to symbolize a disciplined, respectable, and racially pure elite. This was accomplished by conducting racial background checks and purging certain "morally deviant" individuals from the ranks, such as the unemployed, alcoholics, criminals, and homosexuals.

The SS eventually grew into a large and multifaceted organization. Different suborganizations existed within the SS. For example, the Algemeine SS, or "general SS," were a police-like organization and also served as a recruiting pool. Recruits from the Algemeine SS eventually became the first administrators and commanders of SS-run concentration camps. In addition, a "foreign legion" was recruited from Germany's conquered territories to fight for Germany and was placed under Waffen SS command. A surprising number of non-Germans volunteered to serve in these SS units: From the West, volunteers included an estimated 50,000 Dutch, 40,000 Flemings and Walloons (Belgians), 20,000 French, and 12,000 Danes and Norwegians.[12]

The German-manned Waffen SS units were a special military organization, organized around mobile *Panzer* and *Panzergrenadier* (armored and armored infantry) units. They were an elite force, receiving the best equipment, recruits, and training. They were also strictly indoctrinated Nazis, or ideological soldiers, so that their training "adhered to the very roots of National Socialist doctrine: the cult of will, the attachment to 'blood and soil,' the scorn of so-called 'inferior' peoples."[13] Their war (especially in the East) became a racial war, and the war against the Russians was often characterized as a racial crusade. In essence,

Members of the Waffen SS on parade in Nazi Germany. German members of the Waffen SS were specially selected as pure members of the Aryan race. They lived according to a code that allowed for the ruthless treatment of enemies and "subhumans."

Source: Hulton Archive/Getty Images; used by permission.

The consequence of their training was to dehumanize the troops. Ideological indoctrination convinced them that the Russians and other eastern Europeans were Untermenschen, or subhuman, who had no place in the National Socialist world.[14]

The Waffen SS committed many atrocities during the Second World War. For example, in the West during the German invasion of France, an SS unit massacred 100 British soldiers at Paradis-Finistère. During the Normandy campaign, groups of Canadian and British prisoners of war (POWs) were shot.[15] In December 1944, a Waffen SS unit under the command of Jochen Peiper machine-gunned 71 American POWs at Malmédy during the Ardennes campaign (the Battle of the Bulge). On the Eastern Front and in the Balkans, the SS were responsible for killing tens of thousands of military and civilian victims. Behind the front lines, their reprisals against civilians for guerrilla attacks by partisans (resistance fighters) were brutal. For example, during the time of the Normandy invasion in June 1944, Waffen SS troops massacred 642 civilians at Oradour-sur-Glane in France.[16] In August 1944, Waffen SS soldiers massacred 560 Italian civilians in the Tuscan village of Sant'Anna di Stazzena during an antipartisan campaign.[17] In both examples, the villages were destroyed.

Although not all Waffen SS soldiers participated in these atrocities, the organization as a whole was condemned because of this behavior. At the war crimes trials in Nuremberg after the war, their unmatched sadism was the main reason why the Nuremberg tribunal condemned the SS in toto as a criminal organization after the war.[18]

Japan's Code of Bushido

Bushido, or "way of the warrior," formed the core of Japanese military philosophy from the late 16th century to the collapse of the Japanese Empire in 1945. Modern Bushido hearkened back to the origins of Japan's code of the **samurai**. Sometime during the eighth century,[19] the breakdown of central authority motivated Japan's wealthy landowners to establish a feudal system of service that lasted (in principle, if not in fact) until well into the 19th century. Large landowners retained the military services of smaller landowners in times of crisis. An intricate system of loyalty and service evolved, wherein

> a master/servant relationship grew, whose bonds were strong and whose loyalties were local and personal. When trouble threatened the servant would follow his master's lead. . . . Supporters of the powerful landowners called themselves "samurai," which is roughly translatable as "those who serve."[20]

The samurai became a separate martial class, a kind of nobility, who served their masters with unquestioning devotion. *Bushi* is literally translated as "warrior," so that a samurai was a specific type of *bushi,* or warrior. Throughout Japanese history, the samurai were renowned for their bravery, obedience, and discipline. For example, samurai *bushi* twice repulsed Mongol invasions prepared by the Great Khan, Kublai Khan, in the 13th century. Legend holds that during the second invasion, when the samurai faced likely defeat despite fanatical resistance, they prayed to the gods for victory. That night, a small cloud appeared, grew in size to become a great storm, and smashed the Mongol fleet. This storm became known as the Divine Wind, or "**kamikaze.**"[21]

The martial class declined—for many reasons—so that it became almost a social burden by the 17th century. Beginning in that century, a series of philosophers redefined the role of the martial class and rekindled Bushido. They instilled the class with a sense of duty that went beyond martial discipline and required that they set high moral and intellectual examples.[22] It was at this time that modern Bushido began to take shape. By the end of this intellectual rebirth, the Way of the Warrior had become a code of life service. "The main virtues [that Bushido] emphasized are the samurai's bravery, integrity, loyalty, frugality, stoicism and filial piety."[23] Included in Bushido was a zealous code of honor, wherein self-inflicted death—ideally by *seppuku,* an ancient samurai ritual of self-disembowelment—was preferable to dishonor. Cowardice was considered to be contemptible. Surrender was unthinkable.

By the 19th century, Bushido was a well-entrenched credo, so much so that during relentless attempts to modernize Japan, a rebellion occurred in 1877; an army of 15,000 traditionalist samurai refused to accept abolishment of the class and restrictions on the wearing of swords. During the Second World War, imperial Japanese soldiers were indoctrinated with the martial virtues of Bushido. In practice, enemy soldiers who surrendered to the Japanese were often dehumanized and treated harshly. Conquered civilians, particularly in Korea and China, were brutalized. When faced with defeat, Japanese soldiers would often make suicidal charges into enemy lines rather than surrender. Suicide was also common among imperial troops. Toward the end of the war, thousands of Japanese pilots flew planes packed with explosives on missions to crash into American naval vessels. They were called the kamikaze and were considered—under the code of Bushido—to be the new Divine Wind.

Islam's Mujahideen

The **mujahideen,** or "holy warriors," are fighters who have taken a vow to take up arms to defend the faith. They tend to be believers in a fundamentalist interpretation of Islam who have defined their **jihad**, or personal struggle, to be one of fighting and dying on behalf of the faith.

The modern conceptualization of the mujahideen began during the Soviet war in Afghanistan, which dated from the time of the Soviet invasion of the country in December 1979 to their withdrawal in February 1989. Although several Afghan rebel groups (mostly ethnically based) fought the Soviets, they collectively referred to themselves as "mujahideen." To them, their war of resistance was a holy jihad. Significantly, Muslim volunteers from around the world served alongside the Afghan mujahideen. These "Afghan Arabs" played an important role in spreading the modern *jihadi* ideology throughout the Muslim world. The concept of jihad will be explored further in Chapter 8.

Reasons for taking up arms as a *jihadi*[24] vary, depending on one's personal or national context. Some mujahideen recruits answer calls for holy war from religious scholars who might declare, for example, that Islam is being repressed by the West. Others respond to clear and identifiable threats to their people or country, such as the Soviet invasion of Afghanistan. And others may join as mujahideen on behalf of the cause of other Muslims, such as the wars fought by Bosnian Muslims or Algerian rebels. Regardless of the precipitating event, mujahideen are characterized by their faith in several basic values.

The ideology of the modern mujahideen requires selfless sacrifice in defense of the faith. Accepting the title of mujahideen means that one must live, fight, and die in accordance with religious teachings. They believe in the inevitability of victory, because the cause is being waged on behalf of the faith and in the name of God; both the faith and God will prevail. During this defense of the faith, trials and ordeals should be endured without question, because the pain suffered in this world will be rewarded after death in paradise. If one lives a righteous and holy life, for example by obeying the moral proscriptions of the Koran, one can enjoy these proscribed pleasures in the afterlife. Thus, the essence of modern mujahideen ideology is

> a hybrid and simplistic blend of Islamic fundamentalism. This "Islam" seeks to eradicate all forms of Islam other than its own strict literal interpretation of the Koran. It comes packaged with a set of now well-known political grievances . . . and justifies violence as a means of purging nations of corruption, moral degradation, and spiritual torpor.[25]

As applied by the mujahideen, the defensive ideology of jihad holds that when one defends the faith against the unfaithful, death is martyrdom, and through death paradise will be achieved. One oath of commitment made by a recruit to the jihad in Afghanistan read:

> I . . . state in the presence of God that I will slaughter infidels my entire life. . . . And with the will of God I will do these killings in the supervision and guidance with Harkat ul-Ansar. . . . May God give me strength in fulfilling this oath.[26]

Understanding Codes of Self-Sacrifice

As demonstrated by the foregoing cases in point, codes of self-sacrifice are an important explanatory cause for terrorist behavior. Those who participate in movements and organizations similar to the Waffen SS, Bushido, and mujahideen adopt belief systems that justify their behavior and absolve them of responsibility for normally unacceptable behavior. These belief systems "cleanse" participants and offer them a sense of participating in a higher or superior morality.

EXPLANATIONS OF TERRORISM

There are many explanations given for terrorism. Scholars and other experts have devoted a great deal of effort to explaining terrorist behavior. This is not a simple task. Explanatory models consider many factors to explain why a particular group or people choose to employ terrorism. This calculus includes political history, government policy, contemporary politics, cultural tensions, ideological trends, individual idiosyncrasies, and other variables. Although many terrorist environments exhibit similar characteristics—and groups have historically carried out attacks "in solidarity" with each other—explanations for terrorist activity are not readily transferable across national boundaries.

Finding a single explanation for terrorism is impossible. Nevertheless, experts have identified common explanatory characteristics among politically violent groups and individuals. The following discussion summarizes three explanatory categories:

- Acts of political will
- Sociological explanations
- Psychological explanations

The first category (acts of political will) consists of strategic choices made by ideologically motivated revolutionaries who pursue victory by sheer force of will.[27] The other two categories are theoretical explanations for conditions that contribute to terrorist behavior.

Making Revolution: Acts of Political Will

An **act of political will** is an effort to force change. It is a choice, a rational decision from the revolutionaries' perspective, to adopt specific tactics and methodologies to defeat an adversary. These methodologies are instruments of rational strategic choice wherein terrorism is adopted as an optimal strategy. All that is required for final victory is to possess the political and strategic will to achieve the final goal. The selection of terrorism as a strategic methodology is a process based on the experiences of each insurgent group, so that its selection is the outcome of an evolutionary political progression. Thus,

> Perhaps because groups are slow to recognize the extent of the limits to action, terrorism is often the last in a sequence of choices. It represents the outcome of a learning process. Experience in opposition provides radicals with information about the potential consequences of their choices. Terrorism is likely to be a reasonably informed choice among available alternatives, some tried unsuccessfully.[28]

As a result, terrorism is simply a tool, an option, selected by members of the political fringe to achieve their desired goal. Terrorism is a deliberate strategy, and from their perspective success is assured so long as the group's political and strategic will remains strong.

The evolution of Marxist revolutionary strategy illustrates the essence of political will. Karl Marx argued that history and human social evolution are inexorable forces that will inevitably end in the triumph of the revolutionary working class. He believed that the prediction of the eventual collapse of capitalism was based on scientific law. However, Vladimir Ilich Lenin understood that capitalism's demise would not come about without a "push" from an organized and disciplined *vanguard organization* such as the Communist Party. This organization would lead the working class to victory. In other words, the political will of the people can make history if they are properly indoctrinated and led. Vanguard theory (the notion of a revolutionary elite) will be explored further in Chapter 6.

An important conceptual example will help students better understand the theory of revolutionary change through acts of political will. It is a strategy known as **people's war**. The context in which it was first developed and applied was the Chinese Revolution.

Mao Zedong led the Communist Red Army to victory during the Chinese Revolution by waging a protracted war—first against Chiang Kai-shek's Nationalists (*Kuomintang*), then in alliance with the Nationalists against the invading Japanese, and finally driving Chiang's forces from mainland China in 1949. The Red Army prevailed largely because of Mao's military-political doctrine, which emphasized waging an insurgent people's war. His strategy was simple:

- Indoctrinate the army.
- Win over the people.
- Hit, run, and fight forever.

People's war was a strategy born of necessity, originating when the Red Army was nearly annihilated by the Nationalists prior to and during the famous Long March campaign in 1934-1935. During the Long March, the Red Army fought a series of rearguard actions against pursuing Nationalist forces, eventually finding refuge in the northern Shensi province after a reputed 6,000-mile march. After the Long March, while the Red Army was being rested and refitted in Shensi, Mao developed his military doctrine. People's war required protracted warfare (war drawn out over time), fought by an army imbued with an iron ideological will to wear down the enemy.[29]

According to Mao, the Red Army should fight a guerrilla war, with roving bands that would occasionally unite. The war was to be fought by consolidating the countryside and then gradually moving into the towns and cities. Red Army units would avoid conventional battle with the Nationalists, giving ground before superior numbers. Space would be traded for time, and battle would be joined only when the Red Army was tactically superior at a given moment. Thus, an emphasis was placed on avoidance and retreat. In people's war, assassination was perfectly acceptable, and targets included soldiers, government administrators, and civilian collaborators. Government-sponsored programs and events—no matter how beneficial they might be to the people—were to be violently disrupted to show the government's weakness.

A successful people's war required the cooperation and participation of the civilian population, so Mao ordered his soldiers to win their loyalty by treating the people correctly. According to Mao,

> The army is powerful because all its members have a conscious discipline; they have come together and they fight not for the private interests of a few individuals or a narrow clique, but for the interests of the broad masses and of the whole nation. The sole purpose of this army is to stand firmly with the Chinese people and to serve them whole-heartedly.[30]

Mao's contribution to modern warfare—and to the concept of political will—was that he deliberately linked his military strategy to his political strategy; they were one and the same. Terrorism was a perfectly acceptable option in this strategy. The combination of ideology, political indoctrination, guerrilla tactics, protracted warfare, and popular support made people's war a very potent strategy. It was an effective synthesis of political will.

Leftist revolutionaries adopted this strategy elsewhere in the world in conflicts that ranged in scale from large insurrections to small bands of rebels. Terrorism was frequently used as a strategic instrument to harass and disrupt adversaries, with the goal of turning the people against them and forcing them to capitulate. In the end, people's war had mixed success. It was sometimes very successful, such as in China and Vietnam, but failed elsewhere, such as in Malaysia and the Philippines.[31]

The Fruit of Injustice:
Sociological Explanations of Terrorism

Sociological explanations generally hold that terrorism is a product of intergroup conflict that results in collective violence. The sociological approach argues that terrorism is a group-based phenomenon that is selected as the only available strategy by a weaker group. From the perspective of an opponent group, "terrorism and other forms of collective violence are often described as 'senseless,' and their participants are often depicted as irrational."[32] However, this is not an entirely complete analysis, because

> if "rational" means goal directed . . . then most collective violence is indeed rational . . . Their violence is indeed directed at achieving certain, social change-oriented goals, regardless of whether we agree with those goals or with the violent means used to attain them. If "rational" further means sound, wise, and logical, then available evidence indicates that collective violence is rational . . . because it sometimes can help achieve their social goals.[33]

In essence, the disadvantaged group asserts its rights by selecting a methodology—terrorism—that from the group's perspective is its only viable option. The selection process is based on the insurgent group's perceptions and its analysis of those perceptions. To illustrate this point, the following example describes a hypothetical group's analytical progression toward revolution:

- The perception grows within a particular group that the government or social order is inherently brutal or unfair toward the group.
- Because the system does not allow for meaningful social dissent by the group (in the opinion of group members), it concludes that the only recourse is to oust the existing government or order.
- The group perceives that an opportunity for change is available at a particular point in history. To wait longer would likely mean a lost possibility for revolutionary change.
- After analyzing the contemporary political environment, the group perceives that the government or system possesses inherent weaknesses or "contradictions" (to use a Marxist term).[34] All that is needed is a revolutionary "push" to achieve the group's goals.
- An important ingredient in the group's calculation is the perception that the people are ripe for revolution. What is required is for the group to act as a vanguard to politicize the broader masses and lead them to revolution.

The foregoing analytical progression incorporates two theoretical concepts: structural theory and relative deprivation theory.[35] These theories are summarized below.

Structural theory has been used in many disciplines to identify social conditions ("structures") that affect group access to services, equal rights, civil protections, freedom, or other quality-of-life measures. Examples of social structures include government policies, administrative bureaucracies, spatial (geographic) location of the group, the role of security forces, and access to social institutions. Applying this theory to the context of terrorism,

Structural theories of revolution emphasize that weaknesses in state structures encourage the potential for revolution. . . . According to this view, a government beset by problems such as economic and military crises is vulnerable to challenges by insurgent forces. . . . Other governments run into trouble when their . . . policies alienate and even anger elites within the society.[36]

The state is the key actor in structural theories of revolution. Its status is the precipitating factor for popular revolutions. Popular discontent, the alienation of elites, and a pervasive crisis are the central ingredients for bringing a society to the brink of revolution.[37]

Relative deprivation theory essentially holds that "feelings of deprivation and frustration underlie individual decisions to engage in collective action."[38] According to this theory, when a group's rising expectations are met by sustained repression or second-class status, the group's reaction may include political violence. Their motive for engaging in political violence is their observation that they are *relatively* deprived, vis-à-vis other groups, in an unfair social order. This should be contrasted with **absolute deprivation**, when a group has been deprived of the basic necessities for survival by a government or social order. This condition can also lead to political violence.

One observation must be made about relative deprivation theory: Although it was, and still is, a popular theory among many experts, three shortcomings have been argued:

- Psychological research suggests that aggression happens infrequently when the conditions for relative deprivation are met.
- The theory is more likely to explain individual behavior rather than group behavior.
- Empirical studies have not found an association between relative deprivation and political violence.[39]

Cases in Point

Examples of movements that are motivated against a government or social order include ethno-nationalist movements among Basques in Spain, Irish Catholics in Northern Ireland, Palestinians in Israel, and French Canadians in Quebec. Sociological explanations for these movements are summarized below:

Basques in Spain. The Basque region of northern Spain is home to approximately 2.5 million Basques. Nationalism in the region dates to the defeat of Spanish Republicans during the Spanish Civil War of 1936-1939. After the war, Franco's fascist regime suppressed Basque culture, integrated the region into Spain, and banned the Basque language. Spanish culture and language were promoted in the Basque region. Since the late 1950s, Basque nationalists, especially **Basque Fatherland and Liberty (Euskadi Ta Azkatasuna, or ETA)**, have fought for autonomy from Spain and the preservation of their national identity. The Basque cause will be explored further in Chapter 5.

Irish Catholic Nationalism. Irish Catholic nationalism in Northern Ireland dates to the 16th century, when English King James I granted Scottish Protestant settlers land in Ireland, thus beginning a long process of relegating Irish Catholics to second-class status in their own country. Protestant ("Scotch-Irish") and English domination was secured in 1690 at the Battle of the Boyne. Catholic independence was finally won in 1919 and 1920, but the island was formally divided between the independent Irish Republic in the south and the British-administered six-county region of Northern Ireland. Since that time, some Irish republicans in the north, especially the Provisional Irish Republican Army (Provos), have engaged in armed resistance against Protestant and British political domination. They seek union with the southern republic. The Irish republican cause will be explored further in Chapters 5 and 6.

Palestinian Nationalism. Palestinian nationalism dates to the formal creation of the state of Israel on May 14, 1948. The next day, the Arab League (Lebanon, Egypt, Jordan, and

Table 3.1   Nationalism and Sociological Explanations of Terrorism:
Constituencies and Adversaries

Nationalism is an expression of ethno-national identity. Nationalist activism can range in scale from the promotion of cultural heritage to armed insurrection. Its goals can range from a desire for equal political rights to complete national separation.

Some ethno-national groups have engaged in nationalist activism to preserve their cultural heritage and have opposed what they consider to be national and cultural repression. Within these ethno-national groups, violent extremists have engaged in terrorism.

The following table summarizes the constituencies and adversaries of several nationalist movements that have used terrorism to obtain autonomy from social orders they perceive to have repressed their national and cultural aspirations.

Group	*Constituency*	*Adversary*
Irish Republican Army factions	Northern Irish Catholics	British and Ulster Protestants
ETA factions	Spanish Basques	Spaniards
Secular and religious Palestinian groups	Palestinians	Israelis
FLQ	French-speaking residents of Quebec (Québécois)	English-speaking Canadians

Syria) declared war on Israel. Israel was victorious, and in the subsequent consolidation of power, hundreds of thousands of Palestinians either left Israel or were expelled. Since that time, Palestinian nationalists, especially the Palestine Liberation Organization, have fought a guerrilla and terrorist war against Israel to establish a Palestinian state. The Palestinian cause will be explored further in Chapter 5.

French Canadian Nationalism. French Canadian nationalism is centered in Quebec, where French-descended residents (known as the Québécois) predominate. The French identity in Quebec has always been vigorously protected by Québécois against English domination. Some Québécois are nationalists, seeking grater autonomy or independence from English-speaking Canada. Most French Canadian nationalism has been democratic in expression and has been led by the Parti Québécois. However, a separatist group founded in 1963 known as the Front du Liberacion de Québec (FLQ) engaged in a bombing campaign to promote an independent Quebec. Nationalist sentiment increased during the late 1960s when, during a visit by French President Charles de Gaulle in July 1967, he delivered a speech using the now-famous phrase "*vive le Québec libre,*" or "long live free Quebec."

Table 3.1 summarizes the constituencies and enemies of groups promoting the foregoing causes.

Rationality and Terrorist Violence: Psychological Explanations of Terrorism

Psychological approaches to explaining terrorism broadly examine the effects of internal psychological dynamics on individual and group behavior. This kind of analysis incorporates many of the concepts that were discussed previously in this chapter, such as moral convictions and simplified definitions of good and evil.

At the outset, it is useful to examine the presumption held by a number of people—experts, policymakers, and laypersons—that terrorism is a manifestation of *insanity* or *mental illness* or that terrorism is the signature of a *lunatic fringe*. This presumption suggests that terrorism is a priori (fundamentally) irrational behavior and that only deranged individuals or deranged collections of people would select terrorist violence as a strategy. Most experts agree that this blanket presumption is incorrect. Although individuals and groups do act out of certain idiosyncratic psychological processes, their behavior is neither insane nor necessarily irrational.

Those who engage in collective violence are, in many respects, "normal" people:

> How rational are the participants in collective violence? Are they sane? Do they really know what they're doing? . . . The available evidence favors rationality . . . Although some explanations of collective violence stress psychological abnormality among its participants, studies on this issue suggest that in general they're as psychologically normal and rational as the average person.[40]

Individual-Level Explanations

Some experts argue that the decision to engage in political violence is frequently an outcome of significant events in individual lives that give rise to antisocial feelings. They actively seek improvement in their environment or desire redress and revenge from the perceived cause of their condition. Very often,

> Psychological motivation for terrorism derives from the terrorist's personal dissatisfaction with his life and accomplishments. He finds his *raison d'être* in dedicated terrorist action. . . . Terrorists tend to project their own antisocial motivations onto others, creating a polarized "we versus they" outlook. They attribute only evil motives to anyone outside their own group. This enables the terrorists to dehumanize their victims and removes any sense of ambiguity from their minds. The resultant clarity of purpose appeals to those who crave violence to relieve their constant anger.[41]

Research has *not* found a pattern of psychopathology among terrorists. In comparing nonviolent and violent activists, studies reported "preliminary impressions . . . that the family backgrounds of terrorists do not differ strikingly from the backgrounds of their politically active counterparts."[42] There is evidence of some psychosocial commonalities among violent activists. For example, research on 250 West German terrorists reported "a high incidence of fragmented families"; "severe conflict, especially with the parents"; conviction in juvenile court; and "a pattern of failure both educationally and vocationally."[43]

Group-Level Explanations

In a number of social and political contexts, political violence is a familiar social phenomenon for some people. When this process is combined with "the pronounced need to belong to a group,"[44] individuals can in the end "define their social status by group acceptance." Thus, at the group level,

> Another result of psychological motivation is the intensity of group dynamics among terrorists. They tend to demand unanimity and be intolerant of dissent . . . [and] pressure to escalate the frequency and intensity of operations is ever present. . . . Compromise is rejected, and terrorist groups lean towards maximalist positions.[45]

An important outcome of these dynamics is the development of a self-perpetuating cycle of rationalizations of political violence. This occurs because

The psychodynamics also make the announced group goal nearly impossible to achieve. A group that achieves its stated purpose is no longer needed; thus, success threatens the psychological well-being of its members.[46]

Generalized Psychological Explanations

Psychological explanations are fairly broad approaches to the dynamics of terrorist behavior. Both individual and group theories attempt to generalize reasons for the decision to initiate political violence and the processes that perpetuate such violence. These explanations may be summarized as follows:

- Terrorism is simply a choice among violent and less violent alternatives. It is a rational selection of one methodology over other options.
- Terrorism is a technique to maintain group cohesion and focus. Group solidarity overcomes individualism.
- Terrorism is a necessary process to build the esteem of an oppressed people. Through terrorism, power is established over others, and the weak become strong. Attention itself becomes self-gratifying.
- Terrorists consider themselves to be an elite vanguard. They are not content to debate the issues, because they have found a "truth" that needs no explanation. Action is superior to debate.
- Terrorism provides a means to justify political violence. The targets are depersonalized, and symbolic labels are attached to them. Thus, symbolic buildings become legitimate targets even when occupied by people, and individual victims become symbols of an oppressive system.

Case: The Stockholm Syndrome. In August 1973, three women and one man were taken hostage by two bank robbers in Stockholm, Sweden. The botched robbery led to a hostage crisis that lasted for six days. During the crisis, the robbers threatened to kill the four hostages if the authorities tried to rescue them. At the same time, the hostages received treatment from the robbers that they began to think of as kindness and consideration. For example, one hostage was told that he would not be killed, but rather shot in the leg if the police intervened, and that he should play dead. Another hostage, who suffered from claustrophobia, was let out of the bank vault on a rope leash. These were perceived as acts of kindness because the situation was very tense inside the bank:

> The hostages were under extended siege by a horde of police seeking opportunities to shoot the robbers, depriving the group of food and other necessities to force their surrender, and poking holes in walls to gas the robbers into submission. The captors often acted as the hostages' protectors against the frightening maneuvers by the police.[47]

During the six-day episode, all of the hostages began to sympathize with the robbers and gradually came to completely identify with them. They eventually denounced the authorities' attempts to free them. After the situation was resolved, the hostages remained loyal to their former captors for months. They refused to testify against them and raised money for their legal defense. One of the female former hostages actually became engaged to one of the robbers. This was, to say the least, surprising behavior. The question is whether this was an isolated phenomenon or whether it is possible for it to occur in other hostage crises.

Experts are divided about whether the **Stockholm syndrome** is a prevalent condition. Those who contend that it can occur and has occurred in other situations argue that the syndrome sets in when a prisoner suffers a psychological shift from captive to sympathizer.

In theory, the prisoner will try to keep his or her captor happy in order to stay alive whenever he or she is unable to escape, is isolated, and is threatened with death. This becomes an obsessive identification with what the captor likes and dislikes, and the prisoner eventually begins to sympathize with the captor. The psychological shift theoretically requires three or four days to set in. An example of the Stockholm syndrome during the kidnapping of Patricia Hearst is presented in Chapter 12, when Hearst was kidnapped by the terrorist Symbionese Liberation Army and joined them after being psychologically and physically tormented for more than 50 days.

Summing Up. In essence, then, psychological explanations of terrorist behavior use theories of individual motivations and group dynamics to explicate why people first decide to adopt strategies of political violence and why groups continue their campaigns of violence. Among violent extremists,

> It appears that people who are aggressive and action-oriented, and who place greater-than-normal reliance on the psychological mechanisms of externalization and splitting, are disproportionately represented among terrorists.[48]

Pressures to conform to the group, combined with pressures to commit acts of violence, form a powerful psychological drive to carry on in the name of the cause, even when victory is logically impossible. These pressures become so prevalent that achieving victory becomes a consideration secondary to the unity of the group.[49] Having said this, it is inadvisable to completely generalize about psychological causes of terrorism, because "most terrorists do not demonstrate serious psychopathology," and "there is no single personality type."[50]

Case in Point   **Profiles of Terrorists**

The processes that cause people to become political extremists and terrorists are very idiosyncratic. Individuals adopt extremist beliefs and engage in terrorist behaviors for many of the reasons discussed in this chapter.

Profiles of three revolutionaries championing the Palestinian cause are discussed. These are cases that illustrate the origins of the motives and ideologies of politically violent individuals.

Leila Khaled: Self-Proclaimed Freedom Fighter

During the early 1970s, **Leila Khaled** was famous both because of her exploits as a Palestinian revolutionary and because she was for a time the best-known airline hijacker in the world.

Khaled was born in Haifa in Palestine. After the Israeli war of independence, she and her family became refugees in a camp in the city of Tyre, Lebanon, when she was a young child. Khaled has said that she was politicized from a very young age and became a committed revolutionary by the time she was 15. Politically, she was influenced by leftist theory. One of her revolutionary heroes was Ernesto "Che" Guevara, whom she considered to be a "true" revolutionary, unlike other Western radicals.

In August 1969, at the age of 23, Leila Khaled hijacked a TWA flight on behalf of the Popular Front for the Liberation of Palestine (PFLP). The purpose of the hijacking was to direct the world's attention to the plight of the Palestinians. It was a successful operation, and she reportedly forced the pilots to fly over her ancestral home of Haifa before turning toward Damascus. In Damascus, the passengers were released into the custody of the Syrians and the plane was blown up. Afterward, a then-famous photograph was taken of her.

In preparation for her next operation (and because the photograph had become a political icon), Khaled underwent plastic surgery in Germany to alter her appearance. She participated in a much larger operation on September 6 and 9, 1970, when the PFLP attempted to hijack five airliners. One of the hijackings failed, one airliner was flown to a runway in Cairo where it was destroyed, and the remaining three airliners were flown to Dawson's Field in Jordan, where they were blown up by the PFLP on September 12. Khaled had been overpowered and captured during one of the failed attempts on September 6—an El Al (the Israeli airline) flight from Amsterdam. She was released on September 28 as part of a brokered deal exchanging Palestinian prisoners for the hostages.

Leila Khaled published her autobiography in 1973, entitled *My People Shall Live: The Autobiography of a Revolutionary*.[a] She eventually settled in Amman, Jordan, and became a member of the Palestinian National Council, the Palestinian parliament. She has never moderated her political beliefs, has always considered herself to be a freedom fighter, and takes pride in being one of the first to use extreme tactics to bring the Palestinians' cause to the world's attention. Khaled considers the progression of Palestinian revolutionary violence—such as the *intifadeh* ("shaking off," or uprising)—to be a legitimate means to regain Palestine.

Abu Nidal: Ruthless Revolutionary

Sabri al-Banna, a Palestinian, adopted the *nom de guerre* of "**Abu Nidal,**" which has become synonymous with his **Abu Nidal Organization** (ANO). He was a radical member of the umbrella Palestine Liberation Organization (PLO) from an early point in its history. Yasir Arafat's nationalist **Al Fatah** organization was the dominant group within the PLO. Unlike the Fatah mainstream, Abu Nidal was a strong advocate of a dissident ideology that was **pan-Arabist,** meaning he believed that national borders in the Arab world are not sacrosanct. Abu Nidal long argued that Al Fatah membership should be open to all Arabs, not just Palestinians. In support of the Palestinian cause, he argued that Palestine must be established as an Arab state. Its borders must stretch from the Jordan River in the east to the Mediterranean sea. According to pan-Arabism, however, this is only one cause among many in the Arab world.

After the 1973 Yom Kippur war, when invading Arab armies were soundly defeated by Israel, many in the mainstream Al Fatah group argued that a political solution with Israel should be an option. In 1974, Abu Nidal split from Al Fatah and began his "rejectionist" movement to carry on a pan-Arabist armed struggle. He and his followers immediately began engaging in high-profile international terrorist attacks, believing that the war should not be limited to the Middle East. At different periods in his struggle, he successfully solicited sanctuary from Iraq, Libya, and Syria—all of which have practiced pan-Arabist ideologies.

The ANO became one of the most prolific and bloody terrorist organizations in modern history. It carried out attacks in approximately 20 countries and was responsible for killing or injuring about 900 people. The ANO's targets included fellow Arabs, such as the PLO, Arab governments, and moderate Palestinians. Its non-Arab targets included the interests of France, Israel, the United Kingdom, and the United States. Many of these attacks were spectacular, such as an attempted assassination of the Israeli ambassador to Great Britain in June 1982, simultaneous attacks on the Vienna and Rome airports in December 1985, the hijacking of a Pan Am airliner in September 1986, and several assassinations of top PLO officials in several countries. It has been alleged that Abu Nidal collaborated in the 1972 massacre of 11 Israeli athletes by the Black September group at the Munich Olympics.

Abu Nidal remained a dedicated pan-Arabist revolutionary and never renounced his worldwide acts of political violence. His group has several hundred members, a militia in Lebanon, and international resources. The ANO operated under numerous names, including the Al Fatah Revolutionary Council, Arab Revolutionary Council, Arab Revolutionary Brigades, Black September, Black June, and Revolutionary Organization of Socialist Muslims. The group seemingly ended its attacks against Western interests in the late 1980s. The only major attacks attributed to the ANO in the 1990s were the 1991 assassinations of PLO deputy chief Abu Iyad and PLO security chief Abu Hul in Tunis, and the 1994 assassination of the senior Jordanian diplomat Naeb Maaytah in Beirut.

The whereabouts of Abu Nidal were usually speculative, but he relocated to Iraq in December 1998. In August 2002, he was found dead in Iraq of multiple gunshot wounds. The official Iraqi account of Abu Nidal's death was that he committed suicide. Other unofficial accounts suggested that he was shot when Iraqi security agents came to arrest him, dying either of self-inflicted wounds or during a shootout.

Carlos "The Jackal": International Terrorist-for-Hire

Ilich Ramirez Sanchez, popularly known as **Carlos the Jackal,** was a Venezuelan-born terrorist who became notorious during the 1970s for his violence on behalf of the Palestinian cause. He became politically conscious at a very young age, his Marxist father having named him after Vladimir Ilich Lenin (Ilich's brothers were named Vladimir and Lenin). His father indoctrinated Sanchez in Marxist ideology and literature, as well as stories of Latin American rebellion, when he was a boy. Sanchez came from a family of revolutionaries, with an uncle who participated in a coup in 1945 and a grandfather who led an army that overthrew the government in 1899. When he was 14, he joined the Venezuelan Communist Youth. He supposedly received guerrilla training

Ilich Ramirez Sanchez, also known as Carlos the Jackal. He was personally responsible for the deaths of scores of victims.

Source: Hulton Archive/Getty Images; used by permission.

in Cuba. Sanchez then attended Patrice Lumumba University in Moscow, but he rejected the Soviets' doctrinaire brand of communism.

It was in Moscow that Sanchez learned about the PFLP. He traveled to Beirut, Lebanon, in July 1970 and walked into an office of the PFLP. He was immediately accepted into the fold and began training with the PFLP, apparently in Jordan. Sanchez was given the *nom de guerre* of "Carlos" by Bassam Abu-Sharif, a top official in the PFLP. Later, a reporter for the British newspaper *Guardian* appended the new *nom de guerre* of "The Jackal," named for the assassin in Frederick Forsyth's novel *The Day of the Jackal.*

Carlos the Jackal was a terrorist-for-hire, apparently retained by Libya, Iraq, Syria, Cuba, the PFLP, Italy's Red Brigades, and Germany's Red Army Faction. He has been suspected of committing dozens of attacks, including assassinations, bombings, skyjackings, kidnappings, and the taking of hostages. Carlos's most stunning operation was the 1975 kidnapping in Vienna of approximately 70 people attending a meeting by the ministers of the powerful Organization of Petroleum Exporting Countries (OPEC).[b]

The Jackal's career was terminated when the government of Sudan "sold" him to France in August 1994. French intelligence agents, acting on a tip from the U.S. CIA, seized Carlos from a Khartoum hospital room after he was sedated for liposuction surgery; he literally went to sleep in the hospital and awoke on board a French military plane. In 1997, he was prosecuted, convicted, and sentenced to life imprisonment for the deaths of two French counterterrorist operatives. By his own count, Ilich Ramirez Sanchez had personally killed 83 people.

NOTES

a. Khaled, Leila. *My People Shall Live: The Autobiography of a Revolutionary.* London: Hodder & Stoughton, 1973.

b. The OPEC raid is explored further in Chapter 6.

CHAPTER SUMMARY

This chapter introduced students to the theoretical causes of terrorism and presented examples that represent some of the models developed by scholars and other researchers. Individual profiles, group dynamics, political environments, and social processes are at the center of the puzzle of explaining why people and groups adopt fringe beliefs and engage in terrorist behavior. Social movements and dramatic (or "traumatic") events have been identified as two sources of terrorism, with the caveat that they are generalized explanations.

Not all extremists become terrorists, but certainly all terrorists are motivated by extremist beliefs. Motives behind terrorist behavior include a range of factors. One is a moral motivation, which is an unambiguous conviction of the righteousness of one's cause. Terrorists believe that the principles of their movement are unquestionably sound. A second motive is the simplification of notions of good and evil, when terrorists presume that their cause and methods are completely justifiable because their opponents represent inveterate evil. There are no "gray areas" in their struggle. A third factor is the adoption of utopian ideals by terrorists, whereby an idealized end justifies the use of violence. These idealized ends are often very vague concepts, such as Karl Marx's dictatorship of the proletariat. The fourth motive is critical to understanding terrorist behavior. It is the development of codes of self-sacrifice, when an ingrained belief system forms the basis for a terrorist's lifestyle and conduct. Collectively, these factors form a useful theoretical foundation for explaining terrorist motives.

Explanations of terrorism also consist of a range of factors. The theory of acts of political will is a rational model in which extremists choose to engage in terrorism as an optimal strategy to force change. Sociological explanations of terrorism look at intergroup dynamics, particularly conflict that results in collective violence. Perception is an important factor in the decision to engage in collective violence. Psychological explanations broadly explain individual motivations and group dynamics. Psychological theories also help to explicate the cohesion of terrorist organizations and why they perpetuate violent behavior even when victory is logically impossible.

One final point should be considered when evaluating the causes of terrorism: When experts build models and develop explanatory theories for politically motivated violence, their conclusions sometimes "reflect the political and social currents of the times in which the scholars writing the theories live."[51] It is plausible that

> to a large degree, the development of theories . . . reflects changing political and intellectual climates. When intellectuals have opposed the collective behavior of their times . . . they have tended to depict the behavior negatively. . . . When scholars have instead supported the collective behavior of their eras . . . they have painted a more positive portrait of both the behavior and the individuals participating in it.[52]

This is not to say that analysts are not trying to be objective or that they are purposefully disingenuous in their analyses. But it is only logical to presume that the development of new explanatory theories will be affected by factors such as new typologies of terrorism or new ideologies that encourage political violence. The progression of explanations by the social and behavioral sciences in the future will naturally reflect the sociopolitical environments of the times in which they are developed.

KEY TERMS AND CONCEPTS

The following topics were discussed in this chapter and are found in the Glossary:

Absolute deprivation
Abu Nidal
Abu Nidal Organization
Act of political will
Al Fatah
Basque Fatherland and Liberty (Euskadi Ta
  Azkatasuna, or ETA)
Black September
Bloody Sunday
Bushido
Carlos "The Jackal"
Codes of self-sacrifice
The end justifies the means
Jihad
Intifadeh
Jihadi
Kamikaze
Khaled, Leila

Kosovo
Kosovo Liberation Army
Marighella, Carlos
Mini-Manual of the Urban Guerilla
More, Sir Thomas
Mujahideen
Nihilist dissidents
Nihilist dissident terrorism
Pan-Arabism
People's war
Relative deprivation theory
Samurai
Schutzstaffel
Stockholm syndrome
Structural theory
Utopia
Viet Cong
Waffen SS

RECOMMENDED WEB SITES

The following Web sites provide links to examples of the reasons given for political agitation, as explained by activist organizations and movements.

European Federation of Green Parties: www.europeangreens.org
National Alliance (U.S.): www.natvan.com
New Kach Movement: www.newkach.org
Pan Africanist Congress of Azania: www.paca.org.za
Puerto Rican Independence Party: www.independencia.net

WEB EXERCISE

Using this chapter's recommended Internet sites, conduct an online investigation of the causes of extremist agitation and terrorist violence.

- What issues do these groups consider to have unquestioned merit? What reasons do they give for this quality?
- What scenarios do you think might cause these groups to engage in direct confrontation or violence?
- Act as "devil's advocate" and defend one of these causes that you *disagree* with.

For an online search of factors that are commonly cited as causes for terrorist violence, students should activate the search engine on their Web browser and enter the following keywords:

"Intifadeh (or Intifada)"
"Just War"

RECOMMENDED READINGS

The following publications provide discussions about the causes of terrorist behavior.

Djilas, Milovan. *Memoir of a Revolutionary.* New York: Harcourt Brace Jovanovich, 1973.
Khaled, Leila. *My People Shall Live: The Autobiography of a Revolutionary.* London: Hodder & Stoughton, 1973.
Martinez, Thomas, and John Guinther. *Brotherhood of Murder.* New York: Simon & Schuster, 1988.
Perry, Barbara. *In the Name of Hate: Understanding Hate Crimes.* New York: Routledge, 2001.
Reich, Walter, ed. *Origins of Terrorism: Psychologies, Ideologies, States of Mind.* Washington, DC: Woodrow Wilson Center Press, 1998.

Discussion Box	**Bloody Sunday and Black September**

This chapter's Discussion Box is intended to stimulate critical debate about seminal incidents in the history of national groups.

Bloody Sunday

In the late 1960s, Irish Catholic activists calling themselves the Northern Ireland Civil Rights Association attempted to emulate the African American civil rights movement as a strategy to agitate for equality in Northern Ireland. They thought that the same force of moral conviction would sway British policy to improve the plight of the Catholics. Their demands were similar to those of the American civil rights movement: equal opportunity, better employment, access to housing, and access to education. This ended when mostly peaceful demonstrations gradually became more violent, leading to rioting in the summer of 1969, an atmosphere of generalized unrest, and the deployment of British troops. After 1969, the demonstrations continued, but rioting, fire bombings, and gun battles gradually became a regular feature of strife in Northern Ireland.

On January 30, 1972, elite British paratroopers fired on demonstrators in Londonderry. Thirteen demonstrators were killed. After this incident, which was known as **Bloody Sunday,** many Catholics became radicalized and actively worked to drive out the British. The Irish Republican Army received recruits and widespread support from the Catholic community. In July 1972, the Provos launched a massive bombing spree in central Belfast.

Black September

When Leila Khaled and her comrades attempted to hijack five airliners on September 6 and 9, 1970, their plan was to fly all of the planes to an abandoned British Royal Air Force (RAF) airfield in Jordan, hold hostages, broker the release of Palestinian prisoners, release the hostages, blow up the planes, and thereby force the world to focus on the plight of the Palestinian people. On September 12, 255 hostages were released from the three planes that landed at Dawson's Field (the RAF base), and 56 were kept to bargain for the release of seven Palestinian prisoners, including Leila Khaled. The group then blew up the airliners.

Unfortunately for the hijackers, their actions greatly alarmed King Hussein of Jordan. Martial law was declared on September 16, and the incident led to civil war between Palestinian forces and the Jordanian army. Although the Jordanians' operation was precipitated by the destruction of the airliners on Jordanian soil, tensions had been building between the army and Palestinian forces for some time. King Hussein and the Jordanian leadership interpreted this operation as confirmation that radical Palestinian groups had become too powerful and were a threat to Jordanian sovereignty.

On September 19, Hussein asked for diplomatic intervention from Great Britain and the United States when a Syrian column entered Jordan in support of the Palestinians. On September 27, a truce ended the fighting. The outcome of the fighting was a relocation of much of the Palestinian leadership and fighters to its Lebanese bases. The entire incident became known among Palestinians as **Black September** and was not forgotten by radicals in the Palestinian nationalist movement. One of the most notorious terrorist groups took the name Black September, and the name was also used by Abu Nidal.

Discussion Questions:

- What role do you think these incidents had in precipitating the IRA's and PLO's cycles of violence?
- Were the IRA's and PLO's tactics and targets justifiable responses to these incidents?
- What, in your opinion, would have been the outcome in Northern Ireland if the British government had responded to the Irish Catholics' emulation of the American civil rights movement?
- What, in your opinion, would have been the outcome if the Jordanian government had not responded militarily to the Palestinian presence in Jordan?
- How should the world community have responded to Bloody Sunday and Black September?

NOTES

[1] Whittaker, David J., ed. *The Terrorism Reader*. London: Routledge, 2001, p. 14. Explaining the model developed by Crenshaw, Martha. "The Causes of Terrorism." *Comparative Politics* (July 1981): 381-85.

[2] See Simonsen, Clifford E., and Jeremy R. Spindlove. *Terrorism Today: The Past, the Players, the Future*. Upper Saddle River, NJ: Prentice Hall, 2000, pp. 22-24.

[3] *Intifadeh* literally means "shaking off."

[4] Riley, Kevin Jack, and Bruce Hoffman. *Domestic Terrorism: A National Assessment of State and Local Preparedness*. Santa Monica, CA: RAND, 1995, p. 3.

[5] For an analysis of American intervention in Central America and the Caribbean, see Langley, Lester D. *The Banana Wars: United States Intervention in the Caribbean, 1898-1934*. Chicago: Dorsey Press, 1985.

[6] Ibid., pp. 7-8.

[7] See Mallin, Jay. *Terror and Urban Guerrillas: A Study of Tactics and Documents*. Coral Gables, FL: University of Miami Press, 1971.

[8] Marighella's name has been alternatively spelled with one *L* and two *L*'s. Marighella himself alternated between spellings.

[9] Marighella, Carlos. *Mini-manual of the Urban Guerrilla*. Quoted in Mallin, Jay. *Terror and Urban Guerrillas: A Study of Tactics and Documents*. Coral Gables, FL: University of Miami Press, 1971, pp. 70-71.

[10] For an interesting attack against Marxist ideology, see Djilas, Milovan. *The Unperfect Society: Beyond the New Class*. New York: Harcourt, Brace & World, 1969.

[11] Quotation in Ferracuti, Franco. "Ideology and Repentance: Terrorism in Italy." In Reich, Walter, ed. *Origins of Terrorism: Psychologies, Ideologies, Theologies, States of Mind*. Washington, DC: Woodrow Wilson Center Press, 1998, p. 60.

[12] Masson, Philippe. "The SS: Warders of Hitler's Europe." In Taylor, A. J. P., and J. M. Roberts. *20th Century*. London: Purnell Reference Books, 1979, p. 1733.

[13] Ibid., p. 1732.

[14] Ailsby, Christopher. *SS: Hell on the Eastern Front: The Waffen-SS War in Russia 1941-1945*. Oceola, WI: MBI, 1998, p. 19.

[15] Masson (note 12 above), p. 1734.

[16] For a discussion of the French commemoration of the massacre, see Farmer, Sarah. *Martyred Village: Commemorating the 1944 Massacre at Oradour-sur-Glane*. Berkeley: University of California Press, 1999.

[17] The SS soldiers were allegedly overcome by a "bloodlust." See Carroll, Rory. "Revelations of Wartime SS Massacre in Tuscany Haunt Former Ruling Party." *The Guardian*. November 27, 1999.

[18] Lee, Martin A. *The Beast Reawakens*. New York: Routledge, 1997, p. 16.

[19] Dating the origins of the code of Bushido and the samurai is imprecise and must be approximated.

[20] Turnbull, S. R. *The Samurai: A Military History*. New York: Macmillan, 1977, p. 15.

[21] Ibid., pp. 84-94.

[22] Ibid., p. 282.

[23] Ibid., p. 286.

[24] A *jihadi* is one who wages jihad, regardless of whether it is an armed jihad. Mujahideen are *jihadis* who have taken up arms.

[25] Marquand, Robert. "The Tenets of Terror: A Special Report on the Ideology of Jihad and the Rise of Islamic Militancy." *Christian Science Monitor*. October 18, 2001.

[26] Rohde, David, and C. J. Chivers. "Al Qaeda's Grocery Lists and Manuals of Killing." *New York Times*. March 17, 2002.

[27] For a good discussion of terrorism as a product of strategic choice, see Crenshaw, Martha. "The Logic of Terrorism: Terrorist Behavior as a Product of Strategic Choice." In Reich, Walter, ed. *Origins of Terrorism: Psychologies, Ideologies, Theologies, States of Mind*. Washington, DC: Woodrow Wilson Center Press, 1998, pp. 7-24.

[28] Ibid., p. 11.

[29] For a good summary of Mao's political ideology, see Schram, Stuart R. *The Political Thought of Mao Tse-tung*. New York: Praeger, 1974.

[30] Mao Tse-tung. "On Coalition Government." *Selected Works, Volume III,* p. 264. See Mao Tse-tung. *Selected Works.* New York: International Publishers, 1954.

[31] For a summary discussion of the history of irregular warfare, see Keegan, John, and Richard Holmes. *Soldiers: A History of Men in Battle.* New York: Elisabeth Sifton Books, 1986, pp. 241-58.

[32] Barkan, Steven E., and Lynne L. Snowden. *Collective Violence.* Boston: Allyn & Bacon, 2001, p. 6.

[33] Ibid., p. 7.

[34] Maoists and Trotskyites in particular cite "contradictions" in the capitalist democracies—for example, the existence of democratic institutions and ideologies of equality existing alongside entrenched poverty, racism, sexism, and so on.

[35] Relative deprivation theory was pioneered by James C. Davies. See Davies, James Chowning. "Toward a Theory of Revolution." *American Sociological Review* 25 (1962): 5-19.

[36] Barkan and Snowden (note 32 above), p. 53. Citing Goldstone, Jack A. "Introduction: The Comparative and Historical Study of Revolutions." In Goldstone, Jack A., ed. *Revolutions: Theoretical, Comparative, and Historical Studies.* San Diego, CA: Harcourt Brace Jovanovich, 1986, pp. 1-17.

[37] See ibid., p. 55.

[38] Barkan and Snowden (note 32 above), p. 17.

[39] Discussed ibid., p. 18.

[40] Barkan and Snowden (note 32 above), p. 8.

[41] Crenshaw, Martha. "The Causes of Terrorism." *Comparative Politics* (July 1981): 381-385. Quoted in Whittaker, David J., ed. *The Terrorism Reader.* New York: Routledge, 2001, pp. 19-20.

[42] Post, Jerrold M. "Terrorist Psycho-logic: Terrorist Behavior as a Product of Psychological Forces." In Reich, Walter, ed. *Origins of Terrorism: Psychologies, Ideologies, Theologies, States of Mind.* Washington, DC: Woodrow Wilson Center Press, 1998, p. 9.

[43] Ibid., p. 28. Reporting findings of the Ministry of the Interior, Federal Republic of Germany. *Analysen Zum Terrorismus* 1-4. Darmstadt: Deutscher Verlag, 1981, 1982, 1983, 1984; Jäger, H., G. Schmidtchen, and L. Süllwold, eds., *Analysen Zum Terrorismus 2: Lebenlaufanalysen.* Darmstadt: Deutscher Verlag, 1981; and von Baeyer-Kaette, W., D. Classens, H. Feger, and F. Neidhardt, eds. *Analysen Zum Terrorismus 3: Gruppeprozesse.* Darmstadt: Deutscher Verlag, 1982.

[44] Post, p. 28.

[45] Ibid., p. 20.

[46] Ibid.

[47] Bandura, Albert. "Mechanisms of Moral Disengagement." In Reich, Walter, ed. *Origins of Terrorism: Psychologies, Ideologies, Theologies, States of Mind.* Washington, DC: Woodrow Wilson Center Press, 1998, p. 183.

[48] Post (note 42 above), p. 9.

[49] Ibid., pp. 25-42.

[50] Ibid., p. 31.

[51] Barkan and Snowden (note 32 above), p. 27.

[52] Ibid., pp. 27-28.

Part II

THE TERRORISTS

Ulrike Meinhof and Gudrun Ensslin, prominent members of West Germany's Red Army Faction, also known as the Baader-Meinhof Gang. Both committed suicide in prison.

Source: Hulton Archive/Getty Images; used by permission.

Chapter 4

TERROR FROM ABOVE: STATE TERRORISM

T his chapter discusses the characteristics of "terrorism from above"—state terrorism—committed by governments and quasi-governmental agencies and personnel against perceived enemies. State terrorism can be directed externally against adversaries in the international domain or internally against domestic enemies. Students will explore the various types of state terrorism and will acquire an appreciation for the qualities that characterize each state terrorist typology. A state terrorist paradigm will be discussed, and cases in point will be applied to understand what is meant by *terrorism as foreign policy* and *terrorism as domestic policy*.

It is important to understand conceptually that political violence by the state is the most organized, and potentially the most far-reaching, application of terrorist violence. Because of the many resources available to the state, its ability to commit acts of violence far exceeds in scale the kind of violence perpetrated by antistate dissident terrorists. Only communal dissident terrorism (group-against-group violence) potentially approximates the scale of state-sponsored terror.[1] Dissident terrorism will be explored further in Chapter 5.

Why do governments use terrorism as an instrument of foreign policy? What is the benefit of applying terrorism domestically? How do states justify their involvement in either international or domestic terrorism? The answers to these questions generally incorporate the following considerations:

1. *Internationally*, the state defines its interests in a number of ways, usually within the context of political, economic, or ideological considerations. When promoting or defending these interests, governments can choose to behave unilaterally or cooperatively, and cautiously or aggressively.

2. *Domestically,* the state's interests involve the need to maintain internal security and order. When threatened domestically, some regimes react with great vigor and violence.

In both the international and domestic domains, states will choose from a range of overt and covert (secret) options.

Terrorism by states is characterized by official support for policies of violence, repression, and intimidation. This violence and coercion is directed against perceived enemies that the state has determined threaten its interests or security. Although the perpetrators of state terrorist campaigns are frequently government personnel, and directives do originate from government officials, those who carry out the violence are also quite often unofficial agents of the government.

An example illustrating this concept is the violent suppression campaign against the pro-independence movement in the former Indonesian province of East Timor. East Timor comprises the eastern half of the island of Timor, which is located at the southeastern corner of the Indonesian archipelago northwest of Australia. East Timor is unique in the region because it was ruled for centuries as a Portuguese colony and its population is predominantly Roman Catholic. Portugal announced in 1975 that it would withdraw in 1978 after occupying the territory for more than 450 years. The Indonesian army invaded East Timor in December 1975 and annexed the territory in 1976. During the turmoil that followed, more than 200,000 Timorese were killed in the fighting or were starved during a famine. At the same time that the Indonesian army committed numerous atrocities— including killing scores of protesters by firing on a prodemocracy protest in November 1991—the government encouraged the operations of pro-Indonesian paramilitaries. The paramilitaries were armed by the government and permitted to wage an extended campaign of terror for nearly two decades against East Timor's pro-independence movement. This violence became particularly brutal in 1999 as the territory moved toward a vote for independence. For example, in April 1999 a paramilitary murdered about 25 people in a churchyard. The long period of violence ended in September 1999 when Indonesia gave control of East Timor to United Nations peacekeepers. Under UN supervision, East Timor's first presidential elections were held in April 2002, and former resistance leader Xanana Gusmao won in a landslide victory.

The East Timor case illustrates the common strategy of using violent state-sponsored proxies (paramilitaries in this example) as an instrument of official state repression to violently enforce state authority. The discussion in this chapter will review the following:

- Monitoring State Terrorism
- A State Terrorism Paradigm
- State Terrorism as Foreign Policy
- State Terrorism as Domestic Policy

MONITORING STATE TERRORISM

The incidence of state-sponsored terrorism is monitored by public and private organizations. These organizations compile data and publish annual reports on domestic and international state terrorism. They also perform a "watchdog" function and are resources for collecting data on state terrorism. These agencies provide useful standards for identifying and defining terrorist behavior by governments.

In the *international policy domain*, the U.S. Department of State regularly compiles a list of state sponsors of international terrorism. This list includes an annual list of countries that the Department of State has designated as state terrorist sponsors. The following comments from the Department of State's 2001 report summarize the types of behavior it defines as state-sponsored international terrorism:

- *Iran* was considered by the State Department to be the "most active state sponsor of terrorism in 2001." Iran continued its support to numerous terrorist groups, including Hezbollah in Lebanon, Hamas, the Popular Front for the Liberation of Palestine–General Command, and the Palestine Islamic Jihad (PIJ).
- *Iraq* provided safe haven and support to a variety of Palestinian groups, such as the Palestine Liberation Front, the Popular Front for the Liberation of Palestine, and the

Abu Nidal Organization. Iraq also provided bases, weapons, and protection to the Kurdistan Workers' Party and the Mujahedin-e-Khalq (MEK), an Iranian terrorist group that opposes the current Iranian regime.

- *Syria* condemned the September 11, 2001, attacks and pledged to investigate Al Qaeda and other terrorist groups. Nevertheless, Syria continued to provide safe haven in the Syrian-controlled **Beka'a Valley** of Lebanon for the Popular Front for the Liberation of Palestine–General Command, Palestine Islamic Jihad, and Hamas.
- *Libya* repeatedly denounced terrorism after the September 11, 2001, attacks on the United States homeland as part of its ongoing effort to mend its image as a state sponsor of terrorism.
- *Cuba* continued to provide safe haven to Basque Fatherland and Liberty terrorists, members of Colombia's Revolutionary Armed Forces of Colombia and National Liberation Army movements, and several U.S. fugitives.
- *North Korea*'s cooperation in international efforts to curtail international terrorism after the September 11, 2001, attacks was described as "disappointing" by the State Department. In addition, North Korea continued to harbor several hijackers of a 1970s Japanese Airlines flight to North Korea, and evidence suggests that arms may have been sold to terrorist groups.
- *Sudan* condemned the September 11, 2001, attacks and pledged its cooperation in international counterterrorism. Nevertheless, Sudan continued to serve as a safe haven for members of Al Qaeda, Hezbollah, al-Gama'a al-Islamiyya, Egyptian Islamic Jihad, Palestine Islamic Jihad, and Hamas.[2]

It is important to note that the State Department's list includes countries that have significantly reduced their involvement in terrorism, such as North Korea and Cuba. For example, North Korea was at one time quite active in attacking South Korean interests. In November 1987, North Korean operatives apparently destroyed **Korean Airlines Flight 858,** which exploded over Myanmar (Burma). The North Korean government has since renounced its sponsorship of terrorism.

In the *domestic policy domain,* several private agencies monitor political abuses by governments and have catalogued examples of state-sponsored domestic terrorism. These organizations usually refer to these abuses as "human rights violations." One such group, **Human Rights Watch**, was founded in 1978.[3] Human Rights Watch actively monitors the status of human rights throughout the world and maintains field offices in closely monitored countries. It reports in detail on government-sponsored and internecine violations of human rights. Another organization, **Amnesty International**, was founded in 1961. In 1983, Amnesty International published a special report on political killings by governments, which described government political killings as

> unlawful and deliberate killings of persons by reasons of their real or imputed political beliefs or activities, religion, other conscientiously held beliefs, ethnic origin, sex, colour or language, carried out by order of a government with its complicity.[4]

Both Human Rights Watch and Amnesty International promote publicity campaigns from time to time to highlight specific human rights issues. The purpose of these campaigns is to focus the world's attention on particularly urgent human rights issues.

All of these approaches to the analysis of state terrorism are useful for evaluating different types of state-sponsored political violence. To simplify our analysis, the following discussion presents a model for understanding the basic characteristics of state sponsorship of terrorism. It first contrasts state patronage and state assistance for terrorism and then applies this distinction to the international and domestic policy domains.

A STATE TERRORISM PARADIGM

A **paradigm** is "a pattern, example, or model"[5] that is logically developed to represent a concept. Paradigms represent theoretical concepts that are accepted among experts, and they can be useful for practitioners to design policy agendas. When paradigms change—commonly called a "paradigm shift"—it is often because new environmental factors persuade experts to thoroughly reassess existing theories and assumptions. A dissident terrorism paradigm will be presented in Chapter 5.

Experts and scholars have designed a number of models to describe state terrorism. These constructs have been developed to identify distinctive patterns of state-sponsored terrorist behavior. Experts agree that several typologies of state involvement in terrorism can be differentiated. For example, one model[6] describes state-level participants in a security environment as including the following:

- *Sponsors* of terrorism, meaning those states that actively promote terrorism and that have been formally designated as "rogue states" or state sponsors under U.S. law.[7]
- *Enablers* of terrorism, or those states that operate in an environment wherein "being part of the problem means not just failing to cooperate fully in countering terrorism but also doing some things that help enable it to occur."[8]
- *Cooperators* in counterterrorism efforts, including unique security environments wherein "cooperation on counterterrorism is often feasible despite significant disagreements on other subjects."[9]

State terrorism incorporates many types and degrees of violence. The intensity of this violence may range in scale from single acts of coercion to extended campaigns of terrorist violence. One model describes the scale of violence as including the following:

- In **warfare**, the conventional military forces of a state are marshaled against an enemy. The enemy is either a conventional or guerrilla combatant and may be an internal or external adversary. This is a highly organized and complicated application of state violence.
- In **genocide**, the state applies its resources toward the elimination of a scapegoat group. The basic characteristic of state-sponsored genocidal violence is that it does not differentiate between enemy combatants and enemy civilians; all members of the scapegoat group are considered to be enemies. Like warfare, this is often a highly organized and complicated application of state violence.
- **Assassinations** are selective applications of homicidal state violence, whereby a single person or a specified group of people is designated for elimination. This is a lower-scale application of state violence.
- Torture is used by some states as an instrument of intimidation, interrogation, and humiliation. Like assassinations, it is a selective application of state violence directed against a single person or a specified group of people. Although it is often a lower-scale application of state violence, many regimes will make widespread use of torture during states of emergency.[10]

A number of experts consider the quality of violence to be central to the analysis of state terrorism and have drawn distinctions between different types of state coercion. Thus,

Some analysts distinguish between *oppression* and *repression*. Oppression is essentially a condition of exploitation and deprivation . . ., and repression is action against those who are seen to be threats to the established order.[11]

Table 4.1   State Sponsorship of Terrorism

State participation in terrorist and extremist behavior can involve either direct or indirect sponsorship and can be conducted in the international or domestic policy domains. State *patronage* refers to relatively direct linkages between a regime and political violence. State *assistance* refers to relatively indirect linkages. The following table distinguishes state patronage and assistance in the international and domestic policy domains.

Domain	Type of Sponsorship	
	Patronage	*Assistance*
International	International violence conducted on government orders	International violence with government encouragement and support
	Case: Assassination of former Iranian Prime Minister Shahpour Bakhtiar in France	Case: Pakistani assistance for anti-Indian extremists in Jammu and Kashmir (the **Jammu Kashmir Liberation Front**)
Domestic	Domestic repression by government personnel	Domestic repression by progovernment extremists
	Case: Argentina's "Dirty War"	Case: Violence by rightist paramilitaries in El Salvador

Understanding State-Sponsored Terrorism

Linkages between regimes and terrorism can range from very clear lines of sponsorship to very murky and indefinable associations. States that are inclined to use terrorism as an instrument of statecraft are often able to control the parameters for their involvement, so that governments can sometimes manage how precisely a movement or an incident can be traced back to its personnel. For example, the Soviet Union established the **Patrice Lumumba Peoples Friendship University** in Moscow. Named for the martyred Congolese Prime Minister **Patrice Lumumba,** the university recruited students from throughout the developing world. Much of its curriculum was composed of standard higher education courses. However, students also received instruction in Marxist theory, observed firearms demonstrations, and were networked with pro-Soviet "liberation" movements. Patrice Lumumba University was also used by the KGB, the Soviet intelligence service, to recruit students for more intensive training in the intricacies of national liberation. Many graduates went on to become leaders in a number of extremist movements. Many Palestinian nationalists attended the university, as did the Venezuelan terrorist Ilich Ramirez Sanchez, also known as Carlos the Jackal.

Thus, state sponsorship of terrorism is not always a straightforward process. It is frequently a covert, secret policy that allows states to claim "deniability" when accused of sponsoring terrorism. Because of these veiled parameters, a distinction must be made between **state patronage** and **state assistance for terrorism.**

As discussed in the next section, the basic characteristic of state patronage is that the state is overtly and directly linked to terrorist behavior. The basic characteristic of state assistance is that the state is tacitly and indirectly linked to terrorist behavior. These are two subtly distinct concepts that are summarized in Table 4.1.

State Sponsorship: The Patronage Model

State patronage for terrorism refers to active participation in, and encouragement of, terrorist behavior. Its basic characteristic is that the state, through its agencies and personnel, actively takes part in repression, violence, and terrorism. Thus, state patrons adopt policies that *initiate* terrorism and other subversive activities—including directly arming, training, and providing sanctuary for terrorists.

The Foreign Policy Domain

In the *foreign policy domain,* state patronage for terrorism occurs when a government champions a politically violent movement or group—a proxy—that is operating beyond its borders. Under this model, the state patron will directly assist the proxy in its cause and will continue its support even when the movement or group has become known to commit acts of terrorism or other atrocities. When these revelations occur, patrons typically reply to this information with rationalizations. The patron will either

- accept the terrorism as a necessary tactic,
- deny that what occurred should be labeled as "terrorism,"
- deny that an incident occurred in the first place, or
- issue a blanket condemnation of all such violence as unfortunate.

The 1981-1988 United States–directed guerrilla war against the **Sandinista** regime in Nicaragua incorporated elements of the state patronage model.[12] Although it was not a terrorist war per se, the United States' proxy did commit human rights violations. It is therefore a good case in point of state patronage for a proxy that was quite capable of engaging in terrorist behavior.

In 1979, the United States-supported regime of **Anastasio Somoza Debayle** was overthrown after a revolution led by the Sandinistas, a Marxist insurgent group. Beginning in 1981, the Reagan administration began a campaign of destabilization against the Sandinista regime. The most important component of this campaign was U.S. support for anti-Sandinista Nicaraguan counterrevolutionaries, known as the **contras**. During this time,

> The centerpiece of the Reagan administration's low-intensity-warfare strategy was a program of direct paramilitary attacks. Conducted by a proxy force of exiles supplemented by specially trained U.S. operatives, these operations were, ironically, meant to be the covert side of Reagan's policy. Instead, the so-called contra war became the most notorious symbol of U.S. intervention in Nicaragua.[13]

From December 1981 until July 1983, funding and equipment were secretly funneled by the CIA to build training facilities, sanctuaries, and supply bases for the contras along the Nicaraguan-Honduran border. Allied personnel from Honduras and Argentina assisted in the effort. From this base-camp region, the contras were able to be trained, supplied, and sent into Nicaragua to conduct guerrilla missions against the Sandinistas. The contras were sustained by U.S. arms and funding—without this patronage, they would not have been able to operate against the Sandinistas. Unfortunately for the United States, evidence surfaced that implicated the contras in numerous human rights violations. These allegations were officially dismissed or explained away by the Reagan administration.

The Domestic Policy Domain

In the *domestic policy domain,* state patronage of terrorism occurs when a regime engages in direct violent repression against a domestic enemy. Under this model, state patronage is characterized by the use of state security personnel in an overt policy of state-sponsored political violence. State patrons typically rationalize policies of repression by arguing that they are necessary to

- suppress a clear and present domestic threat to national security;
- maintain law and order during times of national crisis;
- protect fundamental cultural values that are threatened by subversives; or
- restore stability to governmental institutions that have been shaken, usurped, or damaged by a domestic enemy.

The Syrian government's 1982 suppression of a rebellion by the **Muslim Brotherhood** is a case in point of the state patronage model. The Muslim Brotherhood is a transnational Sunni Islamic fundamentalist movement that is very active in several North African and Middle Eastern countries. Beginning in the early 1980s, the Muslim Brotherhood initiated a widespread terrorist campaign against the Syrian government. During their campaign, the movement assassinated hundreds of government personnel, including civilian and security officials. They also assassinated Soviet personnel who were based in Syria as advisers.

In 1980, a rebellion was launched (and suppressed) in the city of Aleppo. In 1981, the Syrian army and other security units moved in to crush the Muslim Brotherhood in Aleppo and the city of Hama, killing at least 200 people. Syrian president Hafez el-Assad increased security restrictions and made membership in the organization a capital offense. In 1982, a Muslim Brotherhood revolt broke out in Hama. The Syrian regime sent in troops and tanks, backed by artillery, to put down the revolt; they killed approximately 25,000 civilians and destroyed large sections of the city. Since the suppression of the Hama revolt, the Muslim Brotherhood and other religious fundamentalist groups have posed little threat to the Syrian regime.

State Sponsorship: The Assistance Model

State assistance for terrorism refers to tacit participation in, and encouragement of, terrorist behavior. Its basic characteristic is that the state, through sympathetic proxies and agents, implicitly takes part in repression, violence, and terrorism. In contrast to state patronage for terrorism, state assisters are less explicit in their sponsorship, and linkages to state policies and personnel are more ambiguous. State assistance includes policies that help sympathetic extremist proxies engage in terrorist violence, whereby the state will *indirectly* arm, train, and provide sanctuary for terrorists.

The Foreign Policy Domain

In the *foreign policy domain,* state assistance for terrorism occurs when a government champions a politically violent proxy that is operating beyond its borders. Under this model, state assistance will indirectly help the proxy in its cause, and the state may or may not continue its support if the movement or group becomes known to commit acts of terrorism or other atrocities. When this occurs, state assisters typically weigh political costs and benefits when crafting a reply to these allegations. The ambiguity that the assister has built into its linkages with the proxy is intended to provide it with the option to claim "deniability" when accused of complicity. The assister can

- deny that a linkage exists between the state and the politically violent movement;
- admit that some support or linkage exists but argue that the incident was a "rogue" operation that was outside of the parameters of the relationship;
- admit or deny a linkage but label the alleged perpetrators as "freedom fighters" and assert that their cause is a just one despite unfortunate incidents; or
- blame the movement's adversary for creating an environment that is conducive to, and is the source of, all of the political violence.

The contra insurgency against the Sandinistas was introduced previously as a case in point for the state patronage model—with the caveat that it was not per se a terrorist war. The later phases of the war are also a good example of the state assistance model.

Several incidents undermined the U.S. Congress's support for the Reagan administration's policy in Nicaragua. First, "assassination of civilians and wanton acts of terrorism against nonmilitary targets . . . were . . . well recognized within U.S. national security agencies."[14] Second, an alleged CIA "assassination manual" was discovered and made public. Third, the CIA was implicated in the mining of the harbor in the capital city of Managua. In December 1982, Congress passed the "**Boland Amendment**," which forbade the expenditure of U.S. funds to overthrow the Sandinista government. In mid-1983, Congress appropriated $24 million as the "final" expenditure to support the contras—after it was spent, the CIA was required to end support for the contras. In late 1984, a second Boland Amendment forbade all U.S. assistance to the contras.

These legislative measures were the catalyst for a highly covert effort to continue supplying the contras. Sources of supply had always included an element of covert transfer of arms for the contras. For example, Operation Tipped Kettle sought to funnel arms to the contras that were captured from the PLO by Israel during Israel's 1982 invasion of Lebanon. Another example was Operation Elephant Herd, which sought to transfer surplus U.S. military equipment to the CIA free of charge, to be distributed to the contras.[15]

The most effective effort to circumvent the congressional ban was the resupply network set up by Marine Lieutenant Colonel Oliver North, an official of the National Security Council. While the CIA explored obtaining support for the contras from international sources (primarily allied countries), North and others successfully set up a resupply program that shipped large amounts of arms to the contras—both in their Honduran base camps and inside Nicaragua itself. This program was intended to wait out congressional resistance and was successful, because in June 1986 Congress approved $100 million in aid for the contras. Congressional support for this disbursement was severely shaken when a covert American cargo plane was shot down inside Nicaragua, an American mercenary was captured, and the press published reports about Lt. Col. North's operations. This combination of factors—known as the **Iran-Contra Scandal**—ended congressional support for the contra program. Iran-Contra will be revisited in Chapter 13.

As a postscript to the contra insurgency, it is useful to report the economic and human costs of the war:

Between 1980 and 1989, the total death toll—Nicaraguan military, contra, and civilian—was officially put at 30,865. Tens of thousands more were wounded, orphaned, or left homeless. As of 1987, property destruction from CIA/contra attacks totaled $221.6 million; production losses, $984.5 million. Nicaraguan economists estimated monetary losses due to the trade embargo at $254 million and the loss of development potential from the war at $2.5 billion.[16]

The Domestic Policy Domain

In the *domestic policy domain,* state assistance for terrorism occurs when a regime engages in indirect violent repression against an enemy. Under this model, state assistance is characterized by the use of sympathetic proxies in a policy of state-assisted political violence. The use of proxies can occur in an environment where the proxy violence coincides with violence by state security personnel. Thus, the overall environment may include both state patronage (direct repression) and state assistance (indirect repression). The East Timor case discussed at the beginning of this chapter is an example of a repressive environment characterized by both patronage and assistance. State assisters typically rationalize policies of indirect repression by adopting official positions that

- blame an adversary group for the breakdown of order and call upon "the people" to assist the government in restoring order,
- argue that the proxy violence is evidence of popular patriotic sentiment to suppress a threat to national security,
- call upon all parties to cease hostilities but focus blame for the violence on an adversary group, or
- assure everyone that the government is doing everything in its power to restore law and order but that the regime is unable to "immediately" end the violence.

The **Great Proletarian Cultural Revolution** in China lasted for three and a half years, from 1965 to 1969.[17] It is a good example of state assistance for an ideologically extremist movement. Launched by Mao Zedong and the Chinese Communist Party Central Committee, the Cultural Revolution was a mass movement that mobilized the young post-Revolution generation. Its purpose was to eliminate "revisionist" tendencies in society and create a newly indoctrinated revolutionary generation. The period was marked by widespread upheaval and disorder.

In late 1965 through the summer of 1966, factional rivalries within the leadership of China led to a split between Mao's faction and the "old guard" establishment of the Chinese Communist Party. Members of the establishment were labeled "revisionists" by the Maoist faction. Mao successfully purged these rivals from the Communist Party, the **People's Liberation Army,** and government organs. When this occurred, the pro-Mao Central Committee of the Communist Party launched a full-scale nationwide campaign against revisionism. The Great Proletarian Cultural Revolution had begun.

Maoists mobilized millions of young supporters in the **Red Guards**, who waged an ideological struggle to eliminate the "**Four Olds**": old ideas, old culture, old customs, and old habits.[18] The Red Guards were the principal purveyors of the Cultural Revolution and were strongly encouraged to attack the Four Olds publicly and with great vigor. This led to widespread turmoil. For example, the Red Guards were deeply anti-intellectual and suppressed "revisionist" ideas. They did this by denouncing teachers and professors, destroying books, banning certain music, and forbidding other "incorrect" cultural influences, so that the Chinese education system collapsed. Also, establishment Communist Party leaders were denounced and purged by the Red Guards in public "trials," which led to massive disruption within the ranks of the party. For approximately 18 months, beginning in early 1967, the Red Guards seized control of key government organs. Because they were completely inexperienced in government operations, the government ceased to operate effectively.

During this period, the Maoists kept the People's Liberation Army in check, allowing the Red Guards to wage the ideological war against the Four Olds. It was not until violent infighting began between factions within the Red Guards that Mao ordered an end to the Cultural Revolution and deployed the People's Liberation Army to restore order.

STATE TERRORISM AS FOREIGN POLICY

During the 20th century, military forces have been used by states to pursue policies of aggression, conquest, and cultural or ethnic extermination. The case of the Nazi **Einsatzgruppen** (described in Appendix B, Historical Examples) illustrates the scale of capable violence by military forces. The military have been used repeatedly as

> agents of state violence in the process of invading a foreign country and engaging in killing the enemy. The major wars of the twentieth century are examples of the tremendous levels of state violence.[19]

In the latter half of the 20th century—and especially in the latter quarter of the century—governments frequently used terrorism as an instrument of foreign policy. As a policy option, state-sponsored terrorism is a logical alternative, because states cannot always deploy conventional armed forces to achieve strategic objectives. As a practical matter for many governments, it is often logistically, politically, or militarily infeasible to directly confront an adversary. For example, few states can hope to be victorious in a direct military confrontation with the United States—as was learned by Saddam Hussein's well-entrenched Iraqi army in Kuwait during the Gulf War of 1990-1991. Terrorism thus becomes a relatively acceptable alternative for states pursuing an aggressive foreign policy. A report from Israel's International Policy Institute for Counter-Terrorism noted that

> state-sponsored terrorism can achieve strategic ends where the use of conventional armed forces is not practical or effective. The high costs of modern warfare, and concern about nonconventional escalation, as well as the danger of defeat and the unwillingness to appear as the aggressor, have turned terrorism into an efficient, convenient, and generally discrete [*sic*] weapon for attaining state interests in the international realm.[20]

Most state sponsors of terrorism attempt to conceal their involvement. This is a practical policy decision, because

> if the sponsorship can be hidden, the violence against one's enemy can be safe and unaccountable. The nation that is the target of the terrorism cannot respond, as it might to a direct attack, unless and until it can develop evidence of its enemy's responsibility. Nor can the domestic opposition object to violent adventures for which its government disclaims responsibility.[21]

Therefore, states use terrorism and other means of confrontational propaganda because, from their point of view, it is an efficacious method to achieve their strategic objectives. As a practical matter for aggressive regimes, state terrorism in the international domain is advantageous in several respects:

State terrorism is inexpensive. The costs of patronage and assistance for terrorist movements are relatively low. Even poor nations can strike at and injure a prosperous adversary through a single spectacular incident.

State terrorism has limited consequences. State assisters that are clever can distance themselves from culpability for a terrorist incident. They can cover their involvement, disclaim responsibility, and thereby escape possible reprisals or other penalties.

State terrorism can be successful. Weaker states can raise the stakes beyond what a stronger adversary is willing to bear. Aggressor states that wish to remain anonymous can likewise successfully destabilize an adversary through the use of a proxy movement. They can do this through one or more spectacular incidents or by assisting in a campaign of terror.

As discussed earlier in this chapter, state patrons and assisters overtly and covertly sponsor many subversive causes. These patrons and assisters have available to them a range of policy options that represent different typologies of state backing. For example, Pakistan and India—both nuclear powers—have been engaged in recurrent confrontation in Kashmir, a large mountainous region on the northern border of India and northeast of Pakistan. Conditions are extremely difficult for the combatants, with much of the fighting conducted at very high altitudes in a harsh climate. Nevertheless, Pakistan has used proxies to combat Indian forces in Kashmir. Pakistan has also deployed Pakistani veterans from Afghanistan to the front lines. Although the fighting in Kashmir has sometimes been conventional in nature, some Pakistani-supported groups have engaged in terrorist attacks against the Indians.[22]

One study listed the following categories of support as comprising the range of policy options available to states:

- *Ideological Support.* The terrorist organization is provided with political, ideological, or religious indoctrination via agents of the supporting state or is trained by institutions of the sponsoring state.
- *Financial Support.* A terrorist organization requires large sums of money, which are sometimes unavailable through its own independent resources.
- *Military Support.* The state supplies the terrorist organization with a broad range of weapons, provides military training, organizes courses for activists, and so on.
- *Operational Support.* The direct provision of . . . false documents, special weapons, safe havens, etc.
- *Initiating Terrorist Attacks.* The state . . . gives specific instructions concerning attacks, it initiates terrorist activities, and it sets their aims.
- *Direct Involvement in Terrorist Attacks.* The state carries out terrorist attacks . . . using agencies from its own intelligence services and security forces, or through people directly responsible to them. (italics added)[23]

To simplify matters for the purposes of our discussion, we will discuss the following four policy frameworks. They signify the varied qualities of state-sponsored terrorism in the international domain:

1. Politically sympathetic sponsorship

2. Logistically supportive sponsorship

3. Episode-specific sponsorship

4. Joint operations

Table 4.2 summarizes each of these policy frameworks by placing them within the context of state patronage and state assistance for terrorism.

As the discussion proceeds through the four policy frameworks, it is important to remember that state terrorism in the international domain is not limited to "rogue" states. It has also been used as a covert alternative by democracies. For example,

Table 4.2   State-Sponsored Terrorism: The Foreign Policy Domain

State participation in terrorism in the international domain can involve several types of backing for championed causes and groups. This backing can range in quality from relatively passive political sympathy to aggressive joint operations.

The following table distinguishes state patronage and assistance within four policy frameworks. Each policy framework—a type of state backing—is summarized within the state sponsorship model that distinguishes between patronage and assistance.

	Type of Sponsorship	
Type of State Backing	*Patronage*	*Assistance*
Politically sympathetic	Overt political support and encouragement for a championed group's motives or tactics	Tacit political support and encouragement for a championed group's motives or tactics
	Case: Official Arab governments' political support for the objectives of the PLO	Case: Iran's ideological connection with Lebanon's Hezbollah
Logistically supportive	Direct state support, such as sanctuary, for a championed cause to the group	The provision of state assistance to a group, such as providing *matériel* (military hardware)
	Case: Jordanian facilitation of PLO *fedayeen* bases inside Jordan for raids on Israel prior to Black September	Case: Syria's provision of sanctuary, resupply, and other facilities for extremist movements
Episode-specific	Direct involvement by government personnel for a specific incident or campaign	The provision of state assistance to a group or movement for a specific goal
	Case: Yugoslavia's deployment of Yugoslav Army units to Bosnia during the Bosnian civil war	Case: Iran's attempted delivery of 50 tons of munitions to the PLO in January 2002
Joint operations	Operations carried out by government personnel jointly with its proxy	Indirect state support for a proxy using allied personnel
	Case: The American–South Vietnamese "Phoenix Program" during the war in Vietnam	Case: Soviet deployment of Cuban troops to Ethiopia

During the 1960s the French Intelligence Agency hired an international mercenary to assassinate the Moroccan leader Ben Barka. The French Intelligence Agency in 1985 [also] bombed Greenpeaces [*sic*] flag ship in New Zealand, killing one member of its crew.[24]

Politically Sympathetic Sponsorship

Politically sympathetic sponsorship occurs when a government openly embraces the main beliefs and principles of a cause. This embrace can range in scope from political agreement with a movement's motives (but not its tactics) to complete support for both motives and tactics. Politically sympathetic governments act as ideological role models for their championed group.

An example of this type of support is the patronage and assistance given by Iran to Lebanon's **Hezbollah** movement. Lebanon's Shi'ites, who comprise roughly half of Lebanon's Muslims, have been a historically poorer and less politically influential population among Lebanon's religious groups. The Sunnis, Maronite Christians, and Druze have typically wielded more authority. Hezbollah ("Party of God") is a Shi'ite movement in Lebanon that champions the country's large Shi'ite population. Although it has proven to be an effective guerrilla and terrorist force, it is much more. For example,

> [Hezbollah] provides social services to its followers, such as schools and medical services. It has engaged in a variety of business ventures, including supermarkets, bakeries, building, farming, bookshops, and clothing sales to true believers, partly to finance its terrorist activities.[25]

Hezbollah emerged during the Lebanese civil war and Israel's 1982 invasion as a strongly symbolic champion for Lebanese independence and justice for the Shi'ite population.

Hezbollah has for some time been closely linked to Iran. Hezbollah's leadership, while sometimes guarded about their identification with Iran, has overtly stated that they support the ideals of the Iranian Revolution. Their ultimate goal is to create an Islamic republic in Lebanon, and they consider Israel to be an enemy of all Muslims. Hezbollah tends to consider Iran a "big brother" for their movement. As one leader stated: "Our relationship with the Islamic revolution [in Iran] is one of a junior to a senior . . . of a soldier to his commander."[26] Thus, at their root, the ideological bonds between the movement and the Iranian Revolution are strong.

These bonds allowed Iran's support to extend beyond ideological identification toward overt sponsorship. For example, Iran deployed members of its **Revolutionary Guards Corps** into Lebanon's Beka'a Valley to organize Hezbollah into an effective fighting force. Iran provided training, funding, and other logistical support, which is the topic of our next discussion.

Logistically Supportive Sponsorship

Logistically supportive sponsorship occurs when a government provides aid and comfort to a championed cause. This can include directly or indirectly facilitating training, arms resupply, safe houses, or other sanctuary for the movement. These options are relatively "passive" types of support that allow state sponsors of terrorism to promote an aggressive foreign policy agenda but at the same time deny their involvement in terrorist incidents.

One example of logistically supportive sponsorship is the foreign policy adopted by Syria during the regime of Hafez el-Assad. During his rule (February 1971 to June 2000), Syria fought two wars against Israel, strongly backed the Palestinian cause, occupied the Beka'a Valley in Lebanon, and supported the Lebanese militias Amal and Hezbollah. Assad's regime could certainly be aggressive in the international domain, but despite this activism Syria was rarely linked directly to terrorist incidents. In fact, "There is no evidence that either Syria or Syrian government officials have been directly involved in the planning or execution of international terrorist attacks since 1986."[27]

Assad was very skillful in creating a covert support network for sympathetic terrorist movements in the region. This policy was strictly one of pragmatism. His regime provided safe haven and extensive logistical support for these movements but cleverly maintained official "deniability" when an incident occurred. Syria permitted the presence on its soil of several terrorist organizations, such as Palestine Islamic Jihad and the Popular Front for the Liberation of Palestine–General Command. It also facilitated the presence of the Japanese Red Army, the Abu Nidal Organization, Hamas, and others in the Beka'a Valley and Syria proper. Significantly, Assad permitted the Iranian presence in the Beka'a Valley and established strong links with Hezbollah. All of these groups were very active in targeting Israeli and Western interests in the Middle East and Europe. Nevertheless, the Assad regime was rarely called to account for its activities.

Episode-Specific Sponsorship

Episode-specific sponsorship refers to government support for a single incident or series of incidents. For this type of operation, the government will provide as much patronage or assistance as is needed for the terrorist episode. Sometimes members of the proxy will carry out the episode, and at other times agents of the state sponsor will participate in the assault.

One incident of episode-specific support was the bombing of **Pan Am Flight 103**, which exploded over Lockerbie, Scotland, on December 21, 1988. Two hundred seventy people were killed, including all 259 passengers and crew and 11 persons on the ground. In November 1991, the United States and Great Britain named two Libyan nationals as the masterminds of the bombing. The men—**Abdel Basset al-Megrahi** and **Lamen Khalifa Fhima**—were alleged to be agents of Libya's **Jamahiriya Security Organization (JSO).** This was a significant allegation, because the JSO has been implicated in numerous acts of terrorism, including killing political rivals abroad, laying mines in the Red Sea, attacking Western interests in Europe, and providing logistical support and training facilities for terrorists from around the world. Libyan leader **Muammar el-Qaddafi** denied any involvement of the Libyan government or its citizens.

In 1993, the United Nations Security Council approved enhanced trade sanctions against Libya, and a criminal trial of al-Megrahi and Fhima was held under Scottish law before the International Court of Justice in the Hague, Netherlands. The economic sanctions and the trial are discussed in Chapter 13.

Joint Operations

Joint operations are when government personnel jointly carry out campaigns in cooperation with a championed proxy. Close collaboration occurs, with the sponsor providing primary operational support for the campaign. Joint operations often occur during a large-scale and ongoing conflict.

An example of joint operations is the **Phoenix Program**, a campaign conducted during the Vietnam War to disrupt and eliminate the administrative effectiveness of the communist **Viet Cong**, the communist guerrilla movement recruited from among southern Vietnamese. It was a three-year program that attacked the infrastructure of the Viet Cong. Both American and allied South Vietnamese squads were to wage the campaign by pooling intelligence information and making lists of persons to be targeted. The targets were intended to be hard-core communist agents and administrators, and they were supposed to be arrested rather than assassinated. In essence, the Phoenix Program was to kill, jail, or intimidate into surrender the members of the secret Communist-led government the guerrillas had established in the rural eras of the South. The program . . . resulted in the death or imprisonment of tens of thousands of Vietnamese.[28]

The program was, by some accounts, an initial success. The Viet Cong had suffered severe losses during their 1968 Tet offensive. When the Phoenix Program was launched, they could not adequately protect their cadres, so that many of them were denounced, arrested, and often killed. In theory, this was supposed to be a program to efficiently root out the communist infrastructure. In practice, although the communists were significantly disrupted, many innocent Vietnamese were swept up in the campaign. Also, "despite the fact that the law provided only for the arrest and detention of the suspects, one-third of the 'neutralized agents' were reported dead."[29] Corruption was rampant among South Vietnamese officials, so that they

saw the glitter of extortionist gold in the Phoenix Program, blackmailing innocents and taking bribes not to arrest those they should have arrested. In the rush to fill quotas they posthumously elevated lowly guerrillas killed in skirmishes to the status of VC hamlet and village chiefs. . . . Thousands died or vanished into Saigon's prisons.[30]

Estimates of casualties are that 20,585 Viet Cong were killed and 28,000 captured. It is likely that many of those killed were not Viet Cong members.[31] In the end, the Viet Cong were hurt but not eliminated. Unfortunately for the Viet Cong's status as an independent fighting force, after Tet and the Phoenix Program, the North Vietnamese Army became the predominant communist fighting force in the South.

Thus, terrorism and sponsorship for subversive movements are methods of statecraft that have been adopted by many types of governments, ranging from stable democracies to aggressive and revolutionary regimes. It is certainly true that democracies are less likely to engage in this type of behavior than are aggressively authoritarian states. However, as suggested by the cases of the Phoenix Program and French intelligence operations, democracies have been known to resort to terrorist methods when operating within certain security or political environments.

STATE TERRORISM AS DOMESTIC POLICY

State terrorism as domestic policy refers to the state's politically motivated application of force inside its own borders. The state's military, law enforcement, and other security institutions are used to suppress perceived threats; these institutions can also be supplemented with assistance from unofficial **paramilitaries** and **death squads**. The purpose of domestically focused terrorism is to demonstrate the supreme power of the government and to intimidate or eliminate the opposition. In environments where the central government perceives its authority to be seriously threatened, this use of force can be quite extreme.

An example of the latter environment occurred in South Africa during the final years of **apartheid**, the system of racial separation. When confronted by a combination of anti-apartheid reformist agitation, mass unrest, and terrorist attacks, the South African government began a covert campaign to root out anti-apartheid leaders and supporters. This included support for the Zulu-based **Inkatha Freedom Party** in its violence against the multiethnic and multiracial **African National Congress (ANC)**. The South African government also assigned security officers to command death squads called **Askaris**, who assassinated ANC members both inside South Africa and in neighboring countries:

These officially sanctioned groups targeted in particular African National Congress members suspected of being dissidents or sympathizers, both black and white. The African National Congress claims that police have been involved in the killings of more than 11,000 people [between 1990 and 1994].[32]

Legitimizing State Authority

Every type of regime seeks to legitimize its authority and maintain its conception of social order. Governmental legitimization can be enforced in many ways and often depends on the nature of the political environment that exists at a particular point in a nation's history. Some governments legitimize their authority through intimidation and force of arms.

Violent state repression against reformers and revolutionaries has been a common occurrence that has been justified by rulers since the dawn of the nation-state. For example, during Europe's Age of Absolutism (at its height in the 17th century), each monarchy's legitimacy was indisputable, and deviations from the law were harshly punished as offenses against the authority of the monarch. In the modern era, repression has been a frequent instrument of domestic policy. As a policy option, state-sponsored domestic terrorism and other forms of coercion have been used to quell dissent, restore order, eliminate political opponents, and scapegoat demographic populations.

State authority is legitimized and enforced with varying degrees of restraint. Stable democracies with strong constitutional traditions will usually enforce state authority with measured restraint. Regimes with weak constitutional traditions, or those that are in a period of national crisis, will often enforce state authority with little or no restraint. Examples of state domestic authority can be summarized as follows:

- *Democracy* is a system of elected government wherein authority is theoretically delegated from the people to elected leaders. Under this model, a strong constitution grants authority for elected leaders to govern the people and manage the affairs of government. The power of the state is clearly delimited.
- *Authoritarianism* is a system of government in which authority and power emanate from the state and are not delegated from the people to elected leaders. Law, order, and state authority are emphasized. Authoritarian regimes can have elected leaders, but they have authoritarian power and often rule for indefinite periods of time. Constitutions do not have enough authority to prohibit abuses by the state.
- *Totalitarianism* is a system of total governmental regulation. All national authority originates from the government, which enforces its own vision of an ordered society.
- *Crazy States.*[33] The term **crazy states** refers to states whose behavior is not rational; in such states, the people live at the whim of the regime or a dominant group. Some crazy states have little or no central authority and are ravaged by warlords or militias. Other crazy states have capricious, impulsive, and violent regimes in power that act out with impunity.

Table 4.3 illustrates these typologies of domestic state authority by summarizing sources of state authority and giving examples of the typologies.

The following discussion is a domestic state terrorist model adapted from one originally designed by Peter C. Sederberg.[34] It defines and differentiates broad categories, or typologies, of domestic state terrorism that are useful for critically analyzing the motives and behaviors of terrorist regimes. They signify the varied qualities of state-sponsored terrorism in the domestic domain:

Table 4.3   State Domestic Authority

Several typologies can be identified that illustrate the manner in which state authority is imposed and the degree of coercion that is commonly used to enforce governmental authority. Sources of state authority differ depending on which typology of authority characterizes each regime.

Typologies of State Authority	Sources of State Authority		
	Legitimization of Authority	*Center of Authority*	*Examples of Typologies*
Democracy	Secondary role of security institutions; strong constitution and rule of law	Government with constrained authority	United States, Western Europe, Japan
Authoritarianism	Central role of official security institutions; strong constitution possible	Government with minimally constrained authority	Egypt, Myanmar (Burma), Syria
Totalitarianism	Central role of official security institutions	Government with unconstrained authority	China, North Korea, Taliban regime
Crazy states	Central roles of official and unofficial security institutions	Government with unconstrained authority, or unconstrained paramilitaries, or both	Liberia, Somalia, Uganda under Idi Amin

- Vigilante domestic state terrorism
- Overt official state terrorism
- Covert official state terrorism
- Genocidal state terrorism

Table 4.4 summarizes these policy frameworks by placing them within the context of state patronage and state assistance for terrorism.

Vigilante Domestic State Terrorism

Vigilante terrorism is political violence that is perpetrated by nongovernmental groups and individuals. These groups can receive unofficial support from agents of the state.

Why do regimes encourage vigilante violence? What are the benefits of such support? From the perspective of the state, what are the values that are being safeguarded by the vigilantes? Vigilante violence committed on behalf of a regime is motivated by the perceived need to defend a demographic group or cultural establishment. The overall goal of **vigilante state terrorism** is to violently preserve the preferred order. In a classic terrorist rationalization process, the end of an orderly society justifies the means of extreme violence.

Table 4.4   State-Sponsored Terrorism: The Domestic Policy Domain

State participation in terrorism in the domestic domain can involve several types of support for championed causes and groups. This support can range in intensity from relatively passive encouragement of vigilante political violence to unrestrained genocidal violence. The following table distinguishes state patronage and assistance within four policy frameworks.

	Type of Sponsorship	
Type of State Support	*Patronage*	*Assistance*
Vigilante	Members of the security forces unofficially participate in the repression of undesirables.	Members of the security forces unofficially provide support for the repression of undesirables.
	Case: Social cleansing in Colombia by security personnel	Case: Social cleansing in Colombia by civilian vigilante groups and paramilitaries
Overt official	The state openly deploys its security forces to violently assert its authority.	The state openly provides support for progovernment political violence.
	Case: China's suppression of the **Tiananmen Square** demonstrations	Case: Indonesian army's support for anti-independence gangs in East Timor
Covert official	The state clandestinely uses its security forces to violently assert its authority.	The state clandestinely provides support for progovernment political violence.
	Case: South Africa's assignment of security personnel to eliminate ANC members and supporters	Case: South African security agencies' support for anti-ANC Askari death squads
Genocidal	The resources of the state are deployed to eliminate or culturally suppress a people, religion, or other demographic group.	The state provides support for the elimination or cultural suppression of a people, religion, or other demographic group.
	Case: Iraq's anti-**Kurd** Anfal Campaign	Case: Anti-Semitic pogroms by the Black Hundreds in Czarist Russia

The vigilante terrorists, sometimes alongside members of the state security establishment, unofficially wage a violent suppression campaign against an adversarial group or movement. This type of suppression campaign occurs when civilians and members of the state's security forces perceive that the state is threatened. This perception can occur in

Child soldiers in training. Adults drill armed young boys at a stadium in Angola.

Source: Hulton Archive/Getty Images; used by permission.

warlike environments or when an established order is challenged by an alternative social movement or ideology. Civilians and members of the security establishment who participate in vigilante violence adhere to a code of duty and behavior similar to those discussed in Chapter 3, so that they believe their actions are absolutely justifiable.

Nongovernmental vigilantes often organize themselves into paramilitaries and operate as death squads. Death squads have committed many documented massacres and atrocities, including assassinations, massacres, "disappearances," and random terrorist attacks. One incident reported by Amnesty International illustrates the style of terrorism perpetrated by paramilitaries:

> In February [2000], 200 paramilitary gunmen raided the village of El Salado, Bolivar department, [Colombia], killing 36 people, including a six-year-old child. Many victims were tied to a table in the village sports field and subjected to torture, including rape, before being stabbed or shot dead. Others were killed in the village church. During the three-day attack, military and police units stationed nearby made no effort to intervene.[35]

One disturbing—and common—trend among state-sponsored paramilitaries and other armed groups has been the conscription of children as fighters. **Child soldiers** are a serious humanitarian issue, with "children as young as six . . . being used in combat by government and rebel forces in civil wars throughout the world."[36] Around the world, nearly 300,000 children—both boys and girls—have been recruited as fighters in at least 33 armed conflicts.[37] For example,

- In Liberia, rebel Charles Taylor formed a unit called the Small Boy Unit.[38] Boys were regularly ordered to commit human rights violations against civilians.

Table 4.5   Vigilante Terrorism: The Case of the Paramilitaries

Paramilitaries are armed nongovernmental groups or gangs. Progovernment paramilitaries generally consider themselves to be the defenders of an established order that is under attack from a dangerously subversive counterorder. Some paramilitaries are well armed and receive direct official support from government personnel. Others are semi-independent vigilante groups.

Reactionary right-wing paramilitaries in Latin America have been implicated in numerous atrocities, including massacres and assassinations. Table 4.5 summarizes information about several of these groups.

Paramilitary Group	*Benefactor*	*Target*
United Self-Defense Groups (AUC)	Colombian security services, Colombian landholders	Marxist FARC rebels and suspected supporters
Civil Patrols (CAP)	Guatemalan security services, Guatemalan landholders	Marxist rebels and suspected supporters
Chiapas Paramilitaries	Possibly Mexican security force members; Mexican landholders	Zapatistas and suspected supporters
Argentine Anticommunist Alliance (Triple-A)	Argentine security services	Leftists

- In Sri Lanka, the Liberation Tigers of Tamil Eelam have conscripted boys as young as nine years old. Tamil Tigers have been known to "pull the biggest children out of classes, raid orphanages, and go to homes to demand that families turn over teenage sons and daughters."[39]
- In Mozambique, during its civil war, the Renamo rebel movement used child soldiers extensively.[40]
- In Colombia, both right-wing progovernment paramilitaries and left-wing antigovernment guerrillas conscript children and teenagers.
- In Burundi, the Forces for the Defense of Democracy have kidnapped hundreds of boys for military service in their movement.[41]

Paramilitaries and rebel movements have assigned child soldiers to the front lines. Some children are drugged prior to entering into combat and have been known to commit atrocities under orders.

Table 4.5 identifies several paramilitaries that have operated in Latin America with the support of government security services. Interestingly, some scholars have linked paramilitary activity in Latin America to U.S. training programs during its Cold War rivalry with the Soviet Union. In this regard, it has been argued that that

the death squad made its appearance in ten different Latin America countries in the 1960s and 1970s, all of them recipients of U.S. military and police aid and training, which stressed counterinsurgency and unconventional warfare against subversion from the Kennedy Era onward. In a number of countries . . . death squads appeared immediately following a major U.S. intervention.[42]

The Killing Fields. Skulls are displayed of victims of Cambodia's genocidal Khmer Rouge regime. The Khmer Rouge waged a campaign of domestic terrorism that claimed the lives of at least 1 million Cambodians.

Source: Hulton Archive/Getty Images; used by permission.

Official Domestic State Terrorism

State-sponsored repression and political violence were practiced regularly during the 20th century. Many regimes deliberately adopted domestic terrorism as a matter of official policy, and directives ordering government operatives to engage in violent domestic repression frequently originated with ranking government officials.

Why do regimes resort to official policies of domestic violence? What are the benefits of such programs? From the perspective of the state, who are the people that deserve this kind of violent repression? The goals of **official state terrorism** are to preserve an existing order and to maintain state authority through demonstrations of state power. Regimes that officially selected violent repression as a policy choice rationalized their behavior as a legitimate method to protect the state from an internal threat. Two manifestations of official state terrorism in the domestic domain must be distinguished: overt and covert official state terrorism.

Overt official state terrorism refers to the visible application of state-sponsored political violence. It is a policy of unconcealed and explicit repression directed against a domestic enemy. Overt official terrorism has been commonly practiced in totalitarian societies, such as Stalinist Russia, Nazi Germany, Khmer Rouge Cambodia, and Taliban Afghanistan.

Covert official state terrorism refers to the secretive application of state-sponsored political violence. In contrast to overt state terrorism, it is a policy of concealed and implicit repression directed against a domestic enemy. Covert official terrorism has been commonly practiced in countries with extensive secret police services, such as **Shah Mohammad Reza Pahlavi**'s Iran, President Hafez el-Assad's Syria, General Augusto Pinochet's Chile, and Argentina during the Dirty War.

Soviet leader Joseph Stalin in military regalia. Stalin's totalitarian regime brutally purged and killed many thousands of ideological rivals and sent millions of members of ethno-national groups into internal exile. Millions of others died during famines and in work camps.

Source: Hulton Archive/Getty Images; used by permission.

Iran during the regime of Shah Mohammad Reza Pahlavi is a case in point for the convergence of state-sponsored policies of overt and covert terrorism. The Shah, who ruled Iran from 1953 to 1979, considered himself to be the Shahanshah, or King of Kings. His reign hearkened back to the ancient kings of Persia, his authority was unquestioned, and dissent was impermissible. The Shah regularly used his army and security services to suppress dissidents. His secret police, **SAVAK**, was particularly efficient and ruthless. The army was used to quell demonstrations and other public forms of dissent, frequently firing on protestors to disperse crowds. In one incident in 1963, as many as 6,000 people were killed by the army and SAVAK.[43] The Shah strongly relied on SAVAK's extensive intelligence network to root out potential dissidents and opposition groups. It was permitted to imprison people with virtual impunity, with an estimated annual average of political prisoners reaching 100,000.[44] SAVAK was extremely harsh toward persons detained in its own special prisons, and its torture methods were renowned for their brutality. Despite the Shah's extensive system of repression, he could not defeat a popular uprising in 1978 despite the deaths of thousands of Iranians at the hands of the army and SAVAK. Shah Pahlavi was deposed and forced into exile in 1979 after an Islamic revolution inspired by the **Ayatollah Ruhollah Khomeini.**

Official state terrorism is not always directed against subversive elements. It is sometimes conducted to "cleanse" society of an undesirable social group. These groups are perceived to be purveyors of a decadent lifestyle or immoral values, or are seen as otherwise unproductive drains on society. Chapter Perspective 4.1 discusses how extremist regimes have solved this problem by engaging in so-termed "**social cleansing**" and "**ethnic cleansing.**"

Genocidal Domestic State Terrorism

The word *genocide* was first used by **Dr. Raphael Lemkin** in 1943 and first appeared in print in his influential book *Axis Rule in Occupied Europe,* published in 1944.[45] It is derived from the Greek word *genos,* meaning race or tribe, and the Latin-derived suffix *cide,* meaning killing. Genocide is, first and foremost, generally defined as the elimination of a group as a matter of state policy or communal dissident violence. The latter refers to campaigns of substate, group-against-group terrorism and is explored further in Chapter 5.

Whether perpetrated at the state or communal levels, genocide is considered by the world community to be an unacceptable social policy and an immoral application of force. Genocide has been regarded as a crime under international law since 1946, when the General Assembly of the United Nations adopted Resolution 96(I). In 1948, the General

| **Chapter Perspective 4.1** | **Cleansing Society** |

Among the euphemisms used by propagandists to characterize state-initiated domestic terrorism, perhaps the most commonly applied term is that of "cleansing" society. Conceptually, an image is constructed that depicts an undesirable group as little more than a virus or bacterium that has poisoned society. The removal of this group is considered to be a necessary remedy for the survival of the existing social order.

This imagery has been invoked repeatedly by extremist regimes. An example from Fascist Italy illustrates this point:

"Terror? Never," Mussolini insisted, demurely dismissing such intimidation as "simply . . . social hygiene, taking those individuals out of circulation like a doctor would take out a bacillus."[a]

For society to solve its problems, the bacterium represented by the group must be removed. Acceptance of this characterization makes domestic terrorism palatable to many extremist regimes. The following "cleansing" programs are recent examples of this imagery.

Social Cleansing

Social cleansing refers to the elimination of undesirable social elements. These undesirable elements are considered to be blights on society and can include street children, prostitutes, drug addicts, criminals, homeless people, transvestites, and homosexuals. In Colombia, undesirable social elements are commonly referred to as "disposables."

Social cleansing has occurred in a number of countries. The term was probably coined in Latin America, where social cleansing took on the attributes of vigilante state domestic terrorism in Brazil, Guatemala, Colombia, and elsewhere. Participants in cleansing campaigns have included members of the police and death squads. In societies where social cleansing has occurred, the "disposables" have been killed, beaten, and violently intimidated.

Ethnic Cleansing

The term *ethnic cleansing* was coined during the war in Bosnia in the former Yugoslavia. It refers to the expulsion of an ethno-national group from a geographic region as a means to create an ethnically pure society. During the war in Bosnia, Serb soldiers and paramilitaries initiated a cycle of ethnic cleansing. They systematically expelled, killed, raped, and otherwise intimidated Bosnian Muslims to create Serb-only districts. The most intensive campaigns of Serb-initiated ethnic cleansing in Bosnia occurred in 1992 and 1993. As the war progressed, Croats and Bosnians also engaged in ethnic cleansing, so that there were periods during the war in which all three groups "cleansed" areas populated by members of the other groups.

Since the war in Bosnia, the term has become widely used to describe present and past campaigns to systematically and violently remove ethno-national groups from geographic regions.

a. Hoffman, Bruce. *Inside Terrorism*. New York: Columbia University Press, 1998. p. 24. Quoting Laqueur, Walter. *The Age of Terrorism*. Boston: Little, Brown, 1987, p. 66.

Assembly adopted the Convention on the Prevention and Punishment of the Crime of Genocide. Under Article 2 of the Convention, genocide is formally defined as follows:

Any of the following acts committed with intent to destroy, in whole or in part, a national, ethnical, racial or religious group, such as:

(a) Killing members of the group;
(b) Causing serious bodily or mental harm to members of the group;
(c) Deliberately inflicting on the group conditions of life calculated to bring about its physical destruction in whole or in part;
(d) Imposing measures intended to prevent births within the group;
(e) Forcibly transferring children of the group to another group.[46]

Why do regimes resort to genocidal policies against their fellow countrymen? What are the benefits to a regime of eliminating a particular group? From the perspective of the state, why do some groups deserve to be eliminated? One practical reason for terrorist regimes is that scapegoating a defined enemy is a useful strategy to rally the nation behind the ruling government. The goal is to enhance the authority and legitimacy of the regime by targeting internal enemies for genocidal violence.

States have available to them, and frequently marshal, an enormous amount of resources for use against an undesired group. These resources can include the military, security services, civilian paramilitaries, legal systems, private industry, social institutions, and propaganda resources. When the decision is made to eliminate or culturally destroy a group, state resources can be brought to bear with devastating efficiency. An example of

---

Chapter Perspective 4.2   **The Anfal Campaign: Genocidal State Terrorism**

Political power in Iraq is highly centralized and resides in the **Ba'ath Party**, which is led by **Saddam Hussein.** The Ba'ath Party is a secular Arab nationalist party. Ba'athist functionaries are personally loyal to Hussein and command key government institutions, the military, and the security services. Hussein and the Ba'ath Party legitimize state authority through force of arms. Dissent is severely repressed, and rebellion is dealt with mercilessly. Iraqi armed forces have been unleashed to quell rebellions among the so-called Marsh Arabs in the country's southeastern region and among its Kurdish population in the north.

Iraq's **Anfal Campaign** was a case of genocidal state terrorism waged against the Iraqi Kurdish minority from February to September 1988.

Had history been kinder to the Kurds, they might have established their own sovereign nation of **Kurdistan.** Unfortunately, Kurdistan is a geographic region that is divided between Iraq, Iran, Turkey, and Syria. The Iraqi Kurds have historically sought political self-governance in their region. Some Iraqi Kurds seeking complete independence have resorted to armed insurrection. Iraqi policy during its suppression campaigns against Kurdish rebellions have been brutal and have included the use of poison gas.

In 1987, Saddam Hussein's cousin Ali Hassan al-Majid was assigned the task to secure Iraqi governmental authority in Kurdistan. He carefully planned a campaign that was code-named *al-Anfal,* or "the spoils." The operation was named for passages in the Koran that describe the Prophet Mohammed's revelations after his first great victory. The passages advise the prophet to severely punish unbelievers when necessary. When the Anfal Campaign was launched, it had eight phases, during which civilians were uprooted and many were killed en masse. Males in particular were singled out for death. During the campaign, Iraq dropped chemical weapons on Kurdish villages, including mustard gas and nerve agents.[a] One attack was described as follows:

> The planes dropped bombs. They did not produce a big noise. A yellowish cloud was created and there was a smell of rotten parsley or onions. There were no wounds. People would breathe the smoke, then fall down and blood would come from their mouths.[b]

Between 50,000 and 100,000 Kurds may have died.[c] After the Anfal Campaign, that particular round of the Kurdish rebellion was quelled, and approximately 2.5 million Iraqi Kurds were forced into exile. It is a case in point that illustrates how some regimes—in which state power is centralized in a ruling body—will use terrorism and other means of violent repression to maintain domestic authority.

a. Hoffman, Bruce. *Inside Terrorism.* New York: Columbia University Press, 1998, p. 24. Quoting Laqueur, Walter. *The Age of Terrorism.* Boston: Little, Brown, 1987, p. 66.

b. Quoted in Stern, Jessica. *The Ultimate Terrorists.* Cambridge, MA: Harvard University Press, 1999, p. 107.

c. Human Rights Watch. *Iraq's Crime of Genocide: The Anfal Campaign Against the Kurds.* New York: Human Rights Watch Publications, 1994.

Table 4.6   Genocidal State Terrorism

Genocidal state terrorism is directed against populations within countries that the state declares to be undesirable. When this occurs, extremist regimes have designed policies of elimination that can include cultural destruction, violent intimidation, or complete extermination. Historically, state-initiated genocide is not an uncommon policy selection.

As shown by the summary below, state-initiated genocidal terrorism has occurred in every region of the world.

	Activity Profile		
Country	*Incident*	*Target Group*	*Outcome*
Rwanda	Rwandan president Habyarimana assassinated	Tutsis and Hutu moderates	Genocidal violence; approximately 500,000 people killed by Rwandan army and Hutu militants
Cambodia	Victory on the battlefield by the Khmer Rouge; imposition of a new regime	City dwellers, educated people, upper class, Buddhists, fellow Khmer Rouge	The Killing Fields; up to 2 million deaths
Bosnia	The breakup of Yugoslavia and Serb resistance to the declarations of independence by Slovenia, Croatia, and Bosnia	Muslims living in territory claimed by Serbs	Ethnic cleansing assisted by Serbia, population removals, massacres, systematic rape, and cultural destruction
Germany	Racially motivated genocide by the Nazi regime	German Jews	The Holocaust; deaths of most of Germany's Jewish population
United States	Conquering the frontier and 19th-century frontier wars	Native Americans	Annihilation of some tribes; resettlement of others on reservations

this efficiency is illustrated in Chapter Perspective 4.2, which discusses Iraq's genocidal Anfal Campaign against its Kurdish population in 1988.

Thus, **genocidal state terrorism** occurs when the resources of a nation are mobilized to eliminate a targeted group. The group can be a cultural minority—such as a racial, religious, or ethnic population—or the group can be a designated segment of society—such as believers in a banned ideology or a socioeconomically unacceptable group. Unlike vigilante and official state terrorism, the scale of violence during campaigns of state-sponsored genocidal terrorism can be virtually unlimited. In some cases, no check at all is placed on the use of violence against an adversary group, with the result that the targeted group may suffer casualties in the many thousands or millions.

Table 4.6 identifies several examples of state-sponsored genocidal campaigns directed against domestic groups.

Case in Point **Latin American State Terrorism as *Domestic* Policy and North African/Middle Eastern State Terrorism as *Foreign* Policy**

Latin America

Honduras during the early 1980s was a staging area for American-supported Nicaraguan coun-terrevolutionary guerrillas known as the contras. During this period, the Honduran government actively suppressed domestic dissent. The military established torture centers and created a clan-destine death squad called Battalion 3-16. Battalion 3-16 was allegedly responsible for the disap-pearances of hundreds of students, unionists, and politicians.

In **El Salvador** during the 1980s, a Marxist revolutionary movement fought to overthrow the United States–backed government. To counter this threat, right-wing death squads worked in con-junction with Salvadoran security services to eliminate government opponents, leftist rebels, and their supporters. ORDEN was a paramilitary and intelligence service that used terror against rural civilians. Another death squad, the White Hand, committed numerous atrocities against civilians.

In **Guatemala**, a brutal civil war and related political violence cost about 200,000 lives, includ-ing tens of thousands of "disappeared" people. It was, in part, a racial war waged against Guatemala's Indians, descendants of the ancient Mayas, who make up half the population. The government responded to an insurgency in the Indian-populated countryside with widespread

---

It is important to understand that the "elimination" of a group does not necessarily require their physical extermination. The state's goal might also be to destroy a culture. This can be accomplished through forced population removals or prohibitions against practicing religious, linguistic, or other measures of cultural identification. In fact, the original deliberations that crafted the legal definition of genocide recognized that genocide was much more than physical extermination. Because of the policies of the Nazi regime, it was considered necessary to design a new conceptual category for certain types of state-sponsored practices. It was agreed that

> genocide . . . went beyond the killing of people: it covered such related acts as the prac-tice of [forced] abortion, sterilization, artificial infection, the working of people to death in special labor camps, and the separation of families or of sexes in order to depopulate specific areas. . . . These activities . . . had to be regarded as criminal in intent as well as in execution.[47]

Most cases of state genocide are not examples of a precipitous policy whereby the secu-rity services are suddenly unleashed against a targeted group. More commonly, the methodology and purpose behind genocidal policies require a coordinated series of events, perhaps in phases over months or years. During these phases, cultural or other measures of identification can be suppressed—perhaps with the ultimate goal of physical extermi-nation, but not always.

CHAPTER SUMMARY

This chapter introduced students to the "terror from above" that characterizes state-sponsored terrorism. Students were provided with an understanding of the nature of state terrorism. The purpose of this discussion was to identify and define several typologies of state terrorism, to differentiate state terrorism in the foreign and domestic policy domains, and to provide cases in point of these concepts.

torture, killings, and massacres against Indian villagers. Death squad activity was widespread. One government campaign, called **Plan Victoria 82,** massacred civilians, destroyed villages, and resettled survivors in zones called "strategic hamlets." Plan Victoria 82 was responsible for thousands of deaths by mid-1982.

North Africa/Middle East

Libya was implicated in a number of terrorist incidents during the 1980s, including the attacks at the Rome and Vienna airports in 1985, the bombing of the La Belle Discotheque in Berlin in 1986, and the bombing of Pan Am Flight 103 in 1988. Libya was also implicated in providing support for the Popular Front for the Liberation of Palestine–General Command and the Abu Nidal Organization.

Sudan has been a supporter of regional terrorist groups, rebel organizations, and dissident movements throughout North Africa and the Middle East. It has provided safe haven for Osama bin Laden's Al Qaeda network, the Abu Nidal Organization, Palestine Islamic Jihad, Hamas, and Hezbollah. It has also provided support for rebels and opposition groups in Tunisia, Ethiopia, Uganda, and Eritrea.

Syria has provided safe haven and support for Hezbollah, Palestine Islamic Jihad, Hamas, the Popular Front for the Liberation of Palestine–General Command, and the Abu Nidal Organization. Its occupation of the Beka'a Valley has allowed many extremist groups to operate, including Iranian Revolutionary Guards.

Students were introduced to public and private agencies that monitor state terrorism. The U.S. Department of State's list of sponsors of state terrorism is a useful compilation of information about states that are active in the foreign policy domain. Human Rights Watch and Amnesty International are private activist organizations that have extensive databases on state terrorism in the domestic policy domain.

The state terrorism paradigm identified several approaches that are used by experts to define and describe state terrorism. Included in this discussion was a comparison of the underlying characteristics of the state patronage and state assistance models of terrorism. The patronage model was characterized by situations whereby regimes act as active sponsors of, and direct participants in, terrorism. Under the assistance model, regimes tacitly participate in violent extremist behavior and indirectly sponsor terrorism.

The discussion of state terrorism as foreign policy applied a model that categorized terrorism in the foreign domain as politically sympathetic, logistically supportive, episode-specific, or joint operations. Each of these typologies described different aspects in the scale of support and directness of involvement by state sponsors. Several examples were provided to clarify the behavioral distinctions of these typologies.

In the domestic policy domain, several models of state domestic authority and legitimacy were identified and summarized. The sources of authority and centers of power were contrasted in these models. These models were democracy, authoritarianism, totalitarianism, and crazy states. Because the methodologies of state domestic terrorism differ from case to case, several typologies provide a useful approach to understanding the characteristics of a particular environment. These typologies were vigilante, overt official, covert official, and genocidal state domestic terrorism.

In Chapter 5, students will be introduced to typologies and examples of "terrorism from below" conducted by nongovernmental dissident movements. The discussion will present a dissident terrorism paradigm that will be applied in a similar manner as the state terrorism paradigm. Typologies and cases in point will be presented to explain the causes and contexts of dissident terrorist behavior.

KEY TERMS AND CONCEPTS

The following topics were discussed in this chapter, and are found in the Glossary:

African National Congress (ANC)
al-Megrahi, Abdel Basset
Amnesty International
Anfal Campaign
Apartheid
Askaris
Assassinations
Ba'ath Party
Beka'a Valley
Blacklisting
Boland Amendment
Child soldiers
Contras
Crazy states
Death Squads
Einsatzgruppen
Episode-specific sponsorship
Ethnic Cleansing
Fhima, Lamen Khalifa
Four Olds, The
el-Qaddafi, Muammar
Genocidal state terrorism
Genocide
Great Proletarian Cultural Revolution
Hezbollah
House Un-American Activities Committee
Human Rights Watch
Hussein, Saddam
Inkatha Freedom Party
Iran-Contra Scandal
Jamahiriya Security Organization (JSO)
Jammu Kashmir Liberation Front
Joint operations
Khomeini, Ayatollah Ruhollah

Korean Airlines Flight 858
Kurdistan
Kurds
Lemkin, Dr. Raphael
Logistically supportive sponsorship
Lumumba, Patrice
McCarthy, Senator Joseph
Muslim Brotherhood
Official state terrorism
Pahlavi, Shah Mohammad Reza
Palmer Raids
Palmer, R. Mitchell
Pan Am Flight 103
Paradigm
Paramilitaries
Patrice Lumumba Peoples Friendship
    University
People's Liberation Army
Phoenix Program
Plan Victoria 82
Politically sympathetic sponsorship
Red Guards
Red Scares
Revolutionary Guards Corps
Sandinistas
SAVAK
Social cleansing
Somoza Debayle, Anastasio
State assistance for terrorism
State patronage for terrorism
Tiananmen Square
Viet Cong
Vigilante state terrorism
Warfare

RECOMMENDED WEB SITES

The following Web sites are links to international organizations that provide information about countries and human rights conditions.

Amnesty International: www.amnesty.org
CIA World Factbook: www.odci.gov/cia/publications/factbook
Human Rights Watch: www.hrw.org
Iraq Foundation: www.iraqfoundation.org
State Department: State-Sponsored Terrorism 2001: http://www.state.gov/s/ct/rls/pgtrpt/
    2001/html/10249.htm

Discussion Box   **Authoritarianism and Democracy**

This chapter's Discussion Box is intended to stimulate critical debate about the application of authoritarian methods by democratic governments and the justifications used by these governments for such methods.

Democracies are constrained by strong constitutions from summarily violating the rights of its citizens. Most democracies have due process requirements in place when security services wish to engage in surveillance, search premises, seize evidence, or detain suspects. However, when confronted by serious security challenges, democracies have frequently resorted to authoritarian security measures. Germany, Italy, France, the United Kingdom, and the United States have all adopted aggressive policies to suppress perceived threats to national security.

For example:

In the **United States**, periodic anti-Communist "**Red Scares**" occurred when national leaders reacted to the perceived threat of Communist subversion. Government officials reacted by adopting authoritarian measures to end the perceived threats. The first Red Scare occurred after the founding of the Communist Party–USA in 1919, and a series of letter bombs were intercepted. President Woodrow Wilson allowed Attorney General **R. Mitchell Palmer** to conduct a series of raids—the so-called **Palmer Raids**—against Communist and other leftist radical groups. Offices of these groups were shut down, leaders were arrested and put on trial, and hundreds were deported.

A second Red Scare occurred in the 1930s. This Scare resulted in the creation of the **House Un-American Activities Committee** and the passage of the Smith Act in 1940, which made advocacy of the violent overthrow of the government a federal crime. In the late 1940s Communists were prosecuted, and high-profile investigations were made of people such as Alger Hiss.

A third Red Scare occurred in the 1950s when **Senator Joseph McCarthy** of Wisconsin held a series of hearings to expose Communist infiltration in government, industry, and Hollywood. Hundreds of careers were ruined, and many people were "**blacklisted,**" meaning that they were barred from obtaining employment.

In **Northern Ireland**, the British government has periodically passed legislation to combat terrorism by the IRA. These laws granted British forces authoritarian powers in Northern Ireland. One such law was the 1973 Northern Ireland Emergency Provisions Act, which provided the military with sweeping powers to temporarily arrest and detain people and to search homes in Northern Ireland without warrants. Under the Act, the army detained hundreds of people and searched more than 250,000 homes. This sweep was actually fairly successful, because thousands of weapons were found and seized.

Discussion Questions

- Are authoritarian methods morally compatible with democratic principles and institutions?
- Under what circumstances are authoritarian policies justifiable and necessary, even in democracies with strong constitutional traditions?
- The postwar Red Scare investigations in the United States have been labeled by many as "witch hunts." Were these investigations nevertheless justifiable, considering the external threat from the Soviet Union?
- The British security services detained hundreds of innocent people and searched the homes of many thousands of non-IRA members. Considering the threat from the IRA, were these actions nevertheless justifiable?
- Assume for a moment that some security environments justify the use of authoritarian measures by democracies. What kind of "watchdog" checks and balances are needed to ensure that democracies do not move toward permanent authoritarianism?

WEB EXERCISE

Using this chapter's recommended Internet sites, conduct an online investigation of state terrorism.

- Are there certain governmental or institutional profiles that distinguish repressive regimes from nonrepressive regimes?
- Read the mission statements of the monitoring organizations. Do they reflect objective and professionally credible approaches for monitoring the behavior of states?
- In your opinion, how effective are these organizations?

For an online search of state terrorism, students should activate the search engine on their Web browser and enter the following keywords:

"State Terrorism"
"Terrorist States"

RECOMMENDED READINGS

The following publications provide discussions on state-sponsored terrorism in the international and domestic policy domains.

Dror, Yehezkel. *Crazy States: A Counterconventional Strategic Problem.* New York: Kraus, Milwood, 1980.
Goren, Roberta, and Jillian Becker, eds. *The Soviet Union and Terrorism.* London: Allen & Unwin, 1984.
Bullock, Alan. *Hitler: A Study in Tyranny.* New York: Harper, 1958.
Stohl, Michael, and George Lopez, eds. *The State as Terrorist: The Dynamics of Governmental Violence and Repression.* Westport, CT: Greenwood Press, 1984.
Tucker, Robert C. *Stalin in Power: The Revolution From Above, 1928-1941.* New York: Norton, 1990.

NOTES

[1] The one noncommunal dissident terrorist incident that approximated state terrorism in sheer scale was the September 11, 2001, Al Qaeda attack on the United States.

[2] From U.S. Department of State. "Overview of State-Sponsored Terrorism." *Patterns of Global Terrorism-2001*: http://www.state.gov/s/ct/rls/pgtrpt/2001/html/10249.htm (date accessed: October 23, 2002).

[3] The organization was originally called Helsinki Watch. Its Western Hemisphere branch is called Americas Watch.

[4] Amnesty International. *Killings by Government.* London: Amnesty International, 1983. Quoted in Iadicola, Peter, and Anson Shupe. *Violence, Inequality, and Human Freedom.* Dix Hills, NY: General Hall, 1998, p. 255.

[5] *Webster's New Twentieth Century Dictionary of the English Language, Unabridged*, 2nd ed. New York: Publishers Guild, 1966.

[6] Pillar, Paul R. *Terrorism and U.S. Foreign Policy.* Washington, DC: Brookings Institution Press, 2001, pp. 157-98.

[7] Ibid., p. 157.

[8] Ibid., p. 178.

[9] Ibid., p. 186.

[10] See Iadicola and Shupe (in note 4 above), pp. 276-89.

[11] Sederberg, Peter C. *Terrorist Myths: Illusion, Rhetoric, and Reality.* Englewood Cliffs, NJ: Prentice Hall, 1989, p. 59. Citing Stohl, Michael, and George Lopez. "Introduction." In Stohl, Michael, and George Lopez, eds. *The State as Terrorist: The Dynamics of Governmental Violence and Repression.* Westport, CT: Greenwood Press, 1984, p. 77.

[12] For a good discussion of U.S. policy in Nicaragua, see Walker, Thomas W., ed. *Revolution & Counterrevolution in Nicaragua.* Boulder, CO: Westview Press, 1991.

[13] Kornbluh, Peter. "The U.S. Role in the Counterrevolution." In Walker, Thomas W., ed. *Revolution & Counterrevolution in Nicaragua.* Boulder, CO: Westview Press, 1991, p. 326.

[14] Ibid., p. 331.

[15] Ibid., p. 327.

[16] Ibid., pp. 344-45.

[17] See Fairbank, John King. *The Great Chinese Revolution: 1800-1985*. New York: Harper & Row, 1987, pp. 316-41.

[18] Ibid., p. 317.

[19] Iadicola and Shupe (in note 4 above), p. 269.

[20] International Policy Institute for Counter-Terrorism, Herzliya, Israel. Web site: www.ict. org.il/interter/org.cfm. Quoted in Whittaker, David J., ed. *The Terrorism Reader*. New York: Routledge, 2001, p. 37.

[21] Heymann, Philip B. *Terrorism and America: A Commonsense Strategy for a Democratic Society*. Cambridge: MIT Press, 1998, p. 66.

[22] For further information, see U.S. Department of State. "Asia Overview." *Patterns of Global Terrorism-2000*. Office of the Coordinator for Terrorism, 2001.

[23] Ganor, Boaz. "Countering State-Sponsored Terrorism." International Policy Institute for Counter-Terrorism, Herzliya, Israel: www.ict.org.il/articles/counter.htm (date accessed: October 14, 2002). Quoted ibid., pp. 268-69.

[24] Iadicola and Shupe (in note 4 above), p. 281.

[25] Laqueur, Walter. *The New Terrorism: Fanaticism and the Arms of Mass Destruction*. New York: Oxford University Press, 1999, p. 137.

[26] Kramer, Martin. "The Moral Logic of Hizballah." In Reich, Walter, ed. *Origins of Terrorism: Psychologies, Ideologies, Theologies, States of Mind*. Washington, DC: Woodrow Wilson Center Press, 1998, p. 138. Quoting Interview with Tufayli, *Ettela'at* (Tehran), August 20, 1985.

[27] Hoffman, Bruce. *Inside Terrorism*. New York: Columbia University Press, 1998, p. 195.

[28] Sheehan, Neil. *A Bright Shining Lie: John Paul Vann and America in Vietnam*. New York: Random House, 1988, p. 18.

[29] FitzGerald, Frances. *Fire in the Lake: The Vietnamese and the Americans in Vietnam*. New York: Vintage Books, 1972, p. 549.

[30] Ibid., p. 733.

[31] Schlagheck, Donna M. "The Superpowers, Foreign Policy, and Terrorism." In Kegley, Charles W., ed. *International Terrorism: Characteristics, Causes, Controls*. New York: St. Martin's Press, 1990, p. 176.

[32] Ibid., p. 267.

[33] Dror, Yehezkel. *Crazy States: A Counterconventional Strategic Problem*. New York: Kraus, Milwood, 1980.

[34] Sederberg (note 11 above).

[35] Amnesty International. "Colombia." *Amnesty International Report 2001*. London: Amnesty International Secretariat, 2001.

[36] Iadicola and Shupe (in note 4 above), p. 266.

[37] Human Rights Watch. "Child Soldiers: Facts About Child Soldiers." New York: Human Rights Watch, 2002: www.hrw.org/campaigns/crp/facts.htm

[38] Iadicola and Shupe (in note 4 above).

[39] Crossette, Barbara. "Tamil Rebels Said to Recruit Child Soldiers." *New York Times*. July 17, 2000.

[40] Iadicola and Shupe (in note 4 above).

[41] Agence France-Presse. "In Burundi, Rebels Kidnap Children to Fill Ranks." *New York Times*. November 19, 2001.

[42] Herman, Edward, and Gerry O'Sullivan. *The Terrorism Industry*. New York: Pantheon, 1989, p. 37. Quoted in Iadicola and Shupe (in note 4 above), p. 271.

[43] Iadicola and Shupe (in note 4 above), p. 271.

[44] Ibid.

[45] Lemkin, Raphael. *Axis Rule in Occupied Europe: Laws of Occupation, Analysis of Government, Proposals for Redress*. Washington, DC: Carnegie Endowment for International Peace, 1944. Chapter 9 of Lemkin's book discussed genocide in detail.

[46] Quoted in von Glahn, Gerhard. *Law Among Nations: An Introduction to Public International Law*, 5th ed. New York: Macmillan, 1986, pp. 303-4.

[47] Ibid., p. 303.

Chapter 5

TERROR FROM BELOW: DISSIDENT TERRORISM

This chapter discusses the characteristics of "terrorism from below"—**dissident terrorism**—committed by nonstate movements and groups against governments, ethno-national groups, religious groups, and other perceived enemies. Students will probe the different types of dissident terrorism and develop an understanding of the qualities that differentiate each dissident terrorist typology. A dissident terrorist paradigm will be discussed, and cases in point will be applied to illustrate what is meant by **antistate terrorism** and **communal terrorism**.

It is important to remember that political violence by nonstate actors has long been viewed as a necessary evil by those who are sympathetic to their cause. Revolutionaries, terrorists, and assassins have historically justified their deeds as indispensable tactics that are necessary to defend a higher cause. The methods used to defend the higher cause can range in intensity from large-scale "wars of national liberation"—such as the many anti-colonial wars of the 20th century—to individual assassins who strike down enemies of their cause. In the United States, for example, when Confederate sympathizer **John Wilkes Booth** assassinated President Abraham Lincoln during a play at Ford's Theater in Washington, D.C., he leaped from Lincoln's balcony to the stage after shouting "*sic semper tyrannis!*" ("Thus be it ever to tyrants!").

Why do people take up arms against governments and social systems? What weapons are available to the weak when they make the decision to confront the strong? Do the ends of antistate dissident rebels justify their chosen means? As discussed in Chapter 3, state repression and exploitation are frequently cited as grievances to explain why nonstate actors resort to violence. These grievances are often ignored by state officials, who refuse to act until they are forced to do so.

An example illustrating this concept is the rebellion in Mexico waged by rebels calling themselves the **Zapatista National Liberation Front** (Ejercito Zapatista de Liberacion Nacional). The Zapatistas were leftists who championed the cause of Indians native to Mexico's Chiapas state, where starvation and disease were common and where the government had long supported large landowners in their exploitation of poor Indian peasants. In January 1994, the Zapatistas began attacking Mexican army troops and police stations in Chiapas. During this initial campaign, approximately 145 people were killed before the rebels retreated into the jungle to continue the conflict. A low-intensity **guerrilla** insurgency continued, with the government gradually agreeing to address the grievances of all of Mexico's 10 million Indians. By 2001, the Zapatistas had evolved into an aboveground political movement lobbying for the civil rights of Mexico's Indians and poor peasants. A key reason for the Zapatistas' success was their ability to adopt a "Robin Hood" image for their movement.

The discussion in this chapter will review:

- A Dissident Terrorism Paradigm
- Operational Shifts—The New Morality and the Rise of Terrorist Cells
- Antistate Dissident Terrorism
- Communal Terrorism

A DISSIDENT TERRORISM PARADIGM

As discussed in Chapter 4, a paradigm is "a pattern, example, or model"[1] that is logically developed to represent a concept. Policy experts and academics have designed a number of models that define dissident terrorism. For example, one model places dissident terrorism into a larger framework of "three generalized categories of political action"[2] that include the following:

- *Revolutionary terrorism*—the threat or use of political violence aimed at effecting complete revolutionary change
- *Subrevolutionary terrorism*—the threat or use of political violence aimed at effecting various changes in a particular political system (but not aimed at abolishing it)
- *Establishment terrorism*—the threat or use of political violence by an established political system against internal or external opposition[3]

Other models develop specific types of dissident terrorism, such as "single-issue," "separatist," and "social revolutionary" terrorism.[4] Likewise, "insurgent" terrorism has been defined as violence "directed by private groups against public authorities [that] aims at bringing about radical political change."[5] One comprehensive definition of "nonstate domestic" terrorism describes it as "illegal violence or threatened violence directed against human or nonhuman objects,"[6] conducted under the following five conditions, assuming that the violence

was undertaken with a view to maintaining a putative norm in at least one particular territorial unit . . .

had secretive, furtive, and/or clandestine features that were expected by the participant to conceal their personal identity . . .

was not undertaken to further the permanent defense of some area . . .

was not conventional warfare . . .

was perceived by the participants as contributing to the normative putative goal . . . by inculcating fear of violence in persons other than the immediate target of the actual or threatened violence and/or by publicizing some cause.[7]

To simplify our analysis, the discussion here presents a dissident terrorist model adapted from one designed by Peter C. Sederberg.[8] It defines and differentiates broad categories, or typologies, of dissident terrorism that are useful for critically analyzing terrorist motives and behaviors. Although each category—**revolutionary**, **nihilist**, **nationalist**, and **criminal dissident terrorism**—is specifically defined for the purposes of our discussion, one should keep in mind that the same terms are applied by experts in many different contexts.

Revolutionary Dissident Terrorism: A Clear World Vision

The goals of revolutionary dissidents are to destroy an existing order through armed conflict and to build a relatively well-designed new society. This vision for a new society can be the result of nationalist aspirations, religious principles, ideological dogma, or some other goals.

Revolutionaries view the existing order as regressive, corrupt, and oppressive; their envisioned new order will be progressive, honest, and just. Revolutionary dissident terrorists are not necessarily trying to create a separate national identity; they are activists seeking to build a new society on the rubble of an existing one. Marxist revolutionaries, for example, have a general vision of a Communist Party-led egalitarian classless society with centralized economic planning. Islamic revolutionaries also have a grand vision—that of a spiritually pure culture that is justly based on the application of *Shari'a*, or God's law. The latter case is exemplified by the Hezbollah (Party of God) organization in Lebanon, which is actively agitating for its own vision of a spiritually pure Lebanon; to that end, Hezbollah has its own political movement, armed militia, and social services.

As a practical matter, revolutionary dissidents are often outnumbered and outgunned by the established order. Their only hope for victory is to wage an unconventional war to destabilize the central authority. Terrorism thus becomes a pragmatic tactical option to disrupt government administration and symbolically demonstrates the weakness of the existing regime.

Good cases in point for the selection of terrorism as a legitimate tactic are found in the Marxist revolutionary movements in Latin America during the 1950s to the 1980s. For example, during the Cuban Revolution, which began in 1956, rebels operating in rural areas waged classic hit-and-run guerrilla warfare against the Batista government's security forces. Fidel Castro and Ernesto "Che" Guevara led these rural units. In urban areas, however, terrorist attacks were commonly carried out by the rebels, who successfully disrupted government administration and thereby undermined public confidence in Batista's ability to govern. This model was repeated throughout Latin America by Marxist revolutionaries (usually unsuccessfully), so that urban terrorism became a common phenomenon in many countries during this period. Carlos Marighella, the Brazilian revolutionary and author of *Mini-Manual of the Urban Guerrilla,* detailed the logic of urban terrorism in the Latin American context.[9] The Latin American case and the *Mini-Manual* will be explored further in Chapter 6.

Nihilist Dissident Terrorism: Revolution for the Sake of Revolution

Nihilism was a 19th-century Russian philosophical movement of young dissenters who believed that only scientific truth could end ignorance. They believed that religion, nationalism, and traditional values (especially family values) were at the root of ignorance. Nihilists had no vision for a future society, asserting only that the existing society was intolerable. Nihilism was, at its core, a completely negative and critical philosophy. The original nihilists were not necessarily revolutionaries, but many anarchists (including Petr Kropotkin and Sergei Nechayev) adapted basic nihilist philosophy to anarchist activism.

Modern nihilist dissidents exhibit a similar disdain for the existing social order but offer no clear alternative for the aftermath of its destruction. The goal of modern nihilists is to destroy the existing order through armed conflict with little forethought given to the configuration of the new society; victory is defined simply as the destruction of the old society. Nihilist dissidents, like revolutionary dissidents, define the existing order as regressive, corrupt, and oppressive. Unlike revolutionaries, nihilists believe that virtually anything is better than the current establishment, so that destruction of the establishment alone becomes the ultimate goal. Many modern nihilists do have a vague goal of "justice," but they offer no clear vision for building a just society other than destroying the existing social order.

Because nihilist dissidents have no clear postrevolution societal design, they have been relegated to the political fringes of society. They have never been able to lead broad-based revolutionary uprisings among the people and have never been able to mount sustained guerrilla campaigns against conventional security forces. Thus, the only armed alternative among hard-core nihilists has been to resort to terrorism. Examples of modern nihilist dissident terrorists include the **Red Brigades** in Italy and the **Weather Underground Organization** in the United States, each of which had only a vague model for postrevolutionary society. These cases will be explored further in Chapters 6 and 12, respectively. Another example is the Palestinian terrorist Abu Nidal, who had no postrevolution vision. Arguably, Osama bin Laden's Al Qaeda network fits the nihilist dissident model, because "from the moment it was established during the chaos of the Afghan war, the aim of Al Qaeda was to support, both militarily and financially, oppressed Muslims around the world."[10]

Although Al Qaeda has a generalized goal of defending Islam and fomenting a pan-Islamic revival, the group offers no specific model for how the postrevolution world will be shaped, and its long-term goals are not clearly defined.

Nationalist Dissident Terrorism: The Aspirations of a People

Nationalist dissidents champion the national aspirations of groups of people who are distinguished by their cultural, religious, ethnic, or racial heritage. The championed people generally live in an environment in which their interests are subordinate to the interests of another group or a national regime. The goal of nationalist dissidents is to mobilize a particular demographic group against another group or government. They are motivated by the desire for some degree of national autonomy, such as democratic political integration, regional self-governance, or complete national independence.

Nationalist sentiment has been commonplace—particularly during the 19th and 20th centuries—and can arise in many social or political environments. For example, the championed group may be a minority living among a majority group, such as the Basques of Spain. Or they may be a majority national group living in a region that is politically dominated by the government of another ethnic group, such as the domination of Tibet by the Chinese. The group may be a minority with a separate cultural and linguistic identity, such as the French Canadians in Quebec. Some national groups have a distinct cultural, ethnic, and regional identity that exists within the borders of several countries, such as the Kurds, whose Kurdistan region is divided among Iran, Iraq, Turkey, and Syria.

Although many nationalist dissident factions incorporate ideological or religious agendas into their movements, the core component of their activism is their ethno-national or other identity. For instance, not all Vietnamese nationalists were communists. Those who were led by Ho Chi Minh certainly were communists, but their wars against the Japanese, French, Americans, and South Vietnamese were ultimately fought to unify Vietnam. Likewise, Muslim rebels in the Southwest Asia Kashmir region have fought a long jihad or holy war against India with the support of Pakistan, but their underlying goal is regional independence from India.

Many nationalist dissidents have used terrorism to achieve their goals. This has often been a practical option, because their opponents have overwhelming military and political superiority and would quickly defeat them during a guerrilla or conventional conflict. An example of this type of strategy is that adopted by the **Provisional Irish Republican Army (Provos)** in Northern Ireland. In other contexts, the armed opposition must operate in urban areas, which always favors the dominant group or regime because of the impossibility of maneuver, the concentration of security forces, and sometimes the lack of mainstream support from the championed group. An example of this type of environment is the Basque Fatherland and Liberty (Euskadi Ta Azkatasuna, or ETA) organization in the Basque region of northern Spain. For nationalists, "the basic strategy is to raise the costs to the enemy occupiers until they withdraw."[11]

Criminal Dissident Terrorism: Protecting the Enterprise

Organized crime became a transnational enterprise during the latter quarter of the 20th century. It had always exhibited minimal transnational characteristics in the past, but it in no way resembled the billion-dollar enterprises of modern arms and drug traffickers. Drug traffickers have especially been prone to engage in criminal dissident terrorism—so-called **narco-terrorism**[12]—because their product must be grown, refined, packaged, and transported from production regions within the borders of sovereign nations. Thus, among international criminals, drug traffickers in particular must necessarily establish a political environment that is conducive to their illegal enterprise.

The goal of criminal dissidents is to protect their illegal enterprise. Because they are motivated by sheer profit, criminal dissidents are political only to the extent that they wish to create a safe environment for their enterprise. They are not necessarily interested in active political participation, other than to subvert or co-opt government officials. Thus, governments that are neutral, weak, or ambivalent will likely not be targeted by criminal dissidents. Conversely, those governments that embark on criminal suppression campaigns, such as drug crop eradication, may be victimized by criminal terrorism.

An example of a long campaign of narco-terrorism occurred in Colombia. Drug cartel *narcotraficantes* (drug traffickers), based in the city of Medellin and led by Pablo Escobar, were notorious during the 1980s and early 1990s for their violence against police officers, prosecutors, journalists, and judges who attempted to interfere with cocaine production and trafficking. The Medellin cartel's rival *narcotraficantes* in the city of Cali were also known to react violently when challenged by Colombian officials, though they were more sophisticated in their manipulation of the government through bribery and corruption. Both cartels were eventually dismantled by Colombian law enforcement agencies with the assistance of the United States. However, a new *narcotraficante* model has replaced the cartels—smaller drug gangs in Colombia and new Mexican gangs. These gangs continue to send many tons of cocaine and other drugs north to the United States. Criminal terrorism will be further explored in Chapter 8.

Revolutionaries, Nihilists, and Nationalists: Freedom Fighters?

Table 5.1 gives examples of how terrorists perceive themselves. Regardless of their ideology, methodology, or goals, there is unanimity in positive self-perception. The names adopted by terrorist organizations reflect their self-perception. As indicated in Table 5.1, adopted organizational names often have nothing to do with the reality of the group's actual composition.

OPERATIONAL SHIFTS: THE NEW MORALITY AND THE RISE OF TERRORIST CELLS

The dissident terrorist paradigm is a good model for understanding the typologies, motives, and behaviors of modern terrorism. Categorizing the goals and strategies of dissident

Table 5.1 Self-Perception or Self-Deception?
Dissident Terrorists as Freedom Fighters

Dissident terrorists adopt organizational names that characterize themselves as righteous defenders of a group or principle. These monikers are always positive representations that indicate the "higher purpose" of the group. The following categories and examples illustrate the self-perception of armed dissident groups.

Liberation Fighters	*Military Units*	*Defensive Movements*	*Retribution Organizations*	*Unifying Alliances*
Basque Fatherland and Liberty	Alex Boncayo Brigade	Islamic Resistance Movement	Revolutionary Justice Organization	Aum Supreme Truth
Liberation Tigers of Tamil Eelam	Irish Republican Army	Revolutionary People's Struggle	International Justice Group	Middle Core Faction
Palestine Islamic Jihad	Japanese Red Army	National Council of Resistance	Palestinian Revenge Organization	Al Qaeda ("The Base")
Revolutionary People's Liberation Party	New People's Army	Jewish Defense League	Black September	Orange Volunteers

terrorists as revolutionary, nihilistic, nationalistic, or criminal is a useful method for understanding dissident violence. However, one must remember that terrorism is an evolutionary phenomenon, and terrorist environments are never static. Terrorist methodologies and organizational structures undergo changes over time. In the modern era, these methodologies and organizational structures have continued to evolve.

Toward the end of the 20th century, two important developments came to characterize the terrorist environment, moving it into a new phase in the postwar world.

The New Dissident Terrorist Morality

The morality of dissident terrorism in the latter decades of the 20th century differed from 19th-century anarchist terrorism and other violent movements. The new generation did not share the same moralistic scruples of the previous generation. Terrorism in late 19th- and early 20th-century Russia was "surgical" in the sense that it targeted specific individuals to assassinate, specific banks to rob, and specific hostages to kidnap. In fact, not only did the **Social Revolutionary Party** in Russia (founded in 1900) engage in an extensive terrorist campaign in the early 20th century, but its tactics actually became somewhat popular because its victims were often government officials who were hated by the Russian people.

In contrast, during the postwar era the definitions of who an enemy was, what a legitimate target could be, and which weapons to use became much broader. This redefining of what constitutes a legitimate target, and the appropriate means to attack that target, led to a new kind of political violence. Late 20th-century dissident terrorism was "new" in the sense that it was "indiscriminate in its effects, killing and maiming members of the general public . . . , arbitrary and unpredictable . . . , refus[ing] to recognize any of the rules or conventions of war . . . [and] not distinguish[ing] between combatants and non-combatants."[13]

When terrorists combine this new morality with the ever-increasing lethality of modern weapons, the potential for high casualty rates and terror on an unprecedented scale is very real in the new millennium. This combination was put into practice on September 11, 2001, in the United States, as well as during the long-term terrorist suicide campaign in Israel during the Palestinians' *intifadeh*. Should terrorists obtain high-yield weapons—such as nuclear or biological weapons—the new morality would provide an ethical foundation for their use.

Cells and Lone Wolves

A newly predominant organizational profile—the **cell**—also emerged as the 20th century drew to a close. Terrorist organizations had traditionally been rather clearly structured, many with hierarchical command and organizational configurations. They commonly had aboveground political organizations and covert "military wings."

During the heyday of group-initiated New Left and Middle Eastern terrorism from the 1960s to the 1980s, it was not uncommon for dissident groups to issue formal communiqués. These communiqués would officially claim credit for terrorist incidents committed on behalf of championed causes, and press conferences were held on occasion.

The "vertical" organizational models began to be superceded by less structured "horizontal" models during the 1990s. These cell-based movements have indistinct command and organizational configurations. Modern terrorist networks are often composed of a "hub" that may guide the direction of a movement, but that has little direct command and control over operational units. The operational units are typically autonomous or semi-autonomous cells that act on their own, often after lying dormant for long periods of time as "sleepers" in a foreign country. The benefit of this type of organizational structure is that if one cell is eliminated or its members are captured, they can do little damage to other independent cells. This configuration also permits aboveground supporters to have "deniability" over the tactics and targets of the cells.

A good example of how a cell can be as small as a single individual—the **lone wolf model**—is the case of Richard C. Reid, a British resident who converted to Islam. Reid was detected by an alert flight attendant and overpowered by passengers on December 22, 2001, when he attempted to ignite plastic explosives in his shoe on a Boeing 767 flying from Paris to Miami.[14] Reid was apparently linked to Al Qaeda and had been trained by the organization in Afghanistan.

ANTISTATE DISSIDENT TERRORISM

A good deal of "terrorism from below" is antistate in nature. It is directed against existing governments and political institutions, attempting to destabilize the existing environment as a precondition to building a new society. As discussed previously, antistate dissidents can have a clear vision of the new society (revolutionary dissidents), a vague vision of the new society (nihilist dissidents), national aspirations (nationalist dissidents), or a profit motive (criminal dissidents). Regardless of which typology fits a particular antistate movement, their common goal is to defeat the state and its institutions.

Antistate Terrorist Environments

With few exceptions, antistate terrorism is directed against specific governments or interests and occurs either within the borders of a particular country or where those interests are found in other countries. Thus, antistate terrorist environments are defined by the idiosyncrasies of each country, each dissident movement, and each terrorist organization. The histories of every nation give rise to specific antistate environments that are unique to their societies. A few examples from North America and Europe illustrate this point.

In the United States, leftist terrorism predominated during the late 1960s through the late 1970s, at the height of the anti-Vietnam War and people's rights movements. Acts of political violence—such as bank robberies, bombings, and property destruction—took place when some Black, White, and Puerto Rican radicals engaged in armed protest. This changed in the 1980s, when the leftist remnants either gave up the fight or were arrested. Around this time, rightist terrorism began to predominate when some racial supremacists, religious extremists, and antigovernment members of the Patriot movement adopted strategies of violence.[15]

In the United Kingdom, the terrorist environment was shaped by the sectarian conflict in Northern Ireland. This conflict was characterized by both antistate and communal violence from 1969 until the peace settlement implemented in 1999. The nationalist Provisional IRA[16] was responsible for most acts of antistate political violence directed against British administration in Northern Ireland. During the same period, Protestant Loyalist terrorism tended to meet the criteria for communal terrorism rather than antistate terrorism, as Loyalist paramilitaries targeted pro-IRA Catholics rather than symbols of governmental authority. The IRA responded in kind, so that more than 3,500 people were killed on both sides by 1999, when a cease-fire was implemented.[17]

In West Germany from the late 1960s through the mid-1980s, the leftist **Red Army Faction** (RAF) engaged in a large number of bank robberies, bombings, assassinations, and other acts of antistate violence aimed at destabilizing the West German government. The RAF also targeted the NATO presence in West Germany, primarily focusing on U.S. military personnel. After the fall of the communist Eastern Bloc in 1989 and the reunification of Germany, RAF-style leftist terrorism waned. Around this time, rightist neo-Nazi violence increased—much of it directed against non-German *Gastarbeiters*, or "guest workers." The perpetrators of this violence were often young skinheads and other neo-fascist youths. Many of these rightist attacks occurred in the region that formerly comprised East Germany.

In Italy, the leftist Red Brigades were responsible for thousands of terrorist incidents from the early 1970s through the mid-1980s. Originating in the student-based activism of the late 1960s and early 1970s, Red Brigades members were young urban terrorists whose terrorist campaign can best be described as a nihilist attempt to undermine capitalism and democracy in Italy. By the late 1980s, Italian police had eliminated Red Brigades cells and imprisoned their hard-core members. During this period, Italian neofascists also engaged in terrorist violence, eventually outlasting the leftist campaign, and they remained active into the 1990s.

In Spain, antistate terrorism has generally been nationalistic or leftist. General Francisco Franco, who seized power after leading the fascist revolt against Republican government during the Spanish Civil War of 1936-1939,[18] ruled as a right-wing dictator until his death in 1975. Small, violent leftist groups have appeared in Spain—such as the Anti-Fascist Resistance Group of October First and the Maoist Patriotic and Anti-Fascist Revolutionary Front. Without question the most prominent antistate dissident group in Spain is the nationalist and vaguely Marxist ETA. ETA was founded in 1959 to promote the independence of the Basque region in northern Spain. The Basques are a culturally and linguistically distinct people who live in northern Spain and southwestern France. Although ETA adopted terrorism as a tactic in response to the Franco government's violent repression of Basque nationalism, "of the more than 600 deaths attributable to ETA between 1968 and 1991, 93 per cent occurred after Franco's death."[19] ETA was rife with factional divisions—at least six ETA factions and subfactions have been formed—but their terrorist campaign continued, despite the granting of considerable political rights

Yasir Arafat, chairman of the Palestine Liberation Organization. Arafat successfully united disparate Palestinian nationalist factions under the PLO umbrella. A number of these factions regularly engaged in terrorism against the state of Israel.

Source: Hulton Archive/Getty Images; used by permission.

by the Spanish government and the loss of popular support for ETA among the Basque people. A right-wing terrorist group, Spanish National Action (Accion Nacional Espanila) was formed as a reaction to ETA terrorism.

Sometimes antistate dissident movements, because of their history and political environment, take on elements of both antistate and communal conflict. In Israel, for example, the Palestinian nationalist movement is made up of numerous organizations and movements that have mostly operated under the umbrella of the **Palestine Liberation Organization (PLO),** led by PLO Chairman **Yasir Arafat.** From its inception, the PLO has sought to establish an independent Palestinian state. Because they claim the same territory as the state of Israel, the PLO and its affiliates have attacked targets inside Israel and abroad. Until recently, Palestinian armed resistance was characterized by a series of dramatic hit-and-run raids, hijackings, bombings, rocket attacks, and other acts of violence. Civilians were often targeted. For example, on May 15, 1974, 16 Jewish teenagers were killed and 70 wounded when three Palestinian terrorists seized a school and demanded that Israel free 23 Palestinian prisoners; all of the gunmen were killed when Israeli soldiers stormed the school.

Since September 28, 2000, Palestinian resistance has taken on the characteristics of a broad-based uprising—and communal terrorism. On that date, Israeli General Ariel Sharon visited the Temple Mount in Jerusalem. The Temple Mount is sacred to both Muslims and Jews. Muslims believe that the prophet Mohammed ascended to heaven from the site, upon which was constructed the Al-Aqsa Mosque. Jews believe that the patriarch Abraham prepared to sacrifice his son on the Temple Mount in accordance with God's wishes, and that Judaism's First and Second Temples were located at the site. After Sharon's visit, which was perceived by Palestinians to be a deliberate provocation, enraged Palestinians began a second round of massive resistance, known as the "shaking off," or *intifadeh*. The new dissident environment includes violent demonstrations, street fighting, and suicide bombings. The violence is regularly characterized by bombings, shootings, and other attacks against civilian targets. Thus, the Palestinian nationalist movement has arguably entered a phase distinguished by the acceptance of communal dissident terrorism as a strategy.

Faith in Victory

Why do small groups of individuals violently confront seemingly invincible enemies? Why do they engage powerful foes by force of arms when their envisioned goal

The assassination of the 16th President of the United States, Abraham Lincoln, by actor John Wilkes Booth at Ford's Theatre, Washington, D.C., on April 14, 1865.

Source: Hulton Archive/Getty Images; used by permission.

is often illogical or unattainable? From the perspective of antistate dissidents, their armed struggle is never in vain. They believe that their cause is not only *likely* to end in victory, but that victory is in fact *inevitable.* From the perspective of outside observers of terrorist groups and terrorist campaigns, terrorists are almost certainly fighting a losing battle with a slim-to-none likelihood of eventual victory, and yet the terrorists persist in their war.

Although antistate dissident terrorists avoid direct confrontation out of a pragmatic acceptance of their comparative weakness, they nevertheless believe in the ultimate victory of their cause. They have a utopian vision that not only justifies their means, but also (in their worldview) guarantees the triumph of their idealized ends. Violent confrontation in the present—often horrific in scope—is acceptable because of the promised good at the end of the struggle. Religious antistate dissidents believe that God will assure them final victory. A 1996 pronouncement by an Egyptian terrorist organization, the Islamic Group (al-Gama'at al-Islamiyya), stated

> They plot and plan and God too plans . . . but the best of planners is God . . . [The Islamic Group will] pursue its battle . . . until such time as God would grant victory—just as the Prophet Mohammed did with the Quredish[20] until God granted victory over Mecca.[21]

Nonreligious antistate dissidents also hold an enduring faith in final victory. Some have adopted a strategy similar to the urban terrorist (or "urban guerrilla") model developed by Carlos Marighella. According to Marighella's strategy, rebels should organize themselves in small cells in major urban areas. He argued that terrorism, when correctly

---

Chapter Perspective 5.1   The Palestinian Movement

Some antistate dissident environments are long-standing and have generated many contending factions. A good example of this phenomenon is the Palestinian movement. Palestinian activism against the state of Israel has as its ultimate goal the creation of an independent Palestinian state. The antistate strategies of most of these groups have been replaced by a broad-based communal dissident environment known as the *intifadeh,* or uprising. The following organizations have been prominent in the Palestinian nationalist movement.[a]

Palestine Liberation Organization

Formed in 1964, the Palestine Liberation Organization (PLO) is not a religious movement, but rather a secular nationalist umbrella organization comprising numerous factions. Its central and largest group is **Al Fatah**, founded by PLO chairman Yasir Arafat in October 1959. The PLO is the main governing body for the Palestinian Authority in Gaza and the West Bank. **Force 17** is an elite unit that was originally formed in the 1970s as a personal security unit for Yasir Arafat. It has since been implicated in paramilitary and terrorist attacks. The **Al Aqsa Martyr Brigades** is a "martyrdom" society of fighters drawn from Al Fatah and other factions; it includes suicide bombers.

Abu Nidal Organization

Led by Sabri al-Banna, the **Abu Nidal Organization** (ANO) is named for al-Banna's *nom de guerre.* The ANO split from the PLO in 1974 and is an international terrorist organization, having launched attacks in 20 countries at the cost of 900 people killed or wounded. The ANO has several hundred members and a militia in Lebanon. It has operated under other names, including Fatah Revolutionary Council, Arab Revolutionary Council, and Black September. The ANO has operated from bases in Libya, Lebanon, and Sudan.

Popular Front for the Liberation of Palestine

The **Popular Front for the Liberation of Palestine** (PFLP) was founded in 1967 by George Habash. It is a Marxist organization that advocates a multinational Arab revolution. With about 800 members, the PFLP was most active during the 1970s but has continued to commit acts of terrorism. The PFLP is responsible for dramatic international terrorist attacks. Its hijacking campaign in 1969 and 1970, its collaboration with West European terrorists, and its mentorship of Carlos the Jackal arguably established the model for modern international terrorism.

---

applied against the government, will create sympathy among the population, which in turn forces the government to become more repressive, thus creating an environment conducive to a mass uprising.[22] Although this model has failed repeatedly (the people tend not to rise up, and repressive states usually crush the opposition), it exemplifies the faith held by antistate dissidents in their victory scenarios—no matter how far-fetched those scenarios may be. Thus,

> Comparatively small in number, limited in capabilities, isolated from society and dwarfed by both the vast resources of their enemy and the enormity of their task, secular terrorists necessarily function in an inverted reality where existence is defined by the sought-after, ardently pursued future rather than the oppressive, angst-driven and incomplete present.[23]

Chapter Perspective 5.1 summarizes the coalitional features of the Palestinian movement. Attention should be given to the PLO and its role as an umbrella for numerous ideological factions.

Popular Front for the Liberation of Palestine—General Command

Ahmid Jibril formed the **Popular Front for the Liberation of Palestine–General Command** (PFLP-GC) in 1968 when he split from the PFLP because he considered the PFLP to be too involved in politics and not sufficiently committed to the armed struggle against Israel. The PFLP-GC has several hundred members, is probably directed by Syria, and is responsible for many cross-border attacks against Israel.

Palestine Liberation Front

The **Palestine Liberation Front** split from the PFLP-GC in the mid-1970s and further split into pro-PLO, pro-Syrian, and pro-Libyan factions. The pro-PLO faction was led by **Abu Abbas**, who committed a number of attacks against Israel. It is a small organization, with about 50 members.

Democratic Front for the Liberation of Palestine

The **Democratic Front for the Liberation of Palestine** split from the PFLP in 1969 and further split into two factions in 1991. It is a Marxist organization that believes in ultimate victory through mass revolution. With about 500 members, it has committed primarily small bombings and assaults against Israel, including border raids.

Islamic Resistance Movement (Harakt al-Muqaqama al-Islamiya, or Hamas, meaning "zeal")

Hamas is an Islamic fundamentalist movement founded in 1987, with roots in the Palestinian branch of the Muslim Brotherhood. Hamas is a comprehensive movement rather than simply a terrorist group, providing social services to Palestinians while at the same time committing repeated acts of violence against Israeli interests. Its armed groups operate as semi-autonomous cells and are known as the **Izzedine al-Qassam Brigade** (named for a famous *jihadi* in the 1920s and 1930s). Hamas has always been at the forefront of the communal dissident *intifadeh*.

Palestine Islamic Jihad

The **Palestine Islamic Jihad** is not a single organization but a loose affiliation of factions. It is an Islamic fundamentalist revolutionary movement that seeks to promote jihad, or holy war, to form a Palestinian state. It is responsible for assassinations and suicide bombings. Like Hamas, it is actively promoting the *intifadeh*.

a. Most of these data were found in *Patterns of Global Terrorism 1996*. U.S. Department of State, 1997, pp. 41 ff.

COMMUNAL TERRORISM

Dissident terrorism is not always directed against a state or national symbols. It is often directed against population groups—people who are perceived to be ethno-national, racial, religious, or ideological enemies. It is not unusual for this type of dissident terrorism to be characterized by extreme repression and violence on a massive scale. It is deeply rooted in long cultural memories of conflict. Communal violence sometimes descends into genocidal behavior because

> While the rival combatants often lack the weapons of destruction available to the major powers, they often disregard any recognized rules of warfare, killing and maiming civilians through indiscriminate car bombings, grenade attacks and mass shootings.[24]

Communal terrorism is essentially "group against group" terrorism, whereby subpopulations of society wage internecine (that is, mutually destructive) violence against each other. As with other types of terrorist violence, it occurs in varying degrees of intensity and in many different contexts. Sometimes it can occur on a massive scale, such as the periodic outbreaks of genocidal violence between Hutus and Tutsis in Rwanda and Burundi which have killed hundreds of thousands. At other times—and on a lower scale of intensity—a politically dominant ethnic or racial group may seek to terrorize a subordinate ethnic or racial group into submission, as occurred in the American South from 1882 to 1930 when more than 3,000 Southern African Americans were lynched (publicly murdered) by white mobs and vigilantes.[25] The scale of violence frequently surprises the world, for these conflicts "often do not command the headlines that rivet world attention on international wars and guerrilla insurgencies, but they frequently prove more vicious and intractable."[26]

There are many sources of communal violence, and it is useful to review a few broad typologies and illustrative cases in point. These typologies—ethno-nationalist, religious, and ideological—are presented in the following discussion.

Ethno-Nationalist Communal Terrorism

Ethno-nationalist communal terrorism involves conflict between populations that have distinct histories, customs, ethnic traits, religious traditions, or other cultural idiosyncrasies. Numerous adjectives have been used to describe this type of dissident terrorism, including "separatist, irredentist, . . . nationalist, tribal, racial, indigenous, or minority."[27] It occurs when one group asserts itself against another group—many times to "defend" its cultural identity. This defensive rationale for violent communal behavior is not uncommon and has been used in communal conflicts in Bosnia, the Caucasus, Sri Lanka, Indonesia, and elsewhere. In these conflicts, all sides believe themselves to be vulnerable and use this perception to rationalize engaging in terrorist violence.

Regionally, Africa leads in the number of ethno-nationalist communal conflicts, with ongoing discord in Sierra Leone, Liberia, Nigeria, Chad, Sudan, the Horn of Africa, Congo, Burundi, Rwanda, South Africa, and elsewhere. Typical of the African conflicts is the case of the fighting that occurred during the apartheid era in South Africa between the nationalist African National Conference (ANC) and the Zulu-based Inkatha Freedom Party.[28] South and Central Asia probably ranks second, with ethnic and nationalist sentiment strongest in Chechnya, Afghanistan, Kashmir, and Sri Lanka. The Middle East has several simmering conflicts, such as the Kurdish and Palestinian-Israeli conflicts. East Asia and Southeast Asia also have several armed movements that represent ethnic and nationalist sentiments, such as the Moro National Liberation Front in the Philippines (which has signed a cease-fire but has some renegade fighters) and the Kachin Independence Army in Burma (Myanmar). Latin America has occasionally experienced ethno-nationalist communal violence, with the worst in scale in recent decades occurring during Guatemala's anti-Indian racial violence, which caused approximately 200,000 deaths before officially ending in 1996, after 35 years of genocidal communal conflict. Western Europe, aside from simmering discord in the Basque region of Spain, has been relatively free of ethno-nationalist violence since the Second World War, as has North America (with the exception of violence in Chiapas, Mexico, during the 1990s).

The scale of ethno-nationalist communal violence can vary considerably from region to region, depending on many different factors—such as unresolved historical animosities, levels of regional development, and recurrent nationalist aspirations. It can be waged across national borders (as in the Congo-Rwanda-Burundi region of East Africa), inside national borders (as in Afghanistan), within ethnically polarized provinces (as in the Nagorno-Karabakh territory of Azerbaijan), at the tribal level (as in Liberia), and even at the subtribal clan level (as in Somalia).

Examples of ethno-nationalist communal conflict have occurred in the following countries and regions:[29]

Corsica. France has ruled Corsica since 1796. Migrants from the French mainland have settled in Corsica since its annexation to France. Since the 1960s, separatists from groups such as the Front for the National Liberation of Corsica have attacked the interests of French mainlanders in an ongoing campaign for independence. Several hundred bombings, assaults, and incidents of vandalism occur each year, as separatists have targeted French mainlander businesses, homes, and offices.

Nigeria. Since gaining independence from Britain in 1960, Nigeria has experienced recurrent outbreaks of ethnic, tribal, and religious violence. The overwhelmingly Muslim north and west is populated mostly by Fulanis, Hausas, and Yorubas. The largely Christian south comprises mostly Ibos. During the 1967-1970 civil war, approximately 1 million people died when Ibo separatists unsuccessfully tried to establish the nation of Biafra in southern Nigeria. About 200 people were killed in Kano in northern Nigeria when ethnic and religious riots broke out after the American bombing of Afghanistan began in October 2001.

New Caledonia. In the French overseas territory of New Caledonia, a South Pacific island group east of Australia, Melanesian nationalists sought independence during the 1980s and early 1990s. Violent confrontations occurred between pro-independence and anti-independence Melanesians, as well as European (mostly French) residents.

Religious Communal Terrorism

Sectarian violence refers to conflict between religious groups. It is sometimes one element of discord in a broader conflict between ethno-national groups. Many of the world's ethnic populations define their cultural identity partly through their religious beliefs, so that violence committed by and against them has both ethnic and religious qualities. This linkage is common in regions where ethnic groups with dissimilar religious beliefs have long histories of conflict, conquest, and resistance. In Sri Lanka, for example, the ongoing civil war between the Hindu Tamils and the Buddhist Sinhalese has been exceptionally violent, with massacres and indiscriminate killings a common practice.

Two examples further illustrate this point:

Nagorno-Karabakh Territory, Azerbaijan. After the Soviet bloc collapsed in 1989, fighting in the Nagorno-Karabakh territory of the Caucasus nation of Azerbaijan pitted majority Orthodox Christian Armenians in the territory against minority Muslim Azeri Turks. This conflict is both ethnic and religious, with the Armenians receiving military support for their national aspirations from the Republic Armenia, which eventually occupied 20% of Azerbaijan, including Nagorno-Karabakh. The Azeris have received support from the Republic of Azerbaijan.

Yugoslavia. Some intra-ethnic internecine conflict occurs because of combined nationalist aspirations and regional religious beliefs. The breakup of Yugoslavia led to internecine fighting, the worst of which occurred in Bosnia in 1992-1995. During fighting between Orthodox Christian Serbs, Muslim Bosnians, and Roman Catholic Croats, "ethnic cleansing"—the forcible removal of rival groups from claimed territory—was practiced by all sides. Significantly, all three religious groups are ethnic Slavs.

In both of the foregoing cases, regional nationalism was suppressed under the communist regimes in the Soviet Union and Yugoslavia. However, neither the Soviets nor Josip

Broz Tito's style of Yugoslav nationalist communism could eliminate centuries of ethnic and religious differences. When these regimes ended, those differences led to brutal communal violence.

Israel. In Israel, religion is used by both Jewish and Muslim militants to justify communal violence. For example, militant members of the Jewish settler community have regularly engaged in violence against Palestinians, usually retaliatory in nature. The religious nature of many of these attacks has been encouraged by members of radical organizations such as the late Rabbi Meir Kahane's **Kach** ("thus") movement, which has advocated the expulsion of all Arabs from biblical Jewish territories. Settlers generally rationalize their attacks as reprisals for Palestinian attacks and sometimes cite Jewish religious traditions as a basis for their actions. This kind of justification was used after an attack in 1983; when settlers

> killed an eleven-year-old Palestinian girl in the city of Nablus on the West Bank, a religious text was used in their defense. The chief rabbi of the Sephardic Jewish community referred to the talmudic text, which justified killing an enemy if one can see from a child's eyes that he or she will grow up to be your enemy.[30]

Thus, intractable religious sentiment exists on both sides of the conflict in Israel and Palestine, with Islamic extremists waging a holy war to expel Jews and Jewish settler extremists seeking to reclaim biblical lands and expel Arabs.

Not all religious communal terrorism occurs in an ethno-nationalist context. For example, religious campaigns are sometimes directed against perceived blasphemy to "purify" a religious belief. Religious fundamentalists of many religions have been known to chastise, denounce, and attack members of their own faiths for failing to follow the spiritual path of the fundamentalists. The perceived transgressors can be members of the same ethno-national group who are members of the same religion as the fundamentalists. Thus, the Algerian fundamentalist **Armed Islamic Group** waged a brutal religious communal war against their countrymen that took 75,000 lives. Similarly, the Egyptian fundamentalist Islamic Group, a cell-based organization, targeted fellow Muslims and Egyptian government officials, as well as Coptic Christians.[31]

Examples of religious communal conflict have occurred in the following countries and regions:[32]

Northern Ireland. In Northern Ireland, communal dissident terrorism between Catholic nationalists (Republicans) and Protestant unionists (Loyalists) became common during unrest that began in 1969. Targets included civilian leaders, opposition sympathizers, and random victims. From 1969 to 1989, of the 2,774 recorded deaths, 1,905 were civilians; of the civilian deaths, an estimated 440 were Catholic or Protestant terrorists.[33] Between 1969 and 1993, 3,284 people died. During this period, Loyalist paramilitaries killed 871 people, Republican paramilitaries killed 829 people, and British forces killed 203 people.[34]

Sudan. In Sudan, long-term animosity exists between the mostly Arabized[35] Muslim north and mostly Black Christian and animist (traditional religions) south. Civil war has been a feature of Sudanese political life since its independence in 1956, generally between progovernment Muslim groups and antigovernment Christian and animist groups. The war has been fought by conventional troops, guerrilla forces, undisciplined militias, and vigilantes.

Lebanon. In Lebanon, bloody religious communal fighting killed more than 125,000 people during the 16-year Lebanese civil war that began in 1975. Militias were formed along religious affiliations, so that Maronite Christians, Sunni Muslims, Shi'ite Muslims, and Druze all contended violently for political power. Palestinian fighters, Syrian troops, and Iranian revolutionaries were also part of this environment, which led to the breakdown of central government authority.

Ideological Communal Terrorism

Ideological communal terrorism in the post-World War II era reflected the global rivalry between the United States and Soviet Union. The capitalist democratic West competed with the authoritarian communist East for influence in the postcolonial developing world and in countries ravaged by invading armies during the war. A common pattern was for civil wars to break out after European colonial powers or Axis armies[36] were driven out of a country. These civil wars were fought by indigenous armed factions drawn from among the formerly occupied population. In China, Yugoslavia, Malaysia, and elsewhere, communist insurgents vied with traditional monarchists, nationalists, and democrats for power. Civilian casualties were high in all of these conflicts.

Examples of ideological communal conflict have occurred in the following countries and regions:[37]

Greece. The five-year-long civil war in Greece from 1944 to 1949 was a complicated and brutal affair that in the end took at least 50,000-65,000 lives. It involved fighting among conventional troops, guerrilla groups, gendarmerie (armed police), and armed bands. The Greek Communist Party, which had led a resistance group during the Second World War, fought against the Greek government in several phases after liberation in 1944. The Greek Communist Party eventually lost, in the only attempted communist takeover in postwar Europe to be defeated by force of arms.

Angola. In Angola, former anti-Portuguese allies fought a long conflict after independence in 1975. The ruling Movement for the Liberation of Angola (MPLA) is a Marxist-Leninist movement whose ideology promotes a multicultural and nationalistic (rather than ethnic or regional) agenda. Its principal adversary is National Union for the Total Independence of Angola (UNITA), mostly made up of the Ovimbundu tribal group. Because the MPLA leadership identified with the international ideological left, the Soviet Union, Cuba, the United States, and South Africa supported either the MPLA or UNITA. This is a rare example of conflict between a multicultural ideological movement and a regional ethnic movement.

Indonesia. In Indonesia, the Indonesian Communist Party (PKI) was implicated in an October 1965 abortive coup attempt. While the army rounded up PKI members and sympathizers, many Indonesians took to the streets to purge the communist presence. During a wave of anticommunist communal violence, much of it done by gangs supported by the government, roughly 500,000 communists, suspected communists, and political opponents to the government were killed.

Ideology has been used repeatedly in the 20th century to bind together nations or distinctive groups. It has become, in many conflicts, a means to discipline and motivate members of a movement. When applied to rationalize behavior in communal conflicts, the effect can be devastatingly brutal.

| Chapter Perspective 5.2 | Violence Against Women: Gender Communal Terrorism?[a] |

Violence against women has been an integral feature of wartime atrocities for centuries. In many conflicts, regular armies, irregular fighters, and politically motivated gangs have routinely selected the women of enemies to be kidnapped, raped, or killed. This type of violence has often been committed as a matter of policy and has been both systematic and methodical. As expressed by some violators, one motive behind systematic rape is to impregnate the women of an enemy group—thus "achieving forced pregnancy and thus poisoning the womb of the enemy."

The question is whether these gender-focused atrocities can be defined as **gender communal terrorism.**

The following are examples of communal gender violence against women.

- During the 1992-1995 war in Bosnia, an estimated 20,000 to 50,000 women were raped as part of ethnic cleansing campaigns. "Rape camps" and "rape hotels" were set up by Serb militia forces, where Muslim women were methodically raped, tortured, or killed.
- Hutu troops and militiamen in Rwanda systematically raped Tutsi women during the 1994 genocide.
- During the mid-1990s, the Armed Islamic Group in Algeria kidnapped and raped hundreds of women and young girls.

- During 1998 rioting and looting of ethnic Chinese neighborhoods in Jakarta, Indonesia, hundreds of ethnic Chinese women were allegedly raped by organized gangs.

The following are examples of government-initiated violence against women.

- During World War II, Japan provided "comfort women" to its armed forces. These were women from Korea, China, and other conquered territories who were forced into sexual slavery. In December 1937, thousands of Chinese women were raped, humiliated, and killed during the "Rape of Nanking."
- The Taliban regime in Afghanistan repressed women with edicts that forbade them from working, receiving an education, showing any portion of their body, and even wearing certain kinds of shoes. Reports indicate that some Taliban and tribal commanders kidnapped girls and women to serve as sexual concubines and servants for their fighters.[b]

During investigations and prosecutions of war crimes committed in the Balkans, the United Nations International Criminal Tribunal for the Former Yugoslavia—for the first time in the history of war crimes tribunals—officially recognized rape as a war crime.

a. For an excellent discussion of the international crime of systematic rape, see Crossette, Barbara. "An Old Scourge of War Becomes Its Latest Crime." *New York Times.* June 14, 1998.

b. In Afghanistan, the Revolutionary Association of the Women of Afghanistan was founded in 1977 to combat abuses against women. They actively opposed the Taliban government and have continued to fight for basic civil liberties. Their Web site can be accessed at www.rawa.org.

Source: Crossette, Barbara. "An Old Scourge of War Becomes Its Latest Crime." *The New York Times.* June 14, 1998. Used by permission.

Communal terrorism, like other terrorist typologies, is not static and continues to evolve. Chapter Perspective 5.2 presents the hypothesis that mass violence against women is a type of communal terrorism. As war crimes are redefined to incorporate crimes such as rape conducted by combatants, it is appropriate to consider the inclusion of politically motivated gender-based violence.

Case in Point   **The Tupamaros**

Uruguay is situated on the southeast Atlantic coast of South America. Although poor economic conditions led to labor unrest in the late 1950s, Uruguay, unlike many Latin American countries, had a political tradition of liberal democracy. It was, in fact, the most politically progressive country in South America. When militant unionists demonstrated in the capital city of Montevideo in 1962, a confrontation with the police led the government to denounce the labor activists as Marxists and revolutionaries. Out of this confrontation, the National Liberation Movement—better known as the **Tupamaros**—was formed. They named themselves after Tupac Amaru, the greatest Incan leader to resist the Spanish *conquistadores,* who was executed in 1572.

The Tupamaros were young, idealistic, middle-class rebels. Their enemy was the Uruguayan "oligarchy," and their constituency was the Uruguayan people. They styled themselves as Marxists and sought to redirect government priorities to redistribute wealth and political power to the working class. They sought broad-based public support from among the urban workers and unionists and had a fairly large and active cadre of aboveground supporters. Early in their movement, the Tupamaros realized that they could not directly confront the Uruguayan security forces, so they adopted Carlos Marighella's strategy of waging an "urban guerrilla," or terrorist, war with the immediate objective of forcing the government to adopt repressive measures, thereby causing the general population to rise up in revolt.

The Tupamaros operated widely in Montevideo. They received worldwide media attention, and are the only urban rebel movement to have come close to establishing "liberated zones" inside a major city. About 2,000 fighters were counted at the peak of their war. In the beginning, Tupamaro targets were selective, and they refrained from indiscriminate bombings or shootings. They robbed banks, exploded bombs, and kidnapped prominent Uruguayans for ransom. Later, they began to kill security officers and assassinate officials. In 1972, the Tupamaros kidnapped Sir Geoffrey Jackson, the British ambassador to Uruguay, holding him prisoner in a "people's prison" for eight months. When the British Foreign Office refused to negotiate for his release, the Tupamaros seemed to be at a loss about what to do—killing Jackson or releasing him without a ransom would accomplish nothing. They finally released him when 100 Tupamaros dramatically escaped from prison during a riot.

As anticipated, the Uruguayan government responded harshly—but not with the outcome theorized by Marighella. When the police could not contain the Tupamaros, they resorted to the systematic use of torture as a way to intimidate supporters and eliminate Tupamaro cells. Beatings, rapes, electric shocks, sleep deprivation, murder, and other methods were applied to extract information about Tupamaro operatives and sympathizers. They were successful, and mass arrests followed. When aboveground Tupamaro supporters failed to win any appreciable support at the election polls or from the labor unionists whom they had championed, the Tupamaros were eventually wiped out. Interestingly, popular support for government repression of the Tupamaros was widespread among Uruguayans.

The legacy of the Tupamaros was significant. They became a model for other armed dissidents in the 1960s and 1970s. Many young rebels in Latin America adopted their urban-based application of Marighella's strategy. Outside of Latin America, the Red Army Faction in West Germany, the Irish Republican Army in Northern Ireland, and Weather Underground in the United States all imitated the Tupamaros.

In the end, however, the Tupamaros were unable to accomplish any of the goals they fought for in Uruguay. In fact, their campaign was responsible for temporarily destroying democracy in the only country in Latin America that had never experienced a repressive dictatorship.

CHAPTER SUMMARY

This chapter provided students with an understanding of the nature of dissident terrorism. The purpose of this discussion was to identify and define several typologies of dissident behavior, to classify antistate dissident terrorism, to describe types of communal dissident terrorism, and to provide examples of these concepts.

The dissident terrorist paradigm identified several typologies of dissident terrorism. Included in this model were revolutionary, nihilist, nationalist, and criminal dissident terrorism. These typologies were defined and discussed with the underlying recognition that they are ideal categorizations, and it should be remembered that some terrorists will exhibit characteristics of several typologies. It should also be understood that new models became more common as the 20th century drew to a close—the cell organizational structures and "lone wolf" attacks are now integral elements of the modern terrorist environment.

Antistate dissident terrorism was defined as terrorism directed against existing governments and political institutions, attempting to destabilize the existing environment as a precondition to building a new society. Several antistate terrorist environments were presented as cases in point for understanding why violent antistate agitation may arise. The cases included the United States, several European societies, and a look at the nexus of antistate and communal violence in Israel. The seemingly irrational faith in ultimate victory despite overwhelming odds was examined; this faith in the inevitability of success is at the center of antistate dissident campaigns.

Communal terrorism was defined as "group against group" terrorism, wherein subpopulations of society wage internecine violence against each other. Several typologies were discussed to illustrate differences in motivations, manifestations of violence, and environments conducive to communal conflict. The typologies that were evaluated were ethnonationalist, religious, and ideological communal terrorism. Cases in point were identified that illustrated each concept, including a discussion of gender-focused terrorism.

In Chapter 6, students will review leftist ideologies and terrorist behavior. The discussion will focus on specific cases in point as well as the contexts for armed left-wing dissident movements. Reasons for leftist violence in liberal democracies will also be evaluated.

KEY TERMS AND CONCEPTS

The following topics were discussed in this chapter, and are found in the Glossary:

Abbas, Abu	Kach
Abu Nidal Organization	Lone wolf model
Al Aqsa Martyr Brigades	Narco-terrorism
Al Fatah	Nationalist dissident terrorism
Antistate terrorism	Nihilism
Arafat, Yasir	Nihilist dissident terrorism
Armed Islamic Group	Palestine Islamic Jihad
Booth, John Wilkes	Palestine Liberation Front
Cells	Palestine Liberation Organization
Communal terrorism	Popular Front for the Liberation of Palestine
Criminal dissident terrorism	Popular Front for the Liberation of
Democratic Front for the Liberation of	Palestine–General Command
Palestine	Provisional Irish Republican Army
Dissident terrorism	Red Army Faction
Ethno-nationalist communal terrorism	Red Brigades
Force 17	Religious communal terrorism
Freedom Birds	Revolutionary dissident terrorism
Gender communal terrorism	Sectarian violence
Guerrilla	*Sic semper tyrannis*
Hamas	Social Revolutionary Party
Ideological communal terrorism	Tupamaros
Intifadeh	Weather Underground Organization
Izzedine al-Qassam Brigade	Zapatista National Liberation Front

Discussion Box	**The Tamil Tigers**

This chapter's Discussion Box is intended to stimulate critical debate about the legitimacy of using guerrilla and terrorist tactics by dissident movements.

The Democratic Socialist Republic of Sri Lanka is an island nation in the Indian Ocean off the southeast coast of India. Its population is about 74% Sinhalese and 18% Tamil; the rest of the population is a mixture of other ethnic groups.[a]

In April 1987, more than 100 commuters were killed when terrorists—most likely Tamil Tigers—exploded a bomb in a bus station in the capital city of Colombo. This type of attack was typical in a long war of independence fought by the Liberation Tigers of Tamil Eelam (Tamil Tigers) against the Sri Lankan government. The Tamil Tigers were founded in 1976. They champion the Tamil people of Sri Lanka—Hindus who make up 18% of the population—against the majority Buddhist Sinhalese.

The goal of the movement is to carve out an independent state from Sri Lanka, geographically located in the north and east of the island. To accomplish this goal, the Tamil Tigers have used conventional, guerrilla, and terrorist tactics during the conflict and have attacked government, military, and civilian targets. A unit known as the Black Tigers specializes in terrorist attacks, often committing suicide in the process. Sinhalese forces and irregular gangs have often used extreme violence to repress the Tamil uprising.

About half the members of the Tiger movement have been teenagers. Indoctrination of potential Tigers includes spiritual purity, nationalist militancy, and a glorification of death. At the conclusion of training and indoctrination, young Tiger initiates are given a vial of cyanide, which is worn around the neck and intended to be taken if capture is inevitable. Songs, poetry, and rituals glorify the Tamil people and nation. A higher morality is systematically instilled in Tigers. The Tamil Tigers have been very shrewd with public relations, making extensive use of media such as video and the Internet; they have also established a foreign service presence in numerous countries. They also apparently became adept at transnational organized crime, raising revenue for the cause by trading in arms and drugs.

Estimates of the membership of the Tamil Tigers range from 6,000 to 15,000 fighters. They are well organized and disciplined. Women, called **Freedom Birds**, have taken on important leadership positions, as Tamil male leaders became casualties. About one third of the movement's members are women.

Some Tamil Tiger attacks have been spectacular. In May 1991, a Tamil girl detonated a bomb, killing herself and Indian Prime Minister Rajiv Gandhi. In 1996, Tigers surrounded and annihilated a government base, killing all 1,200 troops. Also in 1996, a Tiger bomb at Colombo's Central Bank killed scores and injured 1,400 others. In 1997, the new Colombo Trade Center was bombed, causing 18 deaths and more than 100 injuries. The Tamil Tigers operate a small naval unit of speedboats (the Sea Tigers) that interdict Sri Lankan shipping. Fighting has centered repeatedly on the Jaffna peninsula in the north, with both sides capturing and losing bases.

By 1997, the war had claimed at least 58,000 military and civilian lives, including 10,000 Tigers. By 2002, the combatants had fought to a stalemate. In early 2002, both sides agreed to Norwegian mediation to negotiate terms for a lasting peace settlement. Several hundred thousand Tamils have fled the island, with more than 100,000 living in India and about 200,000 living in the West.

Discussion Questions

- Is terrorism a legitimate tactic in a war for national independence? Does the quest for national freedom justify the use of terrorist tactics?
- When a cause is considered just, is it acceptable to use propaganda to depict the enemy as uncompromisingly corrupt, decadent, and ruthless, regardless of the truth of these allegations?

- Is suicidal resistance merely fanatical and irrational, or is it a "higher" form of commitment to one's struggle for freedom? Is this type of indoctrination and myth building necessary to sustain this level of commitment to a just cause?
- When a cause is just, are arms smuggling and drug trafficking acceptable options for raising funds?
- Are the Tamil Tigers terrorists or freedom fighters?

NOTE

a. Data are derived from Central Intelligence Agency. *The World Fact Book 2001.* Washington, DC: Central Intelligence Agency, 2001.

Tamil Tigers on parade. Members of the Liberation Tigers of Tamil Eelam stand for review.

Source: Hulton Archive/Getty Images; used by permission.

RECOMMENDED WEB SITES

The following Web sites provide links to dissident revolutionary organizations, movements, and information.

Al-Fatah: www.fateh.net
Foreign Terrorist Organizations: www.state.gov/www/global/terrorism/terror_org.html
Irish Northern Aid (Noraid): http://inac.org
Liberation Tigers of Tamil Eelam: www.eelam.com
Terrorist Profiles: web.nps.navy.mil/~library/tgp/tgpmain.htm

WEB EXERCISE

Using this chapter's recommended Internet sites, conduct an online investigation of dissident terrorism.

- How would you describe the self-images presented by dissident movements?
- Based on the information given by the monitoring organizations, are some dissident movements seemingly more threatening than others? Less threatening? Why?
- Compare the dissident Web sites to the monitoring agencies' sites. Are any of the dissident groups *unfairly* reported by the monitoring agencies?

For an online search of dissident terrorism, students should activate the search engine on their Web browser and enter the following keywords:

"Terrorist Organizations (or Groups)"
"Revolutionary Movements"
The names of specific dissident organizations

RECOMMENDED READINGS

The following publications provide discussions on dissident activism, protest movements, and violence.

Barkan, Steven E., and Lynne L. Snowden. *Collective Violence*. Boston: Allyn & Bacon, 2001.
Bell, J. Boywer. *The IRA 1968 -2000: Analysis of a Secret Army*. London: Frank Cass, 2000.
Jaber, Hala. *Hezbollah: Born With a Vengeance*. New York: Columbia University Press, 1997.
Mallin, Jay, ed. *Terror and Urban Guerrillas: A Study of Tactics and Documents*. Coral Gables, FL: University of Miami Press, 1971.
Wickham-Crowley, Timothy P. *Guerrillas and Revolution in Latin America: A Comparative Study of Insurgents and Regimes Since 1956*. Princeton, NJ: Princeton University Press, 1993.

NOTES

[1] *Webster's New Twentieth Century Dictionary of the English Language, Unabridged*, 2d ed. New York: Publishers Guild, 1966.

[2] Whittaker, David J., ed. *The Terrorism Reader*. New York: Routledge, 2001, p. 33.

[3] Schultz, Richard. "Conceptualizing Political Terrorism." *Journal of International Affairs* 32 (1978): 1, 7-15. Quoted in Whittaker (note 2 above).

[4] Barkan, Steven E., and Lynne L. Snowden. *Collective Violence*. Boston: Allyn & Bacon, 2001, p. 70.

[5] Gurr, Ted Robert. "Political Terrorism: Historical Antecedents and Contemporary Trends." In Gurr, Ted Robert, ed. *Violence in America: Protest, Rebellion, Reform*, vol. 2. Newbury Park, CA: Sage, 1989, p. 204.

[6] Gibbs, J. P. "Conceptualization of Terrorism." *American Sociological Review* 54 (1989): 329-40.

[7] Hamm, Mark S., ed. *Hate Crime: International Perspectives on Causes and Control*. Cincinnati, OH, and Highland Heights, KY: Anderson and Academy of Criminal Justice Sciences, 1994, p. 178. Citing Gibbs (note 6 above).

[8] Sederberg, Peter C. *Terrorist Myths: Illusion, Rhetoric, and Reality*. Englewood Cliffs, NJ: Prentice Hall, 1989.

[9] The *Mini-Manual* is reprinted in Mallin, Jay, ed. *Terror and Urban Guerrillas: A Study of Tactics and Documents*. Coral Gables, FL: University of Miami Press, 1971, pp. 70-115.

[10] Reeve, Simon. *The New Jackals: Ramzi Yousef, Osama bin Laden and the Future of Terrorism*. Boston: Northeastern University Press, 1999, p. 170.

[11] Hewitt, Christopher. "Public's Perspectives." In Paletz, David L., and Alex P. Scmid. *Terrorism and the Media*. Newbury Park, CA: Sage, 1992, p. 182.

[12] For an interesting discussion about drug-related criminal terrorism, see Ehrenfeld, Rachel. *Narco-Terrorism*. New York: Basic Books, 1990.

[13] Crosbie-Weston, R. "Terrorism and the Rule of Law." In Cross, R. W., ed. *20th Century*. London: Purnell Reference Books, 1979, p. 2715.

[14] Associated Press. "Did Shoe Bombing Suspect Act Alone?" *Christian Science Monitor*. December 27, 2001.

[15] An excellent discussion of this progression is found in Smith, Brent L. *Terrorism in America: Pipe Bombs and Pipe Dreams*. Albany: State University of New York Press, 1994.

[16] The Provisional IRA was formed in 1969 when radicals broke from the official IRA, which was more political than military.

[17] For an excellent analysis of the IRA and the "troubles" in Northern Ireland, see Bell, J. Boywer. *The IRA 1968–2000: Analysis of a Secret Army*. London: Frank Cass, 2000.

[18] An interesting compilation of British newspaper reports from the Spanish Civil war is published in Haigh, R. H., D. S. Morris, and A. R. Peters, eds. *The Guardian Book of the Spanish Civil War*. Aldershot, UK: Wildwood House, 1987.

[19] Whittaker, David J. (note 2 above), p. 126.

[20] Also known as the Quaraysh, who were the tribe that the prophet Mohammed was born into. Mohammed split from his tribe to gather together his Muslim followers in 622 during "the migration" (*hijrah*). The Quaraysh never forgave him for leaving the tribe and became his most formidable foes. The Muslims were eventually victorious over the Quaraysh. See Armstrong, Karen. *Islam: A Short History*. New York: Modern Library, 2000, pp. 13-23.

[21] Hoffman, Bruce. *Inside Terrorism*. New York: Columbia University Press, 1998, p. 169.

[22] See Marighella, Carlos. *Mini-Manual of the Urban Guerrilla*. In Mallin, Jay, ed. *Terror and Urban Guerrillas: A Study of Tactics and Documents*. Coral Gables, FL: University of Miami Press, 1971, pp. 110-12.

[23] Hoffman (note 21 above), p. 169.

[24] Podesta, Don. "The Terrible Toll of Human Hatred." *Washington Post National Weekly Edition*. June 8, 1987. Quoted in Schechterman, Bernard, and Martin Slann, eds. *Violence and Terrorism*, 3d ed. Guilford, CT: Dushkin, 1993, p. 33.

[25] Barkan and Snowden (note 4 above), p. 67.

[26] Podesta (note 24 above).

[27] Thomas, Trent N. "Global Assessment of Current and Future Trends in Ethnic and Religious Conflict." In Pfaltzgraff, Robert L., Jr., and Richard A. Schultz, eds. *Ethnic Conflict and Regional Instability*. Carlisle, PA: Strategic Studies Institute, 1994, pp. 33-41. Quoted in Schechterman, Bernard, and Martin Slann, eds. *Violence and Terrorism*, 5th ed. Guilford, CT: Dushkin, 1999, p. 24.

[28] The Inkatha Freedom Party's Web site can be accessed at www.ifp.org.za.

[29] Information from Central Intelligence Agency. *The World Fact Book 2001*. Washington, DC: Central Intelligence Agency, 2001, and Podesta (note 24 above).

[30] Kelly, Robert J., and Jess Maghan. *Hate Crime: The Global Politics of Polarization*. Carbondale and Edwardsville: Southern Illinois University Press, 1998, p. 91.

[31] Copts are Orthodox Christians whose presence in Egypt predates the Arab conquest.

[32] Central Intelligence Agency (note 29 above) and Podesta (note 24 above).

[33] Clutterbuck, Richard. *Terrorism, Drugs and Crime in Europe After 1992*. New York: Routledge, 1990, p. 73.

[34] *Irish News*. November 30, 1993. Reporting on a joint study by the Northern Ireland Economic Research Centre in Belfast and the Economic and Social Research Institute in Dublin.

[35] Some northerners are ethnic Arabs, but many are not. Nevertheless, non-Arab Muslims have been heavily influenced by their Arab neighbors and fellow Muslims and hence have developed an "Arabized" culture.

[36] The Axis powers were an alliance of Germany, Japan, Italy, and their allies.

[37] Podesta (note 24 above).

Chapter 6

CLASS STRUGGLE AND NATIONAL LIBERATION: THE TERRORIST LEFT

This chapter revisits left-wing terrorism, which was first introduced in Chapter 2. Students will recall that the imprecise—and confusing—term *radical* has been used to describe leftist extremism. Rather than strictly applying this term, the important concept to remember is that leftist extremism is future oriented, seeking to reform or destroy an existing system prior to building a new and just society. When leftists champion a particular group, it is one that is perceived to be oppressed unjustly by a corrupt system or government. In this sense, leftist extremism is idealistic.

Fringe-left ideology in the 20th century was usually an extreme application of Marxist ideology, and it generally adopted the doctrines of class warfare or national liberation to justify political violence. On the radical left wing, violence has been seen as a perfectly legitimate option, because the terrorist group considers itself to be at war against an oppressive class, government, or system. The terrorist group pictures itself as a righteous champion of the poor and downtrodden.

One theoretical pattern that has appeared repeatedly on the radical left is the adoption of a "**vanguard strategy**" by leftist activists. This strategy is, in essence, a belief that revolutionary conditions will rarely occur *spontaneously* from within the exploited lower classes or group. Instead, revolutionary conditions must be *created* by a committed and disciplined revolutionary movement, which will build a generalized climate of change. When this happens, the exploited class or group will become "politically conscious" and will accept revolution as a preferable alternative to the existing system. Those activists who would create this climate of change are the "vanguard" of the soon-to-be revolutionary exploited classes or group. Not surprisingly, the vanguard group's membership tended to be drawn from among a young educated elite that became disaffected by what they perceived to be a system of exploitation and privilege.

Vanguard theory was put into practice time after time during the 20th century. Two short cases in point illustrate this pattern:

Russian Vanguard of the Proletariat. The vanguard strategy was adopted by Russian communists during the creation of the first successful Communist Party and was applied worldwide by other communist parties.[1] Lenin and the Bolsheviks (literally, "majoritarians") who built the party required their followers to consider themselves to be the **vanguard of the proletariat** (Marx's term for the working class); they were an elite who would bring about the revolution and build the communist society.

Foquismo. In another application of the vanguard strategy, Latin American revolutionary Ernesto "Che" Guevara believed after the Cuban Revolution that a transnational climate of revolutionary change could be created in South America, and that all of Latin America could be swept by revolution—all that was needed was a revolutionary "push" by a vanguard of dedicated revolutionaries. Guevara and his followers were annihilated in Bolivia while trying to deliver that push in 1967.[2] Guevara's (and the Cuban) variant on this theory was termed *foquismo,* or "armed struggle." It included an emphasis on creating an immediate impact on the general political environment, rather than engaging in a long process of "consciousness building" among the lower classes.

The discussion in this chapter will review:

- Left-Wing Ideology and Activism
- Leftist Terrorism
- The Future of the Violent Left

LEFT-WING IDEOLOGY AND ACTIVISM

Leftist agitation is group oriented. Emphasis has traditionally been placed on creating a collective political consciousness—a class or national consciousness—within the championed group. On the far and fringe left, this collective political consciousness is considered a precondition to successful revolution. Hence, indoctrination has been used by radical leftists to fashion a disciplined and motivated "**cadre group,**" who represent the interests of the class or national group. At the vanguard of the struggle, then, are the political and military cadres—those who have been indoctrinated to engage in political agitation and armed conflict on behalf of the championed group. This concept of a politically disciplined cadre group has been applied by leftist extremists in many contexts, including nonviolent agitation, guerrilla warfare, and terrorist campaigns.

Many leftists, especially Marxists, believe that capitalism inherently causes social and economic inequities that relegate working people and other groups (such as racial minorities)[3] to a subordinate political status. The political agenda on the left frequently reflects this fundamental principle.

The following propositions summarize the quality of activism by modern leftists:

1. Radical leftists tend to emphasize "economic rights" as a priority. Because orthodox Marxists and other radical socialists represent ideological and class interests, "rights" are defined within the context of redistributing the wealth and basic services to lower classes and groups. It was therefore not uncommon for radicals on the left to conclude that political rights are secondary to economic rights. Examples of economic rights include guaranteed health care, a job, enough income to support a household, and retirement benefits. Unlike coalitional political parties in the United States and elsewhere—which build broad demographic bases of political support—communist and socialist parties are usually affiliated with labor unions, minority or exploited demographic groups, or other political and economic interests.

2. Democratic socialism emphasizes reform, not revolution. Democratic socialist political parties—usually called Social Democrat parties—are quite common around the world and are affiliated with one another through the Socialist International. Although socialists seek to redistribute wealth and services to a subordinate group, this is usually done nonviolently. The democratic socialist movement seeks to influence policy democratically, although selective demonstrations or labor strikes are sometimes advocated to pressure the governing authorities. In many democracies—particularly in Europe—Social Democrat parties wield significant political influence and have large delegations in Parliaments and other elected assemblies.

3. Communists traditionally emphasize revolution, not reform. Orthodox communism offers a vision of doing away with the capitalist system completely and reconfiguring society as a model of complete economic equality—ideally with no dominant or subordinate classes. As discussed in Chapter 2, orthodox Marxism claims to be a scientific theory, so that class conflict is inevitable and a future communist society is ensured. Some communist movements and communist parties were violently activist, adopting armed insurgency and terrorism as viable options. In the developing world, this insurgent variant of Marxist activism continued well into the 1980s; some insurgencies in countries such as Colombia and Peru continued through the 1990s. Other communist parties, especially those in Western Europe, adapted to specific democratic environments, so that by the mid-1970s, "democratic communism" became fashionable. In Europe, this phenomenon was known as "EuroCommunism" and was a strategic adaptation of Western communist parties to the generalized prosperity and stability of the West.

4. Because democratic socialists are traditionally reformers, and communists are traditionally revolutionaries, they tend to distrust each other. The history of interaction between communist and democratic socialist parties has been contentious. Although democratic socialist parties have acquired sufficient respectability to become a mainstream force in many countries, communist parties have never acquired lasting mainstream support.

5. Leftist terrorists in Western democracies often considered the working class to be corrupted or co-opted by capitalism. The Weather Underground in the United States and the Red Army Faction in West Germany claimed to fight on behalf of the oppressed of their countries and the exploited people of the developing world. They held little faith that the working classes in their countries would develop a revolutionary class consciousness sufficient for them to identify with the oppressed of the world.

Three subjects of leftist activism are discussed below: class struggle, leftist nationalism, and special-interest extremism.

Class Struggle

Marxists have traditionally focused their attention on being a vanguard movement on behalf of the working class. They faithfully believe that this class struggle will end in victory by the working class.

"Class struggle" refers to more than simply competition between people with different job incomes. In fact, orthodox Marxists would argue that one's income alone does not confer class status. According to Karl Marx, one's class is determined by one's relationship to the **"means of production"** (the historical and evolutionary significance of this relationship was discussed in Chapter 2). Because Marx and Engels wrote *Manifesto of the Communist Party* and other documents[4] during the Industrial Age, one's relationship to the means of production referred to whether one was a wage-earning worker (the **proletariat**), a small-time shop owner or wage-owning manager (the **bourgeoisie**), or an owner of an industrial enterprise. The political power of each group, and the degree of exploitation suffered by each group, was determined by that group's relationship to the means of production.

According to Marx, the owners are the political and economic ruling class, the bourgeoisie are a co-opted middle class, and the proletariat is a class of exploited labor. After the proletarian revolution, he envisioned the creation of a communist society under the

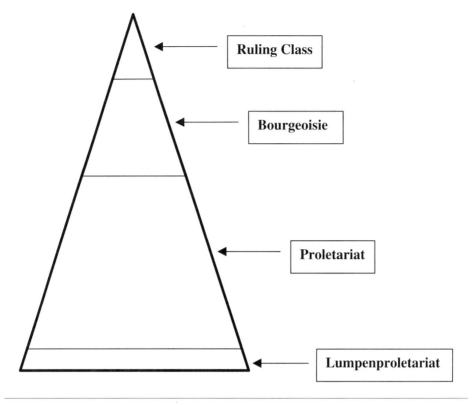

Figure 6.1   Marx: The Industrial Age Class Pyramid

leadership of the working class—a society that he termed the **dictatorship of the prole-tariat**. There was no blueprint for the creation of this new society; instead, Marx believed that the state would simply wither away after the revolution.

Interestingly, Marx championed the industrial working class and dismissed any attempt to mobilize either the peasantry or the marginalized sectors of society (the **lumpen-proletariat**). To Marx, the peasants' relationship to the means of production (agricultural laborers) meant that they were socially and politically isolated from each other. Because of this, they could never develop lasting revolutionary political organization. This analysis was proven wrong. Despite Marx's emphasis on the revolution of the industrial working class, successful Marxist rebellions during the 20th century occurred not in industrialized nations, but in agrarian peasant-based societies in the developing world. This occurred in China, Vietnam, and Nicaragua. Other successful non-Marxist rural-based rebellions in the 20th century occurred in Mexico and Algeria.

Figure 6.1 illustrates the class pyramid during the industrial age, which Marx considered to be the final age of human society prior to the dictatorship of the proletariat.

For the People—Leftist Nationalism

Nationalism is a concept that promotes the aspirations of groups of people who are distinguished by their cultural, religious, ethnic, or racial heritage. It is difficult to apply the categories of the classical ideological continuum (fringe left to fringe right) to nationalist movements, because the guiding motivation behind these movements is national identity. In cases where ideological theory becomes secondary to promoting one's national identity, the labels of "right-wing" and "left-wing" become imprecise.

Examples of this imprecision include the Provisional IRA in Northern Ireland (Provos), UNITA in Angola, and the PLO in Israel. All adopted Marxist rhetoric and theory during their wars, but none of them fit straightforwardly into the Marxist camp. Among these groups,

- The Provisional IRA's leftist political agenda (as opposed to its violent methodology) in the end became no more extreme than other European social democratic agendas, and in fact, the Provos' leftist rhetoric disappeared gradually during the 1980s.
- UNITA began its "war of national liberation" against the colonial Portuguese as a Marxist insurgency. After the Portuguese were driven out and UNITA's civil war began against the pro-Soviet MPLA, its ideological foundation shifted from Marxist to anticommunist. UNITA's cause against the MPLA was supported by South Africa and the United States.
- The PLO's internal political agenda is coalitional. As discussed in Chapter 5, some PLO factions were overtly Marxist and secular. Others were nationalistic but non-Marxist. The PLO as an umbrella organization is best described as a nationalistic organization with a number of Marxist members.

One may conclude from these examples that nationalist movements have selectively applied Marxism as required by their unique circumstances. These movements were, in fact, an adaptation of orthodox Marxist theory to the reality of 20th-century political conflict. For Karl Marx, guerrilla warfare in the developing world did not enter into his calculation for bringing about the workers' revolution, and nationalism was certainly subordinate to class consciousness. In theory, the workers would simply rise up under the leadership of their party (the Communist Party). In practice, nationalists often adopted a political ideology in their struggle for national independence, and Marxism was frequently the ideology of choice.

During the Cold War rivalry between the United States and the Soviet Union, each superpower displayed a persistent pattern of international behavior. The Soviets tended to side with nationalist insurgencies in the developing world, whereas the United States supported the embattled established governments. These insurgencies took on the characteristics of Marxist revolutions, and the embattled governments became, from the perspective of the United States, bulwarks against the spread of communism. The Soviets, and to a lesser extent the Chinese, armed and financed many of these "**wars of national liberation**" against United States-supported regimes.

Nationalism and Marxism were synthesized repeatedly by 20th-century revolutionaries in the developing world. Three of these conflicts—led by Mao Zedong in China, Ho Chi Minh in Vietnam, and Fidel Castro in Cuba[5]—came to symbolize the new phenomenon of leftist nationalism. Left-wing revolutionaries in the West drew on these examples and developed theories of solidarity with Marxist nationalists to justify acts of violence in Western democracies. As discussed later, many New Left revolutionaries in the West were particularly receptive to the theory that their terrorist campaigns in Western democracies were linked to the nationalistic armed insurgencies in the developing world. From their perspective, all of these struggles were part of a worldwide war against capitalism, imperialism, and exploitation.

Special-Interest Extremism

Special-interest extremism is also described as "single-issue" terrorism. Unlike the global scope of Marxist ideology or the nation-building goal of nationalism, special-interest extremism involves agitation on behalf of a narrowly drawn political interest. These political interests are often very specific, so that violence is usually carefully focused. For example, animal rights activists have repeatedly vandalized, or "trashed," laboratories.

The key feature of this type of terrorist behavior is that its motives are confined to the single cause, and its goals are limited. As noted by former Federal Bureau of Investigation (FBI) Director Louis Freeh,

> Special interest terrorism differs from traditional right-wing and left-wing terrorism in that extremist special interest groups seek to resolve specific issues, rather than effect more widespread political change. Special interest extremists . . . conduct acts of politically motivated violence to force segments of society, including the general public, to change attitudes about issues considered important to their causes . . . Some special interest extremists—most notably within the animal rights and environmental movements—have turned increasingly toward vandalism and terrorist activity in attempts to further their causes.[6]

Mainstream special-interest movements on the left include left-wing environmentalism, the peace movement, the antinuclear movement, the civil rights moment, feminism, and alternative lifestyle groups. Extremists within each of these movements include radical animal rights groups, neo-anarchist groups, Black Power advocates, and radical feminist groups. One commonality among modern special-interest extremists is that they believe their narrow issue is universally important and is linked to other "rights" movements. Hence, animal rights and neo-anarchist radicals find common cause on the question of exploitation by international business interests.

For many radicals, political dissent and terrorist violence are necessary to "save" a fundamental truth. For those on the fringes of these movements, the only means to save their fundamental truth may be the destruction of an existing social order or economic system. Thus, ecological and animal rights terrorists have engaged in politically motivated vandalism and arson to "save the planet" from human exploitation. This is obviously a nihilist dissident strategy.

Problems on the Radical Left

The radical left was never a monolithic or united belief system. It was always factionalized and underwent a never-ending process of internecine feuding that ended in ideological and organizational splits. Many of these feuds ended in bloodshed.

A number of theoretical and practical challenges arose on the radical left, several of which have been alluded to. The following four problems are illustrative of these challenges.

The first problem was that Marx and other orthodox socialist revolutionaries assumed that the communist revolution would occur in one or both of the two most industrialized nations of the time—either Great Britain or Germany. Despite this fundamental and "scientific" faith, the first communist revolution occurred in Russia, which was a pre-industrial, peasant-based, semifeudal society. This presented Marxists with a problem, because history was not unfolding as it should. The solution was one that was repeated again and again on the radical left: Simply redesign the basic ideology to reflect the new reality, and reassess the revolution's strategy and tactics. Thus,

- Lenin organized the Communist Party as a vanguard party;
- Stalin consolidated communism in one country, thus rejecting Trotsky's theory of "permanent revolution" (described later);

- Mao designed a revolutionary philosophy and strategy that was adopted extensively in the developing world; and
- Nationalists used Marxism to organize, discipline, and motivate their followers in their quest for national independence.

A second problem was the revolutionary party. Once Lenin and others accepted the need to give the revolution a "push," they designed a revolutionary party as the mechanism to do so. The new Communist Party was a vanguard party and a combat party. It was nothing like traditional political parties in democratic societies. However, the communist movement could not determine what kind of revolutionary party should represent the workers. This question was at the heart of infighting in the communist movement and led to repeated splits in the Communist Party, as dissident factions either broke away or were expelled. As expected, each new faction considered itself to be the true heir of Karl Marx's vision.

The first great split occurred between the followers of Stalin and the followers of Leon Trotsky. **Stalinists** worked to consolidate communism in the Soviet Union, known in the movement as "**socialism in one country**." They also tried to rally all communist parties worldwide under the leadership and inspiration of the Communist Party of the Soviet Union. **Trotskyites** rejected the idea of building socialism in one country and promoted international agitation as a worldwide revolutionary movement—a theory referred to as "**the permanent revolution**." This split in the movement continued into the 21st century, with Trotskyites continuing to refer to the Soviet Union as an excellent example of a "**degenerate workers' state**."

A third problem involved the application of theory to practice. The communist pantheon (leadership in the movement) from the Soviet perspective moved from Marx to Lenin to Stalin. When Stalin died in 1953, the most important figure in the international communist movement was China's Mao Zedong. However, the Soviets never considered Mao to be an heir of Stalin, and another split occurred in the ranks of international communism. Soviet communism was centered in Eastern Europe, with allies among insurgent movements and newly formed leftist regimes such as in Cuba, Angola, and Ethiopia. The Chinese became prominent for their contribution to revolutionary and guerrilla theory in the developing world; they considered the Soviets to be "social imperialists."

A fourth problem was the reality that the working class in the liberal democratic West would likely never acquire a sufficiently revolutionary class consciousness. This realization was a blow to orthodox Marxists and radical leftists, who had long considered the working class to be the true standard bearers of revolution and human progress. The radical left adapted their ideological foundation to allow for the inclusion of peasant-based rural revolutionaries as their new championed class. These "Third World revolutionaries" became iconic on the radical left, and many Western leftists chose these revolutionaries as the new championed group. Additionally, young members of the New Left during the 1960s largely rejected orthodox Marxism and took on the revolutionary theories of Fanon, Marcuse, and Marighella (discussed later in this chapter). Nevertheless, some radical leftists—especially the Trotskyites—maintained the orthodox Marxist fiction that the workers of the world would someday unite.

Case: Required Reading on the "New Left"

In the postwar West, many leftist terrorists were inspired not by orthodox Marxism, but by examples of revolutionaries in the developing world such as Mao, Ho Chi Minh, Castro, and Guevara. Realizing as a practical matter that building guerrilla units in the countryside was impossible—and that the working class was not sufficiently prepared for revolution—many young radicals became nihilistic dissident revolutionaries. They concluded that revolution is a goal in itself, and "revolution for the hell of it"[7] became a slogan and a practice for many left-wing radicals in the West. For them, there was little vision of what kind of society would be built on the rubble of the old. In fact,

> The central question about the rationality of some terrorist organizations, such as the West German groups of the 1970s or the Weather Underground in the United States, is whether or not they had a sufficient grasp of reality . . . to calculate the likely consequences of the courses of action they chose.[8]

Nevertheless, from the perspective of radical activists and intellectuals, nihilist dissident behavior was rational and logical.

Several books inspired radical leftists in the West. These books provided a rational justification for revolutionary agitation against democratic institutions in relatively prosperous societies. They came to define the New Left of the 1960s and 1970s, which rejected the rigid ideological orthodoxy of the "Old Left" Marxists. They created a new interpretation of revolutionary conditions. On the short list of "required reading" among radical activists were three books:[9]

- Frantz Fanon's *The Wretched of the Earth,*
- Herbert Marcuse's *One-Dimensional Man,* and
- Carlos Marighella's *Mini-Manual of the Urban Guerrilla.*

The Wretched of the Earth. In *The Wretched of the Earth,* Fanon analyzed the role of indigenous people living in countries controlled by imperial governments that exploited local resources and imposed a foreign culture and values. He concluded that revolutionary violence was perfectly justifiable under these conditions. In fact, it was required, because, in addition to liberating one's country, one had to liberate oneself as an individual; only "liberating violence" could do this. Young radicals in the West agreed with this analysis, and some concluded that liberating violence in a prosperous society was justified. They also rationalized their violent political behavior by establishing a sense of revolutionary solidarity with "the wretched of the earth."

One-Dimensional Man. Marcuse was a French philosopher who, along with Jean-Paul Sartre, was prominent among existentialist writers. He argued in *One-Dimensional Man* that capitalist society—no matter how prosperous or democratic—creates "manacles" of privilege that keep the public docile and content. He explained that the people's oppression is measured by how much they have been co-opted by the accoutrements of capitalist comfort. Using this analysis, middle-class college students who considered themselves to be Marxists could justify revolutionary activism, even though they were far removed from the working class. Thus, they were rejecting their "manacles" of privilege and fighting in common cause with other revolutionaries worldwide.

Mini-Manual of the Urban Guerrilla. As discussed in Chapter 5, Carlos Marighella's book was extremely influential on leftist revolutionary strategy in Latin America, Western Europe, and the United States. It was a blueprint for revolution in urban societies, and Marighella's guidelines for using urban terrorism to create revolutionary conditions were practiced widely. However, as noted previously, the assumption that the exploited group would join the revolution at the right time rarely happened in practice.

These works of dissident philosophy shaped the ideological justifications for the tactics of many revolutionary movements. For example, the motivation behind West Germany's

Red Army Faction has been described as having three central elements. These elements reflect the revolutionary literature and theory of the time.[10] They were:

- The concept of the "armed struggle" and the model of Third World liberation movements . . .
- The Nazi "connection" and "formal democracy" in the Federal Republic . . . [and]
- The rejection of consumer society.[11]

LEFTIST TERRORISM

Leftist terrorism in its modern context originated after the 1848 revolutions in Europe. Anarchism and Marxism provided the philosophical basis for revolutionary violence, and many who adopted these ideologies engaged in acts of terrorism. Throughout the 20th century, variations of anarchism and Marxism were repeatedly adapted to unique sociopolitical conditions.

Historically, left-wing terrorism has not been a method of first resort. It usually occurred after other options were tried and abandoned, sometimes as an expression of frustration with the pace of change, and other times after the state repressed leftist dissent. In fact, "traditional left-wing doctrine has favored terrorism only in rare cases . . . not because they were humanitarians but because they feared that terrorism opened the door to all kinds of possibilities that might endanger their own cause."[12]

Once the line had been crossed between peaceful dissent and a strategy of violent agitation, terrorism repeatedly became an accepted option among left-wing extremists.

Perspective on the Left:
Two Examples From 19th-Century Europe

Modern left-wing terrorism is not a product of the 20th century. Its ideological ancestry dates to the 19th century, when anarchist and communist philosophers began to advocate the destruction of capitalist and imperial society—what Karl Marx referred to as the "spectre . . . haunting Europe."[13] Some revolutionaries readily encouraged the use of terrorism in the new cause. One theorist, **Karl Heinzen** in Germany, anticipated the late 20th-century fear that terrorists might obtain weapons of mass destruction when he supported the acquisition of new weapons technologies to utterly destroy the enemies of the people. According to Heinzen, these weapons should include poison gas and new high-yield explosives.[14]

During the 19th century, several terrorist movements championed the rights of the lower classes. These movements were prototypes for 20th-century groups and grew out of social and political environments that were unique to their countries. To illustrate this point, the following two cases in point are drawn from early industrial England and the semifeudal Russia context of the late 19th century.

The **Luddites** were English workers in the early 1800s who objected to the social and economic transformations of the Industrial Revolution. Their principal objection was that industrialization threatened their jobs, and so they targeted the machinery of the new textile factories. Textile mills and weaving machinery were disrupted and sabotaged. For example, they attacked stocking looms that mass-produced stockings at the expense of skilled stocking weavers who made them by hand.

A mythical figure, Ned Ludd, was the supposed founder of the Luddite movement. The movement was active from 1811 to 1816 and was responsible for sabotaging and destroying wool and cotton mills. The British government eventually suppressed the movement by passing anti-Luddite laws, including establishing the crime of "machine breaking," which was punishable by death. After 17 Luddites were executed in 1813, the movement gradually died out. Modern anti-technology activists and terrorists, such as the Unabomber Theodore Kaczynski, are sometimes referred to as neo-Luddites.

People's Will (Narodnaya Volya) in Russia was a direct outgrowth of student dissatisfaction with the czarist regime in the late 19th century. Many young Russian university students, some of whom had studied abroad, became imbued with the ideals of anarchism and Marxism. Many of these students became radical reformists who championed the rights of the people, particularly the peasant class. A populist revolutionary society, Land and Liberty (Zemlya Volya), was founded in 1876 with the goal of fomenting a mass peasant uprising by settling radical students among them to raise their class consciousness. After a series of arrests and mass public trials, Land and Liberty split into two factions in 1879. One faction, Black Repartition, kept to the goal of a peasant revolution. The other faction was People's Will, who fashioned themselves into a conspiratorial terrorist organization.

People's Will believed that they understood the underlying problems of Russia better than the uneducated masses of people did, and they concluded that they were therefore better able to force government change. This was, in fact, one of the first examples of a revolutionary vanguard strategy. They believed that they could both demoralize the czarist government and expose its weaknesses to the peasantry. People's Will quickly embarked on a terrorist campaign against carefully selected targets. Incidents of terror committed by People's Will—and other revolutionaries who emulated them—included shootings, knifings, and bombings against government officials. In one successful attack, Czar Alexander II was assassinated by a terrorist bomb on March 1, 1881. The immediate outcome of the terrorist campaign was the installation of a repressive police state in Russia that, although not as efficient as later police states would be in the Soviet Union or Nazi Germany, succeeded in harassing and imprisoning most members of People's Will.

Regional Case: Latin America

Latin America has a long history of political agitation, repression, and rebellion. The postwar era has seen dozens of revolutions, coups, attempted coups, civil wars, military dictatorships, and proxy wars. Terrorism from the right and left has been common.

Armed leftist activism in the postwar era has posed serious challenges to many established governments. Armed Marxist guerrillas have operated in the countryside of several nations, and urban terrorists—who resolutely applied Marighella's *Mini-Manual*—have appeared repeatedly in Latin America. Although leftist nationalism did occur in the postwar era, most leftist insurgents were dedicated Marxists. Some similarities can be found in many of these insurgencies, including the following:

- Virtually all left-wing Latin American revolutionaries applied versions of Marxist ideology to their cause.
- The United States was considered to be an imperialist power that propped up repressive right-wing dictatorships, and thus opposing the United States became central to their "anti-imperialist" wars.
- Many revolutionaries were inspired by the Cuban Revolution.
- Rural rebels tended to train and fight using classic guerrilla tactics and tried to create "liberated zones" as bases for military operations.
- Urban rebels practiced terrorist methodologies that included kidnappings, extortion, bombings, shootings, and other politically motivated criminal behavior.
- Strategies were adopted that used "urban guerrilla warfare" to provoke the state and politicize the lower classes.

Six Latin American cases in point are discussed in the following sections. These armed extremist movements were active in Colombia, Peru, and Argentina. All engaged in terrorist violence to some degree.

Colombia

Colombia has a long history of communal violence. For example, 200,000 people died during a civil war known as *La Violencia*, which lasted from 1946 to 1966. Modern Colombia has experienced a different type of terrorist environment, with dissident violence being committed by left-wing rebels, right-wing paramilitaries ("death squads"), and drug lords (*narcotraficantes*).[15] A culture of political violence and intimidation is now endemic to Colombia, so that likely and unlikely alliances have been formed: The weakened government has been accused of aiding and abetting the work of the paramilitaries; the paramilitaries and *narcotraficantes* have cooperated against the Marxist rebels; and the Marxist rebels have moved into drug-producing regions to generate revenue for their cause. In fact, drug-related income has been a significant factor in securing the financial independence of the Marxist rebellion. The result has been that approximately 3,500 Colombians—the vast majority civilians—die annually in the fighting.

After the breakdown of a cease-fire in early 2002, the Colombian civil war reignited in earnest. On the left, two intractable Marxist insurgencies had continued for decades.[16] The strategies of both insurgent groups allowed for the use of classic guerrilla tactics and terrorism.

Revolutionary Armed Forces of Colombia.[17] The **Revolutionary Armed Forces of Colombia** (Fuerzas Armadas Revolucionarias de Colombia, or FARC) was organized in 1964 as a Marxist rebel organization that operated primarily in the Colombian countryside. Its role in the overall revolution was to operate as the armed wing of the originally pro-Soviet Colombian Communist Party. FARC's anti-imperialist political position labeled the United States as an imperial power and the Colombian government as a right-wing oligarchy. The group historically enjoyed widespread support among many peasants and farmers, and FARC successfully created "liberated zones" in central Colombia, including a large "demilitarized" zone that the Colombian government temporarily ceded to FARC. With about 17,000 fighters,[18] FARC became a formidable fighting force and scored numerous victories using guerrilla tactics against Colombian security forces. FARC's terrorist activities included kidnapping, robberies, assassinations, and other violent tactics. It also conscripted child soldiers into its ranks.[19] In the largest cocaine-producing country in the world, FARC participated in the drug trade to finance its revolution and became independent from outside aid.

National Liberation Army.[20] The **National Liberation Army** (Ejercito de Liberacion Nacional, or ELN) was organized as a pro-Cuban Marxist rebel organization that, like FARC, operated primarily in the countryside of Colombia. Its ideological icons were Fidel Castro and Ernesto "Che" Guevara. Also like FARC, it followed an anti-imperialist line that fought to end what it considered to be United States-backed oppression in Colombia. Unlike FARC, its ideology has been more Maoist in outlook. With 3,000 fighters, the ELN was always smaller than FARC, but it also largely fought the Colombian army to a standstill. The ELN engaged in bombings, extortion, and kidnappings. Targets included foreign businesses and oil pipelines. The ELN also participated in the drug trade.

Peru

The Peruvian government was besieged by a dissident terrorist environment from the 1970s through the 1990s. By the late 1990s, security forces had delivered serious setbacks to the primary terrorist organizations.

Shining Path.[21] **Shining Path** (Sendero Luminoso) is an interesting case because of its uniqueness. It was radically Maoist, but unlike other Latin American revolutionary groups, it did not completely accept orthodox Marxist theory. Nor did Shining Path accept the New Left theories of Fanon, Marcuse, or Marighella. Instead, they considered the teachings of their supreme leader, former university professor Abimael Guzmán, to be the highest evolution of Marxist thought, directly superceding Marx, Lenin, Stalin, Trotsky, and Mao. Guzmán's philosophy is a hybrid of Marxism, Maoism, and native Indian traditionalism that championed Peru's Quechua-speaking Incans and mixed-race mestizos. This racial dimension was melded with a quasi-mystical philosophy that was considered to be the "shining path" to liberation; Guzmán was referred to as the "Fourth Sword of Marxism." In practice, Shining Path's methods paralleled those of the ruthless Khmer Rouge movement in Cambodia, which was responsible for 2 million Cambodian deaths. Shining Path members were racial and xenophobic, rejecting all outside influences—including orthodox Marxist revolutionary theory. Shining Path used brutal intimidation to force support from the Quechua-speaking and mestizo Peruvians whom they championed. They also set about waging a campaign of widespread terror against Peruvian society in cities, towns, villages, and the countryside. Anyone who did not join them was considered to be their enemy. Its campaign cost Peru more than 30,000 lives. In September 1992, Guzmán was captured. Because support for Shining Path largely depended on the cult of personality that was built around him, Shining Path gradually withered after Guzmán's capture and the capture of other leaders. When Guzmán renounced violence in 1993, 5,500 of his followers accepted a government amnesty. Nevertheless, diehards remained active. The group detonated at least two bombs in 2001, and an explosion near the U.S. embassy in March 2002 bore the Shining Path signature.[22]

Tupac Amaru Revolutionary Movement.[23] The **Tupac Amaru Revolutionary Movement** (Movimento Revolucionario Tupac Amaru, or MRTA) was an orthodox Marxist organization that had no connection whatsoever to the Tupamaros of Uruguay. Founded in 1983, MRTA was an anti-imperialist movement that sought to create a Marxist state. It applied Carlos Marighella's strategy to Peru and so engaged in urban terrorism. Its membership was never large, and it operated in urban areas rather than the countryside, which was probably impractical because of the presence of Shining Path. Its most dramatic—and, as it happened, its last—major attack was on December 17, 1996, when they seized the Japanese ambassador's residence in Lima and held hundreds of guests hostage. This feat received worldwide attention. The crisis lasted for four months as negotiations ebbed and flowed, with many hostages being released. Finally, after an impasse—and after the Peruvian army had tunneled beneath the residence—on April 22, 1997, soldiers stormed the residence. They literally burst from tunnels on the grounds, and after about 40 minutes all of the MRTA terrorists were killed and 25 hostages injured. Two soldiers were killed.

Argentina

The complicated political environment of postwar Argentina centered on tension among several movements, including the populism of President Juan Peron, the right-wing military establishment, Spanish-inspired fascism, and leftist activism. Peronism was a populist and nationalist ideology that split into leftist and rightist factions. The Argentine left was primarily Marxist, and several small armed dissident groups appeared in the late 1960s and early 1970s. However, one group, the **Montoneros,** was unique. They were originally young leftist Peronists but eventually came to advocate several distinctly Argentine sentiments: radical Catholic principles of justice, Peronist populism, and leftist nationalism. They were young radicals who championed justice and unity for "the people" in Argentina.

During the early 1970s, these armed dissident movements gradually disbanded or coalesced around the Marxist People's Revolutionary Army and the Montoneros.

Ideology of the Armed Argentine Left. The Montoneros accepted Ernesto "Che" Guevara's theory that a dedicated and focused revolutionary group could bring about a generalized revolutionary environment. Thus, the theory of *foquismo* infused a Cuban-inspired addition into their unique Argentine ideology. The People's Revolutionary Army was originally a Trotskyite group that eventually adopted the Maoist theory of building a revolutionary base in the countryside. Like the Montoneros, they applied Che Guevara's theory of *foquismo*.

Montonero and People's Revolutionary Army Terrorism. The Montoneros inspired young leftists with their slogan "Fatherland or Death." Although the nationalism of the Montoneros attracted a numerous and loyal following, the **People's Revolutionary Army** never became as prominent. Both groups engaged in urban terrorism, à la Carlos Marighella. The Montoneros became skillful kidnappers and extorted an estimated $60 million in ransom payments. Shootings, bombings, and assassinations were also pervasive. Their campaign caused widespread disorder and even spawned a retaliatory right-wing death squad, the Argentine Anti-Communist Alliance, whose brutality caused hundreds of intellectuals to flee the country. When Juan Peron died in 1974, the political situation became precarious. In March 1976, the military seized control in Argentina. Under President Videla, all political opposition was crushed, including the terrorist campaign. Torture, murder, assassinations, and "disappearances" were used. Thousands of Montoneros and People's Revolutionary Army members were killed.

Regional Case: Asia

Asia's regional, ethnic, religious, racial, and cultural diversity produced a significant number of armed insurgencies and terrorist movements during the postwar years. The motives and goals of these conflicts reflect this diversity and represent ideologies that characterize the classical ideological continuum as well as idiosyncratic religious and nationalistic motivations. In essence, Asia is a good example of the development of a wide variety of terrorist environments and organizations.

Leftist extremism in Asia was widespread after the end of the Second World War and was largely nationalistic in quality. Unlike the left in Europe, North America, and most of Latin America, the Asian left fought to end long periods of colonial rule or what they perceived to be corrupt and repressive governments supported by European or American interests. This passion for true national independence united revolutionaries who represented a range of ideological ideals—such as liberal democrats, democratic socialists, ethnic nationalists, and communist revolutionaries.

One pattern that was repeated throughout this period was the gradual domination of national liberation movements by Marxist revolutionaries. This was because the Marxist movements were very adept at linking nationalist sentiment to Marxist ideology. They also skillfully indoctrinated many poorly educated peasants with basic Marxist liberation theory, thus creating a strong ideological motivation to fight "wars of national liberation" against foreign imperialists and local regimes. This was a potent and persuasive strategy, and Marxist revolutionary cadres were often formidable fighters. Interestingly, several Marxist insurgencies resorted to state terrorism as domestic policy after they seized power.

The armed left in Asia exhibited the following commonalities:

- Perceived enemies included European colonial regimes, American "imperialist" interests, and governments dependent on these foreign powers.

- Leaders of insurgencies were often well-educated, having studied in universities in the colonial home country.
- Marxist ideology was very compelling among the leftist leadership, because it blended nationalist aspirations with a worldview of local opposition against global colonial and imperialist interests.
- Marxist movements usually became dominant in armed rebellions.
- "Wars of national liberation" were fought to win the support of large segments of society.
- Strategies for victory required the consolidation of the countryside, disruption of government administration, and gradual isolation of urban areas.
- Tactics for victory included classic guerrilla hit-and-run engagements and the use of terrorism.
- Terrorist tactics included bombings, assassinations, symbolic "executions," sabotage, and kidnappings.

Three Asian cases in point are discussed in the following sections. They are armed movements that arose in Cambodia and the Philippines.

Cambodia

Colonial Cambodia was governed as part of French Indochina, which also included what are now the countries of Laos and Vietnam. In 1944, Vietnamese nationalists led by Ho Chi Minh rebelled against the French colonial regime, which had essentially collaborated with Japanese occupiers during World War II. Cambodian intellectuals and activists joined with the Vietnamese during their resistance against the French. One Cambodian activist was **Pol Pot**, who joined the underground Indochinese Communist Party in about 1946.

When the French withdrew after their defeat in 1954 at Dien Bien Phu[24] in Vietnam, Cambodia became a republican monarchy ruled by Prince Norodom Sihanouk.

Cambodian Communists. Many of the Cambodians who participated in anti-French agitation during World War II were nationalist communists. Some of them gathered abroad after the war, and they established strong ideological bonds. Pol Pot lived and studied in France for four years after the war, where he was an unremarkable student, but where he met with other Indochinese activists and became a dedicated Marxist revolutionary. When Pol Pot returned to Cambodia, he became a member of the People's Revolutionary Party of Kampuchea, a communist revolutionary party. In 1960, the Cambodian Communist Party was founded. Pol Pot became its leader in 1963 and soon fled with his followers into the jungle after Prince Sihanouk suppressed Communist Party activities.

The Khmer Rouge. It was in the jungle in the mid-1960s that the guerrilla movement known as the **Khmer Rouge** ("Red Khmers"—most Cambodians are ethnic Khmers), led by Pol Pot, took up arms. The Khmer Rouge was an extreme left-wing movement that sought to completely redesign and restructure society. In 1967, the Khmer Rouge staged an armed rebellion that was put down by Sihanouk's forces. In 1970, a civil war broke out after a right-wing coup—led by Cambodian Prime Minister Lon Nol and Prince Sirik Matak—toppled the Sihanouk government. Prince Sihanouk eventually joined Pol Pot and the Khmer Rouge to fight against the new regime. Khmer Rouge forces were swelled with new recruits when U.S. forces bombed and invaded Cambodia in 1970.[25] Despite massive U.S. assistance, the Lon Nol government suffered one defeat after another at the hands of the Khmer Rouge.

Year Zero—The Beginning of State Terrorism. In January 1975, the Khmer Rouge seized the capital of Phnom Penh, now swollen by 2 million refugees. They renamed the country Democratic Kampuchea, set the calendar to **Year Zero,** and began a four-year reign of state domestic terror. Their first act was to depopulate Phnom Penh through mass evacuations of the inhabitants to the countryside. There, they toiled in the fields to build the Khmer Rouge's vision of an ideal communist society. The era of the Killing Fields had begun, when hundreds of thousands of Cambodians (possibly as many as 2 million) died in the countryside from executions, starvation, and arduous forced labor.

The Philippines

The Republic of the Philippines has experienced several insurgencies and terrorist campaigns in the postwar era. A nationalistic Muslim rebellion in the southern islands, led by the Moro National Liberation Front, scored a number of military and political successes. The Muslim fundamentalist group Abu Sayyaf has links to international terrorist Osama bin Laden and has been responsible for numerous acts of political violence.

The first serious left-wing rebellion occurred after the Second World War. The rebellion, and the government's response to it, was the only case in Southeast Asia of a major communist insurgency that was defeated without foreign military assistance.

The Hukbalahaps. The **Hukbalahaps**, or **Huks,** were the best-organized and most effective Filipino resistance force to fight against the Japanese during the Second World War. In fact, their name is a contraction in the Tagalog dialect for "People's Anti-Japanese Army." During the war, the Huk terrorists killed many fellow Filipinos whom they considered to be rivals or collaborators. After the war, they overtly declared themselves to be communist guerrillas seeking to create a communist state. They received some support among peasants because of their plan to reform and redistribute the land. Their rebellion was centered in the island of Luzon, with a smaller presence in Panay, and at first they scored a few victories. However, the Huks were never able to spread their movement to other islands, and the government succeeded in geographically containing them, and then crushing them, by the mid-1950s. They reappeared in the late 1960s but were again suppressed in 1970.

New People's Army.[26] The **New People's Army** (NPA) is a Marxist guerrilla group that was founded in 1969. Its ideology is Maoist, and its strategy is to wage a protracted guerrilla insurgency from the countryside with the goal of overthrowing the government and building a communist society. It engages in urban terrorism, such as bombings, shootings, extortion, and assassinations. The NPA has approximately 6,000 to 8,000 fighters and regularly targets Filipino security forces.

Regional Case: Europe

Prior to the opening of the Berlin Wall in 1989, very little terrorism of any kind occurred in the communist Eastern Bloc. However, democratic Western Europe experienced a wave of leftist terrorism that began during the student and human rights movements in the 1960s. This wave of political violence occurred in numerous Western countries. Although some nationalist terrorism occurred—in Northern Ireland and Spain—most terrorist groups were ideologically motivated. The latter style of terrorism exhibited certain similarities across national boundaries, including the following:

- Origins in leftist activism on university campuses
- Origins in youthful members of the middle class

- The application of New Left theories that justified violence committed by middle-class terrorists in prosperous democracies
- Methodologies that included kidnappings, extortion, bombings, shootings, and other politically motivated criminal behavior
- Adoption of strategies similar to those of Latin American terrorists, using "urban guerrilla warfare" to provoke the democratic state and politicize the working class
- Nihilistic dissident activism, with no clear vision for the new postrevolutionary society

Six European cases in point are discussed in the following sections. They are armed movements that were active in Italy, Germany, and Northern Ireland.

Italy[27]

Postwar Italy was a unique democracy. Although its democratic institutions were rarely if ever threatened by street-level unrest, its parliamentary politics were chaotic. Governments rose and fell regularly, and, with one of the few strong communist parties in the West, the left was quite influential in setting the political agenda. As in most Western democracies, the 1960s were a time of political activism among the young generation. In addition to activism on campus, Italy in 1969 experienced significant union unrest in North Italy. Out of this environment arose a strong radical leftist movement, as well as a significant terrorist campaign from the left.

The Red Brigades.[28] In 1969, Italy's most notable leftist terrorist group was formed. It was a Marxist revolutionary movement that sought to create a revolutionary environment by waging a widespread campaign of urban terrorism. It practiced nihilist dissident terrorism and never developed a clear vision of postrevolutionary Italy. Although the Red Brigades operated in solidarity with the goals of other terrorist groups—as well as liberation movements in the developing world—it never collaborated with other organizations to any significant extent. It apparently did receive weapons from Palestinian sources. The Red Brigades' first base of operations was in Milan, but they gradually spread to Rome, Genoa, Turin, and other cities. Aside from the Irish dissident terrorists, the Red Brigades were the most active terrorist group in Europe. During its first 10 years of existence, the Red Brigades committed about 14,000 terrorist attacks.

Years of Lead. The politically violent years of the 1970s and 1980s in Italy have been termed the **"Years of Lead."** During that period, the Red Brigades were exceptionally active. The Red Brigades initially committed symbolic attacks against property. However, beginning in about 1972, they began a campaign of violence that included shootings, bombings, kidnappings, and other violent criminal acts. Kidnap victims included Genoa's Assistant Attorney General Mario Sossi (1974), former Italian Prime Minister Aldo Moro (1978), and American Brigadier General James Dozier (1981). Of these cases, Sossi was released, Moro was executed, and Dozier was rescued from a "people's prison" run by the Red Brigades. During Moro's kidnapping, five of his bodyguards were slain. He was very prominent in Italian politics at the time and would have likely become president of Italy. By the mid-1990s, the Red Brigades had declared an end to "military" operations.

Germany[29]

The partition of Germany after World War II symbolized the Cold War rivalry between the democratic capitalist West and the totalitarian communist Eastern Bloc. The Federal Republic of Germany (West Germany) was pro-Western, and the Soviet troops stationed in the German Democratic Republic (East Germany) ensured that it would be pro-Eastern Bloc. No terrorist movement existed in East Germany, but at least three violent leftist groups emerged in West Germany. These groups were avowedly Marxist or anarchist but practiced nihilist dissident terrorism. They were certainly New Left in orientation, having read and put into practice the theories of Fanon, Marcuse, Marighella, and other new revolutionary thinkers.

An interesting feature of the German groups is the level of collaboration with each other and with Palestinian terrorist groups. The German terrorists included the following groups.

Red Army Faction.[30] The Marxist **Red Army Faction** (RAF, or Baader-Meinhof Gang) was the most prominent terrorist group in Germany in the postwar era. From its beginning in 1970, the RAF committed many politically motivated bank robberies, kidnappings, murders, bombings, and other crimes. They

Prisoner of the Red Brigades. A photograph of former Italian Prime Minister Aldo Moro taken during his captivity by the Red Brigades. Moro was later executed by the terrorists.

Source: Hulton Archive/Getty Images; used by permission.

quickly established links with Palestinian terrorists, and some members received weapons training in the Middle East. This was the beginning of a long collaboration between German and Palestinian terrorists, especially the Marxist Popular Front for the Liberation of Palestine. This collaboration was based on a sense of ideological solidarity, the RAF's internationalist worldview, and their conclusion that the capitalist West and Israel were common foes. Joint operations between the RAF and Palestinian terrorists included the June 1976 hijacking of an Air France airliner to Entebbe, Uganda. Two German terrorists participated in the hijacking. The RAF remained active well into the 1990s, officially ceasing "military" operations in 1998.

June 2nd Movement. The **June 2nd Movement** (Bevegung 2. Juni), founded in West Berlin in 1971, was named for the date in 1967 when a German pacifist, Benno Ohnesorg, was killed by the police during a demonstration in West Berlin. Unlike the RAF and **Revolutionary Cells** (discussed next), June 2nd Movement was more anarchistic in its ideology. It was known for bombings of property targets in West Berlin. June 2nd Movement's most famous action was the 1975 kidnapping of Peter Lorenz, a Berlin mayoral

Prisoner of the Red Army Faction. A photograph of West German industrialist Hanns-Martin Schleyer taken during his captivity by the Red Army Faction (also known as the Baader-Meinhof Gang). The RAF later executed Schleyer.

Source: Hulton Archive/Getty Images; used by permission.

candidate. He was released in one day after four June 2nd comrades were released and flown to Yemen. After the group disbanded in the 1980s, many members joined the RAF.

Revolutionary Cells. Revolutionary Cells (Revolutionär Zelles) is a shadowy Marxist organization that was founded in Frankfurt, probably in 1972 or 1973. They adopted an underground cell-based strategy, believing (correctly) that the RAF's organizational structure made the group easier to penetrate. They disappeared into the middle class by holding jobs, owning homes, and raising families. Their terrorist activity included bombings and other criminal activity. A women's "auxiliary" called **Red Zora** (Rote Zora) was apparently formed and later became independent of Revolutionary Cells.

The RAF—and arguably the other German terrorists—considered itself to be "the vanguard of the exploited and oppressed Third World, terrorism being the only feasible strategy of weak revolutionary movements."[31] Some important events in the history of the violent German left are discussed in the following sections.

Origin of the RAF. Like many other leftist organizations, the RAF grew out of the activism of the 1960s. **Gudrun Ensslin** and her boyfriend **Andreas Baader** were prominent in student protests at Berlin Free University during the 1960s. Both were imprisoned in 1968 when convicted of attempted arson by fire-bombing department stores in the city of Frankfurt. After being released a year later during a grant of temporary amnesty, they fled the country illegally, but Baader was imprisoned when he later returned. In May 1970, Ensslin and **Ulrike Meinhof** collaborated with others on a successful jailbreak of Baader. From that point on, the group was popularly referred to as the **Baader-Meinhof Gang** (although Ensslin was more of a leader than Meinhof). They officially referred to themselves as the Red Army Faction.

Death Night. In 1972, approximately 100 members and supporters of the RAF were arrested and imprisoned, including founders Ensslin, Baader, and Meinhof. In prison,

Ulrike Meinhof hanged herself on May 9, 1976. On October 18, 1977—known as "**Death Night**"—Andreas Baader, Gudrun Ensslin, and Jan-Carl Raspe were shot in prison. West German authorities officially concluded that Ensslin hung herself and that Baader and Raspe shot themselves with guns smuggled into their cells—ostensibly for a jail break. A fourth terrorist (Irmgard Möller) stabbed herself four times with a knife but missed her heart. Many Germans have never believed the official version of their deaths, although attorneys for the RAF are known to have smuggled other illegal contraband into what had been touted as the most secure prison in the world.

The OPEC Raid. On December 21, 1975, members of the RAF, June 2nd Movement, and Revolutionary Cells collaborated with Palestinian terrorists in a hostage-taking raid on the Vienna headquarters of OPEC. The group was led by Carlos the Jackal, the *nom de guerre* for Ilich Ramirez Sanchez. During the course of the raid, the terrorists and some of the hostages were flown to Algiers, Algeria, and then to Tripoli, Tunisia. The hostages were released (and the terrorists disappeared into the Middle East) when a $5 million ransom was paid for Palestinian causes.

Northern Ireland

Most terrorism in the British Isles has been related to the sectarian conflict between Catholics and Protestants in Northern Ireland—commonly termed "**the Troubles**"— which began in West Belfast and Londonderry in 1969. Catholic Republicans had initially tried to emulate Dr. Martin Luther King Jr.'s leadership of the African American civil rights movement in the American south. When this failed in the summer of 1969, Catholic and Protestant extremists organized themselves into a terrorist underground.

Although the violent Catholic groups are included under the category of "left-wing" because of their professed adoption of socialist ideology, it is important to remember that their primary goal is reunification with the Irish Republic. The following groups became prominent during the sectarian fighting:

Provisional Irish Republican Army.[32] The Provos, as the Provisional IRA is often referred to, is a mildly socialist nationalist "military" organization that seeks reunification with the Irish republic. Its leftist rhetoric moderated significantly during the 1980s. The Provisional IRA split in the 1960s from the **Official Irish Republican Army** when the latter group continued to pursue a less militant line than the Provos. The Provos were initially organized to respond to bombings and other attacks on Catholic neighborhoods by Protestant gangs. At first, it was a somewhat disorganized and undisciplined organization, but it eventually became

The Provos at work: Members of the Provisional Irish Republican Army as they prepare for a mission.

Source: Hulton Archive/Getty Images; used by permission.

a highly militarized group organized into three- or four-member cells. Although it never fielded more than 1,000 "soldiers" at any one time, and usually about 250, it became the most notorious armed Catholic dissident group. They engaged in urban terrorist strikes in Northern Ireland and mainland Britain.

Irish National Liberation Army. The **Irish National Liberation Army** (INLA), founded in the early 1970s, grew out of the split in the IRA. The group followed the pattern of many radical nationalist organizations at the time and adopted Marxist theory as its guiding ideology. Like the Provos, the INLA fought to reunite Northern Ireland with Ireland. The INLA is unique in that it envisioned the creation of a socialist Irish republic. In fact, the INLA considered itself to be fighting in unity with other terrorist groups that championed oppressed groups around the world. The INLA's heyday was during the 1970s and mid-1980s. It operated in urban areas, primarily in the cities of Londonderry and Belfast. Although it never fielded more than several dozen "soldiers," it was exceptionally violent and ruthless—arguably more so than the Provos. An internal feud significantly debilitated the group during the 1990s.

Chapter Perspective 6.1 summarizes the championed constituencies and enemies of left-wing terrorists.

THE FUTURE OF THE VIOLENT LEFT

Since its origins in 19th-century Europe, leftist activism has undergone several generational shifts in ideology, methodology, and purpose. Ideologically, New Left and nationalist liberation theories predominated in the postwar era, gradually displacing orthodox Marxism among the new generation of young middle-class activists. Methodologically, Soviet-style communist parties were superceded by nationalist movements and EuroCommunism, and labor agitation was supplanted by student and ethnic and national activism. Additionally, the purpose of leftist activism on the far and fringe left became nihilistic in the West, as activists rationalized their behavior by referencing New Left revolutionary philosophy and solidarity with the developing world.

The driving forces behind political agitation on the left have been, and remain, class struggle, leftist nationalism, and special-interest activism. By the beginning of the 21st century, although vestiges of the armed left continued in some regions of the world, these were mere "pockets" of violent revolutionary sentiment. They did not compare in scale to the revolutionary fervor that existed earlier in the 20th century, nor to the wave of urban guerrilla warfare toward the end of the century. And although a few leftist nationalist and orthodox Marxist insurgencies continued to be fought in the countryside of some countries, they likewise did not compare in scale or frequency to similar wars in the postwar era.

The Defeat of the Urban Guerrillas

The 1960s through the 1980s was the high tide for the theory of urban guerrilla warfare. Ideological revolutionaries applied Carlos Marighella's strategy repeatedly in Latin America, Western Europe, and (to a lesser extent) in the United States. Frantz Fanon's and Herbert Marcuse's theories had allowed middle-class revolutionaries to rationalize armed rebellion in the democratic and relatively prosperous West. The intensity of urban guerrilla violence was significant in several countries, including Italy, West Germany, Argentina, and Uruguay. Nevertheless, the urban guerrillas were ultimately defeated and their strategy discredited.

In the near term, this type of urban violence from the left is unlikely to be replicated, absent new crises of faith and new revolutionary theorists. Left-wing revolutionary

---

| **Chapter Perspective 6.1** | **Terrorism on the Left** |

Although left-wing terrorist groups share similar values and often are rooted in Marxist theory, they arise out of unique political environments that are peculiar to their respective countries. In Latin America and Asia, these movements have fought on behalf of identifiable domestic constituencies against identifiable domestic adversaries. In Europe, regional nationalist movements similarly champion identifiable constituencies against identifiable adversaries. However, the New Left constituencies and adversaries have tended to be ideological conceptualizations.

The following table summarizes the constituencies and adversaries of several politically violent dissident movements.

Latin America

Group	Constituency	Adversary
FARC	Workers, peasants	The oligarchy
National Liberation Army	Workers, peasants	Government, imperialists
Shining Path	Indians, oppressed classes	Government, imperialists
MRTA	Workers, peasants	Government
Montoneros	The people	Government, right wing
People's Revolutionary Army	Workers, peasants	Government, right wing

Asia

Group	Constituency	Adversary
Khmer Rouge	Rural peasantry	Government, old society
Hukbalahaps	Rural peasantry	Government
New People's Army	Workers, peasants	Government

Europe

Group	Constituency	Adversary
Red Brigades	Workers, the oppressed	Government, imperialists
Red Army Faction	Oppressed classes and people	Government, imperialists
June 2nd Movement	Oppressed classes and people	Government, imperialists
Revolutionary Cells	Oppressed classes and people	Government, imperialists
Provisional IRA	Northern Irish Catholics	British, Northern Irish government
Irish National Liberation Army	Northern Irish Catholics	British, Northern Irish government

activism is unlikely to match the scale or scope of the past unless there is a new ideological revolutionary system or movement similar to 20th-century Marxism as a foundation. In the long term, there simply is not a large pool of new revolutionaries, and without a clear vision for the postrevolutionary society, this pool will continue to be small at best.

Rebels in the Hills

By the late 1980s, the wars of national liberation of the postwar era had been largely fought and either won or lost. The postwar rivalry between the Soviet Union and the United

Case in Point   **Supportive Environments on the Left—1968 Paris**

During the late 1960s, France experienced the same left-wing political turmoil that occurred elsewhere in Western Europe and the United States. In Western Europe, the radical student movement produced mass protests in many countries during 1968 and 1969, and this was the turning point toward armed rebellion for a number of young activists. As in those countries, the environment in France was characterized by radical leftist sentiment on university campuses, including intensive demonstrations and rioting in Paris.

President Charles de Gaulle had been an iconic symbol of the French nation. De Gaulle had led the Free French during World War II and had guided the nation through the turmoil of the colonial war in Algeria. However, the Gaullist government he created was often overbearing, and its administrative system was ponderous. At the same time, conditions at universities during the 1960s were poor. Dormitories and classrooms were terribly overcrowded, facilities had become run-down, university administrators were indifferent, and the government did nothing to remedy these poor conditions. To make matters more tense, leftist politics were very strong on campus. Student discontent was pervasive, particularly at the Sorbonne in Paris.

In May and June 1968, *les événéments* ("the events") nearly toppled de Gaulle's government. On May 3 of that year (a Friday), French police broke up a peaceful demonstration at the Sorbonne in Paris. As they arrested the protestors, student onlookers became enraged and began throwing debris and taunting the police, who fired tear gas into the crowd. On the following Monday, the police violently attacked a large demonstration, and 12 hours of street fighting ensued. Protests and street fighting continued, and during the next week Sorbonne students became radicalized, the protests became a general student revolt, and revolutionary students took the initiative.

States ended with the opening of the Berlin Wall in 1989 and the subsequent collapse of Soviet communism. The symbol of developing world revolutionaries rising up against colonial and imperial exploitation waned as developing world countries gained independence and consolidated power.

Although Marxist insurgencies continued through the 1990s in a few countries—such as Colombia and the Philippines—they no longer had strong benefactors in the communist world. Significantly, the record of human rights violations in communist societies became well-known, so that the idealism and leadership from educated elites became much weaker than it had been during the postwar anticolonial period. It is therefore likely that although a few leftist insurgencies will linger, the worldwide political environment will not provide strong support for the same scale of left-wing nationalist fervor as in its heyday.

New Seeds for a Resurgent Left?

Leftist activism has certainly not disappeared. Protests against a globalized economy have rallied activists ranging in ideology from liberal trade unionists to radical anarchists. New symbols—exemplified by demonstrations against meetings of the World Trade Organization—have attracted the attention of a new far-left movement. The "Battle of Seattle" in November 1999 is typical of this new activism, with protesters rallying around perceived inequalities created by exploitation from global corporate and national interests.

The more committed activists have labeled themselves anarchists but have yet to create a generalized activist environment similar to those that occurred after the Bolshevik Revolution or during the 1960s and 1970s. Absent a poignant and overt issue to arouse passions—such as the war in Vietnam or the people's rights movements during the 1960s—it is unlikely that mass far-left activism will become widespread in the near future.

Significantly, the French public supported the students. Nationwide, most university campuses were closed by demonstrations.

In the Latin Quarter of Paris, students erected barricades. At 2:00 a.m. on the morning of May 11, the police began to storm the barricades. The fighting was intense, as nonstudent youth joined the Sorbonne students and as the police hunted and beat young people indiscriminately. French Prime Minister Georges Pompidou withdrew the police and ended their violent repression of the protests. At this point, a nationwide uprising began.

On Monday, May 13, an alliance of students, leftist parties, and workers brought about 800,000 people into the streets to demonstrate against the government. When the police were withdrawn from the Latin Quarter, radical students seized control of the entire area and declared it to be the **Student Soviet.** Shortly thereafter, workers began a series of strikes and factory seizures, continuing until 9 million workers were on strike. The Student Soviet became a center for revolutionary debate about what direction the country should take, and it seemed for a moment that the student-worker rebellion would topple the republic. However, Charles de Gaulle intervened, called for elections, and sent the police into the factories and the Student Soviet. The factories were reoccupied and the Student Soviet ended by June 16. In the general elections held in late June, the Gaullists won handily. The revolt was over.

This kind of environment would normally be ripe for the beginning of a period of violence from the left. However, France never experienced the same degree of nihilist dissident terrorism that existed in Italy and Germany. It did produce one noteworthy leftist terrorist organization—**Direct Action (Action Directe)**—but this group was an anti-American and anti-NATO organization that grew out of the late 1970s rather than the 1960s. Founded in 1979, Direct Action operated mainly in Paris and committed approximately 50 terrorist attacks. It acted in solidarity with the RAF, the Red Brigades, Belgium's Combatant Communist Cells, and Palestinian extremists.

Nevertheless, the seeds of resurgent leftist terrorism could be sown among those who rally against issues such as globalization.

Internationally, the problems of unemployment, poverty, and perceived exploitation have traditionally given rise to leftist sentiment. Thus,

> In the West, the dismantling of the welfare state, especially in Europe, is having a divisive effect on societies with high rates of unemployment. Elsewhere, economic reform and higher rates of economic growth are producing marked disparities in income and a mounting perception of inequality . . . the divide between "haves" and "have nots" is making issues of class and economic opportunity central to political change.[33]

Should these factors stimulate renewed social discontent, with renewed analysis from a reinvigorated leftist intelligentsia, it is possible that a "new" new left may yet arise.

CHAPTER SUMMARY

This chapter provided students with insight into the characteristics of leftist terrorism. Marxism was identified as the principle ideology underlying left-wing terrorist behavior, even though the political environments where Marxism became strongest were not those originally envisioned by Karl Marx. Explanations for this phenomenon included ideological disaffection and nationalism; in both cases, Marxism was used as an insurgent ideology. Examples were presented of leftist insurgencies in weak or repressive political systems, as well as terrorist violence in relatively strong and prosperous democracies. Cases in point of groups and movements were discussed to illustrate the theoretical themes of the chapter.

A key theoretical pattern of the insurgent left was the vanguard strategy used by small, motivated groups of revolutionaries. It effectively consolidated and motivated activist movements in their resistance to established authority. The quality of activism on the left can be summarized in five propositions: The radical left emphasizes "economic rights"; democratic socialism emphasizes reform, not revolution; communists emphasize revolution, not reform; democratic socialists and communists tend to distrust each other; and leftist terrorists in the West considered the working class to be corrupted or co-opted by capitalism.

Key subjects of leftist activism are class struggle, leftist nationalism, and special-interest extremism. Among the theoretical and practical problems on the radical left are: orthodox communist expectations about revolutionary environments, the revolutionary party, the application of theory to practice, and the fact that the working class is unlikely to ever develop a sufficiently revolutionary consciousness. The revolutionary identity of the New Left in the West was defined by "required reading" that included *The Wretched of the Earth* by Frantz Fanon, *One-Dimensional Man* by Herbert Marcuse, and *The Mini-Manual of the Urban Guerrilla* by Carlos Marighella. Regional cases from Latin America, Asia, and Europe illustrate the variety of motivations, methodologies, and strategies of leftist terrorism. Nevertheless, the common ideological bond for the radical left is Marxist revolutionary theory.

In Chapter 7, students will review rightist ideologies and terrorist behavior. The discussion will focus on specific examples as well as the contexts for armed right-wing dissident movements. Reasons for rightist violence in specific political environments will also be evaluated.

KEY TERMS AND CONCEPTS

The following topics were discussed in this chapter and are found in the Glossary:

Baader, Andreas
Baader-Meinhof Gang
Bourgeoisie
Cadre group
Death Night
Degenerate workers' state
Dictatorship of the Proletariat
Direct Action (Action Directe)
Ensslin, Gudrun
Foquismo
(Haks)
Heinzen, Karl
Hukbalahaps
Irish National Liberation Army
June 2nd Movement
Khmer Rouge
Les evenéments
Luddites
Lumpenproletariat
Lumumba, Patrice
Means of production
Meinhof, Ulrike
Montoneros
National Liberation Army
New People's Army
Official Irish Republican Army
One-Dimensional Man

Pan-Africanism
People's Revolutionary Army
People's Will
Pol Pot
Proletariat
Provos
Red Army Faction
Red Zora
Revolutionary Armed Forces of Colombia
   (FARC)
Revolutionary Cells
Shining Path
Socialism in one country
Stalinists
Student Soviet
The permanent revolution
Trotskyites
Troubles, The
Tupac Amaru Revolutionary Movement
   (MRTA)
Vanguard of the proletariat
Vanguard strategy
Viet Minh
Wars of national liberation
Wretched of the Earth, The
Year Zero
Years of Lead

Discussion Box   **Young Nationalist Idealists**

This chapter's Discussion Box is intended to stimulate critical debate about the appeal of leftist ideologies to educated leaders of anticolonial insurgencies in the developing world.

Until 1989, the Cold War rivalry between the communist East and the democratic West dominated the international relations and domestic politics of many nations. Nationalist movements often adopted leftist and Marxist ideology, and the Soviets supported a number of these movements.

The outcomes of these movements and the fates of their leaders are now the subject of history books. The early years of these leaders are intriguing stories and good case studies for our analysis of leftist dissent. The background and questions about three nationalist leaders are presented here.

Patrice Lumumba—Fallen National Hero, or Communist Sympathizer?

Patrice Lumumba was a Congolese nationalist who became a martyred national hero. The first Prime Minister of Congo, he was executed by a rebel faction when he fled a military coup in 1961 that was instigated by Mobutu Sese Seko. Mobutu became dictator of Congo (which he renamed Zaire) for three decades.

Lumumba was born in colonial Belgian Congo in 1925 and was strongly influenced by French existentialism (particularly Jean-Paul Sartre) and Marxism. He was a writer and activist who advocated Congolese independence from Belgium. A leftist, but not a communist, he was president of the National Congolese Movement and became a pan-Africanist. During the anticolonial period in Africa, **pan-Africanism** advocated the unity of all African religions and people.

When the Belgians withdrew under pressure in 1960, Lumumba became prime minister. The new country was torn apart by a secessionist war in Katanga province (where Lumumba was killed), civil war, United Nations intervention, and rogue units of European mercenaries. Lumumba, who tried desperately to create a stabilized economy and government, asked for aid from the Soviet Union. He was thereafter branded a communist by the West. Lumumba, who was declared a national hero in 1966, also became a nationalist hero in the pan-Africanist movement.

Fidel Castro—The Revolutionary in America's Backyard

Fidel Castro seized power in Cuba in 1959 after leading a revolution that successfully waged an urban terrorist and rural guerrilla campaign against the United States-supported government of Fulgencio Batista. He later openly declared himself to be a communist and became an important ally of the Soviet Union.

When young, Castro's observations of Cuban poverty and American condescension toward Cubans shaped his nationalistic beliefs. Castro was a student of Cuban nationalism and history, and when he enrolled at the University of Havana law school, he participated in violent political activism. At this point, he was certainly a leftist, but most likely not a communist. In Havana, he met radical exiles from other Caribbean countries and participated in an abortive attempt to overthrow the dictator of the Dominican Republic. Castro was very active in international Latin American conferences and movements that opposed U.S. hegemony over the region.

In 1951, Castro was still a believer in democratic reform and ran for political office in the Cuban legislature. Unfortunately, Batista led a coup before the election could be held, and this was the end of Castro's belief in democratic change; thereafter, he was an advocate of armed rebellion.

Ho Chi Minh—Master of Guerrilla Warfare

Ho Chi Minh was a committed communist nationalist who fought a long war against Japanese, French, and American adversaries. He successfully applied terrorist and guerrilla tactics, and his forces eventually achieved victory after a conventional invasion of South Vietnam in 1975.

Ho was born in French Indochina in 1890. As a young man, he traveled the world while working on a French steam-liner. It was during this period that he became acquainted with the writings of Karl Marx and the ideals of the French and American revolutions. Ho eventually took residence in Paris, and after World War I he became a founding member of the French Communist Party. After visiting the Soviet Union in 1923, he traveled through China and met other Vietnamese nationalists.

Ho cofounded the Indochinese Communist Party in Hong Kong in 1930. Eventually returning to Vietnam in 1941, he organized the Vietnam Independence Brotherhood League (Viet Nam Doc Lap Dong Minh Hoi)—known as the **Viet Minh**—which began fighting first against the Japanese conquerors of French Indochina and then against the French colonial forces. Its goal was to "overthrow the Japanese and French and their [Vietnamese] jackals."[a] Ho's forces regularly used assassinations and other acts of terrorism as part of their overall military and political strategy.

Discussion Questions

- What are common themes in these case studies of revolutionary nationalists?
- In what ways do these examples differ?
- Were these leaders freedom fighters? Were they terrorists?
- Compare and contrast the points in their lives at which these individuals became radicals.
- Were Fidel Castro and Ho Chi Minh justified in taking up arms against their respective enemies?

NOTE

a. Sheehan, Neil. *A Bright Shining Lie: John Paul Vann and America in Vietnam.* New York: Random House, 1988, p. 159.

RECOMMENDED WEB SITES

The following Web sites provide information about leftist organizations, movements, and goals.

Earth Liberation Front: www.earthliberationfront.com/main.shtml

Popular Front for the Liberation of Palestine: http://members.tripod.com/~freepalestine

Revolutionary Armed Forces of Colombia: www.contrast.org/mirrors/farc

Sinn Féin: http://sinnfein.ie

Socialist International: www.socialistinternational.org

Zapatista National Liberation Front: www.ezln.org

WEB EXERCISE

Using this chapter's recommended Internet sites, conduct an online investigation of left-wing dissident movements.

- How would you describe the self-images presented by left-wing dissident movements?
- Review the goals and objectives of these organizations. Do they seem reasonable to you? Do they justify violent behavior?
- If you were a violent leftist dissident, how would you design your own Web site?

For an online search of violent left-wing dissident movements, students should activate the search engine on their Web browser and enter the following keywords:

"National Liberation"
"Marxist Revolution"
The names of specific dissident organizations

RECOMMENDED READINGS

The following publications give insight into leftist ideologies, movements, and personalities.

Djilas, Milovan. *The New Class: An Analysis of the Communist System.* New York: Praeger, 1957.

Djilas, Milovan. *The Unperfect Society: Beyond the New Class.* New York: Harcourt, Brace & World, 1969.

Fanon, Frantz. *The Wretched of the Earth.* New York: Grove Press, 1963.

Marcuse, Herbert. *One-Dimensional Man.* Boston: Beacon Press, 1964.

Marighella, Carlos. *Mini-Manual of the Urban Guerrilla.* Chapel Hill, NC: Documentary Publications, 1985.

Tucker, Robert C., ed. *The Marx-Engels Reader.* New York: Norton, 1972.

NOTES

[1] A good history of the Russian Revolution is found in Ulam, Adam B. *The Bolsheviks: The Intellectual and Political History of the Triumph of Communism in Russia.* New York: Collier Books, 1965.

[2] For insight into Guevara's Bolivian campaign, see James, Daniel, ed. *The Complete Bolivian Diaries of Che Guevara and Other Captured Documents.* New York: Stein & Day, 1968.

[3] For a Marxist analysis of the African American rights movement, see Thomas, Tony, ed. *Black Liberation & Socialism.* New York: Pathfinder Press, 1974.

[4] For a good compilation of the writings of Marx and Engels, see Tucker, Robert C., ed. *The Marx-Engels Reader.* New York: Norton, 1972.

[5] For further information about Mao's ideology, see Schram, Stuart R. *The Political Thought of Mao Tse-tung.* New York: Praeger, 1974. For a discussion of the Vietnamese and American perspectives during the war in Vietnam, see FitzGerald, Frances. *Fire in the Lade: The Vietnamese and the Americans in Vietnam.* New York: Vintage Books, 1972. For a good analysis of revolution in Cuba, see del Aguila, Juan M. *Cuba: Dilemmas of a Revolution.* Boulder, CO: Westview Press, 1988.

[6] Freeh, Louis J. *Statement for the Record on the Threat of Terrorism to the United States.* U.S. Senate Committees on Appropriations, Armed Services, and Select Committee on Intelligence. May 10, 2001.

[7] The title of a book by the American New Left radical Abbie Hoffman. See Hoffman, Abbie. *Revolution for the Hell of It.* New York: Dell Publishing Company, 1968.

[8] Reich, Walter. *Origins of Terrorism: Psychologies, Theologies, States of Mind.* Washington, DC: Woodrow Wilson Center Press, 1990, p. 9.

[9] Fanon, Frantz. *The Wretched of the Earth.* New York: Grove Press, 1963; Marcuse, Herbert. *One-Dimensional Man.* Boston: Beacon Press, 1964; Marighella, Carlos. *Mini-Manual of the Urban Guerrilla.* Chapel Hill, NC: Documentary Publications, 1985.

[10] Marighella (in note 9 above).

[11] Pridham, Geoffrey. "Terrorism and the State in West Germany During the 1970s: A Threat to Stability or a Case of Political Over-Reaction?" In Lodge, Juliet, ed. *Terrorism: A Challenge to the State.* Oxford, UK: Martin Robinson, 1981. Quoted in Whittaker, David J., ed. *The Terrorism Reader.* New York: Routledge, 2001, pp. 189-91.

[12] Laqueur, Walter. *The New Terrorism: Fanaticism and the Arms of Mass Destruction.* New York: Oxford University Press, 1999, p. 106.

[13] Marx, Karl, and Friedrich Engels. *Manifesto of the Communist Party.* In Tucker, Robert C., ed. *The Marx-Engels Reader.* New York: Norton, 1972, p. 335.

[14] Laqueur (note 12 above), p. 13.

[15] For an interesting discussion of radical Colombian politics and the drug trade, see Ehrenfeld, Rachel. *Narco-Terrorism.* New York: Basic Books, 1990, pp. 74-112.

[16] A third group is the small terrorist April 19 Movement, also known as M-19.

[17] For further information, see "Revolutionary Armed Forces of Colombia (FARC)." *Terrorist Group Profiles.* Dudley Knox Library, Naval War College. Web site: http://web.nps.navy.mil/~library/tgp/farc.htm (date accessed October 15, 2002).

[18] Miller, Christian T. "Colombia, Rebels Set New Talks." *Los Angeles Times*. January 15, 2002.

[19] The global problem of the conscription of child soldiers by extremist rebels is explored further in Chapter 4.

[20] For further information, see "National Liberation Army (ELN)-Colombia." *Terrorist Group Profiles*. Dudley Knox Library, Naval War College. Web site: http://web.nps.navy.mil/~library/tgp/elncol.htm (date accessed: October 15, 2002).

[21] For further information, see "Sendero Luminoso (Shining Path, SL)." *Terrorist Group Profiles*. Dudley Knox Library, Naval War College. Web site: http://web.nps.navy.mil/~library/ tgp/sendero.htm (date accessed: October 15, 2002).

[22] Faiola, Anthony, and Lucien Chauvin. "Peruvian Attaché Raises Fears of Rebel Resurgence." *Washington Post*. March 21, 2002.

[23] For further information, see "Tupac Amaru Revolutionary Movement (MRTA)." *Terrorist Group Profiles*. Dudley Knox Library, Naval War College. Web site: http://web.nps.navy.mil/~library/tgp/tupac.htm (date accessed: October 15, 2002).

[24] France lost 15,000 soldiers at Dien Bien Phu. For a good history of the battle, see Fall, Bernard. *Hell in a Very Small Place: The Siege of Dien Bien Phu*. Philadelphia: Lippincott, 1963.

[25] See Shawcross, William. *Sideshow: Kissinger, Nixon, and the Destruction of Cambodia*. New York: Simon & Schuster, 1979.

[26] For further information, see "New People's Army (NPA)." *Terrorist Group Profiles*. Dudley Knox Library, Naval War College. Web site: http://web.nps.navy.mil/~library/tgp/npa.htm (date accessed: October 15, 2002).

[27] See Clutterbuck, Richard. *Terrorism, Drugs and Crime in Europe after 1992*. New York: Routledge, 1990, pp. 30-45.

[28] For further information, see "Red Brigades (BR)." *Terrorist Group Profiles*. Dudley Knox Library, Naval War College. Web site: http://web.nps.navy.mil/~library/tgp/br.htm (date accessed: October 15, 2002).

[29] See Clutterbuck (note 27 above), pp. 46-52.

[30] For further information, see "Red Army Faction (RAF)." *Terrorist Group Profiles*. Dudley Knox Library, Naval War College. Web site: http://web.nps.navy.mil/~library/tgp/raf.htm (date accessed: October 15, 2002).

[31] Whittaker, David J., ed. *The Terrorism Reader*. New York: Routledge, 2001, p. 29.

[32] For further information, see "Irish Republican Army (IRA)." *Terrorist Group Profiles*. Dudley Knox Library, Naval War College. Web site: http://web.nps.navy.mil/~library/tgp/ira.htm (date accessed: October 15, 2002).

[33] Lesser, Ian. "Countering the New Terrorism: Implications for Strategy." In Lesser, Ian, et al. *Countering the New Terrorism*. Santa Monica, CA: RAND, 1999, p. 103.

Chapter 7

RACE AND ORDER: THE TERRORIST RIGHT

This chapter revisits right-wing terrorism, which was first introduced in Chapter 2. Students may recall that although the term *reactionary* has been affixed to rightist extremism, it can be an imprecise and confusing term. Because of this, the following concept is what should be kept in mind: Rightist ideologies tend to be a reaction against perceived threats to a group's value system and presumption of superiority. Right-wing extremists try to protect their value system and affirm their special status, frequently expressing a desire to return to a time of past glory. In this sense, rightist extremism is nostalgic.

Fringe-right ideology typically promotes an uncompromising belief in ethno-national, ideological, or religious superiority. Terrorist violence is sometimes selected as a justifiable option because an extremist group believes that it is defending the purity of an ethnonational group, rightist ideology, or religion. Right-wing terrorists picture themselves as champions of an ideal order that has been usurped or attacked by inferior ethno-national interests or religious values. They faithfully believe that final victory will result in the natural assumption (or restoration) of power by the favored group or belief. These uncompromising beliefs are typical among right-wing advocates who act on behalf of national groups, regional minorities, religious fundamentalists, or other groups with a distinctive identity. The identity is championed as being more legitimate, more sacred, or otherwise superior to other identities.

The discussion in this chapter will cover the following:

- Right-Wing Ideology and Activism
- Cases in Point of Common Themes on the Right
- Rightist Terrorism
- The Future of the Violent Right

RIGHT-WING IDEOLOGY AND ACTIVISM

Terrorism on the modern right is an outgrowth of fascist, National Socialist (Nazi), Falangist, and other reactionary movements that existed in Europe between the First and Second World Wars. The between-war era was a heyday for mass agitation on the far and fringe right. It was a period in history when rightist nationalism in Europe was very strong—and popular—among large segments of the public. Fascists, Nazis, Falangists, and others were certainly dictatorial, but they adroitly marshaled the nationalistic spirit of millions of Europeans. These were, without question, mass movements that waged a concerted struggle against communism and Western-style democracy.

The interwar history has been nostalgically recaptured in the ideologies and symbolism of reactionaries on the modern right. Modern activists have selectively chosen specific facets of certain right-wing movements for their causes. For example, right-wing ideologies in Latin America have historically promoted fascist and Falangist-style militarism, anticommunism, traditional values, and authoritarian rule. German extremists use neo-Nazi slogans, symbols, and doctrines, as do some racial supremacists in the United States. Italian activists have looked to their between-war past and adopted fascist traditions and values. These and other commonalities (which are discussed later) continue to invigorate the extreme right wing.

Political Parties and Dissident Movements

Political parties and dissident movements on the right reflect the distinctive features of their national environments.

Right-wing political parties are most viable in countries with strong traditions of parties that embody the values of grassroots political movements. These traditions have led to the formation of class-specific and ideology-specific political parties. Thus, rightist parties in Europe and Latin America are often represented in their elected assemblies, but such parties are negligible in the United States, where the political system is coalitional.[1] In Europe, right-wing political parties tend to be nationalistic; they advocate traditional national values, promote national culture, and demand strict limitations on immigration. The British National Party in the United Kingdom, the National Front (Front National) in France, and the National Alliance (Alleanza Nazionale) in Italy are typical right-wing parties in Europe. These parties represent movements that are aboveground and that are "mainstreamed" in the sense that they participate in democratic processes. They are also fascistic in their ideology. For example, Italy's Alleanza Nazionale is considered to be the heir to Mussolini's Fascist Party. In Russia, the neofascist party Russian National Unity was banned in Moscow because of its overtly fascist ideology.

In comparison to the neofascist political parties, the unorganized, or partly organized, right-wing dissident movements have varied in how overtly they state their political agendas. Some are frank in their ideological linkages to reactionary traditions, whereas others use contemporary language and code words for their beliefs. For example, rightists in the United States and Europe make references to "international bankers" as a code phrase for Jewish interests. Many right-wing dissidents in Europe, Russia, the United States, and elsewhere have borrowed or imitated the symbolism and mythology of Nazi Germany and other war-era fascist traditions. It is not uncommon for dissidents to use the stiff-armed fascist salute at demonstrations or to adopt reconfigured swastikas, Nordic runes, or other Nazi-era emblems. For example, South Africa's **Afrikaner Resistance Movement** (Afrikaner Weerstandsbeweging, or AWB), is overtly racist and has adopted as its organizational symbol a reconfigured swastika called the "Three Sevens."[2] It also overtly uses the rhetoric of racial supremacy and purity.

Right Versus Left

Reactionaries on the right and radicals on the left have characteristics peculiar to each ideological extreme. A comparison of these distinguishing qualities is instructive, because unlike the fringe left, the fringe right never developed an orthodox system similar to Marxism as an ideological "anchor." Basic distinguishing characteristics include the following:

- There was no singular event such as the Revolution of 1848 to inspire the rise of a right-wing version of Karl Marx.
- No seminal core document, such as the *Manifesto of the Communist Party,* was written to inspire generations of rightists. Hitler's *Mein Kampf* is the closest comparison, but it was a German fascist document and was never universally adopted on the right as were Marx's theories on the left.
- No leadership pantheon exists on the right that is similar to the Marx–Lenin–Stalin/ Trotsky–Mao pantheon.
- There was never a long-term intellectual evolution of right-wing theory that allowed for its adaptation to history-making events such as the mostly leftist anticolonial and nationalist wars of the postwar era.

The postwar left produced many revolutionary icons who were revered by dissidents and rebels on the left—such as Guevara, Lumumba, Ho, and Castro. The postwar left also produced intellectuals and writers who introduced fairly sophisticated systems of analysis that were operationalized by leftist radicals—such as Marcuse, Fanon, and Marighella. There was no postwar rightist equivalent of these revolutionary icons or intellectuals and writers. In fact, terrorists on the right eschew strong intellectualism, rejecting it in favor of simplistic analyses and conclusions.

In essence, right-wing ideology is less systematic and focused than the left. It tends to be less intellectual in its analysis of environmental conditions, relying instead on racial or other stereotyping of perceived enemies to mobilize followers. Thus,

> Whereas the left-wing terrorists of the 1970s emerged from the clubs and cafeterias of the universities, those of the right have more in common with bars and street corners. While those on the left spent inordinate time in ideological discussions . . . those on the right have not the slightest interest in doctrine, do not include even pseudo-intellectuals, and would have had no time for them were they to encounter them.[3]

Characteristic Trends on the Right

Although right-wing terrorists have a much less sophisticated ideological foundation, their behavior and activism do exhibit common themes. Tendencies among right-wing terrorists at the end of the 20th century included the following:

- *Theory*, in the broadest sense has been far less important for the extreme right . . . , but this has traditionally been true for political movements of the right as well as for terrorist movements.
- There has been a considerably larger incidence of *nonpolitical criminality* among the extreme right . . .
- Much of right-wing terrorism is *single-issue* in character.
- Much terrorism . . . is vigilante or reactive terrorism . . . terrorism not so much aiming at radical change as at *preserving the status quo*.[4]

In a broader context, both violent and nonviolent activism on the extreme right possess basic common characteristics. The following commonalities are typical elements found in right-wing movements and political parties:[5]

Nationalism: Only people belonging to a particular nationality have a right to reside within that group's country. Moreover, all people belonging to that particular group, wherever they reside, should have the right to live within that country's borders.

Racism: The notion that there are natural and permanent differences between groups of people.

Xenophobia: The fear of strangers or foreigners. In its current manifestation, it also posits the superiority of the group to which the fearful belong.

Antidemocracy: An aversion to the democratic rules of the game; a rejection of the principle of equality; opposition to a pluralist conception of society.

Strong state: Support for militarism and for "law and order" against the threat of crime and chaos. However, the American right's adherence to conspiracy theories has made it suspicious of strong central government (this is discussed further later).

Right-wing political parties and dissident movements do not share the same degree of solidarity as seen on the left. Rather, they have maintained an idiosyncratic quality that has not been consolidated into a multinational movement. World circumstances and domestic political environments have not given rise on the right to the same kind of international common cause that was seen on the left for much of the 20th century.

COMMON THEMES ON THE RIGHT

The following discussion incorporates common themes of the fringe right into the following categories:

- Tradition and order
- Right-wing nationalism
- Religion and mysticism

Tradition and Order

Nostalgia for a lost utopia is a common theme on the reactionary right. It is frequently expressed as a desire to reclaim the past supremacy of a championed group. Recapturing past traditions, symbols, and values becomes an important priority to justify their self-perception as defenders of a supreme principle. These traditions, symbols, and values are often portrayed as bulwarks of order against the threat of chaos; they are the keys to a people's supremacy. Thus, whereas leftists might describe their postrevolutionary society as a "people's republic" or "socialist state," rightists are likely to defend their behavior by describing their goals as a "new order" or "**Lebensraum**" (the Nazis' concept of "room to live"). They seek to preserve hallowed traditions and create an idealized order.

A new mythology is frequently created to explain the superior group's fall from glory—a mythology that claims the lost utopia has been stolen (or is threatened) by an enemy group. If the traditional values can somehow be resurrected or preserved, the ascendancy of the group will be assured. Once the "truth" of this new mythology is

Table 7.1   Usurpers of the Chosen People? Scapegoats of the Reactionary Right

Scapegoating is a common theme among right-wing extremists. Reactionaries tend to champion their favored group by creating a mythology of past glory that has been lost to the interests of an unworthy or inferior group. There is also a strong call to defend the championed group against the threat of subjugation or extermination at the hands of the scapegoated group. The following table lists groups that are typically scapegoated in the United States, Germany, and the United Kingdom.

United States	*Germany*	*United Kingdom*
Homosexuals	*Ausländer* (foreigners)	Asians ("Paki-bashing")
Illegal aliens/immigrants	Jews	Blacks
Jews	Leftists	Homosexuals
Hispanics	Racial minorities	Jews
Racial minorities	Turks	Muslims

revealed, many right-wing extremists conclude that their group's rightful status must be recouped from (or protected against) the usurper group. As a result, the usurper group becomes an enemy group, and therefore **scapegoating** is a common trait of the far and fringe right wing. For example, German "guest workers" (*Gastarbeiter*) from Italy, Spain, Greece, Turkey, Morocco, and Portugal were originally invited (dating to the 1950s) to help in postwar recovery.[6] They are now fully integrated into the economy and have a significant presence in many West German cities. This, combined with an influx of 1 million refugees during the 1990s from the Balkans and elsewhere, has created a significant population of non-Germans. These foreigners (***Ausländer***) have been targets of right-wing violence.

Table 7.1 provides a comparison of scapegoated groups in the United States, Germany, and the United Kingdom.

Right-Wing Nationalism

The reactionary right has, at its core, a concept of group loyalty and unity. The basic issue is whether one's primary loyalty should be to country, race, ethno-national identity, or another attribute. In the history of the right, there has been no unanimity on the selection of to which "group" one should pledge loyalty. For example, in the modern era nationalism and racism were commonly invoked as a way to rally the championed group to the cause and to scapegoat a perceived enemy group. However, the Nazis were originally pan-Germanic, militaristic, and virulently anti-Semitic. They did not, however, initially promote a global White supremacist ideology approximating that of modern neo-Nazis until well into their regime. In fact,

> Hitler's original program did not call for racial unity on the basis of a transnational white or Aryan identity. A racially based transnational doctrine with the explicit goal of bringing all Germanic and Nordic nations together in one united Germanic Reich was not developed . . . until 1940-1941.[7]

Thus, although general trends exist on the reactionary right, and although rightist political parties have been formed throughout Europe, some ideological differences exist on the question of group loyalty and nationalism. A brief examination of divergences on this point is instructive. Three cases in point, two European and one from the United States, are discussed in the following paragraphs. One of the cases—Norway—is an interesting example of the characteristics of activism from the reactionary right in Scandinavia.

In Germany, those on the fringe right exhibit affinity with their National Socialist past. Activist associations include political parties, paramilitaries, and a youth subculture.[8]

Prior to the 1980s, the right wing in Germany was suppressed in the West by laws prohibiting the display of Nazi-era symbols and in the East by communist proscriptions against fascist activities. During the 1980s, right-wing parties and organizations began to be organized in the West, and a rightist youth movement began to grow. Around the time of the opening of the Berlin Wall, East Germany experienced a rapid growth in right-wing sentiment. Its isolation from the West and lack of foreigners and ethnic minorities may have been responsible for the relative lack of tolerance for non-Germans in the East. In the East after the opening of the Wall,

> It is the small far-right parties that have taken root and are growing fast. Their message of nationalism, racism, and xenophobia set against a background of high unemployment, reduced wages, and inflation has a wide and growing appeal.[9]

There was, in fact, an outbreak of xenophobic violence in the East after the Wall was opened.[10] Thus, in Germany, the extreme right wing is characterized by xenophobia, nationalism, and secularism.

In Norway, although activism on the right has historically been nationalistic rather than National Socialistic in nature, there has been some divergence in focus among different groups.[11] The modern Norwegian right

> consists of three layers characterized by rather different lifestyles and ideologies: paramilitaries, Nationalist Socialist skinheads, and ideologists . . . the main ideological dimensions that divide the underground [are]: nationalism versus Germanism, culture versus race, and Right versus Left.[12]

For Norwegians, "the paramilitaries are those who best fit the nationalist label,"[13] and the skinhead youth are those who are closest to Nazi-like ideology. Interestingly, racial supremacist **skinheads** have adopted some of the ideological theories of the American racist right wing. For example, many accept the Zionist Occupation Government theory of American neo-Nazis.

In the United States, the nationalist right is by no means monolithic. It has been characterized by a number of movements, including pro-American movements, anticommunist movements, religious extremism, racial supremacy, and opposition to the influx of "foreigners" and their culture.

It is important to understand that the American variant of rightist extremism is highly suspicious of a strong central government. This is because conspiracy theories are common on the American right, with some members of the militia movement arming themselves to prepare for war against the New World Order and international bankers (i.e., Jewish interests). Some add religion to their favored conspiracy theory and actively engage themselves in looking for signs of the Rapture and the Anti-Christ. Neo-Nazis tend to demonize the federal government as having been co-opted by Jewish interests, known as the Zionist Occupation (or "Occupied") Government.

Religion and Mysticism

Religion and mysticism are not universal traits of the fringe right. Even though religious convictions obviously motivate overtly religious right-wingers—such as politicized

A new fascist generation? Youthful racist skinheads in London give the fascist salute.

Source: Hulton Archive/Getty Images; used by permission.

fundamentalist Christians, Muslims, and Jews—the modern neofascist movement (especially in Europe) does not always appeal to a deity or spiritual foundation. However, the Christian church as an institution has been upheld as a symbol of tradition and order. It is not uncommon for neofascists to reference the values of an orthodox religious tradition or to adopt these values as an element in their defense of an overarching value system.

In Europe, the war-era Nazis flirted with mysticism, neopaganism, and the occult by using astrology and reintroducing ancient Nordic ceremonies and rites. This is now rarely part of the European right-wing milieu, with modern European rightists tending to be non-religious. Their affiliations, symbols, and culture are politically secular, and their racial beliefs are essentially nationalistic in character. When referenced at all, religion and the church are simply another institution to be managed in the new order.

By contrast, American rightists have historically used religious and mystical symbols and myths as foundations for their ideology—the burning cross of the Ku Klux Klan is one example, as are the references to God's will by anti-abortion terrorists. Many right-wing American terrorists try to create a supernatural quality for the superiority of their championed cause or group, as evidenced on the American racial supremacist right. The modern supremacist right has adopted a variety of cult-like beliefs, such as Creativity,[14] Christian Identity,[15] and **Ásatrú**.[16] These beliefs will be explored further in Chapter 12.

Thus, although European rightists promote the secular nature of their political parties and street gangs, their American counterparts are likely to appeal to otherworldly authority.

Case: *The Protocols of the Learned Elders of Zion*

It is useful to mention that there often exists a convergence between scapegoating and mysticism on the fringe right. Just as it is common for rightists to assert their natural superiority, it is also common for them to demonize a scapegoated group, essentially declaring that the entire group is inherently evil. One case in point is the promulgation of a document entitled *The Protocols of the Learned Elders of Zion*.[17]

The *Protocols* originated in czarist Russia and were allegedly the true proceedings of a meeting of a mysterious committee of the Jewish faith, during which a plot to rule the world was hatched—in league with the Freemasons. The *Protocols* are a detailed record of this alleged conspiracy for world domination, but they were, in fact, a forgery written by the secret police (**Okhrana**) of Czar Nicholas II around 1895 and later published by professor Sergyei Nilus. Many anti-Semitic groups have used this document to justify the repression of European Jews, and it was an ideological foundation for the outbreak of anti-Jewish violence in Europe, including massacres and **pogroms** (violent anti-Jewish campaigns in eastern Europe).

The National Socialist movement and Adolf Hitler used the *Protocols* extensively. Modern Eurocentric neo-Nazis and Middle Eastern extremists (both secular and religious) continue to publish and circulate the *Protocols* as anti-Semitic propaganda. In 1993, a Russian court formally ruled that the *Protocols* are a forgery.[18] The *Protocols* are quoted in Chapter Perspective 7.1.

RIGHTIST TERRORISM

Right-wing terrorism in the postwar era has not been as well organized, focused, or sustained as left-wing terrorism. There has not been an overarching movement or political environment to support the terrorist right, nor has there been an ideology that bound together dissidents in different countries. Exceptions to this general observation are found in countries with unstable political environments that allow for the operation of armed paramilitaries or "death squads" in long-term campaigns of terror. These paramilitaries have been notoriously brutal, and many were closely affiliated with government security agencies, such as during the Argentine "Dirty War."

Other than the paramilitaries, rightist terrorism has been characterized by indiscriminate attacks carried out by small cells and street toughs. This characterization can be summarized as follows:

Organization. Organizationally, right-wing terrorists normally operate clandestinely in small groups or overtly as street militias and gang-like brawlers. On occasion, the violent right has operated as paramilitaries who attack perceived enemies of the state and established traditions and order, but these incidents are regionally specific. Latin America and Northern Ireland provide examples of paramilitary violence.

Focus. The focus of the violent right is generally much broader than that of leftist terrorists. Right-wing terrorists have typically been indiscriminate in their selection of targets. They have defined members of entire ethno-national groups as enemies and hence have categorized whole civilian populations as legitimate targets. For example, right-wing bombers in Europe during the 1980s were more likely to randomly select targets than their leftist counterparts, with the result being higher casualty counts.

Longevity. It is rare for right-wing terrorist campaigns to be *sustained*. An important exception to this observation is activism by paramilitaries and street militias during times of national crisis when governments are weak or besieged. Other than this kind of deeply unstable political environment, right-wing terrorist campaigns have never had the longevity or staying power seen in leftist terrorist campaigns.

The goals and objectives of dissident right-wing terrorism are best described as nihilistic, because

Chapter Perspective 7.1　　*The Protocols of the Learned Elders of Zion*:
A Conspiracy of the Extreme Right

The Protocols of the Learned Elders of Zion was a forgery written by the Czar Nicholas II's secret police (the Okhrana) around 1895. It was reproduced privately in Russia in 1897 and printed publicly in 1905 by Professor Sergyei Nilus. The document was used by the Okhrana to incite anti-Jewish pogroms. It was widely used by other reactionaries in Russia, including the violently nationalist and anti-Semitic **Black Hundreds** group and later by the White Army counterrevolutionaries during their civil war against the communist Bolsheviks, or Reds. It lists a series of 24 protocols from a fictional meeting of a mysterious group called the Elders of Zion, who allegedly conspired to rule the world in league with ancient freemasonry.

The following excerpts are from the *Protocols.*[a]

From Protocol 1: The political has nothing in common with the moral. The ruler who is governed by the moral is not a skilled politician, and is therefore unstable on his throne. He who wishes to rule must have recourse [*sic*] both to cunning and to make-believe. Great national qualities, like frankness and honesty, are vices in politics, for they bring down rulers from their thrones more effectively and more certainly than the most powerful enemy. Such qualities must be the attributes of the kingdoms of the goyim, but we must in no wise be guided by them.

From Protocol 2: In the hands of the States of to-day there is a great force that creates the movement of thought in the people, and that is the Press. The part played by the Press is to keep pointing out requirements supposed to be indispensable, to give voice to the complaints of the people, to express and create discontent. It is in the Press that the triumph of freedom of speech finds its incarnation. But the goyim States have not known how to make use of this force; and it has fallen into our hands.

From Protocol 3: The people under our guidance have annihilated the aristocracy, who were their one and only defence and foster-mother for the sake of their own advantage which is inseparably bound up with the well-being of the people. Nowadays, with the destruction of the aristocracy, the people have fallen into the grips of merciless money-grinding scoundrels who have laid a pitiless and cruel yoke upon the necks of the workers . . . We appear on the scene as alleged saviours of the worker from this oppression when we propose to him to enter the ranks of our fighting forces— Socialists, Anarchists, Communists—to whom we always give support in accordance with an alleged brotherly rule (of the solidarity of all humanity) . . .

From Protocol 7: The intensification of armaments, the increase of police forces—are all essential for the completion of the aforementioned plans. What we have to get at is that there should be in all the States of the world, besides ourselves, only the masses of the proletariat, a few millionaires devoted to our interests, police and soldiers.

From Protocol 14: When we come into our kingdom it will be undesirable for us that there should exist any other religion than ours of the One God with whom our destiny is bound up by our position as the Chosen People and through whom our same destiny is united with the destinies of the world. We must therefore sweep away all other forms of belief.

The *Protocols* are organized as follows:

Protocol I	The Basic Doctrine
Protocol II	Economic Wars
Protocol III	Methods of Conquest
Protocol IV	Materialism Replace Religion
Protocol V	Despotism and Modern Progress
Protocol VI	Take-Over Technique
Protocol VII	World-Wide Wars
Protocol VIII	Provisional Government
Protocol IX	Re-education
Protocol X	Preparing for Power
Protocol XI	The Totalitarian State
Protocol XII	Control of the Press
Protocol XIII	Distractions
Protocol XIV	Assault on Religion
Protocol XV	Ruthless Suppression
Protocol XVI	Brainwashing
Protocol XVII	Abuse of Authority
Protocol XVIII	Arrest of Opponents
Protocol XIX	Rulers and People
Protocol XX	Financial Programme
Protocol XXI	Loans and Credit
Protocol XXII	Power of Gold
Protocol XXIII	Instilling Obedience
Protocol XXIV	Qualities of the Ruler

a. From the 1906 English translation by Victor E. Marsden, a reporter for the *Morning Post.*

the majority of right-wing groups do not espouse any specific programme of reform, preferring to hide behind vague slogans of strident nationalism, the need for racial purity and the re-assertion of governmental strength.[19]

Nevertheless, as the cases of the paramilitary activity in Latin America and Northern Ireland indicate, in some political environments the goals and objectives of the violent right can be very clear. In these cases, death squad activity seeks to preserve law and order, protect the state, and eliminate dangerous (defined as leftist) movements. Assassinations, massacres, and the terrorizing of civilian populations are considered to be necessary methods to achieve the desired goal.

Regional Case: Latin America

Right-wing terrorism in Latin America has come primarily from two sources: state-level terrorism and right-wing paramilitaries—commonly called "death squads" (*esquadrón muerte*). **Death squads** have been defined as

clandestine and usually irregular organizations, often paramilitary in nature, which carry out extrajudicial executions and other violent acts (torture, rape, arson, bombing, etc.) against clearly defined individuals or groups of people . . . in the rare case where an insurgent group forms them, death squads operate with the overt support, complicity, or acquiescence of government, or at least some parts of it.[20]

Government-initiated and paramilitary sources of right-wing terrorism are not clearly separable, because there is frequently some degree of linkage between the two. Death squads have historically been covertly sanctioned by governments or agents of the government, and government personnel have covertly operated with rightist terrorists. Death squads have had a measure of independence, but connections with government security apparatuses have been repeatedly discovered.

Case studies from four countries are presented in the following sections. They summarize the environments that gave rise to paramilitary activity, as well as types of linkages between governments and death squads.

Colombia

Colombia is a country with a long history of communal strife, military coups, and revolutions. During the latter decades of the 20th century, it became a country beset by armed insurgencies on the left, paramilitary death squads on the right, a weak central government, and the problems of being the world's principal supplier of cocaine. Colombia has been home to death squads since Marxist guerrillas began attacking the interests of rich property owners—and the owners themselves—in the 1960s and 1970s. Guerrillas also extorted money from the owners. In the 1980s, wealthy land owners hired private security units to defend their landholdings. This protective mission became more aggressive as the FARC and ELN rebellions spread (these groups were discussed in Chapter 6).

Colombian Death Squads. Security units hired by wealthy landowners gradually began operating as counterinsurgency paramilitaries, often fighting in units numbering several hundreds. The paramilitaries also engaged in what can only be described as terrorist attacks against suspected FARC members and their sympathizers. It was not uncommon for these squads to commit atrocities to frighten peasants from helping FARC or the ELN. The progression from security units to right-wing death squads included the use of these groups not only by wealthy property owners, but also by *narcotraficantes*. The *narcotraficantes* wished to pacify drug-producing regions by driving away FARC and ELN guerrillas and intimidating local residents. The most prominent paramilitary has been the **United Self-Defense Forces of Colombia** (AUC). Colombian security forces evidently encouraged death squad activity by the AUC and other groups.

Argentina

Early in the 20th century, Argentina was a dynamic country with a thriving economy. Culturally, it has long been a Europeanized country, with significant waves of immigration from Italy, the United Kingdom, Germany, and elsewhere. In the 1960s and 1970s, Argentina was beleaguered by an unstable economy, political turmoil, and an ever-weakening central government. This eventually led to a military *coup d'état* in 1976.

Argentine Anticommunist Alliance. Prior to the 1976 *coup d'état,* Jose Lopez Rega, an advisor to President Juan Peron, organized the **Argentine Anticommunist Alliance (Triple-A).** Rega was a right-wing terrorist and arguably a Nazi-style fascist. The death squad was responsible for numerous acts of violence against leftists, human rights organizers, students, and others. Some of its clandestine operatives were members of the Argentine security apparatus. After the 1976 coup, and the institutionalization of Argentina's "Dirty War," Triple-A was integrated into the Argentine state terrorist apparatus.

El Salvador

Businessmen and wealthy landowners have traditionally built close ties to security and intelligence agencies in El Salvador. The National Guard (Guardia Nacional), founded in 1910, was used repeatedly to suppress peasant organizations. During the 1970s, three leftist guerrilla movements were organized, and by 1980 at least five groups were operational. They formed the Farabundo Martí National Liberation Front. At the same time, student and labor activism spread. The right wing responded violently.

ORDEN. During the late 1960s, army general José Alberto Medrano organized a paramilitary counterinsurgency group known as **ORDEN** ("Order"). Originally affiliated with the National Guard, ORDEN was used to root out unionists, student activists, communists, and other leftists. It evolved into a ruthless death squad. During the Salvadoran civil war, "the military and right-wing terrorists killed approximately 30,000 civilians to stop spreading revolution"[21] in 1980 and 1981 alone. On March 24, 1980, Catholic Archbishop Oscar Romero was assassinated by right-wing terrorists while celebrating mass.

Honduras

During the late 1970s, attempted land reforms had been only marginally successful, and unrest spread among poor peasants. Some leftists organized themselves into revolutionary groups, including the Morazan Honduran Liberation Front. The army, which had positioned itself to be the true center of power, encouraged a right-wing reaction against leftists. It also supported the United States-backed Nicaraguan counterrevolutionary guerrillas based in Honduras. Right-wing paramilitaries were formed and supported by the government. During the 1980s hundreds of civilians were killed by these death squads. One unit, **Battalion 3-16**, had been directly organized by the Honduran military.

Regional Case: Europe

Right-wing violence during the postwar era in Europe has been characterized primarily by a combination of attacks by terrorist cells and hate crimes by individuals or small gangs

The Guardia on patrol. Salvadoran troops patrol a village during the brutal civil war in the 1980s. The Guardia and rightist death squads were responsible for thousands of civilian deaths.

Source: Hulton Archive/Getty Images; used by permission.

of people—many of them racist skinheads. Organized rightist terrorism in Europe never approximated the scale or intensity of leftist terrorism. Operationally, whereas leftist groups were active throughout Western Europe, organized groups on the right have tended to engage in sudden and singular attacks rather than terrorist campaigns. Organizationally, European rightist terrorists operate in small clandestine cells or as gang-like skinhead street toughs. Some neofascists and other rightists have tried to organize themselves into militias, but these groups are apparently not proto-terrorist cells, and true paramilitaries are rare.

One distinguishing characteristic of the right, vis-à-vis the left, is that left-wing terrorists were much more discriminating in choosing their targets. The violent left typically engaged in "surgical" acts of violence such as political assassinations, kidnappings, or symbolic bombings. The violent right was almost nonselective, preferring to plant bombs in public places (as occurred in Italy and Germany during the early 1980s) or to randomly seek out and attack members of unwanted ethno-national groups.

Cases in point from four countries are presented in the following sections. They summarize the types of right-wing terrorist environments common to Europe.

Germany

During the 1970s, most terrorism in Germany came from the radical left. A small number of neo-Nazi groups did exist during the 1970s and 1980s, including the National Democratic Party, but there were relatively few right-wing incidents during those decades. During a peak of right-wing violence in 1980 and 1981, 36 people were killed by bombs, including a bombing at the famous Munich Oktoberfest beer festival in October 1980.[22]

After the opening of the Berlin Wall, the incidence of left-wing violence declined, and right-wing violence increased. This was especially true in the former communist East Germany. Among the reasons given for rightist violence emanating from the East were that East Germans were unaccustomed to living among significant numbers of non-Germans and that the former communist state had never accepted responsibility for Nazi atrocities; they instead ascribed blame to the "fascists" in the West.

Right-wing violence in Germany has come mostly from street-level confrontations rather than from terrorist cells or organizations. It has been random and spontaneous rather than politically focused or part of an ongoing terrorist campaign. The most common type of right-wing violence can be broadly described as hate crime activity. The number of these incidents spiked in the early part of the 1990s, declined in the mid-1990s, and then rose again. During this period,

> The number of right-wing actions rose dramatically . . . to a high of 2,600 in 1992, before falling to 1,489 in 1994 and 781 in 1996, levels still considerably above the average of the 1980s. . . . There was another upswing of right-wing terrorist activities in 1997-98, particularly in eastern Germany.[23]

The targets of this violence were usually *Ausländers* (foreign workers and immigrants), Jews, and occasionally U.S. interests. Those responsible were mostly young street toughs, some of them racist skinheads. These attacks and other harassment were perpetrated by individuals and small groups of racially motivated Germans, not organized terrorist cells or paramilitaries.

Italy

Right-wing terrorism in Italy has been sporadic, but deadly. It is characterized by neo-fascist ideology, randomly placed bombs, and higher body counts than those incurred during leftist terrorist incidents. During the peak years of terrorist violence in Italy (1969-1987), the violent right committed only 27 (7.5%) of the attacks that caused death or injury. However,

> In those 27 attacks, the right killed more victims than the left—193 compared to 145. Of the 193, 85 were killed by a single bomb at Bologna railway station, and 52 in four other indiscriminate bomb attacks in public places.[24]

Despite a spike in right-wing terrorism in the early 1980s, few attacks have occurred since the middle part of that decade. Unlike the rightist environment in Germany, Italy has not experienced a surge of street-level violence from the right. An underlying culture of street toughs and skinheads is not widespread in Italy. Instead, the most significant examples of neofascist violence have come from terrorist cells. Two organizations typify right-wing violence in Italy.

New Order. **New Order** (Ordine Nuovo) carried out several attacks in the late 1960s and early 1970s. On December 12, 1969, New Order bombed the famous Piazza Fontana in Milan, causing 16 deaths and 90 injuries. The group bombed a train in July 1970, killing six people and injuring 90, and in May 1974 New Order detonated a hand grenade in Brescia during an antifascist demonstration, killing eight people.

Armed Revolutionary Nuclei. The **Armed Revolutionary Nuclei** split from New Order. Its most notorious act was the bombing of the main train station in Bologna, which killed 85 and injured 180.

As in Germany, the Italian terrorists on the right seem to be indiscriminate in the selection of their targets. Bombings and other attacks are typically directed against exposed targets with undifferentiated victims.

Turkey

Modern Turkish nationalism dates to the founding of the Republic of Turkey in 1923 under the leadership of Kemal Atatürk. Atatürk created a secular, Westernized republic out of the ruins of the autocratic Ottoman Empire. He was a nationalist who, among other reforms, liberated women, adopted a Western alphabet, promoted Western dress, and ended the designation of Islam as a state religion. His goal was to create a secular, modernized republic. This ideology forms the foundation of Turkey's democracy.

Reactionary right-wing nationalists have been active since the 1980s. The **National Movement Party** (Milliyetci Hareket Partisi, or MHP) is an ultranationalist political movement that was first organized in the 1960s. MHP's ideology centers on unifying all Turkic people and creating **Turan**, or the Great Turkish Empire. This new state would unite Turkic peoples who now live in independent states founded after the collapse of the Soviet Union. Ethnic Turks are demographically significant throughout the Caucasus region and Central Asia in Turkmenistan, Kazakhstan, Azerbaijan, Kyrgyzstan, and Uzbekistan. MHP's ideology also strongly supports the war against the Kurdish rebels in southeastern Turkey, using this conflict to rally its followers around Turkish nationalism. MHP has links to a clandestine paramilitary known as the **Grey Wolves.**

The Grey Wolves. The most prominent organization on the violent right wing in Turkey is the Grey Wolves. The Grey Wolves are named for a mythical she-wolf who led ancient Turks to freedom. Its wolf's-head symbol is displayed by MHP members and other nationalists. Grey Wolves have been implicated in many attacks against leftists, Kurds, Muslim activists, and student organizations. They have also been implicated in attacks supporting the Turkish occupation of Cyprus. **Mehmet Ali Agca,** who was convicted of shooting Pope John Paul II, was a former Grey Wolf.

The Grey Wolves have typically targeted leftists, minority nationalists, religious activists, and others opposed to their nationalist agenda. Attacks have included shootings, bombings, and kidnappings.

Northern Ireland

The armed Catholic dissident groups are nominally "leftist" because of their adoption of variations on socialist ideology. The armed Protestant Loyalist groups—which are arguably paramilitary militias rather than underground terrorist movements—reject reunification with the Irish republic. They operate as a reaction to Catholic Republican nationalism.

Ulster Volunteer Force. The **Ulster Volunteer Force** (UVF) is the main Protestant Loyalist paramilitary and has its roots in the anti-Republican movement of the early 1900s. Its membership since that time has totaled about 40,000. The mission of the modern UVF was to retaliate against, and suppress, Provo violence against Protestants. Its members have frequently resorted to acts of terrorism against Catholics.

Loyalist Volunteer Force. A more violent terrorist fringe group, the **Loyalist Volunteer Force,** split from the UVF because it considered the UVF to have betrayed the Protestant cause when it participated in the peace process. Founded in 1996, it is small and violent. The LVF's goal has been to derail the peace process in Northern Ireland through terrorist violence.

Pope John Paul II lies wounded after being shot by Mehmet Ali Agca. Agca was a member of the Grey Wolves, a fringe right-wing Turkish nationalist group implicated in numerous acts of terrorism.

Source: Hulton Archive/Getty Images; used by permission.

Protestant paramilitaries typically target Catholic activists, suspected IRA sympathizers, and suspected IRA members. They have been implicated in dozens of assassinations and many more acts of violence.

Table 7.2 summarizes the perceived championed constituencies and enemies of right-wing terrorists.

THE FUTURE OF THE VIOLENT RIGHT

Terrorism from the right has generally increased since its spike in activity during the early 1980s. It has also developed several typologies, including terrorist cells, paramilitary death squads, and gang-like hate movements. These typologies differ from region to region and within distinct political environments. The incidence of rightist violence has ebbed and flowed, so that there have not been sustained right-wing terrorist campaigns—with the exception of political environments conducive to paramilitary activity.

Rightist terrorism is likely to continue to be characterized by xenophobic violence in Europe, paramilitary violence in Latin America, and militia-religious-supremacist violence in North America. The current right-wing terrorist environments in North America and Europe will not dramatically change, absent a significant shift in their respective political environments. However, right-wing activism will continue to occur, particularly in the following manner:

Table 7.2   **Terrorism on the Right**

Right-wing terrorist groups have arisen as a reaction against perceived domestic ideological and ethnic enemies. Although they share basic characteristics, their values and ideologies are rooted in their domestic political contexts. They do not share an overarching ideology similar to Marxist theory on the left. In essence, right-wing terrorists develop characteristics that arise out of unique political environments that are peculiar to their respective countries. In Latin America, right-wing terrorists have tended to be paramilitaries that engage in terrorist campaigns arising out of destabilized domestic environments. In Europe, violence on the right has come from either street-level toughs or clandestine terrorist cells.

The following table summarizes the constituencies and adversaries of several politically violent movements.

	Latin America	
Group	*Constituency*	*Adversary*
Colombian death squads	Rich, government, traffickers	FARC, ELN, sympathizers
Argentine Anticommunist Alliance	Right wing, military	Leftists, perceived opponents
ORDEN	Government, right wing	Leftists, sympathizers
Battalion 3-16	Government, military	Leftists, sympathizers

	Europe	
Group	*Constituency*	*Adversary*
German neo-Nazis	Native Germans	*Ausländers*, Jews, United States
New Order	Italian right wing	Anyone not in support
Armed Revolutionary Nuclei	Italian right wing	Anyone not in support
Revolutionary Cells	Oppressed classes and people	Government, imperialists
Grey Wolves	Native Turks, Turkic people	Non-Turks, Nonsupporters
Ulster Volunteer Force	Northern Irish Protestants	Republicans and supporters
Loyalist Volunteer Force	Northern Irish Protestants	Republicans and supporters

Scapegoating. Political and social forces that produced right-wing activism immediately before and after the opening of the Berlin Wall are likely to continue to stimulate a rightist reaction. Immigration and discomfort with influences from nonnative cultures have historically caused rightist reactions, especially during periods of domestic uncertainty. During these periods, terrorists are likely to blame ethno-nationalist, religious, or political scapegoats for domestic problems. Should domestic problems such as unemployment or inflation become severe, right-wing scapegoating and ethno-national chauvinism are also likely to increase in severity.

Rejection of Unpopular Agendas. The fringe right wing has historically reacted to unpopular agendas, considering them to be threatening to traditional values and group supremacy. Even during times of relative prosperity and stability, some domestic policies and programs will stimulate terrorism from the right wing. In North America, tax policy, abortion rights, alternative lifestyles, and subsidy programs for demographic groups have traditionally aroused reactions from the right. In Europe, foreign worker laws, immigration, and European Union issues ("Europeanization") are likely to arouse reaction from the right.

The prospects for an international revolutionary movement on the right—akin to the left-wing environment in the postwar era—are very unlikely. This is because right-wing political environments are uniquely peculiar to specific domestic environments. For example, it is unlikely that American religious extremists will find common cause with European neofascists. Nor will organizations such as the Ku Klux Klan appear in Latin America. At the same time, paramilitary activity similar to the Latin American case is unlikely to take root except in the most unstable of regions, such as the Balkans. Thus, aside from regional trends such as xenophobia in Europe or reactionary sentiment in Latin America, deep-seated international linkage or solidarity is unlikely on the right wing.

In Europe, violence by right-wing terrorists is likely to continue to be xenophobic, selecting as scapegoated enemies foreign workers, Jews, socialists, and immigrants. Neofascist and nationalist political parties and organizations will remain active. Among young right-wing adherents, the strongest and most enduring movement will continue to be the amorphous and nihilistic youth subculture. The music, lifestyle, and lack of organizational focus will provide a supportive environment for a generalized continuation of right-wing sentiment. The type of violence that this is likely to translate into will be street-level hate crimes and other assaults. It is also likely that terrorist cells will occasionally strike.

In the United States, the most likely future scenario is the continuation of sporadic violence from militia members, racial supremacists, and single-issue terrorists. A racist youth culture exists, but it is unlikely to become a significant grassroots youth movement for two reasons: First, the population of right-wing youth has never been as large as its European counterpart, and second, right-wing agitation in the United States has historically come from older activists. Members of militias, racial supremacist groups, and religious terrorists can be expected to occasionally target government symbols, minority groups, and single-issue targets.

In Latin America, unstable political environments will continue to produce paramilitary activity. Should a strong revival of leftist activism emerge, there may very well be a resurgence of rightist reaction from regimes, the armed forces, and paramilitary death squads. However, strong left-wing provocation is unlikely to resurface on the same scale as during the postwar era, except in isolated cases.

Case in Point   **Supportive Environments on the Right— Racist Skinheads**

Skinheads are associations of youths who live a countercultural, and often antisocial, lifestyle. The term *skinhead* is derived from their distinctive appearance, which includes closely cropped hair, suspenders, T-shirts, tattoos, blue jeans, and boots (traditionally manufactured by Dr. Martens). Some skinheads have organized themselves into gangs, but others simply live the lifestyle. Although they have a popular reputation for advocating racial supremacy, the fact is that many have no racial animosity, and some actively confront racist skinheads. An international movement known as **Skinheads Against Racial Prejudice** (SHARP) specifically challenges racist skinhead gangs.

The skinhead movement began in England in the early 1970s among working-class youth as a countermovement to the hippies. They were known for hard drinking (usually beer) and fighting. Some began to engage in racial harassment of, and assaults on, Asians and Blacks. This was the beginning of the racist skinhead movement, which has since adopted supremacist values, Nazi symbols, and Nazi slogans. The movement's lifestyle has become international, with thousands of skinhead youth found in dozens of countries.

Skinhead gangs have been actively courted by extremist organizations in the United Kingdom, Germany, the United States, and elsewhere. They are often viewed as a potential recruitment reservoir that simply requires the discipline of the organized neofascist and neo-Nazi groups and parties. Some of these linkages have been successful, but the movement is by no means directed by organized neofascists.

An important aspect of the racist skinhead lifestyle is an active counterculture. It is expressed through magazines and music. The magazines—called "**skinzines**" or "**zines**"—generally report on skinhead lifestyle and music. Advertising includes standard ads for clothing, flamboyant grooming tips, and music. Skinheads promote a strong music style that is rooted in the punk music that began in the mid-1970s. It is a "hard" rock-and-roll style with driving beats and rhythms and a heavy emphasis on guitars, drums, and racially charged lyrics. Typical of the skinhead music industry is **Resistance Records,** a popular international label owned by the National Alliance, a prominent American neo-Nazi organization.

The following are typical lyrics from the international skinhead music scene:

United Kingdom's Skrewdriver (entitled "White Warriors"):

> Fighting in the city,
> It's a matter of life and death,
> It's as easy as black and white,
> You'll fight till your last breath . . .
> When the battle is over,
> And the victory is won,
> The White man's lands are owned
> By the White people,
> The traitors will be all gone.[a]

Germany's Tonstörung (titled "Doitsche Musik"):

> Sharpen your knife on the sidewalk,
> let the knife slip into the Jew's body.
> Blood must flow
> and we shit on the freedom of this Jew republic . . .
> oiling the guillotine with the Jew's fat.[b]

Hungary's Mos-Oi (titled "Gypsy-Free Zone"):

> We will do away with everything bad;
> Everything base and evil will disappear;
> A blazing gun is the
> Only weapon I can win with.
> I will kill every Gypsy, adult or child . . .
> When the job is done, we can post
> [the sign] "Gypsy-free Zone."[c]

NOTES

a. Quoted in Anti-Defamation League. *The Skinhead International: A Worldwide Survey of Neo-Nazi Skinheads.* New York: Anti-Defamation League, 1995, p. 76.

b. From Anti-Defamation League (note a), p. 38.

c. From Anti-Defamation League (note a), p. 46.

CHAPTER SUMMARY

This chapter instructed students about the nature of right-wing terrorism and presented the purposes and goals of terrorists on the right. Terrorism on the extreme right has increased since the opening of the Berlin Wall in 1989. As terrorism from the left became a shadow of its former self, rightist extremism attracted support from ethno-national, ideological, and religious reactionaries in Europe, North America, and Latin America. Although its historical roots lie in the right-wing movements of Europe in the period between the world wars, modern terrorists have developed their own idiosyncratic qualities.

Comparisons between the radical left and reactionary right indicate that the right wing is much less ideologically centered than the left and is arguably anti-intellectual. Although there is no strong ideology comparable to orthodox Marxism, common themes are identifiable on the right, including nationalism, racism, xenophobia, antidemocracy, and a strong state. Similarly, right-wing terrorism has not been as concerted or sustained as left-wing terrorism in the recent past, other than extensive violence by paramilitaries in politically fractured societies.

In Chapter 8, students will investigate terrorism that is motivated by religious faith and criminal profit. The discussion will focus on motivations of religious and criminal terrorists, and cases in point and contexts for these typologies will be identified. Reasons for religious or criminal violence in specific political environments will also be evaluated.

KEY TERMS AND CONCEPTS

The following topics were discussed in this chapter and are found in the Glossary:

Afrikaner Resistance Movement

Agca, Mehmet Ali

Argentine Anticommunist Alliance (Triple-A)

Armed Revolutionary Nuclei

Ásatrú

Ausländer

Avengers of the Martyrs

Battalion 3-16

Black Hundreds

Death squads

Grey Wolves

Lebensraum

Loyalist Volunteer Force

National Movement Party

New Order

Okhrana

ORDEN

Pogroms

Protocols of the Learned Elders of Zion, The

Resistance Records

Scapegoating

Skinheads

Skinheads Against Racial Prejudice

Skinzines

Turan

Ulster Volunteer Force

United Self-Defense Forces of Colombia

Xenophobia

Zines

RECOMMENDED WEB SITES

The following Web sites provide information about rightist organizations, movements, and goals.

Afrikaner Resistance Movement: www.awb.co.za

Institute for Historical Review: http://ihr.org

Pro-Ulster Protestant Paramilitaries: http://members.lycos.co. uk/uindex/paramilitary/uvf.htm

Resistance Records: www.resistance.com

Stormfront: www.stormfront.org

Discussion Box

Order From Chaos

This chapter's Discussion Box is intended to stimulate critical debate about the role of the military in preserving tradition and order in some societies when civilian governments are unable to do so.

In some political environments, the military has come to symbolize tradition and order. When civilian governments have been unable to preserve a traditional or orderly society, the military has stepped in to "save" the nation. Latin America from the 1960s through the 1980s was often beset by conflict between the right and left. The military was often a violent institutional bulwark on behalf of the right.

The Chilean and Argentine dictatorships of the 1970s and 1980s are discussed here.

Chile

Salvador Allende, a democratic socialist, was elected president of Chile in 1970, the first democratically elected socialist in Latin America. His policies of nationalizing (seizing control of) industries and banking angered many owners and the traditional upper class. His attempt to control the economy by keeping consumer product prices low and raising the minimum wage created rampant inflation, seriously damaging the economy. Demonstrations broke out in the capital of Santiago, as did labor strikes around the country. During his three years in power, Allende also brought in advisers from communist countries, Cubans, Spanish communists, and thousands of leftists from other countries.

The military, led by General Augusto Pinochet, seized control in a bloody *coup d'état* on September 11, 1973. Allende was killed during the coup. General Pinochet was a neofascist, and his rule was brutal. To suppress the left, the government arrested, tortured, and killed suspected subversives. A government-sponsored death squad—the **Avengers of the Martyrs**—operated under the direction of the security forces. More than 3,000 people "disappeared" or were killed during the regime. When Pinochet stepped down in March 1990, the economy had been stabilized, and the left had been crushed.

Argentina

The unstable political environment in Argentina during the early 1970s was exacerbated by the significant activities of the leftist Montonero and ERP urban terrorist movements. With the inability of the Peronist government to curb mass unrest and the Montonero insurgency, the right wing responded violently. The Argentine Anticommunist Alliance paramilitary was encouraged by government agents.

In March 1976, the Argentine military seized power. General Jorge Videla eventually rose to leadership of the new government. A campaign of state-sponsored terror was waged during the military regime, known as the Dirty War. Tens of thousands of people were tortured, made to disappear, or killed. Detention camps were constructed where much of this activity was carried out. During this period, the Montoneros and ERP were eliminated, the left was crushed, and all political opposition was silenced.

Discussion Questions

- Should the mission of the armed forces include stepping in to save the nation, even at the expense of democratic liberties?
- Was the Argentine military *coup d'état* necessary, considering the violent political environment?
- Was the Chilean military *coup d'état* justifiable, considering the damage Allende's policies had caused the economy and the influx of communist aid and left-wing activists?
- What are the reasons for the strong undercurrent of fascism in many Latin American armed forces?
- To what degree did the United States benefit from the coups in Chile and Argentina? To what degree was the United States harmed by these coups?

WEB EXERCISE

Using this chapter's recommended Internet sites, conduct an online investigation of right-wing dissident movements.

- How would you describe the self-images presented by rightist dissident movements?
- Review the goals and objectives of these organizations. Do they seem reasonable to you? Do they justify violent behavior?
- If you were a violent right-wing dissident, how would you design your own Web site?

For an online search of violent right-wing dissident movements, students should activate the search engine on their Web browser, and enter the following keywords:

"Aryan Revolution"
"Neo-Nazism"
The names of specific dissident organizations

RECOMMENDED READINGS

The following publications give insight into rightist ideologies, movements, and personalities.

Anti-Defamation League. *The Skinhead International: A Worldwide Survey of Neo-Nazi Skinheads.* New York: Anti-Defamation League, 1995.

Kaplan, Jeffrey, and Tore Bjørgo, eds. *Nation and Race: The Developing Euro-American Racist Subculture.* Boston: Northeastern University Press, 1998.

Kelly, Robert J., and Jess Maghan, eds. *Hate Crime: The Global Politics of Polarization.* Carbondale: Southern Illinois University Press, 1998.

Lee, Martin A. *The Beast Reawakens: Fascism's Resurgence from Hitler's Spymasters to Today's Neo-Nazi Groups and Right-Wing Extremists.* New York: Routledge, 1999.

Lipstadt, Deborah E. *Denying the Holocaust: The Growing Assault on Truth and Memory.* New York: Plume, 1994.

NOTES

[1] The American Democratic and Republican parties reflect the American political tradition of coalitional political representation. For example, organized labor in the United States has never been represented by a viable political party, although the Socialist Party did have a period of political influence in the early decades of the 20th century.

[2] For a display of AWB symbolism, see www.awb.co.za

[3] Laqueur, Walter. *The New Terrorism: Fanaticism and the Arms of Mass Destruction.* New York: Oxford University Press, 1999, p. 122.

[4] Adapted and quoted from Laqueur (note 3 above), p. 125.

[5] Adapted and quoted from Weinberg, Leonard. "An Overview of Right-Wing Extremism in the Western World: A Study of Convergence, Linkage, and Identity." In Kaplan, Jeffrey, and Bjørgo, Tore, eds. *Nation and Race: The Developing Euro-American Racist Subculture.* Boston: Northeastern University Press, 1998, pp. 7-8. Reporting Mudde, Cas. "Right-Wing Extremism Analyzed." *European Journal of Political Research* 27 (1995): 203-24.

[6] See Harnishmacher, Robert, and Robert J. Kelly. "The Neo-Nazis and Skinheads of Germany: Purveyors of Hate." In Kelly, Robert J., and Jess Maghan. *Hate Crime: The Global Politics of Polarization.* Carbondale: Southern Illinois University Press, 1998, p. 44.

[7] Kaplan and Bjørgo (in note 5 above), p. xi.

[8] See Kühnel, Wolfgang. "Hitler's Grandchildren? The Reemergence of a Right-Wing Social Movement in Germany." In Kaplan and Bjørgo (in note 5 above), p. 148 ff.

[9] Harnishmacher and Kelly (note 6 above), p. 38.

[10] Ibid., pp. 154-56.

[11] See Fangen, Katrine. "Living Out Our Ethnic Instincts: Ideological Beliefs Among Right-Wing Activists in Norway." In Kaplan and Bjørgo (in note 5 above), p. 202 ff.

[12] Ibid., p. 202.

[13] Ibid., p. 214.

[14] An anti-Christian mystical doctrine adopted by World Church of the Creator.

[15] Adapted from an 18th-century doctrine originating in Great Britain called Anglo-Israelism. The belief system reinterprets the biblical creation story and the concept of the Chosen People.

[16] A neopagan belief based on the pantheon of ancient Norse gods.

[17] *The Protocols of the Learned Elders of Zion* has been extensively published on the Internet. They are readily available from Web sites promoting civil liberties, neo-Nazi propaganda, anti-Semitism, and Islamic extremism.

[18] See Hiltzik, Michael A. "Russian Court Rules 'Protocols' an Anti-Semitic Forgery." *Los Angeles Times*. November 28, 1993.

[19] Hoffman, Bruce. *Inside Terrorism*. New York: Columbia University Press, 1998, p. 165.

[20] Campbell, Bruce B. "Death Squads: Definition, Problems, and Historical Context." In Campbell, Bruce B., and Arthur D. Brenner, eds. *Death Squads in Global Perspective: Murder With Deniability*. New York: St. Martin's Press, 2000, pp. 1-2.

[21] LaFeber, Walter. *Inevitable Revolutions: The United States in Central America*. New York: Norton, 1984, p. 10.

[22] Campbell, Bruce B. "Death Squads: Definition, Problems, and Historical Context." In Campbell, Bruce B., and Arthur D. Brenner, eds. *Death Squads in Global Perspective: Murder With Deniability*. New York: St. Martin's Press, 2000. pp. 1-2.

[23] Laqueur (note 3 above), p. 119.

[24] Clutterbuck (note 22 above), p. 26.

Chapter 8

FOR THE FAITH AND PROFIT: RELIGIOUS AND CRIMINAL TERRORISM

This chapter discusses two typologies of terrorism: religious and criminal. Both have strong, but fundamentally different, characteristics that will be investigated. The following attributes characterize the basic idiosyncratic qualities of religious and criminal terrorists:

Religious terrorism is usually motivated by an absolute belief that an otherworldly power has sanctioned—and commanded—the application of terrorist violence for the greater glory of the faith. Acts that are committed in the name of the faith will be forgiven by the otherworldly power and perhaps rewarded in an afterlife. As will be clarified in this chapter, this profile describes the adoption of religion as a *primary* motive for politically violent behavior; other movements use religion as a *secondary* motive.

Criminal terrorism is motivated by sheer profit. This profit can be invested differently, depending on the goals of the criminal enterprise. **Traditional criminal enterprises** (such as the Mafia) accumulate profits from criminal activity for personal pleasure and aggrandizement; they use violence so that the government will leave them alone. In contrast, **criminal-political enterprises** (such as the Tamil Tigers) accumulate profits from criminal activity to sustain their movement; they use violence to advance their cause.

Table 8.1 presents a model that compares the fundamental characteristics of religious and criminal terrorism. The discussion in this chapter will review:

- Religious Terrorism
- Criminal Terrorism

RELIGIOUS TERRORISM

In the modern era, religious terrorism has increased in its frequency, scale of violence, and global reach. At the same time, a relative decline has occurred in secular—nonreligious—terrorism. The old ideologies of class conflict, anticolonial liberation, and secular

Table 8.1   The Characteristics of Religious and Criminal Terrorism

The actions of religious and criminal terrorists and extremists can be contrasted in several ways, as can the actions of traditional criminal enterprises and criminal-political enterprises. When the decision has been made by these extremists to engage in terrorism, their activity profiles become very distinguishable.

The following table illustrates differences between these typologies in their motives, goals, targets, personnel, and degrees of political agitation.

			Activity Profile		
Typology	*Motives*	*Goals*	*Targets*	*Personnel*	*Political Agitation*
Religious movements	Spiritual	New society	Nonbelievers and institutions	True believers	Active and public
Traditional criminal enterprises	Financial	Passive government	Active governments	Criminals	Reactive and anonymous
Criminal-political enterprises	Political	Revolutionary victory	Agents and symbols of oppression	Dissident activists	Active and public

nationalism have been challenged by a new and vigorous infusion of sectarian (religious) ideologies. Grassroots extremist support for religious violence has been most widespread among populations living in repressive societies that do not permit demands for reform or other expressions of dissent. In this regard,

> It is perhaps not surprising that religion should become a far more popular motivation for terrorism in the post-Cold War era as old ideologies lie discredited by the collapse of the Soviet Union and communist ideology, while the promise of munificent benefits from the liberal-democratic, capitalist state . . . fails to materialize in many countries throughout the world.[1]

Table 8.2 summarizes and contrasts the activity profiles of religious and secular terrorist movements.

Primary and Secondary Motives: The Idiosyncratic Quality of Religious Terrorism

Religion as a basis for terrorism has been applied in different ways, depending on the cultural and political environments of each terrorist movement. In some contexts, religion has become the primary motive for terrorist behavior. In other contexts, it is a secondary motive for politically violent movements. For example, the Jewish terrorist group Lohmey Heruth Israel ("Fighters for the Freedom of Israel")—commonly known as the **Stern Gang**—issued the following (mostly nationalistic) rationalization for the group's violence against the British occupation of Palestine:

> Now this is the law of our war. So long as there is fear in the heart of any Jew in the world, so long as there are embers burning under our feet anywhere in the world, so

Table 8.2   Case Comparison: Religious and Secular Terrorism

Religious and secular terrorism have contrasting activity profiles. Both typologies certainly pose threats to targeted systems, but the manifestations of dissent differ in potential scale and scope of impact.

The quality of violence, constituency profile, and relationship to the existing system are summarized in the following table.

| Typology | *Activity Profile* | | | |
	Quality of Violence[a]	*Scope of Violence*	*Constituency Profile*	*Relationship to Existing System*
Religious	Unconstrained scale of terrorist violence	Expansive target definition	Narrow, insular, and isolated	Alienated "true believers"
	Result: Unconstrained choice of weapons and tactics	Result: Indiscriminate use of violence	Result: No appeals to a broader audience	Result: Completely reconfigured social order
Secular	Constrained scale of terrorist violence	Focused target definition	Inclusive, for the championed group	Liberators
	Result: Relative constraint in choice of weapons and tactics	Result: Relative discrimination in use of violence	Result: Appeals to actual or potential supporters	Result: Restructured or rebuilt society

Source: Hoffman, Bruce. *Inside Terrorism*. New York: Columbia University Press, 1998, pp. 94-95.

a. Communal terrorism is rarely constrained and is a case in point of convergence in the quality of violence used by religious and secular terrorism.

long as there is a foreign policeman guarding the gates of our homeland, so long as there is a foreign master over our country, so long as we do not rule our own land, so long shall we be in your way. You will look around you and fear day and night.[2]

This discussion is similar to our discussions in previous chapters about how Marxism has been applied differently, depending on the political environment of each extremist movement. Students will recall that ideological groups such as Italy's Red Brigades were motivated *primarily* by Marxist ideals, but that nationalist movements such as the Viet Cong were motivated *secondarily* by ideology—their primary motivation was their national identity. A comparison of this model to religious motives is instructive and can be summarized as follows:

Primary Religious Motive. For some terrorists, religion is at the very core of their political, social, and revolutionary agendas. Within this context, the religious belief system is the driving force behind their behavior. Examples of this profile are found in the United

States among violent Christian anti-abortionists, in India among Hindu extremists, and in the Middle East and elsewhere among *jihadi* Islamic fundamentalists.

Secondary Religious Motive. For many ethno-nationalist and other revolutionary movements, national independence or some other degree of autonomy forms the primary motivation for their violent behavior. Religious affiliation can be important because it is an element of their ethnic or national identity, but their ultimate goal is grounded in their secular identity. Examples of this profile are found in Northern Ireland among Catholic and Protestant terrorists, in southern Sudan among Christians and believers in traditional faiths, and in pre-independence Israel among Jewish terrorists.

Religious terrorism is thus an idiosyncratic type of terrorism; it originates from countless cultural and historical contexts. Unlike secular terrorism, which usually has an inherent (but fringe) rationality, religious terrorism is often an expression of faith in a supernatural purpose. It is therefore very much contingent upon trends within specific religions, the historical experiences of ethno-national groups, and the unique political environments of nations.

Keeping this idiosyncratic quality in mind, it is arguably necessary to make a sensitive observation—and caveat—about the study of religious terrorism in the modern era. The observation is:

> Popular Western perception equates radical Islam with terrorism. . . . There is, of course, no Muslim or Arab monopoly in the field of religious fanaticism; it exists and leads to acts of violence in the United States, India, Israel, and many other countries. But the frequency of Muslim- and Arab-inspired terrorism is still striking. . . . A discussion of religion-inspired terrorism cannot possibly confine itself to radical Islam, but it has to take into account the Muslim countries' preeminent position in this field.[3]

The caveat is that there is much misunderstanding in the West about the historical and cultural origins of the growth of radical interpretations of Islam. One such misunderstanding is the common belief that the concept of "holy war" is an underlying principle of the Islamic faith. The term *jihad* is widely presumed in the West to refer exclusively to waging war against nonbelievers. This is simplistic and fundamentally incorrect. An Islamic jihad is *not* the equivalent of a Christian crusade. Chapter Perspective 8.1 provides some clarification of the concept of jihad.

Why do some movements and ethno-national groups link their cause to an underlying spiritual principle? Is it accurate to characterize all spiritually rooted violence as terroristic or extremist? What kinds of historical cases illustrate the idiosyncratic qualities of religious violence? To begin, we may observe that faith-based violence exhibits the same qualities of the terrorist typologies discussed in previous chapters. For example, it can be communal, genocidal, nihilistic, or revolutionary. It can be committed by lone wolves, clandestine cells, large dissident movements, or governments. And, depending on one's perspective, there is often debate about whether the perpetrators should be classified as terrorists or freedom fighters.

The following discussion presents several topical areas—organized as cases in point— that illustrate the idiosyncratic nature of religious terrorism. These topical areas include:

- Several historical examples
- Two examples of cult terrorism
- An example of state sponsorship
- An organizational case
- Several regional cases

| Chapter Perspective 8.1 | Struggling in the Way of God |

The concept of *jihad* is a central tenet in Islam. Contrary to misinterpretations common in the West, the term literally means a sacred "struggle" or "effort" rather than an armed conflict or fanatical holy war.[a] Although a jihad can certainly be manifested as a holy war, it more correctly refers to the duty of Muslims to personally strive "in the way of God."[b]

> This is the primary meaning of the term as used in the Quran, which refers to an internal effort to reform bad habits in the Islamic community or within the individual Muslim. The term is also used more specifically to denote a war waged in the service of religion.[c]

Regarding how one should wage jihad,

> The *"greater"* jihad refers to the struggle each person has within him or herself to do what is right. Because of human pride, selfishness and sinfulness, people of faith must constantly wrestle with themselves and strive to do what is right and good. The *"lesser"* jihad involves the outward defense of Islam. Muslims should be prepared to defend Islam, including military defense, when the community of faith is under attack.[d] (italics added)

Thus, waging an Islamic jihad is not the same as waging a Christian Crusade—it has a broader and more intricate meaning. Nevertheless, it is permissible—and even a duty—to wage war to defend the faith against aggressors. Under this type of jihad, warfare is conceptually defensive in nature; in contrast, the Christian Crusades were conceptually *offensive* in nature. Those who engage in armed jihad are known as mujahideen, or holy warriors. Mujahideen who receive "martyrdom" by being killed in the name of the faith will find that

> awaiting them in paradise are rivers of milk and honey, and beautiful young women. Those entering paradise are eventually reunited with their families and as martyrs stand in front of God as innocent as a newborn baby.[e]

The precipitating causes for the modern resurgence of the armed and radical *jihadi* movement are twofold: the revolutionary ideals and ideology of the 1979 Iranian Revolution and the practical application of jihad against the Soviet Union's occupation of Afghanistan.

Some radical Muslim clerics and scholars have concluded that the Afghan jihad brought God's judgment against the Soviet Union, leading to the collapse of its empire. As a consequence, radical *jihadis* fervently believe that they are fighting in the name of an inexorable force that will end in total victory and guarantee them a place in paradise.

a. Armstrong, Karen. *Islam: A Short History*. New York: Modern Library, 2000, p. 201.

b. Burke, Josh, and James Norton. "Q & A: Islamic fundamentalism: A world-renowned scholar explains key points of Islam." *Christian Science Monitor*. October 4, 2001.

c. Armstrong (note a above), p. 201.

d. Burke and Norton (note b above).

e. Laqueur, Walter. *The New Terrorism. Fanaticism and the Arms of Mass Destruction*. New York: Oxford University Press, 1999, p. 100.

Historical Cases in Point:
Fighting, Dying, and Killing in the Name of the Faith

The following cases are historical examples of the idiosyncratic qualities of religious violence. This is a selective survey (by no means exhaustive) that will demonstrate how some examples of faith-based violence are clearly examples of terrorism, how others are not so clear, and how each example must be considered within its historical and cultural context.

Antiquity

Students may recall that the Book of Joshua in the Bible describes the ancient Hebrews' conquest of Canaan. To Joshua and his followers, this was the "Promised Land" of the covenant between God and the chosen people. According to the Bible, the Canaanite cities were destroyed and the Canaanites themselves were attacked until "there was no one left who breathed."[4] Assuming that Joshua and his army put to the sword all the inhabitants of the 31 cities mentioned in the Bible, and assuming that each city averaged 10,000 people, his conquest cost 310,000 lives.[5]

To the ancient Hebrews, the Promised Land had been occupied by enemy trespassers. To fulfill God's covenant, it was necessary from their perspective to drive them from the land, exterminating them when deemed necessary.

Christian Crusades

During the Middle Ages, the Western Christian church launched at least nine invasions of the Islamic east, the first one in 1095. The purpose of the **Crusades** was to capture the holy lands from the Saracen Turks and other Muslim nations. Christian knights and soldiers answered the call for many reasons. The promise of land, booty, and glory were certainly central reasons. Another important reason was the promise, made by **Pope Urban II,** that fighting and dying in the name of the Cross would ensure **martyrdom** and thereby guarantee a place in heaven. Thus, "knights who with pious intent took the Cross would earn a remission from temporal penalties for all his sins; if he died in battle he would earn remission of his sins."[6]

The Church-sanctioned invasions and atrocities were deemed to be in accordance with God's wishes and therefore perfectly acceptable. An extreme and unquestioning faith in the cause led to a series of campaigns of terror against the non-Christian (and sometimes the Orthodox Christian) residents of conquered cities and territories.

A Secret Cult of Murder

In India during the 13th through the 19th centuries, the **Thuggee** cult existed among worshippers of the Hindu goddess Kali, the destroyer. They were called by various names, including Phansigars ("noose operators"), Dacoits ("members of a gang of robbers"), and Thuggees (from which the English word *thug* is derived). Members would strangle sacrificial victims—usually travelers—with a noose called a ***phansi*** in the name of Kali, and then rob and ritually mutilate and bury them. Offerings would be made to Kali. The British eventually destroyed the movement, although the death toll of Thuggee victims was staggering: "This secretive cult is believed to have murdered 20,000 victims a year . . . perhaps dispatching as many as several million victims altogether before it was broken up by British officials."[7]

There are few debatable counterpoints about this cult—the Thuggees waged a campaign of religious terror for centuries.

Modern Arab Islamist Extremism

Postwar activism in the Arab Muslim world has progressed through several phases, most of them secular expressions of nationalism and radical socialism. The secular phases included

- Anticolonialism
- Pan-Arab nationalism (Nasserism)
- Secular leftist radicalism

The conquest of Bethlehem. A depiction of victorious Christian Crusaders, who seized Bethlehem in June 1099 during the First Crusade. The Crusaders subsequently killed virtually all of the town's inhabitants.

Source: Hulton Archive/Getty Images; used by permission.

New movements promoting Islamist extremism overshadowed all of these movements. This should not be surprising, because

> the discrediting of leftist ideologies within the Muslim world, like the earlier loss of respect for Nasserite pan-Arabism . . . has . . . meant that political Islam has become the main vehicle there for expression . . . of strongly held dissent. A young man in a Muslim country who wants to make a forceful statement against the existing order has few avenues for doing so except through membership in a radical Islamic group.[8]

In the post-Cold War political environment, the adoption of Islam as a vehicle for liberation is a logical progression. Arab nationalists—both secular and sectarian—have struggled since the end of the Second World War to resist what they perceive to be Western domination and exploitation. Some tradition-oriented nationalists have interpreted Western culture and values to be alien to Muslim morality and values. The chief symbol of Western encroachment is the state of Israel. When radical secular ideologies and movements achieved minimal progress in resisting the West and Israel, and when secular Arab governments repressed any expressions of domestic dissent, many activists and intellectuals turned to radical interpretations of Islam.

Cult Case: Aum Shinrikyō (Supreme Truth)

Aum Shinrikyō is a Japan-based cult founded in 1987 by **Shoko Asahara**. Their goal under Asahara's leadership was to seize control of Japan, and then the world. The core belief of the cult is that Armageddon—the final battle before the end of the world—is imminent. One component of this belief is that the United States will wage World War III against Japan.[9] As one top member of the cult explained, "This evil [of the modern age] will be shed in a 'catastrophic discharge' . . . [and only those who] repent their evil deeds . . . [will survive]."[10]

At its peak membership, Aum Shinrikyō had perhaps 9,000 members in Japan and 40,000 members around the world—thousands of them in Russia.[11] Asahara claimed to be the reincarnation of Jesus Christ and Buddha and urged his followers to arm themselves if they were to survive Armageddon. This apocalyptic creed led to the stockpiling of chemical and biological weapons, including nerve gas, anthrax, and Q-fever.[12] One report indicated that Aum Shinrikyō members had traveled to Africa to acquire the deadly Ebola virus. Several mysterious biochemical incidents occurred in Japan, including one in June 1994 in the city of Matsumoto, where seven people died and 264 were injured from a release of gas into an apartment building.[13]

The Tokyo Subway Gas Attack. On March 20, 1995, members of Aum Shinrikyō positioned several packages containing sarin nerve gas on five trains in the Tokyo subway system. The trains were scheduled to travel through Tokyo's Kasumigaseki train station. The containers were simultaneously punctured with umbrellas, thus releasing the gas into the subway system. Twelve people were killed and an estimated 5,000 to 6,000 were injured.[14] Tokyo's emergency medical system was unable to adequately respond to the attack, so that only about 500 victims were evacuated, with the remaining victims making their own way to local hospitals. The police were also surprised by the attack, and

> it took . . . several weeks to narrow their search to the Aum sect, locate its leaders, and seize some of their arsenal, despite the fact that Aum was not a secret organization but one that paraded through the streets of Tokyo—albeit in masks that depicted the face of their guru and leader, Shoko Asahara.[15]

The police seized tons of chemicals stockpiled by the cult. Asahara was arrested and charged with 17 counts of murder and attempted murder, kidnapping, and drug trafficking. A new leader, Fumihiro Joyu, assumed control of Aum Shinrikyō in 2000 and renamed the group Aleph (the first letter in the Hebrew and Arabic alphabets). He has publicly renounced violence, and the cult's membership has enjoyed new growth in membership.

Aum Shinrikyō is an example of the potential terrorist threat from apocalyptic cults and sects that are completely insular and segregated from mainstream society. Some cults are content to simply prepare for the End of Days, but others—like Aum Shinrikyō—are not averse to giving the apocalypse a violent "push." The threat from chemical and other weapons of mass destruction will be explored further in Chapter 10.

Cult Case: Mysticism and Rebellion in Uganda[16]

Phase 1: The Holy Spirit Mobile Force. Uganda in 1987 was a hotbed of rebellion, with several rebel groups opposing the new government of President Yoweri Museveni. One rebel group was the **Holy Spirit Mobile Force,** inspired and led by **Alice Lakwena**. Lakwena claimed to be inspired by the Christian Holy Spirit and preached that her movement would defeat Musevani's forces and purge Uganda of witchcraft and superstition. Because her followers championed the Acholi tribe, the Holy Spirit Mobile Force attracted thousands of followers, many of whom were former soldiers from previous Ugandan government armies. In late 1987, she led thousands of her followers against Museveni's army. To protect themselves from death, Holy Spirit Mobile Force fighters anointed themselves with holy oil, which they believed would ward off bullets. When they met Museveni's forces, thousands of Lakwena's followers were slaughtered in the face of automatic weapons and artillery fire. Alice Lakwena fled the country.

Phase 2: The Lord's Resistance Army. **Josef Kony** reorganized the Holy Spirit Mobile Force into the **Lord's Resistance Army.** Kony blended together Christianity, Islam, and witchcraft into a bizarre mystical foundation for his movement. Kony proclaimed to his followers that he would overthrow the government and purify the Acholi people. From its inception, the Lord's Resistance Army was exceptionally brutal and waged near-genocidal terrorist campaigns—largely against the Acholi people that it claimed to champion. The movement destroyed villages and towns, killed thousands of people, drove hundreds of thousands more from the land, abducted thousands of children, and routinely committed acts of rape and banditry. With bases in southern Sudan, the Lord's Resistance Army proved to be extremely difficult for the Ugandan government to defeat in the field.

As in the case of the Thuggees, the Lord's Resistance Army is unquestionably an example of a cultic movement that waged a campaign of religious terrorism.

State Sponsorship Case: Revisiting Sponsorship by Iran

State sponsorship of terrorism is not limited to state sponsorship of ideological or ethno-national movements. It also incorporates state sponsorship of religious revolutionary movements. Iran became a preeminent state sponsor of religious terrorism in the modern era.

Iran's sponsorship of terrorism was introduced in Chapter 4, which discussed its collaboration with Lebanon's Hezbollah. Iran has also been implicated in the sponsorship of a number of other groups, making it a perennial entry on the U.S. Department of State's list of state sponsors of terrorism. The Iranian Revolutionary Guards has a unit—the Qods (Jerusalem) Force—that promotes Islamic revolution abroad. Revolutionary Guards have appeared in Lebanon and Sudan.

Since the early days of the Iranian Revolution, the Iranian regime has never been guarded about its goal to "liberate" Jerusalem. To achieve this goal, Iran has likewise never been guarded about its overt support for Palestinian organizations that reject dialogue and negotiations with the Israelis. It has, in fact, provided significant assistance to the Palestinian cause. For example,

Two militant Islamic organizations—Palestine Islamic Jihad (PIJ) and Hamas (Islamic Resistance Movement)—are Palestinian extremist groups that received important support from Iran. Both groups perpetrated many acts of terrorism, including suicide attacks, bombings, shootings, and other violent assaults.

Students may recall from Chapter 5 that PIJ is not a single organization; rather, it is a loose affiliation of factions. It is an Islamic revolutionary movement that promotes violent jihad to form a Palestinian state. Iranian support to PIJ includes military instruction and logistical support. PIJ members have appeared in Hezbollah camps in Lebanon's Beka'a Valley and in Iran, and planning for terrorist attacks has apparently taken place in these locations. Members who received this training were infiltrated back into Gaza and the West Bank to wage jihad against Israel.

Hamas's roots lie in the Palestinian branch of the Muslim Brotherhood. It operates as both a social service organization and an armed resistance group that promotes jihad. Because of its social service component, Iran's **Fund for the Martyrs** has disbursed millions of dollars to Hamas. Hamas has a representative in Iran who has held a number of meetings with top Iranian officials. Iran has also provided Hamas with the same type of support that it provides PIJ; this includes military instruction, logistical support, training in Hezbollah's Beka'a Valley camps, and training in Iran. Hamas operatives have returned from these facilities to Gaza and the West Bank.

Organization Case: Al Qaeda's Religious Foundation

The modern era's most prominent pan-Islamic revolutionary organization is Saudi national **Osama bin Laden**'s cell-based Al Qaeda (The Base), which seeks to unite Muslims throughout the world in a holy war. Al Qaeda is not a traditional hierarchical revolutionary organization, nor does it call for its followers to do much more than engage in terrorist violence in the name of the faith. Al Qaeda is best described as a movement or a loose network of like-minded Islamic revolutionaries. Compared to other movements in the postwar era, it is a different kind of network, because al Qaeda

holds no territory;

does not champion the aspirations of an ethno-national group;

has no "top-down" organizational structure;

has virtually nonexistent state sponsorship;

promulgates political demands that are vague; and

is completely religious in its worldview.

Experts do not know how many people count themselves as Al Qaeda operatives, but estimates range from 35,000 to 50,000. Of these, perhaps 5,000 received training in camps in Sudan and Afghanistan,[17] others are new recruits from around the Muslim world and Europe, and many others are veteran "**Afghan Arabs**" who fought in the jihad against the Soviets and later against the post-September 11, 2001, American-led coalition in Afghanistan. With a presence in an estimated 50 to 60 countries, it is likely that new recruits will continue to join the Qaeda cause in the aftermath of the September 11, 2001, attacks. The Afghan Arabs and Al Qaeda's involvement in supporting and promoting international terrorism will be explored further in Chapter 9.

Al Qaeda's religious orientation is a reflection of Osama bin Laden's sectarian ideological point of view. Bin Laden's worldview was created by his exposure to Islam-motivated armed resistance. As a boy, he inherited between $20 million and $80 million from his father, with estimates ranging as high as $300 million. When the Soviets invaded Afghanistan in 1979, bin Laden eventually joined with thousands of other non-Afghan Muslims who traveled to Peshawar, Pakistan, to prepare to wage jihad. However, his main contribution to the holy war was to solicit financial and *matériel* (military hardware) contributions from wealthy Arab sources. He apparently excelled at this. The final leg on his journey toward international Islamic terrorism occurred when he and thousands of other Afghan veterans—the Afghan Arabs—returned to their countries to carry on their struggle in the name of Islam. Beginning in 1986, bin Laden organized a training camp that grew in 1988 into the Qaeda group. While in his home country of Saudi Arabia, bin Laden "became enraged when King Fahd let American forces, with their rock music and Christian and Jewish troops, wage the Persian Gulf war from Saudi soil in 1991."[18]

After the Gulf War, bin Laden and a reinvigorated Al Qaeda moved to its new home in Sudan for five years. It was there that the Qaeda network began to grow into a self-sustaining financial and training base for promulgating jihad. Bin Laden and his followers configured the Qaeda network with one underlying purpose: "launching and leading a holy war against the Western infidels he could now see camped out in his homeland, near the holiest shrines in the Muslim world."[19]

Al Qaeda has inspired Islamic fundamentalist revolutionaries and terrorists in a number of countries. It became a significant source of financing and training for thousands of *jihadis.* The network is essentially a nonstate catalyst for transnational religious radicalism and violence.

When Al Qaeda moved to Afghanistan, its reputation as a financial and training center attracted many new recruits and led to the creation of a loose network of cells and "sleepers" in dozens of countries. Significantly, aboveground radical Islamic groups with links to Al Qaeda took root in some nations and overtly challenged authority through acts of terrorism. Two of these groups—Abu Sayyaf in the Philippines and Laskar Jihad in Indonesia— are discussed in the following sections.

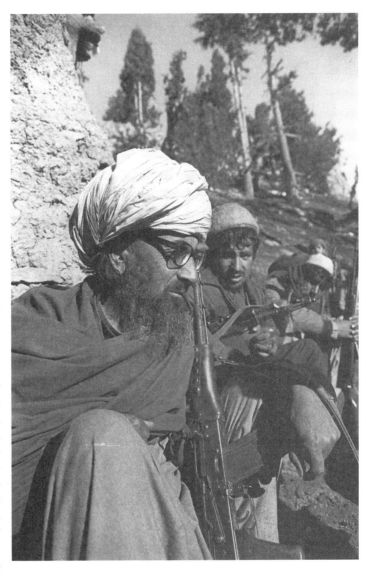

Holy war against communist invaders. Afghan mujahideen during their jihad against occupying Soviet troops.

Source: Hulton Archive/Getty Images; used by permission.

The Abu Sayyaf Group

The religious demographics of the Philippines are roughly 92% Christian, 5% Muslim, and 3% Buddhist.[20] Muslims live on islands in the southern rim of the Philippines. As discussed in Chapter 6, the nation has experienced several left-wing insurgencies and terrorist campaigns. The Philippines is also home to **Abu Sayyaf**, a Muslim insurgency on the island of Basilan with ideological and other links to Al Qaeda. **Abdurajak Janjalani**, who was killed by Filipino police in 1998, founded Abu Sayyaf. Like a few other Filipino Islamic militants, Janjalani fought in the jihad in Afghanistan against the Soviets, where he may have known Osama bin Laden. After the war, he returned to the Philippines to wage jihad to create a Muslim state in the southern Philippines. Al Qaeda funds were apparently sent to Abu Sayyaf, and radical Muslims from the Middle East arrived to provide military and terrorist training for Filipino Muslims.

In April 2000, Abu Sayyaf kidnapped 20 hostages in a Malaysian resort and received $25 million in ransom for their release. The ransom money was used to buy weapons and boats and to recruit and train new fighters. In May 2001, the group kidnapped 20 people, including three American hostages. One of the Americans was beheaded, probably in June 2001. After the September 11, 2001, attacks, the Filipino government—with advice from hundreds of American Special Forces troops—launched a vigorous campaign to wipe out Abu Sayyaf. The government campaign was successful, and hundreds of Abu Sayyaf fighters were killed or captured or went home. In June 2002, Filipino Special Forces troops identified the location of the two surviving Americans and one Filipina nurse who was also held hostage. During a fire fight, one of the Americans and the Filipina were killed, and the other American was wounded.

Laskar Jihad

Under the leadership of Ja'afar Umar Thalib, the armed Islamic group called **Laskar Jihad (Militia of the Holy War)** waged communal holy war in Indonesia. Thousands of fighters joined Laskar Jihad, which was organized in April 2000 to confront Christians in a holy war on Indonesia's Molucca Islands. The Molucca conflict became a communal confrontation between Christians and Muslims in January 1999. The group was based on the island of Java but arrived in the Moluccas in force to champion indigenous Muslims when the fighting broke out. Terrorism and human rights violations became common on both sides—the conflict cost thousands of lives and forced hundreds of thousands of people from their homes.

Although Thalib denied any linkage between Laskar Jihad and Al Qaeda, Western intelligence agencies claimed that the Qaeda link existed. Thalib had in fact met Osama bin Laden in 1987 in Pakistan during the jihad in Afghanistan against the Soviets. However, Thalib argued that bin Laden's interpretation of the Islamic struggle was incorrect and that his war against Islamic governments was wrong. Nevertheless, Thalib and Laskar Jihad do engage in terrorism and have forged ties with Malaysia's terrorist Mujahideen Group.

Regional Case: Pakistan and India

India and Pakistan are seemingly implacable rivals. Much of this rivalry is grounded in religious animosity between the Hindu and Muslim communities. The sponsorship of terrorist proxies has kept the region in a state of nearly constant tension.

Hindus and Muslims in Southwest Asia have engaged in sectarian violence since 1947, when British colonial rule ended. The architect of the movement against British rule was Indian leader Mahatma Gandhi, who led an independence movement based on nonviolence and inclusive principles. Gandhi's deep spiritual convictions could not forestall sectarian confrontation in the new nation. During and after the British withdrawal, communal fighting between Hindus and Muslims led to the partition of British India into mostly Muslim East Pakistan and West Pakistan (now Bangladesh) and mostly Hindu India. During the partition, Hindus and Muslims migrated across the new borders by the hundreds of thousands. Since independence, conflict has been ongoing between Pakistan and India over many issues, including Indian support for Bangladesh's war of independence from Pakistan, disputed borders, support for religious nationalist terrorist organizations, the development of nuclear arsenals, and the disputed northern region of Jammu and Kashmir.

Pakistan, through its intelligence agency, the **Directorate for Inter-Services Intelligence** (ISI), has a long history of supporting insurgent groups fighting against

Indian interests. Religious terrorist groups in the Indian state of Punjab and in Jammu and Kashmir have received Pakistani aid in what is a high-stakes conflict between two nuclear powers that can also field large conventional armies. The Pakistan-India conflict is arguably as volatile as the Arab-Israeli rivalry but with many times the manpower and firepower.

Jammu and Kashmir

In the Jammu and Kashmir region, which is controlled by Pakistan, India, and China, a sustained insurgency supported by the ISI has led to human rights violations and a campaign of terrorism. The fighting was between Pakistani proxies and Muslim Kashmiris on one side and the Indian army on the other side. About 70% of Jammu and Kashmir's population is Muslim; the rest are Hindus, Sikhs, and Buddhists.

Islamic fighters from a number of groups supported by Pakistan have waged war against the Indian presence, using terrorism to attack Indian forces and interests. Their goal is independence for Jammu and Kashmir. The Muslim fighters have included an international assortment of mujahideen (holy warriors) from Pakistan, Afghanistan, Kashmir, and Arab countries. Groups involved in the insurgency and terrorist campaign include:

- **Lashkar e Tayyba**, a large Pakistani proxy based in Pakistan
- **Jammu Kashmir Liberation Front**, a long-standing independence movement
- **Harkat-ul-Ansar**, which kidnapped six Western hostages in 1995
- **Jammu and Kashmir Islamic Front**, another Pakistani proxy supported by the ISI

The Golden Temple Massacre (and Aftermath). Sikhism is a religion that was founded about 500 years ago. One of its fundamental beliefs is that only a single all-powerful God should be worshipped, although its followers accept the existence of lesser gods. With approximately 20 million followers, Sikhism is centered in the Indian state of Punjab. The most sacred temple of the Sikh religion is the Golden Temple in the city of Amritsar, Punjab.

Punjab is rife with discord, originating in Sikh nationalism, the policies of the Indian army, Punjabi interests, and Pakistani agitation. With training and support from Pakistan's ISI, Sikh nationalists have agitated since at least the 1970s for the creation of the Sikh state of Khalistan in Punjab. In May 1984, armed Sikh militants—among them leaders of a terrorist campaign—occupied the Golden Temple. After negotiations failed, the Indian government of Indira Gandhi (no relation to Mahatma Gandhi) sanctioned an assault. When Indian troops stormed the temple in early June 1984, they were met by greater firepower than they anticipated. Tanks and artillery were called in, and hundreds were killed or wounded before the temple was retaken.

The assault on the Golden Temple inflamed tensions in Punjab, leading to communal violence and terrorism between Sikhs and Punjabis. Nationalists declared independence for Khalistan in 1987, but 500,000 Indian troops have violently occupied the Punjab, causing an estimated 250,000 Sikh deaths between 1984 and 1992. Significantly, Indian Prime Minister Indira Gandhi was assassinated in October 1984 by Sikh bodyguards in revenge for the Golden Temple attack. Included among the many Sikh terrorist groups are Dal Khalsa, Bhinderanwala Tiger Force, Saheed Khalsa Force, the Khalistan Liberation Front, and the Khalistan Commando Force.

Regional Case: The Algerian *Jihadis*

Civil War in Algeria

The first multiparty elections in Algeria were scheduled to be held in 1992. When it became apparent that an Islamic movement, the Islamic Salvation Front (Front Islamique de Salut, or FIS), would win the election, the elections were canceled by the government of President Chadli Ben Djedid, a former army colonel. FIS incited violent strikes and demonstrations, and the government responded by declaring a state of emergency, postponing the general elections, and seizing control of FIS offices. An antigovernment campaign of terrorism began, growing into a large-scale insurgency that regularly committed acts of terrorism. Typical of these attacks were indiscriminate bombings in August 1992 at the Algiers airport and in front of the Algiers headquarters of the Sûreté Nationale; the latter bomb killed 42 people and injured 250.[21]

By the mid-1990s, several Islamic terrorist movements were waging a campaign of terror in the countryside and in the cities of Algeria. These groups, which included the Armed Islamic Group (Groupe Islamique Armé) and the **Armed Islamic Movement** (Mouvement Islamique Armé), used exceptionally violent tactics. Thousands of secular teachers, journalists, doctors, academics, and others were assassinated. Foreigners were also singled out for assassination, including French Christian priests, nuns, and monks. In the countryside, bands of Islamic militants swept through villages and towns, killing, kidnapping, and raping noncombatants of all ages. The government responded with a brutal suppression campaign that included massacres and the use of death squads. The government also armed local civilian paramilitary units, many of which included veterans of the anticolonial war against France. Between 1992 and 1997, approximately 120,000 people were killed.[22] In 1999, an amnesty was offered, and about 5,000 militants surrendered.[23]

Spreading the Jihad

Many of Algeria's Islamic militants were veterans of the jihad in Afghanistan. Others had been trained in Al Qaeda camps. During the Algerian insurgency, many Algerians and other North Africans apparently moved abroad to set up support networks for the struggle. The purpose was to establish arms and financing pipelines to the insurgent groups. Some of these support cells apparently became independent "sleeper" cells committed to waging holy war against the West in their home countries. These cells were informally organized and shared "common participants, communications . . . and shared training experiences in Bin Laden-run camps."[24] One such cell plotted to detonate a bomb at Los Angeles International Airport around the time of the 2000 millennial celebrations. It was foiled when **Ahmed Ressem**, an Algerian who lived in Montreal, was arrested as he tried to cross the Canadian border into the United States with bomb-making components.[25] Ressem said that he had been trained in a Qaeda camp.

The Algerian jihad is an example of a nexus of religious terrorism, transnational solidarity among fighters, and the spread of revolutionary fervor beyond Algeria to cells in the West.

Regional Case: The Middle East

The Grand Mosque Incident. The framework for Muslim life is based on the Five Pillars of Islam. The Five Pillars are faith, prayer, *zakat* (alms, or charity), fasting during the month of Ramadan, and the *hajj* (pilgrimage) to the holy city of Mecca, Saudi Arabia, for those who are able. In November 1979 during their *hajj,* 300 radicals occupied the Grand Mosque in Mecca. Their objective was to foment a popular Islamic uprising against the ruling Saud royal family. After nearly two weeks of fighting, the Grand Mosque was reoccupied by the Saudi army, but not before the Saudis called in French counterterrorist commandos to complete the operation. More than 100 radicals were killed, and scores were later executed by the Saudi government. During the fighting, Iranian radio accused the United States and Israel of plotting the takeover, and a Pakistani mob attacked the U.S. embassy, killing two Americans.

The Hebron Mosque Massacre. On February 25, 1994, a New York-born physician, **Baruch Goldstein**, fired on worshippers inside the Ibrahim Mosque at the Cave of the Patriarchs holy site in the city of Hebron, Israel. As worshippers performed their morning prayer ritual, Goldstein methodically shot them with an Israel Defense Forces Galil assault rifle. He fired approximately 108 rounds in about 10 minutes before a crowd of worshippers rushed him and killed him. According to official government estimates, he killed 29 people and wounded another 125;[26] according to unofficial estimates, approximately 50 people died.[27] In reprisal for the Hebron massacre, the Palestinian Islamic fundamentalist movement Hamas launched a bombing campaign that included the first wave of human suicide bombers. Suicide bombers and Hamas's infamous bomb maker known as "The Engineer" are explored further in Chapter 10.

The Rabin Assassination. On November 4, 1995, Israeli Prime Minister Yitzhak Rabin was assassinated by **Yigal Amir**, who had stalked Rabin for about one year.[28] He shot Rabin in the back with hollow-point bullets in full view of Israeli security officers. Amir was a Jewish extremist who said that he acted fully within the requirements of *Halacha*, or the Jewish code. The following account describes the religious justification Amir used for the assassination:

> Asked where he got his ideas, Yigal Amir told the magistrate that he drew on the Halacha, which is the Jewish legal code. "According the Halacha, you can kill the enemy," Amir said. "My whole life, I learned Halacha. When you kill in war, it is an act that is allowed." When asked whether he acted alone, Amir replied: "It was God."[29]

Religious terrorism in the Middle East thus occurs between, and within, local religious groups. Radical true believers of regional faiths do not hesitate to attack "fallen" members of their own religions.

Table 8.3 summarizes the activity profiles of several of the terrorist groups and movements discussed in this section.

CRIMINAL TERRORISM

The modern era has witnessed the growth of a huge system of **transnational organized crime**. Transnational organized crime is an intricate web of illegal enterprise that incorporates both large and small criminal organizations that operate across national borders. Organizationally, some illegal enterprises are unsophisticated and gang-like in their operations, whereas others are highly sophisticated and organized as illicit businesses. The latter organizations have joined together from time to time to create international **criminal cartels** that try to regulate "product lines" such as refined cocaine.

Within this transnational web, criminal organizations have engaged in terrorist violence, the characteristics of which can be summarized with at least two models:

1. Profit-motivated traditional criminal enterprises

2. Politically motivated criminal-political enterprises

Perhaps the most fundamental distinguishing characteristic between the two models (aside from motive) is that **traditional criminal enterprises** are illicit businesses whose participants normally desire a minimal amount of public attention for their activities. In contrast, criminal-political enterprises are dissident movements that frequently desire a high public profile for their activities. As previously indicated in Table 8.1, when the

Table 8.3   Religious Terrorism

Although religious terrorist groups and movements share the general profile of religious identity and often are rooted in similar belief systems, they arise out of unique historical, political, and cultural environments that are peculiar to their respective countries. With few exceptions, most religious movements are grounded in these idiosyncratic influences.

Group	Activity Profile	
	Constituency	*Adversary*
Aum Shinrikyō	Fellow believers	The existing world order
Lord's Resistance Army	Fellow believers and members of the Acholi tribe	Ugandan government and "nonpurified" Acholis
Palestinian Islamic Jihad	Palestinian Muslims	Israel
Hamas	Palestinian Muslims	Israel
Al Qaeda	Faithful Muslims, as defined by Al Qaeda	Secular governments, nonbelievers, the West
Abu Sayyaf	Filipino Muslims	Filipino government, Western influence
Laskar Jihad	Moluccan Muslims	Moluccan Christians
Jammu-Kashmir groups	Jammu-Kashmir Muslims	India
Sikh groups	Punjabi Sikhs	India
Algerian/North African cells	Algerian Muslims and Muslims worldwide	Secular Algerian government, the West

decision is made to engage in extremist violence, the activity profiles of traditional criminal enterprises and criminal-political enterprises are distinguishable in their motives, goals, targets, personnel, and degrees of political agitation.

The Criminal and Political Terrorism Nexus

Before proceeding to discuss the threat of terrorism from traditional criminal and criminal-political enterprises, it is important to understand that there is another dimension to the modern transnational environment that poses an inherent danger to security: that of cooperation and coordination between these groups.

Terrorist groups and criminal enterprises are by their nature secretive, antisocial, and underground. Transnational criminal enterprises are adept at smuggling drugs and weapons to the highest bidder through covert international networks. This black market exists purely for profit and is highly lucrative. Hence, it is acknowledged that transnational criminal enterprises can—and have—covertly provided terrorist groups with arms and other goods. It is likely that terrorists have solicited criminal groups for "special-order" goods, such as certain types of weapons or chemicals. Should a transnational criminal enterprise acquire nuclear, biological, or chemical weapons, it is conceivable that such weapons could be sold on the black market to the highest bidder—all without personal qualms about their use, so long as the price is right. This kind of convergence poses a serious security threat.

Traditional Criminal Enterprises

Examples of traditional criminal enterprises include the Chinese Triads, Japanese Yakuza, American La Cosa Nostra, Colombian drug cartels, Russian Mafia, Italian organized crime, and Southeast Asian drug lords. Most of these enterprises have been politically passive and have engaged in political violence reactively rather than actively. They desire anonymity from public scrutiny. They also desire a stable environment for their enterprise, so that governments that are either too weak to interfere with the enterprise or that lack the motivation to do so are unlikely to be targeted by traditional criminal enterprises. Conversely, some criminal organizations have violently resisted government law enforcement campaigns that interfere with their enterprises. This is by no means a universal reaction, but it is nevertheless one that has occurred repeatedly.

The likelihood of antistate violence by traditional criminal enterprises depends on the social and political environments of their national bases of operation.

Criminal-Political Enterprises

Dissident movements have become increasingly involved in transnational organized crime, having concluded out of pragmatic necessity that there is a benefit to be gained from trading arms or drugs on the illicit market. Some movements have even occupied drug-producing regions as a matter of strategic choice. The reasons for this phenomenon are uncomplicated: Participation in the drug or arms trades is quite lucrative. A dissident movement can guarantee its financial independence from state sponsorship if it can establish its own niche in an illicit trade.

In the modern era, the formerly clear delineation between organized crime, political extremism, and illegal trafficking has become blurred. An overlap between crime and extremist politics has occurred, so that some politically motivated movements and individuals actively participate in the international smuggling of arms and drugs. Alliances are forged between exclusively profit-motivated traditional criminal enterprises and politically violent movements.

Drugs and Terrorism. The drug trade has become particularly prominent in the financing of some extremist movements. Because of the enormous profits derived from the global underground drug trade, terrorists and extremists have become adept traffickers. The concept of *narco-terrorism* describes "the use of drug trafficking to advance the objectives of certain governments and terrorist organizations."[30] Although its original meaning referred to a theorized semimonolithic Marxist (hence, Soviet) control of the trade, narco-terrorism continues to be an important concept in the post-Cold War world.[31] Because of the frequent difficulty in obtaining direct state sponsorship, some indigenous terrorist and revolutionary groups have turned to drug trafficking and arms trading to raise money for their movements. The reality is that there is no grand revolutionary conspiracy to control the drug trade, but rather a very fluid and intricate web that links profit-motivated traditional criminal enterprises to ideologically motivated criminal-political enterprises.

The following regional cases in point illustrate the linkages between terrorism, transnational criminal activity, traditional criminal enterprises, and criminal-political enterprises.

Table 8.4 summarizes the activity profiles of several traditional criminal and criminal-political enterprises.

Regional Case: Asia

Asian drug production is centered on two regions: Southwest Asia and Southeast Asia. The drug-producing regions of Southwest Asia are referred to as the "**Golden Crescent**,"

Table 8.4   Criminal Terrorism

Criminal terrorism, as defined here, refers to traditional criminal enterprises and criminal-political enterprises. They are differentiated primarily by motive, with traditional criminal enterprises motivated by profit and criminal-political enterprises motivated by a dissident cause.

The following table summarizes the activity profiles of several traditional criminal and criminal-political enterprises.

	Activity Profile		
Group	*Criminal Enterprise*	*Motive*	*Quality of Violence*
Taliban	Opium and heroin production	Consolidate the movement; promote jihad	Domestic terrorism; jihad against opponents
Tamil Tigers	Arms and drug trafficking	National independence	Terrorism, insurgency
Myanmar groups	Opium and heroin production	Profit, regional autonomy	Insurgency
Abu Sayyaf	Kidnapping, extortion, drug trafficking	Jihad against the Filipino government	Terrorism, insurgency
Italian organized crime	Broad variety of activities	Profit	Terrorism, extortion, intimidation
Russian Mafia	Broad variety of activities	Profit	Terrorism, extortion, intimidation
Irish dissidents	Drug trade	Republicanism or loyalism	Terrorism
Kosovo Liberation Army/National Liberation Army	Arms and drug trafficking	Albanian nationalism	Terrorism, insurgency
Colombian cartels	Drug trade	Profit	Terrorism
FARC	Drug trade	Revolution	Terrorism, insurgency
Shining Path	Drug trade	Revolution	Terrorism
Arellano-Felix Cartel	Drug trade	Profit	Terrorism

and the drug-producing regions of Southeast Asia are referred to at the "**Golden Triangle**." Dissident terrorists and extremists in both regions have profited from the drug trade. The Golden Triangle—known for its cultivation of opium poppies and the manufacturing of refined opium and heroin—comprises the countries of Myanmar (Burma), Laos, and Thailand. The Golden Crescent—known for its cultivation of opium poppies and the manufacturing of heroin—comprises the countries of Iran, Afghanistan, and Pakistan. Because of the fall of the Soviet Union, the drug production industry in the Golden Crescent has found a lucrative transshipment industry in Central Asia, where

Drugs that fund the revolution. An Afghan fighter sits in a field of ripe opium poppies.

Source: Hulton Archive/Getty Images; used by permission.

organized crime and Islamic extremists have profited from transshipping heroin into the Russian and European drug markets.

Afghanistan

Afghanistan has historically been an important producer of opium and heroin and eventually became the world's chief supplier of illegal opiates. It has also historically been a major supplier of hashish. Warlords, revolutionaries, and holy warriors have all profited from the trade.

Until the Taliban's crackdown on drug production in 2001, Afghanistan's traditional cultivation of opium flourished. The Taliban movement allegedly earned approximately 80% of its income from the opium poppy and heroin trade. They also produced more than 70% of the world's supply of opium after production fell off in the Golden Triangle (discussed later). There have been reports that while in Afghanistan, Osama bin Laden approached opium manufacturers in Afghanistan and Pakistan. The Taliban's radical interpretation of Islam allowed the cultivation of opium poppies but strictly forbade and severely punished the use of opium or heroin.

Sri Lanka

The Liberation Tigers of Tamil Eelam have sustained their movement in part by establishing themselves as middlemen in the illicit arms and drug trades. Evidence suggests that the Tamil Tigers have received drugs and arms "on consignment" from traditional criminal enterprises in Myanmar and India.[32] The Tamil Tigers sell the consigned drugs, pay for the weapons, and repeat the cycle as a method to build their arsenals. This is very similar to the arrangement used by Albanian criminals and dissidents in their management of the Balkan Route (discussed later).

Myanmar (Burma)

Until the mid-1990s, Khun Sa, the commander of the Shan United Army, controlled much of the heroin production coming out of the Golden Triangle. Based in Myanmar, Khun Sa claimed to champion the ethnic Shan people, but in reality he was a traditional warlord, and his army was a renegade force. The Shan United Army waged an occasional insurgency against the government as a way to establish regional autonomy from central control, thus ensuring their profits from the heroin trade.

At its height, the Golden Triangle produced 70% of the world's heroin, largely within the operational area of the Shan United Army. When Khun Sa retired in 1996, a vacuum was created in the trade, so that the drug flow declined significantly from Myanmar's old heroin-producing regions. Taliban-controlled Afghanistan more than made up for this shortfall on the world market. After the Taliban's 2001 crackdown on opium cultivation, the Golden Triangle saw resurgence in production, regaining its prominence as the world's top producer of opium. Groups such as the United Wa State Army, an old splinter group of the Burmese Communist Party, have moved into the Shan United Army's old operational areas in northern Myanmar.

The Philippines

Abu Sayyaf, the southern Filipino Islamic terrorist organization discussed in the first part of this chapter, has been known to engage in criminal enterprise. Although its activities never approximated the scale of other movements, Abu Sayyaf resorted to kidnapping, extortion, and drug trafficking as tactics in its cause of waging a jihad. Reports indicated that it moved into southern Filipino marijuana fields to reap the benefits of the marijuana trade, raising revenues for its war against the Filipino government.[33]

Regional Case: Europe

Europe has a highly active criminal underground. The most historically established criminal enterprises are found in Italy. The most recent enterprises are found in the former communist Eastern Bloc, mainly in Russia. The incidence of terrorism by criminal enterprises occurs to greater or lesser degrees from country to country. The most serious incidence is found in Italy and Russia.

Italian Organized Crime

The word *mafia* is commonly used to describe organized criminal activity anywhere in the world. It correctly refers to traditional organized crime societies in southern Italy and Sicily. The derivation of the word is unknown, although there is some speculation that it is Arabic in origin. Regardless, the original mafia groups were secret associations of Sicilian resistance fighters who opposed the occupation of Sicily by the Spanish and French. A tradition grew out of these origins that demanded the following:

- Secrecy under a code of silence (*omerta*)
- Opposition to, and noncooperation with, security (and law enforcement) agencies and officials
- A code of honor
- Absolute obedience and loyalty toward the respected heads of mafia groups

This concept was adopted throughout southern Italy, so that in Naples a Neapolitan secret society was created called the **Camorra**, and in Calabria the **N'drangheta** was organized. These secret societies have long been criminal enterprises and are best characterized as profit-making traditional organized crime groups. The **Sicilian Mafia,** Camorra, and N'drangheta became entrenched at all levels of southern Italian society, including business and government. One report by Italy's leading trade organization has argued that one business in five has been penetrated by organized crime.[34] Immigrants from these cultures brought these traditions with them to the United States, where **La Cosa Nostra** ("our thing" or "this thing of ours") was organized as "families" in urban areas. La Cosa Nostra has been traditionally associated with the Sicilian Mafia.

The Sicilian Mafia, Camorra, and N'drangheta have used corruption, violence, and extortion to keep opponents not only from interfering with their criminal enterprises, but also from being too public in their criticism. Assassinations, bombings, and other terrorist acts have been committed against politicians, journalists, and law enforcement officials. Examples of this violence include the following:

- In 1971, the Sicilian Mafia assassinated the chief prosecutor in Palermo, Sicily.
- In 1983, the Camorra assassinated a Neapolitan journalist who had written articles criticizing organized crime.
- In July 1992, the Sicilian Mafia assassinated an anti-Mafia judge in dramatic fashion when a bomb exploded outside the judge's mother's home in Sicily, killing him and five bodyguards.
- In 1992, the Sicilian Mafia assassinated the top anti-Mafia prosecutor.
- In 1993, bombs in Florence, Milan, and Rome killed 10 people and wounded 32. One of the bombs damaged the famous Uffizi Gallery in Florence.
- In July 2000, a Calabrian provincial official was assassinated, apparently by the N'drangheta.

The style of these attacks is typical of violence by Italian organized crime. It is usually "surgical" in the sense that specific officials are singled out for intimidation or assassination. However, it has taken a toll in lives. From 1971 to 1991, about 40 judges, law enforcement officers, politicians, and others were assassinated. The death toll has been higher among feuding organized crime groups and civilians. In Sicily alone, an average of 100 people are killed each year by Sicilian Mafia violence.[35]

The Russian Mafia

In the aftermath of the dissolution of the Soviet Union, the **Russian Mafia** has grown into a massive network of criminal enterprise—it is, in fact, the largest organized crime environment in the world. The Russian Ministry of Interior has estimated that as of 1996, the Russian Mafia had 5,000 to 8,000 groups and perhaps 100,000 members.[36] By comparison, the United States has 24 traditional La Cosa Nostra families with an estimated 2,000 members.[37] The Russian Mafia is not a single organization, but rather a loosely organized network of gangs with between 50 and 1,000 members.[38] Some of these gangs are quite large. For example, the **Solntsevskaya Gang,** named after a Moscow suburb, has an estimated 5,000 members.[39] A staggering 40% of private businesses, 60% of state-owned companies, and 80% of banks were estimated to be under Russian Mafia control in 1998.[40] Within the Russian criminal underworld, Georgians and Chechens have become disproportionately prominent.

It is important to understand the quality of violence perpetrated by the Russian Mafia and the nature of their criminal enterprises. The scale and types of violence perpetrated by the Russian Mafia are often terrorist in nature. Gangs have regularly killed private businessmen, journalists, politicians, and others. An estimated 600 murders per year are contract killings, and from 1993 to 1998, 95 bankers were assassinated.[41] The enterprises of the Russian Mafia include arms smuggling, drug smuggling, extortion, murder, racketeering, and other illicit activities. Significantly, there have been indications that the Russian Mafia has transferred weapons to violent organizations and terrorists in the developing world. These transfers have apparently been done with the collaboration of former Soviet KGB (secret service) officers. Because of the KGB connection, many fear that if the Russian Mafia obtains weapons of mass destruction, these weapons will be sold to terrorists on the black market.

Irish Dissidents

Allegations have been made that dissident movements in Northern Ireland have been involved in the illicit sale of drugs. Both Catholic and Protestant groups apparently traded in drugs to generate revenue for their causes. British and Northern Irish law enforcement agencies implicated extremists in the trade, despite protestations from these groups that they were opposed to drug sales and use.

> While publicly crusading against the drug trade in Ireland, there is compelling evidence that the Irish Republican Army (IRA) and its radical offshoot, the Real IRA, are involved in an unholy alliance with the Middle Eastern narcotics industry. . . . The IRA is not the only guilty party in the conflict. Protestant paramilitaries are also heavily involved in using the profits from drug sales to finance their organizations.[42]

The Royal Ulster Constabulary assigned increasing numbers of personnel to narcotics duty and seized significant amounts of marijuana and ecstasy.

The Balkan Route

The fervor of ethnic Albanian nationalism grew dramatically during the collapse of communism in Albania and Yugoslavia. Ethnic Albanians in the southern Yugoslav regions of Kosovo and Macedonia sought independence from Yugoslavia. Macedonia successfully separated and was subsequently pressed by an Albanian rebel force called the National Liberation Army (NLA). Kosovo did not separate from Yugoslavia, but Serb forces were forced by NATO forces to withdraw from the region after prolonged fighting with an Albanian nationalist group called the **Kosovo Liberation Army (KLA)**. Both the NLA and KLA have used terrorism in their wars for independence.

Albanian separatists such as the KLA and Macedonia's NLA have received arms and financing from drug trafficking via the so-called **Balkan Route**. Arsenals stockpiled prior to the fighting in Kosovo and Macedonia were purchased largely with proceeds from the heroin trade.

The Balkan Route is a drug-trafficking crossroads between the European drug-consuming market and the heroin-producing countries of Afghanistan and Pakistan. Approximately 80% of Europe's heroin has historically passed through the former Yugoslavia. Prior to the disintegration of Yugoslavia, Western Europe's heroin was shipped from Turkey through Serbia, Croatia, and Slovenia.[43] Afterward, the Balkan Route shifted through Bulgaria, Hungary, Slovakia, and the Czech Republic. With the rise of Albanian nationalism, the route is again flowing through the former Yugoslavia. European law enforcement experts universally agree that Albanian organized criminal enterprises became the primary traffickers of heroin in Europe during the 1990s. Estimates suggested that Albanian criminal enterprises controlled 70% of the heroin trade in Germany and Switzerland.[44]

Albanian nationalists and drug traffickers have traded in heroin and weapons. Criminal enterprises in Georgia and Chechnya are known to have supplied weapons and heroin to

Albanian traffickers, who sold the heroin in Europe to pay for the arms and then repeated the cycle.[45] This was done in league with traditional criminal enterprises in the West, such as the Italian criminal organizations. This nexus between Albanian nationalism and Albanian organized crime is illustrated by the example of links between illicit Albanian groups and Macedonia's Albanian nationalist Party for Democratic Prosperity (PDP). Top PDP leaders were arrested and prosecuted for crimes that indicated their direct involvement in the smuggling into Macedonia of arms trafficked illegally from Serbia, Albania, Western Europe, and Bulgaria.[46]

Regional Case: Latin America

Colombia's Cartels

Narcotraficantes in Colombia have historically been highly organized, resilient, and terroristic. A *cartel* is "an international syndicate, combine or trust generally formed to regulate prices and output in some field of business."[47] Under this definition, Colombia's traditional criminal enterprises have been classic cartels.

During the 1980s through the mid-1990s, two Colombian cartels dominated the worldwide cocaine trade. These were the Cali and Medellin cartels, named for their home cities. They waged a campaign of terror against anyone opposed to them, frequently targeting government officials. During the 1980s alone, cartel terrorists killed

- 3,000 soldiers and police officers
- More than 1,000 public officials
- 170 judicial employees
- 50 lower judges
- Dozens of journalists
- 12 Supreme Court judges
- Three presidential candidates
- One attorney general
- One newspaper publisher[48]

The cartels were also very adept at co-opting government officials through bribery, extortion, and intimidation. However, perhaps because of the cartels' high profile, the Colombian government was eventually able to dismantle the big cartels with the assistance of the United States. One interesting twist to the offensive against the cartels was a paramilitary terrorist campaign that was waged against the Medellin cartel and its leader, Pablo Escobar. The paramilitary, calling itself **People Persecuted by Pablo Escobar**, or "**Pepes**," assassinated at least 50 cartel members and targeted Escobar's family for assassination.[49] Pepes was apparently a death squad made up of former Medellin operatives and backers with a history of supporting paramilitaries; they claimed that they acted out of a sense of patriotism and a code of vengeance.[50] Escobar was eventually killed in 1993 during a shootout with Colombian troops and police.

After the demise of the Cali and Medellin cartels, the Colombian drug trade was reconfigured around smaller criminal enterprises. These enterprises have kept a lower profile than during the heyday of the cartels and have not engaged in narco-terrorism on the same scale as their predecessors. Cocaine has continued to flow into the American drug consumer market.

FARC's Drug Connection

As discussed in Chapter 6, the Marxist Forces of National Liberation (FARC) and the National Liberation Army (ELN) in Colombia have partly financed their revolutions with drug money. Both groups have used terrorist and guerrilla tactics in their war, and they have become self-sufficient largely through the drug trade.

Since the early period of their insurgency, FARC had permitted cocaine traffickers to operate without interference so long as the *narcotraficantes* paid a "tax" to the movement.[51] This was a pragmatic arrangement. FARC's pragmatism progressed during the 1990s when the rebels cut out the middlemen and began to deal directly with marijuana and coca farmers, trafficking their produce to the Colombian drug cartels. They also protected the trade in their "liberated zones," promising to liberate and protect peasants from exploitation by the drug lords.

FARC established a kind of law, order, and predictability in its liberated zones that became popular among local peasants and small-time drug traders. Because of this new enterprise, "the changes in FARC . . . have been significant. As the revenue from the drug trade . . . expanded, so [did] the power and influence of FARC."[52]

Estimates of FARC's revenues from the cocaine trade were in the hundreds of millions of dollars.[53] There is evidence that the rebel group has forged close ties to the Russian Mafia, supplanting the Colombian drug cartels as clients after the cartels were dismantled and re-formed as smaller drug gangs. Airlifted deliveries of arms were made by the Russian Mafia to FARC in exchange for cocaine, which was then flown back to Russia for distribution to the Russian drug market.[54] There is also evidence of a FARC link to the **Arellano-Felix Cartel** in Tijuana, Mexico.

Shining Path

As discussed in Chapter 6, Peru's Shining Path (*Sendero Luminoso*) regularly engaged in acts of terrorism during its insurgency under the tutelage of Abimael Guzmán, the Fourth Sword of Marxism. Shining Path's ideology had racial and mystical elements to it, championing the Quechua-speaking Indians and mixed-race mestizos. The insurgency gradually withered after Guzmán's capture in 1992, although diehards remained active into the new millennium.

In the mid-1980s, Shining Path aggressively—and violently—vied for a share in Peru's drug trade. During the 1980s, Peru's Upper Huallaga Valley region was the world's richest producer of coca leaf. It was also a top exporter of cocaine paste, which is used to manufacture refined cocaine. Colombian *narcotraficantes* would purchase the coca leaf and cocaine paste for transshipment to Colombia to be refined into cocaine. Shining Path operatives moved into the valley in about 1983, claiming that they were liberating and protecting peasant farmers from exploitation by the Colombian drug cartels and the Peruvian government.[55] In the meantime,

> It is believed that Sendero garnered a minimum of $10 million a year (some estimates range as high as $100 million) between 1987 and 1992 from "taxes" on a large portion of the valley's 80,000 coca growers and from levies of up to $15,000 a flight on the mostly Colombian traffickers as they landed on the scores of clandestine runways in the valley to pick up their cargoes of cocaine paste.[56]

At their height, Shining Path seized control of towns in the Upper Huallaga Valley, expelled government administrators and police, and created their own moralistic model of law and order—which included killing homosexuals and ending prostitution. Before Guzmán's capture, Shining Path had become a self-sufficient terrorist movement, with

Chapter Perspective 8.2	**Violence on the American Border: The Arellano-Felix Cartel**

Criminal gangs in Mexico have historically been involved in banditry and traditional organized criminal activity such as extortion and prostitution. With the rise of the cocaine trade in the 1970s and 1980s, the Colombian cartels hired Mexican gangs to transship cocaine overland to the United States. They were subordinate to the cartels and were initially paid in cash. As Mexican gangs became proficient smugglers, they began to demand marijuana and cocaine as payment, which they then sold to their own customers. The gangs eventually became independent and co-equal partners with the Colombians, growing into criminal cartels.[a] They also became adept at using narco-terrorism to defend their enterprises.

Several large and lucrative criminal enterprises were organized. By 1999, the most important of these were the Carillo Fuentes organization in Juarez, the Caro-Quintero organization in Sonora, and the Arellano-Felix organization in Mexicali and Tijuana. They prospered as drug traffickers, and the Mexican trade in marijuana and cocaine became a $30 billion industry.

The Arellano-Felix group operated on the border with, and inside the territory of, the United States. Their territory centered on the corridor from Mexico to San Diego and Los Angeles. The cartel was considered for some time to be the most profitable and violent of the Mexican organizations. Principally run by brothers Benjamin and Ramon Arellano-Felix, the Arellano-Felix cartel corrupted some government officials, tried to intimidate those whom they could not corrupt, and killed others.[b] Victims of the group included Mexican police chiefs, prosecutors, police officers, journalists, critics, and children. The targeting of civilians was intentional; in one incident in 1998, the group killed three families from a rival enterprise. As one former American drug agent noted about the Arellano-Felix tactics: "If you are late paying the Arellanos, you won't get a nicely worded letter saying your 30 days [are] up. . . . But you might get a finger of your child in the mail."[c]

The Arellano-Felix cartel collapsed when its leaders were eliminated. On February 10, 2002, Ramon Arellano-Felix was killed in a shootout. On March 9 of the same year, his brother Benjamin was arrested. The collapse of the cartel was, however, by no means the end of Mexican narco-terrorism or the drug trade. Unlike their Colombian colleagues, the Mexican criminal enterprises do not cooperate with each other, so that feuding is common, and the demise of one cartel leads to violence over their former turf. At the same time, narco-terrorist activities of the groups continue to include attacks against government officials and critics.

a. Constantine, Thomas A. "DEA Congressional Testimony." Statement before the U.S. Senate Drug Caucus. February 24, 1999.

b. See Kraul, Chris. "The Collapse of Mexico's 'Invincible' Drug Cartel." *Los Angeles Times.* March 16, 2002.

c. Kraul (note b above).

most of its self-sufficiency derived from the drug trade. When a fungus ravaged the Upper Huallaga's coca leaf crop in the mid-1990s, the movement received a final blow, because its primary financial resource was removed.[57]

Chapter Perspective 8.2 discusses the operations and demise of Mexico's Arellano-Felix drug cartel. In its heyday, the cartel was the most profitable and violent of Mexico's drug cartels. It is an important example because it was based on the border with the United States, and had operatives in key distribution centers inside the United States.

Case in Point   **The Beka'a Valley**

The Beka'a Valley is located in the east-central region of Lebanon. It became a nexus of state-sponsored terrorism, religious revolution, drug production, and counterfeiting.

Syria asserted itself as the predominant political and military force in Lebanon when it deployed thousands of troops to the Beka'a Valley. Syria's objective was to influence the behavior of its proxies among Lebanese and Palestinian dissident movements. Adding to the revolutionary environment in the Beka'a was Syria's permission for the presence of members of Iran's Revolutionary Guards; their mission was to sponsor and train Hezbollah and various Palestinian groups who were provided safe haven in the Beka'a. Groups that were based in the valley and protected by the Syrian military presence included Hamas, Palestine Islamic Jihad, Abu Nidal, Popular Front for the Liberation of Palestine–General Command, the Kurdistan Workers' Party, and the Japanese Red Army.

The Beka'a Valley is also a historic center of drug production—primarily hashish and opium. Although its percentage of global drug production has been relatively small, profits from the trade were enough to support the activities of dissident groups in the valley. For example, evidence strongly implicated Hezbollah in the production and sale of drugs to support themselves and to offset reductions in support from Iran.[a] Markets for Lebanese drugs included North Africa, the United States, Israel, and Europe. In an aggressive antidrug campaign, the Lebanese government greatly reduced drug production to negligible levels during the mid-1990s. There is, however, evidence that repeated attempts have been made to reinvigorate drug-related agriculture.

Sophisticated counterfeiting operations were also conducted in the Beka'a Valley. The industry produced a large quantity of high-grade international U.S. dollars. The decision by the United States to redesign its paper currency during the 1990s was due in part to the excellent quality of dollars produced by the Beka'a Valley's counterfeiting industry.

NOTE

a. Cilluffo, Frank. "The Challenge We Face as the Battle Lines Blur." Statement before the U.S. House Committee on the Judiciary, Subcommittee on Crime. December 13, 2000.

CHAPTER SUMMARY

This chapter discussed two typologies of terrorism: religious and criminal. Each has distinguishable motivations and goals in its application of terrorist violence.

Religious movements are generally motivated by a belief that an otherworldly power sanctions and commands their behavior. Some religious terrorists are motivated primarily by faith, whereas other terrorists use religion secondarily. The latter movements are motivated by nationalism or some other ideology as a primary inspiration, but they are united by an underlying religious identity that is incorporated into their belief system. The goals of both primary and secondary religious terrorism are to construct a new society based on their religious or ethno-national identity. The terrorist behavior of both tends to be active and public.

Criminal terrorism is generally motivated by profit. Traditional criminal enterprises have no overarching reason for acquiring profit by illicit means, other than to enjoy the perquisites of accumulated wealth. Newer criminal-political enterprises have an overarching political motivation that guides their behavior. The latter typology uses profits derived from illicit enterprises to finance their cause. The goals of traditional criminal enterprises are simply to generate profit and to be left alone in this endeavor. Their terrorist behavior tends to be reactive. The goals of criminal-political enterprises are revolutionary victory and the reconstruction of society. Their terrorist behavior tends to be active and public. A key concept to understand about criminal terrorism is that there is significant convergence between traditional and criminal-political enterprises. This is an intricate and fluid web of transnational cooperation.

In Chapter 9, students will investigate international terrorism and the concept of terrorist spillovers. The discussion will focus on defining international terrorism, the reasons for international terrorism, and the perceptions of international terrorism. Consideration will also be given to the question of whether international terrorist networks exist and to examples of cooperation between terrorist movements.

KEY TERMS AND CONCEPTS

The following topics were discussed in this chapter and are found in the Glossary:

Abu Sayyaf
Afghan Arabs
Amir, Yigal
Arellano-Felix Cartel
Armed Islamic Group
Armed Islamic Movement
Asahara, Shoko
Aum Shinrikyō
Balkan Route
Bin Laden, Osama
Camorra
Criminal cartels
Criminal-political enterprises
Crusades
Directorate for Inter-Services
    Intelligence (ISI)
Fund for the Martyrs
Golden Crescent
Golden Triangle
Goldstein, Baruch
Greater jihad
Harkat-ul-Ansar
Holy Spirit Mobile Force
Jammu and Kashmir Islamic Front
Jammu Kashmir Liberation Front
Janjalani, Abdurajak

Jewish Defense League
Kach (Kahane Chai)
Kahane, Rabbi Meir
Kony, Josef
Kosovo Liberation Army (KLA)
La Cosa Nostra
Lakwena, Alice
Lashkare Tayyba
Laskar Jihad (Militia of the Holy War)
Lesser jihad
Lord's Resistance Army
Martyrdom
N'drangheta
Narcotraficantes
People Persecuted by Pablo
    Escobar (Pepes)
Phansi
Pope Urban II
Ressem, Ahmed
Russian Mafia
Sicilian Mafia
Solntsevskaya Gang
Stern Gang
Thuggees
Traditional criminal enterprises
Transnational organized crime

RECOMMENDED WEB SITES

The following Web sites provide links to discussions of religious and criminal terrorism and extremism:

Army of God: www.armyofgod.com

Drug Enforcement Administration (DEA): www.usdoj.gov/dea

Islamic Propagation Organization: www.al-islam.org/short/jihad

Muslim Brotherhood Movement: www.ummah.net/ikhwan

Office of National Drug Control Policy (ONDCP): www.whitehousedrugpolicy.gov

Discussion Box   The One True Faith

This chapter's Discussion Box is intended to stimulate critical debate about faith-motivated terrorism within major religions.

Most religious traditions have produced extremist movements whose members believe that their faith and value system is superior to other beliefs. This concept of the "one true faith" has been used by many fundamentalists to justify violent intolerance on behalf of their religion. Religious terrorists are modern manifestations of historical traditions of extremism within the world's major faiths. For example,

- Within *Christianity,* the medieval Crusades were a series of exceptionally violent military campaigns against Muslims, Jews, and heretical Christian sects. Later, during the 16th and 17th centuries, Catholic and Protestant Christians waged relentless wars against each other, which were marked by extreme brutality. In the modern era, Christian terrorists and extremists have participated in communal fighting in numerous countries and in the United States have bombed abortion clinics and committed other acts of violence.
- Within *Judaism,* the Old Testament is replete with references to the ancient Hebrews' faith-based mandate to wage war against non-Jewish occupiers of the Promised Land. In the modern era, the late **Rabbi Meir Kahane**'s **Kach (Kahane Chai)** movement in Israel has likewise advocated the expulsion of all Arabs from Israel. Two members of the **Jewish Defense League** were arrested in the United States in December 2001 on charges of conspiring to bomb Muslim mosques and the offices of a U.S. congressman in Los Angeles.
- Within *Islam,* the relative religious tolerance of the 15th and 16th centuries is counterbalanced against modern intolerance among movements such as Afghanistan's Taliban, Palestine's Hamas, and Lebanon's Hezbollah. There are numerous examples of political and communal violence waged in the name of Islam. Overt official repression has also been imposed in the name of the Islamic faith, as in Saudi Arabia's policy of relegating women to second-class status.

Modern religious extremism is arguably rooted in faith-based natural law. Natural law is a philosophical "higher law" that is theoretically discoverable through human reason and references to moral traditions and religious texts. In fact, most religious texts have passages that can be selectively interpreted to encourage extremist intolerance. To religious extremists, it is God's law that has been revealed to—and properly interpreted by—the extremist movement.

Discussion Questions

- Is faith-motivated activism a constructive force for change?
- At what point does the character of faith-motivated activism become extremist and terrorist?
- Does faith-based natural law justify acts of violence?
- Why do religious traditions that supposedly promote peace, justice, and rewards for spiritual devotion have so many followers who piously engage in violence, repression, and intolerance?
- What is the future of faith-based terrorism?

WEB EXERCISE

Using this chapter's recommended Internet sites, conduct an online investigation of religious extremism. Also conduct an investigation of criminal terrorism as it pertains to narco-terrorism.

- What commonalities can you find among the religious Web sites? What basic values are similar? In what ways do they differ?
- How adequately do the DEA and ONDCP Web sites address the threat from narco-terrorism? Based on the discussion in this chapter, how would you advise these agencies to inform the public online about criminal terrorism?
- Are the religious sites effective propaganda? How would you advise the site designers to appeal to different constituencies?

For an online search of issues pertaining to religious extremism and criminal terrorism, students should activate the search engine on their Web browser and enter the following keywords:

"Christian Crusades"
"Jihad"
"Narco-terrorism"

RECOMMENDED READINGS

The following publications discuss the motives, goals, and characteristics of religious extremism.

Bader, Eleanor J., and Patricia Baird-Windle. *Targets of Hatred: Anti-Abortion Terrorism*. New York: Palgrave, 2001.

Ehrenfeld, Rachel. *Narco-Terrorism*. New York: Basic Books, 1990.

Halevi, Yossi Klein. *Memoirs of a Jewish Extremist: An American Story*. New York: Little, Brown, 1995.

Huband, Mark. *Warriors of the Prophet: The Struggle for Islam*. Boulder, CO: Westview Press, 1999.

Rashid, Ahmed. *Taliban: Militant Islam, Oil and Fundamentalism in Central Asia*. New Haven, CT: Yale Nota Bene, 2001.

Tarazona-Sevillano, Gabriela. *Sendero Luminoso and the Threat of Narcoterrorism*. Westport, CT: Praeger, 1990.

NOTES

[1] Hoffman, Bruce. *Inside Terrorism*. New York: Columbia University Press, 1998, p. 92.

[2] From the Stern Gang's journal, *Hazit*, quoted in Bernhardt, J. *Society and the Assassin: A Background Book on Political Murder*. New York: Parent's Magazine Press, 1970, p. 149.

[3] Laqueur, Walter. *The New Terrorism: Fanaticism and the Arms of Mass Destruction*. New York: Oxford University Press, 1999, p. 129.

[4] Joshua 11, in *The Holy Bible, New Revised Standard Version*.

[5] Iadicola, Peter, and Anson Shupe. *Violence, Inequality, and Human Freedom*. New York: General Hall, 1998, p. 175. Citing Scott, Ralph A. *A New Look at Biblical Crime*. Chicago: Nelson-Hall, 1979, p. 66.

[6] Cohn, Norman. *The Pursuit of the Millennium*. New York: Oxford University Press, 1971, p. 61. Quoted in Iadicola and Shupe (note 5 above), p. 177.

[7] Iadicola and Shupe (note 5 above), p. 181. Citing Haught, James A. *Holy Horrors*. Buffalo, NY: Prometheus Books, 1990, p. 34.

[8] Pillar, Paul R. *Terrorism and U.S. Foreign Policy*. Washington, DC: Brookings Institution Press, 2001, pp. 45-46.

[9] U.S. Department of State. "Aum Supreme Truth (Aum)." *Patterns of Global Terrorism, 2000*. U.S. Department of State, April 2001.

[10] Marshall, Andrew. "It Gassed the Tokyo Subway, Microwaved Its Enemies and Tortured Its Members. So Why Is the Aum Cult Thriving?" *The Guardian*. July 15, 1999.

[11] U.S. Department of State (note 9 above).

[12] Marshall (note 10 above).

[13] Marshall (note 10 above) and Laqueur (note 3 above), p. 54.

[14] Initial reports cited this figure. Later studies suggest that physical injuries numbered 1,300 and that the rest were psychological injuries. U.S. Department of State (note 9 above).

[15] Laqueur (note 3 above).

[16] The discussion has been adapted from Human Rights Watch. *The Scars of Death: Children Abducted by the Lord's Resistance Army in Uganda*. New York: Human Rights Watch, 1997.

[17] McFadden, Robert D. "Bin Laden's Journey from Rich Pious Lad to the Mask of Evil." *New York Times*. September 30, 2001.

[18] Ibid.

[19] Reeve, Simon. *The New Jackals: Ramzi Yousef, Osama bin Laden and the Future of Terrorism*. Boston: Northeastern University Press, 1999, p. 181.

[20] Central Intelligence Agency. "Philippines." *The World Factbook 2001*. www.odci.gov/cia/publications/factbook.

[21] Stone, Martin. *The Establishment of Algeria*. London: Hurst & Co., 1997, pp. 1-3. Quoted in Whittaker, David J., ed. *The Terrorism Reader*. New York: Routledge, 2001, pp. 141-42.

[22] Whitaker (note 21 above).

[23] Daley, Suzanne. "French Leader Visits Algiers to Shore up Terrorism War." *New York Times*. December 2, 2001.

[24] Ibid.

[25] Pyes, Craig, Josh Meyer, and William C. Rempel. "U.S. Sees New Terrorist Threat From North Africa." *Los Angeles Times*. July 8, 2001.

[26] Kelly, Robert J., and Jess Maghan, eds. *Hate Crime: The Global Politics of Polarization*. Carbondale: Southern Illinois University Press, 1998, p. 105.

[27] See Katz, Samuel M. *The Hunt for the Engineer: How Israeli Agents Tracked the Hamas Master Bomber*. New York: Fromm International, 2001, pp. 97-99.

[28] Ibid., p. 225.

[29] CNN. "Rabin's Alleged Killer Appears in Court." *CNN World News*. November 7, 1995.

[30] Ehrenfeld, Rachel. *Narco-Terrorism*. New York: Basic Books, 1990, p. xiii.

[31] Use of the term has been debated, and some controversy regarding its use still exists. See Laqueur (note 3 above), p. 211.

[32] Cilluffo, Frank. "The Challenge We Face as the Battle Lines Blur." Statement before the U.S. House Committee on the Judiciary, Subcommittee on Crime. December 13, 2000.

[33] Ibid.

[34] BBC News. "Mafia 'Gripping Italian Economy.'" November 14, 2000. This report was challenged by Italian officials.

[35] De Gennaro, Giovanni. "The Threat of International Organized Crime and Global Terrorism." Statement before the U.S. House Committee on International Relations. October 1, 1997.

[36] Ibid.; remarks of the Honorable Louis Freeh, Director of the Federal Bureau of Investigation.

[37] Ibid.

[38] BBC News. November 21, 1998.

[39] BBC News. "So Who Are the Russian Mafia?" April 1, 1998.

[40] BBC News (note 38 above).

[41] Cilluffo (note 32 above).

[42] Ibid.

[43] Chazan, Yigal. "Albanian Mafias Find New Drug Routes Around Yugoslavia." *Christian Science Monitor*. October 20, 1994.

[44] Milivojevic, Marko. "The 'Balkan Medellin.'" *Jane's Intelligence Review*. Vol. 7, No. 2. February 1, 1995, p. 68.

[45] James, Barry. "In Balkans, Arms for Drugs." *International Herald Tribune, Paris*. June 6, 1994.

[46] Milivojevic (note 44 above).

[47] *The American College Dictionary.* New York: Harper & Brothers, 1947.

[48] Ehrenfeld (note 30 above), pp. 86-87.

[49] Ambrus, Steven. "Vigilantes Target Drug Chief: Effective Paramilitary Squad Raises Ethical Dilemma for Colombian Government." *Christian Science Monitor.* March 5, 1993.

[50] Cilluffo (note 32 above).

[51] Ibid.

[52] Ibid.

[53] Walters, John. *Press Briefing by Director of the Office of National Drug Control Policy.* February 12, 2002.

[54] Cilluffo (note 32 above).

[55] Ehrenfeld (note 30 above), p. 125.

[56] Scott Palmer, David. "The Revolutionary Terrorism of Peru's Shining Path." In Crenshaw, Martha. *Terrorism in Context.* State College: Pennsylvania State University Press. Quoted in Whittaker, David J., ed. *The Terrorism Reader.* New York: Routledge, 2001, p. 160.

[57] Laqueur (note 4 above), p. 187.

Chapter 9

TERRORIST SPILLOVERS: INTERNATIONAL TERRORISM

This chapter explores the dimensions of international terrorism. International terrorism is terrorism that "spills over" onto the world's stage. Targets are selected because of their value as symbols of international interests. Terrorism in the international arena has been a common feature of political violence since the late 1960s, when political extremists began to appreciate the value of allowing their revolutionary struggles to be fought in a global arena. By doing so, relatively low-cost incidents reaped significant propaganda benefits that were impossible when radicals limited their revolutions to specific regions or national boundaries. Because of their adoption of terrorism on an international scale, revolutionary movements have been very successful in moving terrorism—and their underlying grievances—to the forefront of the international agenda. It is not an exaggeration to conclude that "international terrorism represents one of the defining elements of politics on the world's stage today."[1]

International terrorism affords one of the best examples of ***asymmetrical warfare,*** a term that refers to unconventional, unexpected, and nearly unpredictable acts of political violence. Although it is an old practice, asymmetrical warfare has become a feature of the New Terrorism. In the modern era of asymmetrical warfare, terrorists can theoretically acquire and wield new high-yield arsenals, strike at unanticipated targets, and apply unique and idiosyncratic tactics. The dilemma for victims and for counterterrorism policymakers is that by using these tactics, the terrorists can win the initiative and redefine the international security environment. In this way, the traditional protections and deterrent policies used by societies and the international community can be surmounted by dedicated terrorists. This concept will be explored further in Chapter 10.

When violent dissidents have limited their activism to *domestic* victims and domestic environments, they often have not received a great deal of world attention. This is because the world community usually considers domestic political violence to be a localized issue unless it affects in some way the national interests of other countries. As a matter of domestic policy, some governments will not hesitate to suppress the media's access to information or to mete out swift and brutal reprisals against dissenters. The cumulative impact of repressive government policies toward dissent is that domestic attacks against domestic symbols can become very risky and costly for dissidents, with uncertain prospects for world attention or sympathy.

In the modern era of immediate media attention, small and relatively weak movements have concluded that worldwide exposure can be achieved by committing acts of political violence against international symbols. These groups have discovered that politically motivated hijackings, bombings, assassinations, kidnappings, extortion, and other criminal acts can be quite effective when conducted under an international spotlight. Thus, the international realm guarantees some degree of attention and affords greater opportunities for manipulating the world's political, popular, and media sentiments. In practical terms, this point is illustrated by the case of the Palestinian cause. It is, in fact, the beginning point for understanding modern international terrorism.

Palestinian nationalists were the first revolutionaries to shape the framework for modern international terrorism. Using high-profile international violence such as airline hijackings, shootings, and the taking of hostages, they effectively applied "propaganda by the deed" to force the international community to recognize the plight of the Palestinian people. For many Palestinian nationalists, any means were justifiable—including international terrorism—because their cause was just. From their perspective, the methods that many in the global community condemned as "terrorism" were the legitimate tactics of freedom fighters. As Leila Khaled, who participated in two airline hijackings, wrote:

> Our struggle will be long and arduous because the enemy is powerful, well-organised and well-sustained from abroad. . . . We shall win because we represent the wave of the future . . . because mankind is on our side, and above all because we are determined to achieve victory.[2]

Other nationalist causes emulated the Palestinian model. Radical Kurdish, Armenian, and South Moluccan groups also took their causes into the international arena. These groups committed kidnappings, assassinations, hijackings, and bombings in third countries far from their homelands. In addition, ideological radicals in Europe established common cause with the Palestinians, sometimes carrying out high-profile and dramatic joint operations with them. This created an international terrorist environment during the late 1960s through the 1980s that was dominated by left-wing and ethno-nationalist movements.

Chapter Perspective 9.1 summarizes the changing environments of international terrorism, focusing on the predominant dissident profiles during the latter part of the 20th century.

International terrorism has two important qualities: First, it is a methodology that is specifically selected by violent extremists; and second, it is an identifiable brand of terrorism. International terrorism is, in other words, a tactical-strategic instrument of political violence as well as a category of terrorism. In the discussion that follows, the special features of what gives some terrorist incidents an international quality will be explored—primarily within the following dimensions:

Defining International Terrorism. International terrorism must be defined by identifying the core attributes that make some terrorist acts "international" in character. All incidents of international terrorism exhibit one or more of these core attributes.

Reasons for International Terrorism. A critical examination of international terrorism will naturally raise the question of why extremist violence takes place so frequently—and so publicly—on the world's stage. Several advantages and disadvantages of global terrorism can be identified that enter into the extremists' cost-benefit calculus. Included in this analysis are *perceptions of international terrorism.* One important focus of an inquiry into the attributes of international terrorism is the question of perception—more precisely, how various international actors perceive the legitimacy of using international terrorism as a method of political dissent. For example, Western democracies abhor and denounce

---

Chapter Perspective 9.1   **The Changing Environment of International Terrorism**

International terrorism is in many ways a reflection of global politics, so that the international terrorist environment is dominated at different times by different terrorist typologies. Thus, one may conclude that the profile of international terrorism has progressed through several environmental phases in the postwar era, which can be roughly summarized as follows:[a]

- From the 1960s through the early 1980s, *left-wing* terrorists figured prominently in international incidents. For example, West European groups frequently attacked international symbols "in solidarity" with defined oppressed groups. Only a few leftist groups remain, and most of them (such as Colombia's FARC) do not often practice international terrorism.
- From the beginning of the modern era of international terrorism in the late 1960s, *Palestinian nationalists* were perhaps the leading practitioners of international terrorism. Participating in their struggle were Western European and Middle Eastern extremists who struck targets in solidarity with the Palestinian cause. By the late 1990s, with the creation of the

governing authority on the West Bank and Gaza, Palestinian-initiated terrorism focused primarily on targets inside Israel and the occupied territories. Their radical Western comrades ceased their violent support by the late 1980s, but many Middle Eastern extremists continued to cite the Palestinian cause as a reason for their violent activism.

- Throughout the postwar era, *ethno-national* terrorism occupied an important presence in the international arena. Its incidence has ebbed and flowed in scale and frequency, but ethno-nationalist violence has never completely disappeared. By the late 1990s, these groups operated primarily inside their home countries but continued to occasionally attack international symbols.
- By the end of the 20th century, the most prominent practitioners of international terrorism were *religious* extremists. Although Islamic movements such as Al Qaeda-generated groups were the most prolific international religious terrorists, extremists from every major religion have operated on the international stage.

a. Pillar, Paul R. *Terrorism and U.S. Foreign Policy.* Washington, DC, 2001, pp. 44-45.

---

international terrorism, whereas many regimes and leaders elsewhere in the world have been either weak in their denunciations or have on occasion expressed their approval of international extremist violence.

International Terrorist Networks. Since the days of the Cold War rivalry between the democratic West and the communist East, scholars and policymakers have frequently posed the question of whether cooperation exists between international terrorist groups— and whether international terrorist networks exist.

DEFINING INTERNATIONAL TERRORISM

International terrorism and domestic terrorism differ in both quality and effect. *Domestic terrorism* occurs when several factors are present: The terrorist incident is confined to a domestic venue, the target is a domestic symbol, and the political and psychological "terroristic" impact is primarily domestic. Previous chapters presented a number of cases in point that discussed dissident movements and incidents that were limited in scope to the borders of a country or a region and where domestic targets symbolizing domestic

Table 9.1 Dissident Terrorism on the World's Stage

During the latter half of the 20th century, dissident terrorist groups attacked symbols of international interests many times. Some groups traveled abroad to strike at targets, whereas others attacked domestic symbols of international interests.

The following table summarizes several incidents conducted by dissident terrorist groups.

| | | *Activity Profile* | | |
Dissident Group	*Home Country*	*Incident*	*Target*	*International Effect*
Abu Sayyaf	Philippines	April 2000 kidnapping	20 Asian and European tourists in Malaysia	Increased profile; $20 million ransom
Provos	Northern Ireland	December 1983 bombing	Harrods department store in London	National security crisis in United Kingdom
Shining Path	Peru	March 2002 bombing	Near U.S. Embassy	Renewed profile; domestic spillover
Red Brigades	Italy	December 1981 kidnapping	U.S. Brigadier General James Dozier	Increased profile; NATO security crisis
Black September	Palestinian Diaspora	Summer 1972 kidnapping	Israeli athletes at Summer Olympics	Increased profile; international crisis

interests were attacked. Many of these examples also evaluated state terrorism as domestic policy that was confined within the borders of the nation.

International terrorism occurs when the target is an international symbol and when the political-psychological impact goes beyond a domestic agenda. It will be recalled that state terrorism as foreign policy is often characterized by state sponsorship of dissident movements. In addition, many dissident terrorist groups and extremist movements have regularly acted "in solidarity" with international interests such as class struggle or national liberation. It is not uncommon for domestic groups and movements to travel abroad to attack targets symbolizing their domestic conflict or some broader global issue. And especially in the postwar world, terrorist groups have selected targets that only tangentially symbolize the sources of their perceived oppression. Thus, linkages often exist between seemingly domestic-oriented dissident terrorist groups and international terrorism. Table 9.1 illustrates this point by reviewing the activity profiles of several dissident terrorist groups that were implicated in acts of international terrorism.

Two contexts provide a model for defining international terrorism. The first context is the centrality of the "**spillover effect**," which occurs when violent domestic conflicts are played out internationally, so that revolutionary struggles "spill over" national borders into the global arena. The second context is the interplay between international terrorism and the terrorist typologies discussed in previous chapters. Much of the violence conducted within the framework of these typologies can be classified as international terrorism. Both of these contexts—the spillover effect and the typological interplay—are discussed next.

Concept: The Spillover Effect

Terrorist violence frequently occurs beyond the borders of the countries that are the target of such violence. Those who engage in political violence on an international scale do so with the expectation that it will have a positive effect on their cause at home—thus reasoning that international exposure will bring about compensation for perceived injustices. Using this logic, terrorists will either go abroad to strike at targets or remain at home to strike internationally symbolic targets. The following characteristics distinguish international terrorism as a specific type of terrorism:

- Domestic attacks against victims with an international profile
- Operations in a foreign country
- Unambiguous international implications

Domestic Attacks Against Victims With an International Profile

Most experts would agree that international terrorism by definition does not require terrorists to leave their home countries; they can strike domestically, depending on the symbol represented by the target. As a result, terrorist spillovers do not always occur in third countries. They are frequently domestic targets that signify international interests. In this way, domestic extremist movements can commit acts of international terrorism by selectively attacking internationally symbolic targets.

Examples of domestic targets with symbolic international links include diplomats, businessmen and women, and tourists. An important and disturbing result of these attacks has been a trend in which terrorists recognize no qualitative difference between their victim group and the enemy interest that it represents. Thus, innocent business travelers, civilians, academics, and military personnel are considered to be legitimate targets and fair game for terrorist violence.

The long Lebanese Civil War in the 1970s and 1980s is a good example of domestic attacks against victims with an international profile. During the war, militant Islamic groups targeted symbols of international interests with great drama. The Shi'ite group Hezbollah was responsible for most of these incidents, but claims for responsibility were usually made under different names, such as **Islamic Jihad**, **Organization of the Oppressed**, and the **Revolutionary Justice Organization**. Examples of terrorist attacks included the bombing of the U.S. embassy and attacks against French and American peacekeeping troops in Beirut. In addition, the kidnapping of foreign nationals by Islamic extremists came to be a prominent characteristic of the civil war. Kidnapping victims included non-Lebanese (many of them American and French) journalists, academics, an envoy of the Archbishop of Canterbury, a station chief of the U.S. Central Intelligence Agency, and others. Some hostages were kept in captivity for years, and others were executed.

Other examples of domestic attacks against victims symbolizing international interests include the following:

- In Rwanda on January 18, 1997, Hutu militants shot and killed three Spanish workers from the international aid society Doctors of the World.[3] One American aid worker was seriously wounded, requiring his leg to be amputated.

- In Colombia on February 7, 1997, FARC guerrillas kidnapped two German and two Austrian tourists from a park and demanded $15 million in ransom for their release. On March 4, Colombian soldiers spotted them and attacked. During the firefight, FARC rebels killed two of the hostages, and the army killed four rebels.

Operations in a Foreign Country

The history of terrorism is replete with examples of extremists who deliberately travel abroad to strike at an enemy. Their targets often include nationals that the terrorists symbolically associate with the policies of their perceived enemy. Some are representatives of these policies, such as diplomats or political officials, whereas others are only minimally linked to national policy, such as business travelers, tourists, or other civilians. For example, the Algerian Armed Islamic Group launched a terrorist campaign in metropolitan France from July to October 1995. Eight people were killed and 180 injured during bombings of trains, schools, cafes, and markets. In another example, the IRA in June 1996 fired three mortar rounds into a British army barracks at Osnabreuck, Germany.

In the modern era of the New Terrorism, terrorist plots have taken on a decidedly multinational dimension, with cells linked to each other across several countries. Extremist groups have deliberately positioned terrorist operatives and autonomous cells in foreign countries. Their purpose is to attack enemy interests with a presence in those countries. For example, Latin American and U.S. security officials identified an apparent threat in Latin America, which suggests that Middle Eastern cells became active in the 1990s along the triangular border region where Brazil, Argentina, and Paraguay meet. These concerns arose in part from two incidents in July 1994. In the first incident, the Lebanese Shi'ite movement Hezbollah was suspected of committing a deadly suicide bombing at the Argentine-Israeli Mutual Association in Buenos Aires, Argentina, where about 100 people were killed and 200 injured. Although the media reported that a group calling itself **Ansar Allah** claimed credit, Hezbollah (using the name Islamic Jihad) had previously claimed responsibility for the 1992 bombing of the Israeli embassy in Buenos Ares. In the second incident, an apparent suicide bomb exploded aboard a Panamanian airliner, killing 21 people, 12 of whom were Jewish.

The extent of transnational operations in foreign countries is illustrated by the following examples of investigations that occurred in the aftermath of the attacks against the United States on September 11, 2001:

- According to the U.S. Department of Justice, a terrorist cell based in Hamburg, Germany, included three of the September 11 hijackers and three others who were implicated in the attacks.[4] The cell had apparently been positioned in Hamburg since 1999.
- In November, 2001, a Spanish judge indicted several alleged members of a Qaeda cell that had apparently begun to organize in Spain in 1994. The indictment was based on wire taps of conversations between the Spanish cell, the Hamburg cell, and others who may have been linked to the September 11 attack.[5]
- On March 3, 2002, Macedonian security officers killed seven members of an apparent terrorist cell that was allegedly planning to bomb the American, British, and German embassies the capital city of Skopje. They were a multinational cell, with most members coming from Pakistan or the Middle East. In February 2002, Macedonian police had arrested two Jordanians and two Bosnians and had seized computer disks that contained information about embassies and Macedonian government offices.[6]

Unambiguous International Implications

Regardless of whether political violence is directed against domestic targets that are international symbols or take place in third countries, the fundamental characteristic of international terrorism is that international consequences are clearly apparent. For example, the February 1993 terrorist attack on the World Trade Center in New York City had clear international consequences, as did the terrorist attacks of September 11, 2001. Foreign terrorist cells and the Qaeda network had used transnational resources to position terrorist operatives in the United States, their targets were prominent symbols of international trade and power, and their victims were citizens from many countries.

Case: Hijackings as International Spillovers

A good example of terrorist spillovers is the selection of international passenger carriers as targets by terrorists. They are relatively "soft" targets that easily garner international media attention when attacked. The passengers on these carriers are considered to be legitimate symbolic targets, so that terrorizing or killing them is justifiable in the minds of the terrorists.

Beginning in the late 1960s, terrorists began attacking international ports of call used by travelers. International passenger carriers—primarily airliners—became favorite targets of terrorists. In the beginning, the hijackings were often the acts of extremists, criminals, or otherwise desperate people trying to escape their home countries to find asylum in a friendly country. This profile changed, however, when the Popular Front for the Liberation of Palestine (PFLP) staged a series of hijackings as a way to publicize the cause of the Palestinians before the world community. The first successful high-profile PFLP hijacking was Leila Khaled's attack in August 1969. The PFLP struck again in September 1970, when they attempted to hijack five airliners, succeeding in four of the attempts. As discussed in Chapter 3, these incidents certainly directed the world's attention to the Palestinian cause, but they also precipitated the Jordanian army's Black September assault against the Palestinians. Nevertheless, passenger carriers have since been frequent targets of international terrorists. The selection of international passenger carriers will be explored further in Chapter 10.

International Terrorism and Terrorist Typologies

Many of the terrorist cases in point that were presented in previous chapters were international in character, but they were evaluated within other contexts. It is therefore useful to briefly revisit terrorism typologies discussed previously. International terrorism may be summarized as follows:

State Terrorism

Many governments have used terrorism as an instrument of foreign policy. These policies have been characterized by state sponsorship of terrorist movements and direct state involvement in terrorist incidents or campaigns. Although international state terrorism in the modern era has mostly involved the use of proxy groups by radical regional powers, it has also been used by global powers. For example, during the Cold War the superpowers engaged in behavior that can be labeled as international terrorism. As discussed in Chapter 4, the United States carried out the Phoenix Program in cooperation with its South Vietnamese allies. It was a three-year program that was arguably militarily successful, but there were also many civilian deaths attributable to the campaign. The Soviet Union regularly supported dissident "national liberation" movements that used terrorism, giving rise to a theory in the West that the Soviets and their allies were the primary sources of international terrorism. This theory of a monolithic (single-source) conspiracy is discussed later in this chapter.

Dissident Terrorism

As has been discussed previously, many examples exist of dissident terrorists selecting domestic targets that have a symbolic international connection. Some of these attacks are carried out as a way to express solidarity with foreign movements or demographic groups; other attacks have been directed against perceived foreign enemies. For example, during the late 1970s and early 1980s, the Cuban American terrorist group **Omega 7** was responsible for "more than fifty bombings and assassination attempts in the United States against Cuban diplomats and businesses involved with Cuba."[7] Omega 7 is a good case in point of a domestic dissident terrorist group that engaged in international terrorism. Its targets included

- the Venezuelan Consulate in New York City in 1975;
- the Cuban delegation to the United Nations in 1976;
- a Soviet ship docked at the New Jersey coast [in] 1976;
- several travel agencies in New Jersey in 1977 and 1978;
- New York City's Lincoln Center in 1978; and
- both the Cuban Mission to the United Nations and a Soviet airlines ticket office in New York in 1979.[8]

Left-Wing Terrorism

Many armed left-wing movements resorted to international terrorism, and in fact, these movements significantly shaped the international environment from the 1960s though the 1980s. It was not uncommon for leftist groups to attack Western "imperialist" targets in the groups' home country or in countries far afield from the root causes of the groups' revolutionary movement. For example, Latin American leftists initiated a cycle of kidnappings of American and other nations' businessmen and diplomats during the 1960s and 1970s. The kidnappers sometimes profited handsomely from ransoms that were paid for the hostages' release. These targets were interpreted by leftist groups to be symbols of repression; they were considered to represent the economic and political supports that were propping up enemy domestic governments.

Right-Wing Terrorism

The incidence of international terrorism by right-wing movements has been rather low. Unlike left-wing terrorism, there has not been a consistent cycle of rightist terrorism on an international scale. As discussed in Chapter 7, right-wing terrorist movements have been idiosyncratic in the sense that they are strongly rooted in the political and cultural environments of their home countries. There has not been a transnational rightist movement since the fascist movement of the 1930s and 1940s, so that modern right-wing extremists do not have a common ideological source that has motivated them to form a global movement. Hence, they have rarely engaged in terrorist violence as a way to express solidarity with each other, nor have they established important international terrorist networks. In essence, dissident right-wing terrorism has not been a significant factor in the international arena.

Religious Terrorism

Religious terrorism began to epitomize the international terrorist environment of the 1990s and the new millennium. Much of the religion-motivated international violence is a result of growth in radical Islamic ideologies. This resurgence has grown out of the rejection of traditional secular ideologies such as Marxism, as well as disillusionment with pan-Arab nationalist sentiment. The examples of the Iranian Revolution and the international mujahideen in Afghanistan inspired a number of movements in predominantly Muslim countries. The result has been that a new revolutionary consciousness is promoting a sense of common cause among revolutionary brethren throughout the world. Operationally, pan-Islamic networks such as Al Qaeda have significantly influenced the growth of transnational radical Islamic terrorist cells.

Criminal Terrorism

Traditional criminal terrorists have occasionally engaged in international terrorism, but these incidents are exceptions to the general pattern of refraining from international exposure. As discussed in Chapter 8, traditional criminal terrorists tend to be reactive and anonymous in their political agitation. They rarely seek out high-profile attention for their activities, unless threatened by governments that aggressively try to repress their activity. Traditional criminal terrorism has not been a factor in the international arena.

Table 9.2 summarizes the interplay between international terrorism and terrorist typologies.

REASONS FOR INTERNATIONAL TERRORISM

Extremist groups and movements resort to international terrorism for a number of reasons. Some movements act in cooperation with other groups, waging an international campaign against a perceived global enemy. For example, France's Direct Action, Germany's Red Army Faction, and Italy's Red Brigades frequently attacked symbolic targets as expressions of solidarity with international causes. Other groups were motivated by idiosyncrasies that were unique to the group or movement. For example, the **Armenian Secret Army for the Liberation of Armenia (ASALA),** the **Justice Commandos of the Armenian Genocide**, and the **Armenian Revolutionary Army** waged a campaign of international terrorism against Turkish interests in Europe and the United States during the 1970s and 1980s. To support their demands for autonomy for the Armenian region of Turkey, these groups bombed Turkish interests, killed and wounded Turkish diplomats, and bombed airports. One such bomb, at Orly airport near Paris, killed about 10 people and wounded 70.

The following discussion summarizes several underlying reasons for the selection of international terrorism as a strategy by extremists. It evaluates the following underlying reasons for international terrorism:

- Ideological Reasons: Modern "isms" and International Revolutionary Solidarity
- Practical Reasons: Perceived Efficiency
- Tactical Reasons: Adaptations of Revolutionary Theory to International Operations
- Historical Reasons: Perceptions of International Terrorism

Ideological Reasons: Modern "Isms" and International Revolutionary Solidarity

As discussed previously, conflict in the postwar era was largely a by-product of resistance in many countries against former colonial powers. These indigenous "wars of national liberation" were global in the sense that insurgents established a common cause

Table 9.2   International Terrorism and Terrorist Typologies

Although cases of international terrorism exist for most terrorist typologies, right-wing and traditional criminal terrorists tend to refrain from violence in the international arena.

The following table identifies incidents of international terrorism within the framework of several terrorist typologies.

	Activity Profile			
Typology	*Incident*	*Perpetrator*	*Target*	*International Effect*
State	Car bomb in Washington, D.C.	Chile Security Service, **DINA**	Orlando Letelier	Minimal effect; domestic spillover
Dissident	Bomb in London	Irish Republican Army	Canary Wharf	Significant effect; ended IRA's cease-fire
Left-wing	Hostages taken in Lima, Peru	Peru's Tupac Amaru Revolutionary Movement	Japanese ambassador's residence	Minimal effect; domestic spillover
Right-wing	Arson attacks in former East Germany	Neo-Nazis and supporters	Foreign "guest workers"	Minimal effect
Religious	Attacks of September 11, 2001	Al Qaeda cells	World Trade Center, Pentagon	Significant effect; international crisis and war
Criminal	Kidnapping, murder	Mexican *narcotraficantes*	U.S. DEA Special Agent Enrique Camarena	Significant effect; enhanced war on drugs

among themselves against what they perceived to be domination by repressive and exploitative imperial powers and their local allies. Marxism and generalized leftist sentiment provided a common bond among radicals in the developing world and among Western dissidents.

Reasons for this resistance included, of course, the overt presence of foreign troops, administrators, and business interests in the newly emerging countries. From a broader global perspective, other reasons included the policies and ideologies of the Western powers. These policies and ideologies were given negative labels that insurgents affixed to the Western presence in the developing world. If one were to apply Marxist interpretations of class struggle and national liberation, these indigenous wars could easily be interpreted as representing an internationalized struggle against global exploitation by the West. The conceptual labels commonly used by violent extremists include the following:

"Imperialism." Postwar dissidents fought against what they considered to be the vestiges of European colonial empires. Western powers had traditionally deemed empire building

to be a legitimate manifestation of national prestige and power. For example, the European "scramble for Africa" during the late 19th century was considered to be completely justifiable. During the wars of national liberation, foreign interests and civilians were attacked because they were labeled as representatives of imperial powers.

"Neocolonialism." **Neocolonialism** referred to exploitation by Western interests, usually symbolized by **multinational corporations**. Even when Western armies or administrators were not present and when indigenous governments existed, insurgents argued that economic exploitation still relegated the developing world to a subordinate status. From their perspective, the wealth of the developing world was being drained by Western economic interests. Domestic governments thus became targets because they were labeled as dupes of Western interests. Multinational corporations and other symbols of neocolonialism became targets around the world, so that facilities and employees were attacked internationally.

"Zionism." **Zionism** historically refers to an intellectual movement that sought to establish the proper means, conditions, and timing to resettle Jews in Palestine. Zionism was recognized by the Balfour Declaration of November 2, 1917; this was a statement by the British government that favored the establishment of a Jewish nation in Palestine as long as the rights of non-Jewish residents were guaranteed. The concept has become a lightning rod for resistance against Israel and its supporters. One significant difference in the international character of anti-Zionist terrorism—vis-à-vis resistance against **imperialism** and neocolonialism—is that international terrorists have attacked Jewish civilian targets around the world as symbols of Zionism. This adds a religious and ethno-national dimension to anti-Zionist terrorism that does not necessarily exist in the other concepts just discussed.

Symbols of the foregoing concepts have been attacked repeatedly by dissident terrorists. They have also been the objects of state-sponsored terrorism by enemy governments. An unfortunate consequence of this type of labeling is that diplomats have been victimized as imperialists, bankers have been attacked as neocolonialists, and Jewish civilians have been singled out as Zionists.

Practical Reasons: Perceived Efficiency

One basic (and admittedly simplified) reason for the high incidence of international terrorism is that it is perceived by many extremists to be "a highly efficient (if repugnant) instrument for achieving the aims of terrorist movements."[9] Whether or not this is an accurate assessment, the extremists' calculation to engage in international terrorism certainly incorporates this *perception* of efficiency.

Using this rationale of perceived efficiency as a core motivation, other reasons for international terrorism include several factors:

The Potential for Maximum Publicity. Terrorists practice "propaganda by the deed" and understand that international deeds will reap maximum media exposure. The media has never been reluctant to move dramatic terrorist attacks to the top of their reporting agenda; international terrorism is always depicted as "important" news. After the American embassy was attacked in Tehran, Iran, in November 1979, 53 Americans were held hostage until January 1981, a total of 444 days. During that time, Iran was at the center of media attention, and the revolutionaries manipulated the press to publicize their revolutionary agenda. They also embarrassed the most powerful nation in the world.

The Potential for Inflicting Maximum Psychological Anxiety. Terrorism against enemy interests on a global scale theoretically creates security problems everywhere that the target commands a political or economic presence. When travelers, airliners, and diplomats are attacked internationally, an enemy will give attention to the grievances of the movement that is the source of the violence.

Pragmatism. Demanding concessions from adversaries who become the focus of worldwide attention has occasionally been successful. Terrorists and extremists have sometimes secured ransoms for hostages, prisoner releases, and other concessions.

Thus, international terrorism is a functional operational decision that offers—from the perspective of the terrorists—greater efficiency in promoting the goals of the cause.

Tactical Reasons: Adaptations of Revolutionary Theory to International Operations

Students may recall from previous discussions that Mao Zedong, Carlos Marighella, and Frantz Fanon provided influential analyses of the practicality of revolutionary violence; one may observe that international extremists continue to apply modern adaptations of their ideas. It is therefore instructive to revisit their advice from an international perspective.

Theoretical Adaptation 1: With the continuing trend toward globalization, national, information, and communication barriers have been dramatically altered. Members of dissident movements are now able to reside in multiple countries while remaining in regular contact with each other. Adapting Mao Zedong's maxim to the international arena, terrorists can become "fish swimming in the sea of the world community." It is much more difficult to root out a movement that uses cells prepositioned in several countries, as became apparent during the post-September 11, 2001, war against terrorism.

Theoretical Adaptation 2: Relatively weak groups continue to attempt to provoke governments into reacting in ways that would be detrimental to the governments' interests. By doing so, new supporters will arise to join the cause. Adapting Carlos Marighella's theory of provoking a powerful adversary into overreacting—and thus creating a heightened revolutionary consciousness among the people—international terrorists can now seek to provoke a nation on a global scale. These provocations can provide effective propaganda if the offending nation can be depicted as an international bully. This is not difficult to do, because modern information technology allows for images and messages to be disseminated worldwide. During the 2001-2002 coalition forces campaign against the Taliban in Afghanistan, images of wounded and killed civilians were broadcast throughout the Muslim world.

Theoretical Adaptation 3: It is apparent that terrorists continue to believe that they represent a superior calling and morality. Modern religious extremists in particular believe that killing or dying in defense of the faith will assure them a place in paradise. On an international scale, this superior calling, morality, and promised reward is a kind of "liberation." Adapting Frantz Fanon's analysis that oppressed people psychologically need to engage in revolutionary resistance against their oppressor, terrorists can use the international arena as a means to "liberate" themselves and to thereby obtain vengeful justice against an adversary.

Historical Reasons: Perceptions of International Terrorism

Governments in developing countries do not always share the West's interpretations when political violence is used in the international arena. Western democracies regularly abhor and denounce international terrorism, whereas many regimes and leaders elsewhere in the world have been either weak in their denunciations or have on occasion expressed their approval of international extremist violence.

Three factors illustrate why terrorism is *unacceptable* from the perspective of Western governments:

1. First, Western governments have adopted an ideology of democratic justice as a norm. A *norm* is an accepted standard for the way societies ought to behave. Within the context of these norms, terrorism is perceived to be criminal behavior.

2. Second, the West is often a target of terrorism. This is a practical consideration.

3. Third, the West recognizes accepted methods of warfare. These include rules that define which modes of conflict constitute a legal manner to wage war. If possible, so-called collateral damage (unnecessary casualties and destruction) is to be avoided.

In the developing world, wars waged to gain independence or to suppress political rivals were commonly fought by using "irregular" tactics. Combatants often used guerrilla or terrorist tactics against colonial opponents or against indigenous adversaries during civil wars. In fact, many of the statesmen who rose to prominence after the formation of the new nations were former insurgents who were previously referred to by their adversaries as terrorists. From their perspective, terrorism and other violent methods were necessary weapons for waging "poor man's warfare" against enemies that were sometimes many times stronger than themselves.

Three factors demonstrate why terrorism is often *acceptable* from the perspective of governments in the developing world:

1. Many anticolonial extremists became national leaders. They were freedom fighters in the eyes of their people. A large number of revolutionaries became national leaders in Asia, Africa, and the Middle East.

2. Terrorism was used as a matter of practical choice during necessity. It provided armed propaganda, sowed disorder, and demoralized their adversaries. At some point in many postwar conflicts, the cost of war simply became unacceptable to the colonial powers.

3. Many developing world insurgents crafted an effective fusion of ideology and warfare. Terrorism was a justifiable and legitimate method of warfare as long as the cause was just and the fighters were cadres who understood why they were fighting.

The massacre of 11 Israeli athletes by Black September terrorists at the 1972 Munich Olympics exemplifies how divergent the foregoing perspectives can be. In the aftermath of the tragedy, Western and developing world members of the United Nations engaged in sometimes acrimonious debate about the use of political violence in the international arena. The debate centered around whether "terrorist acts" should be defined by making reference to the perspectives of the victims or the assailants. There were important differences between the positions of the developing world nations and those of the Western members, especially NATO countries[10]: "[Western countries contended that] murder, kidnapping, arson and other felonious acts constitute criminal behavior, but many non-Western nations have proved reluctant to condemn as terrorist acts what they consider to be struggles for national liberation."[11]

Some Arab, African, and Asian nations considered the underlying motives for the Munich attack to be the determining criteria for whether the assault was a terrorist incident. Thus, because of the status of some ethno-national groups, one developing world delegate observed, "The term 'terrorist' could 'hardly be held to apply to persons who were denied the most elementary human rights, dignity, freedom and independence, and whose countries objected to foreign occupation.'"[12]

INTERNATIONAL TERRORIST NETWORKS

The concept of an international terrorist network naturally presumes one or more of the following environments:

- Terrorist groups talk to each other.
- Terrorist groups support each other.
- Governments sponsor terrorists.
- The international terrorist environment is basically conspiratorial.

Using these characteristics as criteria for determining whether or not there is such a thing as an "international terrorist network," one can conclude that networks have existed and continue to exist. As discussed in previous chapters, dissident terrorist movements—such as European leftists and Palestinian nationalists—have cooperated with each other. They frequently establish common cause and act in solidarity to promote a generalized global struggle against "imperialism," "Zionism," or other perceived forces of oppression. In addition, governments (such as those of Iraq and Iran) have sponsored terrorist movements as instruments of foreign policy. There are many cases of terrorist incidents or movements that owe their operational viability to linkages with government sponsors.

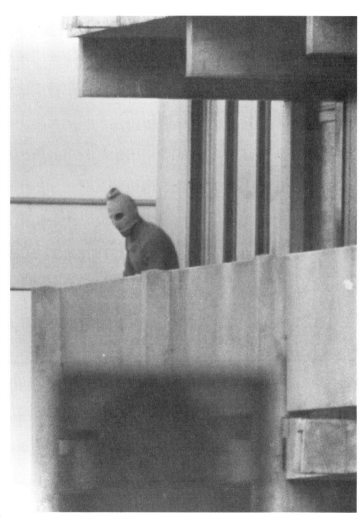

The 1972 Munich Olympics. A hooded Black September terrorist peers over a balcony during the tragic crisis that ended with the deaths of all of the Israeli hostages.

Source: Hulton Archive/Getty Images; used by permission.

| Chapter Perspective 9.2 | The Japanese Red Army and the Lod (Lydda) Airport Massacre |

The **Japanese Red Army** (JRA) was a nearly fanatical international terrorist organization founded in about 1970. It participated in a series of terrorist incidents, including assassinations, kidnappings, and airline hijackings. The JRA on one occasion tried to occupy the U.S. Embassy in Kuala Lumpur, Malaysia. On another occasion, the group bombed a United Service Organizations club in Naples, Italy. Members have been arrested in a number of countries, including one who was caught with explosives on the New Jersey Turnpike. Others who were not arrested are thought to have joined Latin American revolutionaries in Colombia and Peru.

The JRA committed a number of terrorist acts in cooperation with other terrorist groups. On May 30, 1972, three members of the organization fired assault rifles into a group of religious pilgrims and other travelers at Israel's Lod (Lydda) Airport. The death toll was high—26 people were killed and about 80 were wounded. Most of the injured were travelers from Puerto Rico on a religious pilgrimage. During the firefight that ensued, two of the terrorists were killed by security guards, and one was captured. The Japanese terrorists had been retained by the Popular Front for the Liberation of Palestine (PFLP) for the attack, and the PFLP had sent the three operatives on their mission on behalf of the Palestinian cause.

The attack is a remarkable example of international terrorism in its purest form: Leftist Japanese terrorists killed Christian pilgrims from Puerto Rico arriving on a U.S. airline at an Israeli airport on behalf of the nationalist Popular Front for the Liberation of Palestine.

As a postscript, the one survivor of the Lod attack—Kozo Okamoto—was tried and sentenced to life imprisonment in Israel but was later released in a 1985 prisoner exchange with other Palestinian prisoners. He lived in the Beka'a Valley until 1997 but was arrested by the Lebanese with four other members of the JRA. After serving three years in prison, all five members were freed in 2000.

Chapter Perspective 9.2 discusses an interesting example of cooperation between Japanese ideological terrorists and a Palestinian nationalist terrorist group.

Background: Cold War Terrorist-Networking Theory

During the Cold War rivalry between the Western allies and the Eastern bloc, many experts in the West concluded that the communist East was responsible for sponsoring an international terrorist network.[13] The premise was that the Soviet Union and its allies were at least an indirect—and often a direct—source of most international terrorism. Under this scenario, state-sponsored terrorism was a significant threat to world security and was arguably a manifestation of an unconventional World War III. It was a global network of state-sponsored revolutionaries whose goal was to destabilize the democratic West and its allies in the developing world (referred to at that time as the **Third World**).

The Western democracies were able to cite evidence to support their claim that global terrorism related back to a Soviet source. One source of evidence was the fact that the Soviets never denied that they supported revolutionary groups. However, they labeled them as freedom fighters waging wars of national liberation rather than as terrorists. Another source of evidence was the truism that the West was the most frequent target of international terrorism; Soviet interests were rarely attacked. Perhaps the most credible evidence was that a number of regimes were clearly implicated in supporting terrorist movements or incidents. Many of these regimes were pro-Soviet in orientation, or at least recipients of Soviet military aid. Thus, when Soviet- or Chinese-manufactured weapons were found in terrorist arms caches, it was clear that these regimes were conduits for Soviet support for radical movements.

Despite these indications, one significant problem with the Soviet-sponsorship scenario was that most of the evidence was circumstantial and inconclusive. For instance, many of the world's terrorist movements and extremist governments were either non-Marxist in orientation or only secondarily Marxist. They were comfortable with accepting assistance from any willing donor, regardless of the donor's ideological orientation. Although some nationalist movements, such as the Palestine Liberation Organization, certainly had Marxist factions that received training and support from the Soviets, and although some governments, such as those of Cuba and Syria, received Soviet military and economic aid, it is questionable how much actual *control* the Soviets had over their clients. And, very significantly, many dissident movements and state sponsors of terrorism—such as the Provisional Irish Republican Army and revolutionary Iran—were completely independent of Soviet operational or ideological control.

Thus, the belief that terrorism was part of a global conflict between democracy and communism (and hence an unconventional World War III) was too simplistic. It did not take into account the multiplicity of ideologies, motivations, movements, or typologies that represented international terrorism. Having said this, there was without question a great deal of state sponsorship of terrorism that emanated at least indirectly from the East. Ideological indoctrination (for example, at Patrice Lumumba People's Friendship University), material support, and terrorist training facilities did provide revolutionary focus for extremists from around the world. Therefore, although there was not a communist-directed terrorist network, and the Soviets were not a "puppet master" for a global terrorist conspiracy, they did actively inflame terrorist behavior.[14]

International Terrorist Environments

Several terrorist environments are theoretically possible at different times and in different regional contexts. These are not, of course, exclusive descriptions of every aspect of international terrorism. They are, however, useful models for framing a generalized interpretation of international terrorism. The following discussion summarizes four environments that range in structure and cohesion from tightly knit single-sourced threats to loosely linked multiple-source threats.[15] The four environments are:

- Monolithic terrorist environments
- Strong multipolar terrorist environments
- Weak multipolar terrorist environments
- Cell-based terrorist environments

Monolithic Terrorist Environment

The emphasis in the **monolithic terrorist environment** model is on state-centered behavior. The old model of a global Soviet-sponsored terrorist threat described a terrorist environment wherein terrorism was a monolithic (singular) threat emanating from a single source. This presupposed that Soviet assistance and Marxist ideology were binding motivations for international terrorism. As a matter of counterterrorism policy, if this had been correct, combating the threat would have been uncomplicated, because in theory the source (i.e., the Soviets) might be induced or co-opted to reduce or end their sponsorship.

Strong Multipolar Terrorist Environment

In the **strong multipolar terrorist environment**, the emphasis is also on state-centered behavior. This model presumes that state sponsorship guides terrorist behavior but that several governments support their favored groups. It also presumes that there are few truly autonomous international terrorist movements; they all have a link to a state sponsor. Unlike the theory of a monolithic Soviet-sponsored threat, this scenario suggests that regional powers use terrorism to support their own agendas and that many proxies exist. To counter this type of environment, the several sources would theoretically each have to be co-opted independently of the others.

Weak Multipolar Terrorist Environment

The model of the **weak multipolar terrorist environment** shifts the emphasis away from the state toward the terrorist movements. Unlike the strong multipolar model, the weak multipolar model presupposes that state sponsorship exists but that the terrorist groups are more autonomous. Under this scenario, several governments support their favored groups, but many of these groups are relatively independent international terrorist movements. The terrorist groups would be content with *any* state sponsor so long as they received enough assistance to continue their revolutionary struggle. Countering this environment is more difficult than countering the monolithic or strong multipolar models, because the dissident movements are more flexible and adaptable. Cutting off one source of assistance would theoretically have little effect other than to cause a temporary disruption in operations.

Cell-Based Terrorist Environment

In the model of the **cell-based terrorist environment,** the emphasis is centered on the terrorist movement. This model presumes that state sponsorship may exist to some extent but that the revolutionary movement is independent of governmental constraints. It is a kind of "free-floating" revolution that maintains its autonomy through its own resources. In this kind of environment, the movement is based on the viability of small cells that are loosely affiliated with each other. Thus, the movement will prevail even when some of its cells are destroyed or otherwise compromised. Because of the fluid character of its organizational structure, this environment is the most difficult to counter.

Table 9.3 summarizes the activity profiles for the foregoing international terrorist environments.

Movement Case: The International Mujahideen

The Afghan Arabs

The series of wars in Afghanistan produced a large cadre of hardened Islamic fighters. The 1979 Soviet invasion and occupation of Afghanistan by conventional forces led to a sustained guerrilla insurgency that eventually forced the Soviet Army to withdraw after losing 15,000 of its men. The war was considered by the insurgents to be a jihad, and they declared themselves to be mujahideen in a holy war against nonbelievers.

Muslims from around the world volunteered to fight alongside or otherwise support the Afghani mujahideen. This created a pan-Islamic consciousness that led to the creation of the Qaeda network and domestic *jihadi* movements as far afield as the Philippines, Malaysia, Central Asia, and Algeria. The Arab volunteers—called **"Afghan Arabs"**— became a legendary fighting force among Muslim activists. It is not known exactly how many Afghan Arabs fought in Afghanistan during the anti-Soviet jihad. However, reasonable estimates have been calculated:

[A former] senior CIA official . . . claims the number is close to 17,000, while the highly respected British publication *Jane's Intelligence Review* suggests a figure of

Table 9.3   Understanding International Terrorist Environments

International terrorism occurs within the context of international social and political environments. These environments are not static and can vary from time to time and region to region.

The following table suggests a model for understanding the features of several international terrorist environments.

| Environment | *Activity Profile* | | | |
	Foremost Participant	*State Control*	*Group Autonomy*	*Difficulty in Countering*
Monolithic	Single state sponsor	Strong and direct	Minimal	Clear options; easiest to counter
Strong multipolar	Several state sponsors	Strong and direct	Minimal	Clear options
Weak multipolar	Dissident groups; several state sponsors	Weak and insecure	Strong	Problematic and unpredictable
Cell-based	Dissident groups	Weak	Strong	Problematic and unpredictable; most difficult to counter

more than 14,000 (including some 5,000 Saudis, 3,000 Yemenis, 2,000 Egyptians, 2,800 Algerians, 400 Tunisians, 370 Iraqis, 200 Libyans, and scores of Jordanians).[16]

After the Soviet phase of the war, many of the Afghan Arabs (and other non-Arab mujahideen) carried on their jihad in other countries, becoming **international mujahideen.** For example, many Algerians returned home to fight on the side of Muslim rebels in the brutal Algerian insurgency during the 1990s. Others fought in Bosnia and gained a reputation for their fervor, fighting skills, and brutality. Many Afghan Arabs traveled to Muslim communities in Asia and Africa, assisting indigenous Muslim groups in their causes. They provided technical assistance and other resources to these groups. For example, Filipino and Indonesian *jihadis* have had frequent interaction with the Qaeda network and Afghan Arabs. Afghan Arabs have also fought in Chechnya, and some Chechens subsequently fought on behalf of the Taliban in Afghanistan.

Mujahideen in Bosnia

The first wars that were fought after the breakup of Yugoslavia were between the Serbs, Croatians, and Bosnian Muslims. When Bosnia declared independence, it precipitated a brutal civil war that at times had all three national groups fighting against each other simultaneously. The war between the Bosnians and Serbs was particularly violent and involved genocidal "ethnic cleansing" that was initiated by the Serbs and imitated later by other national groups. Ethnic cleansing was explored in Chapter 4.

From the beginning, the Bosnian Muslims were severely pressed by their adversaries and were nearly defeated as town after town fell to the Serbs. Overt international arms shipments were prohibited, although some Islamic countries did provide covert support. Into this mix came Muslim volunteers who fought as mujahideen on behalf of the Bosnians. Most were Middle Eastern Afghan Arabs. An estimated 500 to 1,000 mujahideen fought alongside the Bosnians, coming from nearly a dozen countries. Many came from Afghanistan, Algeria, Egypt, Tunisia, and Yemen. Although the international mujahideen were motivated by religious zeal, the Bosnians are traditionally secular Muslims, so that they were motivated by nationalist zeal. [17] This was a cause for some friction, but a handful of Bosnians also took an oath to become mujahideen.

Since the end of the war, mujahideen have maintained a presence in Bosnia, as has Al Qaeda. Some have been active in hatching plots to attack U.S. and Western interests, including one conspiracy to attack Eagle Base, the main facility for 3,000 American peace-keeping troops that were stationed in the country.[18] Evidence suggests that Bosnia and neighboring regions have developed a fairly well-entrenched mujahideen and al Qaeda presence. The following are examples of such evidence:

- After the Bosnian war, at least 200 mujahideen remained in Bosnia, some working for relief agencies or other social services.
- In 1998, Talaat Fouad Qassem, a member of Egypt's Islamic Group, was seized in Croatia and flown to Egypt. He had been traveling to Bosnia from Denmark.[19]
- In October 2001, 10 suspected mujahideen terrorists were arrested in Bosnia; at least five of them were Algerians.[20]
- In January 2002, five Algerians and a Yemeni were seized by U.S. forces in Bosnia and flown to the U.S. detention camp at Guantanamo Bay, Cuba.[21]

Organization Case:
Al Qaeda and International Terrorism

Students may recall from Chapter 8 that Al Qaeda is not an organization, but a loose network of Islamic revolutionaries; it is unique compared with other movements because it

holds no territory,

does not champion the aspirations of an ethno-national group,

has no "top-down" organizational structure,

has virtually nonexistent state sponsorship, and

promulgates political demands that are vague at best.

Al Qaeda is a transnational movement with members and supporters from throughout the Muslim world. It is, at its very core, an international revolutionary movement that uses terrorism as a matter of routine. Al Qaeda has two overarching goals: to link together Muslim extremist groups throughout the world into a loose pan-Islamic revolutionary network and to expel non-Muslim (especially Western) influences from Islamic regions and countries. As discussed in Chapter 8, Osama bin Laden established training camps in Sudan and Afghanistan where an estimated 5,000 men received direct training. Other Al Qaeda operatives are drawn from a pool of new recruits from Muslim and European countries and the "Afghan Arab" veterans who fought in Afghanistan.

International Cells

Operatives who were trained or inspired by Al Qaeda established cells in dozens of countries and regions. For instance, cells and larger groups became resident in the following predominantly Muslim countries and regions: Afghanistan, Algeria, Bosnia, Chechnya, Indonesia, Iraq, Kosovo, Lebanon, Malaysia, Pakistan, the southern Philippines, Somalia, Sudan, the West Bank, and Yemen. Other cells were apparently

Death in Kenya: A Kenyan man is lifted out of the rubble of the American embassy in Nairobi, Kenya. On August 7, 1998, the U.S. Embassy in Nairobi was bombed by an Al Qaeda cell, which coordinated the assault with an attack conducted by another cell against the American embassy in Dar es Salaam, Tanzania.

Source: U.S. Department of State.

covertly positioned in the following Western and non-Muslim countries: Britain; France; Germany; Israel; Spain; United States; and the border region of Argentina, Brazil, and Paraguay.

Members communicate with each other using modern technologies such as tele-facsimiles, the Internet, cell phones, and e-mail. Most Al Qaeda cells are small and self-sustaining and apparently receive funding when activated for specific missions. For example, the bombings of the American embassies in Kenya and Tanzania may have cost $100,000.[22] Not all cells are "**sleeper cells**," defined as groups of terrorists who take up long-term residence in countries prior to attacks. For example, most of the September 11, 2001, hijackers entered the United States for the express purpose of committing terrorist acts; they were never prepositioned as sleepers to be activated at a later date.

Al Qaeda has been rather prolific in its direct and indirect involvement in international terrorism. Its operatives or sympathizers have been implicated in numerous terrorist incidents, including the following plots:

1994: A Filipino airliner was bombed.

1994-1995: Filipino security thwarted an ambitious plot that included bombing airliners and assassinations of President Clinton and Pope John Paul II during state visits.

1995: An assassination attempt was made against Egyptian President Hosni Mubarak during a state visit to Ethiopia.

1995: A car bomb was detonated in Saudi Arabia at a Saudi National Guard facility.

2002: An attempted bombing of a Paris-to-Miami airline flight was thwarted; the plan was to ignite explosives hidden inside a shoe.

The rubble of Khobar Towers. An indication of the destruction in the aftermath of a 1996 terrorist attack against the American military facility in Dharan, Saudi Arabia.

Source: U.S. Department of State.

The group was also implicated in the following attacks against American interests:

1993: Bombing of the World Trade Center in New York City

1998: Bombings of two American embassies in East Africa

2000: Attack on the destroyer **USS *Cole*** in Aden, Yemen

2001: Attacks on the World Trade Center in New York City and the Pentagon in Washington, D.C.

The following cases of international al Qaeda terrorist activity illustrate the scope, skill, and operational design of the network.

The Hijacking of Air France Flight 8969

In December 1994, **Air France Flight 8969** was hijacked in Algeria by an Algerian Islamic extremist movement, the Armed Islamic Group (GIA). The GIA apparently has ties to Al Qaeda, and many members of its movement are Afghan Arab war veterans. After hijackers killed three passengers, the plane was permitted to depart the Algerian air-field and made a refueling stop in Marseilles. Intending to fly to Paris, the hijackers demanded three times the amount of fuel needed to make the journey.[23] The reason for this demand was that they planned to blow up the aircraft over Paris—or possibly crash it into the Eiffel Tower—thus killing themselves and all of the passengers as well as raining flaming debris over the city. French commandos disguised as caterers stormed the plane in Marseilles, thus bringing the incident to an end. The assault was played out live on French television.

The Singapore Plot

During December 2001 and January 2002, security officers in Singapore, Malaysia, and the Philippines arrested more than three dozen terrorist suspects. Thirteen were arrested in Singapore, 22 in Malaysia, and 4 in the Philippines. The sweep apparently foiled a significant plot by Al Qaeda to attack Western interests in Singapore. The arrests were made after Northern Alliance forces in Afghanistan captured a Singaporean of Pakistani descent who was fighting for the Taliban. The prisoner gave details about "plans to bomb U.S. warships, airplanes, military personnel and major U.S. companies in Singapore [as well as] American, Israeli, British and Australian companies and government offices there."[24]

Members of the Singaporean cell had been trained by Al Qaeda in Afghanistan, and Al Qaeda operatives had traveled to Singapore to advise some of the suspects about bomb construction and other operational matters. During their preparations for the strike, the cell had sought to purchase 21 tons of ammonium nitrate—by comparison, Timothy McVeigh's ANFO (ammonium nitrate and fuel oil) truck bomb had used only two tons of ammonium nitrate. The Singaporean cell organized itself as the Islamic Group (Jemaah Islamiah). The Malaysian cell called itself the Kumpulan Militan Malaysia. In an interesting twist, the Malaysian group apparently had indirect ties to the October 2000 bombing of the USS *Cole* in Yemen; the September 11, 2001, attacks; and perhaps to Zacarias Moussaoui, the French Moroccan implicated as the one surviving member of the September 11 cells.[25]

POSTSCRIPT: THE "STATELESS REVOLUTIONARIES"

Some terrorist movements operate exclusively on an international scale and have little or no domestic presence in a home country. There are different reasons for this strategy: Some groups espouse a global ideological agenda that requires them to fight on behalf of a vague concept of "the oppressed" of the world. Other groups operate within an environment that mandates as a matter of practicality that they operate internationally. They strike from operational havens across state borders and often move around from country to country.

These movements are essentially "stateless" in the sense that they either have no particular home country that they seek to liberate; or there is no homeland to use as a base; or their group has been uprooted from the land that they are fighting for. Among these stateless extremist movements are secular ideological revolutionaries, sectarian radicals fighting on behalf of a faith, and representatives of stateless ethno-national groups. Examples of **stateless revolutionaries** include the following familiar cases:

The Japanese Red Army. The JRA represents an example of a *secular* stateless revolutionary movement. Although the JRA claimed that one of its core goals was to overthrow the Japanese monarchy and end Japanese capitalism, its activity profile suggests that they had a more global outlook. They considered themselves to be international revolutionaries fighting on behalf of the oppressed of the world against international capitalism, imperialism, and Zionism. Operationally, they acted in coordination with other terrorist groups and extremist movements to promote their global revolutionary agenda.

Al Qaeda. The Qaeda network is an example of a *sectarian* stateless revolutionary movement. Pan-Islamist ideologies began to transcend limitations imposed by national

Case in Point   **Cooperation Between Terrorists:**
                 An Overview of the European Connection

Terrorists have cooperated with each other for a variety of reasons. Some considered their revolutionary struggle to be part of a global war against a particular nation, interest, or ideology. For example, France's Direct Action directed its violence against American interests and "in solidarity" with the Palestinian cause. Many other groups likewise cooperated with each other as a matter of revolutionary solidarity. Some, like the Japanese Red Army, allowed themselves to be "retained" by groups such as the PFLP. Others, such as the Red Army Faction or the June 2nd Movement, regularly collaborated on missions with other movements.

The PFLP established strong links with European terrorist groups. Beginning in the late 1960s, the PFLP provided secure training and networking facilities in Jordan. Its working relationships with Germany's Red Army Faction and the June 2nd Movement were very strong, and members of these groups were welcomed and trained in the PFLP's camps, as were members from Spain's Basque Fatherland and Liberty. The PFLP served as a mentor for Ilich Ramirez Sanchez, also known as Carlos the Jackal, who cooperated extensively with a variety of terrorist groups.

The December 1975 kidnapping in Vienna of the ministers of OPEC was a dramatic example of cooperation. Led by Venezuelan terrorist Carlos, German and Palestinian terrorists carried out a well-planned and coordinated assault and then escaped safely.

From 1985 to 1987, European terrorists attempted to create an "anti-imperialist" umbrella group in Europe similar to the Palestine Liberation Organization. They hoped to replicate the PLO's success by targeting NATO and European capitalism. The RAF, Direct Action, Italy's Red Brigades, and Belgium's Communist Combat Cells joined forces for approximately two years in a temporary united front of European terrorist groups. However, arrests and political changes in Europe kept the new movement from producing anything like a PLO-style environment.

In the aftermath of the decline and dissolution of the leftist terrorist environment, a new cell-based network of cooperation emerged. The new model was inspired by Al Qaeda, which became the most extensive—albeit loosely structured—international network to date.

---

boundaries in the 1980s and 1990s. This new revolutionary consciousness was a direct result of the Iranian Revolution and the jihad against the Soviet Union in Afghanistan. The Qaeda network epitomizes the emerging profile of a transnational revolutionary consciousness among Islamic radicals.

Palestinian Nationalism. The Palestinian cause prior to the establishment of the governing authority in Gaza and on the West Bank exemplified a stateless ethno-national revolutionary movement. Until their strategy for revolution shifted to an internal *intifadeh* (uprising) inside the old borders of Palestine, Palestinian nationalists were forced to operate from bases in third countries. These countries included Jordan, Lebanon, Tunisia, Syria, and Iraq. Acts of terrorism usually occurred in the international arena, originating from the safe havens provided by these sympathetic governments. The movement was essentially stateless until the Palestinian Authority was established, which allowed relatively steady internal operations to be conducted against Israel.

Table 9.4 summarizes the activity profiles of secular, sectarian, and ethno-national "stateless revolutions."

Table 9.4   The Stateless Revolutionaries

Some movements operate almost exclusively in the international arena. The reasons for this include ideologies of transnational revolution, global spiritual visions, or simple practicality brought on by their political environment.

The following table describes the activity profiles of three such radical movements.

Political Orientation	*Activity Profile*				
	Group	*Constituency*	*Adversary*	*Benefactor*	*Goal*
Secular	Japanese Red Army	Oppressed of the world	Capitalism, imperialism, Zionism	Unclear; probably PFLP, maybe Libya	International revolution
Sectarian	Al Qaeda	Muslims of the world	Foes of Islam	Self-supporting; maybe radical states	International Islamic revolution
Ethno-nationalist	Palestinian nationalists	Palestinians	Israel	Government sponsors	Palestinian nation

CHAPTER SUMMARY

This chapter provided students with a critical assessment of international terrorism. International terrorism was defined from the point of view of the motives of the perpetrators and the symbolism of their selected target; terrorists who choose to operate on an international scale select targets that symbolize an international interest. In order to further define international terrorism, students were reintroduced to the terrorist typologies discussed in previous chapters. These typologies were evaluated from the perspective of the international venue.

Within the framework of the reasons that were identified for international terrorism—ideological, practical, tactical, and historical reasons—students were asked to apply adaptations of revolutionary theory to international operations. Recalling previous discussions about Mao's doctrine for waging guerrilla warfare as "fish swimming in the sea of the people" and Marighella's strategy for destabilizing established governments, it is no surprise that modern terrorists would carry variations of these themes onto the international stage.

International terrorist networks have been a facet of international terrorism since the 1960s. The models presented in this chapter are useful for understanding the networking features of terrorist environments and typologies. The cases of Al Qaeda and the international mujahideen illustrate the nature of modern terrorist networks.

In Chapter 10, students will be introduced to the tactics and targets of terrorists. The discussion will center on terrorist objectives, methods, and targets. The discussion will also ask whether, and to what extent, terrorism is effective.

KEY TERMS AND CONCEPTS

The following topics were discussed in this chapter and are found in the Glossary:

Afghan Arabs
Air France Flight 8969
Ansar Allah
Armenian Revolutionary Army
Armenian Secret Army for the Liberation of
    Armenia (ASALA)
Asymmetrical warfare
Cell-based terrorist environment
DINA
Imperialism
International Mujahideen
Islamic Jihad
Japanese Red Army
Justice Commandos of the Armenian Genocide

Monolithic terrorist environment
Multinational corporations
Neocolonialism
Omega 7
Organization of the Oppressed
Revolutionary Justice Organization
Sleeper cells
Spillover effect
Stateless revolutionaries
Strong multipolar terrorist environment
Third World
USS *Cole*
Weak Multipolar Terrorist Environment
Zionism

RECOMMENDED WEB SITES

The following Web sites provide links to organizations that report research on or discuss international terrorism.

Global Development Center: www.globaldisaster.org

International Policy Institute for Counter-Terrorism: www.ict.org.il

Naval Postgraduate School: web.nps.navy.mil/~library/terrorism.htm

South Asia Terrorism Portal: www.satp.org

Terrorism Research Center: www.terrorism.com/index.shtml

WEB EXERCISE

Using this chapter's recommended Internet sites, conduct an online investigation of international terrorism.

- From your review of these Web sites, how significant do you think the threat is from international terrorist groups?
- Which groups do you think pose a serious threat of international terrorism? Which groups do you think present less serious threats?
- Critique the Web sites of the international monitoring organizations. Are some more helpful than others?

For an online search of international terrorism, students should activate the search engine on their Web browser and enter the following keywords:

"International Terrorism (or International Terrorists)"
"Global Terrorism"

Discussion Box	**Understanding Terrorist "Spillovers": The Case of Middle Eastern/ North African Spillovers in Europe**

This chapter's Discussion Box is intended to stimulate critical debate about whether spillover incidents are a legitimate expression of grievances.

Terrorist spillovers have occurred regularly since the 1960s. The most common sources of spillovers since that time have been from the Middle East and North Africa, and the most frequent venue for these spillovers has been Western Europe. For example, during the 1980s hundreds of Middle Eastern and North African terrorist incidents occurred in more than a dozen countries, causing hundreds of deaths and hundreds of people wounded. Outside of the Middle East and North Africa, Europe is the favored theater of operations.

There are several types of Middle Eastern and North African spillovers in Europe: Some result from the foreign policies of governments; others are PLO-affiliated groups; and others are attacks by Islamic revolutionaries.

The motives behind these incidents have included:

- The silencing or intimidating of exiles
- Attempts to influence European policies
- Retaliation against a person or state
- "Solidarity" attacks by indigenous European groups

Europe has been an attractive target for many reasons, including:

- The presence of large Middle Eastern and North African communities
- Many "soft" targets
- Immediate publicity
- Open borders and good transportation
- Proximity to the Middle East and North Africa

These attacks have been widespread geographically, and many have been indiscriminate.

Discussion Questions

- Is the international arena a legitimate venue for the expression of grievances?
- Is Europe an appropriate venue for conflicts originating in the Middle East or North Africa?
- Are some grievances more legitimate, or more acceptable, for spillovers?
- What is the likely future of spillover attacks in Europe?
- Since Europe has historically been perceived to be an easy battlefield with soft targets, should the European Union "harden" itself?

RECOMMENDED READINGS

The following publications provide discussions about the nature of international terrorism and cases in point about international terrorists.

Follain, John. *Jackal: The Complete Story of the Legendary Terrorist, Carlos the Jackal.* New York: Arcade, 1998.

Herman, Edward S. *The Real Terror Network: Terrorism in Fact and Propaganda.* Boston: South End Press, 1982.

Kegley, Charles W., Jr., ed. *International Terrorism: Characteristics, Causes, Controls.* New York: St. Martin's Press, 1990.

Pillar, Paul R. *Terrorism and U.S. Foreign Policy.* Washington, DC: Brookings Institution Press, 2001.

Reeve, Simon. *The New Jackals: Ramzi Yousef, Osama bin Laden and the Future of Terrorism.* Boston: Northeastern University Press, 1999.

NOTES

[1] Kegley, Charles W., Jr. "The Characteristics, Causes and Controls of International Terrorism: An Introduction." In Kegley, Charles W., ed., *International Terrorism: Characteristics, Causes, Controls.* New York: St. Martin's Press, 1990, p. 3.

[2] Khaled, Leila. *My People Shall Live: The Autobiography of a Revolutionary.* London: Hodder & Stoughton, 1973, p. 209. Quoted in Hoffman, Bruce. *Inside Terrorism.* New York: Columbia University Press, 1998, p. 169.

[3] The Doctors of the World Web site may be accessed at www.doctorsoftheworld.org.

[4] Associated Press. "Ashcroft Says Terrorist Cell Based in Germany Included Hijackers." *New York Times.* October 23, 2001.

[5] Dillon, Sam. "Indictment by Spanish Judge Portrays a Secret Terror Cell." *New York Times.* November 20, 2001.

[6] Finn, Peter. "Macedonian Police Kill 7 in Suspected Terror Cell." *Washington Post.* March 3, 2002.

[7] Barkan, Steven E., and Lynne L. Snowden. *Collective Violence.* Boston: Allyn & Bacon, 2001, p. 75.

[8] Ibid., pp. 75-76.

[9] Kegley (note 1 above) p. 21.

[10] At that time made up of the Western democracies, excluding France.

[11] North Atlantic Assembly Papers, Sub-Committee on Terrorism. *Terrorism.* Brussels: International Secretariat, January 1989, p. 34. Quoted in Hoffman, Bruce. *Inside Terrorism.* New York: Columbia University Press, 1998, p. 32.

[12] Sofaer, Abraham D. "Terrorism and the Law." *Foreign Affairs* 64 (Summer 1986): 904. Quoted in Hoffman, ibid.

[13] See Sterling, Claire. *The Terror Network: The Secret War of International Terrorism.* New York: Holt, Rinehart & Winston, 1981. See also Cline, Ray S., and Yonah Alexander. *Terrorism: The Soviet Connection.* New York: Crane Russak, 1984.

[14] For an argument that the Soviet-sponsorship theory was simply a new Red Scare, see Herman, Edward S. *The Real Terror Network: Terrorism in Fact and Propaganda.* Boston: South End Press, 1982.

[15] See Sederberg, Peter C. *Terrorist Myths: Illusion, Rhetoric, and Reality.* Englewood Cliffs, NJ: Prentice Hall, 1989, p. 117 ff.

[16] Reeve, Simon. *The New Jackals: Ramzi Yousef, Osama bin Laden and the Future of Terrorism.* Boston: Northeastern University Press, 1999, p. 3.

[17] Bruce, James. "Arab Veterans of the Afghan War." *Jane's Intelligence Review* 7 (April 1, 1995): p. 175 ff.

[18] Purvis, Andrew. "The Suspects: A Bosnian Subplot." *Time.* November 12, 2001.

[19] Chandrasekaran, Rajiv, and Peter Finn. "U.S. Behind Secret Transfer of Terror Suspects." *Washington Post.* March 11, 2002.

[20] Ibid.

[21] Ibid.

[22] McNeil, Donald G. "What Will Rise if bin Laden Falls?" *New York Times.* December 2, 2001.

[23] MSNBC. "The Lesson of Air France Flight 8969." MSNBC.com: www.msnbc.com/news/635213.asp?cp1=1 (date accessed: September 30, 2001).

[24] From Paddock, Richard C., and Bob Drogin. "A Terror Network Unraveled in Singapore." *Los Angeles Times.* January 20, 2002. Quoted with permission.

[25] Ibid.

Part III

THE TERRORIST TRADE

A dramatized depiction of a 19th-century "scientific anarchist" constructing a bomb in his apartment.

Source: Hulton Archive/Getty Images; used by permission.

Chapter 10

TOOLS OF THE TRADE: TACTICS AND TARGETS OF TERRORISTS

This chapter investigates terrorist objectives, methods, and targets. It focuses on the rationale behind the calculation of terrorists' ends and means—*what* terrorists are trying to do and *how* they try to do it. Weaponry is, of course, an integral factor in the evaluation of ends and means, so attention will also be given to the terrorists' arsenal.

Terrorism—however defined—is usually officially condemned, even by movements and governments that most of the global community would consider to be terrorists (they, of course, consider themselves to be freedom fighters or the champions of freedom fighters). This is because much of the discussion about the objectives and methods of politically violent movements is a *moralistic debate*, centering on whether one can legitimately select certain methods as an expression of dissent. When terrorists adopt methods that will inevitably cause the deaths of defined enemies—including innocent civilians—a process of "moral disengagement" occurs that allows them to justify their actions.[1] Thus,

> The conversion of socialized people into dedicated combatants is not achieved by altering their personality structures, aggressive drives, or moral standards. Rather, it is accomplished by cognitively restructuring the moral value of killing.[2]

Previous chapters have stressed the importance of *perspective* in the debate about the morality of extremists' tactics and targets. Students may remember from Chapter 3 the important role of codes of self-sacrifice, which essentially "cleanse" those who follow the code, regardless of the scale of the violence committed in support of the cause. Recall also how *dramatic events* in the unique histories of ethno-national and religious groups can lead them to adopt terrorist methods. And remember our discussion in Chapter 1 of the following concepts:

- "It became necessary to destroy the town to save it."[3]
- "Extremism in defense of liberty is no vice."[4]
- "One person's terrorist is another person's freedom fighter."
- "One man willing to throw away his life is enough to terrorize a thousand."[5]

Ironically, many people sympathize with the goals and objectives of extremist movements but oppose the means they use to accomplish those ends. The problem for some sympathizers is the seeming senselessness of certain types of violence. To most onlookers, many methods appear to be senseless and random; however, from the perspective of terrorists, these methods are neither senseless nor random. Two commonalities must be remembered about terrorist violence from the perspective of terrorists:

Terrorist violence is not senseless. It is usually well thought-out and not an exercise in irrationality. Within the context of their circumstances, extremists conclude that terrorist methods make perfect sense. Regardless of the ultimate scale of violence applied or the number of civilian casualties, these are considered to be logical and sensible consequences of waging a just war.

Terrorist violence is not random. Targets are specifically selected and represent the outcome of careful deliberation. An element of randomness occurs when "targets of opportunity" are attacked without a period of careful preplanning.

Extremist movements justify the selection of terrorist methods in different ways. Among extremists, there is an almost universal acceptance that terrorist violence is a kind of "poor man's warfare" used by the weak against stronger opponents. According to this rationale, terrorism is a weapon used by the downtrodden poor against brutally intransigent regimes. There is also a rationale that politically violent groups have no recourse other than to engage in terrorism, because their opponents are unreceptive (perhaps violently so) to peaceful or democratic methods of dissent. As a matter of practicality, terrorist methods are adopted by extremists for several reasons:

- Terror tactics are relatively easy to employ and therefore commend themselves to an organization that may lack sophisticated weapons or popular support.
- Terrorism produces a disproportionate amount of publicity, a commodity highly prized by a separatist movement of political faction that may feel it has no other way of seizing the world's attention.
- Spectacular atrocities illustrate that the government's ability to rule is weakened and provoke exasperated security forces into overreaction.[6]

Based on these types of justifications and practical considerations, terrorists have selected methods and targets from a menu of options that are derived from their interpretation of their environment. Many terrorists in the past were known to be quite discriminating in their selection of methods and targets. Conversely, practitioners of the New Terrorism are apt to wield any available weapon against broadly defined enemy interests.

The discussion in this chapter will review:

- Terrorist Objectives
- Terrorist Methods
- Terrorist Targets
- The Outcome—Is Terrorism Effective?

TERRORIST OBJECTIVES

Objectives and goals are theoretical concepts that help explain the actions taken by extremist groups and movements during the course of their struggle; they are descriptions of processes that move toward final outcomes. An *objective* is an incremental step in the overall process that leads to an ultimate goal. A *goal* is the final result of the process, the terminal point of a series of objectives. Thus, a desired objective in a revolutionary campaign could be the overthrow of an enemy government or social order; the goal could be the establishment of a new society. During a revolutionary campaign, many objectives would have to be achieved to reach the final goal.

Typical Objectives

Similarities in objectives can be identified among politically violent groups and movements. These objectives tend to fall somewhere within the range of minimal and optimal desirability: "For most terrorists, the *minimal* objective is increased public recognition that they are a political actor to contend with. The *optimal* objective is movement toward achieving their communal, revolutionary, or other political objective"[7] (italics added).

The following discussion identifies a few commonalities in objectives. The selected list is by no means common to all violent extremists at all phases of their campaigns, and this is not an exhaustive analysis of every objective.[8] However, it is instructive to review a few central objectives.[9] These common objectives are the following:

- Changing the existing order
- Psychological disruption
- Social disruption
- Publicizing the cause
- Creating a revolutionary environment

Changing the Existing Order

At some level, all terrorists seek to change an existing order, even if it is simply a short-term objective to disrupt the normal routines of society by inflicting maximum casualties. When evaluating what it means to "change" an existing order, one must take into consideration the different profiles of terrorist movements, their motives, and the idiosyncrasies of individual terrorists. For example:

- *Ethno-nationalist* terrorists seek to win recognition of their human rights, or a degree of national autonomy, from the present order.
- *Nihilists* wish to destroy systems and institutions without regard for what will replace the existing order.
- *Religious* terrorists act on behalf of a supernatural mandate to bring about a divinely inspired new order.
- *"Lone wolves"* have a vague and sometimes delusional assumption that their actions will further a greater cause against a corrupt or evil social order.

Psychological Disruption

An obvious objective is to inflict maximum psychological damage by applying dramatic violence against symbolic targets. "From the terrorists' perspective, the major force of terrorism comes not from its physical impact but from its psychological impact."[10] When terrorist violence is applied discerningly, the weak can influence the powerful, and the powerful can intimidate the weak. Cultural symbols, political institutions, and public leaders are examples of iconic (nearly sacred) targets that can affect large populations when attacked.

Although it is seemingly simplistic to state that terrorists strike these targets to "spread terror," this is not an inaccurate characterization of the trauma that follows from a particularly dramatic terrorist incident. For example, many New Yorkers exhibited strong manifestations of stress and anxiety long after the September 11, 2001, attacks.[11]

Social Disruption

Social disruption is an objective of propaganda by the deed. The ability of terrorists and extremists to disrupt the normal routines of society demonstrates both the weakness of the government and the strength of the movement; it provides terrorists with potentially very effective propaganda. When governments fail to protect the normal routines of society, discontent may spread throughout society, thus making the population susceptible to manipulation by a self-styled vanguard movement (discussed in Chapter 6). For example, social disruption could be accomplished—and government weakness could be demonstrated—by bombing attacks on public transportation systems. These kinds of attacks have occurred many times in Israel, including a Jerusalem attack in February 1996 when Hamas bombed a bus, killing 22 Israelis. In another scenario, a targeted group could be attacked specifically to deter them from traveling through a region or territory; this group could be an ethno-national group or simply an economic group, such as the customers of a tourism industry.

Publicizing the Cause

As discussed in previous chapters, terrorists practice propaganda by the deed as a way to achieve exposure for their cause. When successfully manipulated, specific populations, governments, or other interests will focus on the extremists and their grievances. In the modern era, this means that a great deal of terrorist violence is **media-oriented terrorism**. Live broadcasting of violent incidents and their aftermath is de rigueur for media networks that wish to remain competitive in the global audience market. Television can bring terrorism, warfare, or other violence into hundreds of millions of households within seconds. Thus, with proper planning, terrorists can succeed not only in publicizing their cause but also in causing significant psychological disruption. In this way, the cause receives maximum exposure, and the target audience becomes victimized. All that is required is to attack a symbol that moves the targeted audience. The role of the media will be explored further in Chapter 11.

Creating a Revolutionary Environment

Dissident extremists understand that they cannot hope to win in their struggle against the state without raising the "revolutionary consciousness" of the people. Theoretically, this objective can be achieved through the cumulative effect of the objectives just discussed. For many terrorists, propaganda by the deed is considered to be the most direct method for creating a broad-based revolutionary environment, so that "the destruction of one troop transport truck is more effective propaganda for the local population than a thousand speeches."[12] As discussed in previous chapters, revolutionary theorists predicted that terrorism would force the state to overreact, the people would understand the true repressive nature of the state, and a mass rebellion would occur—led by the revolutionary vanguard movement.

Playing to the Audience:
Objectives, Victims, and Constituencies

Terrorists adapt their methods and selection of targets to the characteristics of their championed group and the idiosyncrasies of their environment. Targets are selected for specific symbolic reasons, with the objectives of victimizing specific groups or interests and sending symbolic messages to the terrorists' constituency. In a sense, the targeted groups or interests serve as conduits to communicate the extremist movement's message. Thus,

The act of victimizing captures the attention of particular audiences and allows the terrorist to communicate more specific messages tailored to each one. . . . The use of threat and violence against victims—the kidnappings, the bombings, the assassinations, the killings—serves to transmit specific demands to certain targets and different messages to other targets.[13]

If skillfully applied, propaganda by the deed can be manipulated to affect specific audiences. These audiences can include the following segments of society:[14]

Politically Apathetic People. The objective of terrorist violence directed toward this group is to force an end to their indifference and, ideally, to motivate them to petition the government for fundamental changes.

The Government and Its Allied Elites. Terrorists seek to seriously intimidate or distract a nation's ruling bodies to force them to deal favorably with the underlying grievances of the dissident movement.

Potential Supporters. An important objective of propaganda by the deed is to create a revolutionary consciousness in a large segment of society. This is more easily done within the pool of those who are sympathetic to the extremists' objectives but who do not yet approve of their methods.

Confirmed Supporters. Terrorists seek to assure their members and confirmed supporters that the movement continues to be strong and active. They communicate this through acts of symbolic violence.

Depending on whom they claim to champion, extremist movements adapt their tactics to their environment as a way to communicate with (and attract) their defined constituency. Consider, for example, the perspective from three familiar typologies:

Ethno-nationalist terrorists have tended to be focused and surgical, with the important exception of extreme examples of communal violence. Their objectives are to win improved conditions or autonomy for their championed group. Even when the scale of violence has escalated to the point of near civil war, the enemy group has usually been clearly (if broadly) defined, and the targeted symbols have been interpreted as representations of the enemy group. Attacks against rival ethno-national groups certainly cause civilian casualties, but these civilians have been defined as legitimate targets because of their ethno-national affiliation. Thus, aside from extreme communal terrorist environments,

> These terrorist movements . . . see themselves as a revolutionary vanguard—if not in classic Marxist-Leninist terms, at least as a spearhead, similarly using violence to "educate" fellow members of their national or ethnic group about the inequities imposed upon them by the ruling government and the need for communal resistance and rebellion.[15]

Left-wing terrorists historically tended to be focused and relatively surgical in their objectives and methods. Their overriding objective has been to use propaganda by the deed to create a revolutionary consciousness in their championed group and thereby to attract the championed group to the cause. Leftists have traditionally been careful about attacking clearly symbolic targets such as buildings, offices, interests, and officials. Based on their interpretation of the existing social and political environment, "the overriding tactical—and indeed ethical—imperative for left-wing terrorists has been the deliberate tailoring of their violent acts to appeal to their perceived 'constituencies.'"[16]

Right-wing terrorists have been much less likely to be either focused or surgical in their political objectives. This is perhaps because their objectives are often quite vague, and

Table 10.1   Constituencies and Enemies: Selecting Tactics and Targets

Terrorists select their methods within the context of their social and political environments. They appeal to specific constituencies and justify their choice of methods by championing the political cause of their constituencies. Their targeted interests (that is, enemy interests) can be defined narrowly or broadly, so that civilian populations can be included as legitimized targets.

The following table summarizes the constituencies, objectives, methods, and targeted interests of several terrorist groups and movements.

Group or Movement	*Activity Profile*			
	Constituency	*Objectives*	*Methods*	*Targeted Interest*
Al Aqsa Martyr Brigades	Palestinians	Palestinian state	Suicide bombings; small-arms attacks	Israeli civilians; Israeli military
Al Qaeda	Muslims	Worldwide Islamic revolution	Well-planned bombings; indigenous insurrections	The West; secular Islamic governments
Provos	Irish Catholics	Union with the Irish Republic	Small-arms attacks; bombings	British; Ulster Protestants
Bosnian Serb Militias	Bosnian Serbs	Serb state	Ethnic cleansing; communal terrorism	Bosnian Muslims; Bosnian Croats
Tamil Tigers	Sri Lankan Tamils	Tamil state	Terrorist attacks; guerrilla warfare	Sri Lankan government; Sinhalese

their constituencies are not clearly defined. As discussed in Chapter 7, right-wing ideology is very idiosyncratic to specific national political environments, and rarely is there a global philosophy that seeks to bind together the violent right. Within the context of terrorist objectives, right-wing terrorist violence has been described as nothing more than

> an egocentric pleasure derived from brawling and bombing, preening or parading in 1940s-era Nazi regalia . . . given that the majority of right-wing groups do not espouse any specific programme of reform, preferring to hide behind vague slogans of strident nationalism, the need for racial purity and the re-assertion of governmental strength.[17]

Thus, with a few exceptions, appeals to specific constituencies are commonly made by terrorists and extremists. These appeals are peculiar to the environment and idiosyncrasies of the movement, although leftists and ethno-nationalists have sometimes championed the same groups out of a sense of revolutionary solidarity. Table 10.1 illustrates the relationship between several extremist groups and their constituencies, objectives, methods, and targeted interests.

Ethnic cleansing. A mother and child lie dead after a "cleansing" sweep by paramilitaries in Bosnia.

Source: U.S. Department of State.

The New Terrorism and New Objectives

Students may recall from Chapter 2 that the New Terrorism is different from previous models because it is characterized by vaguely articulated political objectives, indiscriminate attacks, attempts to achieve maximum psychological and social disruption, and the potential use of weapons of mass destruction. There is also an emphasis on building "horizontally" organized, semi-autonomous cell-based networks.

*Weapons of Mass Destruction and
the Objectives of the New Terrorism*

Terrorist violence is, at its core, symbolic in nature. With notable exceptions, methods and targets have tended to be focused and relatively surgical, and they have been modified to accommodate the terrorists' definitions of who should be labeled as a championed group or as an enemy. However, within the context of the redefined morality of the New Terrorism, the potential now exists for methods to include high-yield weapons and for targets to include large populations. Symbolic targets and enemy populations can now be hit much harder than in the past; all that is required is the will to do so.

Why would terrorists deliberately use high-yield weapons? What objectives would they seek? Depending on the group, many reasons have been suggested, including the following general objectives:[18]

- *Attracting Attention.* No one can ignore movements that carry out truly devastating attacks. This is the ultimate manifestation of armed propaganda and propaganda by the deed.
- *Pleasing God.* Divinely inspired terrorists seek to carry out what they believe to be a mandate from God. For example, Christian terrorists believing in the inevitability

of the apocalypse might wish to hasten its arrival by using a weapon of mass destruction.

- *Damaging Economies.* This could be accomplished by the destruction of food or other consumer products. A few poisoning events or other acts of consumer-focused sabotage could damage an economic sector.
- *Influencing Enemies.* Terrorists may be moved to wield exotic weapons as a way to influence a large population. After using these weapons, their demands and grievances would receive serious scrutiny.

In the era of the New Terrorism, terrorists may strike with the central objective of killing as many people as possible. They are not necessarily interested in overthrowing governments or changing policies as their primary objectives. Rather, their intent is simply to deliver a high body count and thereby terrorize and disrupt large audiences. For example, the two attacks on the World Trade Center in New York City, the **sarin nerve gas** attack in Tokyo, and the bombing in Oklahoma City were all intended to kill as many civilians as possible and to demonstrate the vulnerability of society. There was little if any consideration given to changing government policies.

The following examples are cases in point of attempted and actual acquisitions of **chemical agents** by extremists. They demonstrate how the underlying characteristic of groups willing to use these weapons is that their objectives (often very vague) permit indiscriminate targeting. These groups also exhibit a minimal intention to pursue concrete political objectives.

The Covenant, the Sword, and the Arm of the Lord. **The Covenant, the Sword, and the Arm of the Lord (CSA)** was an apocalyptic religious and racial supremacist survivalist community in the Ozark Mountains of Arkansas. The group was effectively disbanded in 1985 after prosecutions by federal authorities for, among other charges, possessing a large quantity of poisonous **potassium cyanide**. CSA had intended to use the toxin to poison water supplies in U.S. cities.[19] Their objective was to fulfill their apocalyptic vision of hastening the end of time and the coming of a new racial and religious age. It is an important example of the threat from committed fringe communities (a number of which exist in the United States) and how such communities can easily acquire chemical agents if motivated to do so.

Ramzi Yousef. Students may recall that Yousef masterminded the first World Trade Center attack in February 1993. Some authorities claimed that he had incorporated toxic **sodium cyanide** into the bomb, intending to create a toxic chemical cloud.[20] This is unlikely,[21] but Yousef apparently did attempt to procure chemical agents prior to the attack but was unable to do so. Yousef's case confirms that some activists in the new international terrorist environment have no compunction about using chemical agents (if available) to inflict as high a death toll as possible. This kind of objective is purely terroristic in character.

Aum Shinrikyō. As discussed in Chapter 8, the Aum Supreme Truth cult released sarin nerve gas into the Tokyo subway system in March 1995, killing 12 and injuring thousands. The Aum example is significant because it provides several important lessons: First, the attack was easily planned; second, the attack was easily carried out; third, the chemical agent was easily manufactured; fourth, the potential death toll from this kind of attack is massive; and fifth, the emergency medical systems of major cities may be unable to respond effectively to this kind of attack.

TERRORIST METHODS

The terrorist environment in the new millennium is shaped by advances in technology, information, and transnational interconnectivity. This new environment has given rise to new possibilities in terrorist methodology. Two factors in particular are believed by experts to contribute significantly to the distinctiveness of the New Terrorism. The first is "the diffusion of information technology and advanced communications":

> The concern about chemical, biological, radiological, or nuclear . . . terrorism is based partly on the increased ease of finding pertinent information on [the] Internet. The principal impact of the new electronic technologies, however, has not been to move the terrorists toward more exotic methods of attack, but rather . . . to improve the efficiency of all of their activities. . . . Computers and satellite phones have become standard equipment in terrorist groups.[22]

A second distinctive factor of the New Terrorism is the "increased movement, and ease of movement, across international boundaries":

> The terrorists' greater ability to operate over long distances has manifested itself [in] . . . the building by several terrorist groups of globe-circling infrastructures [and] . . . the rise of ad hoc terrorists—small cabals of extremists who do not belong to any larger, established, previously known group.[23]

The following discussion reviews common methods used by terrorists to achieve their objectives, including their selection of weapons.

Concept: Asymmetrical Warfare

The concept of **asymmetrical warfare** has been adapted to the characteristics of contemporary political violence.[24] Students may recall from Chapter 9 that modern asymmetrical warfare refers to the use of unconventional, unexpected, and nearly unpredictable methods of political violence. Terrorists intentionally strike at unanticipated targets and apply unique and idiosyncratic tactics. In this way, they can seize the initiative and redefine the international security environment. Traditional protections and deterrent policies used by societies and the international community can be surmounted by dedicated terrorists using asymmetrical tactics.

The Appeal of Asymmetrical Conflict

Asymmetrical warfare as a method of confrontation arose "from the perception that the United States, and the West (including Israel) more generally, have developed an unassailable capacity for conventional warfare."[25] Because of this reality, state-level rivals must resort to unconventional and subversive methods to confront U.S. and Western interests. At the same time, dissidents must adopt unorthodox methods that can deliver maximum propaganda and symbolic blows against the seemingly overwhelming power of enemy states or societies. Hence, the New Terrorism is characterized by the threat of asymmetrical warfare, which allows for the use of weapons of mass destruction, indiscriminate attacks, maximum casualties, technology-based terrorism, and other exotic and extreme methods.

This methodology is particularly appealing to antistate movements. Dissident terrorists are quantitatively and qualitatively weaker than conventional security forces. In the modern security environment, they simply cannot prevail in a conventional confrontation or last indefinitely in an urban-based guerrilla campaign. Modern terrorists who understand this are more willing than before to deploy unconventional weapons and use highly destructive tactics. Through the adoption of asymmetrical methods, "the weaker forces are seeking total war, encompassing all segments of society."[26] These weaker forces seek to break the enemy's will to resist through whatever means are at their disposal.

Netwar: A New Organizational Theory

The New Terrorism incorporates maximum flexibility into its organizational and communications design. Semi-autonomous cells are either prepositioned around the globe, or they travel to locations where an attack is to occur. They communicate using new cyber and digital technologies. An important concept in the new terrorist environment is the notion of *netwar*, which refers to

an emerging mode of conflict and crime . . . in which the protagonists use network forms of organization and related doctrines, strategies, and technologies attuned to the information age. These protagonists are likely to consist of dispersed small groups who communicate, coordinate, and conduct their campaigns in an internetted manner, without a precise central command.[27]

The new "internetted" movements are modern adaptations of the following organizational models:[28]

Chain Networks. People, goods, or information move along a line of separated contacts, and end-to-end communication must travel through the intermediate nodes.

Star, Hub, or Wheel Networks. A set of actors is tied to a central node or actor and must go through that node to communicate and coordinate.

All-Channel Networks. There is a collaborative network of small militant groups, and every group is connected to every other group.

Case: The "Martyr Nation" as an Asymmetrical Strategy

An example of the application of asymmetrical warfare is found in the conflict between the Palestinians and Israelis during 2001-2002. The doctrine of engagement used by Palestinian nationalists called for incessant confrontation with the Israelis, using guerrilla, terrorist, and suicidal "martyrdom" tactics to strike unexpectedly at soft civilian targets. As one Palestinian leader said, "Our ability to die is greater than the Israelis' ability to go on killing us." Nationalists contended that "Israel is confronting a martyr 'nation,' not just individual fanatics or militant groups."[29] Thus, the Maoist concept of *people's war* arguably has had an asymmetrical application in the "martyrdom" tactics used by Palestinian extremists, because it suggests that an entire people is willing to sacrifice a great deal to achieve its goals. This concept of a **martyr nation** as a doctrine for engagement is an example of modern asymmetrical warfare.

An Introduction to Common Methods of Terrorists

Methods adopted by modern terrorists reflect the idiosyncrasies of their political environments, so that no single factor explains the adoption of specific tactics by different groups. For example, some methods can become routine among a number of groups but are then rarely employed by other groups. Nevertheless, some commonalities do exist, and a number of tactics and weapons are recurrently encountered:

- *Bombings* are a very common terrorist method, because they allow the extremist movement to inflict maximum physical and psychological damage with minimum casualties.
- *Side arms* (pistols and rifles) are likewise commonly employed to ambush, assassinate, or otherwise inflict casualties on an enemy.
- *Kidnappings* are conducted for different reasons; they are done sometimes to extort ransoms and at other times for purely propaganda purposes. In the latter scenario, the hostages are sometimes executed.
- *Hijackings* of airliners, seagoing vessels, trains, and other modes of transportation are generally conducted for maximum propaganda effect. This is because they generally have an international profile and are conducted in conjunction with seizing hostages.

Methods have occasionally become "signatures" of terrorist movements. These are methods that become closely affiliated with the operational activities of specific extremist groups. An example of a **signature method** is a technique used by the Irish Republican Army, Irish Protestant loyalists, and Italy's Red Brigades known as "**kneecapping**." The technique involved shooting a victim in the back of the knee joint, thus shooting off the kneecap. Other signature methods have included kidnappings (Abu Sayyaf in the Philippines), hijackings (Popular Front for the Liberation of Palestine), and **suicide bombings** (Liberation Tigers of Tamil Eelam).

The weapons employed by terrorists are integral features of their overall methodologies. Firearms and explosives have historically been the weapons of choice for terrorists. This has not appreciably changed in the modern era, although available firepower has greatly increased, and the selection of targets has arguably become more indiscriminate. Weapons typically include small arms, commercial- and military-grade explosives, rocket-propelled grenades, and vehicular (car and truck) bombs. Sophisticated weapons have occasionally been used, such as **precision guided munitions** (shoulder-fired anti-aircraft rockets) and high-technology triggering devices for bombs. Very few examples exist of the use of weapons of mass destruction, such as chemical, biological, radiological, or nuclear devices. Although the *threat* from terrorists' acquisition of weapons of mass destruction increased during the 1990s, the overarching profile of terrorists and extremists is that they typically wield conventional firearms and explosives.

Weapons Old and New

In the modern era, weaponry can be classified along a sliding scale of technological sophistication and threat potential. This scale includes a high, medium, and low range, summarized as follows:[30]

High Range. The New Terrorism is defined in part by the threatened acquisition of chemical agents, **biological agents**, or **nuclear weapons.** This threat includes the development of **radiological agents** that spread highly toxic radioactive materials by detonating conventional explosives. The first case of widespread use of a biological agent by terrorists occurred when **anthrax** was deliberately sent through the mails in the United States in the aftermath of the September 11, 2001, attacks.

Medium Range. Terrorists currently have extensive access to military-style weaponry. These include automatic weapons, rocket launchers, and military-grade explosives of many varieties. Sympathetic state sponsorship and the international arms black market permit the procurement of a virtually unlimited array of conventional small arms and munitions. These arms have been the weapons of choice for terrorists in innumerable examples.

Low Range. Often forgotten in the discussions about the threat from medium- and high-range weaponry are the powerful homemade weapons that can be manufactured from commercial grade components. For example, ammonium nitrate and fuel oil (ANFO) bombs can be easily manufactured from readily available materials.

Contrary to popular assumptions, terrorists and extremists have historically been selective about their choice of weapons and reserved about their use. They have not, as a rule, been particularly adventurous about the quality of violence that they employ. Although modern terrorists have utilized improvements in the technology of firearms and explosives, they are similar to their violent predecessors in the basic kinds of weaponry that they elect to use:

Previously, most terrorists had shown an aversion to the esoteric and exotic weapons of mass destruction. . . . Radical in their politics, the majority of terrorists were equally conservative in their methods of operation. Indeed, from the time of the late nineteenth-century Russian revolutionaries and the [Irish] Fenian dynamiters . . . terrorists have continued to rely almost exclusively on the same two weapons: the gun and the bomb.[31]

Firearms

Small arms and other handheld weapons have been, and continue to be, the most common types of weapons employed by terrorists. These are light and heavy infantry weapons and include pistols, rifles, submachine guns, assault rifles, machine guns, **rocket-propelled grenades,** mortars, and precision guided munitions. Typical firearms found in the hands of terrorists include:

Submachine Guns. Originally developed for military use, **submachine guns** are now mostly used by police and paramilitary services. Although new models have been designed, such as the famous Israeli Uzi and the American Ingram, World War II-era models are still on the market and have been used by terrorists.

Assault Rifles. Usually capable of both automatic (repeating) and semi-automatic (single-shot) fire, **assault rifles** are military-grade weapons that are used extensively by terrorists and other irregular forces. The **AK-47**, invented by **Mikhail Kalashnikov** for the Soviet Army, is the most successful assault rifle in terms of production numbers and its widespread adoption by standing armies, guerrillas, and terrorists. The American-made **M-16** has likewise been produced in large numbers and has been adopted by a range of conventional and irregular forces.

Rocket-Propelled Grenades. Light self-propelled munitions are common features of modern infantry units. The **RPG-7** has been used extensively by dissident forces throughout the world, particularly in Latin America, the Middle East, and Asia. The weapon was manufactured in large quantities by the Soviets, Chinese, and other communist nations. It is an uncomplicated and powerful weapon that is useful against armor and fixed emplacements such as bunkers or buildings.

Precision Guided Munitions. Less commonly found among terrorists, but extremely effective when used, are weapons that can be guided to their targets by using infrared or other tracking technologies. The American-made **Stinger** is a shoulder-fired surface-to-air missile that uses an infrared targeting system. It was delivered to the Afghan mujahideen during their anti-Soviet jihad and was used very effectively against Soviet helicopters and other aircraft. The Soviet-made **SA-7**, also known as the **Grail**, is also an infrared-targeted surface-to-air missile. Both the Stinger and the Grail pose a significant threat to commercial airliners and other aircraft.

Common Explosives

Terrorists regularly use explosives to attack symbolic targets. Along with firearms, explosives are staples of the terrorist arsenal. The vast majority of terrorists' bombs are self-constructed improvised weapons rather than premanufactured military-grade bombs. The one significant exception to this rule is the heavy use of military-grade **mines** by the world's combatants. These are buried in the soil or rigged to be detonated as "booby traps." Antipersonnel mines are designed to kill people, and antitank mines are designed to destroy vehicles. Many millions of mines have been manufactured and are available on the international market.

Some improvised bombs are constructed from commercially available explosives such as **dynamite** and **TNT**, whereas others are manufactured from military-grade compounds. Examples of compounds found in terrorist bombs include the following:

Plastic Explosives. **Plastic explosives** are putty-like explosive compounds that can be easily molded. The central component of most plastic explosives is a compound known as **RDX**. Nations that manufacture plastic explosives often use chemical markers to "tag" each batch that is made. The tagged explosives can be traced back to their source if used by terrorists. In December 2001, Richard Reid, the "shoe bomber" aboard American Airlines Flight 63, attempted to detonate a bomb crafted from plastic explosives molded into his shoe.

Semtex. **Semtex** is a very potent plastic explosive of Czech origin. During the Cold War, Semtex appeared on the international market, and a large quantity was obtained by Libya. It is popular among terrorists. For example, the IRA has used Semtex-based bombs in Northern Ireland and England.

Composite-4 (C-4). Invented in the United States, **Composite-4 (C-4)** is a high-grade and powerful plastic explosive. It is more expensive and more difficult to obtain than Semtex. The availability of C-4 for use by terrorists became apparent when a renegade CIA agent was convicted of shipping 21 tons of the compound to Libya during the 1970s. About 600 pounds of C-4 was used in the attack against the USS Cole in Yemen, and it was evidently used to bomb the American facility at Khobar Towers in Dharan, Saudi Arabia, in 1996.

ANFO explosives are manufactured from common ammonium nitrate fertilizer that has been soaked in fuel oil. Using ammonium nitrate as a "base" for the bomb, additional compounds and explosives can be added to intensify the explosion. These devices require hundreds of pounds of ammonium nitrate, so they are generally constructed as car or truck bombs. ANFO explosives were used by the IRA in London in 1996; Timothy McVeigh used a two-ton device in Oklahoma City in 1995. The Tamil Tigers have also used ANFO-based devices.

Triggers

Regardless of the type of explosive that is used, some bomb makers construct sophisticated triggering devices and are able to shape explosive charges to control the direction of the blast. Examples of triggering devices include:

Timed Switches. Time bombs are constructed from acid-activated or electronically activated triggers. They are rigged to detonate after the passage of a period of time.

Fuses. A very old and low-technology method to detonate bombs is to light a fuse that detonates the explosives. It can be timed by varying the length of the fuse. Shoe bomber Richard Reid was overpowered after a flight attendant smelled burning matches as he tried to light a fuse in his shoe.

Pressure Triggers. Using **pressure triggers,** weapons such as mines are detonated when physical pressure is applied to a trigger. A variation on physical pressure triggers are trip-wire booby traps. More sophisticated pressure triggers react to atmospheric (barometric) pressure, such as changes in pressure when an airliner ascends or descends.

Electronic Triggers. Remotely controlled bombs are commonly employed by terrorists. **Electronic triggers** are activated by a remote electronic or radio signal.

High-Technology Triggers. Some sophisticated devices may use triggers that are activated by motion, heat, or sunlight.

Types of Bombs

Gasoline Bombs. The most easily manufactured (and common) explosive weapon used by dissidents is nothing more than a gasoline-filled bottle with a flaming rag for its trigger. It is thrown at targets after the rag is stuffed into the mouth of the bottle and ignited. Tar, Styrofoam, or other ingredients can be added to create a gelling effect for the bomb, which causes the combustible ingredient to stick to surfaces. These weapons are commonly called "**Molotov Cocktails,**" named for **Vyacheslav Molotov,** the Soviet Union's foreign minister during the Second World War. During the war, Red Army soldiers and partisans (guerrillas) hurled **gasoline bombs** at German tanks.

Pipe Bombs. These devices are easily constructed from common pipes, which are filled with explosives (usually gunpowder) and then capped on both ends. Nuts, bolts, screws, nails, and other shrapnel are usually taped or otherwise attached to pipe bombs. Many hundreds of pipe bombs have been used by terrorists. In the United States, pipe bombs were used in several bombings of abortion clinics and at the 1996 Summer Olympics in Atlanta. Modified pipe bombs have also been used by Palestinian suicide bombers during their *intifadeh.*

Vehicular Bombs. Ground vehicles that have been wired with explosives are a frequent weapon in the terrorist arsenal. **Vehicular bombs** can include car bombs and truck bombs; they are mobile, are "covert" in the sense that they are not readily identifiable, are able to transport large amounts of explosives, and are rather easily constructed. They have been used on scores of occasions throughout the world. Examples of groups that have regularly used vehicular bombs include Sendero Luminoso in Peru, the Irish Republican Army, the Tamil Tigers in Sri Lanka, Palestinian groups, the ETA in Spain, and Lebanese groups. Some of these attacks have been quite devastating:

- February 1993. Four hundred people were killed and 1,000 wounded in 13 simultaneous vehicular bombings in Bombay, India. The attacks were carried out to avenge an attack on a Muslim shrine by Hindus.
- April 1995. One hundred sixty-eight people were killed, including 19 children, when American extremist Timothy McVeigh used a truck bomb to destroy the Murrah Federal Building in Oklahoma City.
- June 1996. A truck bomb killed 19 people in an attack on the U.S. Air Force barracks in Dharan, Saudi Arabia. Anti-Saudi Islamic revolutionaries were responsible.
- August 1998. Twenty-nine people were killed and more than 220 were injured when a car bomb exploded in the town of Omagh, Northern Ireland. The Real Irish Republican Army claimed credit for the attack in an attempt to derail peace negotiations.
- 2000-2001. The Basque terrorist group ETA ended its cease-fire and began a bombing campaign in Spain. A number of these bombs were car bombs.

Barometric Bombs. These bombs use triggers that are activated by changes in atmospheric pressure. An altitude meter can be rigged to become a triggering device when a specific change in pressure is detected. Thus, an airliner can be blown up in midair as the cabin pressure changes. These are sophisticated devices.

Case: Weapons of Mass Destruction

Within the context of threats from high-range weapons, it is important to understand the basic differences between four types of weapons: biological agents, chemical agents, radiological agents, and nuclear weapons.

Biological Agents. These weapons are "living organisms . . . or infective material derived from them, which are intended to cause disease or death in man, animals, and plants, and which depend on their ability to multiply in the person, animal, or plant attacked.'"[32] Viruses, fungi, and bacteria are all labeled as "biological" weapons, although bacteria are not living organisms and hence technically cannot be considered biological weapons. Nevertheless, experts generally agree that the most likely biological agents (whether bacteria or not) to be used by terrorists would be the following:

- *Anthrax.* Anthrax is a disease that afflicts livestock and humans. It can exist as spores or suspended in aerosols. Humans contract anthrax either through cuts in the skin (cutaneous anthrax), through the respiratory system (inhalation anthrax), or by eating contaminated meat. Anthrax-infected letters were sent through the mails in the eastern United States immediately after the September 11, 2001, attacks. Those who died from anthrax exposure suffered from inhalation anthrax.
- *Smallpox.* Eradicated in nature, **smallpox** is a virus that exists only in laboratories. Its symptoms appear after about 12 days of incubation and include flu-like symptoms and a skin condition that eventually leads to pus-filled lesions. It is a highly contagious disease and can be deadly if it progresses to a hemorrhagic (bleeding) stage known as the "black pox."
- ***Botulinum Toxin (Botulism).*** Botulism is a rather common form of food poisoning. It is a bacterium rather than a virus or fungus and can be deadly if inhaled or ingested even in small quantities.
- ***Bubonic Plague.*** A bacterium leads to the disease known as the Black Death in medieval Europe; the disease is spread by bacteria-infected fleas that infect hosts when bitten. The disease is highly infectious and often fatal.

Chemical Agents. These weapons are "chemical substances, whether gaseous, liquid, or solid, which are used for hostile purposes to cause disease or death in humans, animals, or plants, and which depend on direct toxicity for their primary effect."[33] Some chemical agents, such as pesticides, are commercially available. Other chemical agents can be manufactured by extremists using available instruction guides. Examples of chemical agents include the following:

- **Phosgene gas** causes the lungs to fill with water, choking the victim.
- **Chlorine gas** destroys the cells that line the respiratory tract.
- **Mustard gas** is actually a mist rather than a gas. It is a blistering agent that blisters skin, eyes, and the nose and can severely damage the lungs if inhaled.
- **Nerve gases**, such as sarin, tabun, and VX, block (or "short-circuit") nerve messages in the body. A single drop of a nerve agent, whether inhaled or absorbed through the skin, can shut down the body's neurotransmitters.

Radiological Agents. These weapons are materials that emit radiation that can harm living organisms. In order to become threatening to life or health, these radioactive substances must be "ingested, inhaled, or absorbed through the skin" in sufficient quantities.[34] Non-weapons-grade radiological agents could theoretically be used to construct a toxic "dirty bomb" that would use conventional explosives to release a cloud of radioactive contaminants. Radioactive elements that could be used in a dirty bomb include plutonium, uranium, cobalt 60, strontium, and cesium 137.[35] Conceptually, radiological weapons are not unlike chemical or biological weapons in the sense that the effectiveness of each is based on contaminating or infecting living organisms.

Nuclear Weapons. Nuclear weapons are high-explosive military weapons using weapons-grade plutonium and uranium. Nuclear explosions devastate the area within their blast zone, irradiate an area outside the blast zone, and are capable of sending dangerous radioactive debris into the atmosphere that descends to earth as toxic **fallout**. Nuclear devices are sophisticated weapons that are difficult to manufacture. Modern nuclear arsenals include large strategic weapons powerful enough to lay waste to large areas and smaller, relatively compact tactical nuclear weapons that were originally developed to support ground troops. Although it is conceivable that terrorists could construct a nuclear device, most threat scenarios envision the acquisition of tactical nuclear weapons such as artillery shells. The Soviets apparently developed several so-called suitcase bombs—nuclear weapons that are quite compact.

Case: The Suicide Bombers

"Human bombs" have become an accepted method of political violence in a number of conflicts. Although some examples of suicidal behavior by ideological extremists can be found, most incidents have been committed by ethno-national and religious terrorists. When considering the tactical and symbolic value of suicide attacks, it is instructive to recall the words of the Chinese military philosopher Wu Ch'i: "One man willing to throw away his life is enough to terrorize a thousand."[36] In the modern era, the attraction for deploying suicide squads is simply stated: Human bombs

possess an intelligence and flexibility that other weapons do not have;

inflict significant psychological damage on an enemy;

are relatively "cheap" weapons, so long as the reservoir of volunteers is maintained; and

exact a high human toll from an enemy while at the same time incurring acceptable losses.

In some conflicts, suicide bombings have rarely occurred. For example, the IRA, the ETA, and European leftists and rightists did not use suicidal violence. In other conflicts, suicide attacks became a common method of waging war against the defined enemy. The Tamil Tigers in Sri Lanka, Hezbollah (Islamic Jihad) in Lebanon, several Palestinian groups in Israel, and Al Qaeda are all examples of movements that have regularly used this tactic. The following cases in point illustrate this behavior:

Sri Lanka. The civil war between the Sri Lankan government and Tamil separatists involved the extensive use of terrorist methods by the Tamil Tigers. Throughout the 1990s, the movement committed a series of assassinations, detonated a number of car and truck bombs, and regularly engaged in suicide bombing incidents. Tens of thousands of people died during this period. Some suicide incidents have been significant events during the course of the war. For example:

- In May 1991, former Indian Prime Minister Rajiv Gandhi was assassinated in India by a Tamil woman who detonated a bomb as she stood next to Gandhi. She was a Tamil and was probably affiliated with Sri Lanka's Tamil Tigers movement. In 1998, 26 people were sentenced to death by an Indian court for complicity in the assassination.
- In May 1993, Sri Lankan Prime Minister Ramasinghe Premadasa was assassinated by a suicide bomber.
- In December 1999, Sri Lankan President Chandrika Kumaratunga was injured and narrowly escaped death when a suicide bomber attempted to assassinate her at an election rally.

The Lebanon Model. Lebanon descended into anarchy for approximately 15 years during the 1970s and 1980s. The fighting was mostly religious, among contending paramilitaries drawn from the Shi'ite, Sunni, Druze, and Christian communities. The Palestine Liberation Organization also had a strong presence. During the war, these factions carved out de facto fiefdoms that were secured by the paramilitaries. Terrorism and atrocities regularly occurred, and methods included suicide bombings.

The group that pioneered suicide bombing as an effective method of terrorist violence in the Middle East was Lebanon's Hezbollah.[37] As described in Chapter 4, Hezbollah is a Lebanese Shi'ite movement that has historically received significant state support from Iran and Syria. The group conducted a series of suicide bombings in 1983 through 1985 against Israeli, American, and French interests. Credit for the bombings was usually taken by a group calling itself **Islamic Jihad**, a radical splinter group from Hezbollah. The October 1983 suicide attacks against the French and American peace-keeping troops in Beirut were particularly effective—the attackers killed 58 French paratroopers and 241 American Marines, forcing the withdrawal of the peacekeepers. This tactic continued through the 1990s during Hezbollah's campaign against the Israeli occupation of Lebanon's southern border region. These attacks were directed against Israeli troops and Israel's proxy, the mostly Christian South Lebanon Army.

An important aspect of the Lebanese example is that each suicide bomber was later glorified as a "martyr." This concept of *martyrdom* is an important motivation behind the recruitment of young suicide bombers. In Israel, Hamas, Palestine Islamic Jihad, and Al Aqsa Martyr Brigades have all cited the Lebanon model as the inspiration for their renewed *intifadeh* against the Israelis.

Israel. Hamas was the first Palestinian group to initiate a suicide bombing campaign. It launched the campaign in retaliation for the February 1994 Hebron massacre when Dr. Baruch Goldstein killed and wounded scores of Muslim worshippers at the Ibrahim

Peacekeeping in Beirut. Two U.S. Marines survey the rubble of the Marine Corps barracks, which had been destroyed by a Lebanese suicide bomber. More than 200 of their comrades died in the attack.

Source: U.S. Department of State.

Mosque on the holy site of the Cave of the Patriarchs. Goldstein's attack was discussed in Chapter 8. Hamas recruited human-bomb candidates into its Izzedine al-Qassam Brigade cells, with the specific mission to attack Israeli civilian targets—primarily at commuter transportation sites. The suicide bombers used shrapnel-laden vehicular bombs, satchel charges (bagged bombs), and garment-strapped bombs designed by the bomb maker **Yehiya Ayyash**, also known as "**The Engineer**." These attacks inflicted significant damage on Israel in terms of the number of Israeli casualties. For example, four Hamas bombers killed 59 people in 1996.[38] Ayyash and Hamas are explored further in this chapter's Case in Point.

Beginning in 2001, suicide bombers from sectarian Hamas and the secular PLO-affiliated Al Aqsa Martyr Brigades carried out dozens of attacks against civilian targets, killing scores of people. The targets were selected to disrupt everyday life in Israel. This was not the first suicide bombing campaign in Israel, but it was by far the most sustained and lethal campaign. During the 18-month period beginning in the winter of 2001, nearly 100 suicide bombings occurred. The following timeline illustrates the marked increase in the number of suicide attacks in 2001:[39]

- 1993: 13 attacks
- 1994: 7 attacks
- 1995: 8 attacks
- 1996: 4 attacks

- 1997: 4 attacks
- 1998: 2 attacks
- 1999: 0 attacks
- 2000: 4 attacks
- 2001: 36 attacks

Al Qaeda. Operatives of Osama bin Laden's Al Qaeda network have demonstrated a propensity for suicidal violence. Members of the network have committed a series of highly destructive suicide bombing attacks against American interests. They have also been known to carry out attacks against rival factions. Examples of these methods include the following incidents:

- August 7, 1998: Suicide bombers struck the American embassies in Nairobi, Kenya, and Dar es Salaam, Tanzania, killing over 200 people and wounding 5,000.
- October 12, 2000: The American destroyer USS Cole was severely damaged by two suicide bombers while berthed in the port of Aden, Yemen. The bombers detonated a boat bomb next to the Cole, killing themselves and 17 crew members and wounding 39 other Navy personnel.
- September 9, 2001: Ahmad Shah Massoud was assassinated by two Arab suicide bombers posing as a film crew for an interview. Massoud was a highly regarded Afghani commander who fought very well during the anti-Soviet jihad. He was also the most effective commander fighting against the Taliban movement. The bombers were Afghan Arabs who used a booby-trapped camera.
- April 11, 2002: A natural gas truck exploded on Djerba Island in Tunisia at the oldest synagogue in North Africa. Seventeen people, 12 of them German tourists, were killed.[40]

Interestingly, Al Qaeda apparently designed an internal consensus about how to conduct terrorist operations. Members of the network committed to writing what are best described as terrorist protocols; these procedures were discovered during searches of Al Qaeda hideouts in the aftermath of the attacks of September 11, 2001. The protocols were published in a Qaeda "terrorism manual" found in the dwelling of a Qaeda suspect in Manchester, England. Other similar manuals were found in locations as diverse as Chechnya, the United States, and Afghanistan. A six-volume, 1,000-page manual on CD-ROM was also discovered. Chapter Perspective 10.1 presents sample guidelines designed for Al Qaeda operatives.

Table 10.2 summarizes the scale of violence experienced during the suicide bombing campaign waged by the Palestinians during their *intifadeh.*[41] It is important to consider that the targets were almost exclusively civilians and that the death toll was "acceptable" from the perspective of the terrorists—200 people were killed during this timeline, at a cost of 13 "human bombs."

TERRORIST TARGETS

Brazilian revolutionary Carlos Marighella advocated the adoption of terrorism and **armed propaganda** as justifiable tactics in waging urban guerrilla warfare. He wrote that armed propaganda is a symbolic process in which targets should be chosen after a period of careful deliberation about the effect an attack will have on a larger audience. In his *Minimanual of the Urban Guerrilla*, Marighella recommended specific targets to be attacked for maximum propaganda effect. He suggested that careful selection would psychologically damage an enemy and attract supporters to the cause. Marighella wrote,

| Chapter Perspective 10.1 | Al Qaeda "Terrorist Manual" |

In May 2000, an Arabic document was found during the search of the home of an alleged Al Qaeda member in Manchester, England. The document was a manual, approximately 180 pages in length, entitled "Military Studies in the Jihad Against the Tyrants." It is essentially an operations manual, or blueprint, for engaging in cell-based terrorist activities in foreign countries. Excerpts from the manual include the following passages:

Goals and Objectives

The confrontation that we are calling for with the apostate regimes does not know Socratic debates, . . . Platonic ideals, . . . nor Aristotelian diplomacy. . . . But it knows the dialogue of bullets, the ideals of assassination, bombing and destruction, and the diplomacy of the cannon and machine gun.

Missions Required: The main mission for which the Military Organization is responsible is the overthrow of the godless regimes and the replacement with an Islamic regime. Other missions consist of the following:

- Kidnapping enemy personnel, documents, secrets and arms.
- Assassinating enemy personnel as well as foreign tourists.
- Freeing the brothers who are captured by the enemy.
- Blasting and destroying the places of amusement, immorality, and sin; not a vital target.
- Blasting and destroying the embassies and attacking vital economic centers.
- Blasting and destroying bridges leading into and out of the cities.

Source: The Al Qaeda "Terrorist Manual," U.S. Department of Justice Web site.

The following security precautions should be taken:

- All documents of the undercover brother, such as identity cards and passport, should be falsified.
- The brother who has special work status . . . should have more than one identity card and passport.
- The photograph of the brother in these documents should be without a beard . . .

Operations

Cell or cluster methods should be adopted by the Organization. It should be composed of many cells whose members do not know one another. . . .

Facsimile and wireless: . . . Duration of transmission should not exceed five minutes in order to prevent the enemy from pinpointing the device location. . . .

Measures that should be taken by the undercover member:

Not reveal his true name to the Organization's members who are working with him . . .

Have a general appearance that does not indicate Islamic orientation (beard, tooth-pick, book, long shirt, small Koran).

Be careful not to mention the brothers' common expressions or show their behaviors . . .

Avoid visiting famous Islamic places . . .

Not park in no-parking zones and not take photographs where it is forbidden.

Important note: Married brothers should observe the following: Not talking with their wives about Jihad work.

Bank assaults, ambushes, desertions and diverting of arms, the rescue of prisoners, executions, kidnappings, sabotage, terrorism, and the war of nerves, are all cases in point. . . . Airplanes diverted in flight by revolutionary action, moving ships and trains assaulted and seized by guerrillas, can also be solely for propaganda effect.[42]

Terrorists select their targets because of the expectation that any moral ambiguities of the deed will be outweighed by the target's propaganda value. Terrorists must calculate that they can manipulate the incident into a positive propaganda context. The following sampling of typical targets indicates that terrorists and extremists must rely on a process

Table 10.2   The *Intifadeh* Suicide Bombers

The Palestinian *intifadeh* increased in scale and ferocity during 2001 and 2002. Fighting in Gaza and the West Bank became pitched battles between Palestinian guerrillas and the Israeli military. Street fighting broke out in Bethlehem, Nablus, Ramallah, and other ancient cities. At the same time, a deadly and unpredictable new weapon was applied extensively by the Palestinians—the human bomb.

Initially used by radical Islamic movements such as Hamas and Palestine Islamic Jihad, suicide bombing became a regular weapon of secular Palestine Liberation Organization fighters. The Al Aqsa Martyr Brigades was a secular "martyrdom" society linked to the mainstream Fatah organization of the PLO.

The following table is a snapshot of the activity profiles of several human bombing incidents.

| *"Martyr" Profile* | *Activity Profile* | | |
	Date	*Target*	*Fatalities*
22-year-old male Jordanian	June 1, 2001	Tel Aviv discothèque	20 killed
23-year-old male Hamas activist	August 9, 2001	Jerusalem pizzeria	15 killed, including 7 children
48-year-old man, first known Arab Israeli bomber	September 9, 2001	Train depot	3 killed
21-year-old man, engaged to be married	December 2, 2001	Haifa passenger bus	15 killed
28-year-old woman, first female suicide bomber	January 27, 2002	Jerusalem shopping district	1 elderly man killed
21-year-old female English student	February 27, 2002	Israeli roadblock	3 hurt
19-year-old man	March 2, 2002	Bar Mitzvah celebration	9 killed
20-year-old man	March 9, 2002	Café near Prime Minister Ariel Sharon's residence	11 killed
20-year-old man	March 20, 2002	Commuter bus	7 killed
23-year-old man, wanted fugitive	March 27, 2002	Passover celebration (Seder)	21 killed
18-year-old woman, engaged to be married	March 29, 2002	Jerusalem supermarket	2 killed
23-year-old man	March 30, 2002	Tel Aviv restaurant	32 hurt
22-year-old man	March 31, 2002	Haifa restaurant	15 killed

SOURCE: Primarily from Ripley, Amanda. "Why Suicide Bombing Is Now All the Rage." *Time.* April 15, 2002. Used with permission.

of redefining who constitutes an enemy group, thereby turning them into a legitimate target. Terrorists

take innocent civilians hostage—if the civilian is a symbolic person, they have not hesitated to execute them;

attack and murder third-country military personnel who have no direct connection to their cause;

indiscriminately attack civilians as part of terrorist and reprisal campaigns against enemy interests; and

regularly target symbolic buildings such as embassies.[43]

In many terrorist campaigns, the objective has been to disrupt society to the point where the routines of life cannot be managed and the government cannot maintain order. In order to accomplish this, some terrorist movements have incrementally adapted their methods to new targets. This point is exemplified by Algeria's Armed Islamic Group and Armed Islamic Movement (both are discussed in Chapter 8), which escalated their terrorist campaign by gradually shifting their emphases to new targets, managing to move through several phases during their insurgency:[44]

Beginning in 1992, the first targets were security forces, who were ambushed in the countryside and in towns. Civilians were also targeted to keep them from revealing where the rebels were based.

Next, assassinations were carried out. Suspected collaborators (broadly defined), government officials, party officials, and professionals were killed.

Beginning in 1993, the terrorists redefined who their enemies were and began killing family members of government officials.

Terrorists also began to target foreign workers and tourists in 1993.

Women became specific targets for assassination. These victims included professionals and female family members of government officials.

Indiscriminate bomb attacks began in 1994, escalating into a campaign of suicide bombings in Algiers in June 1995.

The Symbolism of Targets

In light of our previous discussions about terrorist groups, typologies, and incidents, one conclusion should now be readily apparent: Terrorists select their targets because of their symbolic and propaganda value. High-profile, sentimental, or otherwise significant targets are chosen with the expectation that the terrorists' constituency will be moved and that the victims' audience will in some way suffer. The following targets are often selected because terrorists conclude that they offer a high return in propaganda value.

Embassies and Diplomatic Personnel

The symbolism of embassy attacks can be quite profound. Embassies represent the sovereignty and national interests of nations. Diplomatic personnel are universally recognized as official representatives of their home countries, and attacks on embassy buildings or embassy personnel are conceptually the same as direct attacks on the nations they represent. Assaults on embassies also guarantee a large audience. For example, the 1996-1997 attack and hostage seizures by Peru's Tupac Amaru Revolutionary Movement (MRTA) on the Japanese ambassador's residence in Lima, Peru, garnered worldwide attention. The incident ended with the deaths of the MRTA members and dealt a severe blow to the movement, but it demonstrated how a relatively small dissident movement can otherwise score significant propaganda successes.

International Symbols

Many nations deploy military representatives to other countries. They also encourage international investment by private corporations, which consequently set up offices and other facilities. These interests are understandable targets for terrorists because they can be manipulated symbolically to depict exploitation, imperialism, or other representations of repression. Thus, terrorists and extremists redefine military facilities, corporate offices, military personnel, and company employees as enemy interests and legitimate targets. For example, Colombian leftists attacked U.S. business interests and Mormon missionaries— and took American citizens hostage—during the country's 1994 election season. In another example, during the winter of 1991, the Greek terrorist group **Revolutionary Organization November 17** carried out a series of attacks against international businesses in Greece. Their targets symbolized the interests of the international coalition opposing Iraq during the Gulf War.[45]

Symbolic Buildings and Sites

Buildings and sentimental sites often represent the prestige and power of a nation or the identity of a people. These sites can evoke strong psychological and emotional reactions from people who revere them. Terrorists and extremists select these cultural symbols because they know that the target audience will be affected. Interestingly, the target audience can be affected without the use of violence against symbolic buildings and sites—the perception (by the target audience) of these sites as having been "desecrated" can involve nothing more than a show of strength at a cultural site. For example, in September 2000 Israeli leader Ariel Sharon, who was at that time the chairman of the opposition Likud Party, made a politically motivated visit to Jerusalem's Al Aqsa Mosque (also known as the Temple Mount). A strong opponent of the negotiation process that led to the Oslo [Peace] Accords, Sharon arrived at the site surrounded by 1,000 Israeli security officers. Palestinians became enraged by the symbolism of the incursion, and the Al Aqsa *intifadeh* began. The *intifadeh* became a mass uprising marked by reprisals and terrorism.

Symbolic People

Terrorists frequently assault individuals because of the symbolic value of their status. Security personnel, political leaders, journalists, business executives, and others are often selected as targets. Kidnappings and physical violence are common methods used by terrorists against human symbols. In kidnapping and hostage situations, videotapes and photographs are sometimes released for propaganda purposes. For example, in September 1977 the leftist Red Army Faction/Baader-Meinhof Gang kidnapped German industrialist Hanns-Martin Schleyer. He was murdered by the group in October 1977 (see Appendix B).

Passenger Carriers

From the perspective of terrorists, passenger carriers are logical targets. If the carrier is big, such as an airliner, it provides a large number of potential victims or hostages who are confined inside a mobile prison. International passenger carriers readily lend themselves to immediate international media and political attention. For example, the nationalist

---

Chapter Perspective 10.2   The Symbolism of Targets:
Terrorist Attacks Against the United States

Many targets are selected because they symbolize the interests of a perceived enemy. This selection process requires that these interests be redefined by extremists as representations of the forces against whom they are waging war. This redefinition process, if properly communicated to the terrorists' target audience and constituency, can be effectively used as propaganda on behalf of the cause.

The following attacks were launched against American interests.

Embassies

- June 1987: A car bombing and mortar attack were launched against the U.S. embassy in Rome, most likely by the Japanese Red Army.
- February 1996: A rocket attack was launched on the American embassy compound in Greece.

International Symbols

- April 1988: A USO club in Naples, Italy, was bombed, most likely by the Japanese Red Army. Five people were killed.
- November 1995: Seven people were killed when anti-Saudi dissidents bombed an American military training facility in Riyadh, Saudi Arabia.

Symbolic Buildings and Sites

- January 1993: Two were killed and three injured when a Pakistani terrorist fired at

employees outside the CIA headquarters in Langley, Virginia.
- February 1993: The World Trade Center in New York City was bombed, killing six and injuring more than 1,000.
- September 2001: Attacks in the United States against the World Trade Center and the Pentagon killed approximately 3,000 people.

Symbolic People

- May 2001: The Filipino Islamic revolutionary movement Abu Sayyaf took three American citizens hostage. One of them was beheaded by members of the group in June 2001.
- January 2002: An American journalist working for the *Wall Street Journal* was kidnapped in Pakistan by Islamic extremists. His murder was later videotaped by the group.

Passenger Carrier Attacks

- August 1982: A bomb exploded aboard Pan Am Flight 830 over Hawaii. The Palestinian group 15 May committed the attack. The plane was able to land.
- April 1986: A bomb exploded aboard TWA Flight 840. Four were killed and nine injured, including a mother and her infant daughter who fell to their deaths when they were sucked out of the plane. Flight 840 landed safely.

Popular Front for the Liberation of Palestine repeatedly used airline hijackings to achieve maximum propaganda exposure for their movement.

Chapter Perspective 10.2 summarizes the foregoing discussion by describing several symbolic attacks against American interests.

THE OUTCOME: IS TERRORISM EFFECTIVE?

Does terrorism work? When we consider the effectiveness of terrorism, the basic question to be answered is: Do the methods used by terrorists against their selected targets promote their goals and objectives? Terrorism is arguably "effective"—however defined—in some manner to someone.[46] The key (for terrorists) is to establish a link between terrorist methods and incidents and desirable outcomes. There is a tendency for terrorists to use unconventional factors as measures for their effectiveness. For example, terrorists have been known to declare victory using the following criteria:

- Acquiring global media and political attention
- Having an impact on a target audience or championed constituency
- Forcing concessions from an enemy interest
- Disrupting the normal routines of a society
- Provoking the state to overreact

The following discussion reviews these criteria. This is not an exhaustive evaluation of measures of effectiveness, but it demonstrates commonalities found among modern terrorists.

Media and Political Attention

At times, the focusing of world attention on the terrorists' cause is itself a measure of success. One central fact in the age of instantaneous media attention is that

> for the terrorist, success . . . is most often measured in terms of the amount of publicity and attention received. Newsprint and airtime are thus the coin of the realm in the terrorists' mindset: the only tangible or empirical means they have by which to gauge their success and assess their progress. In this respect, little distinction or discrimination is made between good or bad publicity.[47]

Many terrorist groups engage in violence that is, at least in part, media oriented. As one Red Army Faction/Baader-Meinhof Gang member[48] reflected after his "retirement" from the terrorist trade: "We always immediately looked how the newspapers, especially in Berlin, reacted to our actions, and how they explained them, and thereupon we defined our strategy."[49] The June 1985 hijacking of **TWA Flight 847**, with its odyssey through several countries and the hijackers' manipulation of the world's media, is a classic example of a media-oriented terrorist incident. The epic case of Flight 847 and the role of the media will be explored further in Chapter 11.

Having an Impact on an Audience

Terrorists often use propaganda by the deed to affect audiences, hoping to rouse them to action or incite a society-level response. Victim audiences, neutral audiences, and championed groups can all be affected by a terrorist event. When an incident occurs, extremists and their supporters assess reactions from these audiences. From the terrorists' perspective, the effectiveness of an attack requires successful manipulation of various audiences' reactions. If, for example, a victim audience is successfully manipulated, members of the audience

> change [their] travel habits or [their] vacation destinations out of fear of becoming victims. The rationale for this fear is small . . . but the fear of victimization is real, especially among heavy media consumers . . . A process of identification takes place not only with former victims and likely future victims but with all those in the audience who share some "victim characteristics."[50]

An unusual example of an *unsuccessful* campaign to generate this measure of effectiveness is found in the motives of South Africa's **People Against Gangsterism and Drugs** (PAGAD). Founded in 1996, PAGAD waged a campaign of violence to protest the values of what it considered to be an immoral South African society. Originally a vigilante anticrime group, PAGAD evolved into a dissident terrorist group. It espoused an antigovernment and anti-Western ideology, supposedly on behalf of South Africa's

Muslim population, but its attacks focused largely on "moral" targets. PAGAD selected these targets—primarily in Cape Town—as a way to promote moralistic Islamic values and to cleanse society. Targets included fast-food restaurants, gay bars, tourist sites, and other symbols of Western decadence and immorality. Unfortunately for PAGAD, South Africa's population was minimally affected, and there was not a societal reaction to PAGAD's attacks (other than revulsion). Interestingly, PAGAD promoted its cause in part by maintaining a Web site.[51]

Forcing Concessions From an Enemy Interest

Enemy interests—broadly defined—will sometimes concede to the demands of a politically violent movement. Concessions vary in magnitude. They can be made as short-term and immediate concessions or as long-term and fundamental concessions whereby an entire society essentially concedes to a movement. At the level of immediate concessions, accommodations could include ransoms paid by companies for the release of employees who are being held hostage. At the societal level, laws might be changed or autonomy granted to a national group. One repeated method used by terrorists to force concessions is **kidnapping/hostage-taking**. This is because

> hostage takers may influence the government's decision by promising rewards for compliance. . . . The release of hostages unharmed when ransom is paid underwrites a promise in the future. Sequential release of selected hostages makes promises credible. Maintaining secrecy about a government's concessions is an additional reward for compliance.[52]

For example, in 1969 two radical Brazilian organizations—National Liberation Action and MR-8—collaborated in the kidnapping of the American ambassador to Brazil, Charles Burke. They demanded and received radio airtime in exchange for his release. The groups were permitted to broadcast their indictment of Brazil's authoritarian government to a broad audience.

Disruption of Normal Routines

An obvious measure of effectiveness is whether the normal routines of society can be affected or halted by a terrorist incident or campaign. Some targets—such as the commercial transportation industry—can be selectively attacked to the point where their operations will be disrupted. When this happens, the daily habits of individuals and routines of society will change. In this way, large numbers of people in the broader society in essence respond to the tactics of a relatively weak movement. For example, the American airline industry lost $2.2 billion during the first quarter of 2002 as a direct result of changes in Americans' travel behavior following the September 11, 2001, attacks.[53]

Provoking the State to Overreact

One outcome that terrorists allude to as a measure of effectiveness is the state's imposition of violent security countermeasures in response to a terrorist environment. This notion of "enraging the beast" is common across the spectrum of terrorist typologies and has been discussed in previous chapters. Terrorists, of course, anticipate that the state will become violently repressive, the people will suffer, and the masses will rise up in rebellion after experiencing the true nature of the enemy. This theory has had only mixed success, as evidenced in the following (now familiar) cases in point.

Viable Movements

Some movements proved to be viable after provoking the state, as demonstrated by the examples of the Irish Republican Army and the Palestine Liberation Organization:

Northern Ireland's Irish Republican Army fought in an environment wherein Irish Catholics were subjected to violence perpetrated by Protestant paramilitaries, British security forces, and the Royal Irish Constabulary. The IRA had a significant amount of popular support. Because of this support—and because their opponents could not end the violence—the aboveground Sinn Féin party was welcomed as an equal partner by the British during several rounds of peace talks, also known as the "**decommissioning**" process.

The Palestine Liberation Organization survived countless crises that might have defeated other movements. It maintained a consistent level of international and domestic violence directed against Israel for decades. Despite significant applications of force by the Israelis—including assassinations, surgical reprisals, reprisal campaigns, and conventional warfare—the PLO continued to garner worldwide attention and regional support from sympathetic governments.

Unviable Movements

Some movements proved to be unviable after provoking the state, as demonstrated by the examples of the Montoneros and Tupamaros:

Argentina's Montoneros were effective according to several measures: They successfully received media and political attention, affected target audiences, received concessions from enemy interests, and disrupted societal routines. Unfortunately for the Montoneros, they were wiped out during the Argentine military's repressive "Dirty War" after having provoked the state into using authoritarian methods.

Uruguay's Tupamaros were likewise successful in achieving the first four measures of effectiveness. And, like the Montoneros, they provoked the state into adopting violent security measures; the group was annihilated during a somewhat popular suppression campaign waged by the Uruguayan military.

Table 10.3 summarizes the foregoing measures of effectiveness, the cited terrorist incidents, and outcomes.

Effective Terrorism: The King David Hotel Bombing

The 1946 **King David Hotel Bombing** by the Jewish terrorist group **Irgun** was a successful terrorist operation because the attack produced all five of the measures of effectiveness and desired outcomes presented earlier.

After the dissolution of the Ottoman Turk Empire following the First World War, the British Empire occupied and governed Palestine. During the 1930s, communal violence between Palestinian Arabs and Jews led to an unsuccessful rebellion by Arabs. In 1937, a Jewish organization calling itself the Irgun began engaging in revenge attacks against Palestinian Arabs. When the Irgun's leaders, **Vladimir Jabotinsky** and **David Raziel**,

Table 10.3 Measures of Effectiveness

When extremist movements adopt terrorism as a methodology, they measure the effectiveness of their violent behavior by linking the incident to identifiable outcomes. These measures of effectiveness are unconventional in the sense that they are frequently media oriented and audience oriented.

The following table summarizes measures of effectiveness by illustrating the linkage between terrorist incidents and outcomes.

	Activity Profile	
Measure of Effectiveness	*Incident*	*Outcome*
Media and political attention	Hijacking of TWA Flight 847	Global media and political attention
Impact on an audience	PAGAD's moralist terrorist campaign	Failed campaign to bring about a societal response
Concessions from an enemy interest	Kidnapping of U.S. ambassador to Brazil	Broadcast of terrorists' political manifesto
Disruption of societal routines	Suicidal hijackings of four airliners on September 11, 2001	Fewer Americans traveled via airlines; industry suffered revenue losses
Provoke the state	Viable: Provocations by IRA and PLO	Government methods failed to eradicate opposition
	Unviable: Provocations by Montoneros and Tupamaros	Violent military governments crushed the opposition

were killed in 1940 and 1941, a young **Menachem Begin** and other leaders reinvigorated the Irgun's violent resistance in 1944. Irgun's membership was small, so its strategy was to engage in urban terrorist attacks against British institutions, such as immigration department, land registry, and taxation offices, as well as British security forces.

The King David Hotel in Jerusalem housed the headquarters of the British military and the government secretariat. On July 22, 1946, the Irgun bombed the hotel, killing 91 persons and wounding 45 others.[54] Its victims included civilians, Jews, Palestinian Arabs, and British.

The bombing achieved worldwide attention and began a debate in Great Britain about the failure of the British administration to bring peace to Palestine. The British responded with an increase in the authoritarian policies that it had already imposed prior to the bombing. These policies included mass arrests of Jews, military road blocks, random personal and dwelling searches, and curfews. These measures were unpopular in Britain and the United States and led to a gradual shift in political opinion against the British occupation.

When the British executed three Irgun members, the Irgun retaliated in July 1947 by beating and hanging two British sergeants, photographing their hanged corpses, and then releasing the pictures to the media. The effect was the final straw for British public opinion, which turned irrevocably against Britain's administration of Palestine.

The rubble of the King David Hotel in Jerusalem. The hotel, which housed British administrative offices for their Palestine mandate, was bombed by the Jewish terrorist group Irgun.

Source: Hulton Archive/Getty Images; used by permission.

On May 15, 1948, the British mandate in Palestine ended. The Irgun, a small, determined, urban terrorist group, had successfully implemented Carlos Marighella's strategy of pushing the state to the point of unacceptable authoritarian measures that ultimately resulted in the state's inability to sustain its rule.

As a postscript, Menachem Begin served as prime minister in Israel from 1977 to 1983.

Case in Point   **The Engineer**

The Islamic Resistance Movement, better known as Hamas,[a] is a Palestinian Islamic fundamentalist movement founded in December 1987 when the first Palestinian *intifadeh* broke out. Hamas's "military wing" is the Izzedine al-Qassam Brigade, which first appeared in January 1992.

Hamas made a concerted effort from 1994 to 1996 to establish itself as the preeminent Palestinian liberation organization. At that time, the PLO was deeply committed to the peace process, and Hamas was equally committed to sabotaging the process. The movement conducted a significant number of bombings, shootings, and acts of sabotage. It was during this period that Hamas set the precedent—and honed the methodology—for Palestinian suicide bombings.

In 1995 and 1996, Hamas's bombing campaign became more deadly as their bombs became more sophisticated. This was the handiwork of an electrical engineer named Yehiya Ayyash, a master bomb maker better known as "The Engineer."

The Engineer was a typical activist within Hamas's cell-based organizational structure. Unlike PLO-style groups, Hamas required its operatives to organize themselves into small semi-autonomous units. Ayyash was an al-Qassam cell (and later a "brigade") commander, but he had very few outside contacts and built his bombs in an almost solitary setting. He taught others to make bombs and how suicide bombers should position themselves for maximum effect. The Engineer's first bomb was a Volkswagen car bomb that was used in April 1993. When Hamas began its suicide bombing campaign after the February 1994 Hebron massacre, Ayyash was the principal bomb maker. His bombs were sophisticated and custom made for each mission. They were particularly powerful compared to others designed by Hamas.

Ayyash was killed in January 1996. The cell phone he was using to carry on a conversation with his father had been booby-trapped by Israeli security agents and was remotely detonated. The assassination occurred as follows:

> Fifty grams of RDX [plastic] explosives molded into the battery compartment of a telephone had been designed to kill only the man cradling the phone to his ear. The force of the concentrated blast caused most of the right side of Ayyash's face to implode . . . The booby-trapped cellular phone had been . . . so target specific, that the left side of Ayyash's face had remained whole. The right hand which held the telephone was neither burnt or damaged.[b]

The Engineer had been directly and indirectly responsible for killing approximately 150 people and injuring about 500 others.

NOTES

   a. Recall that Hamas means "zeal" and is an acronym for *Harakt al-Muqaqama al-Islamiya.*
   b. Katz, *The Hunt for the Engineer,* pp. 260-61.
Source: Primarily from Katz, Samuel M. *The Hunt for the Engineer: How Israeli Agents Tracked the Hamas Master Bomber.* New York: Fromm International, 2001. Used with permission.

CHAPTER SUMMARY

This chapter discussed terrorist objectives, methods, and targets. It also discussed the effectiveness of terrorism.

Typical objectives included the terrorists' desire to change the existing order, to promote the psychological and social disruption of a society, to publicize their cause through propaganda by the deed, and to create a generalized revolutionary environment. In order to accomplish their objectives, terrorists have traditionally directed their attention to the manipulation of specific audiences. In the era of the New Terrorism, objectives have become characterized by vagueness, and methods have included indiscriminate attacks and the possibility of the use of weapons of mass destruction.

Modern terrorist methods reflect the changing global political environment and are characterized by asymmetrical warfare and new, cell-based organizational models. However, most terrorists rely on age-old methods that can be accomplished by using such conventional weapons as firearms and explosives. Modern technologies such as rocket-propelled grenades, precision guided munitions, and barometric bombs are updated variations on the same theme. Nevertheless, threats from biological, chemical, radiological, and nuclear weapons are unprecedented in the possible arsenals of terrorists.

Terrorist targets are selected because of their symbolic value and the impact they will have on affected audiences. Typical targets include embassies, international symbols, symbolic buildings and sites, symbolic people, and passenger carriers. These targets are selected because they represent the interests of a defined enemy.

The effectiveness of terrorist attacks is measured by unconventional criteria. From the terrorists' perspective, these criteria include gaining media and political attention, affecting targeted audiences, gaining concessions from an enemy interest, disrupting normal routines, and provoking the state to overreact.

In Chapter 11, students will assess the role of the media. The discussion will illustrate how the media can be used to manipulate information, what it means to consider the media to be a "weapon," the language of reporting terrorism, and issues involved in regulating the media.

KEY TERMS AND CONCEPTS

The following topics were discussed in this chapter and are found in the Glossary:

AK-47	Mines
Anthrax	Molotov cocktail
Armed propaganda	Molotov, Vyacheslav
Assault rifles	Mustard gas
Asymmetrical warfare	Nerve gas
Ayyash, Yehiya	Nuclear weapons
Begin, Menachem	People Against Gangsterism and Drugs
Biological agents	Phosgene gas
Botulinum toxins (Botulism)	Plastic explosives
Bubonic plague	Potassium cyanide
Chemical agents	Precision guided munitions
Chlorine gas	Pressure trigger
Composite-4 (C-4)	Radiological agents
Covenant, the Sword, and the Arm	Raziel, David
of the Lord, The (CSA)	RDX
Dynamite	Revolutionary Organization
Electronic trigger	November 17
Fallout	Rocket-propelled grenades
Fuses	RPG-7
Engineer, The	SA-7
Gasoline bomb	Sarin nerve gas
Grail	Semtex
Irgun	Signature method
Islamic Jihad	Smallpox
Jabotinsky, Vladimir	Sodium cyanide
Kalashnikov, Mikhail	Stinger
Kidnapping/hostage-taking	Submachine guns
King David Hotel Bombing	Suicide bombings
M-16	TNT
Martyr nation	TWA Flight 847
Media-oriented terrorism	Vehicular bomb

Discussion Box   **Attacks Against the U.S. Marine**
                                  and French Paratrooper Headquarters in Beirut

This chapter's Discussion Box is intended to stimulate critical debate about how determined terrorist attacks can affect the policies of nations.

In September 1982, 5,000 elite French paratroopers, Italian *Bersaglieri*, and American Marines were sent into Beirut, Lebanon, as members of the peace-keeping Multinational Force (MNF). The purpose of the MNF was to restore order to the city in the midst of a civil war and an Israeli invasion that had been launched to drive the Palestine Liberation Organization from Lebanon.

Members of radical Lebanese Islamic militia movements, specifically the Sunni Amal and Shi'ite Hezbollah groups, viewed the MNF as an invasion force. From their perspective, the West supported the Lebanese Christian Phalangists and the Israelis. They at first waged low-intensity resistance against the Western presence. A gradual escalation then occurred, with Amal and Hezbollah fighters becoming more aggressive in their opposition. In response to casualties incurred by Marines and French Paratroopers, the United States began shelling Syrian-controlled positions from naval vessels.

On October 23, 1983, two suicide bombers driving vehicular bombs simultaneously struck the U.S. Marines' and French paratroopers' headquarters in Beirut; 241 Marines and 58 paratroopers were killed. The terrorist group Islamic Jihad—probably a splinter group of the Lebanese Shi'ite movement Hezbollah—claimed credit for the attacks. The bombings were hailed by Amal and Hezbollah leaderships (who were careful to deny any responsibility for the attacks) as legitimate resistance by patriots against occupying armies.

After the attacks, the United States began using air power and naval artillery to shell hostile positions. However, public opinion had turned against the increasingly complicated "peace-keeping" mission, and MNF troops were withdrawn in early 1984.

Discussion Questions

- Were the Lebanese militia fighters terrorists or freedom fighters?
- Is terrorism "poor man's warfare" and therefore a legitimate option for waging war?
- Were the suicide bombings acceptable methods for opposing the deployment of the MNF?
- Was the presence of Western soldiers indeed an understandable precipitating cause of Amal's and Hezbollah's resistance?
- Were the targets—the French and American headquarters—logical targets for relatively weak opposition forces?

RECOMMENDED WEB SITES

The following Web sites provide links to discussions and data about terrorist objectives, methods, and targets.

Al Qaeda "Training Manual": www.usdoj.gov/ag/trainingmanual.htm

Anarchist's Cookbook, The: Search engine, enter: Anarchist's Cookbook

Center for Defense Information: www.cdi.org

Jaffe Center for Strategic Studies (Tel Aviv): www.tau.ac.il/jcss/lmas.html#Terror

Patterns of Global Terrorism (State Department): http://www.state.gov/s/ct/rls/

Terrorist's Handbook, The: Search engine, enter: Terrorist's Handbook

WEB EXERCISE

Using this chapter's recommended Internet sites, conduct an online investigation of terrorist objectives, methods, and targets.

- What common patterns of behavior and methods can you identify across regions and movements?
- Conduct a search for other Web sites that offer advice for organizing terrorist cells and carrying out terrorist attacks. Do you think that the online terrorist manuals and weapons advice are a danger to global society?
- Compare the Web sites for the monitoring organizations. How would you describe the quality of their information? Are they providing a useful service?

For an online search of terrorist tactics and targets, students should activate the search engine on their Web browser and enter the following keywords:

"Terrorist Weapons"
"Terrorist Manuals"

RECOMMENDED READINGS

The following publications provide discussions on terrorist objectives and methods.

Bergen, Peter L. *Holy War, Inc.: Inside the Secret World of Osama bin Laden*. New York: Simon & Schuster, 2001.

Katz, Samuel M. *The Hunt for the Engineer: How Israeli Agents Tracked the Hamas Master Bomber*. New York: Fromm International, 2001.

Powell, William. *The Anarchist Cookbook*. New York: Lyle Stuart, 1971; assigned to Barricade Books, 1989.

Stern, Jessica. *The Ultimate Terrorists*. Cambridge, MA: Harvard University Press, 1999.

Tucker, Jonathan B., ed. *Toxic Terror: Assessing Terrorist Use of Chemical and Biological Weapons*. Cambridge: MIT Press, 2000.

NOTES

[1] For a discussion of moral disengagement in the use of political violence, see Bandura, Albert. "Mechanisms of Moral Disengagement." In Reich, Walter, ed. *Origins of Terrorism: Psychologies, Ideologies, Theologies, States of Mind*. Washington, DC: Woodrow Wilson Center Press, 1998, pp. 161 ff.

[2] Ibid., p. 164.

[3] Students will recall that this quotation was more widely reported after the war as "we had to destroy the village to save it." The accuracy and source of the statement has been debated by journalists, scholars, and policymakers. See Oberdorfer, Don. *Tet!* Garden City, NY: Doubleday, 1971, pp. 184-85, 332. See also Sheehan, Neil. *A Bright Shining Lie: John Paul Vann and America in Vietnam*. New York: Random House, 1988, p. 719.

[4] A statement made by Republican Senator Barry Goldwater of Arizona during his bid for the presidency in 1964 against President Lyndon Johnson.

[5] A statement made by Chinese military philosopher Wu Ch'i.

[6] See Keegan, John, and Richard Holmes. *Soldiers: A History of Men in Battle*. New York: Elisabeth Sifton Books, 1986, pp. 252-53.

[7] Weimann, Gabriel, and Conrad Winn. *The Theater of Terror: Mass Media and International Terrorism*. New York: Longman, 1994, p. 173.

[8] For a good discussion of the objectives of states vis-à-vis dissidents, see Sederberg, Peter C. *Terrorist Myths: Illusion, Rhetoric, and Reality*. Englewood Cliffs, NJ: Prentice Hall, 1989, pp. 92 ff.

[9] Another inventory of objectives is presented by Pillar, Paul R. *Terrorism and U.S. Foreign Policy*. Washington, DC. Brookings Institution Press, 2001, pp. 130-31.

[10] Heymann, Philip B. *Terrorism and America: A Commonsense Strategy for a Democratic Society*. Cambridge: MIT Press, 1998, p. 9.

[11] Kershaw, Sarah. "Even 6 Months Later, 'Get Over It' Just Isn't an Option." *New York Times*. March 11, 2002.

[12] Debray, Regis. *Revolution in the Revolution?* Westport, CT: Greenwood, 1967. Quoted in Hewitt, Christopher. "Public's Perspectives." In Paletz, David L., and Alex P. Schmid, eds. *Terrorism and the Media*. Newbury Park, CA: Sage, 1992, p. 189.

[13] Crelinsten, Ronald D. "Victims' Perspectives." In Paletz, David L., and Alex P. Schmid, eds. *Terrorism and the Media*. Newbury Park, CA: Sage, 1992, p. 212.

[14] See Heymann (note 10 above), pp. 10-11.

[15] Ibid., p. 161.

[16] Hoffman, Bruce. *Inside Terrorism*. New York: Columbia University Press, 1998, p. 158.

[17] Ibid., p. 165.

[18] See Stern, Jessica. *The Ultimate Terrorists*. Cambridge, MA: Harvard University Press, 1999, pp. 70 ff.

[19] See Stern, Jessica Eve. "The Covenant, the Sword, and the Arm of the Lord (1985)." In Tucker, Jonathan B., ed. *Toxic Terror: Assessing Terrorist Use of Chemical and Biological Weapons*. Cambridge: MIT Press, 2000, pp. 139-57.

[20] See Judge Kevin T. Duffy. Sentencing Statement. *United States of America v. Mohammad A. Salameh, et al.*, S593CR.180 (KTD), May 24, 1994, p. 36. Quoted in Parachini, John V. "The World Trade Center Bombers (1993)." In Tucker, Jonathan B., ed. *Toxic Terror: Assessing Terrorist Use of Chemical and Biological Weapons*. Cambridge: MIT Press, 2000, pp. 185-86.

[21] See Parachini, ibid., pp. 186-87.

[22] Pillar (note 9 above), p. 47.

[23] Ibid., pp. 48-49.

[24] The term was used in a study conducted by the National Defense Panel titled "Transforming Defense: National Security in the 21st Century." The 1997 report warned that "unanticipated asymmetries" in the international security environment would likely result in an attack on the American homeland. Leiby, Richard. "Rueful Prophets of the Unimaginable: High-Level Studies Warned of Threat." *Washington Post*. September 22, 2001.

[25] Lesser, Ian O. "Countering the New Terrorism: Implications for Strategy." In Lesser, Ian O., Bruce Hoffman, John Arquilla, David Ronfeldt, and Michele Zanini. *Countering the New Terrorism*. Santa Monica, CA: RAND, 1999, p. 94.

[26] Haselkorn, Avigdor. "Martyrdom: The Most Powerful Weapon." *Los Angeles Times*. December 3, 2000.

[27] Arquilla, David Ronfeldt, and Michele Zanini. "Networks, Netwar, and Information-Age Terrorism." In Lesser, Ian O., Bruce Hoffman, John Arquilla, David Ronfeldt, and Michele Zanini. *Countering the New Terrorism*. Santa Monica, CA: RAND, 1999, p. 47.

[28] See ibid., p. 49.

[29] Haselkorn (note 26 above).

[30] See Hoffman, Bruce. "Terrorism Trends and Prospects." In Lesser, Ian O., Bruce Hoffman, John Arquilla, David Ronfeldt, and Michele Zanini. *Countering the New Terrorism*. Santa Monica, CA: RAND, 1999, pp. 28 ff.

[31] Hoffman, Bruce (note 16 above), p. 121.

[32] Stern (note 19 above), citing U.N. General Assembly. *Report of the Secretary-General on Chemical and Bacteriological (Biological) Weapons and the Effects of Their Possible Use*. U.N.G.A. A/7575, 1969, p. 6.

[33] Ibid., pp. 21-22.

[34] Ibid., p. 26.

[35] For a discussion of the nuclear threat, see Laqueur, Walter. *The New Terrorism: Fanaticism and the Arms of Mass Destruction*. New York: Oxford University Press, 1999, pp. 70 ff.

[36] Sun Tzu. *The Art of War*. New York: Oxford University Press, 1963, p. 168.

[37] For a good discussion of Hezbollah's rationale in deploying suicide bombers, see Kramer, Martin. "The Moral Logic of Hezbollah." In Reich, Walter, ed. *Origins of Terrorism: Psychologies, Ideologies, Theologies, States of Mind*. Washington, DC: Woodrow Wilson Center Press, 1998, pp. 131 ff.

[38] The 1996 attacks by Hamas led to the election of a hawkish Israeli administration.

[39] From Ripley, Amanda. "Why Suicide Bombing Is Now All the Rage." *Time*. April 15, 2002.

[40] MacFarquhar, Neil. "Qaeda Says Bin Laden Is Well, and It Was Behind Tunis Blast." *New York Times*. June 23, 2002.

[41] See Ratnesar, Romesh. "Season of Revenge: The Inside Story of How Israel Imprisoned Arafat—and Why the Rage Keeps Burning." *Time*. April 8, 2002; and ibid.

[42] Marighella, Carlos. "Mini-Manual of the Urban Guerrilla." In Mallin, Jay, ed. *Terrorism and Urban Guerrillas: A Study of Tactics and Documents*. Coral Gables, FL: University of Miami Press, 1971, pp. 103-04.

[43] See Hoffman (note 16 above), pp. 34-35.

[44] See Stone, Martin. *The Establishment of Algeria*. London: Hurst & Co., 1997. In Whittaker, David J., ed. *The Terrorism Reader*. New York: Routledge, 2001, pp. 146-47.

[45] November 17, a Marxist terrorist movement, had a long history of attacks against NATO and American interests. The group was finally suppressed in 2002 after a series of arrests by Greek security officers.

[46] For a discussion of several "myths" about terrorism, including the notion that it is highly effective, see Laqueur, Walter. "The Futility of Terrorism." In Kegley, Charles W., Jr., ed. *International Terrorism: Characteristics, Causes, Controls*. New York: St. Martin's Press, 1990, pp. 69 ff. Another good discussion of effectiveness is found in Sederberg, Peter C. *Terrorist Myths: Illusion, Rhetoric, and Reality*. Englewood Cliffs, New Jersey: Prentice Hall, 1989, pp. 96 ff; and also Heymann, Philip B. *Terrorism and America: A Commonsense Strategy for a Democratic Society*. Cambridge: MIT Press, 1998, pp. 12 ff.

[47] Hoffman (note 16 above), p. 176.

[48] The Red Army Faction/Baader-Meinhof Gang were discussed in Chapter 6.

[49] Weimann, Gabriel, and Conrad Winn. *The Theater of Terror: Mass Media and International Terrorism*. New York: Longman, 1994, p. 59.

[50] Schmid, Alex P. "Terrorism and the Media: Freedom of Information vs. Freedom from Intimidation." In Howard, Lawrence, ed. *Terrorism: Roots, Impact, Responses*. New York: Praeger, 1992, pp. 101-02.

[51] www.pagad.co.za

[52] Crenshaw, Martha. "The Logic of Terrorism: Terrorist Behavior as a Product of Strategic Choice." In Reich, Walter, ed. *Origins of Terrorism: Psychologies, Ideologies, Theologies, States of Mind*. Washington, DC: Woodrow Wilson Center Press, 1998, p. 22.

[53] *Time*. April 11, 2002.

[54] Menachem Begin said later that the Irgun placed at least three telephone calls warning of the attack—to the hotel, the French consulate, and the Jerusalem Post newspaper.

Chapter 11

THE ROLE OF THE MEDIA

This chapter will introduce students to the role of the media in a terrorist environment. There is frequent interplay between media reporting and the use of violence by extremist movements. If terrorism is a strategy characterized by symbolic attacks on symbolic targets, it is also a strategy characterized by the intentional manipulation of the news media. Since the inception of the modern era of terrorism, "terrorist attacks are often carefully choreographed to attract the attention of the electronic media and the international press."[1] In the modern era, the truism that "**information is power**" is very clearly understood by the media and governments; it is also understood by terrorists, their audiences, and their adversaries.

The ability of modern news agencies to use satellite and digital technologies to broadcast events as they happen "live"—and graphically—to a global audience has not been lost on violent extremists. Terrorists understand that instantaneous media exposure for their grievances simply requires a dramatic incident to attract the world's press. Terrorists seeking publicity are likely to garner a large audience if they dramatically carry out targeted hijackings, bombings, hostage takings, assassinations, or other acts of violence. The press has its own incentives to report major terrorist incidents. From the media's point of view—and aside from its fundamental responsibility to objectively report the news—drama guarantees increased attention from potential viewers.

A brief introduction to two perspectives is useful for understanding the role of the media. These perspectives will be developed further in this chapter. The first is from the media's perspective, and the second is from the perspective of governments.

THE MEDIA'S PERSPECTIVE

For journalists, the time-honored professional ideal is to report the news objectively, without placing too much "spin" on the information. The concept of **media spin** refers to the inclusion of subjective (opinionated) interpretations when reporting the facts. Interpretation is, of course, very desirable at some point during a terrorist incident, but there is an urge within the media to immediately create a mood or a dramatized atmosphere when reporting the news. This is typical of many news outlets and reflects the modern trend toward "tabloid" talk radio, "reality" shows, and "family-oriented" television news—even in major urban outlets. The fact is that a **news triage** (selection process) does occur, so that some news items are given a higher priority than others. Editors must decide what information to report and how it should be reported. As a consequence, dramatic news such as terrorist incidents often reflects the biases of editors and reporters and contains a great deal of emotional "human interest" content.

Because the news triage is a significant factor in the processing of information by audiences, it can be a critical element in the audience's analysis of a particular terrorist environment. For example, editors generally focus on and report terrorist violence without critical analysis of the terrorists' cause or the symbolic message conveyed by their behavior. This can leave the recipient audience with an incomplete understanding of the terrorist environment, and it gives rise to misperceptions and misinterpretations of the terrorists, the grievances of their championed group, and government responses.

THE PERSPECTIVE OF GOVERNMENTS

Policymakers are challenged to develop coherent and consistent policies to respond to acts of terrorism. They are also challenged to develop popular policies that are accepted by the public. When democratic governments try to create a national consensus, they seek to control the media's spins on the terrorist incident. Unfortunately for policymakers, the media can be—and usually are—a source of concern. This is because the press is adept at creating political environments that can sway public opinion. In societies that pride themselves on protecting freedom of the press,

> Terrorism . . . can cause enormous problems for democratic governments because of its impact on the psychology of great masses of citizens. . . . Terrorist bombings, assassinations, and hostage-taking have, in nations with a free press, the ability to hold the attention of vast populations.[2]

For this reason, some level of contention or animosity is frequently present in the relationship between government officials and members of the media when terrorism moves to the forefront of public discourse. In the United States, this tension occurs at all levels of government interaction with the media, from the president's spokespersons, to cabinet-level federal representatives, to local law enforcement officials. At each level, there is often an instinctive (and noticeable) attempt by officials to either keep the media at "arm's length" or to manipulate the conditions for media access to information.

The discussion in this chapter will review:

- An Introduction to the Role of the Media
- A New Battleground: The War for the Information High Ground
- The Public's Right to Know: Regulating the Media

AN INTRODUCTION TO THE ROLE OF THE MEDIA

In societies that champion freedom of the press, a tension exists between the media's professional duty to objectively report the news and the terrorists' desire to use the media to promote their cause. This is a tension between the necessity to keep the public informed and deliberate attempts to manipulate the world's media to disseminate **propaganda**. *Propaganda* is defined as "any systematic, widespread, deliberate indoctrination or plan for such indoctrination."[3] It is used by organizations, movements, and governments to spread their interpretations of the truth or to invent a new truth. Propaganda can incorporate elements of *truth*, *half-truths*, and *lies*. Underlying all extremist propaganda is a particular political agenda.

The media sometimes tread a fine line between providing news and disseminating the terrorists' message. This happens when they report the details of terrorist incidents, broadcast interviews with terrorists and their extremist supporters, or investigate the merits of the terrorists' grievances. In *theory*, the media will be mindful of this fine line and will carefully weigh what news to report and how to do so. In *practice*, some media outlets are blatantly sympathetic to one side of a conflict and completely unsympathetic to the other side. In authoritarian states, this occurs as a matter of routine, because the government heavily regulates the media. In democracies, the **free press** enjoys the liberty to apply whatever spin is deemed desirable in their reporting practices. Some media purposely use provocative language and photographs to attract an audience.

The following discussion will review several factors one should consider when evaluating the role of the media. They are:

- Publicizing the cause
- Mass communications and the terrorists' message
- Mass communications and the "new media"
- The reporting of terrorism

Publicizing the Cause

Terrorists frequently try to publicize their cause, hoping to reach as broad an audience as possible. They do this by adapting their tactics so that their methods are accredited in a public environment. *Media-oriented terrorism* refers to terrorism that is purposely carried out to attract attention from the media, and consequently the general public.[4] Methods and targets are selected because they are likely to be given high priority by news outlets. The purpose of media-oriented terrorism is to deliver the terrorists' message. Thus, "terrorism . . . may be seen as a violent act that is conceived specifically to attract attention and then, through the publicity it generates, to communicate a message."[5]

Terrorists and extremist movements that seek broad exposure have been known to directly and indirectly cultivate relationships with reporters and to establish aboveground organizations that promote media relations. For example, the mainstream Irish Republican political party Sinn Féin has long had a sophisticated information operation, which has historically included close relationships with the print and broadcast media.[6] Some terrorists and rebel movements have also cast themselves as the "military wing" of political movements. For example, Colombia's FARC (discussed in Chapter 6) was originally founded as the armed wing of the Colombian Communist Party in 1964. Both Sinn Féin and the Colombian Communist Party engaged in aboveground political public relations while the Irish Republican Army and FARC waged armed rebellion.

For terrorists concerned about delivering their message, the question is: How can the dissident group communicate its grievances to the world (or a regional) community? Which institutions are most likely to publish the underlying reasons for the group's revolutionary violence? Governments and other targeted interests are highly unlikely to "get the word out" about the merits of the cause—if anything, they will denounce the incident and the cause. Governments and targeted interests are also quite likely to try to control the flow of information and to craft their comments in a manner that will sway an audience against the extremist movement. The best solution to this problem is for terrorists to access and use the technologies of **mass communications**. They can do this in a number of ways, including

appropriation of technologies for their own use to personally send their message to the public (perhaps through aboveground sympathizers), and

skillful "packaging" of their message, hoping to send it through international media outlets.

By cleverly manipulating these technologies and the world's press, terrorists can create a mood among target audiences that can lead to public pressure for the government or other adversary to "do something"—perhaps even grant concessions to the movement. For example, when the media focuses on terrorist victimization (which it usually does), "it is clear that media coverage of victimization can aid in the generation of messages from terrorists to their various target audiences."[7] At the same time, media attention can affect the behavior of target governments: "By stimulating and exacerbating public reaction to victim suffering and family tragedy, it is clear that media coverage can also increase pressure on targets of demands."[8]

Thus, when a message is filtered into the intended audience, and this message has been manipulated in an advantageous manner, the terrorists have successfully publicized their cause.

Mass Communications and the Terrorists' Message

Mass communications is the technological ability to convey information to a large number of people. It includes technologies that allow considerable amounts of information to be communicated through printed material, audio broadcasts, video broadcasts, and expanding technologies such as the Internet. Modern revolutionaries consider mass communications an invaluable tool for achieving the goals of their cause. In fact, the theories of "armed propaganda" are partly technology driven. For example, in his influential discussion of armed propaganda, Carlos Marighella wrote:

> The urban guerrilla must never fail to install a clandestine press and must be able to . . . produce small clandestine newspapers, pamphlets, flyers, and stamps for propaganda and agitation against the dictatorship. . . . The urban guerrilla engaged in clandestine printing facilitates enormously the incorporation of large numbers of people into the revolutionary struggle. . . . Tape recordings, the occupation of radio stations, and the use of loudspeakers, drawings on the walls . . . are other forms of propaganda.[9]

For terrorists, efficiency and timeliness are critical components to mass communication. *Efficiency* is necessary so that one's message will be delivered in an orderly (as opposed to garbled or chaotic) manner and received in an intelligible and easily understood form. *Timeliness* is also necessary, because the message must be received while it is still fresh and relevant. It makes little sense to send a message before an issue has had an opportunity to ripen; it likewise makes little sense to send a message after an issue has become moot. Chapter Perspective 11.1 demonstrates the importance of delivering a coherent message that is easily understood by a target audience.

Thus, if one's message is delivered efficiently and in a timely manner, it will have a stronger impact on the target audience. In fact, if the terrorists can successfully create identification between the audience and some sympathetic symbol of a terrorist incident, the audience could become a factor in resolving the incident. For example, when American hostages were taken during the 1980s in Lebanon and during the hijacking of **TWA Flight 847** (discussed later), an interesting dynamic occurred:

> Powerful pressure groups [were] created, demanding the safe return of the victims of kidnappings at almost any price. . . . The release of [the Lebanon] hostages was a major reason why the U.S. president sent arms to Iran. In the case of the hijacked TWA Flight 847 (June 14-30, 1985) the media exposure of the hostages generated enough pressure for the American president to make concessions.[10]

Chapter Perspective 11.1   **Delivering the Message**

Extremist movements will often use coded language to convey their message. This language is sometimes peculiar to the particular group or ideological movement. From the point of view of laypersons and people not attuned to this language, the group's message is not always easily processed. The following example demonstrates how an extremist group's propaganda can become lost in its own rhetoric.[a]

**Against Social-Democracy
and Liquidationism—
For Steadfast Revolutionary Work!**

Reformism does not mean improving the conditions of the masses; on the contrary, the vital role that reformism has played in the capitalist offensive shows that reformism means collaborating with the bourgeoisie in suppressing the mass struggle and implementing the capitalist program. . . .

The work of the Marxist-Leninist Party has been a beacon against the opportunism of the liquidationist and social-democratic trends. The Marxist-Leninist Party has persevered in steadfast revolutionary struggle, while the opportunists, as fair-weather "revolutionaries," are reveling in despondency and renegacy, are denouncing the revolutionary traditions from the mass upsurge that reached its height in the 1960s and early 1970s, and are cowering behind the liberals, labor bureaucrats and any bourgeois who is willing to throw them a crumb.[b]

Communiqué on the Second
Congress of the Marxist-Leninist
Party, USA, Fall 1983

NOTES

   a. See Sargent, Lyman Tower, ed. *Extremism in America: A Reader.* New York: New York University Press, 1995, pp. 85 ff.
   b. *Communiqué on the Second Congress of the MLP, USA.* Ibid., pp. 88-89.

Source: Sargent, Lyman Tower, ed. *Extremism in America: A Reader.* New York: New York University Press, 1995, pp. 85 ff. Used with permission.

Since the advent of printing presses using industrial-age technologies in the 19th century, terrorists and extremist movements have used virtually every available mass communications technology. The following technologies are commonly used by modern political extremists:

- **Print media**
- Radio
- Television
- The Internet

Print Media

Printed news and propaganda have been used extensively since the 19th century, when the printing press was perfected using steam power and then electric power. These technologies permitted the mass production of multiple-page documents. Privately owned newspapers became common, as did the dissemination of politically critical publications and propaganda.

Dissident movements relied on the printed word throughout the 20th century to disseminate their message. Sympathetic publishers and clandestine printing presses were instrumental in promulgating propaganda on behalf of dissident causes. Governments readily understood the power of the press to sway public sentiment, and there are many cases of crackdowns on aboveground newspapers. There are also many examples of the deployment of security forces to locate and shut down clandestine presses.

Radio

Radio broadcasts were used by many dissident movements prior to the advent of television. Many 20th-century movements continued to issue radio broadcasts in societies where large numbers of people were unable to receive uncensored television broadcasts and where shortwave radio was widely used. Students may recall from Chapter 10 that in 1969 the Brazilian groups National Liberation Action and MR-8 kidnapped the American ambassador to Brazil and successfully demanded that their manifesto be broadcast over the radio. Historically, clandestine radio broadcasts have been instrumental in publicizing the cause to selected audiences, including potential supporters. As has been the case with dissident printing presses, governments have used security forces to root out clandestine radio stations.

Television

The first widespread television broadcasts during the 1950s included news broadcasts. Prior to that time, the only visual images of political issues were broadcast in movie houses as newsreel footage. Newsreels were often little more than short propaganda films that presented the government's and mainstream society's points of view; they were useless to extremists unless their movements were depicted as the favored side in the broadcast. With the advent of mass broadcasts during the 1960s, news of the day was received relatively quickly in people's homes. For example, the Vietnam War became the modern era's first "television war," and for the first time unflattering and even horrific images were regularly seen in American households.

Television has since become the medium of choice for terrorists, especially in the era of cable and digital feeds. It provides immediate visibility and increases the size of the audience. Television also allows for the broadcast of dramatic images.

Television news breaks very quickly—often within minutes of an incident—and is broadcast worldwide. Satellite feeds can be linked from almost anywhere in the world. Television has thus become quite useful for promulgating the terrorists' message both visually and with dramatic, on-the-scene audio. All that is required is for them to manipulate the media into broadcasting a sympathetic spin for their grievances. The terrorists

> use television as the main instrument for gaining sympathy and supportive action for their plight by presenting themselves as risking their lives for the welfare of a victimized constituency whose legitimate grievances are ignored.[11]

If successful, terrorists can bring images of their war into the homes of hundreds of millions of people worldwide nearly instantaneously—possibly with sentimental content that can potentially sway large audiences to their side.

The Internet

Computer technology is now used extensively by many terrorist groups and extremist movements. It is not uncommon for Web sites to be visually attractive, user-friendly, and interactive. Music, photographs, videos, and written propaganda are easily posted on Web pages. Many of these postings portray the sense of a peaceful and rich culture of a downtrodden group. Graphic, gory, or otherwise moving images are skillfully posted, sometimes as photo essays that "loop" for continuous replay. E-mail addresses, mailing addresses, membership applications, and other means to contact the movement are also common.

Mass Communications and the "New Media"

The traditional and new resources just discussed are not the only media outlets. In the United States, there is a growing market in, and consumer demand for, the so-called **New Media**. New Media use existing technologies and alternative broadcasting formats to analyze and disseminate information. These formats include talk-show models, tabloid (sensational) styles, celebrity status for hosts, and blatant entertainment spins. Strong and opinionated political or social commentary make up a significant portion of New Media content. These qualities represent a distinctive media style:

New media are mass communication forms with primarily nonpolitical origins that have acquired political roles. These roles need not be largely political in nature; in some instances they are only tangentially so. What distinguishes these communication forms . . . is the degree to which they offer political discussion opportunities that attract public officials, candidates, citizens, and even members of the mainstream press corps.[12]

Common types of New Media include "political talk radio . . . television talk . . . electronic town meetings . . . television news magazines . . . MTV . . . and print and television tabloids."[13] These media are innovative in their formats and sensational in their delivery. They do not hesitate to make provocative and completely biased statements. An important quality of the New Media is that they are very innovative and frequently experiment with untried formats and issues. Some extremist groups have appeared in the New Media, but terrorists have not been particularly active in attempting to manipulate this resource.

The Reporting of Terrorism

The print and broadcast media have shown a propensity for giving priority to terrorist incidents in their news reports. This is understandable, given the influence terrorism can have on policymaking and domestic or international political environments. However, the media have not been consistent about which incidents they report or how these incidents are reported. The news triage will frequently give extensive coverage to some acts of political violence but will provide little if any information about other incidents. Similarly, media reports attach inconsistent labels to the perpetrators of political violence. There is also a disproportionate media interest in the sheer violent nature of terrorism, without an exploration of the underlying causes of this violence.

Market Competition

The news media are owned and controlled by large corporations that are largely motivated by market shares and profits. This affects the style, content, and reporting practices of the modern media. The fact is that objective reporting is often outweighed by other factors, such as trying to acquire a larger share of the viewing market vis-à-vis competitors. The "scoop" and the "news exclusive" are prized objectives. Thus, coverage can be quite selective, often allowing public opinion and government pronouncements to set the agenda for how the news will be spun. In this type of political and market environment, the media will often forgo criticism of counterterrorist policies. Coverage can also be quite subjective, with the biases of executives, editors, and commentators reported to the public as if they were the most salient features of a particular issue.

The following discussion illustrates the conflict between theoretical objectivity in news reporting and actual inconsistency when these reports are released. It summarizes the dilemma of *which* incidents are reported and *how* they are reported.

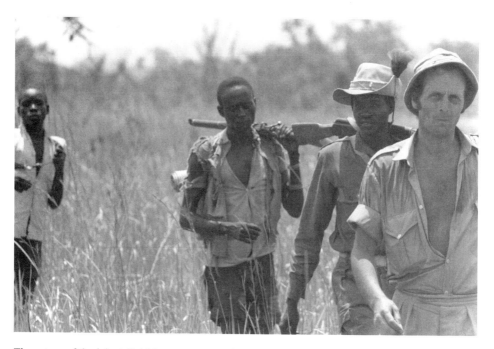

The nature of the job. A British war correspondent travels with southern Sudanese rebels. The rebels, who practiced Christianity or traditional religions, fought a long and brutal war against the northern Islamic government.

Source: Hulton Archive/Getty Images; used by permission.

Deciding Which Incidents to Report

The process for deciding which events to report (the news triage) is often driven by evaluating what kind of news is likely to attract a viewing audience. If it is decided that dramatic incidents will bring in sizable shares of viewers, the modern media will not hesitate to give such incidents a high priority for the day's editions or broadcasts. The media can be highly selective about which terrorist incidents to report. The ultimate decision tends to weigh in favor of news that affects the media's readers or viewing public. In a striking example of this phenomenon,

> Twelve people fell victim to terrorist attacks in Israel in 1985, two British soldiers were killed in Northern Ireland the same year, and the number of Americans killed by terrorists in 1982 was seven. There was great publicity in all these cases, whereas the tens of thousands killed in Iran and Iraq, in the Ugandan civil war, and in Cambodia (where hundreds of thousands were killed) went virtually unreported, because Western media either had no access or were not interested.[14]

The personal stories of participants in a terrorist environment are particularly appealing to the media. Strong emotions such as outrage, grief, and hatred play well to many audiences. Certain kinds of terrorist incidents are particularly susceptible to the media's use of "human interest" spins, because readers and viewers more readily identify with the victims of these incidents. For example, "hostage takings, like kidnappings, are human dramas of universal fascination."[15] Personal identification will always attract the public. The key task for the media is to find personal stories that resonate well with their readers or viewers. When this happens, the personal stories that do not resonate are likely to be left out of the news.

How to Report Incidents

The process of deciding how to report terrorist incidents is, from the readers' or viewers' perspective, seemingly a subjective exercise. Media reports have never been consistent in their descriptions of the perpetrators of terrorist incidents, nor have they been consistent in characterizing examples of extremist violence as terrorism per se. **Labeling** by reporters vacillates in connotation from the pejorative term *terrorist* to somewhat positive terms such as *commando*. These decisions in semantics sometimes reflect social norms. For example, "democratic societies value compromise and moderation so that the term *extremist* tends to be opprobrious."[16] This point is further demonstrated by the following sequence of reporting that occurred in 1973:

> One *New York Times* leading article . . . [described] it as "bloody" and "mindless" and [used] the words "terrorists" and "terrorism" interchangeably with "guerrillas" and "extremists." . . . The *Christian Science Monitor* reports of the Rome Pan Am attack . . . avoided "terrorist" and "terrorism" in favour of "guerrillas" and "extremists"; an Associated Press story in the next day's *Los Angeles Times* also stuck with "guerrillas," while the two *Washington Post* articles on the same incident opted for the terms "commandos" and "guerrillas."[17]

These labels reflect a tendency to use euphemistic (indirect or vague) language to describe what might otherwise be appalling behavior.[18] Euphemisms are also used by governments, policymakers, and others to apply words outside of their normal meaning to mask or soften the language of violence. This practice is deliberately media oriented so that the press and general public will more easily accept an incident or policy. Recent examples of **euphemistic language** used by government officials and soldiers at war include the following:

"Collateral damage"—dead civilians

"Deniability"—ability to plead ignorance

"Jihad"—holy war

"KIA"—dead soldiers

"Neutralize" or "suppress"—destroy or otherwise eliminate

"Preventive reaction strike"—air raid

"Robust"—aggressively violent

"Terminate with extreme prejudice"—assassinate

"Waste"—kill

"Wet work"—assassinations

"WIA"—wounded soldiers

A Word About Terrorist-Initiated Labeling

Terrorist groups also engage in labeling and adopt euphemistic language. They primarily do this in two circumstances: first, when they label enemy interests as potential targets, and second, when they engage in self-labeling. This language is promulgated in communiqués to supporters and journalists.

Table 11.1   Public Relations: The Organizational Titles of Violent Extremists

Terrorists seek to project an image that casts them in the role of liberators and soldiers. They are often conscious of their public image and can become quite media savvy.

The following table illustrates how organizational titles reflect terrorists' self-designations as military organizations, the purpose of their movements, and their championed groups.

Organizational Title	Self-Designation	Purpose	Championed Group
Popular Front for the Liberation of Palestine	A united front; a forward position in a war	Liberation of a people	Palestine and Palestinians
Irish Republican Army	An army; members are soldiers	Republican unification	Northern Irish Catholics
New People's Army	An army; members are soldiers	The continuation of a people's liberation movement	The people
Party of God (Hezbollah)	Movement representing God's will	Carry out God's will on earth	The faithful
Liberation Tigers of Tamil Eelam	Warriors possessing the fierceness of tigers	Liberation	Tamils
Quebec Liberation Front	A united front; a forward position in a war	Liberation of a people	Quebec and people of Quebec

Labeling of Enemies and Targets. Students will recall that terrorists use symbolism to dehumanize potential targets. This is a universal trait of violent extremists regardless of their ideology. For example, leftists might recast Western business travelers as *imperialists.* Or Armenian nationalists could symbolically hold Turkish diplomats to account for the Armenian genocide of the early 20th century. Or anti-Semitic and religious terrorists might label a Jewish Community Center as a *Zionist interest.* In the era of the New Terrorism, Al Qaeda and its sympathizers denounce Western culture and values as being contrary to Islam and the values of the faithful. This labeling process creates important qualifiers for acts of extreme violence, allowing terrorists to justify their behavior even though their victims are often noncombatants.

Self-Labeling. Choosing organizational or movement titles is an important task for terrorists. Those who engage in political violence consider themselves to be an elite—a vanguard—that is waging war against an implacable foe. They consciously use labels and euphemisms to project their self-image. Members of the cause become self-described *martyrs, soldiers,* or *freedom fighters.* Hence, organizational and movement titles always project an image of freedom, sacrifice, or heroism; negative or cowardly images are never conveyed. This pattern is universal among groups on the extremist fringe and is likely to continue. Table 11.1 surveys a few examples of self-labeling and euphemistic language.

A NEW BATTLEGROUND:
THE WAR FOR THE INFORMATION HIGH GROUND

Mass communications technologies can become weapons of war in modern conventional and asymmetrical conflicts. Because the mass media deliver vast amounts of information to large audiences, this informational battleground has become a front line in modern conflicts. Propaganda has, of course, been used by adversaries since the dawn of organized conflict. However, new technologies provide new opportunities and dangerous pitfalls for combatants. The following discussion surveys the manipulation of the media in terrorist environments.

Adversaries in a terrorist environment frequently try to shape the character of the environment by manipulating the media. *For terrorists*, the media serve several useful purposes: First, the media permit the dissemination of information about their cause; second, the media facilitate the delivery of messages to their supporters and adversaries; and third, the media serve as a "front" in their war to shape official governmental policies or influence the hearts and minds of their audience. *For governments*, the media can be a powerful tool for the suppression of terrorist propaganda and for the manipulation of the opinions of large segments of society. This is why every regime will intensively deliver selective information to the media or, as in the case of authoritarian regimes, officially suppress the reporting of some stories.

Revisiting the Participants in a Terrorist Environment

Students may recall from Chapter 2 that the participants in a terrorist environment adopt a multiplicity of interpretations of political violence. Depending on their role when an incident occurs, these participants often provide different assessments of the motives, methods, and targets of violent extremists. Subjective considerations commonly affect how an incident will be interpreted. Adversaries in a terrorist environment view participants as audiences that can be manipulated by effective propaganda or other selective information. The media are an obvious conduit for delivering this information. In many ways, the hearts and minds of the participants in a terrorist environment can become a virtual battleground.

It is instructive to summarize each participant group's role on the informational battlefield.

The Terrorist

Terrorists seek attention and legitimacy for their cause by engaging in media-oriented violence. Propaganda by the deed, if properly carried out, will deliver symbolic messages to a target audience and to large segments of an onlooker audience. One message could be, for example, to "show their power preeminently through deeds that embarrass their more powerful opponents."[19] Terrorists also attempt to cast themselves as freedom fighters, soldiers, and martyrs. If successful, their image will be that of a vanguard movement representing the just aspirations of an oppressed people. When this occurs, political and moral pressure can be brought against their adversaries, possibly forcing them to grant concessions to the movement.

The Supporter

Supporters and patrons of terrorists often help with "spinning" the terrorists' cause and manipulating the reporting of incidents. Supporters with sophisticated informational departments—such as Northern Ireland's Sinn Féin or Lebanon's Hezbollah—can successfully use the media to deliver their message to a wide audience. And in societies with a free press—or with supportive authoritarian regimes—sympathetic reporters and editors might lend a hand in portraying the terrorists as freedom fighters. Supporters will always defend the underlying grievances of the extremists and will often allude to these grievances as the reason for the group's decision to use terrorist methods. The key for activist supporters is to convey to the audience the impression that the terrorists' methods are understandable under the circumstances. If they can do this successfully, public opinion "can provide the movement with a feeling of legitimacy."[20]

The Victim

Media-oriented terrorist violence can be used to spin incidents so that they symbolize punishment or chastisement for injustices. From the terrorists' point of view, high-profile attacks that victimize an audience are useful as "wake-up calls" for the victims to understand the underlying grievances of the movement. Although victims rarely sympathize with the perpetrators who cause their suffering, terrorists believe that they can become educated through propaganda by the deed. Because they are the innocent "collateral damage" of a conflict, victims—with help from media commentators—will often question why they have become caught up in a terrorist environment. This process can theoretically cause public opinion shifts.

The Target

Media-oriented attacks select targets that symbolize the interests of the terrorists' adversaries. Of course, attacks on some targets—such as symbolic buildings—frequently risk inflicting casualties on large numbers of people. With the proper symbolic spin, terrorists can achieve "the lowering of the opponent's morale and the boosting of the self-confidence of its own constituency."[21] Terrorists can also garner sympathy, or at least a measure of understanding, if they can successfully use the media to disseminate their reasons for selecting the target. Targeted interests engage in an assessment process similar to that of victims and are likewise assisted by media commentators. The difference is that the investigatory process is conducted with the understanding that they have been specifically labeled as an enemy interest. In many circumstances, targeted audiences can have a significant impact on public opinion and government policy.

The Onlooker

Onlookers to terrorist incidents observe the dynamics of the attack, public reactions to the event, and political and media analyses of the incident. They can be directly or indirectly affected by the incident, and the media play a significant role in how the onlooker receives information. Depending on who is successful in the battle for information, the result can be that the onlooker will sympathize with the terrorists' grievances, oppose them, or remain indifferent. If the government engages in repression and terrorists or their supporters can spin this to their advantage, "one positive effect of repression is that it can supply the movement with new volunteers."[22]

The Analyst

The media play a strong role as interpreters of the terrorist incident. They also play a role in how other (nonmedia) analysts will have their views broadcast to a larger audience.

Political leaders, experts, and scholars all rely on the media to promulgate their expert opinions. Aside from contact with these analysts, journalists are prominently—and consistently—in communication with other participants in the terrorist environment. Journalists and other media analysts investigate perspectives, interpret incidents, and have significant input on the labeling process. Media analysts often define who is—or is not—a terrorist.

Practical Considerations: Using the Media

Terrorists and their supporters use time-honored techniques to attract media attention. In the tradition of mainstream media-savvy organizations (and aside from acts of dramatic violence), terrorists have invited the media to press conferences, issued press releases, granted interviews, released audio and video productions, and produced attractive photographic essays. They have also come to understand that they can adapt their methods and styles of violence to attract the media.[23] These adaptations can include

the degree of violence applied,

the use of symbolism, and

the performance of very spectacular or special deeds.[24]

These techniques have created environments wherein the media have been eager to receive the terrorists' message. There is a tendency for the media to sensationalize information, so that broadcasts of terrorist audio and video recordings, news conferences, or written statements often take on an entertainment quality.

Terrorists' Manipulation of the News "Scoop"

A competition takes place among news outlets in which they try to preempt the newsworthiness of their competitors' stories by means of **media scoops,** that is, "scooping" their rivals as the first to report breaking news. Even when there is no breaking news, news outlets will often spin human interest or background stories to give the audience an impression of urgency and drama. To accomplish this, journalists will frequently probe the feelings of participants in terrorist environments, including the terrorists themselves and their supporters. "This is a situation that, however unwittingly, is tailor-made for terrorist manipulation and contrivance."[25] There have been a number of occasions when terrorists and other radicals have successfully manipulated this propensity for scooping and sensationalization. For example:

Daniel Pearl. Pearl was kidnapped and later murdered by Pakistani Islamic terrorists, but not before they disseminated photographs and videotapes to the international media.

Source: U.S. Department of State.

- Ilich Ramirez Sanchez, also known as Carlos the Jackal, did not make his escape during the December 1975 OPEC hostage crisis until the television cameras arrived. After their arrival, he dramatically and publicly made his getaway from Vienna to Algeria with 35 hostages in tow.[26]
- During the November 1979 to January 1981 seizure of the American embassy in Iran, there were several incidents of Iranian crowds playing to the cameras. Crowds would come alive when the cameras were on them, so that some sections of the crowd would act temporarily militant while other sections of the crowd were rather quiescent.[27]
- In May 1986, ABC News broadcast a short interview with Abu Abbas, the leader of the Palestine Liberation Front (PLF). The PLF was notorious at the time because a PLF terrorist unit had carried out the October 1985 hijacking of the *Achille Lauro* cruise ship, in which American passengers were terrorized and one was murdered. During the interview, Abbas threatened to carry out acts of terrorism in the United States and referred to President Reagan as "enemy number one." The case of the *Achille Lauro* will be explored further in Chapter 13.

One former member of the leftist West German June 2nd Movement terrorist group made the following argument for the manipulation of the media by West German terrorists:

The RAF [Red Army Faction] has said, this revolution will not be built up by political work, but through headlines, through its appearance in the press, which reports again and again that *guerrilleros* are fighting here in Germany.[28]

Points of Criticism

Because of these and other examples of overt manipulation of the media by terrorists, critics have identified a number of problems in the reporting of the news. These include the following:

First, critics argue that journalists sometime cross the line between reporting the news and disseminating terrorist propaganda. The theoretical problem is that propaganda can be spread even when the media objectively report the motives of terrorists. When motives are broadcast, events can be intellectually rationalized.

Second, critics argue that the media's behavior sometimes shifts from objectivity to sensational opinion during particularly intense incidents. Journalists' urge to create a mood or to adopt roles other than as news reporters—such as de facto negotiators—can complicate terrorist environments.

Third, critics argue that the ability of the mass media to reach large audiences, when combined with the foregoing factors, can lead to realignments within the political environment. The concern is that strongly symbolic attacks by terrorists—in combination with skillful publicity operations by aboveground supporters—may be interpreted by audiences as the acts of rightfully desperate people. This could affect the dynamics of the terrorists' behavior and the government's policymaking options.

A possible outcome of these problems is that some types of reporting can interfere with official efforts to resolve crises. In the case of the United States, for example,

The media contribute to the process of transforming an international issue into a domestic political crisis for the president. There is perhaps no other type of situation that subjects the president to such intense scrutiny, and the president is aware that his image as a decisive and effective leader is constantly at risk.[29]

Thus, in the aftermath of the September 11, 2001, attacks, political and media critics hotly debated whether the media should continue to broadcast feeds from the Persian Gulf state of Qatar's **Al Jazeera** news service. Al Jazeera is one of the rare independent news services in the Middle East, and it broadcast extensive footage of injured Afghani civilians during the Afghan phase of the war on terrorism. Al Jazeera also aired film clips of Osama bin Laden that were released by Al Qaeda. The fear in the United States was that uninterpreted broadcasts could spread enemy propaganda or send messages to sleeper cells. For this reason, American news services were asked to limit Al Jazeera coverage.

Applying these concerns to our model of participants in a terrorist environment, it is conceivable that interviews with terrorists, media scooping, and other reporting practices may

> send messages to *terrorists,* possibly encouraging or suggesting targets for further acts of political violence;
>
> encourage *supporters,* thus improving morale and strengthening the terrorists' base of support for ongoing operations;
>
> cause *victims* to react, possibly demoralizing them or forcing shifts in public opinion and perceptions;
>
> engage the *target* in a global (rather than domestic) forum—this can hurt the target politically and can possibly lead to international pressure to moderate its behavior toward the terrorists' championed group;
>
> elicit sympathy—or at least understanding—from *onlookers*; and
>
> convince political and journalistic *analysts* to affix favorable labels to the group or movement. This may affect the world's perception of the terrorists, possibly transforming them into heroic *guerrillas* or *freedom fighters.*

Counterpointing the Criticism

As a counterpoint to the foregoing criticisms, and in defense of journalistic reporting of terrorist incidents, some proponents of the free press argue that full exposure of terrorism and the terrorists' grievances should be encouraged. In this way, the public can become completely informed about the nature of terrorism in general and about the motives of specific terrorists. Thus, "defenders of media coverage feel that it enhances public understanding of terrorism and reinforces public hostility toward terrorists."[30]

Information Is Power: The Media as a Weapon

The notion that information is power is a concept that politicians, governments, dictators, and extremists have accepted for some time. Controlling informational spins and the mechanisms of distribution are critical components for success, regardless of whether one wishes to sell a product, promote a political agenda, or impose an ideology. As pointed out in previous discussions, information outlets have been purposely sought out to spread the extremists' message, so that the manipulation of information has become a primary strategy in the modern era.

For terrorists and other extremists, information can be wielded as a weapon of war, so **"media as a weapon"** is an important concept. Because symbolism is at the center of most terrorist incidents, the media are explicitly identified by terrorists as potential supplements

TWA Flight 847. A terrorist waves a gun to cut short a press interview with TWA pilot John Testrake during the hijacked airliner's odyssey around the Mediterranean. The terrorists skillfully manipulated the international press.

Source: U.S. Department of State.

to their arsenal. When terrorists successfully—and violently—manipulate important symbols, relatively weak movements can influence governments and entire societies. Even when a terrorist unit fails to complete its mission, intensive media exposure can lead to a propaganda victory. For example, during the 1972 Munich Olympics attack by Black September terrorists, "an estimated 900 million persons in at least a hundred different countries saw the crisis unfold on their television screens."[31] As one PLO leader later observed, "World opinion was forced to take note of the Palestinian drama, and the Palestinian people imposed their presence on an international gathering that had sought to exclude them."[32]

Case: The Hijacking of TWA Flight 847

On June 14, 1985, three Lebanese Shi'ite terrorists hijacked TWA Flight 847 as it flew from Athens to Rome. It was diverted to Beirut, Lebanon, and then to Algiers, Algeria. The airliner was flown back to Beirut, made a second flight to Algiers, and then flew back to Beirut. During the odyssey, the terrorists released women, children, and non-Americans, until 39 American men remained on board the aircraft. At the final stop in Beirut, the American hostages were offloaded and dispersed throughout the city.

As the hijacking unfolded, the media devoted an extraordinary amount of airtime to the incident. ABC, CBS, and NBC broadcast almost 500 news reports, or 28.8 per day, and devoted two thirds of their evening news programs to the crisis.[33] "During the 16 days of the hijacking, CBS devoted 68% of its nightly news broadcasts to the event while the corresponding figures at ABC and NBC were 62% and 63% respectively."[34]

The hijackers masterfully manipulated the world's media. They granted carefully orchestrated interviews, held press conferences, and selected the information they permitted the news outlets to broadcast. It was reported later that the terrorists had offered to arrange tours of the airliner for the networks for a $1,000 fee, and an interview with the hostages for $12,500.[35] After the hostages were dispersed in Beirut, **Nabih Berri**, the leader of Lebanon's Syrian-backed Shi'ite **Amal** movement (an ally and occasional rival of the Shi'ite Hezbollah movement), was interviewed by news networks as part of the negotiations to trade the hostages for concessions. In the end, the terrorists' media-oriented tactics were quite effective. They successfully broadcast their grievances and demands to the world community and achieved their objectives. "[The] media exposure of the hostages generated enough pressure for the American president to make concessions."[36] In effect,

> The most pernicious effect of the crisis was its validation of terrorism as a tactic. The Reagan administration, driven by intense domestic pressure generated by the hostages' plight, in turn compelled Israel to accede to the hijackers' demands and release 756 Shi'a.[37]

The hostages were released on June 30, 1985.

As a postscript—which was sometimes forgotten during the episode—a U.S. Navy diver had been severely beaten, shot, and thrown down to the Beirut airport's tarmac by the terrorists. The murder occurred during the second stopover in Beirut. The leader of the terrorist unit, Imad Mughniyah, and three others were later indicted by U.S. prosecutors for the killing. One hijacker, Mohammed Ali Hamadi, was convicted in Germany of the Navy diver's murder and sentenced to life in prison.

The Contagion Effect

The ***contagion effect*** refers to the theoretical influence of media exposure on the future behavior of other like-minded extremists.[38] This concept can also be applied "to a rather wide range of violent behavior [other than terrorism], including racial disturbances."[39] In theory, when terrorists successfully garner wide exposure or a measure of sympathy from the media and their audience, other terrorists may be motivated to replicate the tactics of the first successful incident. This may be especially true if concessions have been forced from the targeted interest. Assuming that contagion theory has merit (the debate on this point continues), the question becomes the extent to which the contagion effect influences behavior. Examples of the contagion effect arguably include cycles of

> diplomatic and commercial kidnappings for ransom and concessions in Latin America during the 1960s and 1970s,
>
> hijackings on behalf of Middle East–related causes (usually Palestinian) from the late 1960s to the 1980s,
>
> similarities in the tactics of left-wing Western European ideological terrorists during their heyday from the late 1960s to the 1980s, and
>
> the taking of Western hostages in Lebanon during the 1980s.

Past assessments of the contagion effect produced some consensus that the media do have an effect on terrorist cycles. For example, empirical studies have indicated a correlation between media coverage and time lags between terrorist incidents.[40] These studies have not definitively *proven* that contagion is a behavioral fact, but they do suggest that the theory may have some validity.

The era of the New Terrorism arguably presents an unprecedented dynamic for contagion theory, because transnational cell-based movements are arguably a new model for— and may suggest new assessments of—the theory. Organizations such as Al Qaeda should be presumed to engage in a learning process from the lessons of attacks by its operatives around the world. The advent of new communications technologies such as telefacsimiles, cellular telephones, pagers, e-mail, and the Internet—when used in combination with focused manipulation of the media—means that the terrorists' "learning curve" can become a fast and efficient process. Hence, in theory the contagion effect may be enhanced within New Terrorist movements on a global scale.

The Risk of Backlash

As the examples of TWA Flight 847 and other incidents demonstrate, terrorists purposefully try to force concessions or environmental shifts through the media. In a terrorist environment,

> The media, then, do more than inform us when reporting on terrorism. They give tiny numbers of violent men access to millions of homes and allow the terrorist newsmakers to horrify us by sudden unprovoked killings of innocents.[41]

Unfortunately for terrorists, this widespread exposure does not always work to their advantage. Governments are also experts at spinning the nature of terrorist violence to the media. When the violence is truly horrific, and when the victims, targets, or onlooker audiences recoil in popular disgust, the terrorists can significantly diminish their influence over their adversary. They can, in effect, actually strengthen the adversary's resolve. Hence,

> A vital factor in gaining access to the media, lethality, can sow the seeds of a terrorist group's own destruction. Terrorist groups can experience an irremediable backlash, even among supporters, as a result of doing injury to innocents.[42]

Public opinion among victims, targets, and onlooker audiences is critical to the success of media-oriented terrorism. However, one should bear in mind that terrorists often play to their supporter audiences, so that "success" is always a relative term in the battle for the media.

THE PUBLIC'S RIGHT TO KNOW: REGULATING THE MEDIA

Freedom of the press is an ideal standard—and arguably an ideology—in many democracies. The phrase embodies a conceptual construct that suggests that the press should enjoy the liberty to independently report information to the public, even when this information might be unpopular. News editors and journalists, when criticized for their reports, frequently cite "the people's right to know" as a justification for publishing unpleasant information. The counterpoint to absolute freedom of the press is *regulation* of the press. This issue arises when the media publish unpleasant facts (often in lurid prose) about subjects that the public or the government would rather not consider. Regulation is also a genuine option when matters of national security are at stake. When these and other concerns arise, regimes and societies are challenged to address the following policy questions:

- Should the media be regulated?
- If regulation is desirable, how much regulation is acceptable?

The following discussion addresses these questions within the contexts of the free press and the **state-regulated press**.

The Free Press

The international media operate under many rules that emanate from their cultural environments. Some media operate with few if any codes of professional self-regulation, whereas others have adopted rather strict self-standards.[43] For example, the Netherlands Broadcasting Corporation has traditionally had no formal code of operations, whereas the British Broadcasting Corporation operates under a detailed set of rules.[44] Consensus exists that ethical standards should be observed when reporting terrorist incidents. These include the following:

[Do not] serve as a spokesman/accomplice of the terrorists . . .

[Do not] portray terror as attractive, romantic, or heroic; honest portrayal of motives of terrorists . . .

Hold back news where there is clear and immediate danger to life and limb.

Avoid . . . unchallenged terrorist propaganda . . .

Never try to *solve* a situation.[45]

Gatekeeping

In societies that champion freedom of the press, one model professional environment is that of **journalistic self-regulation**. Journalistic self-regulation is sometimes referred to as "**media gatekeeping**." If conducted under established standards of professional conduct, self-regulation obviates the need for official regulation and censorship. In theory, moral arguments brought to bear on the press from political leaders and the public will pressure them to adhere to model standards of fairness, accuracy, and objectivity.

This is, of course, an *ideal* free press environment; in reality, critics argue that journalistic self-regulation is a fluid and inconsistent process. As discussed previously, the media report terrorist incidents using certain labels and often create a mood by spinning their reports. Some media—acting in the tabloid tradition—sensationalize acts of political violence, so that very little self-regulation occurs. Chapter Perspective 11.2 illustrates this criticism by contrasting different standards of gatekeeping by the American media at several points in time when reporting news about several U.S. presidents.

Regulation of the Free Press

Many governments occasionally regulate or otherwise influence their press community while at the same time advocating freedom of reporting. Governments selectively release information, or release no information at all, during terrorist incidents. The rationale is that the investigation of these incidents requires limitations to be placed on which information is made available to the public. This occurs as a matter of routine during wartime or other national crises.

A number of democracies have state-run and semiprivate radio and television stations. For example, Great Britain, France, Germany, and other European democracies all have government-affiliated networks. These networks are expected to promote accepted standards of professional conduct and to practice self-regulation for the sake of good taste and national security. In some democracies, the law permits the government to suppress the reporting of news. For example:

- In Great Britain, the televised media were prohibited from broadcasting the statements of Irish terrorists or their supporters. No broadcasts were permitted of the

Chapter Perspective 11.2   An Examination of Self-Regulation and the American Media

Gatekeeping is a process of self-regulation by the press, using professional standards of restraint and industry guidelines about fair and objective journalism. The American media have traditionally practiced self-regulation with relatively little hindrance from government regulators, except in times of war (particularly during World War II).

Reporters working in the White House press pool, or otherwise reporting on the U.S. presidency, have developed gatekeeping standards that until recently ensured that the personal lives of presidents would not become front-page news. This "hands-off" approach to reporting details of presidential personal qualities has not been consistent. For example:

The reporting of *Franklin Delano Roosevelt's* (FDR) administration was highly self-censored. FDR was the United States' only president with a limiting disability. His legs were paralyzed, and he used a wheelchair from the age of 39. President Roosevelt wore thick braces on his legs to prop him up when he delivered speeches. And yet, no photographs were published of him in his wheelchair by the media, most likely because American culture at the time was biased against people with disabilities. During his last years in office, he has

been described as a dying man. Nevertheless, his declining health was never reported extensively to the public. The press also never reported persistent rumors about FDR's alleged long-term extramarital affair.

Likewise, the reporting of *John F. Kennedy's* (JFK) administration was self-censored. JFK symbolized the youth and idealism of a new generation. However, he suffered from poor health during much of his adult life. For example, he had Addison's disease, severe allergies, and congenital spinal problems, and he contracted malaria during the Second World War in the South Pacific. The media were captivated by JFK, portraying him as a man of great vigor and youth. As was the case with FDR, the press never reported rumors of alleged extramarital affairs.

In contrast, the reporting of *Bill Clinton's* personal life was lurid and long-term. Extramarital rumors were reported, interviews were broadcast of his accusers, and the Monica Lewinsky episode was front-page news around the world. For Bill Clinton, the media's self-regulatory gatekeeping practices were virtually nonexistent—particularly in comparison with the reporting of the personal lives of previous presidents.

Marxist Irish National Liberation Army. Even aboveground and somewhat mainstreamed broadcasts were banned, so that television broadcasts of interviews with Sinn Féin leader Gerry Adams were proscribed.

- Also in Great Britain, the **Official Secrets Act** permitted the prosecution of individuals for the reporting of information that was deemed to endanger the security of the British government.
- The Canadian Official Secrets Act proscribes any communication of information that may be prejudicial to the safety or interests of Canada.

The State-Regulated Press

State-regulated media exist in environments where the state routinely intervenes in the reporting of information by the press. This can occur in societies that otherwise have a measure of democratic freedoms. For example, Turkey has frequently suppressed its media and has one of the worst records among democracies. Hundreds of journalists were prosecuted in the past, receiving harsh sentences for writing offensive articles. In another example, the state-regulated presses of most countries in the Middle East led many people in those countries to believe that the September 11, 2001, attacks either were not the work of Al Qaeda or were the work of "the Jews." Some media commentators reported and supported a popular conspiracy theory that anonymous telephone calls warned thousands of Jewish workers in the World Trade Center to leave the buildings before the attack.

Different scales of intervention can emanate from the state, ranging from permitting independent (but regulated) newspapers to creating government-controlled propaganda enterprises. Some examples follow:

Under authoritarianism,[46] the press can be privately owned and may be granted some latitude in reporting the news. However, information is sometimes officially censored, and the publication of unfavorable articles can be punished. Singapore (a democracy) has a history of suppressing articles that make "libelous" accusations against the government.

Under totalitarianism,[47] the government operates on a more restrictive scale of intervention. In totalitarian systems, the state controls all information reported in the media, and the press is relegated to a state-controlled enterprise. For example, the People's Republic of China permits no independently published criticism from the media. During the bloody June 1989 suppression of the Tiananmen Square protests in Beijing, the Western press interviewed a number of Chinese civilians, eliciting some criticism of the government's actions. The interviewees were reportedly arrested.

In **authoritarian** and **totalitarian regimes**, terrorists have no chance to rely on the media to sensationalize their deeds. In these societies, the media serve to promote the government's interests and often to disseminate government propaganda. There are no gripping stories that might sway an audience. The general public is never privy to sympathetic human interest stories or to an extremist manifesto's call to arms. When terrorist incidents occur, they are either underreported by the government or manipulated to the absolute advantage of the regime. As a result,

> One of the reasons for the virtual absence of terrorism in totalitarian states and other effective dictatorships, besides the efficacy of the police forces, is the suppression of publicity. Unless the terrorists succeed in killing the dictator, which would be impossible to ignore, their deeds will pass unheralded.[48]

In very restrictive societies, the media are used as outlets for propaganda on behalf of the existing regime. For example, Iraqi dictator Saddam Hussein created an extensive **cult of personality** not unlike that of former dictators Joseph Stalin in the Soviet Union or North Korean dictator Kim Il Sung. Cults of personality are used by dictatorial regimes to promote the leader or ruling party as the source of absolute wisdom, truth, and benevolence. Likenesses of the leader are widely distributed, usually in a variety of symbolic poses. Saddam Hussein, for example, is regularly depicted as a visionary, a warrior, the good father, a common citizen, and a devout Muslim. Hussein, Stalin, and Kim promoted themselves, their regimes, and their policies by completely controlling the dissemination of information.

Case in Point　Media-Oriented Terror and Lebanon's Hezbollah

The Lebanese Shi'ite Hezbollah (Party of God) movement was responsible for hundreds of incidents of political violence during the 1980s and 1990s. These incidents included kidnappings of Westerners in Beirut, suicide bombings, attacks against Israeli interests in South Lebanon, and attacks against Israel proper. They operated under various names, such as Islamic Jihad and Revolutionary Justice Organization.

Hezbollah is a good case in point for a number of issues, including the following:

- Proxies for state-sponsored terrorism
- Practitioners of religious dissident terrorism
- Participation in international terrorism
- Application of asymmetrical methods such as high-profile kidnappings and suicide bombings

Hezbollah is also an interesting case in point for media-oriented terrorism. The group has historically promoted itself to the media in a number of ways, including disseminating its grievances as press releases, filming and photographing moving images of its struggle, compiling "human interest" backgrounds of Hezbollah fighters and Shi'ite victims, and packaging their attacks as valiant assaults against Western and Israeli invaders and their proxies. This has been done overtly and publicly, and incidents were sometimes manipulated to generate maximum publicity and media exposure. For example, the January 1987 kidnapping in Beirut of Terry Waite, the Archbishop of Canterbury's envoy, was broadcast globally. He was released in November 1991.

Hezbollah was skillful at conducting extraordinary strikes, some of which ultimately affected the foreign policies of France, Israel, and the United States. In the aftermath of these attacks, Hezbollah leaders and supporters—sometimes including the influential Lebanese Sunni Amal militia—would engage in public relations campaigns. Press releases were issued and interviews granted. Statements were made to the world press claiming, for example, that attacks against French and U.S. interests were in reprisal for their support of the Lebanese Christian **Phalangist** militia and the Israelis. This public linkage between terrorist attacks and a seemingly noble cause served to spin the violence favorably and thereby justify it.

Hezbollah would intentionally package its strikes as representing heroic resistance against inveterate evil and exploitation. They produced audio, photographic, and video images of their resistance for distribution to the press. For example, some of Hezbollah's attacks against the Israelis in South Lebanon were videotaped and sent to the media—with images of dead Israeli soldiers and stalwart attackers.

Young Hezbollah suicide bombers recorded videotaped messages prior to their attacks. These messages explained in very patriotic terms why they intended to attack Israeli interests as human bombs. These tapes were widely distributed, and the suicidal fighters were cast as martyrs in a righteous cause. Photographs and other likenesses of many Hezbollah "martyrs" have been prominently displayed in Hezbollah-controlled areas.

Hezbollah continues to maintain an extensive media and public relations operation and has posted a Web site.[a] The Web site contains a great deal of pro-Hezbollah information, including political statements, reports from the "front," audio links, video links, photographs, and e-mail links.

NOTE

a. See www.hizbollah.org.

CHAPTER SUMMARY

This chapter investigated the role of the media in terrorist environments. Particular attention was given to efforts by terrorists to **publicize the cause**, the manipulation of mass communications by terrorists, and the potential impact of the New Media. Issues regarding the reporting of terrorism by the media include questions about *which* incidents to report and *how* to report those incidents. The concepts of "information is power" and "media-oriented terrorism" were defined and explored as critical considerations for understanding the role of the media.

Evaluation of the new battleground for information requires that students first explore this issue from the perspectives of participants in terrorist environments. Practical considerations for terrorists' treatment of the media include their manipulation of the media's desire to "scoop" their competitors. The contagion effect and the example of the hijacking of TWA Flight 847 demonstrate how media exposure can become a weapon in the terrorists' arsenal.

Regulation of the media is a challenge for every government. For authoritarian and totalitarian regimes, this challenge is easily resolved by simply prohibiting certain kinds of reporting practices. It is a more complex issue in most democratic systems, although most have adapted by adopting laws and practices that restrict media access to operational information.

In Chapter 12, students will review terrorism in the United States. The discussion will investigate domestic sources of terrorism from the right and left, as well as cases of nationalist and international terrorism. Consideration will be given to terrorist typologies and the reasons for terrorism in the United States.

KEY TERMS AND CONCEPTS

The following topics were discussed in this chapter and are found in the Glossary:

Al Jazeera
Amal
Authoritarian regimes
Berri, Nabih
Contagion effect
Cult of personality
Euphemistic language
Free press
Information is power
Journalistic self-regulation
Labeling
Mass communications
Media as a weapon

Media gatekeeping
Media scoops
Media spin
New Media
News triage
Official Secrets Act
Phalangists
Print media
Propaganda
Publicize the cause
State-regulated press
Totalitarian regimes
TWA Flight 847

RECOMMENDED WEB SITES

The following Web sites are links to the online addresses of major media resources that regularly report news about terrorism:

Al Jazeera (Qatar): www.aljazeera.net

BBC (Britain): www.bbc.co.uk

CNN (USA): www.cnn.com

Dawn (Pakistan): www.dawn.com

New York Times: www.nytimes.com

Discussion Box	**Freedom of Reporting and Security Issues**

This chapter's Discussion Box is intended to stimulate critical debate about how to balance freedom of the press with the protection of national security.

During times of crisis, governments restrict media access to information about matters that affect security policy. The logic is quite understandable: Governments believe that the war effort (or counterterrorism policy) requires limitations to be imposed to prevent information from helping the enemy and to prevent the enemy from spreading its propaganda. For example, the British Official Secrets Act was designed to manage the flow of information both *from* adversaries and *to* adversaries.

The challenge for democracies is to strike a balance between governmental control over information—for the sake of national security—and unbridled propaganda. The following examples illustrate how the United States and Great Britain managed the flow of information during international crises:

- During the *War in Vietnam,* journalists had a great deal of latitude in the field to visit troops in the field and observe operations. Vietnam was the first "television war," so violent and disturbing images were broadcast into American homes on a daily basis. These reports were one reason why American public opinion turned against the war effort.
- During the *Falklands War,* news about operations was highly controlled and censored by the British government. Press briefings were strictly controlled by the government, under the rationale that useful information could otherwise be received by the Argentines and jeopardize the war effort.
- During the *Gulf War,* news was likewise highly controlled. Unlike during the Vietnam War, the media received their information during official military press briefings. They were not permitted to travel into the field except under highly restrictive conditions.
- During the Afghan phase of the *War on Terrorism,* news was also highly restricted. Official press briefings were the norm, and requests were made for cooperation in not broadcasting enemy propaganda.

Discussion Questions

- Should the United States adopt information-control regulations similar to Britain's Official Secrets Act?
- What are the policy implications of permitting journalists to have the same degree of access to information as occurred during the Vietnam War?
- What are the policy implications of permitting journalists to have the same degree of access to information as occurred during the Gulf War?
- Under what circumstances should the state increase restrictions on the media? How would you justify these restrictions?
- Do you think that the media in democracies are more prone to manipulation by terrorists? Or is this a myth?

WEB EXERCISE

Using this chapter's recommended Internet sites, conduct an online investigation of the reporting of terrorism by the media.

- Compare and contrast the reporting of political violence by the referenced media services. What patterns of reporting can you identify?
- To what extent are the media services biased in their reporting? How so?
- To what extent are the media services objective in their reporting? How so?

For an online search of reporting of terrorism by the media, students should activate the search engine on their Web browser and enter the following keywords:

"Media and Terrorism"
"Propaganda and Terrorism"

RECOMMENDED READINGS

The following publications provide discussions for evaluating the role of the media in the reporting of terrorism, national conflict, and political dissent.

Davis, Richard, and Diana Owen. *New Media and American Politics*. New York: Oxford University Press, 1998.

Gitlin, Todd. *The Whole World Is Watching: Mass Media in the Making & Unmaking of the New Left*. Los Angeles: University of California Press, 1980.

Knightley, Phillip. *The First Casualty: The War Correspondent as Hero and Myth Maker From the Crimea to Kosovo*. Baltimore: Johns Hopkins University Press, 2002.

Paletz, David L., and Alex P. Schmid, eds. *Terrorism and the Media*. Newbury Park, CA: Sage, 1992.

Weimann, Gabriel, and Conrad Winn. *The Theater of Terror: Mass Media and International Terrorism*. New York: Longman, 1994.

NOTES

[1] Jenkins, Brian. Quoted in Hoffman, Bruce. *Inside Terrorism*. New York: Columbia University Press, 1998, p. 132.

[2] Heymann, Philip B. *Terrorism and America: A Commonsense Strategy for a Democratic Society*. Cambridge: MIT Press, 1998, p. 9.

[3] *Webster's New Twentieth Century Dictionary of the English Language, Unabridged* (2d ed.) New York: Publishers Guild, 1966.

[4] See Weimann, Gabriel, and Conrad Winn. *The Theater of Terror: Mass Media and International Terrorism*. New York: Longman, 1994.

[5] Hoffman (note 1 above), p. 131.

[6] See Laqueur, Walter. *The New Terrorism: Fanaticism and the Arms of Mass Destruction*. New York: Oxford University Press, 1999, p. 44.

[7] Paletz, David L., and Alex P. Schmid, eds. *Terrorism and the Media*. Newbury Park, CA: Sage, 1992, p. 214.

[8] Ibid., p. 215.

[9] Marighella, Carlos. *Mini-Manual of the Urban Guerrilla*. In Mallin, Jay. *Terror and Urban Guerrillas: A Study of Tactics and Documents*. Coral Gables, FL: University of Miami Press, 1971, p. 104.

[10] Schmid, Alex P. "Terrorism and the Media: Freedom of Information vs. Freedom From Intimidation." In Howard, Lawrence, ed. *Terrorism: Roots, Impact, Responses*. New York: Praeger, 1992, p. 102.

[11] Bandura, Albert. "Mechanisms of Moral Disengagement." In Reich, Walter, ed. *Origins of Terrorism: Psychologies, Ideologies, Theologies, States of Mind*. Washington, DC: Woodrow Wilson Center Press, 1998, p. 172.

[12] Davis, Richard, and Diana Owen. *New Media and American Politics*. New York: Oxford University Press, 1998, p. 7.

[13] Ibid., pp. 9-15.

[14] Laqueur (note 6 above).

[15] Sick, Gary. "Taking Vows: The Domestication of Policy-Making in Hostage Incidents." In Reich, Walter, ed. *Origins of Terrorism: Psychologies, Ideologies, Theologies, States of Mind*. Washington, DC: Woodrow Wilson Center Press, 1998, p. 241.

[16] Weimann and Winn (note 4 above), p. 176.

[17] Hoffman (note 1 above), pp. 36-37.

[18] See Bandura (note 11 above), p. 169.

[19] Gerrits, Robin P. J. M. "Terrorists' Perspectives: Memoirs." In Paletz, David L., and Alex P. Schmid, eds. *Terrorism and the Media*. Newbury Park, CA: Sage, 1992, p. 36.

[20] Ibid., p. 39.

[21] Ibid., p. 38.

[22] Ibid.

[23] See ibid., pp. 45-49.

[24] Ibid., p. 46.

[25] Hoffman (note 1 above), p. 142.

[26] Ibid.

[27] See ibid.

[28] Schmid (note 10 above), p. 98. Quoting Schmid, Alex P., and Janney De Graaf. *Insurgent Terrorism and the Western News Media*. Leiden: Center for the Study of Social Conflicts, 1980, p. 48.

[29] Sick (note 15 above), p. 242.

[30] Barkan, Steven E., and Lynne L. Snowden. *Collective Violence*. Boston: Allyn & Bacon, 2000, p. 84.

[31] Hoffman (note 1 above), p. 74. Citing Taylor, Peter. *States of Terror: Democracy and Political Violence*. London: Penguin, 1993, p. 8.

[32] Ibid., p. 73. Quoting Iyad, Abu, with Eric Rouleau (Trans. Linda Butler Koseoglu). *My Home, My Land: A Narrative of the Palestinian Struggle*. New York: Time Books, 1981, pp. 111-12.

[33] Hoffman (note 1 above), p. 132.

[34] Weimann and Winn (note 4 above), p. 1.

[35] Barkan and Snowden (note 30 above).

[36] Howard, Lawrence, ed. *Terrorism: Roots, Impact, Responses*. New York: Praeger, 1992, p. 102.

[37] Weimann and Winn (note 4 above), p. 133.

[38] For a discussion of the contagion effect and additional discussions, see Weimann and Winn (note 4 above), pp. 157-60 and 211 ff.

[39] Ibid, p. 158. See also Spilerman, C. S. "The Causes of Racial Disturbances." *American Psychological Review* 35 (1970): 627-49; and Berkowitz, L., and J. Macaulay. "The Contagion of Criminal Violence." *Psychometry* 34 (1971): 238-60.

[40] See ibid., pp. 219 ff.

[41] Schmid (note 10 above), p. 101.

[42] Weimann and Winn (note 4 above), p. 144.

[43] See Paletz, David L., and Laura L. Tawney. "Broadcasting Organizations' Perspectives." In Paletz, David L., and Alex P. Schmid, eds. *Terrorism and the Media*. Newbury Park, CA: Sage, 1992, pp. 105 ff.

[44] Ibid., pp. 107 and 109.

[45] See ibid., p. 126.

[46] Defined in Chapter 4 as "A system of government in which authority and power emanate from the state, and are not delegated from the people to elected leaders. Law, order, and state authority are emphasized. Authoritarian regimes can have elected leaders, but they have authoritarian power and often rule for indefinite periods of time. Constitutions do not have enough authority to prohibit abuses by the state."

[47] Defined in Chapter 4 as, "A system of total governmental regulation. All national authority originates from the government, which enforces its own vision of an ordered society."

[48] Laqueur (note 6 above), p. 44.

Part IV

FINAL ANALYSIS

A Rewards for Justice program poster disseminated by the U.S. Department of State's Diplomatic Security Service. It depicts the aftermath of the 1993 bombing of the World Trade Center in New York City.

Source: U.S. Department of State.

Chapter 12

TERRORISM IN THE UNITED STATES

This chapter applies concepts introduced in previous chapters to the case of the United States. The focus of the discussion will be on contemporary terrorism—defined here as political violence occurring after the Second World War.

The quality of postwar ideological extremism in the United States reflects the characteristics of the classical ideological continuum, which was discussed in Chapters 1 and 2. Students may recall that the classical ideological continuum incorporates political tendencies that range from the fringe left to the fringe right. Students may also recall that many examples of nationalist and religious terrorism do not fit squarely within the categories of the continuum. However, the United States is an idiosyncratic subject, and most terrorism in the postwar era originated from the left- and right-wing spectrums on the classical ideological continuum.

Unlike many terrorist environments elsewhere in the world, where the designations of *left* and *right* are not always applicable, most political violence in the United States falls within these designations. Even nationalist and religious sources of domestic political violence have tended to reflect the attributes of leftist or rightist movements. It is only when we look at the international sources of political violence that the left and right designations begin to lose their precision in the United States.

It is instructive to briefly survey the American left, the American right, and international terrorism.

The *American left* traditionally refers to political trends and movements that emphasize group rights. Several trends characterize the American left: labor activism, "people's rights" movements, single-issue movements, and antitraditionalist cultural experimentation. For example:

Labor Activism. Historically, labor activism and organizing promoted ideals that are often found on the left. The labor movement of the late 19th and early 20th centuries was often violent, with violence emanating from management, the unions, and the state. Socialist labor activists such as Samuel Gompers were quite active in organizing workers. However, the mainstream American labor movement was distinctive, in comparison with European labor movements, in that the dominant labor unions generally rejected Marxist or other socialistic economic ideologies.[1]

People's Rights. There have been a number of "people's rights" movements on the American left. In the modern era, activism on the left has generally promoted the interests of groups that have historically experienced discrimination or a lack of opportunity. Examples of people's rights movements include the civil rights, **Black Power**, and **New Left** movements.

Single-issue movements such as the environmentalist and peace movements have also been common on the left.

Questioning Traditions. One facet of the left has been a tendency toward antitraditionalist cultural trends. Manifestations of this trend have included experimentation with alternative lifestyles and the promotion of countercultural issues such as drug legalization.[2]

On the far and fringe left, one finds elements of Marxist ideology and left-wing nationalist principles. Terrorist violence from the left has usually been ideological or ethnonationalist in nature. It has typically been carried out by covert underground organizations or cells that link themselves (at least ideologically) to leftist "rights" movements. Although there have been human casualties as a direct result of leftist terrorism, most violence has been directed at nonhuman symbols such as unoccupied businesses, banks, or government buildings. Law enforcement officers were also occasionally targeted, usually by ethno-nationalist terrorists. The heyday of leftist terrorism in the United States was from the late 1960s to the mid-1980s.

The *American right* traditionally encompasses political trends and movements that emphasize conventional and nostalgic principles. On the mainstream right, traditional values are emphasized. Examples include family values, educational content, and social order ("law and order") politics. It is also common on the American right (unlike the European right) to find an infusion of fundamentalist or conservative religious principles.

On the far and fringe right, one finds that racial, mystical, and conspiracy theories abound; one also finds a great deal of antigovernment sentiment, with some fringe extremists opting to separate themselves from mainstream society. Terrorist violence has usually been racial, religious, or antigovernment in nature. With few exceptions, terrorism from the right has been conducted by self-isolated groups, cells, or individual **"lone wolves."** Unlike most leftist attacks, many of the right's targets have intentionally included people and occupied symbolic buildings. Most ethnocentric hate crimes—regardless of whether one considers them to be acts of terrorism or aggravated crimes[3]—come from the far and fringe right wing. This type of ethnocentric violence has a long history in the United States:

> Since the middle of the nineteenth century, the United States has witnessed several episodic waves of xenophobia. At various times, Catholics, Mormons, Freemasons, Jews, blacks, and Communists have been targets of groups . . . seeking to defend "American" ideals and values.[4]

Right-wing terrorism has occurred within different political and social contexts, from **Ku Klux Klan** violence during the civil rights movement of the 1950s and 1960s, to neo-Nazi violence in the 1980s, to antigovernment and **single-issue terrorism** in the 1990s.

International terrorism in the United States has included anti-Castro movements, Jewish groups opposing the former Soviet Union's emigration policy, Irish Provos, and sporadic spillovers from conflicts around the world. Since the collapse of the Soviet Union, most international terrorism in the United States has come from spillovers originating in Middle Eastern conflicts. Attacks such as the September 11, 2001, homeland attacks indicate that practitioners of the New Terrorism have specifically targeted the United States as an enemy interest. Operatives carrying out Middle East–related attacks have been foreign nationals who attack symbolic targets, specifically intending to kill people. These attacks have usually been carried out by prepositioned cells. The members of these cells were drawn from groups such as Hamas and Islamic Jihad, which have had operatives and supporters living in the United States. Collaborative efforts by these and other

Table 12.1   Features of Terrorism in the United States

In the United States, terrorism has typically been conducted by groups and individuals espousing leftist or rightist ideologies or those who engage in international "spillover" conflicts. These interests are motivated by diverse ideologies, operate from different milieus, possess distinctive organizational profiles, and target a variety of interests.

The following table summarizes these typologies and activity profiles.

	Activity Profile			
Typology	*Ideological Profile*	*Bases of Operation*	*Organizational Profile*	*Typical Targets*
Leftist	Marxist; left-wing nationalist	Urban areas; suburbs	Clandestine groups; movement-based	Symbolic structures; avoidance of human targets
Rightist	Racial supremacist; antigovernment; religious	Rural areas; small towns	Self-isolated groups; cells; lone wolves	Symbolic structures; human targets
"Old" international terrorism	Ethno-nationalist	Urban areas	Clandestine groups	Symbols of enemy interest
"New" international terrorism	Religious	Urban areas	Cells	Symbolic structures; human targets

groups illustrate the internationalization of the New Terrorism, its loose organizational structure, and its potential effectiveness inside the United States.

Table 12.1 summarizes and contrasts the basic characteristics of contemporary left-wing, right-wing, and international political violence in the United States.[5] This is not an exhaustive profile, but it is instructive for purposes of comparison.

Cults are an important, though rare, source of terrorist violence. Few terrorist incidents occur in the United States that do not originate from the left, right, or international terrorist typologies. However, there have been a few examples of cult-initiated violence that do not easily fall within the classical ideological continuum and that cannot be described as international terrorist incidents. Although this type of violence is uncommon, a few incidents have been the result of rather fantastic political agendas that are rooted in cultic mysticism. Chapter Perspective 12.1 illustrates this point by summarizing three examples of violence emanating from American cults.

The discussion in this chapter will review:

- Background to Political Violence on the Left and Right
- Left-Wing Terrorism in the United States
- Right-Wing Terrorism in the United States
- The New Millennium and International Terrorism in the United States
- Prospects for Terrorism in the United States

Chapter Perspective 12.1   American Cults and Terrorist Violence

Cults are self-isolated mystical communities that claim to have definitive answers for societal and personal problems. They are usually tightly knit groups of people who follow a spiritual belief that is a product of some "higher" mystical insight. These beliefs are often based on extreme interpretations of existing religions. Many cults are led by a single charismatic spiritual leader. The Tokyo subway terrorist attack by the Japanese cult Aum Shinrikyō was discussed in Chapter 8.

Most American cults have not directed violence against nonmembers. However, some cults—such as the apocalyptic **People's Temple of the Disciples of Christ**—have committed acts of extreme violence against their own members, as well as nonmembers who challenged their authority. Founded and led by **Jim Jones**, the People's Temple was originally based in California. In the late 1970s, hundreds of its members migrated to Guyana to establish a compound called Jonestown. They relocated after Jones and others became obsessed with conspiracy theories about government oppression and the imminence of the Apocalypse (a time of global trial and warfare). During a November 1978 visit to Jonestown by a delegation led by U.S. Congressman Leo Ryan, a number of cult members decided to leave the People's Temple. They accompanied Ryan's party to an airfield. At the airfield, they were assaulted by heavily armed members of the People's Temple; Ryan and several others were killed. Jones and hundreds of his followers committed suicide—mostly by drinking flavored sugar water that had been poisoned, although some shot themselves. A number of members were apparently murdered by gunshots or injections of the poison. Jim Jones audiotaped the episode, in which 914 people died, including more than 200 children.

Another cult—the **Black Hebrew Israelites**—is a counterpart to the neo-Nazi Christian Identity faith, with the distinction that it promotes African racial supremacy. Branches of the cult have called themselves the Tribe of Judah, Nation of Yahweh, and Temple of Love.

Black Hebrew Israelites believe that the ancient Hebrews were Africans, and that these Chosen People migrated to West Africa during the Diaspora (scattering) of the ancient Jewish people. The descendents of these migrants were brought to the Western Hemisphere as slaves by Europeans during the 400-year African slave trade. Thus, Africans in general—and African Americans in particular—are the true Chosen People of God. This "truth" has been rediscovered by followers of the Black Hebrew Israelite movement. One branch was established in Miami in 1979 by **Hulon Mitchell, Jr.**, who adopted the name of Yahweh Ben Yahweh (God, Son of God). This branch became highly insular, and members followed Mitchell's authority without question. Disobedience was dealt with harshly, so that when some members tried to leave the group they were assaulted, and some were beheaded. Mitchell also taught that Whites are descendants of the devil and worthy of death. Mitchell and some of his followers were eventually prosecuted and imprisoned after the group dispatched death squads known as the Death Angels to murder Whites in the Miami area. The group was linked to at least 14 murders.

In the Pacific Northwest, followers of the **Bhagwan Shree Rajneesh** committed at least one act of biological terrorism. The group occupied a rural area in Oregon where their leader—the Bhagwan—was revered as the source of ultimate spiritual truth and enlightenment. Their mystical belief system was loosely based on Hinduism. Cult members, known as **Rajneeshees**, were expected to renounce their previous lifestyles and totally devote themselves and their livelihoods to their group and the Bhagwan. For example, they expressed great pride in the Bhagwan's fleet of Rolls Royce sedans. In September 1984, the group poisoned the salad bars of 10 Oregon restaurants with *Salmonella* bacteria. More than 700 people fell ill. It was an experiment to test options for how they could influence a local election in which the Rajneeshees hoped to elect members of the cult.

BACKGROUND TO POLITICAL VIOLENCE ON THE LEFT AND RIGHT

An examination of the origins of activism on the modern left and right provides insight into the social trends and political environments that eventually produced terrorist violence. Understanding the background to terrorism on the American left and right is instructive for evaluating why some members of social movements adopted terrorism as a means toward an end. Although only a small core of activists engaged in terrorism, their decisions to do so originated in uniquely American political environments.

The following discussion surveys the origins of several social and political movements on the left and right. It is not an exhaustive survey, but the predominant activist trends are identified. Most members of these movements did not rationalize, support, or otherwise advocate political violence. Nevertheless, some of them developed extremist tendencies and began to aggressively challenge the nation's basic political and cultural institutions. Factions within a few of these movements concluded that terrorist violence was necessary and then acted on this decision. The following discussion frames the social and ideological background to the origins of terrorist violence in the postwar United States.

Leftist Issues and Movements

The modern American left is characterized by several movements that grew out of the political fervor of the 1960s. These movements were fairly interconnected, so that understanding their origins provides instructive insight into the basic issues of the left. One should bear in mind that none of these movements was fundamentally violent in nature, and they were not terrorist movements. However, extremist trends within these movements sometimes espoused violent confrontation, and a few of these trends eventually produced factions that engaged in terrorist violence.

Origins of the Modern Civil Rights Movement[6]

The modern civil rights movement initially centered on the struggle to win equality for African Americans in the South. This was not the only regional emphasis of the movement, but its momentum came out of the battle to end racial segregation and legalized inequality in the South. During the early 1950s, the movement—at first led by the National Association for the Advancement of Colored People—forced an end to segregation on trains and interstate busses by successfully appealing several federal lawsuits to the U.S. Supreme Court. Despite these victories, Southern state laws still allowed segregation on *intra*state transportation.

In December 1955 in Birmingham, Alabama, Rosa Parks was arrested for refusing to give up her seat to a White man and move to the back of the bus, which is where African Americans were required to sit. The Reverend Martin Luther King, Jr., led a bus boycott in Birmingham that lasted for 13 months. A Supreme Court decision, combined with lost revenues, forced the bus company to capitulate. This was the beginning of the application of civil disobedience using a strategy known as **collective nonviolence**. King and his followers adopted this strategy from the Indian leader Mahatma Gandhi's successful movement to end British rule in India. The theory was that massive resistance, coupled with moral suasion and peaceful behavior, would lead to fundamental change.

A great many other civil rights protests occurred during the 1950s and 1960s, with official and unofficial violence being directed against the movement. There were numerous anti–civil rights bombings, shootings, and beatings in the South during this period. Under the leadership of King and others, the strategy of collective nonviolence—and targeted lawsuits by civil rights attorneys (including future Supreme Court justice Thurgood Marshall)—finally held sway in the South. However, not every member of the civil rights movement accepted collective nonviolence as a fundamental principle, and the strategy was not particularly effective outside of the Southern context.

The Rise of Black Power

As a direct result of the violence directed against the nonviolent civil rights movement, an emerging ideology of African American empowerment took root among many activists. It began in June 1966, when civil rights activist **James Meredith** planned to walk through Mississippi to demonstrate that African Americans could safely go to polling places to register to vote. He was ambushed, shot, and wounded early in his walk. The incident caused Martin Luther King and other national civil rights activists to travel to Mississippi to finish Meredith's symbolic march. One of the leaders was **Stokely Carmichael**, chairman of the Student Nonviolent Coordinating Committee (SNCC).

Carmichael renounced collective nonviolence. He also disagreed with the civil rights movement's strategy of working within mainstream political parties (primarily the Democratic Party). As the SNCC became more radicalized, the group expelled its White members, many of whom went on to become activists in the New Left movement. At a rally in Mississippi, Carmichael roused the crowd to repeatedly shout "Black power!" and adopted the clenched fist as a symbol of defiance. The slogan caught on, as did the clenched-fist symbol, and the Black Power movement began.

It is important to note that the Black Power movement occurred at a time when the violence in the South was paralleled by urban activism, unrest, and rioting in the impoverished African American ghettos of the North, Midwest, and West. In the Northeast, prior to Carmichael's Black Power rally, former Nation of Islam spokesman Malcolm X had eloquently challenged African Americans to empower themselves economically and culturally. To do so, Malcolm X argued that economic self-sufficiency was essential for African American communities and that it was necessary for African Americans to culturally unite internationally with the emerging independence movements in Africa, as well as with the descendents of African slaves in the Americas. His autobiography has become an influential document within the greater body of African American literature.[7]

The ideology of Black Power advocated political independence, economic self-sufficiency, and a cultural reawakening. It was expressed in Afrocentric political agendas; experiments in economic development of African American communities; and cultural chauvinism that was expressed in music, art, and dress (the **Black Pride** movement). Some members of the movement were radicalized by the violence in the South and began to advocate Black Nationalism. This led to the formation of overtly nationalist and militant organizations such as the **Black Panther Party for Self-Defense** (discussed later in the chapter and in Chapter Perspective 12.3).

Growth of the New Left

The "old left" was characterized by orthodox Marxist ideologies and political parties, dating from the time of the Russian Revolution. Other tendencies of the old left included anarchism and traditional socialist ideologies. After revelations about Stalinist brutality, the Soviet Union's suppression of the Hungarian Revolution in 1956, and frustration with the failure of socialist organizing in the United States, the old left movement became discredited among young activists. New issues galvanized a new movement among educated young activists, primarily on the nation's university campuses.

The New Left arose in the mid-1960s when a new generation of activists rallied around the antiwar movement, the civil rights movement, and other political and social causes.

New student organizations such as **Students for a Democratic Society** (SDS) advocated a philosophy of **direct action** to confront mainstream establishment values (SDS is discussed later in the chapter). In the fall of 1964, participants in the Free Speech Movement at the University of California, Berkeley, seized an administration building on the campus. This was a wakeup call for adopting direct action as a central tactic of the fledgling New Left.

New Left movements still reflected the ideals of the new generation of activism even when they revisited orthodox Marxism. For example, one faction of SDS—the **Revolutionary Youth Movement II (RYM II)**—tailored the orthodox ideologies of the old left to the political environment of the 1960s. RYM II argued that the youth movement should be organized

> not as a cultural phenomenon but as members of the working class who had experienced "proletarianization" in schools and the army. In these institutions, the young found themselves in the same boat as the oppressed black community, slaves to the lords of war and industry.[8]

RYM II (and the New Left in general) adapted their ideological motivations to the political and social context of the 1960s. As discussed in Chapter 6, many young radicals turned to the ideas of a new generation of radical thinkers, such as Herbert Marcuse, Frantz Fanon, and Carlos Marighella. They also championed contemporary revolutionaries and movements, such as the Cuban, Palestinian, and Vietnamese revolutionaries. At its core, "the [American] New Left was a mass movement that led, and fed upon, growing public opposition to U.S. involvement in Vietnam."[9] The collective term applied by the New Left to the mainstream American political and cultural establishment was the "**military-industrial complex.**" This term had been used by President Dwight D. Eisenhower to warn against the possible threat to democratic values from corporate and military interests.

Just as the Black Power movement incorporated a cultural agenda, so too did the New Left. Many young Americans experimented with alternative lifestyles, drugs, and avant-garde music. They also challenged the values of mainstream American society, questioning its fundamental ideological and cultural assumptions. This component of the New Left was commonly called the **counterculture**. There was also a genuinely idealistic belief that activist youth could bring justice to the world. This period was marked by many experiments in youth-centered culture.

Rightist Issues and Movements

The modern American right is characterized by several trends that developed from cultural and grassroots sources. Unlike the left, whose characteristics reflected the activism of the 1960s, the right is characterized more by self-defined *value systems*. These value systems have been perceived by many on the right to be under attack, and hence in need of protection—often by resorting to activist defense. This tendency is rooted in newly emergent trends such as antigovernment and religious activism, as well as in historical cultural trends such as racial supremacy. The following discussion surveys the modern (postwar) characteristics of these trends. They provide a background to contemporary terrorism on the right.

Religious Politics and the "Christian Right"

The movement commonly termed the *Christian Right* is a mostly Protestant fundamentalist movement that links strict Christian values to political agendas. The Christian Right is certainly not unique in making this connection; the civil rights movement was also led by members of the religious community. In both examples, activists sought the "moral high ground" on issues, thus framing the political debate as one of moral urgency rather than political expediency. The modern origins of the Christian Right lie in the conservative political environment of the 1980s. During the 1980s, President Ronald Reagan and other conservative leaders actively embraced many principles of the movement's political agenda.

The Christian Right is not an inherently violent movement, and some activists have practiced variations of collective nonviolence and direct action by blockading and protesting at the offices of abortion providers. The movement has sometimes been highly active and has successfully mobilized voters and other activists at both the national and local levels. There has also been some success in lobbying politicians for support, particularly among conservative members of Congress who represent conservative religious constituencies. Rallying issues include the promotion of traditional family values, denunciations of homosexuality, and opposition to abortion. The ultimate goal of the Christian Right is to make Christian religious values an integral part of the nation's social and political framework.

Far- and fringe-right members of the movement have adopted a highly aggressive and confrontational style of activism. For example, a number of blockades and protests at abortion clinics involved harassment and threats directed against employees and patients. Some clinics received death threats, and violence was occasionally directed against facilities—including bombings and shootings. One significant aspect of the more reactionary tendency within the movement is the promotion of a specifically *Christian* agenda, thus rejecting agendas that are secular or nonfundamentalist Christian.

Rise of the Antigovernment Patriots

The Patriot movement came to prominence during the early 1990s. The movement considers itself to represent the true heirs of the ideals of the framers of the U.S. Constitution. They hearken back to what they have defined as the "true" American ideals of individualism, an armed citizenry, and minimum interference from government. For many Patriots, government in general is not to be trusted, the federal government in particular is to be distrusted, and the United Nations is a dangerous and evil institution. To them, American government no longer reflects the will of the people; it has become dangerously intrusive and violently oppressive. The Patriot movement is not monolithic, and numerous tendencies have developed, such as the Common Law Courts and Constitutionalists.

Conspiracy theories abound within the Patriot movement. Some of them have long and murky origins, having been developed over decades. Two events from the 1990s have served to invigorate paranoid political activism on the Patriot right and have given rise to new conspiracy theories. These events are the tragedies at **Ruby Ridge**, Idaho, and **Waco**, Texas.

Ruby Ridge. In August 1992 at Ruby Ridge, Idaho, racial supremacist Randy Weaver and his family, with compatriot Kevin Harris, were besieged by federal agents for Weaver's failure to reply to an illegal weapons charge. Two members of the Weaver family were killed during the standoff, as was a U.S. marshal. Weaver's teenaged son Sammy and Marshal William Degan were killed during a shootout that occurred when Sammy, Randy, and Harris were confronted as they walked along a path. Weaver's wife Vicky was later fatally shot by an FBI sniper as she held her baby in the doorway of the Weaver home. The sniper had previously fired shots at Randy Weaver and Harris. Members of the Patriot movement and other right-wing extremists cite this incident as evidence of a broad government conspiracy to deprive freedom-loving "true" Americans of their right to bear arms and other liberties. Randy Weaver's story has inspired Patriots and other members of the extreme right.

Waco. In 1993 at Waco, Texas, federal agents besieged the Branch Davidian cult's compound after a failed attempt in February to serve a search warrant for illegal firearms had ended in the deaths of four federal agents and several cult members. On April 19, 1993,

Chapter Perspective 12.2   Conspiracy Theories on the Right

The modern far and fringe right have produced a number of conspiracy theories and rumors. Although they may seem fantastic to nonmembers of the Patriot (and other) movements, many adherents of these theories live their lives as if the theories were an absolute reality.

Communist Invaders
During the Cold War

- Rumors "confirmed" that Soviet cavalry units were preparing to invade Alaska across the Bering Strait from Siberia.
- Thousands of Chinese soldiers (perhaps an entire division) had massed in tunnels across the southwestern border of the United States in Mexico.
- Thousands of Vietcong and Mongolian troops had also massed in Mexico across the borders of Texas and California.

The New World Order
Replaces the Communist Menace

- Hostile un-American interests (which may already be in power) include the United

Nations, international Jewish bankers, the Illuminati, the Council on Foreign Relations, and the Trilateral Commission.
- Assuming it is Jewish interests who are in power, the U.S. government has secretly become the Zionist Occupation Government (ZOG).
- The government has constructed concentration camps that will be used to intern Patriots and other loyal Americans after their weapons have all been seized (possibly by African American street gangs).
- Invasion coordinates for the New World Order have been secretly stuck to the backs of road signs.
- Sinister symbolism and codes have been found in the Universal Product Code (the bar lines on consumer goods), cleaning products, cereal boxes, and dollar bills (such as the pyramid with the eyeball).
- Sinister technologies exist that will be used when ZOG or the New World Order make their move. These include devices that can alter the weather and scanners that can read the plastic strips in American paper currency.

during an assault led by the FBI, about 80 Branch Davidians—including more than 20 children—died in a blaze that leveled the compound. As with Ruby Ridge, Patriots and other rightists consider this tragedy to be evidence of government power run amuck.

Rightist conspiracy theories range from the fanciful to the paranoid. For example, Patriots cite evidence that non-American interests are threatening to take over—or have already taken over—key governmental centers of authority. This is supposedly part of an international plot to create a one-world government called the **New World Order**. According to one version of this conspiracy theory:

- New World Order troops may already have been prepositioned inside the United States—as evidenced by sightings of **black helicopters**.
- The black helicopters are possibly United Nations troops conducting reconnaissance in preparation for their seizure of power.
- The tragedies at Ruby Ridge and Waco were trial runs for imposing the New World Order on the United States.
- Background information databases, especially gun registrations, will be used to round up and oppress loyal patriotic Americans.

The New World Order and black helicopters conspiracy is not the only one created by "true believers" on the extreme right. Chapter Perspective 12.2 summarizes several conspiracy theories emanating from the right.

With these and other conspiracy theories as an ideological foundation, many within the Patriot movement organized themselves into citizens' **militias**. Scores of militias were organized during the 1990s. At their peak, it is estimated that 50,000 Americans were militia members, drawn from 5 to 6 million adherents of the Patriot movement.[10] Some members joined to train as weekend "soldiers," whereas other militias organized themselves as paramilitary survivalists. **Survivalism** originated during the Cold War, when many people believed that a nuclear exchange between the superpowers was inevitable. They moved into the countryside, stocked up on food and weapons, and prepared for the nuclear holocaust. Many militias adapted this expectation to the New World Order conspiracy theory. Militia members who became survivalists went "**off the grid**" by refusing to have credit cards, drivers' licenses, Social Security cards, or government records. The purpose of going off the grid was to disappear from the prying eyes of the government and the New World Order. Several principles are common to most militias:

- The people are sovereign. When necessary, they can resist the encroachment of government into their lives. They can also reject unjust government authority.
- Only an armed citizenry can counterbalance the authority of an oppressive government.
- The U.S. government has become oppressive, so the time is right to organize citizens' militias.
- It is necessary for citizens' militias to train and otherwise prepare for the day when an oppressive government or the New World Order moves in to take away the sovereignty of the people.

The potential for political violence from some members of the armed, conspiracy-bound Patriot movement has been cited by experts and law enforcement officials as a genuine threat.

Racial Supremacy: An Old Problem With New Beginnings

The history of racial supremacy in the United States began during the period of African chattel slavery and continued with the policy to remove Native Americans from ancestral lands. The racial dimensions of these practices became norms (accepted features) of the early American nation. As the nation grew, what had originated before the Civil War as a cultural *presumption* of racial supremacy became entrenched as cultural and political *policy* after the war. For example, African Americans were legally relegated to second-class citizenship, which meant that racial exclusion and discrimination were practiced with impunity. Most Native Americans were simply removed from society and resettled on reservations.

After the Civil War and prior to the Second World War, the United States became a highly segregated country. Housing patterns, cultural institutions (such as sports), and national institutions (such as the armed forces) were racially segregated as a matter of policy. The effort to win equality for African Americans was slow, arduous, and often dangerous. As often as not, racial equality was politically unpopular among large blocs of White Americans. Organized supremacist organizations such as the Ku Klux Klan enforced the racial code of separation and White dominance. After the Second World War, the tide turned against overt and unquestioned racial supremacy. The civil rights movement won significant legal victories before the Supreme Court and found many allies among prominent White political and social leaders. However, supremacist tendencies continued to win adherents in the postwar era.

Modern organized racial supremacist groups include the modern Ku Klux Klan, neo-Nazi movements, and racist skinhead youth gangs. The new non-Klan groups came into their own during the 1980s, when **Aryan Nations**, **White Aryan Resistance**, and the **National Alliance** (explored further in Chapter Perspective 12.4) actively disseminated information about supremacist ideology. Members of the new supremacist groups created their own mythologies and conspiracy theories. For example, the novel ***The Turner Diaries***[11] is considered by many neo-Nazis to be a blueprint for the Aryan revolution in America. The book inspired the terrorist group the Order (discussed later in the chapter) in its terrorist campaign. Also on the racist right, the **Fourteen Words** have become a rallying slogan. Originally coined by David Lane, a convicted member of the terrorist group the Order, the Fourteen Words are: "We must secure the existence of our people and a future for White children." The Fourteen Words have been incorporated into the Aryan Nations' "declaration of independence" for the White race, and the slogan is often represented by simply writing or tattooing *14*.

There were terrorist incidents and abortive terrorist plots during the 1980s rebirth, and since then violent racial supremacists have committed a number of hate crimes. For example, a typical racially motivated assault occurred in November 1988, when a group of racist skinheads in Portland, Oregon, beat to death an Ethiopian immigrant. They had been influenced by White Aryan Resistance.

Racial Mysticism

Recall that in Europe neofascist movements and political parties are decidedly secular. They reference religion and the organized Christian church only to support their political agendas; they do not adopt Christian or cult-like mystical doctrines as spiritual bases to justify their legitimacy. In the United States, members of far- and fringe-right movements frequently justify their claims of racial supremacy and cultural purity by referencing underlying spiritual values. Racial supremacists in particular have developed mystical foundations for their belief systems, many of which are cult-like. Two of these cultish doctrines are the following.

World Church of the Creator. The **World Church of the Creator**, founded by **Ben Klassen** in 1973, practices a faith called **Creativity**. It is premised on a rejection of the White race's reliance on Christianity, which Klassen believed was created by the Jews as a conspiracy to enslave Whites. According to Creativity, the White race itself should be worshipped.

Ásatrú. **Ásatrú** is a neopagan movement that worships the pantheon of ancient Norse (Scandinavian) religions. In its most basic form—which is not necessarily supremacist—Ásatrú believers worship the Norse pantheon of Odin, Thor, Freyr, Loki, and others. In its more activist and racist form, Ásatrú believers link variants of Nazi ideology to the Nordic pantheon. Variations on the Ásatrú theme include Odinism, which venerates the Norse god Odin (Wotan) as the chief god of all gods.

Race and the Bible:
The Christian Identity Creation Myth

Christian Identity is the Americanized strain of an 18th-century quasi-religious doctrine called **Anglo-Israelism** that was developed by **Richard Brothers**. Believers hold that Whites are descended from Adam and are the true Chosen People of God, that Jews are biologically descended from Satan, and that non-Whites are soulless beasts (also called the "**Mud People**"). Christian Identity adherents have developed two cultish creation stories that are loosely based on the Old Testament. The theories are called **One-Seedline Christian Identity** and **Two-Seedline Christian Identity**.

One-Seedline Identity accepts that all humans regardless of race are descended from Adam. However, only Aryans (defined as northern Europeans) are the true elect of God. They are the Chosen People whom God has favored and who are destined to rule over the rest of humanity. In the modern era, those who call themselves the Jews are actually descended from a minor Black Sea ethnic group and therefore have no claim to Israel.

Two-Seedline Identity rejects the notion that all humans are descended from Adam. Instead, their focus is on the progeny of Eve. Two-seedline adherents believe that Eve bore Abel as Adam's son but bore Cain as the son of the Serpent (that is, the devil). Outside of the Garden of Eden lived non-White, soulless beasts who are a separate species from humans. They are the modern non-White races of the world and are often referred to by Identity believers as Mud People. When Cain slew Abel, he was cast out of the Garden to live among the soulless beasts. Those who became the descendants of Cain are the modern Jews. They are thus biologically descended from the devil and are a demonic people worthy of extermination. There is an international conspiracy by the Jewish devil-race to rule the world. The modern state of Israel and the Zionist Occupation Government in the United States are part of this conspiracy.

LEFT-WING TERRORISM IN THE UNITED STATES

As New Left and Black Power movements and organizations became radicalized, many individuals and groups began to advocate active resistance against the "Establishment"—defined as mainstream American political and social institutions. This resistance included explicit calls for civil disobedience and confrontation with the authorities. Many within these movements referred to themselves as revolutionaries, and some advocated the overthrow of the military-industrial complex. Prototypical revolutionary organizations began to form in the late 1960s, and a few of these groups produced cadres or factions that became terrorist organizations. All of this occurred in a generalized environment of activism and direct action. Social tensions were quite volatile during the first half of 1970, as indicated by the following incidents that occurred before the summer college break:

- On May 4 at Kent State University in Ohio, four students were killed and nine wounded by the Ohio National Guard after several days of violent antiwar demonstrations against the U.S. incursion into Cambodia.
- Just after midnight on May 15 at Jackson State University in South Carolina (a historically African American university), one student and one passerby were killed when police fired into a crowd of African American protestors. At least a dozen students were hospitalized.
- Approximately 30 Reserve Officer Training Corps (ROTC) buildings were burned or bombed.
- More than 500 colleges closed early because of student protests.

There were also a large number of politically motivated bombings, shootings, and assaults during this period. The Senate Committee on Government Operations reported the following statistics:[12]

In 1969, there were 298 explosive and 243 incendiary bombings.

From January to July 1970, there were 301 explosive and 210 incendiary bombing incidents.

Chapter Perspective 12.3   Seeds of Terrorism: Radicals on the Left

Two militant case studies are discussed here—the Black Panthers and the radicalized Students for a Democratic Society. Within each movement were groups of cadres who advocated violent revolution.

Case: The Black Panthers

The Black Panther Party for Self-Defense was organized in 1966 in Oakland, California. The name was selected from an African American organization founded in Alabama called the Lowndes County Freedom Organization. The Lowndes County group had used the symbol of a black panther on voter ballots, ostensibly so that illiterate voters would know who their candidates were.

The Oakland Black Panthers initially imitated a tactic that had been used by the Los Angeles–based Community Alert Patrol, which had been formed after the Watts riot in August 1965.[a] The Community Alert Patrol would dispatch observers to scenes of suspected harassment by the Los Angeles Police Department and observe police stops. In Oakland, the Black Panthers took this tactic one step further and arrived on the scene openly carrying law books and shotguns or rifles (legal at the time in California).[b] The symbolism of young African Americans projecting a paramilitary image in poor urban ghettos attracted members to the Black Panthers around the country. More than 40 chapters were formed, with a total of more than 2,000 members. By 1968 the group made

worldwide headlines and came to symbolize the Black Power movement. Public demonstrations by the Black Panthers maximized the use of paramilitary symbolism, with members marching and chanting slogans in precision and wearing black berets and black leather jackets.

Ideologically, the Black Panthers were inspired by Malcolm X,[c] Frantz Fanon, and Mao Zedong. They were advocates of Black Nationalism and encouraged economic self-sufficiency and armed self-defense in the Black community. Black Panther self-help initiatives included free breakfasts for poor schoolchildren in urban areas. The police (at that time all male and mostly White in most cities) were especially singled out and labeled as a kind of "occupation" force in African American communities.

The group's militancy attracted the attention of federal and local law enforcement agencies, who considered the organization to be a threat to national security. The revolutionary and antipolice rhetoric of Black Panther leaders and the militant articles in its newspaper *The Black Panther* increased their concern. FBI Director J. Edgar Hoover stated that the Black Panthers were the most significant threat to domestic security in the United States. A series of arrests and shootouts at Black Panther offices occurred. The leadership of the organization was decimated by arrests, police raids, and a successful "**disinformation**" campaign that sowed distrust among central figures. Internal feuds between leaders Huey Newton and Eldridge Cleaver also disrupted the group.

From January 1968 to June 1970, there were 216 ambushes against law enforcement personnel and headquarters.

Also from January 1968 to June 1970, there were 359 total assaults against the police, causing 23 deaths and 326 injuries.

Chapter Perspective 12.3 presents two examples of radicalized organizations—one from the New Left (Students for a Democratic Society) and the other from the Black Power movement (the Black Panthers). The story of both groups illustrates the evolutionary process of left-wing revolutionary cadres and factions that eventually advocated political violence.

The following discussion evaluates four trends and one case in point on the violent left. They are:

Although the Black Panthers continued to be active into the late 1970s—after significantly moderating its militancy by the mid-1970s—its heyday as a paramilitary symbol of Black Nationalism was during the late 1960s and early 1970s. As it declined under relentless internal and external pressures, some of its more radical members joined the revolutionary underground.

Case: Students for a Democratic Society

In June 1962, a group of liberal and mildly leftist students, known as Students for a Democratic Society, or SDS, many from the University of Michigan, met to draft a document that became known as the **Port Huron Statement**. In this document, SDS harshly criticized the values of mainstream American society and called for the establishment of a "new left" movement in the United States. The Port Huron Statement was a critique and a call for action directed to middle-class students. At this time, SDS was liberal and leftist, but hardly revolutionary. SDS espoused "direct action," which originally referred to peaceful and nonviolent confrontation.

By 1965, SDS had moved to the radical left, and when the bombing of North Vietnam began, its national membership soared. By 1966, its focal point was the war in Vietnam and support for the Black Power movement (SDS's membership comprised mostly White students). In 1967, SDS (in a classic Marcuse-like interpretation) cast activist American youth as a "new working class" oppressed by the military-industrial complex. By 1968, SDS's leadership was revolutionary. An SDS-led takeover of Columbia University occurred during the 1968 spring term, when students seized five buildings for five days. When the police were called in, a riot ensued; more than 700 people were arrested, and nearly 150 were injured. A student strike—again led by SDS—closed Columbia. SDS also led dozens of other campus disturbances in 1968.

In June 1968, SDS factionalized because of ideological tensions within the group. Some members formed a prototypical Revolutionary Youth Movement, others aligned themselves with developing world revolutionary heroes, and others (sometimes called Crazies) espoused violent revolution. At its next meeting in June 1969 in Chicago, SDS split along doctrinal and tactical lines into the Maoist **Progressive Labor Party** (also known as Worker-Student Alliance), Revolutionary Youth Movement II, and the violent revolutionary **Weatherman** group.

NOTES

a. The toll for the Watts disturbance was high; 34 people were killed, more than 1,000 injured, and nearly 4,000 arrested. Approximately 200 businesses were destroyed and about 700 damaged. For a study of the Watts riot, *see* Conot, Robert. *Rivers of Blood, Years of Darkness*. New York: Bantam Books, 1967.

b. The armed patrols ended when California passed a law prohibiting the open display of firearms.

c. For more information about Malcolm X, see X, Malcolm. *The Autobiography of Malcolm X*. New York: Grove Press, 1964.

- New Left Terrorism
- Ethno-Nationalist Terrorism on the Left
- Leftist Hard Cores
- Case: The United Freedom Front
- Single-Issue Violence on the Left

New Left Terrorism

The New Left was deeply affected by the war in Vietnam, the civil rights movement, and the turmoil in inner-city African American communities. A number of terrorist groups and cells grew out of this environment. Although the most prominent example was the Weatherman group, other groups such as the Symbionese Liberation Army also engaged in terrorist violence. The United Freedom Front, discussed later in the chapter as a special case, proved to be the most enduring of all terrorist groups of the era.

The Weatherman/Weather Underground Organization

The Weatherman group—known as the **Weatherman**—jelled at the June 1969 Students for a Democratic Society national convention in Chicago, when SDS splintered into several factions. The Weathermen were mostly young, White, educated members of the middle class. They represented in stark fashion the dynamic ideological tendencies of the era, as well as the cultural separation from the older generation. Although they and others were sometimes referred to collectively as the "Crazies," they operated within a supportive cultural and political environment. The following description of this environment is typical:

> Only a handful of the New Left were alienated enough to embrace revolutionary strategies, but many of them agreed with the objectives, if not the tactics, of the militant Weather People, and some provided support for them. . . . Testimony to the effectiveness of that support network is the fact that no Weather People were arrested during the early 1970s or after the voluntary cessation of their bombing campaign in 1975.[13]

From the beginning, the Weathermen were violent and confrontational. In October 1969, they distributed leaflets in Chicago announcing what became known as their "**Days of Rage**" action. They justified their action by declaring,

> We move with the people of the world to seize power from those who now rule. We . . . expect their pig lackeys to come down on us. We've got to be ready for that. This is a war we can't resist. We've got to actively fight. We're going to bring the war home to the mother country of imperialism. AMERIKA: THE FINAL FRONT.[14]

The Days of Rage lasted for four days and consisted of acts of vandalism and running street fights with the Chicago police. In December 1969, the Weathermen held a "war council" in Michigan. Its leadership, calling itself the **Weather Bureau**, advocated bombings, armed resistance, and assassinations. One leader, **Bernardine Dohrn**, praised the murders committed by the Charles Manson cult, referring to it as a revolutionary act and calling the cult's victims "pigs." In March 1970, an explosion occurred in a Greenwich Village townhouse in New York City that was being used as a bomb factory. Three Weathermen were killed, several others escaped through the New York subway system, and hundreds of members went underground to wage war.

By the mid-1970s, the Weathermen—renamed the **Weather Underground Organization**—had committed at least 40 bombings, including the following targets:

- The Pentagon
- The United States Capitol (possibly—see United Freedom Front later in chapter)
- Police stations
- National Guard facilities
- ROTC buildings
- The Harvard war research center in Cambridge, Massachusetts
- The Gulf Oil corporate headquarters in Pittsburgh, Pennsylvania

Aside from these actions, the Weather Underground also freed counterculture guru Timothy Leary from prison,[15] published a manifesto called *Prairie Fire*, and distributed an underground periodical called *Osawatomie*. They established an aboveground support network of **Weather Collectives** organized by a group called the **Prairie Fire Organizing**

Committee. Their underground network of safe houses and rural safe collectives—which served to hide themselves and New Left fugitives from the law—was never effectively infiltrated by law enforcement agencies. By the mid-1970s, members of the Weather Underground began to give up their armed struggle and returned to aboveground activism—a process that they called "inversion." Those who remained underground (mostly the East Coast wing) committed acts of political violence into the 1980s, and others joined other terrorist organizations.

The Symbionese Liberation Army

The Symbionese Liberation Army (SLA) was a violent terrorist cell that gained notoriety for several high-profile incidents in the mid-1970s. The core members were led by **Donald DeFreeze**, who took the *nom de guerre* Cinque (named for the leader of a 19th-century rebellion aboard the slave ship *Amistad*). Members trained in the Berkeley hills, rented safe houses, and obtained weapons. In November 1973, the Oakland school superintendent was assassinated when he was shot eight times; five of the bullets were cyanide-tipped. In a communiqué, the SLA took credit for the attack, using a rhetorical phrase that became its slogan: "Death to the fascist insect that preys upon the people!"

In February 1974, newspaper heiress Patricia Hearst was kidnapped by the cell. She was kept bound and blindfolded in a closet for more than 50 days while under constant physical and psychological pressure, including physical abuse and intensive political indoctrination. She broke down under the pressure, and a tape recording was released in which she stated that she had joined the SLA. In April 1974 Hearst participated in a bank robbery in San Francisco. This was a classic case of Stockholm syndrome, which was explored in Chapter 3.

In May 1974, five of the SLA's core members, including DeFreeze, were killed in a shootout in a house in the Watts neighborhood of Los Angeles.

Patricia Hearst was a fugitive for approximately one year. She was hidden—probably by the Weather Underground—and traveled across the country with compatriots. By 1975, the SLA had a rebirth with new recruits and was responsible for several

A photograph of kidnapping victim Patricia Hearst, sent to a Berkeley, California, radio station by the Symbionese Liberation Army. On the accompanying audio message, Hearst claimed to support the SLA cause.

Source: Bettman/Corbis, April 1974; used with permission.

bank robberies and bombings in California. They referred to themselves as the **New World Liberation Front**. Hearst was captured in September 1975 in San Francisco, along with another underground fugitive. Most of the other members either were captured or disappeared into the underground. One member of the renewed SLA, Kathy Soliah, was arrested in July 1999 in a Minneapolis suburb. She had changed her name and become a typical community-oriented "soccer mom." Soliah was convicted in California on 20-year-old charges of plotting to blow up two Los Angeles Police Department patrol cars.

Ethno-Nationalist Terrorism on the Left

Ethno-national violence—which is distinguishable from racial supremacist violence—has been rare in the United States. This is primarily because activist environments have not historically supported nationalist terrorism. Exceptions to this general observation grew out of the political environment of the 1960s, when nationalist political violence originated in African American and Puerto Rican activist movements. There have been few nationalist movements outside of these examples. One isolated example of nationalist violence did occur on the island of St. Croix in the territory of the U.S. Virgin Islands. In 1972, eight people—seven Whites and one African American employee—were shot execution-style at the Fountain Valley Golf Club by Virgin Islands nationalists seeking independence from the United States. This incident (known as the **Fountain Valley Massacre**) was isolated and idiosyncratic and did not develop into an underground revolutionary movement as did the Puerto Rican and mainland African American movements.

The following discussion evaluates ethno-national political violence committed by adherents of the Black Liberation and Puerto Rico independence movements. In both examples, the underlying ideological justifications for the violence were Marxist-inspired.

The Black Liberation Movement

Racial tensions in the United States were extremely high during the 1960s. African Americans in the South directly confronted southern racism through collective nonviolence and the burgeoning Black Power ideology. In the urban areas of the North and West, cities became centers of confrontation between African Americans, the police, and state National Guards. Many Black Power advocates in the North and West became militant as the summers became seasons of urban confrontation. During what became known in the 1960s as the "**long hot summer**," many cities were social and political powder kegs, and hundreds of riots occurred during the summers from 1964 to 1969. When President Lyndon Johnson and the U.S. Senate organized inquiries into the causes of these disorders, their findings were disturbing. Table 12.2 describes the quality of these findings, which indicate the severity of tensions in urban areas during the mid-1960s.

Within this environment grew cadres of African American revolutionaries dedicated to using political violence to overthrow what they perceived to be a racist and oppressive system. The most prominent example of African American nationalist terrorism is the **Black Liberation Army** (BLA).

The Black Liberation Army

The BLA was an underground movement whose membership included former members of the Black Panthers and Vietnam veterans. BLA members were nationalists who were inspired in part by the 1966 film *Battle of Algiers,* a semidocumentary of an Algerian urban terrorist uprising against the French during their colonial war in Algiers. In the film, Algerian rebels organized themselves into many autonomous cells to wage urban guerrilla

Table 12.2 Racial Conflict in America: A Snapshot of Urban Rioting During the 1960s

The urban disturbances in the United States during the 1960s caused an unprecedented period of communal discord. The disturbances were widespread and violent and were a culmination of many factors. One factor was the deeply rooted racial polarization in American society. The presidential-appointed National Advisory Commission on Civil Disorders (known as the **Kerner Commission**) reported in 1968 that

> segregation and poverty have created in the racial ghetto a destructive environment totally unknown to most white Americans. What white Americans have never fully understood—but what the Negro can never forget—is that white society is deeply implicated in the ghetto. White institutions created it, white institutions maintain it, and white society condones it.[a]

The following table reports data from a Senate Permanent Subcommittee on Investigations inquiry into urban rioting after the serious disturbances in the summer of 1967.[b] The table summarizes the environment during three years of civil disturbances.[c]

	Activity Profile		
Incident Report	*1965*	*1966*	*1967*
Number of urban disturbances	5	21	75
Casualties (killed)	36	11	83
Injured	1,206	520	1,897
Legal sanctions (arrests)	10,245	2,298	16,389
Convictions	2,074	1,203	2,157
Costs of damage (in millions of dollars)	$40.1	$10.2	$664.5

NOTES

a. *Report of the National Advisory Commission on Civil Disorders.* New York: Bantam Books, 1968, p. 2.
b. In 1967, the Senate passed a resolution ordering the Senate Permanent Subcommittee on Investigations to investigate what had caused the 1967 rioting and to recommend solutions.
c. Senate Permanent Subcommittee on Investigations. Data reported in *Ebony Pictorial History of Black America,* vol. 3. Chicago: Johnson Publishing Company, Inc., 1971, p. 69.

warfare against the French. The actual Battle of Algiers is considered by many to be a prototypical example of cell-based irregular and asymmetrical warfare.

There were at least two cells (or groups of cells) of the BLA—the East Coast and West Coast groups. Although the BLA was likely active in late 1970 and early 1971, both cells became known later, and in similar fashion, to law enforcement agencies and the media:

East Coast Cell. In May 1971 two New York City police officers were ambushed and killed by .45-caliber fire. A package delivered to the *New York Times* containing, among other items, a communiqué and a .45 bullet claimed credit for the shootings on behalf of the BLA. This was the beginning of a number of known and suspected BLA attacks in the New York City region.

West Coast Cell. In August 1971 similar attacks were made against police officers in San Francisco. In one ambush, the police were attacked by .45-caliber machine-gun fire; two BLA "soldiers" were captured after a shootout in this incident.

The BLA is suspected to have committed a number of attacks prior to and after these attacks in both New York and California. They are thought to have been responsible for numerous bombings, ambushes of police officers,[16] and bank robberies to "liberate" money to support their cause. Their areas of operation were California and New York City, although some BLA members apparently received training in the South.

The symbolic leader of the BLA was JoAnne Chesimard, a former Black Panther who later changed her name to **Assata Shakur**. She was described by admirers as the "heart and soul" of the BLA. In May 1973, a gunfight broke out when she and two other BLA members were stopped on the New Jersey Turnpike by a New Jersey State Trooper. The trooper was killed, as was one of the occupants of the automobile. Shakur was captured, tried, and eventually convicted in 1977. She was sentenced to life imprisonment but was freed in 1979 by members of the **May 19 Communist Organization** (discussed later in the chapter) and spirited to Cuba. She remains there under the protection of the Cuban government.

Most members of the BLA were eventually captured or killed. Those who were captured were sentenced to long prison terms. Unlike the Weather Underground's network, the BLA network was successfully penetrated and infiltrated by the FBI, using informants. Those who escaped the FBI net re-formed to join other radical organizations. Interestingly, the only known White member of the BLA, Marilyn Buck, was a former member of the radicalized SDS who had disappeared into the revolutionary underground.

Puerto Rican Independencistas

Puerto Rico is a commonwealth of the United States, meaning that it is self-governed by a legislature and an executive (a governor) and has a nonvoting delegate to Congress. The island is exempt from the Internal Revenue Code, and its residents are ineligible to vote in presidential elections. Opinion about the island's political status is divided among a majority who wish for it to remain a commonwealth, a large number who favor statehood, and a minority who desire national independence. Those who desire independence are nationalists called *independencistas*. Most *independencistas* use democratic institutions to promote the cause of independence; they are activists but are not prone to violence. Many are intellectuals and professionals who are working to build pro-independence sentiment. For example, the Puerto Rico Independence Party is a fairly mainstreamed leftist political movement in Puerto Rico.

Some *independencistas* are revolutionaries, and a small number have resorted to violence. Nationalist violence on the mainland United States has a history dating to the postwar era. Two incidents from the 1950s illustrate this history:

In November 1950, nationalists attacked Blair House in Washington, D.C., in an attempt to assassinate President Harry Truman. Two people were killed—one terrorist and one Secret Service agent.

In March 1954, five members of the U.S. House of Representatives were wounded when four nationalists opened fire from the visitors' gallery overlooking the House floor. All of the attackers were captured, tried, and convicted.

President Jimmy Carter granted executive clemency to the perpetrators of these incidents, freeing them from prison.

Modern violent nationalists pattern themselves after Cuban nationalism and view the United States as an imperial and colonial power. Cuba has, in fact, provided support for violent *independencista* groups, especially during the 1980s.

There have been several Puerto Rican *independencista* terrorist organizations. These organizations include the **Macheteros** ("Machete-Wielders"), the **Organization of Volunteers for the Puerto Rican Revolution**, and the **Armed Forces of Popular Resistance**. Although most violent *independencistas* carried out their operations in Puerto Rico, one group—the **Armed Forces for National Liberation (Fuerzas Armadas de Liberación Nacional, or FALN)**—was based on the mainland and was highly active from the 1970s through the mid-1980s. The Macheteros were also responsible for attacks on the mainland.

The FALN

The FALN[17] was a very active terrorist organization that concentrated its activities on the U.S. mainland, primarily in Chicago and New York City. One important fact stands out about the FALN: They were the most prolific terrorist organization in U.S. history. The group became active in 1974, and from 1975 to 1983, approximately 130 bombings were linked to the FALN or the Macheteros, with the vast majority being the responsibility of the FALN. Most attacks by the FALN were symbolically directed against buildings, although some of their attacks were deadly. For example, in January 1975 the FALN detonated a bomb at the trendy restaurant Fraunces Tavern in New York, killing four people and wounding more than 50. In another incident in 1983, three New York City police officers were maimed while trying to defuse explosives at the New York police headquarters. The group was also responsible for armored car and bank robberies.

Aside from their attacks, the political and legal issues surrounding the FALN were high-profile and significant. Two cases in point are instructive:

In 1977, leader William Morales was captured by the police after being injured in an explosion at a FALN bomb factory in New York City. In 1979, Morales was freed from a hospital in New York by the May 19 Communist Organization, the same group that freed BLA leader Assata Shakur. He escaped to Mexico, where he remained hidden until 1983. In 1983, Morales was captured by Mexican authorities at an international telephone; he was also convicted *in absentia* of sedition by a federal district court in Chicago for participation in 25 bombings. In 1988, Mexico refused to extradite Morales to the United States, and he was allowed to move to Cuba, where he remains under the protection of Cuban authorities.

In 1980, more than a dozen FALN members were convicted of terrorist-related crimes. Sentences were imposed for seditious conspiracy, possession of unregistered firearms, interstate transportation of a stolen vehicle, interference with interstate commerce by violence, and interstate transportation of firearms with intent to commit a crime. None of these charges were linked to homicides. FALN members' sentences ranged from 15 to 90 years, and they considered themselves to be prisoners of war.

In August 1999, President Bill Clinton proposed executive clemency for 16 imprisoned FALN members. President Clinton offered to commute their sentences if the prisoners agreed to meet three conditions: First, sign agreements to renounce violence; second, admit that they had committed criminal acts; and third, agree not to reestablish their associations with one another after release. In September 1999, 12 members accepted clemency, and 2 refused the offer. Under the terms of the clemency agreement, 11 were released, and 1 accepted a grant of parole in 2004. This process was opposed by the FBI, the U.S. Bureau of Prisons, two U.S. Attorneys, local law enforcement agencies, and the families of victims of FALN attacks. It was supported by human rights officials (who argued that the sentences were too harsh), mainstream Puerto Rican politicians, and members of the Puerto Rican nationalist movement. It was also popular among large constituencies on the island and mainland.

Leftist Hard Cores[18]

The left-wing revolutionary underground re-formed after the decline of groups like the Weather Underground and the BLA. These new groups were made up of die-hard former members of the Weather Underground and BLA, as well as former activists from other organizations such as the radicalized SDS and the Black Panthers. Two cases in point illustrate the character of the reconstituted revolutionary left in the 1980s.

May 19 Communist Organization

The May 19 Communist Organization (M19CO) derives its name from the birthdays of Malcolm X and Vietnamese leader Ho Chi Minh. The symbolism of this designation is obvious—it combines domestic and international examples of resistance against self-defined U.S. racism and imperialism. The group was composed of remnants of the Republic of New Africa (described later in the chapter), the BLA, the Weather Underground, and the Black Panthers. These cadres included the founders of the Republic of New Africa and the most violent members of the Weather Underground. Many of its members were people who had disappeared into the revolutionary underground for years.

M19CO was fairly active, engaging in bank and armored car robberies, bombings, and other politically motivated actions. Its more spectacular actions included the following incidents:

Responsibility for freeing BLA leader Assata Shakur from a New Jersey prison in 1979. M19CO hid Shakur for months before spiriting her to Cuba.

Responsibility for freeing FALN leader William Morales from a New York City hospital in 1979. The group hid Morales and arranged his flight to Mexico.

Participation in the October 1981 robbery of a Brinks armored car in suburban Nyack, New York. During the robbery, one security guard was killed. After an automobile chase and shootout at a roadblock, four M19CO members were captured. Two police officers had died at the roadblock shootout. One person captured was Kathy Boudin, daughter of prominent attorney Leonard Boudin.[19] She had been one of the survivors of the explosion at the Weatherman group's Greenwich Village townhouse in 1970. Also captured was Donald Weems, a former BLA member and later member of the New African Freedom Fighters.

M19CO adopted several different names when claiming responsibility for its attacks. These aliases included Red Guerrilla Resistance, **Revolutionary Fighting Group**, and **Armed Resistance Unit**. After the Nyack incident, M19CO remained active and engaged in several bombings. The group was finally broken when its remaining members were arrested in May 1985.

The New African Freedom Fighters

The **New African Freedom Fighters** were the self-defined "military wing" of a nationalist organization called the **Republic of New Africa**. The objective of the Republic of New Africa was to form a separate African American nation from portions of several southern states. Many of the Republic of New Africa's activities were aboveground, and many of its members were educated intellectuals. Some members opted to engage in political violence under the name of the New African Freedom Fighters. The group included former members of the BLA and the Black Panthers. They operated in collaboration with other members of the revolutionary underground. The group was eventually broken up in

1985 after members were arrested for conspiring to free from prison Donald Weems, the group's Nyack armored car robbery comrade; bomb the courthouse; and commit other acts of political violence. Interestingly, most of them had been educated professionals.

Case: The United Freedom Front[20]

One case is unique in comparison with other New Left, nationalist, or hard-core groups. Formed in 1975, the **United Freedom Front** (UFF) was underground and active for approximately 10 years. It was a New Left terrorist organization that grew out of a program by former SDS members to educate prison inmates about the "political" nature of their incarceration. This effort was similar to other radical programs that defined incarcerated African Americans as political prisoners. Activists across the country went into the prisons to develop the revolutionary consciousness of what they perceived to be an oppressed group—much as orthodox Marxist revolutionaries had long used vanguard strategies to politicize the working class and peasantry.

In 1975, the UFF detonated a bomb at the Boston State House under the name of the **Sam Melville-Jonathan Jackson Unit**, named for two politicized inmates. The group was never very large but it was very active, peaking in activity during the early 1980s. The UFF is suspected to have committed at least 25 bombings and robberies in New York and New England. Their attacks were primarily intended to exhibit anticorporate or antimilitary symbolism. A group calling itself the Armed Resistance Unit detonated a bomb on the Senate side of the U.S. Capitol building on November 6, 1983, to protest the U.S. invasion of Grenada. It is possible that the Armed Resistance Unit was the UFF operating under a different name.

The UFF exhibited a great deal of discipline in their activities—for example, taking copious notes at regular meetings that they called "sets." Members went underground in the American suburbs, immersing themselves in the middle class and adopting covers as nondescript residents. The UFF was broken when its members were arrested in late 1984 and early 1985. Few leftist groups had survived by remaining both underground and active for as long as did the UFF.

Single-Issue Violence on the Left

The left has produced violent single-issue groups and individuals who focus on one particular issue to the exclusion of others. To them, their championed issue is the central point—arguably the political crux—for solving many of the world's problems. For example, recall from Chapter 1 that Ted Kaczynski, also known as the Unabomber, protested the danger of technology by sending and placing bombs that killed three people and injured 22 others during a 17-year campaign.

Typical of leftist single-issue extremism is the fringe environmental movement. Groups such as the **Animal Liberation Front** (ALF) and the **Earth Liberation Front** (ELF) have committed numerous acts of violence, such as arson and vandalism. Their activity profiles are summarized as follows:

The ALF favors direct action to protest animal abuse, with the objective of saving as many animals as possible. There is no hierarchy within the movement, and they have operated in small groups.

The ELF was founded in England by activists who split from the environmentalist group Earthfirst! because of its decision to abandon criminal activities. It is potentially more radical than the ALF.

For the most part, both the ALF and ELF have been nonviolent toward humans, but they have committed many incidents of property destruction. Their targets have included laboratories and other facilities where animals are kept. Other actions have included

- Destruction of a forest station in Oregon
- Poisoning Mars candy bars
- Destruction of a University of California, Davis, livestock research laboratory
- Tree "spiking," which involves pounding metal staves into trees in logging areas The purpose is to destroy or damage logging equipment.
- The "liberation" of minks in Wisconsin
- Arson at the Vail, Colorado, ski resort

The ALF and ELF have coordinated their activities. Several joint claims have been made about property damage and other acts of vandalism, and it is likely that the two groups share the same personnel.

RIGHT-WING TERRORISM IN THE UNITED STATES

Right-wing terrorism in the United States is usually motivated by racial supremacism and antigovernment sentiment. Unlike the violent left, terrorist campaigns by underground rightist organizations and networks have been rare. Massive bombings such as the Oklahoma City attack have also been rather uncommon. It is more common for the right to be characterized by small-scale, cell-based conspiracies within the Patriot and neo-Nazi movements. In comparison with the left, the violent right has been less organized and less consistent.

The activity profile of the violent right reflects a long history of vigilante behavior, so that most acts of rightist terrorism have been communal incidents, ambushes, and low-yield bombings. Historically, the Ku Klux Klan and its supporters used vigilante communal violence as the preferred model for its terrorism. Vigilante **lynch mobs** came to symbolize the racial nature of right-wing terrorism in the United States during the late 19th century and continuing well into the 20th century. Lynchings are discussed in this chapter's Case in Point. These incidents were directed primarily against African American men, although a few lynching victims were African American women, White immigrants, Jews, or criminals.

Chapter Perspective 12.4 on page 331 summarizes several examples of racial supremacist activity on the right in the modern era. These examples illustrate how potentially violent members of the right wing can find organizations to provide direction and structure for their underlying animosity toward target groups.

The following discussion explores the terrorist right by investigating the following subjects:

- The Legacy of the Ku Klux Klan
- Neo-Nazi Terrorism
- Patriot Threats
- Case: Moralist Terrorism

The Legacy of the Ku Klux Klan

The Ku Klux Klan is a racist movement that has no counterpart among international right-wing movements—it is a purely American phenomenon. Its name comes from the

Table 12.3   The Fraternal Klan

From its inception in 1866, the Ku Klux Klan has used fraternity-like greetings, symbolism, and rituals. These behaviors promote secrecy and racial bonding within the organization. Examples of Klan language include the following greeting: Ayak? (Are you a Klansman?), and Akia! (A Klansman I am!). The language used for regional offices is also unique, as indicated by the following examples:

- Invisible Empire = the KKK national organization
- Realm = the KKK state organization
- Klavern = the KKK local organization

The following table summarizes the official Klan organizational designations.

Klan Official	Duties	Scope of Authority	Symbolic Identification
Imperial Wizard	National leader	Invisible Empire	Blue stripes or robe
Grand Dragon	State leader	Realm	Green stripes or robe
Exalted Cyclops	County leader	Klaverns within county	Orange stripes or robe
Nighthawk	Local security and administration	Klavern	Black robe
Klonsel	General counsel	Invisible Empire	White robe
Citizen	Member	Klan faction	White robe

Greek word **kuclos**, or "circle." The KKK is best described as an enduring movement that developed an ideology with the following components:

- Racial supremacy
- Protestant Christian supremacy
- American cultural nationalism (also known as **nativism**)
- Violent assertion of Klan racial doctrine
- Ritualistic symbolism, greetings, and fraternal behavior

Klan terminology in many ways is an exercise in racist secret fraternal bonding. Table 12.3 samples the exotic language of the Ku Klux Klan.

Ku Klux Klan terrorism has been characterized by different styles of violence in several historical periods. Not every Klansman has been a terrorist, nor has every Klan faction practiced terrorism. However, the threat of violence and racial confrontation has always been a part of the Klan movement. In order to understand the nature of Klan violence, it is instructive to survey the historical progression of the movement. There have been several manifestations of the KKK, which most experts divide into five eras.

First-Era Klan

The KKK was founded in 1866 in the immediate aftermath of the Civil War. Some sources date its origin to Christmas Eve, 1865, whereas others cite the year 1866. According to most sources, the KKK was first convened in Pulaski, Tennessee, by a group of Southerners who initially formed the group as a fraternal association.

They originally simply wore outlandish outfits and played practical jokes but soon became a full civic organization. Their first Imperial Wizard, or national leader, was former

Communal terrorism in America. The lynchings of Tommy Shipp and Abe Smith in Marion, Indiana, on August 7, 1930. The crowd is in a festive mood, including the young couple holding hands in the foreground.

Source: Hulton Archive/Getty Images; used by permission.

Confederate general and slave trader Nathan Bedford Forrest. Military-style rankings were established, and by 1868 the KKK was a secretive and politically violent underground. Their targets included African Americans, Northerners, and Southern collaborators. Northern victims were those who traveled south to help improve the conditions of the former slaves, as well as profiteering "carpetbaggers." Southern victims were collaborators derisively referred to as "Scalawags." The KKK was suppressed by the Union Army and the anti-Klan "Ku Klux laws" passed by Congress. Nathan Bedford Forrest ordered the KKK to be officially disbanded, and their robes and regalia were ceremoniously burned. It has been estimated that the Klan had about 400,000 members during its first incarnation.

Second-Era Klan

After the Reconstruction era (after the departure of the Union Army from the South and the end of martial law), the KKK re-formed into new secret societies and fraternal groups. It wielded a great deal of political influence and successfully helped restore racial supremacy and segregation in the South. African Americans lost most political and social rights during this period, beginning a condition of racial subjugation that did not end until the civil rights movement in the mid-20th century. The targets of Klan violence during this period were African Americans, immigrants, Catholics, and Jews.

Third-Era Klan

During the early part of the 20th century, and continuing into the 1920s, the KKK became a broad-based national movement. In 1915 they gathered at Stone Mountain, Georgia, and

---

Chapter Perspective 12.4   **Seeds of Terrorism: Reactionaries on the Right**

Three reactionary case studies are discussed here—Aryan Nations, White Aryan Resistance (WAR), and the National Alliance. Each case has directly or indirectly influenced activists on the racial supremacist right.

Aryan Nations

The "Reverend" **Richard Butler** established the Aryan Nations organization as a political counterpart to his Christian Identity sect, called the Church of Jesus Christ Christian. Aryan Nations established its spiritual and political headquarters in a compound at Hayden Lakes, Idaho. Residents of the compound were overtly neo-Nazi. They adopted a rank hierarchy, established an armed security force, trained as survivalists, worshipped as Identity believers, and took to wearing uniforms. A number of people who passed through the Aryan Nations group eventually engaged in political and racial violence, a pattern that included violence by the Order and **Buford Oneal Furrow.** This pattern led to its financial ruin. In a celebrated lawsuit brought by the Southern Poverty Law Center, Aryan Nations lost its title to the Hayden Lakes property in September 2000 when a $6.3 million verdict was decided. During the trial, the Southern Poverty Law Center successfully linked Aryan Nations security guards to the terrorizing of a family who had driven to the compound's entrance.

White Aryan Resistance

White Aryan Resistance—WAR—is an overtly racist organization founded and led by Tom Metzger. Based in California, WAR publishes neo-Nazi propaganda, manages an active Web site, and has tried to recruit and organize racist skinheads. Implicit in its message is the notion that skinheads should be mobilized as Aryan shock troops in the coming Racial Holy War. WAR has used popular culture and music to appeal to potential skinhead recruits, and its Web site is largely marketed to racist youth. In October 1990, WAR lost a $12.8 million verdict after the Southern Poverty Law Center litigated a case on behalf of the family of an Ethiopian immigrant who was beaten to death by WAR-inspired racist skinheads.

National Alliance

The National Alliance is historically linked to the now-defunct American Nazi Party, which had been founded and led by George Lincoln Rockwell prior to his assassination. **William Pierce**, the founder and leader of the National Alliance, was long considered by experts and members of the neo-Nazi movement to be the most prominent propagandist of the movement. Prior to his death in July 2002, Pierce authored *The Turner Diaries* (under the *nom de plume* **Andrew MacDonald**), published a magazine called the *National Vanguard*, made regular radio broadcasts, and managed an active Web site. The National Alliance is headquartered in a compound in rural Hillsboro, West Virginia, and Pierce's followers continue in his tradition. Although some violent neo-Nazis or other reactionaries may have been inspired by the National Alliance's message (recall that *The Turner Diaries* was found in the possession of Timothy McVeigh), no acts of terrorism or hate crimes have been directly linked to the group.

---

formed a movement known as the Invisible Empire. The Klan was glorified in the novel *The Clansman* and in the 1915 film *Birth of a Nation*, which was shown in the White House during the administration of President Woodrow Wilson. During this period, the Invisible Empire had between 3 and 4 million members. In 1925, 45,000 Klansmen and women paraded down Pennsylvania Avenue in Washington, D.C. Also during this period, Klan and Klan-inspired violence was widespread. Thousands of people—mostly African Americans—were victimized by the KKK. Many acts of terrorism were ritualistic communal lynchings.

Fourth-Era Klan

After a decline because of revelations about Third-Era violence and corruption, the Klan was reinvigorated in 1946—once again at Stone Mountain, Georgia. At this gathering, the

Invisible Empire disbanded, and new independent Klans were organized at local and regional levels. There was no longer a single national Klan, but rather autonomous Klan factions. During the civil rights movement, some Klan factions became extremely violent. The White Knights of Mississippi and the United Klans of America (mostly in Alabama) committed numerous acts of terrorism to try to halt progress toward racial equality in the American South. This era ended after several successful federal prosecutions on criminal civil rights charges, although the Klan itself endured.

Fifth-Era Klan

Violence during the Fifth Era has been committed by lone wolves rather than as organized Klan actions. The modern era of the Ku Klux Klan is characterized by two trends:

The Moderate Klan. Some Klansmen and women have tried to moderate their image by adopting more mainstream symbolism and rhetoric. Rather than advocating violence or paramilitary activity, they have projected an image of law-abiding activists working on behalf of White civil rights and good moral values. Those who promote this trend have eschewed the prominent display of Klan regalia and symbols. For example, former neo-Nazi and Klansman David Duke has repeatedly used mainstream political and media institutions to promote his cause of White civil rights. He is the founder of the National Association for the Advancement of White People.

The Purist Klan. A traditional and "pure" Klan has emerged that hearkens back to the original traditions and ideology of the KKK. This group has held a number of aggressive and vitriolic rallies—many in public at county government buildings. Their rhetoric is unapologetically racist and confrontational. Some factions of the purist trend prohibit the display of Nazi swastikas or other non-Klan racist symbols at KKK gatherings.

Ku Klux Klan membership has ebbed and flowed in the Fifth Era, in part because of changes in the nation's cultural and political environment, but also because of competition from other racial supremacist movements such as the racist skinhead and neo-Nazi groups. There was also fresh competition beginning in the late 1990s from the neo-Confederate movement.

Neo-Nazi Terrorism

In the modern era, most non-Klan terrorism on the right wing has come from members of the neo-Nazi movement. Recall that the American version of Nazism has incorporated mystical beliefs into its underlying ideology of racial supremacy. This mysticism includes Christian Identity, Creativity, and Ásatrú. Neo-Nazi terrorism is predicated on varying mixes of religious fanaticism, political violence, and racial supremacy. Their worldview is predicated on the superiority of the Aryan race, the inferiority of non-Aryans, and the need to confront an evil global Jewish conspiracy. Another common theme is the belief that a **racial holy war**—called **"Rahowa"**—is inevitable.

Although most violence emanating from these beliefs has been expressed as lone wolf terrorism and hate crimes, several groups have embarked on violent sprees. For example, a group calling itself the **Aryan Republican Army** (ARA) operated in the Midwest from 1994 to 1996.[21] Inspired by the example of the Irish Republican Army, the ARA robbed 22 banks in seven states before they were captured. Their purpose had been to finance racial supremacist causes and to hasten the overthrow of the Zionist Occupation Government. Some members also considered themselves to be Christian Identity fundamentalists called Phineas Priests, who are discussed later in the chapter. The following case in point further illustrates the nature of neo-Nazi violence.

Oklahoma City. The rubble of the Alfred P. Murrah Federal Building in the aftermath of a bomb attack by right-wing members of the Patriot movement. This was the worst terrorist incident on American soil prior to the September 11, 2001, homeland attacks. It remains the worst domestic terrorist incident carried out by Americans.

Source: Federal Emergency Management Agency (FEMA).

The Order

The Order was a covert, underground, and violent group that was inspired by a fictional secret organization depicted in the novel *The Turner Diaries*. In the book, the Order was a heroic inner circle and vanguard for the Aryan revolution in the United States. **Robert Jay Mathews**, a racial supremacist activist, was the founder of the actual Order in 1983.

The Order's methods for fighting the war against the Zionist Occupation Government were counterfeiting, bank robberies, armored car robberies, and occasional murders.[22] Their area of operation was primarily in the Pacific Northwest. Its first action in 1983 was a small heist in Spokane, Washington, that netted the group slightly more than $300. Mathews later robbed the Seattle City bank of $25,000. In April 1984, the group bombed a synagogue in Boise, Idaho. In March 1984, members of the Order seized $500,000 from a parked armored car in Seattle; the group detonated a bomb at a theater as a diversion. In May 1984, a peripheral member, Walter West, was executed because he was indiscreet about the group's secrecy. In June 1984, Alan Berg, a Jewish talk-radio host, was murdered in Denver; he had regularly lambasted the neo-Nazi movement. Also in June, a Brinks armored car was robbed near Ukiah, California, with disciplined precision, and the Order made off with $3.6 million. The end of the Order came when the FBI traced a pistol that Mathews had left at the scene of the Brinks robbery. He was eventually tracked to Whidbey Island in Washington in December 1984, and he died when his ammunition exploded and caused a fire during an FBI-led siege. More than 20 members of the Order were prosecuted and imprisoned in December 1985.

Some members of the potentially violent racial supremacist right consider Mathews to be a martyr and interpret the Order's terrorist spree as a "premature" endeavor. Two subsequent incidents with links to the Order are instructive:

In March 1998, federal agents arrested members of the self-styled **New Order** in East St. Louis, Illinois. They had modeled themselves after the Order and were charged with planning to bomb the Anti-Defamation League's New York headquarters; the headquarters of the Southern Poverty Law Center in Birmingham, Alabama; and the Simon Wiesenthal Center in Los Angeles.

In August 1999, Buford Oneal Furrow went on a shooting spree in the Los Angeles area, including an attack at a Jewish community center in which five people were wounded. He had been an Aryan Nations member and security officer and had married the widow of Robert Jay Mathews in a Christian Identity ceremony.

Patriot Threats

Although the Patriot movement attracted a significant number of adherents during the 1990s, and although militias at one point recruited tens of thousands of members, no underground similar to that of the radical left was formed. Few terrorist movements or groups emanated from the Patriot movement—largely because many members were "weekend warriors" who did little more than train, and because law enforcement agencies successfully thwarted a number of true plots. Thus, despite many implicit and explicit *threats* of armed violence from Patriots, conspiracies were rarely carried to completion.

In 1992 former Ku Klux Klan member Louis Beam began to publicly advocate "**leaderless resistance**" against the U.S. government. Leaderless resistance is a cell-based strategy requiring the formation of "**phantom cells**" to wage war against the government and enemy interests. Dedicated Patriots and neo-Nazis believe that leaderless resistance and the creation of phantom cells will prevent infiltration from federal agencies. The chief threat of violence came from the armed militias, which peaked in membership immediately prior to and after the Oklahoma City bombing. After the Oklahoma City bombing, federal authorities broke up at least 25 Patriot terrorist conspiracies. Examples of threatened and actual violence from the Patriot movement include the following incidents from the mid-1990s:[23]

October 1992: A gathering was held at the Estes Park, Colorado, resort to respond to the Ruby Ridge incident. The meeting attracted an assortment of rightists, supremacists, Christians, and Christian Identity members. They called for a united front against the government. The militia movement quickly grew, as did the theory of leaderless resistance.

August 1994: Members of the Minnesota Patriots Council were arrested for manufacturing ricin, a potentially fatal toxin.

April 1995: A large truck bomb destroyed the Alfred Murrah Federal Building in Oklahoma City, Oklahoma, killing 168 people.

November 1995: Members of the Oklahoma Constitutional Militia were arrested for conspiring to bomb several targets, including gay bars and abortion clinics.

July 1996: Members of the Viper Team militia in Arizona were arrested for plotting to bomb government buildings. They had diagrams and videos of possible targets and had trained using ANFO explosives.

October 1996: Members of the Mountaineer Militia in West Virginia were arrested for conspiring to bomb the FBI Criminal Justice Information Services building in Clarksburg, West Virginia.

The number of militias declined during the period between the aftermath of the April 1995 Oklahoma City bombing and the American homeland attacks of September 11, 2001.[24] By 2000, the number of Patriot organizations was only one fourth of the 1996 peak.[25] This general decline continued after the September 11, 2001, homeland attacks.[26]

Case: Moralist Terrorism

Moralist terrorism refers to acts of political violence that are motivated by a moralistic worldview. Most moralist terrorism in the United States is motivated by an underlying religious doctrine, and this is usually a fringe interpretation of Christianity. Abortion clinics and gay bars have been targets of moralist violence. Examples of moralist terrorism and threats against abortion providers include the following incidents:

June and December 1984: An abortion clinic was bombed twice in Pensacola, Florida.

March 1993: A physician was shot and killed outside an abortion clinic in Pensacola.

July 1994: A physician and his bodyguard were killed outside an abortion clinic in Pensacola.

October 1997: A physician was wounded by shrapnel in Rochester, New York.

October 1998: A physician was killed in Amherst, New York.

1998-2000: Scores of letters with notes claiming to be infected with anthrax bacteria were sent to abortion clinics in at least 16 states.

Post-September 11, 2001: During the actual anthrax attacks in the period following the homeland attacks, scores of letters were sent to abortion clinics in a number of states claiming to be infected with anthrax.

Examples of violent moralist movements include the **Army of God** and the **Phineas Priesthood**. They are both shadowy movements that apparently have little or no organizational structure, operate as lone wolves or cells, and answer to the "higher power" of their interpretations of God's will. They seem to be belief systems in which like-minded activists engage in similar behavior. The Phineas Priesthood is apparently a "calling" (divine revelation) for Christian Identity fundamentalists, and the Army of God membership is perhaps derived from fringe Christian fundamentalists. These profiles are speculative, and it is possible that they are simply manifestations of terrorist contagion (copycatting). There has also been speculation that both movements are linked. Nevertheless, it is instructive to review their activity profiles.

Army of God

The Army of God is a cell-based and lone wolf movement that opposes abortion and homosexuality. Its ideology is apparently a fringe interpretation of fundamentalist Protestantism, although it has also exhibited racial supremacist tendencies. The methodology of the Army of God has included the use of violence and intimidation—primarily in attacks against abortion providers and gay and lesbian targets. The Army of God posted a Web site with biblical references and grisly pictures of abortions, and the manifesto disseminated by the group included instructions for manufacturing bombs.

The Army of God first appeared in 1982 when an Illinois abortion provider and his wife were kidnapped by members of the group. It has since claimed responsibility for a number of attacks, primarily against abortion providers.

February 1984: A clinic in Norfolk, Virginia, where abortions were performed was firebombed.

February 1984: A clinic in Prince George's County, Maryland, where abortions were performed was firebombed.

January 1997: A clinic in Atlanta, Georgia, where abortions were performed was bombed.

February 1997: A nightclub in Atlanta was bombed. Its patrons were largely gays and lesbians.

January 1998: An abortion clinic in Birmingham, Alabama, was bombed, killing a police officer and severely wounding a nurse.

One apparent affiliate of the Army of God—**Eric Robert Rudolph**—became a fugitive after he was named as a suspect in the Birmingham bombing and the Atlanta bombings. Rudolph was also wanted for questioning for possible involvement in the July 1996 bombing at Centennial Olympic Park in Atlanta during the Summer Olympic Games. He was also linked to a militia group in North Carolina.

Phineas Priesthood

Phineas Priests were first described in the 1990 book *Vigilantes of Christendom: The History of the Phineas Priesthood*.[27] The book is a fundamentalist interpretation of Christian Identity. In the book, the alleged history of the Phineas Priesthood is traced from biblical times to the modern era. The name is taken from the Bible at chapter 25, verse 6 of the Book of Numbers, which tells the story of a Hebrew man named Phineas who killed an Israelite man and his Midianite wife in the temple. According to the Book of Numbers, this act stayed the plague from the people of Israel.

Phineas Priests believe that they are called by God to purify their race and Christianity. They are opposed to abortion, homosexuality, interracial mixing, and Whites who "degrade" White racial supremacy. Members also believe that acts of violence—called **Phineas Actions**—will hasten the ascendancy of the Aryan race. It is important to note that the Phineas Priesthood is a calling for men only, so that no women can become Phineas Priests. The calling also requires an absolute and fundamentalist commitment to Christian Identity mysticism. Some acts of political violence have been inspired by this doctrine. These incidents include the following:

In 1991, **Walter Eliyah Thody** was arrested in Oklahoma after a shootout and chase. Thody claimed to be a Phineas Priest and stated that fellow believers would also commit acts of violence against Jews and others.

In 1993, Timothy McVeigh apparently "made offhand references to the Phineas Priesthood" to his sister.[28]

From 1994 to 1996, the Aryan Republican Army robbed 22 banks throughout the Midwest. Members of the ARA had been influenced by *Vigilantes of Christendom* and the concept of the Phineas Priesthood.[29]

In October 1996, three Phineas Priests were charged with bank robberies and bombings in Washington State. They had left political diatribes in notes at the scenes of two of their robberies. The notes included their symbol, "**25:6**," which denotes chapter 25, verse 6 of the Book of Numbers.

Because the Phineas Priesthood has been a lone wolf and cell-based phenomenon, it is impossible to estimate its size or even whether it has ever been much more than an example of the contagion effect. Nevertheless, the fact is that a few true believers have considered themselves to be members of the Phineas Priesthood, and the concept of Phineas Actions was taken up by some adherents of the moralist and racial supremacist right.

THE NEW MILLENNIUM AND INTERNATIONAL TERRORISM IN THE UNITED STATES

International terrorism has been relatively rare in the United States, and the number of international terrorist incidents is much lower than in other countries, such as the United Kingdom and France.

The Spillover Effect in the United States

During most of the postwar era (prior to the 1990s), international incidents in the United States were spillovers from conflicts in other Western countries and were directed against foreign interests with a domestic presence in the United States. Most of these spillovers ended after a single incident or a few attacks, such as in the following examples:

In September 1976, a bomb in Washington, D.C., killed former Chilean Foreign Minister Orlando Letelier and his American assistant Ronni Moffitt. He had been assassinated on orders from DINA, the right-wing Chilean government's secret police.

In August 1978, Croatian terrorists took hostages in the West German consulate in Chicago. In September of the same year, they killed a New York City policeman when they detonated a bomb. The terrorists hijacked a TWA jet, forcing it to fly over London and Paris.

Some terrorist spillovers were ongoing campaigns. As was the case with the short-term incidents, these campaigns were directed primarily against non-American interests. Examples include the following.

Omega 7

During the late 1970s and early 1980s, anti-Castro Cuban terrorists actively targeted Cuban interests in the United States. Members of **Omega 7** were Cuban-born exiles who fled Cuba for the United States after the 1959 victory of Fidel Castro's forces during the Cuban Revolution. Omega 7 is thought to have been responsible for at least 50 attacks against Cuban businessmen and diplomats, including attempted assassinations and bombings. Their targets included the Venezuelan consulate in New York City, a Soviet ship in New Jersey, travel agencies in New Jersey, Lincoln Center in New York City, and the Cuban mission to the United Nations. The group's founder, **Eduardo Arocena**, was arrested in July 1983 and sentenced to life imprisonment for murdering a Cuban diplomat.

Provisional Irish Republican Army

The Provos did not wage a terrorist campaign in the United States. Rather, members of the IRA in the United States and their American supporters were implicated in the purchase and transshipment of armaments to Northern Ireland. The Provo presence was a support operation for terrorist cells in Northern Ireland. For example, in 1984, weapons were seized aboard a vessel off the coast of Ireland. The weapons had been transported to Irish waters aboard a vessel (the *Valhalla*) whose point of origin was the United States. In another incident in 1986, supporters of the Provos were arrested in a plot to fly weapons into Belfast, including a shoulder-fired Redeye anti-aircraft missile.

Jewish Defense League

The **Jewish Defense League** (JDL) is an example of American extremists who targeted international interests in the United States. The organization was founded in 1968 in New York City by **Rabbi Meir Kahane** as a militant youth-based Jewish movement. It favored active—and sometimes violent—defense of the Jewish community and a militant variant of Zionism that advocates the expulsion of Arabs from Israel. Kahane was assassinated in November 1990 in New York City by **El-Sayyid Nosair**, a radical Egyptian Islamic revolutionary.

The JDL Legacy

The JDL's offshoots in Israel are the right-wing Kach ("Only Thus") and Kahane Chai ("Kahane Lives") movements. Both receive support from American and European supporters, and both share common objectives. During the early 1980s in the United States, the JDL and a shadowy group called the **United Jewish Underground** were responsible for several acts of terrorism. These attacks were directed primarily against Soviet targets, such as the offices of the Soviet national airline Aeroflot, and were conducted to protest that government's treatment of Soviet Jews. Their bombings were sometimes lethal, and a number of deaths were attributed to JDL attacks. The movement ended its attacks in the mid-1980s and shifted its political emphasis to militant Zionist activism in Israel, although it is still in existence in the United States. For example, in December 2001 two JDL members (including the group's leader) were indicted in Southern California for plotting to attack the offices of a Lebanese American Congressman and two Islamic centers.

The New Terrorism in the United States

The activity profile changed during the 1990s, when American interests began to be directly attacked within the American homeland by international terrorists. A new threat emerged from religious radicals who considered the United States a primary target in their global jihad. After the September 11, 2001, homeland attacks, the activity profile of international terrorism in the United States shifted to cell-based religious terrorist spillovers originating in the Middle East. The American people and government became acutely aware of the destructive potential of international terrorism from the following incidents.

February 1993. In the first terrorist attack on the World Trade Center, a large vehicular bomb exploded in a basement parking garage; it was a failed attempt to topple one tower into the other. Six people were killed, and more than 1,000 were injured. The mastermind behind the attack was the dedicated international terrorist Ramzi Yousef. His motives were to support the Palestinian people, to punish the United States for its support of Israel, and to promote an Islamic jihad. Several men, all *jihadis*, were convicted of the attack.

October 1995. Ten men were convicted in a New York federal court of plotting further terrorist attacks. They allegedly conspired to attack New York City landmarks, such as tunnels, the United Nations, and the George Washington Bridge.

September 11, 2001. The most significant incident of domestic international terrorism in the United States was the homeland attacks in New York City, Washington, D.C., and rural Pennsylvania. It was also one of the most significant single attacks in modern history because of its coordination, audacity, high death toll, and global consequences.

At the dawn of the 21st century, these incidents herald the emergence of a threat to homeland security that has not existed since the Second World War. The practitioners of the New Terrorism apparently concluded that assaults on the American homeland are desirable and feasible. The key preparatory factors for making these attacks feasible were the following:

They were carried out by prepositioned terrorist cells.

The cells had entered the United States, lived among the civilian population, and planned their attacks.

Members of the cells performed their tasks with dedication and efficiency.

The support apparatus profile in the United States for this was not entirely unknown, because militants have been known to be in the United States since the 1980s and 1990s. For example, aboveground organizations were established to funnel funds to the Middle East on behalf of Hamas, Hezbollah, and other movements. These organizations—and other social associations—were deliberately established in many major American cities. The fact is that since at least the late 1980s, anti-American *jihadi* sentiment has existed within the United States among some fundamentalist communities. And significantly, jihad has been overtly advocated by a number of fundamentalist leaders who took up residence in the United States.[30]

The threat from the New Terrorism in the American homeland includes the very real possibility of a terrorist campaign using high-yield weapons to maximize civilian casualties. The potential scale of violence was demonstrated by an anthrax attack after the September 11, 2001, attacks, which made use of the U.S. postal system. For the first time in its history, the threat of chemical, biological, and radiological terrorism became a reality in the United States.

Case in Point   **Lynching—Vigilante Communal Terrorism in the United States**

Lynchings were public communal killings. They were usually racially motivated hangings or burnings of African American males. Lynch mobs would typically abduct the victim, drag him to the place of execution, physically abuse him (often gruesomely), and then publicly kill him. The activity profile of lynchings included the following elements:

- White mobs
- Killings of African Americans (usually men) and others
- Physical abuse, including torture, mutilations, and the taking of "souvenirs" from the corpses (bones, toes, etc.)
- Symbolic protection of the White community
- Symbolic "warnings" to the African American community

Photography was commonly used to record lynchings, and it was not uncommon for members of lynch mobs to pose proudly next to the corpses. This is significant, because

the use of the camera to memorialize lynchings testified to their openness and to the self-righteousness that animated the participants. Not only did photographers capture the execution itself, but also the carnival-like atmosphere and the expectant mood of the crowd.[a]

The term *lynching* is based on Charles Lynch, a colonial-era Virginia farmer who, during the Revolution, acted as a judge who hung outlaws and Tories (pro-British colonials). From 1882 to 1968, nearly 5,000 African Americans are known to have been lynched. Some had been accused of crimes, but most were simply innocent sacrificial victims.

NOTE

a. Litwack, Leon F. "Hellhounds." In Allen, James, Hilton Als, Congressman John Lewis, and Leon Litwack, eds. *Without Sanctuary: Lynching Photography in America.* Santa Fe, NM: Twin Palms Publishers, 2000, pp. 10-11.

CHAPTER SUMMARY

This chapter investigated political violence in the United States. Both domestic and international terrorism were discussed. The sources of domestic terrorism were identified as extremist tendencies that grew out of movements and cultural histories, and the sources of international terrorism were identified as terrorist spillover activity.

On the left, modern terrorism originated in the social and political fervor of the 1960s and 1970s. Some members of activist movements became radicalized by their experiences within the context of their environment. A few became dedicated revolutionaries and chose to engage in terrorist violence. Members of New Left and nationalist terrorist groups waged terrorist campaigns until the mid-1980s. Single-issue and nascent anarchist tendencies have replaced the now-defunct Marxist and nationalist movements on the left.

On the right, the long history of racial violence continued into the 21st century. The Ku Klux Klan is a uniquely American racist movement that has progressed through five eras, with terrorist violence occurring in each era. Modern Klansmen, neo-Nazis, and moralists have also engaged in terrorist violence. Threats of potential political violence come from antigovernment movements and emerging "heritage" movements. The activity profile of the modern era is primarily a lone wolf and cell-based profile. It has become rare for racial supremacist and moralist terrorists to act as members of established organizations.

International terrorism in the postwar era began as spillover activity directed against non-American targets with established interests in the United States. Most of this activity was of short duration, although several movements waged terrorist campaigns. Fringe Cuban, Irish, and Jewish organizations waged violent campaigns against their perceived enemies but did not target American interests. This profile changed dramatically during the 1990s, when revolutionary Islamic groups began to target American interests inside the United States.

In Chapter 13, students will be introduced to counterterrorist policy options. Theoretical options and responses will be augmented by examples of successful and failed measures. The discussion will investigate legalistic, repressive, and conciliatory responses to terrorism.

KEY TERMS AND CONCEPTS

The following topics were discussed in this chapter and are found in the Glossary:

25:6	Aryan Nations
Anglo-Israelism	Aryan Republican Army
Animal Liberation Front	Ásatrú
Armed Forces for National Liberation (Fuerzas Armadas de Liberación Nacional, or FALN)	Bhagwan Shree Rajneesh
	Black Hebrew Israelites
Armed Forces of Popular Resistance	Black helicopters
Armed Resistance Unit	Black Liberation Army
Army of God	Black Panther Party for Self-Defense
Arocena, Eduardo	Black Power

RECOMMENDED WEB SITES

The following Web sites provide information about extremist movements, terrorist ideologies, and "watchdog" agencies in the United States.

Anti-Defamation League Militia Watchdog: www.militia-watchdog.org

Hate Directory: www.bcpl.net/~rfrankli/hatedir.htm

Prairie Fire Organizing Committee: www.prairie-fire.org

U.S. Department of Homeland Security: www.whitehouse.gov/homeland

White Aryan Resistance: www.resist.com

Discussion Box   **Domestic Terrorism in the American Context**

This chapter's Discussion Box is intended to stimulate critical debate about the idiosyncratic nature of domestic terrorism in the United States.

The case of domestic terrorism in the United States is arguably a study in idiosyncratic political violence. Indigenous terrorist groups reflected the American political and social environments during historical periods when extremists chose to engage in political violence.

In the modern era, left-wing and right-wing political violence emerged under very different circumstances. Leftist violence evolved from a uniquely American social environment that produced the civil rights, Black Power, and New Left movements. Rightist violence grew out of a combination of historical racial and nativist animosity, combined with modern applications of religious and antigovernment ideologies.

At the beginning of the 21st century, threats continued to emanate from right-wing antigovernment and racial supremacist extremists. Potential violence from leftist extremists remained low in comparison with the right. After the September 11, 2001, attacks created a new security environment, the question of terrorism originating from domestic sources remained open and uncertain; this was especially true after the anthrax attacks on the American East Coast.

Discussion Questions:

- Assume that a nascent anarchist movement continues in its opposition to globalism. How should the modern leftist movement be described? What is the potential for violence originating from modern extremists on the left?
- Keeping in mind the many conspiracy and mystical beliefs of the American right, what is the potential for violence from adherents of these theories to the modern American environment?
- As a matter of policy, how closely should hate and antigovernment groups be monitored? What restrictions should be imposed on their activities? Why?
- Is the American activity profile truly an *idiosyncratic* profile, or can it be compared with other nations' environments? If so, how? If not, why not?
- What is the likelihood that the new millennium will witness a resurgence of a rightist movement on the scale of the 1990s Patriot movement? What trends indicate that it *will* occur? What trends indicate that it *will not* occur?

WEB EXERCISE

Using this chapter's recommended Internet sites, conduct an online investigation of terrorism in the United States.

- How would you describe the typologies of groups that predominate in the United States?
- Conduct a Web search of American monitoring organizations, read their mission statements, and assess their services. Which organizations do you think provide the most useful data? Why?
- If you were an American dissident extremist (leftist or rightist), how would you design your own Web site?

For an online search of terrorism in the United States, students should activate the search engine on their Web browser and enter the following keywords:

"Homeland Security"
"Domestic Terrorism"

RECOMMENDED READINGS

The following publications discuss the nature of terrorism in the United States and the root causes of political violence in American society.

George, John, and Laird Wilcox. *American Extremists: Militias, Supremacists, Klansmen, Communists, and Others.* Amherst, NY: Prometheus Books, 1996.

MacDonald, Andrew. *The Turner Diaries.* New York: Barricade Books, 1978.

Ridgeway, James. *Blood in the Face: The Ku Klux Klan, Aryan Nations, Nazi Skinheads, and the Rise of a New White Culture.* New York: Thunder's Mouth Press, 1990.

Sargent, Lyman Tower, ed. *Extremism in America: A Reader.* New York: New York University Press, 1995.

Stern, Kenneth S. *A Force Upon the Plain: The American Militia Movement and the Politics of Hate.* New York: Simon & Schuster, 1996.

Smith, Brent L. *Terrorism in America: Pipe Bombs and Pipe Dreams.* Albany: State University of New York Press, 1994.

NOTES

[1] For a good history of the American labor movement, see Brooks, Thomas R. *Toil and Trouble: A History of American Labor.* New York: Dell, 1971.

[2] Some of the lifestyle issues, such as drug legalization, have been endorsed by libertarian conservatives.

[3] See a discussion of the definitional debate about hate crimes in the Chapter 2 Case in Point.

[4] Kelly, Robert J. "The Ku Klux Klan: Recurring Hate in America." In Kelly, Robert J., and Jess Maghan, eds. *Hate Crime: The Global Politics of Polarization.* Carbondale and Edwardsville: Southern Illinois University Press, 1998, p. 54.

[5] See Smith, Brent L. *Terrorism in America: Pipe Bombs and Pipe Dreams.* Albany: State University of New York Press, 1994, pp. 35 ff.

[6] For good histories of the civil rights movement, see Branch, Taylor. *Parting the Waters: American in the King Years, 1954-63.* New York: Simon & Schuster, 1988. See also Hampton, Henry, and Steve Fayer. *Voices of Freedom: An Oral History of the Civil Rights Movement From the 1950s Through the 1980s.* New York: Bantam Books, 1990.

[7] See Malcolm X. *The Autobiography of Malcolm X.* New York: Grove Press, 1964. See also Breitman, George, ed. *Malcolm X Speaks.* New York: Grove Press, 1965.

[8] Jacobs, Ron. *The Way the Wind Blew: A History of the Weather Underground.* New York: Verso, 1997, p. 21. Citing Mellen, Jim. "More on Youth Movement." *New Left Notes.* May 13, 1969.

[9] Gurr, Ted Robert. "Terrorism in Democracies: Its Social and Political Bases." In Reich, Walter, ed., *Origins of Terrorism: Psychologies, Ideologies, Theologies, and States of Mind.* Washington, DC: Woodrow Wilson Center Press, 1998, p. 89.

[10] Hoffman, Bruce. *Inside Terrorism.* New York: Columbia University Press, 1998, p. 107. These numbers declined during the late 1990s and then rebounded after the September 11, 2001, attacks on the U.S. homeland. For a discussion of the militia movement in retrospect, see Southern Poverty Law Center. *Intelligence Report.* Summer 2001.

[11] Many in the racial supremacist movement consider *The Turner Diaries* to be a blueprint for the Aryan revolution. A copy was found with Timothy McVeigh when he was arrested after the Oklahoma City bombing in 1995. See MacDonald, Andrew. *The Turner Diaries.* New York: Barricade Books, 1980. "Andrew MacDonald" is a *nom de plume* for William Pierce, leader of the National Alliance.

[12] Data are derived from *Riots, Civil and Criminal Disorders—Hearings Before the Permanent Subcommittee on Investigations of the Committee on Government Operations, United States Senate,* Part 25. Washington, DC: Government Printing Office, 1970. Cited in Prosser, George. "Terror in the United States: 'An Introduction to Elementary Tactics' and 'Some Questions on Tactics.'" In Mallin, Jay, ed. *Terror and Urban Guerrillas: A Study of Tactics and Documents.* Coral Gables, FL: University of Miami Press, 1971, p. 52.

[13] Gurr (note 9 above).

[14] Sprinzak, Ehud. "The Psychopolitical Formation of Extreme Left Terrorism in a Democracy: The Case of the Weathermen." In Reich, Walter, ed. *Origins of Terrorism: Psychologies, Ideologies, Theologies, States of Mind*. Washington, DC: Woodrow Wilson Center Press, 1998, p. 65. Quoting Thomas, Tom. "The Second Battle of Chicago." In Jacobs, Harold, ed. *Weatherman*. Berkeley, CA: Ramparts Press, 1970, p. 197.

[15] A former professor, Leary was best known for his recreational and spiritual experimentation with the hallucinogenic drug LSD, which he advocated as a "consciousness-raising" drug.

[16] Possibly 26 police officers died in BLA ambushes. Gurr, Ted Robert. "Political Terrorism: Historical Antecedents and Contemporary Trends." In Gurr, Ted R., ed. *Violence in America: Protest, Rebellion, Reform*, vol. 2. Newbury Park, CA: Sage, 1989.

[17] See Smith, Brent L. *Terrorism in America: Pipe Bombs and Pipe Dreams*. Albany: State University of New York Press, 1994, for sources and further discussion of the FALN.

[18] See Smith, ibid., for sources and further discussion of left-wing hard cores.

[19] Boudin was denied parole at her first parole hearing in 2001. See Associated Press. "Kathy Boudin, 60s Radical, Denied Parole." *New York Times*. August 22, 2001.

[20] See Smith (note 17 above) for sources and further discussion of the United Freedom Front.

[21] For a discussion of the Aryan Republican Army, see Hamm, Mark. *In Bad Company: America's Terrorist Underground*. Boston: Northeastern University Press, 2002.

[22] The chronology of the order's terrorist spree is adapted from Anti-Defamation League. *Danger: Extremism. The Major Vehicles and Voices on America's Far-Right Fringe*. New York: Anti-Defamation League, 1996, pp. 270-71.

[23] Timeline adapted from Southern Poverty Law Center, Intelligence Project. *Intelligence Report*. Winter 2000.

[24] Southern Poverty Law Center, Intelligence Project. *Intelligence Report*. Summer 2001.

[25] Ibid.

[26] See "Patriot Free Fall." Southern Poverty Law Center. *Intelligence Report*. Summer 2002.

[27] Hoskins, Richard Kelly. *Vigilantes of Christendom: The History of the Phineas Priesthood*. St. Louis, MO: Virginia, 1995.

[28] Hamm (note 21 above), p. 147.

[29] See Hamm (note 21 above), p. 147.

[30] For a documentary discussion of this subject, see *Terrorists Among Us: Jihad in America*. Prod. SAE Productions, Videocassette. SAE Productions, 2001.

Chapter 13

RESPONDING TO TERROR: THE OPTIONS

This chapter reviews policy options for responding to acts of political violence. The question of how to respond is traditionally regarded as a choice between so-called hard-line and soft-line responses. Hard-line responses include using military and paramilitary measures to punish or destroy the terrorists. No compromise is desired, and no negotiations are accepted. Soft-line responses are a more complicated approach. They incorporate diplomacy, compromise, and social reforms as possible options. Regardless of which category a particular policy option falls under, the key consideration for policymakers is the *practicality* of the counterterrorist option. In other words, will the option work? Will the terrorists' behavior change? Can the terrorist environment be co-opted or suppressed?

Before addressing these bottom-line questions, it is important to consider what is meant by *responding* to terrorism and engaging in *counterterrorism* or *antiterrorism.*

Responding to terrorism is defined here as any action taken by a targeted interest in reply to a terrorist incident or terrorist environment. These actions range in scale from very passive to highly active responses. For example, options can be as passive as simply doing nothing, thus calculating that the terrorists will be satisfied by inaction. More intensive responses include covert campaigns to disrupt or otherwise destabilize hostile movements. Very intensive responses include symbolic military strikes against groups and their sponsors, as well as campaigns to completely incapacitate the terrorists.

Counterterrorism refers to proactive policies that specifically seek to eliminate terrorist environments and groups. Regardless of which policy is selected, the ultimate goal of counterterrorism is clear: to save lives by proactively preventing or decreasing the number of terrorist attacks. As a corollary, *antiterrorism* refers to target hardening, enhanced security, and other defensive measures seeking to deter or prevent terrorist attacks.

Much of our discussion will focus on categories of responses. These are theoretical groupings of policy options that experts have identified as possible responses to terrorist incidents. Categories of responses should not be considered exact templates for every terrorist contingency, for there are no exact theories of responses or counterterrorism. The fact of the matter is that terrorist environments are in many ways idiosyncratic, as are many terrorist groups. The implications of this for counterterrorist policy are that some methods will be successful in only a few cases, whereas others will be adaptable to many cases. Significantly, some policy options often seem to make perfect theoretical sense when they are developed, but subsequently they make little practical sense. Nevertheless, the categories of available options are fairly clearly drawn; it is the *adaptation* of these options to specific scenarios that can become less certain.

Most experts agree that counterterrorist options can be grouped into several policy categories. Examples of these categories include:

- Diplomacy, financial controls, military force, intelligence, and covert action[1]
- Legal, repressive, and conciliatory responses to terrorism[2]
- Targeted and untargeted prevention[3]

OVERVIEW OF OPTIONS

Regardless of which label is attached to an option, or which categories are developed, there is consensus among policymakers that they have available to them several basic counterterrorist options and sub-options. These options and sub-options can be organized as follows:

Use of Force

This is a hard-line option that allows policymakers to use the force of arms against terrorists and their supporters. The objectives of deploying military and paramilitary assets can range from symbolic punitive attacks to destruction of terrorist personnel and infrastructure. The following are examples of military and **paramilitary repressive options:**

- **Coercive covert operations** include assassinations, sabotage, kidnapping, and other "extralegal" methods. The purpose is to wage low-level and secretive war against terrorist movements.
- **Suppression campaigns** are ongoing strikes against targets affiliated with terrorists. The purpose of these strikes is to destroy or severely disrupt terrorist personnel and infrastructure.
- **Punitive strikes** and **preemptive strikes** are attacks that are intended to punish terrorist targets. The former occur in *response to* terrorist attacks, and the latter occur in *anticipation of* terrorist attacks. Both can be symbolic strikes that cause limited damage or that are launched to destroy specific facilities or personnel.

Operations Other Than War: Repressive Options

Repressive responses include military operations other than war and nonmilitary operations other than war. Military operations include raids by special operations units, air strikes, missile strikes, and other actions that fall short of full-scale deployment. Military operations other than war are discussed in detail later in the chapter.

Nonmilitary operations include a range of repressive options that are flexible and can be adapted to specific terrorist environments. Examples of nonmilitary repressive options include the following:

- **Covert operations** are secretive operations. They form a category that includes a number of possible counterterrorist measures, such as infiltration, **disinformation**, and **cyberwar**. Covert programs require creative and imaginative methods that are adapted to each terrorist environment.
- **Intelligence** refers to the collection of data. Its purpose is to create an informational database about terrorist movements and to predict their behavior. This process is not unlike that of criminal justice investigators who work to resolve criminal cases.

- **Enhanced security** refers to the hardening of targets to deter or prevent terrorist attacks. Security barriers, checkpoints, and surveillance are typical security measures. These are critical components of antiterrorism.
- **Economic sanctions** are used to punish or disrupt state sponsors of terrorism. Sanctions can either selectively target specific economic sectors or generally restrict trade. The purpose is to pressure state sponsors to modify or end their support for terrorism.

The successful use of nonmilitary and nonparamilitary assets to suppress terrorism requires the effective deployment of technological and organizational resources. The primary objective of using nonmilitary resources is to disrupt and deter terrorist organizations and their support apparatuses. Nonmilitary options thus require the development of creative security measures and the use of new technologies.

Operations Other Than War: Conciliatory Options

Conciliatory responses are "soft-line" options that allow policymakers to develop a range of options that do not involve the use of force or other repressive methods. The objectives of nonrepressive responses depend on the characteristics of the terrorist environment. Examples of these responses include the following:

- **Diplomacy** refers to different degrees of capitulation to the terrorist which refers to engaging with the terrorists to negotiate an acceptable resolution to a conflict. Diplomatic solutions can be incident specific, or they can involve sweeping conditions that may completely resolve the conflict.
- **Social reform** is an attempt to address the grievances of the terrorists and their championed group. The purpose is to resolve the underlying problems that caused the terrorist environment to develop.
- **Concessionary options.** Concessions can be incident specific, in which immediate demands are met, or generalized concessions in which broad demands are accommodated.

Legalistic Responses

Nations have developed legal protocols to employ in dealing with terrorism. Some of these protocols have been implemented to promote international cooperation, and others have been adopted as matters of domestic policy. The overall objective of **legalistic responses** is to promote the rule of law and regular legal proceedings. The following are examples of these responses:

- **Law enforcement** refers to the use of law enforcement agencies and criminal investigative techniques in the prosecution of suspected terrorists. This adds an element of *rule of law* to counterterrorism.
- Counterterrorist laws attempt to criminalize terrorist behavior. This can be done, for example, by declaring certain behaviors to be criminal terrorism or by enhancing current laws such as those that punish murder.
- **International law** relies on cooperation among states. Those who are parties to international agreements attempt to combat terrorism by permitting them no refuge or sanctuary for their behavior. In some cases, terrorists may be brought before international tribunals.

Table 13.1 summarizes activity profiles for these counterterrorist policy categories.

Table 13.1   Counterterrorist Options: General Policy Categories

Experts have developed generalized categories for counterterrorist options. These categories have been given a variety of labels, but they refer to similar concepts. Each of the generalized categories has been divided into subcategories.

The following table illustrates the activity profiles of general counterterrorist categories.

Counterterrorist Category	*Rationale*	*Activity Profile*	
		Practical Objectives	*Typical Resources Used*
Use of force	Symbolic strength	Punish or destroy the terrorists	Military assets Paramilitary assets
Operations other than war: repressive options	Deterrence	Disruption of the terrorists	Technologies
	Prediction Destabilization	Intelligence Coercion of supporters	Covert operatives Security forces
Operations other than war: conciliatory options	Resolve underlying problems	End immediate crises	Social resources
		Forestall future crises	Economic assets Negotiators
Legalistic options	Rule of law	International cooperation	International organizations
		Prosecution, conviction, and incarceration of terrorists	Law enforcement agencies
			Domestic legal establishments

The discussion in this chapter will review the following responses to terrorism:

- Counterterrorism and the Use of Force
- Operations Other Than War: Repressive Options
- Operations Other Than War: Conciliatory Options
- Legalistic Responses

COUNTERTERRORISM AND THE USE OF FORCE

The use of force is a hard-line approach used by states and their proxies to violently suppress terrorist environments. The goals of this approach are case specific, so that the decision to use violent suppression is based on policy calculations peculiar to each terrorist environment. When states decide to use force against terrorists and their supporters, coercion and violence are considered to be justifiable and desirable policy options. The underlying rationale for many decisions to use force is to demonstrate the state's ability to disrupt the operational capabilities of terrorists and, if necessary, to eliminate them. The process of *eliminating* terrorists refers to incapacitating them by disrupting, isolating, capturing, and killing as many cadres as possible.

This policy option requires the deployment of military or paramilitary assets to punish, destabilize, or destroy terrorists and their supporters. "Military assets" are defined as the recognized and official armed forces of a nation. "Paramilitary assets" are defined as un-official and irregular armed units or individuals that are supported or organized by regimes. Paramilitaries include irregular civilian "home guard" units armed by the government and stationed in their home villages and towns. Paramilitaries also include government-supported death squads, which were discussed in Chapters 4 and 7. A paramilitary asset can also be an individual trained in the use of explosives, small arms, assassination techniques, and other applications of violence.

States have waged military and paramilitary counterterrorist operations domestically and internationally. A comparison of these operational venues may be summarized as follows:

Domestic operations involve the coercive use of military, police, and other security forces against domestic threats. States justify this type of deployment as being necessary to restore order. Unfortunately, historical examples show that a great deal of civilian "collat-eral damage" occurs in these environments. As discussed in previous chapters, a number of governments have readily used domestic force when threatened by dissident insurgents, terrorist campaigns, or other antigovernment political movements. In extreme circum-stances, some governments have adopted official policies of indiscriminate repression and state-sponsored terrorism.

International operations involve the overt or covert deployment of security assets abroad. These deployments can include ground, air, or naval forces in large or very small opera-tional configurations. The scale of the deployment is, of course, dependent on the goals of state policies and the type of counterterrorist action to be carried out. In some cases, units will be deployed to an allied country that is willing to serve as a base of operations. If a host country is unavailable, or if they impose restrictive conditions on the deployment, nations with sufficient military resources (such as the United States) will use naval units as seaborne bases for launching military strikes. Or air assets can be flown over long distances from home bases or friendly third countries to attack designated targets.

The following discussion explores several use-of-force options that are commonly adopted by nations.

Coercive Covert Operations

Coercive covert operations seek to destabilize, degrade, and destroy terrorist groups. Targets include individual terrorists, terrorist networks, and support apparatuses. Although covert assets have been developed by nations to wage "shadow wars" using special oper-atives, conventional forces have also been used to surreptitiously resolve terrorist crises. The following case in point illustrates the latter type of operation:

Case: The Achille Lauro

The Italian cruise ship ***Achille Lauro*** was hijacked in October 1985 by four Palestinian terrorists belonging to the Palestine Liberation Front faction of the PLO. During the hijacking, an elderly wheelchair-bound American was executed and thrown into the

Mediterranean Sea. Other Americans were terrorized aboard the ship—for example, being forced to hold a live hand grenade after the pin had been removed. The cruise ship eventually stopped in Egyptian waters, where the hostages were released and the terrorists were taken to Port Said. When the United States demanded that the terrorists be extradited, Egyptian President Hosni Mubarak claimed that they had already left the country.

In fact, the terrorists were still in Egypt and had been secretly placed aboard an aircraft to fly them out of the country and to safety. Also aboard the aircraft was the Palestine Liberation Front's leader, Abu Abbas. U.S. and Israeli intelligence knew where the aircraft was and when it was in flight. Two U.S. warplanes intercepted the Egyptian aircraft and forced it to fly to Sicily. The final resolution of the *Achille Lauro* crisis is described later in the chapter in the section discussing legalistic responses.

Other types of coercive covert operations are more lethal, as indicated in the following case in point of using assassinations as a policy option.

Case: Assassinations

Counterterrorist assassination is easily defined: It involves the intentional killing of terrorist leaders, cadres, and supporters. The underlying rationale for using assassinations as a counterterrorist option is uncomplicated: Because terrorism is itself a human action, the terrorism will end or diminish if the terrorists and their supporters are eliminated. The argument is that because this option is a terminal solution, those targeted for assassination will be permanently removed as a threat. It is debatable whether this is an accurate assumption, because there is little evidence supporting the supposition that assassinations have ever had an appreciable deterrent effect on determined terrorists. Terrorists who operate within supportive environments and who enjoy the approval of a championed group are likely to be viewed as heroes by supporters. A terrorist's death at the hands of a sworn enemy is likely to elevate the terrorist to martyr status. As discussed in previous chapters, symbolic martyrdom is actively manipulated by terrorist movements to rally their followers and recruit new fighters.

Needless to say, assassination is highly controversial as a matter of policy. It is always covertly implemented—one does not broadcast when an assassination will take place. Government "deniability" is usually incorporated into these operations, and most nations will readily disavow involvement in assassinations. A comparison of the American and Israeli approaches is instructive.

After the Vietnam War, the United States officially declared that it would no longer use assassination as a tool of statecraft. In December 1981, President Reagan's **Executive Order 12333** expressly prohibited employees of the United States from assassinating adversaries. This prohibition, which followed President Gerald Ford's prohibition outlined in Executive Order 11905, also forbade U.S. personnel from using anyone hired as an agent to commit assassinations. This prohibition was applied during the political and terrorist environment that existed prior to the September 11, 2001, homeland attacks.

In comparison, Israel has used assassinations repeatedly in its war against terrorism, primarily targeting Palestinian nationalists. This policy has been in place for many years, and it has often been administered by the **Mossad**, Israel's intelligence and covert operations agency. For example, on July 11, 1970, the Israelis attempted to assassinate two prominent members of the Popular Front for the Liberation of Palestine. Israeli covert operatives identified a safe house used by the PFLP in an apartment in Beirut. They rented an apartment across the street from the safe house and rigged six Katyusha rockets on a timer to fire into the PFLP apartment. Their targets were PFLP cofounder Wadi Haddad and young Leila Khaled (discussed in Chapter 3's Case in Point). Four rockets fired as planned, but Haddad and Khaled survived the attack.

A covert Israeli unit known as **Wrath of God** (Mivtzan Elohim) was responsible for tracking and assassinating Black September terrorists after the 1972 Munich Olympics massacre. At least 20 Palestinians were assassinated in Europe and the Middle East. The Wrath of God program went awry in 1973 when Israeli agents mistakenly shot to death a North African waiter in Norway while his wife looked on; they had mistaken him for a Black September operative.

In October 1995, Israeli agents were the likely assassins of a leader of Palestine Islamic Jihad in Malta. During the Palestinian *intifadeh*, Israeli personnel targeted for assassination many terrorists, insurgents, and activist leaders. A famous case was the January 1996 assassination of Yehiya Ayyash, also known as the Engineer, who was discussed in Chapter 10. An infamous case was the highly publicized September 1997 assassination attempt on a top Hamas leader in Amman, Jordan. When the attempt failed rather publicly, the Israeli government was embarrassed, Mossad was disgraced, and Israeli-Jordanian relations became severely strained. Nevertheless, the assassination campaign against *intifadeh* leaders and operatives continued. In one particularly bloody incident in July 2002, an Israeli rocket attack assassinated top Hamas leader Sheik Salah Shehadeh. The attack also killed Shehadeh's wife and three children, as well as hitting an apartment building. A total of 14 civilians were killed in the attack.

Suppression Campaigns

Counterterrorist campaigns can be undertaken by military and paramilitary forces. These are long-term operations directed against terrorist cadres, their bases, and support apparatuses. Suppression campaigns are uniquely adapted to the conditions of each terrorist environment and are usually of indeterminate duration. They are launched within the policy contexts of war or quasi-war and are often waged with the goal of utterly defeating the terrorist movement.

Military Suppression Campaigns

Nations sometimes resort to the use of conventional units and special operations forces to wage war against terrorist movements. The goal is to destroy their ability to use terrorism to attack the nation's interests. Military campaigns require the deployment of troops to bases in friendly countries or (in the case of nations with significant seaborne capability)[4] offshore aboard naval vessels. The following examples illustrate the nature of military suppression campaigns:

Operation Peace for Galilee. In June 1982, the Israeli army invaded Lebanon for the second time to root out PLO bases of operation.[5] The operation was called **Operation Peace for Galilee** and was launched in reply to ongoing PLO attacks from its Lebanese bases. During the invasion, the Israelis fought and won a war with Syria that lasted six days and drove through Lebanon to West Beirut by mid-June. The city was surrounded, and a three-month siege of trapped PLO and Syrian troops began. The United States brokered an agreement that allowed the PLO and Syrians to withdraw from Beirut in August. The outcome of this phase of the invasion was the successful neutralization of PLO forces south of Beirut. Many Lebanese opposed to the PLO presence had welcomed the Israelis, but this good will ended in mid-September. When Israeli troops entered West Beirut, Christian Phalangist militiamen massacred hundreds of Palestinian civilians for three days in the Sabra and Shatila refugee camps. The Israeli army did not intervene, their army remained in Lebanon, and Lebanese resistance against the Israeli presence began to grow. The Israelis eventually withdrew from most of Lebanon in 1985, establishing an occupation zone in South Lebanon that was maintained until their withdrawal in July 2000.

Operation Enduring Freedom. The United States declared itself to be at war against global terrorism after the September 11, 2001, homeland attacks. The United States was joined by a number of allies who agreed to commit their armed forces and domestic security services to the new war. Dubbed **Operation Enduring Freedom** (renamed from **Operation Infinite Justice**), the operation was defined from the beginning as a long-term suppression campaign. It was also made clear from the outset that the war against terrorism would require extended deployments of U.S. and allied troops around the world, as well as an intensive use of special operations forces, commandos, Marines, and other elite units. The immediate objectives of Enduring Freedom were to destroy Al Qaeda's safe havens in Taliban-controlled Afghanistan, collect intelligence, disrupt the terrorist network around the world, and capture or kill as many cadres as possible. The long-term goal of the campaign—which policymakers expect will take years to achieve—is to degrade or destroy the operational capabilities of international terrorists.

Paramilitary Suppression Campaigns

In some suppression campaigns, military and paramilitary units actively coordinate their operations. A typical policy used in this type of counterterrorist environment has been the government's arming and support of paramilitaries in areas where the military does not have a strong presence. The following examples illustrate the nature of paramilitary suppression campaigns:

Algeria. As discussed in Chapter 8, Algeria was beset by intensive terrorist violence from *jihadis* belonging to several radical Islamic groups. The Algerian government was unsuccessful in suppressing the rebels and was accused of committing human rights violations. Many thousands of civilians were killed, mostly at the hands of the *jihadis*. During the suppression campaign, the government organized and armed paramilitary home guard units.[6] These units, which were used as local self-defense forces, effectively staved off attacks from the rebels, thus reducing their operational effectiveness in the countryside. In part because of the paramilitary policy, as well as government-initiated programs and brutal suppression, the rebellion eventually ended in a negotiated amnesty settlement in 1999.

Colombia. As discussed in Chapter 7, paramilitaries such as the United Self-Defense Forces of Colombia (AUC) fought against Marxist FARC and ELN rebels using guerrilla tactics and death squad terrorism. Paramilitaries such as the AUC received overt and covert support from the government and wealthy Colombians. A typical example of the AUC's operational role and the Colombian army's cooperation occurred in May 2002, when AUC and FARC units fought a pitched battle in the town of Bellavista. Approximately 400 AUC fighters passed through several Colombian army checkpoints on their way to the town to recapture it from FARC. During intense fighting, a FARC homemade mortar crashed through the roof of a church, killing 119 civilians (including 46 children) and wounding more than 100. The Colombian army did not arrive at the village until five days after the fighting ended.[7]

Punitive and Preemptive Operations

Short-duration military and paramilitary operations are usually conducted for a specific purpose under specific rules of engagement. These actions are designed to send a clear symbolic message to terrorists. The following two types of short-duration operations have been used:

Punitive strikes are attacks that are launched as reprisals against terrorists for incidents that have already taken place. Successful punitive strikes require the attacker to symbolically and politically link the attacks to the terrorist incident.

Preemptive strikes are attacks that are undertaken to hurt terrorists prior to a terrorist incident. Preemptive operations are launched as a precautionary measure to degrade the terrorists' ability to launch future attacks. Symbolic and political linkage between the attacks and a real threat is often difficult.

Punitive strikes are used more commonly than preemptive strikes. These attacks can be justified to some extent, as long as links can be established between the attacks and a terrorist incident. Linkage must also be made between the specific targets of the reprisal and the alleged perpetrators of the incident. This latter consideration sometimes goes awry. For example, when the United States launched cruise missiles against targets in Sudan and Afghanistan in August 1998 (in retaliation for the bombings of the U.S. embassies in Tanzania and Kenya), the legitimacy of one of the targets was called into question. A Sudanese pharmaceutical factory was destroyed by the missiles. The United States claimed that it was a Qaeda operation that produced chemicals that could be used in chemical weapons. Many observers questioned this assertion, thus reducing the veracity of the Americans' claim that the target was linked to the terrorist attacks.

Preemptive strikes are used less frequently than punitive strikes, partly because preemption by definition means that the attack is a unilateral action conducted in response to a *perceived* threat. Such attacks are therefore not as easily justified as punitive operations, which is an important consideration for regimes concerned about world opinion. Unless a threat can be clearly defined, it is unlikely that preemptive actions will receive widespread support from friends or neutral parties. Nevertheless, some nations have adopted preemptive operations as a regular counterterrorist method. Israel has for some time preemptively attacked neighboring countries that harbor anti-Israeli terrorists and dissidents. For example, Israeli air, ground, and naval raids into Lebanon frequently target PLO and Hezbollah bases.

Chapter Perspective 13.1 presents an example of a large punitive operation launched by the United States against Libya in 1986.

Special Operations Forces

Special operations forces are defined here as highly trained military and police units that specialize in unconventional operations. These units are usually not organized in the same manner as conventional forces, because their missions require them to operate quickly and covertly in very hostile environments. Operations are frequently conducted in small teams of operatives, although fairly large units can be deployed if required by circumstances. Depending on their mission, special operations forces are trained for long-range reconnaissance, surveillance, "surgical" punitive raids, hostage rescues, abductions, and liaisons with allied counterterrorist forces. Their training and organizational configurations are ideally suited to counterterrorist operations.

Most nations have included specially trained units in their domestic security and national defense commands. Many of these operatives belong to the armed forces, but not all special operations forces are military units—many are elite police forces trained to conduct paramilitary operations. Examples of these units are summarized later in the chapter.

Special Operations Forces: Military Units

In the modern era, special operations forces have become fully integrated into the operational commands of national armed forces worldwide. Their value in counterterrorist

On April 14, 1986, the United States bombed targets in Libya using Air Force bombers based in Great Britain and Navy carrier-borne aircraft based in the Mediterranean. The attacks occurred at the height of tensions between the United States and Libya, which were precipitated by a radically activist Libyan government and its partnership with the Soviet Union.

Background

During the 1980s, Libya established strong ties with the Communist Eastern Bloc (Soviet-dominated Eastern Europe). It also declared itself to be a champion of people "oppressed" by the West and Israel. Libyan leader Muammar el-Qaddafi permitted the Libyan government to build camps to train terrorists from around the world, to stockpile weapons far in excess of Libya's needs, to acquire large amounts of plastic explosives (including powerful Czech-made Semtex), and to directly engage in state-sponsored international terrorism.

In March 1986, the U.S. Mediterranean fleet sailed into a disputed exclusionary zone off the coast of Libya. Qaddafi responded to the American show of force by declaring that a "line of death" had been drawn in the disputed waters—which the U.S. Sixth Fleet then purposefully crossed. Two terrorist bombings blamed on Libya subsequently occurred in Europe. The first bomb killed four Americans aboard a TWA airliner in Greece, and the

second bomb killed one U.S. serviceman at La Belle Discotheque in West Berlin. The American punitive raids—dubbed **Operation El Dorado Canyon**—were ostensibly in retaliation for these bombings, but they probably would have occurred in any event.

Aftermath

More than 100 Libyans were killed in Benghazi and Tripoli, including Qaddafi's young adopted daughter. American policymakers considered the attacks to be successful, because Libya thereafter temporarily scaled back its international adventurism and Qaddafi reduced his inflammatory rhetoric. Libya then entered a second, shorter period of international activism and then pulled back—this time for an extended period of time.

It should be noted that the strike force based in Britain was forced to detour around France and the Iberian Peninsula (Spain and Portugal) and enter the Mediterranean through the Straits of Gibraltar, which separate Europe and Africa. This was necessary because the French and Spanish governments refused to permit the bombers to fly over their airspace. The American air strike was unpopular in Europe. After the attack, demonstrations occurred in several countries, and many Europeans expressed outrage over the bombings. In Beirut, one American and two British hostages were murdered in retaliation for the attack on Libya.

operations has been proven many times in the postwar era. The following cases in point illustrate the mission and configuration of special operations forces commands.

United Kingdom. The **Special Air Service** (SAS) is a secretive organization in the British Army that has been used repeatedly in counterterrorist operations. Organized at a regimental level, but operating in very small teams, the SAS is similar to the French 1st Navy Parachute Infantry Regiment and the American Delta Force (discussed later in the chapter). The SAS has been deployed repeatedly to assignments in Northern Ireland and abroad, as well as to resolve domestic terrorist crises such as rescuing hostages in May 1980 inside the Iranian embassy in London. The **Special Boat Service** (SBS) is a special unit under the command of the Royal Navy. It specializes in operations against seaborne targets and along coastlines and harbors. They are similar to the French Navy's special assault units and the American SEALs (discussed later in the chapter). The **Royal Marine**

French commandos at Orly Airport outside Paris. The group had just secured the release of
hostages held by terrorists in January 1975.

Source: Hulton Archive/Getty Images; used by permission.

Commandos are rapid-reaction troops that deploy in larger numbers than the SAS and
SBS. They are organized around units called commandos, which are roughly equivalent
to a conventional battalion. Royal Marines were deployed to Afghanistan in the hunt for
Al Qaeda cadres and Taliban troops.

France. The **1st Navy Parachute Infantry Regiment** (1RPIMa) is similar to the British
SAS and American Delta Force. Within the 1RPIMa, small **RAPAS** (intelligence and special operations) squads are trained to operate in desert, urban, and tropical environments.
Along with the special police unit GIGN (discussed later in the chapter), they form the
core of French counterterrorist special operations forces. 1RPIMa has been deployed to
crises around the world, particularly in Africa. Five **French Navy Special Assault Units**
have been trained for operations against seaborne targets, coastlines, and harbors. Their
mission is similar to that of the British SBS and American SEALs. When large elite combat
forces must be deployed, the French use their all-volunteer **11th Parachute Division
(Paras)** and the commando or parachute units of the famous French **Foreign Legion**.[8]

Israel. The Sayaret are reconnaissance units that were organized early in the history of the
Israel Defense Force (IDF). Several *Sayaret* exist within the IDF, the most noted of which
is **Sayaret Matkal**, a highly secretive formation that is attached to the IDF General
Headquarters. Operating in small units, it has skillfully (and often ruthlessly) engaged
in counterterrorist operations. For example, in April 1973 a Sayaret Matkal unit killed
several top PLO leaders in Beirut in reprisal for the Munich Olympics massacre. It also

directed the Entebbe operation. The **Parachute Sayaret** has been deployed in small and large units, often using high mobility to penetrate deep into hostile territory. They participated in the Entebbe operation and were used extensively in Lebanon against Hezbollah. The IDF has also deployed undercover agents against suspected terrorist cells. When large elite combat forces must be deployed, the **Golani Brigade** and its Sayaret are frequently used. The Golani Brigade was used extensively against Hezbollah in South Lebanon.

United States. U.S. Special Operations Forces are organized under the U.S. **Special Operations Command**. The **Delta Force (1st Special Forces Operational Detachment—Delta)** is a secretive unit that operates in small teams. Similar in mission to the British SAS and French 1RPIMa, Delta Force operates covertly outside of the United States. Its missions probably include abductions, reconnaissance, and punitive operations. **Green Berets (Special Forces Groups)** usually operate in units called A Teams. These teams comprise specialists whose skills include languages, intelligence, medicine, and demolitions. The traditional mission of the A Team is "force multiplication"; that is, they are inserted into regions to provide military training to local personnel, thus multiplying their operational strength. They also participate in reconnaissance and punitive raids. U.S. Navy **Sea Air Land Forces (SEALs)** are similar to the British SBS and the French Navy's Special Assault Units. Their primary mission is to conduct sea-borne, riverine, and harbor operations, although they have also been used extensively on land. When large elite combat units must be deployed, the United States relies on the Army's **75th Ranger Regiment** and units from the U.S. Marine Corps. The Marines have formed their own elite units, which include force reconnaissance and long-range reconnaissance units (referred to as "Recon"). These units are organized into teams, platoons, companies, and battalions.

Special Operations Forces: Police Units

Many nations have special units within their police forces that participate in counterterrorist operations. In several examples, these units have been used in a semimilitary role.

France. The **GIGN (Groupe d'Intervention Gendarmerie Nationale)** is recruited from the French *gendarmerie*, the military police. GIGN is a counterterrorist unit with international operational duties. In an operation that foiled what was arguably a precursor to the September 11, 2001, attacks, the GIGN rescued 173 hostages from an Air France Airbus in December 1994. Four Algerian terrorists had landed the aircraft in Marseilles, intending to fly to Paris to crash or blow up the plane over the city.

Germany. **GSG-9 (Grenzschutzgruppe 9)** was organized after the disastrous failed attempt to rescue Israeli hostages taken by Black September at the 1972 Munich Olympics. It is a paramilitary unit that has been used domestically and internationally as a counterterrorist and hostage rescue unit. GSG-9 first won international attention in 1977 when the group freed hostages held by Palestinian terrorists in Mogadishu, Somalia.

Israel. The **Police Border Guards** are an elite force that is frequently deployed as a counterterrorist force. Known as the **Green Police**, it operates in two subgroups. **YAMAS** is a covert group that has been used extensively during the Palestinian *intifadeh*. It has been used to neutralize terrorist cells in conjunction with covert IDF operatives. **YAMAM** was specifically created to engage in counterterrorist and hostage rescue operations.

Spain. In 1979, the Spanish National Police organized a counterterrorist and hostage rescue force called **GEO (Grupo Especial de Operaciones)**. Its training has allowed it to be used in both law enforcement and counterterrorist operations. Most of the latter—and

Table 13.2   Counterterrorist Options: The Use of Force

The purpose of repressive responses is to attack and degrade the operational capabilities of terrorists. This can be done by directly confronting terrorists or destabilizing their organizations.

The following table summarizes basic elements of the use of force.

Counterterrorist Option	*Rationale*	*Activity Profile*	
		Practical Objectives	*Typical Resources Used*
Punitive covert operations	Symbolic strength	Disruption of the terrorists	Military assets
	Destabilization	Deterrent effect on potential terrorists	Paramilitary assets
Suppression campaigns	Symbolic strength	Destruction of the terrorists	Military assets
	Destabilization	Disruption of the terrorists	Military assets
Punitive and preemptive strikes	Symbolic strength	Disruption of the terrorists	Military assets
	Destabilization	Deterrent effect on potential terrorists	Paramilitary assets
	Prevention		

a significant proportion of its operations—have been directed against the Basque ETA terrorist movement.

United States. At the national level, the United States has organized several units that have counterterrorist capabilities. These are paramilitary groups that operate under the administrative supervision of federal agencies and perform traditional law enforcement work. Perhaps the best known federal unit is the FBI's **Hostage Rescue Team**. Not as well known, but very important, is the Department of Energy's **Emergency Search Team**. Paramilitary capabilities have also been incorporated into the Treasury Department's Bureau of Alcohol, Tobacco and Firearms and Secret Service. At the local level, American police forces also deploy units that have counterterrorist capabilities. These units are known by many names, but the most commonly known designation is Special Weapons and Tactics (SWAT).

Table 13.2 summarizes the activity profile of counterterrorist options that sanction the use of force.

OPERATIONS OTHER THAN WAR: REPRESSIVE OPTIONS

Nonmilitary and nonparamilitary **repressive responses** can be effective in the suppression of terrorist crises and terrorist environments. The purpose of these responses is to disrupt and deter terrorist behavior. They are unlikely to bring a long-term end to terrorism, but they can reduce the scale of violence by destabilizing terrorist groups and forcing them to be "on the run."

Covert Operations

Covert operations encompass a number of options, and they are often quite creative. They are inherently secretive, and their value lies in manipulating terrorist behavior and surreptitiously taking terrorist groups by surprise. For example, covert manipulation can create internal distrust, fear, infighting, and other types of discord. The outcome might also be a reduction in operational focus, momentum, and effectiveness. Typical covert operations include the following options.

Infiltration

The successful infiltration of operatives into extremist groups can result in the disruption of terrorist operations. Ideally, infiltration will increase the quality of intelligence prediction, as well as the possible betrayal of cadres to counterterrorist forces. However, in the era of the New Terrorism, infiltration of terrorist organizations is more difficult because of their cell-based organizational profiles. There is no hierarchy to penetrate, cells are usually autonomous, and they have few links beyond their immediate operational group.

Disinformation

The manipulation of information can be a powerful counterterrorist tool. Disinformation uses information to disrupt terrorist organizations. It is used to selectively create and deliver data that are calculated to create disorder within the terrorist group or its support apparatus. For example, disinformation could be developed to create dissension and distrust, or to otherwise manipulate the group's behavior. It can also be used to spread damaging propaganda about terrorist organizations and cadres.

Cyberwar

In the digital age, information is recorded and transferred in forms that can be intercepted, altered, and destroyed. Bank accounts, personal records, and other data are no longer stored on paper, but instead in digital databases. Terrorist movements that maintain or send electronic financial and personal information run the risk of having that information intercepted and compromised. Thus, new technologies have become imaginative counterterrorist weapons.

Intelligence

Intelligence agencies involve themselves with the collection and analysis of information. The underlying purpose of intelligence is to construct an accurate activity profile of terrorists. Data are collected from overt and covert sources and evaluated by expert intelligence analysts. This process—intelligence collection and analysis—is at the heart of counterterrorist intelligence. The outcome of high-quality intelligence collection and analysis can range from the construction of profiles of terrorist organizations to tracking the movements of terrorists. An optimal outcome of counterterrorist intelligence is the ability to *anticipate* the behavior of terrorists and to thereby predict terrorist incidents. However, exact prediction is relatively rare, and most intelligence on terrorist threats is generalized rather than specific. For example, intelligence agencies have had success in uncovering threats in specific cities by specific groups, but less success in predicting the exact time and place of possible attacks.

Signal Intelligence

Intelligence collection and analysis in the modern era requires the use of sophisticated technological resources. These technological resources are used primarily for the interception of electronic signals—known as SIGINT. **Signal intelligence** is used for a variety of purposes, such as interceptions of financial data, monitoring communications such as cell phone conversations, and reading e-mail messages. The use of satellite imagery is also commonly used by intelligence agencies, and sophisticated computers specialize in code breaking. However, the practicality of these technologies as counterterrorist options is limited in the era of the New Terrorism. Because of the cellular organizational structure of terrorist groups and their insular interactions (based on personal relationships), technology cannot be an exclusive counterterrorist resource. Human intelligence is also a critical component.

Human Intelligence

The collection of **human intelligence,** also referred to as HUMINT, is often a cooperative venture with friendly intelligence agencies and law enforcement officials. This sharing of information is a critical component of counterterrorist intelligence gathering. Circumstances may also require the covert manipulation of individuals affiliated with terrorist organizations or their support groups, with the objective of convincing them to become intelligence agents. The manipulation process can include making appeals to the potential spy's sense of justice or patriotism, paying them with money and other valuables, or offering them something that they would otherwise be unable to obtain (such as asylum for their family in a Western country). One significant problem with finding resources for human intelligence is that most terrorist cells are made up of individuals who know each other very well. Newcomers are not openly welcomed, and those who may be potential members are usually expected to commit an act of terrorism or other crime to prove their commitment to the cause. In other words, intelligence agencies must be willing to use terrorists to catch terrorists.

Intelligence Agencies

In many democracies, intelligence collection is traditionally divided between agencies that are separately responsible for domestic and international intelligence collection. This separation is often mandated by law. For example, the following agencies roughly parallel each others' missions:

- In Great Britain, **MI-5** is responsible for domestic intelligence, and **MI-6** is responsible for international collection.
- In the United States, the **Federal Bureau of Investigation (FBI)** performs domestic intelligence collection, and the **Central Intelligence Agency (CIA)** operates internationally.
- In Germany, the **Bureau for the Protection of the Constitution** shares a mission similar to MI-5 and the FBI, and the **Military Intelligence Service** roughly parallels MI-6 and the CIA.

The United States has attempted to coordinate intelligence collection and analysis by creating a theoretically cooperative **intelligence community**. This philosophy of cooperation is the primary conceptual goal of the American counterterrorist intelligence effort.

In practice, of course, there have been very serious bureaucratic rivalries. Members of the American intelligence community include the following agencies:

Central Intelligence Agency. The CIA is an independent federal agency. It is the theoretical coordinator of the intelligence community. The agency is charged to collect intelligence outside of the borders of the United States, which is done covertly using human and technological assets. The CIA is legally prohibited from collecting intelligence inside the United States.

Defense Intelligence Agency. The **Defense Intelligence Agency (DIA)** is a bureau within the Department of Defense. It is the central intelligence bureau for the U.S. military. Each branch of the military coordinates its intelligence collection and analysis with the other branches through the DIA.

Federal Bureau of Investigation. The FBI is a bureau within the Department of Justice. It is a law enforcement agency that is charged in part with conducting domestic surveillance of suspected spies and terrorists. The agency also engages in domestic intelligence collection and has been deployed to American embassies around the world. Foreign counterintelligence investigations have included an FBI presence at the sites of the 1998 bombings of the U.S. embassies in Kenya and Tanzania.

National Security Agency. The **National Security Agency (NSA)** is the technological arm of the U.S. intelligence community. Using state-of-the-art computer and satellite technologies, the NSA's primary mission is to collect communications and other signal intelligence. It also devotes a significant portion of its technological expertise to code-making and code-breaking activities. Much of this work is done covertly from secret surveillance facilities positioned around the globe.

Problems of Intelligence Coordination

The collection and analysis of intelligence is a covert process that does not lend itself easily to absolute cooperation and coordination between countries, or between members of domestic intelligence communities. National intelligence agencies do not readily share intelligence with allied countries; they usually do so only after careful deliberation. The same is true of intelligence communities within countries. For example, prior to the September 11, 2001, homeland attacks, dozens of federal agencies were involved in the collection of intelligence about terrorism. This led to overlapping and competing interests. A case in point is the apparent failure by the FBI and CIA to collaboratively process, share, and evaluate important intelligence between their agencies. In the case of the FBI, there was also an apparent failure of coordination between the agency's field and national offices. These problems precipitated a proposal in June 2002 by President George W. Bush to completely reorganize the American homeland security community. This concept of centralized homeland security in the United States is explored further in Chapter 14.

An example of successful intelligence cooperation occurred in May 2002 between American and Moroccan intelligence agencies. In February 2002, Moroccan intelligence officers interrogated Moroccan Al Qaeda prisoners held by the Americans at its naval base in Guantanamo Bay, Cuba. They received information from one of the prisoners about a Qaeda operative in Morocco and also received information about the operative's relatives. Moroccan officials obtained a sketched description of the man from the relatives and showed the sketch to the Guantanamo prisoner, who confirmed his likeness. The Moroccans located the suspect (a Saudi), followed him for a month, and eventually arrested him and two Saudi accomplices. The suspects eventually told the Moroccans that they were Al Qaeda operatives trained in Afghanistan and that they had had escaped during the anti-Taliban campaign after receiving orders to engage in suicide attacks against maritime targets in Gibraltar. They had begun the process of inquiring about speed boats, and their ultimate targets were to be U.S. Navy ships passing through Gibraltar.[9]

An Intelligence Postscript

It is important to remember that intelligence collection and analysis is not always an exact or low-risk science. It can reflect only the quality and amount of data that are available. Because of the nature of counterterrorist intelligence collection and analysis, some experts in the United States have concluded that

the inherent difficulties in both collection and analysis of intelligence on terrorism mean that there will never be tactical warning of most attempted terrorist attacks, or even most major attempted attacks against U.S. targets.[10]

Enhanced Security

Target "hardening" makes potential targets more difficult to attack. This is a key component of antiterrorism, which attempts to deter or prevent terrorist attacks. Enhanced security is also intended to deter would-be terrorists from selecting hardened facilities as targets. These measures are not long-term solutions for ending terrorist environments, but they serve to provide short-term protection for specific sites. Target hardening includes increased airport security, the visible deployment of security personnel, and the erection of crash barriers at entrances to parking garages beneath important buildings. Typical examples of target hardening include the following:

- Vehicular traffic was permanently blocked on Pennsylvania Avenue in front of the White House because of the threat from high-yield vehicular bombs in the aftermath of the 1993 World Trade Center and 1995 Oklahoma City bombings. The area became a pedestrian mall.
- During the 1990s, Great Britain began to make widespread use of closed-circuit surveillance cameras in its urban areas. The police maintain these cameras on city streets, at intersections, and on highways. The purpose of this controversial policy is to monitor suspicious activities, such as abandoned packages or vehicles.

Two examples of target hardening on a grand scale involved the building of extensive security walls around entire regions:

Morocco's Desert Wall. The region now known as Western Sahara in Northwest Africa was called Spanish Sahara until 1975, when Spain agreed to withdraw from this last imperial outpost in Africa. After Spain's withdrawal in 1976, the territory was divided between Mauritania and Morocco. Saharan nationalists, called **Polisario**, fought a guerrilla war against the division, eventually forcing Mauritania to withdraw its claim. Morocco then occupied the entire Western Sahara, and Polisario began a protracted guerrilla war against the Moroccans' claim. In order to defend its occupied territory, Morocco began building a long fortified sand and earthen wall in 1981. The wall stretched for more than 1,200 miles, encircled most of the Western Sahara, and included strong points and electronic sensors. Polisario was unable to effectively breach the wall. The parties began a long period of negotiations after a 1991 cease-fire agreement.

Israel's Wall on the Border. During the initial stages of its conflict with the PLO, Israel built a network of fences and posts along its border with Jordan to prevent Palestinian fighters from infiltrating into Israel. Later, during the *intifadeh*, Israel adapted this concept to its border with the West Bank after scores of bombings and other attacks killed hundreds of Israelis. A long fence was constructed to seal off the West Bank, which had become the main infiltration route for suicide bombers. The Police Border Guards (discussed earlier in the chapter) had primary operational jurisdiction. Both the Jordanian and West Bank fences used mounds of razor wire, electronic sensors, patrol roads, and high electronic fences. There were also strips of soft sand to aid in the detection of footprints.

Economic Sanctions

Although counterterrorist policy is largely aimed at terrorist organizations, the problem of terrorist states must also be addressed. It is agreed that counterterrorism policy must take into account states that "support, facilitate, or practice terrorism, or whose help is needed in combating it."[11] Economic sanctions are a common counterterrorist method directed against governments. *Economic sanctions* are defined as trade restrictions and controls that are imposed to pressure sanctioned governments to moderate their behavior. Used as a counterterrorist option, sanctions serve several purposes:

- Sanctions symbolically demonstrate strong condemnation of the behavior of the sanctioned regime.
- Sanctions are an exercise of the power of the sanctioning body.
- Sanctions potentially bring to bear considerable pressure on the sanctioned regime.

Unlike many other counterterrorist options, sanctions inherently require sanctioning nations to commit to a long timeline to ensure success. The reason for this commitment is easily understood: Economic pressure is never felt immediately by nations, unless they are already in dire economic condition. Trade restrictions require time to be felt in a domestic market, particularly if the nation produces a commodity that is desired on the international market. For example, economic sanctions were imposed against Iraq during the 1990s, but Iraq is a major producer of oil. This caused trade "leaks" to occur.

Conditions for Success of Economic Sanctions

In order for economic sanctions to be effective, they must be imposed in an environment of long-term cooperation. Examples of these conditions for success include the following requirements:

- International cooperation must remain firm.
- Trade leaks in the economic sanctions must be controlled.
- The sanctioned *regime* must be made to suffer.

When evaluating these conditions, one can readily ascertain several fundamental problems inherent in using economic sanctions as a counterterrorist option. These problems include the following:

Sanctioned regimes rarely suffer—it is their people who suffer. Because these regimes are often violently authoritarian, there is no mechanism for the people to petition for changes in policy. Sanctions against Iraq did not appreciably diminish the government's authority or its ability to suppress dissension.

The remains of Pan Am Flight 103 after being bombed in the skies over Lockerbie, Scotland. The attack led to economic sanctions against Libya and the trial of two members of the Libyan security service.

Source: Hulton Archive/Getty Images; used by permission.

Sanctions coalitions do not always remain firm. In fact, economic sanctions sometimes become nothing more than symbolic condemnation, because the sanctioning nation or nations are alone in their demonstrations of disapproval. U.S. sanctions against Cuba were not strongly coalitional, so trade and tourism kept the Cuban economy from completely destabilizing.

Leaks in trade embargoes are difficult to control, and sanctioning policies sometimes become quite porous. The attempted cultural and trade embargoes against South Africa during the apartheid (racial separation) era failed because there was never broad support from the world community or private industry.

An example of an apparently successful policy of economic sanctions is found in the case of Libya. Economic sanctions imposed against Libya were led by Great Britain and the United States in the aftermath of Libyan sponsorship of international terrorism during the 1980s, including the 1988 bombing of Pan Am Flight 103 over Lockerbie, Scotland. When Libya refused to extradite two men suspected of having planned the Lockerbie bombing, the United Nations Security Council imposed economic sanctions. In May 2002, Muammar el-Qaddafi offered to pay $10 million in compensation for each victim of the bombing, provided that all economic sanctions were lifted.

Table 13.3 summarizes the conditions for success, and problems that commonly arise, when attempting to impose economic sanctions.

Table 13.4 summarizes the activity profile of repressive counterterrorist options other than war.

Table 13.3   Economic Sanctions: Conditions for Success and Problems

Economic sanctions can theoretically pressure state sponsors of terrorism to moderate their behavior. However, successful sanctions require certain conditions to be in place and to remain firm during the sanctioning process.

The following table summarizes several representative conditions, problems, and case studies.

Conditions for Success	*Common Problems*	*Cases*
Bring pressure to bear on sanctioned regime	Economic pressure is passed on to a politically powerless population.	Sanctions against Iraq beginning in the early 1990s; regime remained strong
Maintain strong international cooperation	International cooperation can weaken or dissolve.	U.S. sanctions against Cuba; perceived by world community to be a relic of the Cold War
Control leaks in the sanctioning policy	When leaks occur, they cannot be controlled.	Uncoordinated sanctions movement against South Africa during apartheid era; failed to affect South African policy

Table 13.4   Counterterrorist Options: Operations Other Than War: Repressive Options

The purpose of repressive responses other than war is to attack and degrade the operational capabilities of terrorists. The following table summarizes basic elements of repressive options.

Counterterrorist Option	*Rationale*	*Activity Profile*	
		Practical Objectives	*Typical Resources Used*
Covert operations	Deterrence	Deterrent effect on potential terrorists	Paramilitary and covert operatives
	Destabilization	Disruption of the terrorists	Technology
	Prediction		
Intelligence	Prediction	Calculating the activity profiles of terrorists	Technology Covert operatives
Enhanced security	Deterrence	Hardening of targets	Security personnel Security barriers Security technology
Economic sanctions	Deterrence	Long-term destabilization and deterrence of sanctioned states	National economic resources
	Destabilization		Coalitional diplomacy

OPERATIONS OTHER THAN WAR: CONCILIATORY OPTIONS

Conciliatory responses are soft-line approaches for ending terrorist environments. They apply policies designed to resolve underlying problems that cause people to resort to political violence. Diplomatic options such as negotiations and social reform are typical policy options and can sometimes be very effective. There are also concessionary options, but these are more problematic.

Diplomatic Options

Diplomatic options refer to the use of "channels of communication" to secure a counterterrorist objective. These channels range in degree from direct talks with dissidents to formal diplomatic overtures with nations that can influence the behavior of terrorist groups. The characteristics of these overtures are case specific, so the style of interaction and communication between the parties is unique to each example. Peace processes and negotiations are typical diplomatic options used to establish channels of communication.

Peace Processes

In regions with ongoing communal violence, long-term diplomatic intervention has sought to construct mutually acceptable terms for a cease-fire. **Peace processes** often involve long, arduous, and frustrating proceedings. Contending parties are always suspicious of each other, and they do not always represent all of the factions within their camps. For example, the peace process between Israel and the Palestinian Authority (governing body) during the 1990s was condemned by hard-liners on both sides. Hamas tried repeatedly to violently derail the process. The same was true of the Northern Ireland peace process of the late 1990s and early 2000s, when the Real Irish Republican Army and Continuity Irish Republican Army factions rejected the peace process.

A comparison of the cases of the Israeli-Palestinian and Northern Ireland peace processes is instructive.

Israeli-Palestinian Peace Process. It should now be evident from the discussions of previous chapters that the Israeli-Palestinian peace process began to fall apart in 2000, and it completely collapsed during the escalating violence of 2001 and 2002. The cycle of suicide bombings and Israeli reprisals led to hundreds of deaths and made the peace process an irrelevant consideration for most people on both sides. As civilians on both sides bear the brunt of the violence, distrust and hatred are becoming generalized in both communities. Hard-line factions have been quite successful in exploiting and exacerbating tensions between the two communities.

Northern Ireland Peace Process. In contrast to the Middle East, the peace process in Northern Ireland enjoyed a significant turning point in May 1998 when the so-called **Good Friday Agreement** of April 10, 1998, was overwhelmingly approved by voters in the Irish Republic and Northern Ireland. It signaled the mutual acceptance of a Northern Ireland assembly, and the disarmament, or "**decommissioning**," of all paramilitaries. Although groups emerged that tried to derail the peace process—the Real Irish Republican Army killed 28 and injured scores in the August 1998 Omagh bombing—the Good Friday Agreement began a long-term process of building a nonviolent political framework in the troubled North. In July 2002, the Irish Republican Army surprised all parties in the peace process by issuing a formal apology for all of the people it killed during The Troubles.[12]

A lost chance for peace? U.S. president Bill Clinton with Israeli Prime Minister Benjamin Netanyahu and PLO chairman Yasir Arafat. Clinton had hoped to establish a framework for an ongoing peace process, but the process collapsed amid the fighting of the Palestinian *intifadeh*.

Source: Hulton Archive/Getty Images; used by permission.

Negotiations

Conventional wisdom in the United States and Israel holds that one should never negotiate with terrorists, never consider their grievances as long as they engage in violence, and never concede to any demand. The rationale for this hard-line approach is that perceived concessionary behavior on the part of a targeted interest will simply encourage terrorists to commit further acts of violence. Nevertheless, history has shown that case-specific negotiations can resolve immediate crises. Not all negotiations end in complete success for either side, but they sometimes do provide a measure of closure to terrorist crises. These crises include hostage situations and manhunts for fugitive terrorists.

The following cases are examples of negotiations between states, terrorists, and third parties that successfully secured the release of hostages:

The OPEC hostage crisis of December 1975 in Vienna, Austria, was resolved when the terrorists were permitted to fly to Algiers, Algeria, with a few hostages in tow. The hostages were released when a $5 million ransom was paid for Palestinian causes, and the terrorists were permitted to escape. This case was explored in Chapter 6.

The odyssey of TWA Flight 847 in June 1985 ended with the release of the remaining hostages after negotiations were conducted through a series of intermediaries. The Lebanese Shi'ite hijackers used the media and the Lebanese Sunni Amal militia as intermediaries to broadcast their demands. The hostages were freed after the United States negotiated with Israel the release of more than 700 Shi'ite prisoners. This case was explored further in Chapter 11.

The following cases are examples of negotiations (and bribery) between states that successfully secured the capture of terrorist suspects:

Ilich Ramirez Sanchez, better known as Carlos the Jackal, was "purchased" by the French government from the government of Sudan in August 1994. When the French learned that the Sudanese had given Carlos refuge, they secretly negotiated a bounty for permission to capture him, which they did from a Khartoum hospital room. Sanchez was eventually sentenced to life imprisonment for murdering two French *gendarmes*. The career of Carlos was explored further in Chapter 3.

Johannes Weinrich, a former West German terrorist, was also purchased—this time by the German government from the government of Yemen. Weinrich was sent to Germany in June 1995 to stand trial for the 1983 bombing of a French cultural center in Berlin, in which one person was killed and 23 others were wounded. Weinrich, who had been a very close associate of Carlos, was convicted in January 2000 and sentenced to life imprisonment. The bounty paid for his capture was presumed to be $1 million.

Abdel Basset al-Megrahi and Lamen Khalifa Fhima, alleged members of Libya's state security agency, were suspected by Great Britain and the United States of being responsible for the bombing of Pan Am Flight 103. After years of negotiations and United Nations sanctions, an agreement was signed in 1998 between Libya, the United States, and Great Britain to try al-Megrahi and Fhima. The two men were tried under Scottish law before a three-judge Scottish court at Camp Zeist near the Hague, Netherlands. In January 2001, al-Megrahi was sentenced to life imprisonment, and Fhima was acquitted. The Lockerbie incident was explored further in Chapter 4.

Social Reform

Under the assumption that the causes of terrorism lie in political conflict between contending ideologies, ethno-national groups, and religions, it is logical to conclude that solutions to terrorism lie in resolving these political conflicts. A reduction in sources of tensions that lead to intergroup violence would seem to be a long-term solution to political violence. Thus, social reforms attempt to undercut the precipitating causes of national and regional conflicts. Reforms can include the improvement of economic conditions, increased political rights, government recognition of ethno-nationalist sentiment, and public recognition of the validity of grievances.

It should be noted that social reforms are rarely the only stratagem used by states to end terrorist campaigns. They are usually used in conjunction with other counterterrorist responses, including violent options. The following cases are examples of social reforms that successfully reduced the severity of terrorist environments.

Peru

Social reform was one element in the government's response to Shining Path's terrorist campaign. As discussed in Chapter 6, when Shining Path's leader, Abimail Guzmán, was captured in 1992, he subsequently renounced violence, and thousands of his followers accepted the terms of a government amnesty. The Peruvian government also began a social reform campaign in the countryside. Programs included land reforms, political rights, and rural improvements. These new programs successfully undercut peasant support for Shining Path.

Spain

Ethno-national sentiment in the Basque region had been repressed during the regime of Francisco Franco.[13] After his death in 1975, Spanish democracy was restored, and Basque semi-autonomy was granted. Nationalism was permitted to be openly discussed, political groups were recognized, labor organizations became independent, and civil liberties were protected. ETA's political party was legalized. Nevertheless, ETA's most violent period occurred immediately following the restoration of democracy. ETA has since continued to strike from time to time, but Basque sentiment turned against the group during the 1980s. In addition, many ETA members returned to civilian life after accepting the terms of a reintegration program during the mid-1980s. Over time, Spanish commitment to social reforms undercut Basque support for ETA.

Concessionary Options

Granting concessions to terrorists is widely viewed as a marginally optimal counterterrorist response. The reason for this is obvious: Giving terrorists what they want is likely to encourage them to replicate their successful operation or perhaps to increase the stakes in future incidents. In other words, many extremists and those in the general population should be expected to conclude that concessions simply *reward* extremist behavior. Concessions include the following policy decisions:

- Payment of ransoms
- Releases of imprisoned comrades
- Broadcasts or other publications of extremist propaganda
- Political amnesty for dissidents

An interesting example of concessionary behavior is the Iran-Contra Scandal, which was first introduced in Chapter 4. It is a study in how a nation with a publicly strong counterterrorist position (the United States) secretly tried to appease a country that it had defined as a state sponsor of terrorism (Iran).[14]

Case: The Iran-Contra Scandal Revisited

The United States was embarrassed in November 1986 when a Lebanese magazine revealed that high-ranking officials in the Reagan administration had secretly agreed to sell arms to Iran. The operation, which was under way in August 1985, involved the sale of arms to Iran in exchange for help from the Iranian government to secure the release of American hostages held by Shi'ite terrorists in Lebanon. Profits from the sales (reportedly $30 million) were used to support Nicaraguan contras in their war against the Sandinista government. This support was managed by National Security Adviser John Poindexter and Lt. Colonel Oliver North. The administration's embarrassment was aggravated by the fact that the United States had previously adopted a get-tough policy against what it deemed to be terrorist states, and Iran had been included in that category. Soon after American captives were released (apparently as a result of the weapons deal), Lebanese terrorists seized more hostages.

Table 13.5 summarizes the activity profile of the conciliatory counterterrorist options just discussed.

LEGALISTIC RESPONSES

Legalistic responses are law enforcement and law-related approaches for ending terrorist environments. These apply policies designed to use norms of criminal justice and legal

Table 13.5 Counterterrorist Options: Operations Other Than War: Conciliatory Options

The purpose of conciliatory options is to resolve the underlying grievances of the terrorists. This can be done by addressing immediate or long-term threats.

The following table summarizes basic elements of conciliatory options.

Counterterrorist Option	*Rationale*	*Activity Profile*	
		Practical Objectives	*Typical Resources Used*
Diplomatic options	Resolve terrorist crises	Negotiate case-specific agreements	Direct contacts
		Negotiate long-term agreements	Intermediary contacts
Social reform	Degrade terrorist environments	Win support from potential terrorist supporters	Targeted economic programs
		Decrease effectiveness of terrorist propaganda	Intensive political involvement
Concessionary options	Resolve terrorist crises	Satisfy the demands that motivate the terrorists	Negotiators
	Degrade terrorist environments		Economic concessions
			Political concessions

procedures to investigate and punish those who commit acts of political violence. Legislation, criminal prosecutions, and incarceration are typical policy measures.

The "law enforcement" approach to combating terrorism has had some success in disrupting conspiratorial networks, and it has brought closure to criminal cases arising out of terrorist attacks. For example, law enforcement investigations in the United States quickly and effectively brought to justice the key perpetrators of the 1993 World Trade Center bombing, the 1995 Oklahoma City attack, and the 1998 bombings of the American embassies in Tanzania and Kenya. In another investigation, the FBI used an informant to break up a *jihadi* conspiracy to bomb landmarks in New York City in 1993. International cooperation between law enforcement officials has also proven to be effective. For example, in the aftermath of the September 11, 2001, attacks, European and Southeast Asian police uncovered a number of Al Qaeda and other *jihadi* cells in Spain, Germany, Singapore, and elsewhere.

Law Enforcement and Counterterrorism

Because acts of terrorism are considered inherently criminal behaviors under the laws of most nations, law enforcement agencies often play a major role in counterterrorist

Chapter Perspective 13.2   The Capture of Mir Aimal Kansi

On the morning of January 25, 1993, a man armed with an AK-47 assault rifle began firing on employees of the Central Intelligence Agency who were waiting in their cars to enter the CIA's headquarters in Langley, Virginia. Two people were killed, and three were wounded.

The person responsible for the attack was **Mir Aimal Kansi**, a Pakistani who had been a resident of the United States since 1991. After the shootings, he immediately fled the United States for sanctuary in Pakistan and Afghanistan. He apparently traveled between the two countries, although he found refuge among relatives and local Pakistanis in Quetta.

The United States posted a $2 million reward for Kansi's capture and distributed wanted posters throughout the region. His photograph was distributed on thousands of matchbooks, printed in newspapers, and placed on posters. The hunt was successful, because still-unidentified individuals contacted U.S. authorities in Pakistan and arranged Kansi's capture. In June 1997, Kansi was arrested by a paramilitary FBI team and, with the permission of the Pakistani government, flown to the United States to stand trial in a Virginia state court.

At his trial, prosecutors argued that Kansi had committed the attack in retaliation for U.S. bombings of Iraq. He was convicted of murder on November 10, 1997, and was executed by lethal injection at the Greensville Correctional Center in Virginia on November 14, 2002.

operations. The organizational profiles of these agencies vary from country to country, with some countries having large national police establishments and others relying more on local police. Internationally, there is no enforcement mechanism for violations of international criminal law, other than treaties and other voluntary agreements between nations. Nevertheless, many nations have become members of the **International Criminal Police Organization**, more commonly known as **INTERPOL.** INTERPOL is an international association of more than 140 nations that agree to share intelligence and provide assistance in the effort to suppress international crime. The association is based in Ste. Cloud, France, and each member nation has a bureau that serves as a liaison with INTERPOL. INTERPOL is more of an investigative consortium than a law enforcement agency. Its value lies in the cooperative sharing of information between members, as well as the coordination of counterterrorist and criminal investigations.

Law enforcement agencies often take the lead in investigating incidents of domestic terrorism, with other agencies performing a support role to assist in resolving cases. For example, in the United States, the FBI has primary jurisdiction over domestic counterintelligence and counterterrorist surveillance and investigations. The CIA is not a law enforcement agency and therefore officially performs a supportive role in domestic counterterrorist investigations. Other federal agencies, such as the U.S. **Diplomatic Security Service,** also assist in tracking suspects wanted for acts of terrorism. The Diplomatic Security Service is a security bureau within the U.S. Department of State that manages an international bounty program called the **Rewards for Justice Program**. The program offers cash rewards for information leading to the arrest of wanted terrorists. These bounty programs are sometimes successful. As discussed in Chapter Perspective 13.2, a cash bounty led to the capture and arrest of Mir Aimal Kansi, a Pakistani terrorist who attacked CIA employees in 1993 outside the CIA's headquarters in Northern Virginia.

The Police and Terrorist Environments

Prior to the formation of terrorist environments, the primary mission of police agencies is to serve in a *law enforcement* capacity. After terrorist environments become established, the law enforcement mission of the police is transformed into an *internal security* mission. In these cases, the police become responsible for day-to-day civil protection operations. Internal security missions require law enforcement units to be stationed at strategic locations and to perform security-focused (rather than crime-focused) patrols. These responsibilities are sometimes threat specific and mirror the terrorist environment of the times. For example, because of the threat of airline hijackings, many nations commonly place law enforcement officers aboard aircraft to act as **sky marshals**. Other security duties include promoting airport security, securing borders, tracking illegal immigrants, looking out for fugitives and other suspects, and conducting surveillance of groups and people who fit terrorist profiles.

In many environments, police officers are the front line in the war on terrorism because they are the first officials to respond to terrorist incidents. This role became quite common in the terrorist environments that existed in Italy, Germany, the United Kingdom, Israel, and many other countries. In the United States, 60 New York City police officers died during the September 11, 2001, homeland attacks when they were deployed to the World Trade Center site.[15] The police are also the first to stabilize the immediate vicinity around attack sites and are responsible for maintaining long-term order in cities suffering under terrorist campaigns. Thus, the role of law enforcement agencies varies in scale and mission depending on the characteristics of their environment, and can include

traditional police work, in which criminal investigations are carried out by detective bureaus;

specialized services, in which duties require special training (e.g., defusing and removing explosive ordinance by bomb disposal units);

order maintenance (e.g., securing attack sites and stabilizing terrorist environments with large and visible deployments of police personnel); and

paramilitary deployment using highly trained units that include hostage rescue units and SWAT teams.

Police Repression

Ideally, the security role of the police will be carried out professionally, within the context of constitutional constraints, and with respect for human rights. However, the reality is that many police agencies around the world are highly aggressive and sometimes abusive—particularly those in authoritarian and weakly democratic countries. They are less concerned about *human rights* than about *order maintenance*. This is a key distinction, because policies protecting human rights also constrain the behavior of the police, whereas policies of order maintenance are more concerned with protecting the integrity of the state.

The consequences of ideologies of order maintenance are that police agencies operating in authoritarian environments perform a very different mission compared with the professionalized police forces found in most stable democracies. For example, police in Brazil and Colombia have been implicated in practicing "social cleansing" against undesirables. Social cleansing involves the intimidation of a range of defined social undesirables, including political dissidents, supporters of political dissidents, morals criminals (such as prostitutes and drug users), and marginal demographic groups (such as homeless children). Deaths and physical abuse have been documented during social cleansing campaigns.

Case: The United Kingdom

In the United Kingdom, where factions of the Irish Republican Army were highly active in London and other cities, the British police were considered to be the front line against IRA terrorism. They usually displayed a high degree of professionalism without resorting to repressive tactics and consequently enjoyed widespread popular support. For example, London's Metropolitan Police (also known as "The Met") became experts in counterterrorist operations when the Irish Republican Army waged a terrorist campaign during the 1970s. The Met's criminal investigations bureau generally used high-quality detective work rather than authoritarian techniques to investigate terrorist incidents. The British criminal justice system also generally protected the rights of the accused during trials of IRA suspects. However, in the rush to stop the IRA's terrorist campaign (especially during the 1970s), miscarriages of criminal justice did occur. Examples of these miscarriages include the following examples:

Guildford Four. Four people were wrongfully convicted of an October 1974 bombing in Guildford, England. Two of them were also wrongfully sentenced for a bombing attack in Woolwich. The **Guildford Four** served 15 years in prison before being released in 1989 when their convictions were overturned on appeal. The group received a formal apology from Prime Minister Tony Blair in June 2000 and received monetary awards as compensation. The case was made famous by the American film *In the Name of the Father.*

Birmingham Six. Six men were convicted for the November 1974 bombings of two pubs in Birmingham, England, that killed 21 people and injured 168. On appeal, the court ordered the release of the **Birmingham Six** after it ruled that the police had used fabricated evidence. The men were released in 1991 after serving 16 years in prison.

Case: Terrorist Profiling in the United States

Prior to September 11, 2001, the American approach to domestic counterterrorism was a law enforcement approach; after the attacks, the new terrorist environment called for a more security-focused approach. The FBI and other agencies created a **"terrorist profile"** that was similar to standard **criminal profiles** used in law enforcement investigations. Criminal profiles are descriptive composites that include the personal characteristics of suspects, such as their height, weight, race, gender, hair color, eye color, and clothing. Suspects who match these criminal profiles can be detained for questioning. The composite of the new terrorist profile included the following characteristics: Middle Eastern heritage, temporary visa status, Muslim faith, male gender, and young adult age. Based on these criteria—and during a serious security crisis—the FBI and Immigration and Naturalization Service administratively detained hundreds of men fitting this description. Material witness warrants were used from the outset to detain many of these men for questioning.

As the investigations continued, and in the wake of several warnings about possible terrorist threats, the U.S. Department of Justice expanded the FBI's surveillance authority. New guidelines were promulgated in May 2002 that permitted field offices to conduct surveillance of religious institutions, Web sites, libraries, and organizations without an a priori (before the fact) finding of criminal suspicion.

These detentions and guidelines were criticized. Critics argued that the detentions were improper, because the vast majority of the detainees had not been charged with violating the law. Critics of the surveillance guidelines contended that it gave too much power to the state to investigate innocent civilians. Many also maintained that there was a danger that these investigations could become discriminatory **racial profiling**, involving the detention of people because of their ethno-national or racial heritage. Nevertheless, the new security policies continued to use administrative detentions and enhanced surveillance as counterterrorist methods.

Domestic Laws and Counterterrorism

An important challenge for lawmakers in democracies is balancing the need for counterterrorist legislation against the protection of constitutional rights. In severely strained terrorist environments, it is not uncommon for nations—including democracies—to pass authoritarian laws that promote social order at the expense of human rights. Policymakers usually justify these measures by using a "balancing" argument, in which the greater good is held to outweigh the suspension of civil liberties. As illustrated in the following examples, severe threats to the state are sometimes counteracted by severe laws.

Suspending Civil Liberties in Northern Ireland

After the British army was deployed to Northern Ireland, they became severely pressed by an IRA terrorist campaign. The **Northern Ireland Act**, passed in 1993, created conditions of quasi-martial law. The Act suspended several civil liberties. It empowered the British military to engage in warrantless searches of civilian homes, temporarily detain people without charge, and question suspects. The military could also intern (remove from society) suspected terrorists and turn over for prosecution those for whom enough evidence had been seized. Nearly a quarter of a million warrantless searches were conducted by the army, which resulted in the seizure of thousands of arms and the internment or imprisonment of hundreds of suspects.

Another program aimed at prosecuting and imprisoning Irish terrorists was implemented during the 1980s. This was the "**supergrass**" program, which was a policy of convincing Provos and members of the Irish National Liberation Army (INLA) to defect from their movements and inform on their former comrades. Many decided to participate in supergrass. Based on these informants, British-led authorities were able to successfully prosecute and imprison a number of Provos and INLA members. However, many of these dissidents were released in the late 1980s when cases taken up on appeal successfully challenged the admissibility of supergrass testimony. In the end, supergrass disrupted Irish militant groups during the 1980s (particularly the INLA) but did not have a long-term impact on Northern Ireland's terrorist environment.

Counterterrorist Courts in Algeria

Students may recall from Chapter 8 that during the 1990s several Islamic terrorist movements waged a campaign of terror against the Algerian government. By the time the most severe fighting ended in 1999 (when an amnesty was offered), more than 120,000 Algerians had died. During the emergency, special courts were established by the government to prosecute suspected Islamic terrorists and their supporters. The purpose of these courts was to establish a nonmilitary option in their war against terrorism. During a two-year period from October 1992 to October 1994,

13,770 persons had been judged by the special courts and 3,661 of them, or 25 per cent of those appearing, had been acquitted. There had been 1,551 sentences of death, 1,463 of which had been passed *in absentia*, and 8,448 sentences of imprisonment.[16]

The special courts and special prosecutions were used in conjunction with a brutal suppression campaign. It can be argued that the Islamic rebels had been forced into an untenable no-win situation by the time the 1999 amnesty was offered.

Qualified Amnesty in Italy

Italy suffered thousands of terrorist attacks during the heyday of the Red Brigades terrorist campaign in the 1970s and 1980s. As part of its effort to combat the Red Brigades, the Italian government adopted a two-pronged strategy:

1. The first prong required the Italian law enforcement establishment to continue to root out terrorist cells.

2. The second prong offered Red Brigades cadres terms and conditions for reductions in their sentences; all that was required of them was that they "repent" their terrorist past.

The latter prong—the so-called **repentance laws**—offered Red Brigades members qualified amnesty for demonstrations of repentance for their crimes. Repentance could be established by cooperating within a sliding scale of collaboration. Thus, those who collaborated most generously had a proportionally large amount of time removed from their sentences, whereas those whose information was less useful had less time removed. A significant number of the roughly 2,000 imprisoned Red Brigades terrorists accepted repentance reductions in their sentences.

The USA Patriot Act in the United States

In the aftermath of the September 11, 2001, homeland attacks, the U.S. Congress quickly passed legislation with the intent to address the new security threat. On October 26, 2001, President George W. Bush signed this legislation into law. It was labeled the Uniting and Strengthening America by Providing Appropriate Tools Required to Intercept and Obstruct Terrorism Act, also known as the USA Patriot Act. Examples of USA Patriot Act provisions include the following:

- Revisions of the standards for government surveillance, including federal law enforcement access to private records
- Enhancement of electronic surveillance authority, such as tapping into e-mail, electronic address books, and computers
- The use of "roving wiretaps" by investigators, which permit surveillance of an individual's telephone conversations on any phone anywhere in the country
- Requiring banks to identify sources of money deposited in some private accounts and requiring foreign banks to report on suspicious transactions
- The use of nationwide search warrants
- Deportation of immigrants who raise money for terrorist organizations
- The detention of immigrants without charge for up to one week on suspicion of supporting terrorism

Civil liberties watchdog organizations immediately questioned whether these provisions would erode constitutional protections. In order to address some of these concerns, lawmakers included a sunset provision mandating that the USA Patriot Act's major provisions will automatically expire in 2004 unless officially extended. Lawmakers also required the Department of Justice to submit periodic reports on the impact of the Act on civil liberties.

The 1996 Anti-Terrorism Act in the United States

In 1996, the United States passed its first comprehensive counterterrorism legislation, entitled the **Anti-Terrorism and Effective Death Penalty Act**. The purpose of the

Anti-Terrorism Act was to regulate activity that could be used to mount a terrorist attack, provide resources for counterterrorist programs, and punish terrorism. The Act included the following provisions:

- A federal death penalty for deaths that result from acts of terrorism
- The inclusion of so-called "taggant" agents in plastic explosives, which mark the time and place of their manufacture
- The ability to prosecute crimes against federal employees while on duty as federal (rather than state) offenses
- Funding for terrorism prevention, counterterrorism, and counterintelligence
- Stronger procedural controls on asylum, deportation, and entry into the country
- A prohibition on government and private business financial transactions with terrorist states
- Authority for the secretary of state to designate private groups as terrorist organizations and forbid them from raising funds in the United States

The Anti-Terrorism and Effective Death Penalty Act was passed after the terrorist attack at the Atlanta Olympics and the explosion of TWA Flight 800 near Long Island, New York. Although the Flight 800 disaster was later concluded not to be an act of terrorism, officials considered the Anti-Terrorism Act to be a milestone in responding to domestic terrorism.

Case: The Achille Lauro Revisited

It is instructive to review the aftermath of the seemingly successful resolution of the *Achille Lauro* crisis. American warplanes had intercepted an Egyptian aircraft that was transporting Palestine Liberation Front terrorists to safety, and the aircraft was diverted to an airport in Sicily. In Sicily, U.S. counterterrorist troops were flown in to take control of the plane and its passengers.

After the Egyptian plane landed, an American special operations unit disembarked from their aircraft and rushed toward the Egyptian craft. Italian troops and security officers on the ground positioned themselves between the U.S. troops and their target. The Italians refused to permit American special operations troops to take control of the airliner or its passengers. Tensions ran high during the standoff. The terrorists were eventually placed in Italian custody and tried before an Italian court. Their leader, Abu Abbas, successfully claimed diplomatic immunity and was permitted to leave Italy for Yugoslavia. Three of the hijackers received long sentences, and Abu Abbas was sentenced *in absentia*. When one of the terrorists (who had been sentenced to 30 years' imprisonment) was later released on parole for good behavior, he promptly fled the country.

An Italian judge made sympathetic comments in open court about the plight of the Palestinian defendants. He essentially said that their behavior was understandable because they had been forced to grow up in harsh conditions in the Palestinian refugee camps. He also noted that they had no prior criminal record. The judge's comments and Abu Abbas's release occurred within the context of a political environment in Italy that granted the PLO diplomatic status. Technically, Abbas's release was legal (and even mandated) under Italian law, and the terrorists' criminal culpability was considered to be a matter for Italian courts to resolve. The Italian government's refusal to transfer the prisoners into American custody was fully within their legal purview, regardless of whether the decision angered the Americans.

International Law:
Legalistic Responses by the World Community

International law is based on tradition, custom, and formal agreements between nations. It is essentially a cooperative concept, because there is no international enforcement mechanism that is comparable to domestic courts, law enforcement agencies, or crimes codes. All of these institutions exist in some form at the international level, but it should be remembered that nations voluntarily recognize their authority. They do this through formal agreements. Bilateral (two-party) and multilateral (multiple-party) agreements are used to create an environment that is conducive to legalistic order maintenance. These formal agreements include treaties, which are defined as

> contracts or bargains which derive all their force and obligation from mutual consent and agreement; and consequently, when once fairly made and properly concluded, cannot be altered or annulled by one of the parties, without the consent and concurrence of the other.[17]

Nations enter into treaties to create predictability and consistency in international relations. When threats to international order arise—such as hijackings, kidnappings, and havens for wanted extremists—the international community often enters into multilateral agreements to manage the threat. The following examples illustrate the nature of multi-lateral counterterrorist agreements.

International Conventions on Hijacking Offenses

In response to the spate of airline hijackings that occurred in the late 1960s and early 1970s, the world community enacted a number of international treaties to promote cooperation in combating international terrorism directed against international travel services. These treaties included the following:

Tokyo Convention on Offences and Certain Other Acts Committed on Board Aircraft. Enacted in 1963 as the first airline crimes' treaty, it required all signatories to "make every effort to restore control of the aircraft to its lawful commander and to ensure the prompt onward passage or return of the hijacked aircraft together with its passengers, crew, and cargo."[18]

Hague Convention of 1970. This treaty required signatories to extradite "hijackers to their country of origin or to prosecute them under the judicial code of the recipient state."[19]

Montreal Convention of 1971. This treaty extended international law to cover "sabotage and attacks on airports and grounded aircraft, and laid down the principle that all such offenses must be subject to severe penalties."[20]

Protecting Diplomats

In reply to the spate of attacks on embassies and assaults on diplomats in the late 1960s and early 1970s, several international treaties were enacted to promote cooperation in combating international terrorism against diplomatic missions. These treaties included the following:

Convention to Prevent and Punish Acts of Terrorism Taking the Form of Crimes Against Persons and Related Extortion That Are of International Significance. This was a treaty among members of the Organization of American States that "sought to define attacks against internationally protected persons as common crimes, regardless of motives."[21] The purpose of the agreement was to establish common ground for recognizing the absolute inviolability of diplomatic missions.

Prevention and Punishment of Crimes Against Internationally Protected Persons, Including Diplomatic Agents. This was a multilateral treaty adopted by the United Nations in 1973.[22] It sought to establish a common international framework for suppressing extremist attacks against those who are protected by internationally recognized status.

Extradition Treaties

Nations frequently enter into treaties that allow law enforcement agencies to share intelligence and operational information that can be used to track and capture terrorists. An example of this collaboration is INTERPOL, which was discussed earlier in the chapter. Another example is **extradition treaties**, which require parties to bind over terrorist suspects at the request of fellow signatories. Strong extradition treaties and other criminal cooperation agreements are powerful tools in the war against terrorism.

When properly implemented, extradition agreements can be quite effective. However, these treaties are collaborative and are not easily enforceable when one party declines to bind over a suspect or is otherwise uncooperative. When this happens, there is little recourse other than to try to convince the offending party to comply with the terms of the treaty. For example, recall from Chapter 12 that when FALN leader William Morales was captured by Mexican authorities, the government refused to extradite him to the United States. Morales was allowed to seek asylum in Cuba.

International Courts and Tribunals

The United Nations has established several institutions to address the problems of terrorism, genocide, torture, and international crime. The purpose of these institutions is to bring the perpetrators of crimes against humanity to justice. They are international courts, and their impact can be significant when nations agree to recognize their authority. Examples of United Nations authority include the following institutions:

International Court of Justice. The **International Court of Justice** is the principal judicial arm of the United Nations. Its 15 judges are elected from among member states and sit for nine-year terms. The court hears disputes between nations and gives advisory opinions to recognized international organizations.

International Criminal Court. The **International Criminal Court** (ICC) was established to prosecute crimes against humanity, such as genocide. Its motivating principal is to promote human rights and justice. In practice, this has meant that the ICC has issued arrest warrants for the prosecution of war criminals.

International Criminal Tribunal for the Former Yugoslavia. The **International Criminal Tribunal for the Former Yugoslavia** (ICTY) has investigated allegations of war crimes and genocide arising out of the wars that broke out after the fragmentation of Yugoslavia during the 1990s. The fighting among Croats, Muslims, and Serbs was exceptionally brutal and occasionally genocidal. Several alleged war criminals, including former Yugoslavian president Slobodan Milosevic, have been brought before the court. Others remain at large but under indictment.

Table 13.6   Counterterrorist Options: Legalistic Responses

The purpose of legalistic responses is to provide protection to the general public, protect the interests of the state, and criminalize the behavior of the terrorists. The following table summarizes basic elements of legalistic responses.

| Counterterrorist Option | Activity Profile | | |
	Rationale	Practical Objectives	Typical Resources Used
Law enforcement	Enhancement of security apparatus	Day-to-day counterterrorist operations	Police personnel
	Demilitarization of counterterrorist campaign	Bringing terrorists into the criminal justice system	Specialized personnel
Domestic laws	Criminalization of terrorist behavior	Enhancement of criminal penalties for terrorist behavior	Criminal justice system
		Bringing terrorists into the criminal justice system	Legislative involvement
International law	International consensus and cooperation	Coalitional response to terrorism	International organizations
			State resources

International Criminal Court for Rwanda. Like the ICTY, the **International Criminal Court for Rwanda** has investigated allegations of war crimes and genocide that resulted from the breakdown of order in Rwanda during the 1990s. Hundreds of thousands died during the campaign of terror waged by mobs and paramilitaries. The indictments against suspected war criminals detail what can only be described as genocide on a massive scale.

Table 13.6 summarizes the activity profile of legalistic counterterrorist options.

Case in Point   **Hostage Rescues**

When hostage rescue operations succeed, they seem to be almost miraculous victories against terrorism. There have been a number of hostage rescue operations in which well-trained elite units have dramatically resolved terrorist crises. However, there have also been cases when elite units have failed because of poor planning or overly complicated scenarios. The fact is that when they fail, the consequences are disastrous.

The following cases illustrate the inherently risky nature of hostage rescue operations.

The Munich Olympics

In September 1972, members of the Black September terrorist organization captured nine Israeli Athletes and killed two others at the Olympic Village during the Munich Olympics. They demanded the release of Palestinian and Red Army Faction prisoners, as well as one Japanese Red Army member. West German officials permitted the terrorists to transport their hostages to an airport, using the ruse that they would be flown out of the country. In reality, the plan called for five Bavarian police snipers to shoot the terrorists when they were in the open. At the airport, five terrorists, one police officer, and all of the hostages were killed in a firefight with the Bavarian police. Three terrorists were captured and imprisoned in West Germany, but they were later released and flown to Libya. Israel's Wrath of God program later hunted down and assassinated two of the terrorists.

Entebbe

In June 1977, an Air France Airbus was hijacked in Athens while en route from Tel Aviv to Paris. Seven terrorists—two West Germans and five PFLP members—forced the plane to fly to Entebbe in Uganda. There were 248 passengers, but 142 were released. The remaining 106 passengers were Israelis and Jews, who were kept as hostages. Israeli troops, doctors, and nurses flew 2,620 miles to Entebbe, attacked the airport, killed at least seven of the terrorists and 20 Ugandan soldiers, and rescued the hostages. Three hostages and one Israeli commando died. One British-Israeli woman who had become ill was moved to a Ugandan hospital, where she was murdered by Ugandan personnel.

Mogadishu

In October 1977, a Lufthansa Boeing 737 was hijacked in mid-air while en route from Mallorca, Spain, to Frankfurt. The hijackers took the aircraft on an odyssey to Rome, the Persian Gulf, the Arabian Peninsula, and East Africa. The four Palestinian terrorists demanded a ransom[a] and the release of imprisoned Palestinian and West German terrorists. The plane eventually landed in Mogadishu, Somalia. Throughout its odyssey, the aircraft had been shadowed by a plane bearing elite West German GSG-9 police commandos. In Mogadishu, the unit landed, attacked the hijacked aircraft, killed three of the terrorists, and rescued the hostages. None of the hostages or rescuers was killed, and only one person was injured. As a postscript, several imprisoned West German terrorists committed suicide when they learned of the rescue—these suicides, known as Death Night, were discussed in Chapter 6.

Force 777

In 1977, Egypt organized **Force 777** as a small elite counterterrorist special operations unit. Soon after its creation, Force 777 was twice used to assault aircraft hijacked to other countries by Palestinian terrorists. In the first incident, the PFLP landed a hijacked Cyprus Airways airliner in Nicosia, Cyprus. The Egyptian government dispatched Force 777 but neglected to inform Cypriot authorities. When the Egyptians landed and rushed the hijacked airliner, Cypriot police and other security personnel opened fire, thinking that the commandos were reinforcements for the terrorists. During an 80-minute firefight, more than 15 Egyptians and Cypriots were killed. In the second incident, Abu Nidal Organization terrorists landed Egyptair Flight 648 in Malta in retaliation for the Egyptian government's failure to protect the *Achille Lauro* terrorists.[b] The Egyptian government again dispatched Force 777, this time in larger numbers and after notifying Maltese officials. Unfortunately, the assault plan called for explosive charges to blow a hole in the aircraft's roof so that Force 777 commandos could jump into the cabin. The charges were much too strong, and the explosion immediately killed approximately 20 passengers. During the ensuing six-hour firefight, a total of 57 passengers were killed. Reports alleged that Egyptian snipers shot at passengers as they fled the aircraft.

Operation Eagle Claw

During the consolidation of the Iranian Revolution in November 1979, Iranian radicals seized the American embassy in Tehran. Some hostages were soon released, but more than 50 were held in captivity. In April 1980, the United States launched a rescue attempt that was led by the Delta Force but that included units from all branches of the military. The plan was to establish a base in the Iranian desert, fly commando teams into Tehran, assault the embassy compound, ferry the hostages to a soccer field, have helicopters land to pick them up, shuttle them to an airfield secured by Army Rangers, and then fly everyone to safety. Gunships and other aircraft would provide air cover during the operation. The operation did not progress beyond its first phase. As helicopters approached the desert site—dubbed Desert One—they flew into a massive dust storm. Because they were under orders to not exceed 200 feet, they tried to fly through the storm; two helicopters were forced out of the operation, as was a third helicopter that later malfunctioned. On the ground, a helicopter drove into one of the airplanes, and both exploded. Eight soldiers were killed, and the mission was ordered to be cancelled.

NOTES

a. The ransom demand was directed to the son of industrialist Hanns-Martin Schleyer, who was in the hands of West Germany's Red Army Faction.

b. During the *Achille Lauro* crisis, Flight 648 was the same aircraft that had transported the PLF terrorists when it was diverted by U.S. warplanes to Sicily.

CHAPTER SUMMARY

This chapter discussed options for responding to terrorism within the context of several categories and subcategories. The decision-making process for selecting counterterrorist options is predicated on several key factors:

- The characteristics of the terrorist movement
- The nature of the overall terrorist environment
- The political goals of the counterterrorist actor

When assessing the practical utility of resorting to the use of force, it is important to remember that many of these responses are inconsistently effective against determined terrorists in the long term. Successes have been won against domestic terrorists—especially when governments have been unconstrained in their use of force and coercion—but this is not a universal outcome. Internationally, short-term successes have resulted in the resolution of specific terrorist incidents. However, long-term successes have sometimes been difficult to achieve. Nevertheless, the use of force has produced some success in disrupting terrorist groups and reducing the intensity of terrorist environments.

Repressive operations other than war include a number of options. Intelligence collection and analysis is extremely useful for building activity profiles of terrorist groups and for understanding the dynamics of terrorist environments. Intelligence is also useful for generalized prediction but is less useful for predicting the precise location and timing of specific terrorist attacks. Regarding enhanced security, because target hardening usually involves the erection of fixed barriers, surveillance technologies, and security posts, determined terrorists can design methods to circumvent these precautions. Nevertheless, there is an increased potential for failure from the terrorists' perspective, and it should be presumed that enhanced security deters less determined and less resourceful terrorists.

Conciliatory responses have achieved both short-term and long-term success in ending terrorist environments. There have also been a number of failed conciliatory operations. Diplomatic options have enjoyed marked success in some cases but have been frustrated by entrenched hostilities and uncooperative parties in other cases. Social reforms have enjoyed long-term success when reforms are gradually accepted as legitimate by target populations. Concessionary options are risky because of the perception of appeasement of the terrorists, but these options are sometimes successful.

Legalistic responses are in many ways the front line for counterterrorist policies. Law enforcement agencies are usually the first responders to incidents, and they are responsible for ongoing civil security and investigations. Problems arise when repression or miscarriages of justice discredit police agencies. Nevertheless, security-oriented police duties have successfully resolved or controlled terrorist environments. Domestic laws are adaptations of legal systems to domestic terrorist crises. Some of these adaptations—both authoritarian and democratic—have been quite successful. International laws and institutions have likewise enjoyed some success, but because they are inherently cooperative in nature, parties to treaties and other agreements must comply with their terms. Otherwise, international laws and institutions have very little enforcement authority.

KEY TERMS AND CONCEPTS

The following topics were discussed in this chapter and are found in the Glossary:

11th Parachute Division (Paras)
1st Navy Parachute Infantry Regiment
75th Ranger Regiment
Achille Lauro
Antiterrorism
Anti-Terrorism and Effective Death
    Penalty Act
Birmingham Six
Bureau for the Protection of the Constitution
Central Intelligence Agency (CIA)
Coercive covert operations
Concessionary options
Conciliatory responses
Convention to Prevent and Punish Acts of
    Terrorism Taking the Form of Crimes
    Against Persons and Related Extortion That
    Are of International Significance
Counterterrorism
Covert operations
Criminal profiles
Cyberwar
Decommissioning
Defense Intelligence Agency (DIA)
Delta Force (1st Special Forces Operational
    Detachment–Delta)
Diplomacy
Diplomatic Security Service
Disinformation
Economic sanctions
Emergency Search Team
Enhanced security
Executive Order 12333
Extradition treaties
Federal Bureau of Investigation (FBI)
Force 777
Foreign Legion
French Navy Special Assault Units
GEO (Grupo Especial de Operaciones)
GIGN (Groupe d'Intervention Gendarmerie
    Nationale)

Golani Brigade
Good Friday Agreement
Green Berets (Special Forces Groups)
Green Police
GSG-9 (Grenzschutzgruppe 9)
Guildford Four
Hague Convention of 1970
Hostage Rescue Team
Human intelligence
Intelligence
Intelligence community
International Court of Justice
International Criminal Court
International Criminal Court for Rwanda
International Criminal Police Organization
    (INTERPOL)
International Criminal Tribunal for the Former
    Yugoslavia
International law
Kansi, Mir Aimal
Law enforcement
Legalistic responses
MI-5
MI-6
Military Intelligence Service
Military repressive options
Montreal Convention of 1971
Mossad
National Security Agency (NSA)
Nonmilitary repressive responses
Northern Ireland Act
Operation Eagle Claw
Operation El Dorado Canyon
Operation Enduring Freedom
Operation Infinite Justice
Operation Peace for Galilee
Parachute *Sayaret*
Paramilitary repressive options
Peace process
Police Border Guards

Polisario
Preemptive strikes
Punitive strikes
Racial profiling
RAPAS
Repentance laws
Repressive responses
Rewards for Justice Program
Royal Marine Commandos
Sayaret
Sayaret Matkal
Sea Air Land Forces (SEALs)
Signal intelligence
Sky marshals

Social reform
Special Air Service
Special Boat Service
Special Operations Command
Special operations forces
Supergrass
Suppression campaigns
Terrorist profiles
Tokyo Convention on Offences and Certain
    Other Acts Committed on Board Aircraft
Weinrich, Johannes
Wrath of God
YAMAM
YAMAS

RECOMMENDED WEB SITES

The following Web sites provide information and data about counterterrorist policies and options.

Coordinator for Counterterrorism, Department of State: www.state.gov/www/global/terrorism

Diplomatic Security Service, Rewards for Justice: www.rewardsforjustice.net

International Rescue Committee: www.intrescom.org

United Nations International Court of Justice: www.icj-cij.org

War Criminal Watch: www.igc.org/wcw

WEB EXERCISE

Using this chapter's recommended Internet sites, conduct an online investigation of counterterrorism.

- Compare and contrast the services described online by the referenced organizations. How do their services differ?
- How important are the services provided by organizations that monitor terrorist behavior and fugitives? Why?
- In what ways do you think the Internet will contribute to the counterterrorist effort in the future?

For an online search of counterterrorism, students should activate the search engine on their Web browser and enter the following keywords:

"Terrorism and Counterterrorism"
"Antiterrorism"

RECOMMENDED READINGS

The following publications provide information about counterterrorist units and intelligence agencies.

Andrew, Christopher. *Her Majesty's Secret Service: The Making of the British Intelligence Community.* New York: Penguin Books, 1987.

Bamford, James. *Body of Secrets: Anatomy of the Ultra-Secret National Security Agency, From the Cold War Through the Dawn of a New Century.* New York: Doubleday, 2001.

Coulson, Danny O., and Elaine Shannon. *No Heroes: Inside the FBI's Secret Counter-Terror Force.* New York: Picket Books, 1999.

Harclerode, Peter. *Secret Soldiers: Special Forces in the War Against Terrorism.* London: Cassel, 2000.

Thomas, Gordon. *Gideon's Spies: The Secret History of the Mossad.* New York: St. Martin's Press, 1999.

Discussion Box   The Utility of Elite Counterterrorist Units

This chapter's Discussion Box is intended to stimulate critical debate about the purpose of elite antiterrorism units.

Elite military and police counterterrorism units have been mustered into the security establishments of many nations. Many of these units include highly trained professionals who can operate in a number of environments under extremely hazardous conditions. Their missions include hostage rescues, punitive strikes, abductions, and reconnaissance operations.

When elite units perform well, the outcomes include rescued hostages, resolved crises, and disrupted terrorist environments. However, these units sometimes find themselves involved in ambiguous political situations or tenuous operational conditions. In other words, special operations are often high-risk, high-gain situations.

Nevertheless, proponents of elite counterterrorist units argue that conventional forces are not trained or configured to fight "shadow wars"—only special operations forces can do so. Critics of these units argue that conventional forces can accomplish the same objectives and goals and that, aside from the very good special operations units, other elite units have not proven themselves to be very effective.

Historical examples suggest that the deployment of special operations forces is a high-risk and high-gain option.

Discussion Questions:

- How necessary are elite counterterrorism units? Why?
- How effective do you think these elite units are?
- What other counterterrorist options do you think can be effective without resorting to the deployment of elite units?
- Which counterterrorist options work most efficiently in conjunction with elite units? Which options work least efficiently?
- In the long term, what impact will elite units have in the war against international terrorism?

NOTES

[1] Pillar, Paul R. *Terrorism and U.S. Foreign Policy*. Washington, DC: Brookings Institution Press, 2001, p. 73 ff.

[2] Sederberg, Peter C. *Terrorist Myths: Illusion, Rhetoric, and Reality*. Englewood Cliffs, NJ: Prentice Hall, 1989, p. 136 ff.

[3] Heymann, Philip B. *Terrorism and America: A Commonsense Strategy for a Democratic Society*. Cambridge: MIT Press, 1998, p. 80 ff.

[4] Only the United States, Great Britain, Russia, and France have the capability to deploy large numbers of seaborne troops.

[5] The first invasion occurred in 1978 with the same goal of driving out PLO fighters. A third Israeli invasion took place in 1996 and was directed against Hezbollah.

[6] Whittaker, David J., ed. *The Terrorism Reader*. New York: Routledge, 2001, pp. 144-45.

[7] Miller, Christian T. "A War-Torn Village Finds No Sanctuary." *Los Angeles Times*. May 19, 2002.

[8] For a history of the Foreign Legion, see Geraghty, Tony. *March or Die: A New History of the French Foreign Legion*. New York: Facts on File Publications, 1986.

[9] Finn, Peter. "Arrests Reveal Al Qaeda Plans." *Washington Post*. June 16, 2002.

[10] Pillar (note 1 above), p. 115.

[11] Pillar (note 1 above), p. 157.

[12] See Reid, T. R. "IRA Issues Apology for All Deaths It Caused." *Washington Post*. July 17, 2002.

[13] See Chapter 3 for a discussion of the Falangist code of self-sacrifice.

[14] For the complete text of the findings of Senate investigations into the scandal, see New York Times. *The Tower Commission Report*. New York: Bantam Books and Times Books, 1987.

[15] New York Police Memorial Web site: www.cire.com/nypd.

[16] United Nations General Assembly. *Report of the Panel Appointed by the Secretary-General to Gather Information on the Situation in Algeria* [. . .] (report of the Eminent Panel). July-August 1998. Quoted in Whittaker (note 6 above), p. 148.

[17] Franck, Thomas M. *Foreign Relations and National Security Law: Cases, Materials and Simulations*. St. Paul, MN: West, 1987, p. 97.

[18] Wilkinson, Paul. "Fighting the Hydra: Terrorism and the Rule of Law." In Kegley, Charles W., ed. *International Terrorism: Characteristics, Causes, Controls*. New York: St. Martin's Press, 1990, p. 255.

[19] Ibid.

[20] Ibid.

[21] Ibid.

[22] Ibid.

Chapter 14

WHAT NEXT?
THE FUTURE OF TERRORISM

Previous chapters provided students with a great deal of information about the causes of terrorism, the motives behind political violence, terrorist typologies, and counterterrorist responses. Examples of postwar terrorist movements and environments were presented to illustrate theoretical concepts and trends. The discussion in this chapter synthesizes many of these concepts, trends, and typologies, and projects emerging trends that are likely to characterize terrorist environments in the near future.

There is one concept that must be understood at the outset: Projecting future trends is not synonymous with predicting specific events, and the two should be differentiated as follows:

- *Projections* involve theoretical constructs of trends based on available data.
- *Predictions* are practical applications of data (that is, intelligence) to anticipate specific behaviors by extremists.

As indicated in Chapter 13, predicting terrorist threats is the rather difficult work of intelligence agencies. Making accurate predictions is problematic, because most uncovered threats involve generalized rather than specific forewarnings. Thus, intelligence agencies can learn about real threats to specific interests or in specific cities, but they often do not have details about the timing or location of attacks. For example, the U.S. Department of Justice issued many threat warnings after the September 11, 2001, attacks, but very few described specific threats against specific targets.

One must develop a logical longitudinal framework in order to evaluate the future of political violence. A *longitudinal framework* uses past history and trends to project future trends. It allows scholars, students, and practitioners to "stand back" from immediate crises and contemporary terrorist environments to try to construct a reasonable picture of the near future. These projections must be made with the understanding that the more near-term a forecast is, the more likely it is to be a realistic projection. Conversely, far-term forecasts are less likely to be realistic, because projections must be consistently updated using contemporary data.

NEAR-TERM PROJECTIONS OF TERRORISM

It can be argued that the sources of extremist behavior in the modern era will remain unchanged in the near future. Terrorism will continue to occur because of the following reasons:

- People who have been relegated to the social and political margins—or who believe that they have been so relegated—often form factions that resort to violence.
- Movements and nations sometimes adopt religious or ethno-national supremacist doctrines that they use to justify aggressive political behavior.
- Many states continue to value the "utility" of domestic and foreign terrorism.

These factors are not, of course, the only sources of terrorism and extremist sentiment, but they are certainly among the most enduring sources. However, these enduring sources have precipitated the new trends in terrorist behavior that began to spread during the 1990s and early 2000s. These new trends include

- increasing use of communications and information technologies by extremists;
- adaptations of cell-based organizational and operational strategies by global revolutionary movements; and
- efforts to construct or obtain weapons of mass destruction or, alternatively, to convert existing technologies into high-yield weapons.

TERRORISM BY STATES AND DISSIDENTS

State terrorism is always a possibility when regimes are threatened from within by dissident movements or when regimes conclude that their foreign policy will benefit from covert aggression. Authoritarian regimes have historically emphasized the maintenance of order over human rights, and this is unlikely to change in the near future. The use of proxies is likely to continue in regions where states believe that they can destabilize neighboring rivals, such as in the Middle East and along the India-Pakistan border region. In the near future, states will continue to conclude that domestic or foreign terrorism serves their interests.

Dissident terrorism will continue to be a problem as long as violent dissidents find safe haven in supportive environments, such as Gaza and the West Bank during the Palestinian *intifadeh*. There is also a distinct possibility that stateless revolutionaries and other independent internationalist movements will continue to engage in terrorist violence on behalf of a variety of vague causes. Terrorism will also be used as a violent option in countries where ethno-national and religious conflicts remain unresolved.

Counterpoints exist to the continuation of dissident political violence in the near future. One counterpoint is that support for, and the momentum of, domestic terrorist movements can be undercut by genuine social reform. Recent history has demonstrated that these reforms can reduce and even end political violence, as long as they are pursued with determination despite setbacks and sabotage. A second counterpoint is the utility of international counterterrorist cooperation. Several terrorist conspiracies were thwarted, and a number of terrorists were captured or kept on the run, as a direct result of cooperation among intelligence, law enforcement, and security agencies. A third counterpoint is that there is no single binding or common ideological foundation for political violence. Unlike during the heyday of traditional terrorism, there is no modern equivalent to revolutionary Marxism. Religious extremism is self-isolating, and there is no longer an international "solidarity movement" for ethno-nationalist violence. It remains to be seen what the long-term impact will be on terrorist violence, but it is unlikely that there will be an ideological "glue" to bind together extremist sentiment in the near future.

Table 14.1   Supplanting the Old with the New

Traditional terrorism was, in many ways, symmetrical and predictable. It was not characterized by terrorist environments exhibiting massive casualty rates or indiscriminate attacks. Its organizational profile was also characterized by traditional organizational configurations.

The following table contrasts selected attributes of the activity profiles for traditional terrorism and New Terrorism.

			Activity Profile		
Terrorist Environment	*Target Selection*	*Casualty Rates*	*Organizational Profile*	*Tactical/ Weapons Selection*	*Typical Motives*
Traditional terrorism	Surgical and symbolic	Low and selective	Hierarchical and identifiable	Conventional and low to medium yield	Leftist and ethnocentric
New Terrorism	Indiscriminate and symbolic	High and indiscriminate	Cell-based	Unconventional and high yield	Sectarian

WHITHER THE "OLD TERRORISM"?

Traditional terrorism was characterized by the typologies, organizational profiles, and methods developed during the postwar era. These characteristics included the following commonalities:

- Leftist ethno-nationalist motives
- Leftist ideological motives
- Surgical and symbolic selection of targets
- Deliberate media manipulation and publicized incidents
- Relatively low casualty rates
- Identifiable organizational profile
- Hierarchical organizational profile
- Full-time professional cadres

Although traditional terrorism did not become a relic of the past during the 1990s, it ceased to be the primary model for terrorist movements and environments in the 2000s. The relatively clear objectives and motives of traditional terrorism certainly continued to fuel many conflicts, but many modern terrorists began to promote vaguely articulated objectives and motives. The new terrorists also became cell-based stateless revolutionaries, unlike traditional terrorists, who tended to organize themselves hierarchically and had state sponsors. Even though the number of international incidents declined during the era of the New Terrorism, the casualty rates were higher in comparison with traditional terrorism. This is not to say that traditional terrorism has disappeared from the world scene or will do so in the near future. It will continue alongside a growing—and more aggressive—threat from the New Terrorism.

Table 14.1 compares several key characteristics of the Old and New Terrorisms.

The discussion in this chapter will review the future of political violence from the following perspectives:

- The Future of Terrorism
- Controlling Terrorism
- Prospects for Terrorism in the United States

THE FUTURE OF TERRORISM

The sources of extremist behavior have not changed in the recent past and will not change in the near future. As in the recent past, intense expressions of intolerance and resentment are likely to motivate many extremists to blame entire systems, societies, and groups of people for their problems. Under these conditions, political violence will continue to be seen by many people as a justifiable option. The likelihood of political violence will remain high as long as intolerance and blaming are motivated by passionate feelings of national identity, racial supremacy, religious dogma, or ideological beliefs. Both state and dissident terrorists will continue to exploit these tendencies for their own purposes.

Many characteristics of terrorism from the past will remain relevant well beyond the immediate future. For example, it is likely that future terrorism will exhibit the same moralist characteristics discussed in previous chapters. At the core of terrorist moralism are the conceptual perspectives quoted in Chapter 1, which are summed up by the following slogans:

"One person's terrorist is another person's freedom fighter." (Unknown)

"One man willing to throw away his life is enough to terrorize a thousand." (Wu Ch'i)

"Extremism in defense of liberty is no vice." (Senator Barry Goldwater)

"It became necessary to destroy the town to save it." (allegedly an American officer in Vietnam)

These perspectives, and other behavioral attributes such as codes of self-sacrifice, are central and enduring features of modern terrorism.

Terrorist Typologies in the New Millennium

State-Sponsored Terrorism

State-sponsored terrorism will not soon disappear and will remain a feature of future terrorist environments. Authoritarian states will continue to use terrorism as domestic policy, and aggressive states will continue to foment acts of international terrorism as foreign policy.

Domestically, political repression is—and long has been—a common practice by regimes more interested in protecting the authority of the state than human rights. The old instruments of repression will continue to be common tools of authoritarian government. These instruments include security institutions such as police, military, and paramilitary forces. One should expect the pervasiveness of security institutions to be augmented by the continued improvement of surveillance and communications technologies. One should also expect that some of the world's more ruthless regimes will occasionally deploy weapons of mass destruction against dissident ethno-national groups, as the regime of Saddam Hussein did against Iraqi Kurds.

Internationally, aggressive regimes in the postwar era frequently supported sympathetic proxies to indirectly confront their adversaries. This practice was often a safe and low-cost alternative to overt conflict. It is reasonable to assume that some regimes will continue this practice in the near future, especially in regions where highly active proxies have the opportunity to severely press their sponsoring regime's rivals. For example, in early 2002 a ship bearing Iranian arms was intercepted by Israeli security forces before it could offload the arms. The weapons, which were bound for Palestinian nationalist fighters, were almost certainly part of a proxy operation by the Iranian government.

Dissident Terrorism

Patterns of dissident terrorism during the late 1990s and early 2000s were decreasingly ideological and increasingly "cultural." Ethno-nationalist terrorism continued to occur on a sometimes grand scale, and religious terrorism spread among radical Islamic groups. In addition, stateless international terrorism began to emerge as the predominant typology in the global arena. These trends are likely to continue, as vestiges of the East-West ideological competition give way to patterns of religious extremism and seemingly interminable communal conflicts.

The Terrorist Left and Right

Few ideologically motivated insurgencies survived into the 2000s. Most ideological terrorist environments and wars of national liberation were resolved during the 1980s and 1990s. Nevertheless, a few Marxist insurgencies persisted in the early 2000s, and Western democracies witnessed the growth of neofascist and anarchistic movements. Violence from neofascists tended to consist of relatively low-intensity hate crimes, mob brawls, and occasional low-yield bombings. Violence from the new anarchists usually involved brawls with the police at international conferences or occasional confrontations with racist skinheads. Right-wing movements and groups are likely to persist and grow in the near term. With the growth of aboveground neofascist parties in Europe, they could become a vanguard or "armed wing" of a renewed fascist movement.

Religious Terrorism

Terrorism motivated by religion has become a global problem. Religious terrorism spread during the 1980s and grew to challenge international and domestic political stability during the 1990s and early 2000s. The frequency of, and casualties from, sectarian attacks grew quickly during this period. Religious terrorists also became adept at recruiting new members and organizing themselves as semi-autonomous cells across national boundaries.

The trends that developed toward the end of the 20th century suggest that religious violence will continue to be a central aspect of terrorism in the 21st century. *Internationally*, religious terrorists of many nationalities have consistently attacked targets that symbolize enemy interests. Unlike the relatively surgical strikes of secular leftists in previous years, religious terrorists have proven to be particularly homicidal. For example, as discussed in Chapter 10, Al Qaeda was responsible in April 2002 for the explosion of a fuel tanker truck at a synagogue in Tunisia, killing 17 people—12 of them German tourists. This kind of lethality has become a central element to international religious terrorism. *Domestically*, terrorist movements in Pakistan, Israel, Malaysia, the Philippines, and elsewhere have actively sought to overthrow or destabilize their governments and damage symbols representing foreign interests. For example, Western civilians were taken as hostages by radical Islamic antigovernment Abu Sayyaf terrorists in the Philippines during 2001 and 2002.

Criminal Terrorism

Traditional criminal enterprises such as the Russian Mafia, La Cosa Nostra, Sicilian Mafia, and the Mexican drug gangs will continue to ply their trades as long as there is a market for their services. Drugs, arms, and other goods will be illegally transported and sold in the international market regardless of attempts by governments to suppress these transactions. Because of the versatility of these enterprises, it is unlikely that there will soon be an end to criminal terrorist violence directed against law enforcement personnel who challenge them.

Terrorist violence from criminal-political enterprises is also unlikely to end in the near future. With the reduction in support from sympathetic states and the concomitant viability of the drug trade, it is quite possible that more extremist movements will attempt to become self-sustaining through transnational crime. For example, during the 1990s and early 2000s, Colombian, Southeast Asian, and South Asian groups continued to involve themselves in the opium-heroin trade and, to a lesser degree, the arms trade. Thus, it is logical to presume that past trends linking political extremism to transnational crime will continue for the foreseeable future.

The World in Conflict: Future Sources of Terrorism

During the 20th century, seemingly unmanageable regional and internal conflicts raged for years, and often decades, before the warring parties made peace with each other. An enormous amount of carnage occurred during communal conflicts, and millions of people died. Terrorism on a massive scale was not uncommon during this period. It was also during this period that high-profile acts of international terrorism became a familiar feature of the international political environment.

During the 1990s and early 2000s, contending nations and communities continued to engage in significant levels of violence. Terrorism and violent repression were used by many adversaries, who claimed them as necessary methodologies to resolve the problems of their political environments. This trend is unlikely to abate in the near future, and it is reasonable to project that some conflicts may increase in intensity.

The following cases are projected sources and targets of terrorist violence in the near future.

Africa

Ethno-national communal conflict has been a recurring feature in Africa. In East Africa, periodic outbreaks of violence have claimed hundreds of thousands of lives. Similar outbreaks have occurred in West Africa. Another pattern of conflict in Sub-Saharan Africa has been the use of state-sponsored domestic terrorism by authoritarian regimes to suppress dissident ethno-nationalist and political sentiment. Some internal conflicts—such as in Sudan, Somalia, Liberia, and Sierra Leone—are likely to flare up periodically in the near future. These conflicts have been characterized by many examples of terrorism on a large scale. In North Africa, radical Islamic movements have proven themselves motivated to commit acts of terrorism, and they are very capable of doing so. Algerian, Moroccan, and Egyptian members of Al Qaeda and other fundamentalist movements have attacked foreign interests, religious sites, and government officials as part of a vaguely defined international jihad. Libya, a former sponsor of international terrorism, is unlikely to become a reinvigorated source of terrorism.

Asia

Past patterns of ethno-national conflict and domestic terrorism suggest that some Asian nations and regions will continue to experience outbreaks of political violence. These outbreaks are likely to range from small-scale attacks to large-scale conflicts. Ethno-national groups continue to wage war in Sri Lanka, Kashmir, the Caucasus, and elsewhere.

Terrorism is an accepted method of armed conflict among many of these groups. Ideological rebellions are less common than during the postwar era, but pockets of Marxist rebellion are still to be found, such as in Nepal and the Philippines. These leftist remnants have occasionally used terrorist tactics rather effectively. Radical Islamic movements, inspired in part by Al Qaeda internationalism, have appeared in several Asian countries, including Indonesia, the Philippines, Malaysia, India, Pakistan, and the Central Asian republics. Some of these movements have demonstrated their willingness to engage in terrorism.

Europe

International terrorists have long used Europe as a battleground. This is unlikely to change, particularly in light of the post-September 11, 2001, arrests of suspected Al Qaeda operatives in several Western European countries. Domestically, there is a possibility that followers of neofascist movements may target immigrant workers or other people they define as undesirables. There are also pockets of ethno-nationalist conflict remaining in Spain and the United Kingdom, although there is virtually no likelihood that these conflicts will escalate. The Balkans remains the most unstable region in Europe, and sporadic violence is likely to occur from time to time. However, the large-scale communal conflicts and genocidal behavior that resulted from the breakup of Yugoslavia have been suppressed by NATO and United Nations intervention. Russia's conflict in Chechnya will continue to be a source of sporadic terrorism, as well as a possible source of radical Islamic activism. The potential for exceptional violence in this conflict is illustrated by an incident that occurred in October 2002. Approximately 50 Chechen terrorists seized about 750 hostages during the performance of a musical in a Moscow theater. During the 57-hour crisis, the Chechens wired the theater with explosives and threatened to destroy the entire building with everyone inside. Several of the female terrorists also wired themselves with explosives. Russian commandos eventually pumped knockout gas (possibly manufactured with opiates) into the theater. Initial reports indicated that 115 people died from the effects of the gas, but the official toll gradually increased to over 125 victims. Nearly all of the Chechens were shot by the commandos as they swept through the theater during the rescue operation.

Latin America

Most of the conflicts in Central and South America were resolved by the late 1990s. Violent leftist dissidents and repressive rightist regimes were no longer prominent features of the Latin American political environment. However, some conflicts remained unresolved in the early 2000s. The worst scenario for near-term terrorism is found in Colombia, where a weak central government has long exercised minimal control over a society beset by leftist rebels, rightist paramilitaries, and unchecked *narcotraficantes*. In Peru, the Marxist MRTA and Shining Path movements were largely dismantled by the early 2000s, but some vestiges of these groups continued to engage in low-intensity political violence. Aside from these pockets of political violence, near-term *indigenous* terrorist violence (as opposed to *international* threats) will likely be sporadic and on a lower scale of intensity than during the period from the end of the Second World War to the early 1990s.

Case: Palestine and Israel

Palestinian nationalism entered its second generation during the *intifadeh*. The *intifadeh* became a war fought by young gunmen, terrorists, and suicide bombers who grew up amidst the turmoil of the 1960s, 1970s, and 1980s. Black September, the PLO expulsion from Lebanon, the airline hijackings, and many other incidents occurred when members of the new generation were children and teenagers. The new generation unhesitatingly began a new round of violence against Israel, one that was to prove more lethal and more pervasive.

Aside from violence growing out of the *intifadeh*, the state of Israel has long been a unifying target for secular nationalists and religious extremists throughout the Middle East. Extremist movements and regimes have used the existence of Israel to attract and motivate prospective supporters. This pattern continued into the era of the New Terrorism, as radical Islamic movements cited Western support for Israel as a rallying issue. For example, Osama bin Laden's initial grievances were the supposed "desecrations" of Islam's holy sites by the Saudi government and the deployment of foreign troops to Saudi Arabia. His symbolic concepts of Christian "Crusaderism" and the royal Saud family as enemies were later augmented by a newly professed concern for the plight of the Palestinians. Thus, Al Qaeda found common cause with Hamas, Hezbollah, Iran, and other movements and countries that considered Israel to be an implacable enemy.

Case: The United States and the West

During the Cold War, the United States and its Western allies were frequent targets of leftist terrorism. As discussed in previous chapters, the reasons for this were rather uncomplicated: In the ideological conflict between the Marxist East and democratic West, and in the anticolonial wars of national liberation, revolutionaries associated the West with repression and exploitation. In the modern era, the United States and the West have become targets of the practitioners of the New Terrorism. International terrorists still associate them with international exploitation, but they add other dimensions to the new terrorist environment, such as fundamentalist religion, anti-Semitism, and a willingness to use new technologies and weapons of mass destruction. Symbolic targets have been attacked worldwide, and these include embassies, military installations, religious sites, tourists, and business visitors to foreign countries. In the late 1990s and early 2000s, attacks against Western interests were symbolic, high profile, and very lethal. In the modern era, attacks became highly destructive and caused a significant number of casualties.

Table 14.2 summarizes several examples of ongoing conflict that are likely to result in terrorist violence in the near future.

New Technologies

New technologies allow terrorists to communicate efficiently, broaden their message, and wield unconventional weapons in unexpected ways. This is a central characteristic of asymmetrical warfare. Because of incremental improvements in communications and computer technologies, it is reasonable to conclude that the trend among terrorists and their supporters will be to use them extensively. This is also true of the increasing availability of weapons components for weapons of mass destruction, as well as the continuing softening of terrorists' reluctance to use them.

Information Technologies

The Internet provides opportunities for commercial, private, and political interests to spread their message and communicate with outsiders. The use of the Internet by extremists has already become a common feature of the modern era. Information technologies are being invented and refined constantly and will continue to be central to the New Terrorism. These technologies will facilitate networking between groups and cells and will permit propaganda to be spread widely and efficiently. The Internet and e-mail are certain

Table 14.2   A World Still in Conflict: Projected Sources of Political Violence

Regional and domestic conflicts are certain to engender terrorist movements in the near future. Some of these conflicts are long-term disputes that have been ongoing for decades and that are often characterized by international spillovers.

The following table summarizes several long-term conflicts that have increased and diminished in scale and intensity during decades of confrontation. One new conflict—actually a recent typology—is also included.

| *Conflict* | *Opposing Parties* | *Activity Profile* | |
		Contending Issues	*Duration*
Palestinians/ Israelis	Palestinian nationalists, Palestinian fundamentalists, Israelis	Palestinian state, Israeli security	Decades, from late 1940s and Israeli Independence
Northern Ireland	Catholic Unionists, Protestant Loyalists, British administration	Union with Irish Republic, loyalty to United Kingdom	Decades, from late 1960s and first Provo campaign
India/ Pakistan	Kashmiri *jihadis*, India, Pakistan	Status of Kashmir, *jihadi* terrorism, border disputes	Decades, from late 1940s and end of British Empire
Colombia	Marxist rebels, *narcotraficantes*, paramilitaries, Colombian government	Social revolution, drug trade, state authority	Decades, from 1960s
Typology: Stateless "New Terrorism"	Internationalist terrorists, targeted interests	Vague goals, international stability	New model, from 1990s

to be used to send instructions about overall goals, specific tactics, new bomb-making techniques, and other facets of the terrorist trade. Both overt and covert information networks will permit widely dispersed cells to exist and communicate covertly.

It should be remembered that information and computer technologies can also be used offensively. The adoption of cyberwar techniques by extremists is quite possible, in which new technologies are used by terrorists to destroy information and communications systems. Two examples from October 1998 illustrate the potential damage that can be wrought by motivated activists:

- Animal liberation activists dropped an "e-mail bomb" on the server of Sweden's Smittskydinstitute. Its entire database crashed when 2,000 e-mail messages were sent on one day, followed on a second day by 3,000 messages. The institute was targeted because of its use of monkeys in medical experiments.

- A three-week e-mail campaign targeted approximately 100 Israeli Internet sites, resulting in the destruction of data. The campaign was launched by Lebanese Americans living in Texas.

Cyberterrorism may very well become a central facet of the terrorist environment in the near future. As one possible scenario suggests,

A variation on [the] theme of terrorism as an asymmetric strategy goes further to suggest that unconventional modes of conflict will stem . . . from a shift in the nature of conflict itself. In this paradigm, unconventional terrorist attacks on the sinews of modern, information-intensive societies will become the norm, replacing conventional conflicts over the control of territory or people.[1]

Weapons of Mass Destruction

The scenario of terrorists acquiring **weapons of mass destruction** is no longer the stuff of novels and films. Nor is the very real possibility that terrorists may use such weapons on a previously unimaginable scale:

In the near future it will be technologically possible to kill thousands, perhaps hundreds of thousands, not to mention the toll the panic that is likely to ensue may take.[2]

There are incentives for international terrorists to construct and use weapons of mass destruction in lieu of conventional weapons. The psychological and economic impact of such devices can easily outweigh the destructive effect of the initial attack (which might be relatively small). For example, regarding terrorists' use of radiological weapons,

Such a bomb would cause very few deaths from cancer. But the economic and psychological costs would be formidable. If a bomb with some six pounds of plutonium exploded in Washington, D.C., 45,000 people might have to stay indoors for an undefined period afterward to avoid being exposed to fallout.[3]

Terrorists are making concerted efforts to acquire the requisite components for constructing weapons of mass destruction. The acquisition of these components and the assembly of effective weapons is probably just a matter of time. Terrorists who are motivated by race or religion (or both) are likely to have little compunction about using chemical, biological, or radiological weapons against what they define as "subhumans" or nonbelievers. It will be recalled that the Japanese "doomsday" cult Aum Shinrikyō acquired and used Sarin nerve gas in Tokyo's subway system to hasten their vision of the Apocalypse. Aum also apparently attempted to obtain samples of the deadly Ebola virus. A member of Aryan Nations in the United States tried to obtain bubonic plague bacteria via mail order; fortunately, his behavior was amateurish, and the sample was not delivered to committed racial supremacist terrorists. These examples from the 1990s should be interpreted as precursors to terrorist

An anthrax-laced letter sent to Senator Patrick J. Leahy's Capitol Hill office. Several letters were mailed during the immediate aftermath of the September 11, 2001, homeland attacks.

Source: U.S. Federal Bureau of Investigation.

Anthrax containment. FBI and Environmental Protection Agency specialists sift through evidence transported from affected Capitol Hill offices to a secured containment facility.

Source: U.S. Federal Bureau of Investigation and U.S. Environmental Protection Agency.

efforts in the very near future. For example, the anthrax attack in the United States in late 2001 illustrates how toxins or chemicals can be delivered to intended targets.

As an alternative to the construction of weapons of mass destruction, terrorists have demonstrated their ability to convert available technologies into high-yield weapons. The destructive and psychological consequences of turning a nation's technology into a high-yield weapon have not been lost on modern terrorists. A case in point is the fact that modern airliners were used as ballistic missiles during the September 11, 2001, attacks. In another case, which was a precursor to the successful American homeland attacks, elite French GIGN counterterrorist police thwarted Algerian terrorists from using an airliner as a missile over Paris.

Exotic Technologies

Some technologies can theoretically be converted into weapons by terrorists who have a high degree of scientific knowledge and training. These exotic technologies include the following:

Electromagnetic Pulse Technologies. **Electromagnetic pulse (EMP) technologies** use an electromagnetic burst from a generator that can disable electronic components such as microchips. If used on a sizable scale, EMP could destroy large quantities of military or financial information. High-energy radio frequency devices are another type of generator that can disable electronic components.

Plastics. Weapons constructed from plastics and other materials such as ceramics could possibly thwart detection from metal detectors. Handguns, rifles, and bullets can be constructed of these materials.

Liquid Metal Embrittlement. Some chemicals can theoretically weaken metals when applied. They can *embrittle*, or make rigid, various metals. Should **liquid metal embrittlement** technology be obtained by motivated extremists, it would be easily transportable and could conceivably be applied to vehicles and aircraft.

Tech-Terror: Feasibility and Likelihood

The *feasibility* of terrorists' acquiring and using emerging technologies must be calculated by addressing the availability of these technologies. New and exotic technologies frequently require specialized access and knowledge to acquire, and hence not all technologies are readily available. Having said this, the old adage that "where there is a will there is a way" is very relevant, because some practitioners of the New Terrorism (such as Al Qaeda) have exhibited great patience and resourcefulness. They have also proven to be meticulous in their planning.

Technical instructions for manipulating new information technologies are readily available. In fact, a great deal of useful information is available for terrorists on the Internet, including instructions for bomb assembly, poisoning, weapons construction, and mixing lethal chemicals. Extremists who wish to use computer and Internet technologies to attack political adversaries can also obtain the technical knowledge to do so. For example, information about how to engage in computer "hacking" is easy to acquire—instructions have been published in print and posted on the Internet. There is also an underground of people who create computer viruses for reasons that range from personal entertainment to anarchistic sentiment.

The feasibility of obtaining weapons of mass destruction has increased in recent years. This has occurred in part because the scientific knowledge needed for assembling these weapons is available from a number of sources, including the Internet. Some weapons assembly requires expertise, but not necessarily extensive scientific training; an example would be radiological weapons, which are relatively unsophisticated devices because they simply require toxic radioactive materials and a dispersion device. Other devices, such as nuclear weapons components, have so far been exceedingly difficult to assemble or steal. Nevertheless, the feasibility of obtaining weapons of mass destruction has increased not only because of the dissemination of technical know-how, but also because terrorists do not necessarily need to acquire new or exotic technologies. Older technologies and materials—such as pesticides, carbon monoxide, and ammonium nitrate and fuel oil (ANFO)—can be used to construct high-yield weapons. Aerosols and other devices can also be used as relatively unsophisticated delivery systems.

The *likelihood* that new technologies will be acquired and used is perhaps a moot consideration, because modern terrorists have already acquired and used many of these technologies. For example, apparently apolitical and anarchistic hackers—some of them teenagers—have vandalized information and communications systems, thus demonstrating that cyberwar is no longer an abstract concept. There is little reason to presume that this trend will diminish and many good reasons to presume that it will increase. The increasing availability of new technologies, when combined with the motivations and morality of the New Terrorism, suggests very strongly that technology will be an increasingly potent weapon in the arsenals of terrorists.

Endnote: Soft Targets and Symbolism

Terrorists throughout the postwar era tended to select targets that were both symbolic and "soft." **Soft targets** include civilians and passive military targets, which are unlikely to offer resistance until after the terrorists have inflicted casualties or other destruction. This tactic was sometimes quite effective in the short term and occasionally forced targeted interests to grant concessions.

This trend continued unabated into the early 2000s, even as new movements and the New Terrorism supplanted the previous terrorist environment. Those who practice the New Terrorism have regularly selected soft targets that symbolize enemy interests. These targets are chosen in part because of their symbolic value but also because they are likely to result in significant casualties. Suicide bombers have become particularly adept at maximizing casualties. For example, in May 2002, 14 people (11 of them French workers) were killed by a suicide bomber outside a hotel in downtown Karachi, Pakistan.

Thus, regardless of terrorist motives or typologies, it is highly likely that violent extremists will continue to attack passive symbolic targets.

CONTROLLING TERRORISM

Counterterrorist experts in the modern era will be required to concentrate on achieving several traditional counterterrorist objectives. These objectives can realistically, and in a practical sense, only minimize rather than eliminate the terrorist threats of the near future. Objectives include the following:

- Disrupting and preventing terrorist conspiracies from operationalizing their plans
- Deterring would-be terrorist cadres from crossing the line between extremist activism and political violence
- Implementing formal and informal international treaties, laws, and task forces to create a cooperative counterterrorist environment
- Minimizing physical destruction and human casualties

It is clear that no single model or method for controlling terrorism will apply across different timelines or terrorist environments. Because of this reality, the process for projecting counterterrorist models must include a longitudinal framework based on both theory and practical necessity. The *theoretical* models used in the near future will continue to reflect the same categories of responses seen in the recent past. These include the use of force, operations other than war, and legalistic responses (all discussed at length in Chapter 13). The *practicality* of these models will require them to be continually updated and adapted to emerging terrorist threats. With these adaptations, perhaps terrorism will be controlled to some degree by keeping dissident terrorists off balance and state terrorists isolated—thereby preventing them from having an unobstructed hand in planning and carrying out attacks or other types of political violence.

New Fronts in a New War

Counterterrorism must adapt to the fact that terrorist typologies in the early 2000s will reflect the ability of extremists to operate within emerging political environments. During this adaptation process, it is important to remember that [counterterrorist] instruments are complementary, and the value of using them should be—and generally are—more than just the sum of the parts. If the process is not properly managed, the value may be less than the sum of the parts, because of the possibility of different instruments working at cross purposes.[4]

Thus, as some terrorist environments continue to be characterized by the New Terrorism, one projection for near-term counterterrorism stands out: Models must be flexible enough to respond to new environments and must avoid stubborn reliance on methods that "fight the last war." This reality is particularly pertinent to the war against terrorism that was declared in the aftermath of the September 11, 2001, attacks on the United States. Unlike previous wars, the new war was declared against *behavior* as much as against terrorist groups and revolutionary cadres. The "fronts" in the new war are amorphous and include the following:

Covert "Shadow Wars." These are fought outside of public scrutiny using unconventional methods. **Shadow wars** require the deployment of military, paramilitary, and coercive covert assets to far regions of the world.

Homeland Security Measures. These are required to harden targets, deter attacks, and thwart conspiracies. Internal security requires the extensive use of nonmilitary security personnel, such as customs officials, law enforcement agencies, and immigration authorities.

Counterterrorist Financial Operations. These operations are directed against bank accounts, private foundations, businesses, and other potential sources of revenue for terrorist networks. Intelligence agencies can certainly "hack" into financial databases, but a broad-based coalition of government and private financial institutions is necessary for this task.

Global Surveillance of Communications Technologies. This requires surveillance of technologies including telephones, cell phones, and e-mail. Agencies specializing in electronic surveillance, such as the American National Security Agency, are the most capable institutions to carry out this mission.

Identifying and Disrupting Transnational Terrorist Cells and Support Networks. This requires international cooperation to track extremist operatives and "connect the dots" on a global scale. Primary responsibility for this task lies with intelligence communities and law enforcement agencies.

The new fronts in the new war clearly highlight the need to continuously upgrade physical, organizational, and operational counterterrorist measures; flexibility and creativity are essential. Failure to do so is likely to hinder adaptation to the terrorist environment of the early 2000s. Thus, for example, the inability to control and redress long-standing bureaucratic and international rivalries could be disastrous in the new environment.

The Continued Utility of Force

Violent coercion will continue to be a viable counterterrorist option. The dismantling of terrorist cells, especially in disputed regions where they enjoy popular support, cannot be accomplished solely by the use of law enforcement, intelligence, or nonmilitary assets. Situations sometimes require a warlike response by military assets ranging in scale from small special operations units to large deployments of significant air, naval, and ground forces. The stark use of force, when successfully used against terrorists, has a demonstrated record that is relevant for coercive counterterrorist policies in the near future. This record includes the following successes:

Elimination of terrorist threats. This occurred, for example, in the successful hostage rescue operations by West German and Israeli Special Forces in Mogadishu and Entebbe, respectively, in 1977.

General deterrence *by creating a generalized climate in which the risks of political violence outweigh the benefits.* An example of this is Saddam Hussein's use of the Iraqi military to suppress armed opposition from Iraqi Kurds in the north and the so-called Marsh Arabs in the south—this sent an unmistakable message to other would-be opponents.

Specific deterrence *against a specific adversary that communicates the high risks of further acts of political violence.* One example is the American air raids against Libya during Operation El Dorado Canyon in 1986.

Demonstrations of national will. We see this, for example, in the deployment of hundreds of thousands of Indian troops to Kashmir in 2002 after a series of terrorist attacks and provocations by Kashmiri extremists, some of whom acted as Pakistani proxies.

History has shown, of course, that military and paramilitary operations are not always successful. As discussed in previous chapters, some of these operations have ended in outright disaster. Others have been marginally successful. It is therefore likely that future uses of force will likewise fail on occasion. Nevertheless, the past utility of this option, and its symbolic value, are certain to encourage its continued use throughout the modern counterterrorist era. Absent a viable threat of force, states are highly unlikely to dissuade committed revolutionaries or aggressive states from committing acts of political violence.

Countering Terrorist Financial Operations

Mohammed Atta, the leader of the September 11 cell, was closely affiliated with Al Qaeda members operating in several countries. He apparently received wire transfers of money in Florida from operatives in Egypt and was in close contact with Syrians who managed financial resources in Hamburg, Germany.[5] Estimates suggest that the total cost of the attack was $300,000, which is a small sum for the amount of destruction and disruption that resulted.[6] Very few if any of these funds came from state sponsors. They instead came from private accounts run by Al Qaeda operatives.

It is very clear from the Atta example that Al Qaeda—and logically, other practitioners of the New Terrorism—have successfully established themselves as "stateless revolutionaries." It may be recalled from Chapter 9 that stateless revolutionaries are minimally dependent on the largesse of state sponsors. Some financial support does, of course, covertly emanate from state sponsors, but the modern terrorist environment exhibits less *dependency* than previous environments on state sponsorship. Stateless revolutionaries have, in fact, demonstrated that the world's financial systems and profits from transnational crime provide resources that can ensure their financial (and hence, operational) independence. This profile is unlikely to change in the near future.

Finding Hidden Fortunes

Terrorists and their extremist supporters have amassed sizable amounts of money from a variety of sources, including the following:

- Transnational crime—for example, the trafficking and smuggling activities of Colombian and Sri Lankan groups
- Personal fortunes—for example, Osama bin Laden's personal financial resources
- Extortion—for example, the criminal profits of Abu Sayyaf
- Private charities and foundations—for example, front organizations that support Hezbollah and Hamas

Large portions of these assets were deposited in anonymous bank accounts, thus allowing funds to be electronically transferred between banking institutions and other accounts internationally in mere minutes. During the months following the September 11, 2001, attacks, government agencies from a number of countries made a concerted effort to identify and trace the terrorists' banking accounts. Law enforcement and security agencies also began to closely scrutinize the activities of private charities and foundations in an attempt to determine whether they were "front groups" secretly funneling money to supporters of terrorist organizations.

These investigative practices have not been without controversy, and they will continue to provoke serious debate in the immediate future. For example, one problem encountered in the United States came from local coordinators of private charities and foundations, who argued vehemently that their groups were not fronts for terrorist-support groups. Another problem encountered on a global scale involved the tradition and policy of **customer anonymity** found in some banking systems, such as those of the Cayman Islands and Switzerland. Many mainstream executives and policymakers were very hesitant to endorse an abrogation of the sanctity of customer anonymity. Their rationale was straightforward: Individual privacy and liberty could be jeopardized if security officers were permitted to peruse the details of hundreds of thousands of bank accounts looking for a few terrorist accounts that might or might not exist. From a practical business perspective, customers could reconsider doing business with financial institutions that could no longer guarantee their anonymity, thus causing these institutions to lose customers. These tensions will not abate in the near future and will require that a balance be developed between the need for international security and the need to preserve the sanctity of long-standing banking practices.

Terrorist Adaptations

Terrorists adapted quickly to the new focus on financial counterterrorist measures. Implementing a process that apparently began during the global crackdown after September 11, 2001, terrorists and their supporters began to transfer their assets out of international financial institutions, where they were vulnerable to seizure. This is an adaptation that serves as a strong indicator for terrorist behavior in the near future.

Operatives removed assets from financial institutions and began investing in valuable commodities such as gold, diamonds, and other precious metals and gems.[7] From the perspective of counterterrorist officials, this tactic can potentially cripple the global effort to electronically monitor, track, and disrupt terrorist finances. From the perspective of terrorists and their supporters, the chief encumbrance of this adaptation is the fact that they could become literally burdened with transporting heavy suitcases filled with precious commodities. However, this is an acceptable encumbrance, because it is very difficult for counterterrorist agents to identify and interdict couriers or to locate and raid repositories. It is likely that this adaptation will continue to be made as circumstances require, perhaps making it virtually impossible to trace terrorists' assets that have been skillfully hidden.

Another adaptation used by terrorists is through an ancient practice known as *hawala*. *Hawala* is a transnational system of brokers who know and trust each other. Persons wishing to transfer money approach *hawala* brokers and, for a fee, ask the broker to transfer money to another person. Using the name and location of the recipient, the initial broker will contact a broker in the recipient's country. The recipient of the money contacts the local *hawala* broker, who delivers the money. In order to prevent fraud, the sending broker gives the recipient broker a code number (such as the string of numbers on a $20 bill). The recipient (who receives the code from the sender) must give the broker this code number in order to pick up his funds. No records are kept of the transaction, thus assuring anonymity. This is a useful system, because it relies on an "honor system" to succeed, and money is never physically moved.

Countering Extremism

Extremist ideologies and beliefs are the fertile soil for politically violent behavior. Ethnocentrism, nationalism, ideological intolerance, racism, and religious fanaticism are core motivations for terrorism. History has shown that coercive measures used to counter these tendencies are often only marginally successful. The reason is uncomplicated: A great deal of extremist behavior is rooted in passionate ideas, long histories of conflict, and codes of self-sacrifice (explored in Chapter 3). It is difficult to forcibly reverse these tendencies, and although coercion can eliminate cadres and destroy extremist organizations, sheer repression is a risky long-term solution.

Government Responses

Assuming that policymakers in the early 2000s grasp the limitations of exclusive reliance on coercive methods, it is likely that alternative measures will be developed. Operations other than war, explored in Chapter 13, include conciliatory options. These options may provide long-term solutions to future extremism. Past reliance on conciliatory options such as peace processes, negotiations, and social reforms had some success in resolving both immediate and long-standing terrorist crises. If skillfully applied, future adaptations of these options could present extremists with options other than political violence. In the past, these options were usually undertaken with the presumption that some degree of coercion would be kept available should the conciliatory options fail; this is a pragmatic consideration that is likely to continue.

Societal Responses

Because extremism has historically originated primarily from domestic conflict (but sometimes from national traumas such as invasions), it is important that future efforts to counter extremist ideas incorporate societal and cultural responses. It is also important that new societal and cultural norms reflect demographic changes and political shifts. As discussed in previous chapters, dissent can certainly be repressed, but it is rarely a long-term solution absent social reforms and political inclusion. This is an ideal that is likely to succeed in democratic systems rather than under authoritarian regimes.

The United States is a good subject for evaluating these concepts. In the aftermath of the political turmoil of the 1960s and 1970s, the United States underwent a slow cultural and ideological shift that began to promote concepts such as *multiculturalism* and *diversity.* These concepts were adaptations to the fact that the United States has gradually become a country in which no single demographic group will be a majority of the population in the near future, probably by the mid-21st century.[8] This is a significant ideological shift from the "melting pot" ideology of previous generations, when new immigrants, racial minorities, and religious minorities were expected to accept the cultural values of the American mainstream.

Also in the United States, grassroots efforts to promote inclusion have become common features of the social and political environment (although not without political opposition). For example, private "watchdog" organizations monitor extremist tendencies such as right-wing and neofascist movements. Some of these organizations, such as the Southern Poverty Law Center and the Anti-Defamation League, have implemented programs to promote community inclusiveness. In the public sector, government agencies have long been required to monitor and promote inclusion of demographic minorities and women in government-funded programs. Also in the public sector, the trend among local police forces shifted toward practicing variants of community-oriented policing, which in practice means that the police operationally integrate themselves as much as possible within local communities.

Societal responses must, of course, be adapted to the idiosyncrasies of each nation and region. This is difficult in many cases—and seemingly nothing more than impossibly idealistic in other cases—because a great many regimes and contending groups have little interest in reducing social tensions and often try to manipulate these tensions to their benefit.

The Case for International Cooperation

Cooperation between nations has always been essential to counterterrorist operations. International treaties, laws, and informal agreements were enacted during the postwar era to create a semblance of formality and consistency to global counterterrorist efforts. However, cooperation at the operational level was not always consistent or mutually beneficial, as illustrated by the case of the prosecution of the *Achille Lauro* terrorists, discussed in Chapter 13. In the post-September 11, 2001, era of the New Terrorism and international counterterrorist warfare, international cooperation at the operational level has become a central priority for policymakers. A good example of this priority is found in the new frontline missions of intelligence and criminal justice agencies.

Intelligence and Law Enforcement

The world's intelligence communities and criminal justice systems have always been important counterterrorist instruments. After the September 11 attacks, these institutions were tasked with increased responsibilities in the global war against terrorism—largely because of their demonstrated ability to incapacitate and punish terrorists. These institutions, perhaps more so than military institutions, are also able to apply steady and long-term pressure on terrorist networks. Intelligence and law enforcement agencies are in many cases more adept than military assets at keeping terrorists "on the run" over time. This is not to say that these institutions are a panacea for future terrorism, but international cooperation between intelligence and law enforcement agencies does provide the means to track operatives, identify networks, and interdict other assets on a global scale.

International law enforcement cooperation in particular provides worldwide access to extensive criminal justice systems that have well-established **terminal institutions** (such as prisons) for use against terrorists. Counterterrorist terminal institutions—under the jurisdiction of criminal justice and military justice systems—provide final resolution to individual terrorists' careers after they have been captured, prosecuted, convicted, and imprisoned. Applying a concept familiar to students of the administration of justice, these institutions can effectively incapacitate terrorists by ending their ability to engage in political violence or propaganda. When faced with the prospect of lifelong incarceration, terrorists are likely to become susceptible to manipulation wherein, for example, favors can be exchanged for intelligence information. In a cooperative environment, these intelligence data may be shared among allied governments.

Several important objectives are attainable through enhanced international cooperation between intelligence, law enforcement, and security institutions. These objectives—which are certain to be central considerations for counterterrorist policymakers and analysts well into the near future—include the following:

- Destabilization of terrorist networks
- Disruption of terrorist conspiracies
- Collection of intelligence from captured terrorist operatives
- Incapacitation of imprisoned operatives

An example from early 2002 illustrates how international intelligence and security cooperation can achieve these objectives.[9] Mohammed Haydar Zammar, a Hamburg-based Syrian German, was held by Syrian authorities after his capture in Morocco. Zammar had been part of the Hamburg cell that recruited Mohammed Atta, the leader of the September 11 hijackers' cell. Zammar had legally left Germany in October 2001 and traveled to Morocco, allegedly to divorce his Moroccan wife. He was captured and detained by Moroccan authorities, who deported him to Syria with the knowledge of American authorities. During his interrogation in Syria, Zammar provided very useful information about the Hamburg cell, the planning of the September 11, 2001, attacks, and details about Al Qaeda. The Germans lodged mild protests against Morocco and Syria, arguing that under international law and extradition treaties, Germany should have at a minimum been notified about Zammar's detention, deportation, and imprisonment. Nevertheless, the operation was successful.

PROSPECTS FOR TERRORISM IN THE UNITED STATES

The threat of terrorism in the United States emanates from domestic and international sources. Domestic sources of terrorism include threats from right-wing racial supremacist groups and movements that have succeeded the Patriots. Potential threats from left-wing sources come primarily from single-issue groups, such as radical environmentalists. International sources of terrorism emanate primarily from cell-based religious extremist networks that replicate the Qaeda model.

The Future of International Terrorism in the United States

During the years immediately preceding and following the turn of the millennium, it has become very clear that the near future of international terrorism in the United States will be considerably threatening. Trends suggest that the United States will be a preferred target for international terrorists both domestically and abroad. Although this is not a new phenomenon, the modern terrorist environment has made the American homeland vulnerable to attack for the first time in its history. International terrorism has, of course, occurred in the United States—many of these incidents were presented in previous discussions. However, the asymmetrical nature of new threats and the destructive magnitude of newly obtainable weapons are unlike the threats inherent in previous terrorist environments. The existence of prepositioned "sleeper" agents has proven to be a real possibility. For example, an alleged Hezbollah cell was broken up in July 2000 when 18 people were arrested in Atlanta, Georgia.

Violence emanating from international sources will continue to come from Middle Eastern spillovers during the beginning of the 21st century. It is unlikely that the previous activity profile in the United States—threats from groups like Omega 7, the Provos, and the Jewish Defense League—will re-emerge on the same scale. The most significant spillover threat of the early 21st century comes from religious extremists. It is also conceivable that spillover activity from nationalists with an anti-American agenda will occur in the American homeland; these would likely be cases of the contagion effect, with newcomers imitating previous homeland incidents committed by other terrorists. Regardless of the source of international terrorism, the activity profile is almost certain to be that of the New Terrorism.

The Future of the Violent Left in the United States

The future of the terrorist left in the United States is not encouraging for would-be violent extremists. The modern political and social environment does not exhibit the same mass fervor as existed during the era that spawned the New Left, civil rights, and Black Power movements. Nor is there strong nationalism within American ethno-national communities. Perhaps most important, radical Marxism and its contemporary applications are no longer relevant to the American activist community.

Single-issue extremism is certain to be a feature of the radical left. Radical environmentalists have attracted a small but loyal constituency. New movements have also shown themselves to be adept at attracting new followers. For example, a nascent anarchist movement has taken root in the United States and other Western democracies. This movement is loosely rooted in an antiglobalist ideology that opposes alleged exploitation by prosperous nations of poorer nations in the new global economy. It remains to be seen whether violent tendencies will develop within this trend. Sporadic incidents from single-issue terrorists are likely to occur from time to time.

The Future of the Violent Right in the United States

Trends found in the recent past suggest that extremists on the fringe and far right will continue to promulgate conspiracy theories and attract a few true believers to their causes. Reactionary activists continued to attract a number of people to their causes during the 1990s and early 2000s. For example, extremist anti-abortion activism continued sporadically, and its viability was sustained by a core of dedicated true believers.

The future of the politically violent right comes from a potential weak network/weak sponsor scenario. By advocating leaderless resistance, the violent Patriot and neo-Nazi right learned the lessons of 1980s cases of terrorist groups such as the Order. Thus, conspiracies that were uncovered by law enforcement authorities beginning in the mid-1990s exhibited a covert and cell-based organizational philosophy. Possible threats also exist from religious extremists who could reinvigorate the violent moralist movement. An extremist pool still resides within the remnant Patriot movement, racial supremacist communities, and newer movements such as the neo-Confederate movement. There has also been a continued proliferation of antigovernment and racial conspiracy theories. Publications such as *The Turner Diaries*[10] and *The Myth of the Six Million*[11] continue to spread racial and anti-Semitic extremism. The promulgation of these theories keeps reactionary tendencies alive on the right.

Chapter Perspective 14.1 describes Holocaust denial, a conspiracy belief that claims to debunk the Nazi Holocaust. It is an example of reactionary sentiment illustrating the conspiracy mythology that continues to be characteristic of racial supremacist extremism.

Chapter Perspective 14.1   **Holocaust Denial[a]**

Among the many conspiracy theories found on the far and fringe right wing and among Middle Eastern extremists is the argument that the **Nazi Holocaust** (genocide against European Jews) never occurred. The underlying belief is that the Holocaust is a hoax, that the Nazis never systematically murdered any ethnic group, and that death camps such as Auschwitz were merely detention or work facilities. Holocaust denial has become a fundamental tenet for many tendencies on the reactionary right and has been repeated by fairly high-profile individuals. There have been publications and Web sites dedicated to this theory.

In the United States, this is an anti-Semitic conspiracy theory that was promulgated by two right-wing organizations—the Liberty Lobby and the Institute for Historical Review—beginning in the late 1970s and early 1980s. Neo-Nazi groups, Ku Klux Klan factions, and Patriot survivalists have all been known to cite the "hoax" of the Holocaust to justify their anti-Semitic conspiracy theories. Although Holocaust denial is mostly a White racial supremacist phenomenon in the United States, it has been endorsed by other domestic groups such as the Nation of Islam, which has historically promoted Black racial supremacy.

The conspiracy theory has found an international audience among Western neofascists, anti-Zionists, and extremist groups in the Middle East. Many of these groups and movements have adopted overtly anti-Semitic rhetoric. Holocaust denial should be considered to be a facet of broader anti-Semitic tendencies, such as the promulgation of *The Protocols of the Learned Elders of Zion*, a forgery discussed in Chapter 7.

a. For an excellent discussion of Holocaust denial, see Lipstadt, Deborah E. *Denying the Holocaust: The Growing Assault on Truth and Memory.* New York: Plume, 1994.

The Reorganization of Homeland Security in the United States

Strong proposals were made to revamp the American homeland security community within nine months of the September 11, 2001, attacks. This occurred because of the apparent failure of the pre-September 11 domestic security community to adapt to the new terrorist environment, as well as because of highly publicized operational problems.

Prior to the domestic attacks of September 11, the United States had relied on administratively separated federal law enforcement and services agencies to provide homeland security. These agencies are defined for our purposes as follows:

Law Enforcement Agencies. These are bureaus within large Cabinet agencies charged with enforcing federal criminal laws. The FBI; Drug Enforcement Administration; and Bureau of Alcohol, Tobacco, and Firearms are examples of federal law enforcement agencies. Prior to the September 11, 2001, attacks, these agencies investigated security threats in the same manner that they investigated crimes—by working cases and making arrests.

Services Agencies. These agencies regulate and manage services for the general population. Service agencies include large Cabinet agencies, regulatory agencies, and independent agencies. The departments of Health and Human Services, Energy, and Defense and the Central Intelligence Agency are examples of services agencies. Prior to the September 11 attacks, these agencies had a variety of missions, including regulating immigration, inspecting nuclear facilities, and responding to emergencies.

An abandoned ambulance sits amid the rubble of the World Trade Center in New York City after the September 11, 2001, homeland attacks.

Among law enforcement agencies, the FBI was one of the few agencies that performed a quasi-security mission, explicitly adopting as one of its primary missions the protection of the United States from foreign intelligence and terrorist threats. The FBI did this through one of its five functional areas, the Foreign Counterintelligence functional area. The FBI also established missions in several U.S. embassies to coordinate its investigations of cases with international links. Among the services agencies, several bureaus performed a variety of security missions. For example, the Secret Service (part of Treasury) protected the president, and the Federal Emergency Management Agency responded to natural and human disasters.

As discussed in Chapter 13, an ideal policy framework would have required the FBI and CIA to coordinate and share counterterrorist intelligence in a spirit of absolute cooperation. In theory, the FBI would focus on investigating possible domestic security threats, and the CIA would pass along foreign intelligence that might affect domestic security. Table 14.3 summarizes the pre-September 11, 2001, security duties of several U.S. federal agencies.

One problem that became quite clear during the year following the September 11, 2001, homeland attacks was that the old organizational model did not adapt well to the new security crisis. This failure to adapt proved to be operationally damaging; it was politically embarrassing, and it projected an image of disarray. A series of revelations and allegations called into question previous assertions by the FBI and CIA that neither agency had prior intelligence about the September 11 homeland attacks. For example, it was discovered that

- the FBI had been aware for years prior to September 2001 that foreign nationals were enrolling in flying lessons, and
- the CIA had compiled intelligence data about some members of the Qaeda cell that carried out the attacks.

These allegations were compounded by a leak to the press of a memorandum from an FBI field agent that strongly condemned the FBI Directors' and headquarters' handling of field intelligence reports about **Zacarias Moussaoui**. Moussaoui was alleged to have been a member of the September 11, 2001, Al Qaeda cell; he had been jailed prior to the attacks. Moussaoui had tried to enroll in flying classes, in which he was apparently interested only in how to *fly* airplanes and uninterested in the *landing* portion of the classes.

Policymakers and elected leaders wanted to know why neither the FBI nor the CIA had "connected the dots" to create a single intelligence profile. Serious interagency and internal problems became publicly apparent when a cycle of recriminations, press leaks, and congressional interventions damaged the "united front" image projected by the White House. Policymakers determined that problems in the homeland security community included the following:

- Long-standing interagency rivalries
- Entrenched and cumbersome bureaucratic cultures and procedures
- No central coordination of homeland security programs

Table 14.3 Federal Agencies and Homeland Security:
Before the September 11, 2001, Organizational Crisis

Prior to the September 11, 2001, organizational crisis, homeland security was the responsibility of a number of federal agencies. These agencies were not centrally coordinated, and they answered to different centers of authority. Cooperation was theoretically ensured by liaison protocols, special task forces, and oversight. In reality, there was a great deal of functional overlap and bureaucratic "turf" issues.

The following table summarizes the activity profiles of several bureaus prior to the post-September 11 organizational crisis.

	Activity Profile		
Agency	*Parent Organization*	*Mission*	*Enforcement Authority*
Central Intelligence Agency	Independent agency	Collection and analysis of foreign intelligence	No domestic authority
Coast Guard	Department of Transportation	Protection of U.S. waterways	Domestic law enforcement authority
Customs	Department of the Treasury	Examination of people and goods entering the United States	Domestic inspection, entry, and law enforcement authority
Federal Bureau of Investigation	Department of Justice	Investigating and monitoring criminal and national security threats	Domestic law enforcement authority
Federal Emergency Management Agency	Independent agency	Responding to natural and human disasters	Coordination of domestic emergency responses
Immigration and Naturalization Service	Department of Justice	Managing the entry and naturalization of foreign nationals	Domestic inspection, monitoring, and law enforcement authority
Secret Service	Department of the Treasury	Establishing security protocols for president, vice president, and special events	Domestic protection of president and vice president and special law enforcement authority (including counterfeiting)

Internationally known as symbols of U.S. financial power, the two towers of the World Trade Center burn before collapsing after the September 11, 2001, terrorist attack.

Source: "Here Is New York," Image 6327 by Limarie Cabrera; used with permission.

- Fragmentation of counterterrorist operations
- Poor coordination of counterterrorist intelligence collection and analysis
- Disconnect between field offices and Washington headquarters
- "Turf"-based conflict between the FBI and CIA

In order to remedy the highly publicized political and operational disarray of the domestic security effort, President George W. Bush in June 2002 initiated a process that completely reorganized the American homeland security community. The process led to the enactment of the Department of Homeland Security Act of 2002, which was signed into law by President Bush on November 25, 2002. The new law created a large Cabinet-level **Department of Homeland Security**, which is an organizational and conceptual expansion of the existing **Office of Homeland Security**. Because of the operational fragmentation of homeland intelligence and security—and the important fact that the original Office of Homeland Security had no administrative authority over other federal agencies—the new Department absorbed the functions of several large federal agencies.[12] The result of this massive reorganization was the creation of the third largest federal agency, behind only the Department of Veterans Affairs and the Department of Defense in size.

Table 14.4 summarizes the security duties of several U.S. federal agencies after the creation of the new department.

Table 14.4 Federal Agencies and Homeland Security:
After the September 11, 2001, Organizational Crisis

During the post-September 11, 2001, organizational crisis, the Bush administration moved to subsume the homeland security duties of several federal agencies under the jurisdiction of a new Department of Homeland Security. The purpose behind the reorganization was to bring about central operational coordination and to put an end to unproductive overlapping duties.

The following table summarizes the activity profiles of bureaus affected by the creation of the new department. It is a good case study of a nation's reorganization of national security made in response to a significant shift in a terrorist environment. It is also an example of how two security agencies that arguably precipitated the organizational crisis—the FBI and CIA—were able to maintain their independence.

| | *Activity Profile* | | |
Agency	*New Parent Organization*	*New Directorate*	*New Directorate's Duties*
Central Intelligence Agency	No change: independent agency	No change	No change: collection and analysis of foreign intelligence
Coast Guard	Department of Homeland Security	Border and Transportation Security	Coordination of all national entry points
Customs	Department of Homeland Security	Border and Transportation Security	Coordination of all national entry points
Federal Bureau of Investigation	No change: Department of Justice	No change	No change: investigating and monitoring criminal and national security threats
Federal Emergency Management Agency	Department of Homeland Security	Emergency Preparedness and Response	Coordination of national responses to terrorist incidents
Immigration and Naturalization Service	Department of Homeland Security	Border and Transportation Security	Coordination of all national entry points
Secret Service	Department of Homeland Security	Secret Service	Establishing security protocols for president and special events

Case in Point   **The Technology of Surveillance**

Electronic surveillance has moved far beyond the days when law enforcement officers literally tapped the telephone wires of criminal suspects. In the modern era, digital technologies, fiber optics, and satellite communications now allow state security agencies to enter the realm of technology-based surveillance. For example, digital **biometric technology** allows digital photographs of faces to be matched against those of wanted suspects. Biometrics was used at American football's 2001 Super Bowl championship, when cameras scanned the faces of fans as they entered the stadium and matched their digital images against those of criminal fugitives and terrorists. The game became derisively known as the "Snooperbowl."

Some of these technologies are visible and taken for granted by residents of major cities. For example, remote cameras have now become common features on London thoroughfares and at Los Angeles intersections. Other technologies are neither visible nor well known, and they have also caused concern among policy experts, politicians, and civil liberties organizations. Two of these technologies are summarized here.

Carnivore

In July 2000, it was widely reported that the FBI possessed a surveillance system that could monitor Internet communications. Called **Carnivore**, the system was said to be able to read Internet traffic moving through cooperating internet service providers. All that was required was for Carnivore to be installed at the facilities of the service providers. Under law, the FBI could not use Carnivore without a specific court order under specific guidelines, much like other criminal surveillance orders.

The FBI received a great deal of negative publicity after it was reported that the agency had evaded demands for documents in the aftermath of a Freedom of Information Act (FOIA) request filed by the Electronic Privacy Information Center, a privacy rights group. Concern was also raised by critics when it was reported in November 2000 that Carnivore had been successfully tested and that it had exceeded expectations. This report was not entirely accurate. In fact, Carnivore did not operate properly when it was used in March 2000 to monitor a criminal suspect's e-mail; it had inadvertently intercepted the e-mail of innocent Internet users. This glitch embarrassed the Department of Justice (DOJ) and angered the DOJ's Office of Intelligence Policy and Review.

Despite the political row, which continued well into 2002 (in part because of the continued FOIA litigation), Carnivore was cited as a potentially powerful tool in the new war on terrorism. Interestingly, the FBI gave Carnivore a less ominous sounding new name, redesignating the system **DCS-1000.**

Echelon

The United States' National Security Agency (NSA) manages a satellite surveillance network called **Echelon**. The NSA's network is apparently managed in cooperation with its counterparts in Australia, Canada, Great Britain, and New Zealand. Its purpose is to monitor voice and data communications.

Echelon is a kind of global "wiretap" that filters through communications using antennae, satellite, and other technologies. Internet transfers, telephone conversations, and data transmissions are the types of communications that can reportedly be intercepted. It is not publicly known how much communications traffic can be intercepted or how it is done, but the network is apparently very capable. How the traffic is tapped is unknown, but it is likely done with technologies that can pinpoint keywords and interesting Web sites. It can also be done the old-fashioned way: In 1982, an American listening device was reportedly found on a deep-sea communications cable; it was never reported whether this was an Echelon-style operation.

CHAPTER SUMMARY

This chapter explored trends that suggest the near-term future of terrorism. An underlying theme throughout this discussion was that the near future will reflect the emerging profile of the New Terrorism. Traditional terrorism is certainly still a factor, but it is no longer an exclusive or predominant model. These trends can be analyzed within the context of past terrorist typologies, with the caveat that these typologies will continue to adapt to emerging political environments. The near future of terrorism will be shaped by ongoing regional conflicts, new technologies, and renewed attacks against symbolic soft targets.

Counterterrorism in the post-September 11, 2001, era will have to adapt to new fronts in the war against terrorism. These new fronts require creative use of overt and covert operations, homeland security measures, intelligence, and cooperation among counterterrorist agencies. Disruption of terrorist financial operations will prove to be one of the most important, and challenging, priorities in the new war. Regarding prospects for terrorism in the United States, most threats in the near future will come from international religious extremists, domestic rightists, and single-issue leftists. Because of revelations about bureaucratic inefficiency in the aftermath of the September 11, 2001, attacks, the United States implemented a restructuring of its homeland security community.

A Final Thought

There is one final perspective that is worth contemplating. Throughout history, violent dissidents have claimed the lives of countless innocent people whom they labeled as enemies. Among these "enemies" have been reformers, defined as those who genuinely tried to resolve the problems and grievances that gave rise to extremist sentiment in the first place. Many of these reformers have sympathized with the plight of the groups championed by the dissidents, especially when the championed group has been in fact exploited or otherwise oppressed.

Some terrorist movements have made special work of killing and terrorizing reformers, labeling them pejoratively as "collaborators" or some other term. Why do terrorists harm these people? What possible threat can emanate from those who try to better the conditions of extremists' championed groups? The answers to these questions are straightforwardly addressed in the following quotation:

> The best defense against terrorism is a government which has the broad popular support to control terrorist activities through normal channels of law enforcement without resorting to counter-terror. Terrorists often correctly perceive that their greatest enemy is the moderate who attempts to remedy whatever perceived injustices form the basis for terrorist strength. It is often these moderates who are targets of assassinations.[13]

Thus, the true terrorist *wants* to "enrage the beast" within the state and is encouraged when the enemy becomes a genuine instrument of repression. In contrast, the true reformer understands that terrorists will not long survive when—to paraphrase Mao Zedong—the state successfully dries up the sea of the people's support for the extremists. This is a perspective that is worth remembering, but one that is too frequently forgotten when nations must reestablish stability and normalcy after terrorists strike.

Discussion Box   **Toward Big Brother?**

This chapter's Discussion Box is intended to stimulate critical debate about the possible use, by democracies and authoritarian regimes, of antiterrorist technologies to engage in surveillance.

Electronic surveillance has become a controversial practice in the United States and elsewhere. The fear is that civil liberties can be jeopardized by unregulated interception of telephone conversations, e-mail, and telefacsimiles. Detractors argue that government use of these technologies can conceivably move well beyond their legitimate application against threats from crime, espionage, and terrorism. Absent strict protocols to rein in these technologies, a worst-case scenario envisions state intrusions into the everyday activities of innocent civilians. Should this happen, critics foresee a time when privacy, liberty, and personal security become values of the past.

Discussion Questions

- How serious is the threat from abuses in the use of new technologies?
- How should new technologies be regulated? Can they be regulated?
- Is it sometimes necessary to sacrifice a few freedoms to protect national security and to ensure the long-term viability of civil liberty?
- Should the same protocols be used for domestic electronic surveillance and foreign surveillance? Why?
- What is the likelihood that new surveillance technologies will be used as tools of repression by authoritarian regimes in the near future?

KEY TERMS AND CONCEPTS

The following topics were discussed in this chapter and are found in the Glossary:

Biometric technology	Liquid metal embrittlement
Carnivore	Moussaoui, Zacarias
Customer anonymity	Nazi Holocaust
Cyberterrorism	Office of Homeland Security
DCS-1000	Shadow wars
Department of Homeland Security	Soft targets
Echelon	Specific deterrence
Electromagnetic pulse (EMP) technologies	Terminal institutions
General deterrence	Weapons of mass destruction
Hawala	

RECOMMENDED READINGS

The following publications are an eclectic assortment of recommendations that provide classic—and arguably timeless—insight into the nature of dissident resistance, ideologies of liberty, state manipulation, and revolution.

Hamilton, Alexander, John Jay, and James Madison. *The Federalist: A Commentary on the Constitution of the United States.* New York: Modern Library, 1937.

Koestler, Arthur. *Darkness at Noon.* New York: Macmillan, 1963.

Mill, John Stuart. *On Liberty,* David Spitz, ed. New York: Norton, 1975.

Moore, Barrington, Jr. *Social Origins of Dictatorship and Democracy: Lord and Peasant in the Making of the Modern World.* Boston: Beacon Press, 1966.

Orwell, George. *Animal Farm.* New York: Harcourt Brace Jovanovich, 1946.

NOTES

[1] Lesser, Ian O. "Countering the New Terrorism: Implications for Strategy." In Lesser, Ian O., Bruce Hoffman, John Arquilla, David Ronfeldt, and Michele Zanini. *Countering the New Terrorism.* Santa Monica, CA: RAND, 1999, p. 95.

[2] Laqueur, Walter. *The New Terrorism: Fanaticism and the Arms of Mass Destruction.* New York: Oxford University Press, 1999, p. 4.

[3] Stern, Jessica. *The Ultimate Terrorists.* Cambridge, MA: Harvard University Press, 1999, p. 3.

[4] Pillar, Paul R. *Terrorism and U.S. Foreign Policy.* Washington, DC: Brookings Institution Press, 2001, p. 123.

[5] Cohen, Adam. "Following the Money." *Time.* October 8, 2001.

[6] One Hamas leader bragged that suicide bombings were cheap—costing approximately $1,500 each in 2001 dollars.

[7] DeYoung, Karen, and Douglas Farah. "Al Qaeda Shifts Assets to Gold." *Washington Post.* June 18, 2002.

[8] In mid-2001, California became the first major state to become demographically diverse, meaning that no single racial or ethnic group formed a majority population.

[9] From Finn, Peter. "Key Figure in Sept. 11 Plot Held in Secret Detention in Syria." *Washington Post.* June 18, 2002.

[10] MacDonald, Andrew [William Pierce]. *The Turner Diaries.* New York: Barricade Books, 1996.

[11] Anderson, E. L. [David L. Hoggan]. *The Myth of the Six Million.* Newport Beach, CA: Noontide Press, 1969.

[12] The Department of Homeland Security absorbed the Immigration and Naturalization Service, the Coast Guard, the Customs Service, the Federal Emergency Management Agency, and many other smaller bureaus.

[13] Hurwood, Bernhardt J. *Society and the Assassin: A Background Book on Political Murder.* New York: Parents' Magazine Press, 1970, p. 146. Quoting Kirkham, James F., Sheldon Levy, and William J. Crotty. *Assassination and Political Violence.* Staff Report to the National Commission on the Causes and Prevention of Violence, vol. 8, Supplement F. Leiden, Carl. "Assassination in the Middle East," Part 3. Washington, DC: Government Printing Office, 1969, p. 4.

Appendix A

Map References

Afghanistan. After the invasion of the country by the Soviet Union, a jihad was waged to drive out the Soviet Army. Muslims from throughout the world joined the fight, forming prototypical revolutionary movements that culminated in the creation of organizations such as Al Qaeda. Al Qaeda remained active in the region bordered by Pakistan's Northwest Frontier province and along the border in Afghanistan's Paktia region.

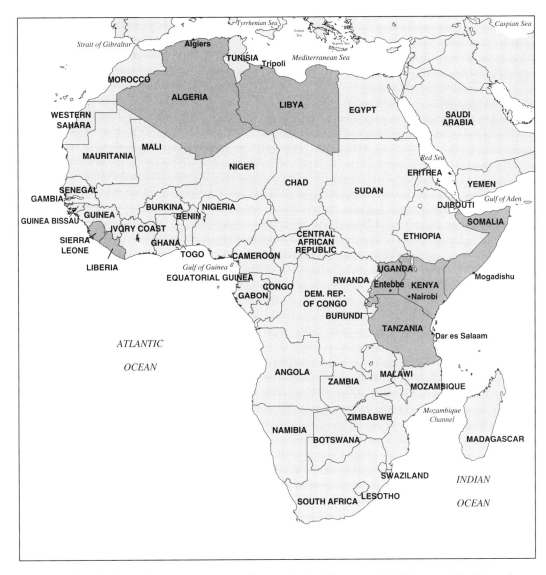

Africa. Africa has been home to most terrorist typologies. For example, Libya practiced terrorism as foreign policy. Religious dissident terrorism occurred in Algeria. Communal terrorism broke out in Rwanda. Communal and paramilitary terrorist violence became common in Somalia, Liberia, and Sierra Leone after the complete breakdown of government authority. International terrorist attacks occurred in Kenya and Tanzania.

Europe. Terrorist violence in Europe originated from ideological, ethno-nationalist, and Middle Eastern sources. The Balkans, Northern Ireland, and the Basque region of Spain have been sources of ethno-nationalist terrorism. Ideological terrorism peaked in Germany and Italy during the 1970s, while Middle Eastern spillovers continued into the new millennium.

Opposite: Central America and the Caribbean. Most terrorist violence originated in Cold War proxy conflicts and was waged by rebels, paramilitaries, and state security forces. Civil wars in El Salvador and Guatemala were markedly brutal, as was the contra insurgency in Nicaragua. The Zapatista insurgency in Mexico championed Chiapas Indians. Cuba was an active partner with the Soviet Union, fomenting and participating in conflicts in Africa and Latin America. The American base at Guantanamo Bay became the primary destination for suspected Al Qaeda members.

Indian Subcontinent. Several areas of confrontation resulted in terrorist violence. Conflicts in Sri Lanka, Kashmir, and Afghanistan have been particularly active, with ethnic and religious violence taking many thousands of lives.

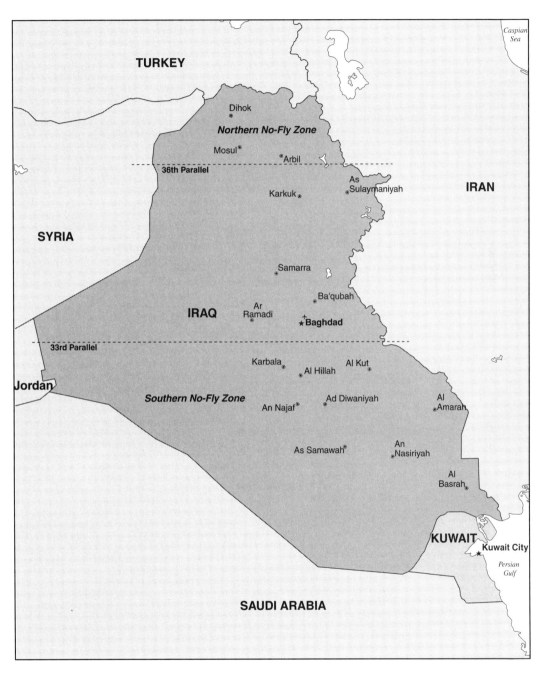

Iraq. The regime of Saddam Hussein sponsored both domestic and international state terrorism, using terror as a regular instrument of state policy. During the Anfal campaign against ethnic Kurds in northern Iraq, the Iraqi army used chemical weapons against civilians. Iraq also invaded Iran and Kuwait, and provided safe haven for terrorist operatives. After the Gulf War, American and British air forces patrolled "no-fly" zones in northern and southern Iraq to suppress Iraqi military flights.

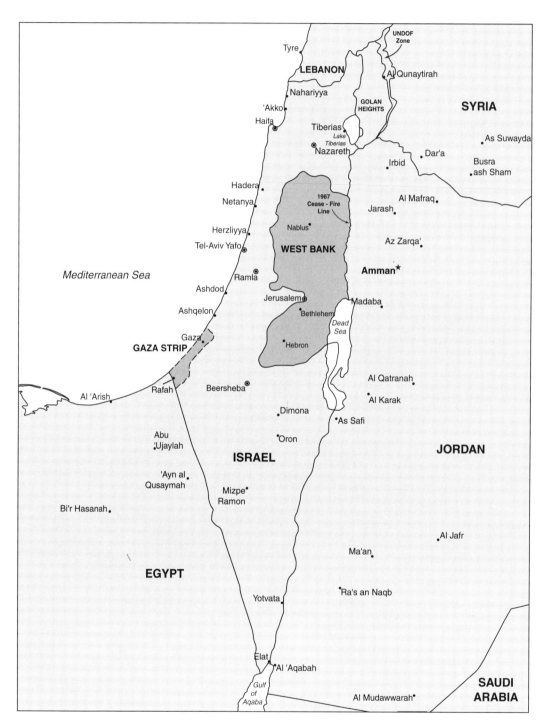

Israel, the West Bank, and Gaza. Although a geographically small region, the area has been a center for communal conflict that has frequently spilled over into the international domain and brought nations to the brink of war.

Middle East. Religious and ethno-nationalist terrorism have plagued the region for decades in innumerable conflicts.

South America. This continent has been a source for many case studies on terrorist typologies. Cases include urban guerrillas in Montevideo and Buenos Ares; state repression in Chile, Argentina, and Uruguay; dissident terrorism in Peru; and criminal terrorism in Colombia.

Southeast Asia. Terrorism has typically originated from ethno-nationalist, ideological, state, and religious sources. Significant cases of dissident and state conflict occurred during and after the Cold War era, with religious terrorists becoming prominent in the Philippines, Indonesia, and elsewhere. The killing fields of Cambodia are a special case of exceptional state-sponsored violence.

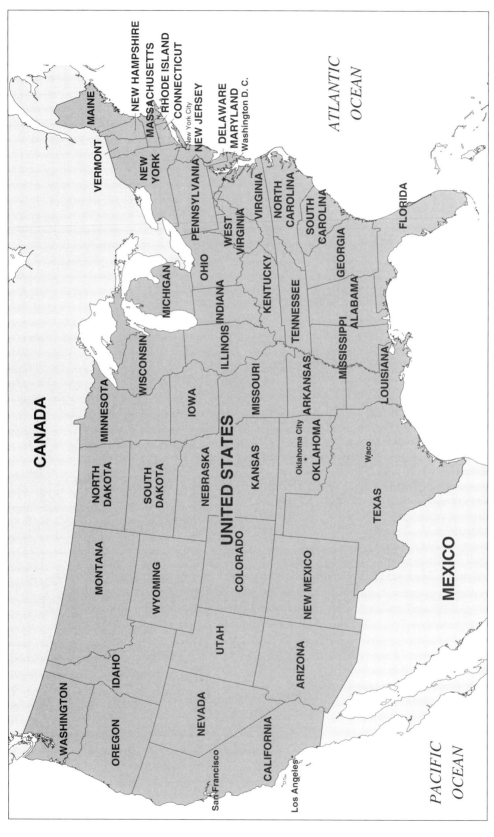

United States. Most terrorism in the United States has been characterized by low-intensity violence in urban areas, with the exceptions of the Oklahoma City bombing and the September 11, 2001 attacks.

APPENDIX B

HISTORICAL EXAMPLES

The following historical examples illustrate concepts discussed in previous chapters. They indicate the historical sweep of terrorism, the sources of terrorism, perspectives, and issues arising out of terrorist environments.

1st Century A.D.   The Zealot sect, founded in about A.D. 6 in what is now Israel, participated in communal fighting against Greeks and in the Jewish rebellion against Roman occupation. They were distinguished by their use of clandestine hit-and-run tactics.

1st Century A.D.   Zealot rebels used a traditional dagger called a sica to dispatch enemies during their rebellion against Roman occupation.

60-61   A revolt against Roman rule in eastern Britain took place, led by Queen Boudicca. Before being defeated by the Romans, the Britons destroyed Londinium, Colchester, and Verulamium, killing 70,000 inhabitants. Roman reprisals were a campaign of terror.

11th Century   The Assassin movement attempted to purge the Islamic faith and resist Crusader occupation in the Middle East by engaging in clandestine assassinations and attacks against opponents.

July 1099   During the First Crusade, Christians of the Western Church entered Jerusalem. They massacred thousands of Muslim and Orthodox Christian residents. An embellished Crusader letter sent to the Pope in Rome boasted that the blood of the Saracens reached the bridles of the Crusaders' horses.

13th Century   During the brutal Albigensian Crusade in southern France, legend holds that concerns were raised about loyal and innocent Catholics who were being killed along with members of the enemy Cathar sect. The pope's representative, Arnaud Amaury, allegedly replied, "Kill them all, God will know his own."

1298-1303; 1336-38   Anti-Jewish communal violence, known as the Rindfleisch and Armleder Massacres, occurred in Central Europe.

13th-19th Centuries   The Thuggee cult in India used a traditional noose called a *phansi* to strangle perhaps millions of victims in tribute to the goddess Kali, the destroyer.

14th-15th Centuries   Christian Europeans conducted many massacres ("pogroms") of Jews. Superstitious accusations used to justify these pogroms included: the ritual killings of Christian children during Jewish holidays (the Blood Libel), spreading the Black Plague, and desecration of the Host (holy bread and wine).

1469-1600s   Ferdinand of Aragon and Isabella of Castile united Spain and revivified the Catholic Inquisition (1478). During the Spanish Inquisition, monarchs and the church rooted out "heresies" such as Protestantism and ordered the execution of heretics during public burnings called autos-da-fé (literally, acts of faith). They also expelled Jews and Muslims (in 1492) and destroyed Moorish culture in south Spain (1609).

August 24, 1572   Catholic forces massacred thousands of French Huguenot Protestants in what became known as the St. Bartholomew's Day Massacre. It occurred during Counterreformation wars to suppress Protestant "heresies."

1604-1605   In England, Guy Fawkes hatched the Gunpowder Plot with other conspirators, intending to blow up Westminster palace on 11/5/1605 when King James I, the king's council, and Parliament would all be present. Thirty-six barrels of gunpowder had been painstakingly smuggled and placed in a cellar beneath the palace. Unfortunately for Fawkes, the plot was accidentally discovered, and he and his coconspirators were tortured and executed.

March 5, 1770   In Boston, Massachusetts, a crowd of Bostonians jeered a unit of British soldiers. They threw rocks and snowballs at the troops and dared them to shoot. Some in the crowd struck the soldiers' muskets. The British unit fired on the crowd, killing five and wounding six. The incident—called the Boston Massacre—was a precipitating event for the American Revolution.

19th Century   Russian revolutionaries became the first antistate dissidents to extensively use the printing press to publicize their cause. Leaflets and other printed documents were produced by People's Will (Narodnaya Volya) and other dissident groups.

19th Century   The United States forcibly removed American Indians from ancestral lands and resettled them on reservations. Tens of thousands of Native Americans were killed during a series of wars, resettlement campaigns, and massacres.

1808-1814   The Spanish people fought a brutal war against French military occupation and the installation of Napoleon Bonaparte's brother as king. Atrocities were common on both sides. The term *guerrilla*, or "little war," was coined to describe the hit-and-run tactics of the Spanish rebels.

1811-1816   The Luddite Riots occurred in England when unorganized factory workers rioted against unemployment and the high price of wheat, which many could not afford. The Luddites were noted for sabotaging and destroying machinery in factories, which they believed were a cause of their unemployment and misery.

1848   A series of liberal revolutions occurred in France, Austria, Hungary, Italy, and Germany. All were crushed, and authoritarian regimes were re-established. The revolutions were directed against absolutism and the conservative reaction against the liberalism that grew after the French Revolution.

February 1848   Karl Marx and Friedrich Engels published the *Manifesto of the Communist Party*.

1865 or 1866   The first Ku Klux Klan was founded in the United States in Pulaski, Tennessee, by former Confederate general Nathan Bedford Forrest and other upper-class southerners. By the 21st century, the KKK had evolved through five eras.

1870s   The Molly Maguires, a secret organization of Irish coal miners in Pennsylvania, committed acts of sabotage and terrorism against mining companies. These included assassinations and bombings.

July 1879   The Russian populist society Land and Liberty (Zemlya Volya) split into two factions—Black Repartition and People's Will (Narodnaya Volya). People's Will embarked on a campaign of terrorism and assassination, arguing that a violent intellectual elite could force government reforms.

1882-1968   Nearly 5,000 African Americans (mostly men) were "lynched" by mobs or smaller groups of White Americans. The aftermaths of these killings were often festive, with people posing for photographs near the hanged or burned corpses, and for a short time tourist-like postcards were made with pictures of the bodies.

May 3, 1886   Demonstrations and outdoor meetings by striking labor unionists in Chicago turned violent when, at one meeting that was addressed by anarchists, a bomb was thrown at the police, killing one officer. During the Haymarket Riot that ensued, several more police officers and demonstrators were killed. Seven of the anarchist speakers were sentenced to death, and four were eventually executed.

About 1900   The Black Hundreds was founded in Russia. A right-wing nationalist group, it was dedicated to defending Russia's traditional heritage. At the center of its ideology was strong and violent anti-Semitism.

20th Century   Revolutionaries commonly resorted to terrorism as part of overall strategies to overthrow existing governments and to defeat ideological rivals. Successful revolutions using terrorism occurred in Russia, China, Cuba, and Iran.

January 9, 1905   Russian police in St. Petersburg fired repeatedly on a peaceful march of 200,000 demonstrators. Hundreds were killed or wounded. They had come to present a petition of grievances to the czar. This massacre—called Bloody Sunday—was a precipitating event for the Revolution of 1905.

October 1910   The *Los Angeles Times* building was bombed, killing 21 people. Another bomb exploded at the home of the *Times*'s owner. Suspects who were prosecuted for the bombing were members of the Typographical Union and the International Union of Bridge and Structural Workers.

June 28, 1914   Gavrilo Princip, a student and member of the Serb terrorist organization Black Hand, assassinated Austrian Archduke Ferdinand and his wife in Sarajevo, Bosnia, thus igniting a series of political events leading to World War I.

1915   Ottoman Turkey committed genocide against its Armenian population. Approximately 1 million Armenians were killed. In the modern era, Armenian terrorist groups have sought revenge for the genocide, periodically attacking Turkish interests. These groups have included the Armenian Secret Army for the Liberation of Armenia, the Justice Commandos of Armenian Genocide, and the Armenian Revolutionary Army.

April 24-29, 1916   The Easter Rebellion occurred in Ireland when 2,000 men seized control of the post office in Dublin and then moved to control much of the city. The rebels declared Irish independence, but the revolt ended when British troops forced them to surrender. Fifteen Irish leaders were tried before a British court martial and executed by firing squad.

1920-1922   American automobile industrialist Henry Ford, Sr., published a series of anti-Semitic articles in *The Dearborn Independent*. The articles formed the foundation for his book *The International Jew: The World's Foremost Problem.* More than 500,000 copies were sold in the United States.

September 1920   A bomb was detonated on Wall Street in New York City. It exploded in a horse cart across the street from the House of Morgan. Thirty-five people were killed, and hundreds were injured. Anarchists or communists were suspected, but the facts of the incident were never determined.

1930s-1940s   During political purges in the ranks of the Communist Party and Red Army, Soviet leader Joseph Stalin ordered the arrests and executions of thousands of party members and army officers.

February 27, 1933   The German Reichstag (Parliament building) was set on fire. Although the fire may have been set by a single individual, Adolph Hitler blamed the communists. Many were rounded up and sent to unofficial (and brutal) "wild man camps." Several communists were tried and executed for the arson.

November 9, 1938   The German government planned and instigated anti-Jewish rioting in an evening that became known as *Kristallnacht* (the "Night of Glass"). Approximately 200 synagogues were burned, 170 Jewish homes were burned, 7,000 Jewish-owned shops were looted, 36 Jews were killed, 20,000 were arrested (most were sent to concentration camps), and countless others were injured.

August, 20, 1940   Leon Trotsky was assassinated by a blow to the head from a mountaineer's pickaxe in Coyoacan, Mexico. He had been killed on the orders of Joseph Stalin.

May 1941   Ho Chi Minh, born into an aristocratic Vietnamese family, organized the Communist-led Vietnam Independence Brotherhood League (Viet Nam Doc Lap Dong Minh Hoi)—the Viet Minh. Ho's long war ended in 1975 when the American-supported Republic of Vietnam (South Vietnam) fell.

July 1941   German Einsatzgruppen (literally, "work groups") began operating in the Eastern occupied territories. These were special squads that systematically killed Russian Jews and other Soviet nationals. By early 1943, these units had killed 1 million Jews and hundreds of thousands of other Soviet civilians.

1946-1966   Two hundred thousand people died during a period of communal violence in Colombia known as La Violencia; 112,000 were killed during La Violencia's peak in 1948-1950.

Late 1960s   ORDEN was organized in El Salvador. Originally formed by government security officers as a counterinsurgency paramilitary, ORDEN became a notorious death squad during the Salvadoran civil war.

1961-1996   Approximately 150,000 to 160,000 Guatemalans were killed, and 40,000 to 50,000 disappeared, during a 35-year civil war that included state-sponsored massacres and extensive activity by state-sponsored death squads.

1965-April 1969   Mao Zedong and the Chinese Communist Party's Central Committee waged the Great Proletarian Cultural Revolution. Purges, public humiliations, and violence were common during this ideological upheaval. Its purpose was to attack "revisionism" and create a new revolutionary generation.

March 1965   Members of the United Klans of America shot to death Viola Liuzzo in Alabama and wounded a traveling companion. Liuzzo was a northern White worker for the Southern Christian Leadership Conference.

6/2/1967   During protests in West Berlin against a visit by the Shah of Iran, German police shot to death a young pacifist named Benno Ohnesorg. He was attending his first demonstration and immediately became a martyr. Many leftists were radicalized, beginning a process that led to the formation of violent organizations such as the Baader-Meinhof Gang.

October 1967   Venezuelan revolutionary Ernesto "Che" Guevara was captured and shot by Bolivian security forces. A hero of the Cuban revolution, Guevara sought to spark a general revolution throughout Latin America. He became an icon of the far left.

April 4, 1968   The Reverend Dr. Martin Luther King, Jr., was assassinated in Memphis, Tennessee. Rioting broke out in about 125 American cities. In Washington, D.C., 11 people were killed, 1,200 injured, and 7,600 arrested. Nationwide, approximately 22,000 people were arrested, and more than 68,000 troops were mobilized to quell the disturbances. These events advanced the radicalization of the Black Power movement and were the worst episode of urban rebellion in American history.

May 1968   Several days of violent clashes occurred between students and the police at the Sorbonne in Paris. Students established the Student Soviet when the police were withdrawn from the embattled Latin Quarter.

1969-1986   Nearly 15,000 right- and left-wing terrorist attacks occurred in Italy.

June 1969   Brazilian revolutionary Carlos Marighella completed the *Mini-Manual of the Urban Guerrilla.*

August 1969   Palestinian nationalists associated with the Popular Front for the Liberation of Palestine hijacked an airliner shortly after it took off from Rome. It was flown to Damascus, Syria, where it was blown up. Leila Khaled participated in the attack, saying that it was done to publicize the Palestinian cause.

October 1969   A bomb in Chicago destroyed a monument dedicated to the Chicago police. The leftist Weatherman group was responsible for the attack.

Early 1970s   The Argentine Anti-Communist Alliance was founded by an adviser to President Juan Peron. It operated as a death squad until the 1976 military *coup d'état,* when it was integrated into Argentina's repressive security apparatus.

September 1970   Jordanian troops drove the Palestine Liberation Organization out of Jordan in a campaign against Palestinian refugee and terrorist camps. The operation became known as Black September, the name later adopted by a Palestinian terrorist organization.

1971-1979   Idi Amin ruled Uganda with an iron fist. He was responsible for the forcible expulsion of Uganda's Indian and Pakistani merchant class, as well as the deaths of at least 100,000, and perhaps as many as 500,000, Ugandans.

January 30, 1972   Elite British paratroopers fired on Irish Catholic demonstrators in Londonderry, Northern Ireland. The incident became known as Bloody Sunday. This was a seminal incident in the armed conflict waged by the Provisional Irish Republican Army.

September 1972   Eight members of Black September captured nine Israeli Athletes and killed two others at the Olympic Village during the Munich Olympics. Five terrorists and all nine athletes were killed during a rescue attempt by the Bavarian police.

1974   The Weather Underground Organization in the United States disseminated its manifesto, *Prairie Fire.* It also began disseminating a periodical, *Osawatomie.* The purpose of these publications was to establish an underground revolutionary press to support their movement.

Fall 1974   The Provisional Irish Republican Army launched a bombing campaign in England. Targets included pubs in Guildford and Woolwich, a telephone exchange in Coventry, military clubs in the West End, post office boxes, locations in Chelsea and Belgravia, Harrods Department Store, and the Tower of London. Dozens were killed or injured.

1975-1979   The communist Khmer Rouge governed Cambodia with extreme brutality. During their rule, up to 2 million Cambodians (30% of the population) died from executions, starvation, exhaustion, and torture.

1975 to mid-1980s   The Spanish government implemented democratic social reforms in the northern Basque region that gradually undermined Basque support for the ETA terrorist group.

December 1975   Terrorist Carlos the Jackal and his comrades seized 70 hostages at an OPEC ministers' meeting in Vienna, Austria. The terrorists eventually flew to Algeria with 35 hostages, but not before they could do so in front of television cameras.

December 2, 1975   South Moluccan terrorists seized a train near Beilen, Netherlands, taking passengers as hostages. They were nationalists seeking independence from Indonesia for the Molucca Islands. Three people were killed in the incident.

June 27, 1976   An Air France Airbus was hijacked to Entebbe, Uganda, by pro-Palestinian terrorists. Israeli passengers were taken hostage. The terrorists included five members of the Popular Front for the Liberation of Palestine and two West German members of Revolutionary Cells. They held the hostages until their rescue by Israeli commandos on July 4.

July 4, 1976   Israeli commandos attacked an airport in Entebbe, Uganda, to rescue 103 hostages taken when an Air France Airbus was hijacked by Palestinian and West German terrorists. Three hostages and the commander of the Israeli unit were killed. All of the terrorists were eliminated by being either killed or possibly captured.

September 10, 1976   Croatian terrorists exploded a bomb in New York, killing a policeman. They then hijacked a TWA jet en route from New York to Canada. They forced the plane to fly over London and Paris, dropping propaganda leaflets.

September 21, 1976   Orlando Letelier, the exiled former foreign minister for Chilean president Salvador Allende, was assassinated in Washington, D.C. A bomb exploded in his car in Embassy Row, killing him and Ronni Moffitt, his American aid. DINA, the Chilean secret police, was implicated in his murder.

September 5, 1977   Members of the German Red Army Faction kidnapped industrialist Hanns-Martin Schleyer, killing four people during the incident. On October 19, a note announcing Schleyer's execution was received. His body was found in the trunk of a car.

October 1977   West German commandos attacked an airport in Mogadishu, Somalia, to rescue 87 hostages taken when a Lufthansa Boeing 737 was hijacked by Palestinian supporters of Red Army Faction prisoners held in West German prisons. Three terrorists were killed, and all of the hostages were rescued.

1978-1995   During a 17-year FBI manhunt, Theodore Kaczynski, also known as the Unabomber, killed three people and injured 22 in a series of bombings.

March 16, 1978   Former Italian Prime Minister Aldo Moro was kidnapped in Rome by the Red Brigades. After the Italian government refused to release jailed Red Brigades members, Moro's body was found in the trunk of a parked car on May 9 after a telephone tip.

August 1978   Croatian terrorists seized hostages at the West German consulate in Chicago, Illinois.

September 11, 1978   Dissident Bulgarian writer and radio broadcaster Georgi Markov died in London. He had been assassinated by an agent of the Bulgarian communist regime of Todor Zhikov. On September 7, the assassin had injected a poisoned pellet into Markov's right thigh with a specially constructed umbrella that had a built-in spring gun.

November 4, 1979   The U.S. embassy in Tehran, Iran, was attacked by Islamic revolutionaries. All personnel inside the embassy were taken hostage, the last of whom were released 444 days later.

December 1979   The Soviet Army invaded Afghanistan and quickly occupied the major population centers. Afghani rebels, calling themselves mujahideen (holy warriors), took to the countryside and waged a guerrilla war that killed approximately 15,000 Soviets before they withdrew. Fighting alongside the Afghani mujahideen were thousands of "Afghan Arabs," including Osama bin Laden.

1980s   Violence escalated in Peru's Upper Huallaga Valley between Peruvian *narcotraficantes* (drug traffickers), Marxist rebels, and security forces. All sides vied for dominance in the valley, which had become the primary coca-producing region in the world.

1980s   Colombian drug cartels killed hundreds of public officials, including police officers, judges, presidential candidates, and criminal justice employees.

April 1980   An attempt to rescue American hostages held in the U.S. embassy in Tehran, Iran, was aborted when several rescue aircraft (which were to rendezvous in the Iranian desert) developed mechanical and other problems. Disaster occurred when a helicopter collided with an aircraft on the ground in Iran. Eight personnel were killed.

August 1980   In Bologna, Italy, a bomb at a train station killed 85 people and wounded 180. The bomb had been detonated by neofascists calling themselves the Armed Revolutionary Nuclei.

October 1980   German neo-Nazis detonated a bomb in Munich during the city's Oktoberfest beer festival, killing 17 people.

May 1981   A Brinks armored car was robbed in Nyack, New York. The perpetrators were former members of the Weather Underground Organization, Students for a Democratic Society, Black Panther Party, the Republic of New Africa, and the Black Liberation Army.

December 17, 1981   U.S. Army Brigadier General James Dozier was kidnapped in Milan by the Red Brigades. He was rescued on 1/28/1982 by Italian security forces.

April 1983   A neo-Nazi group calling itself the Order initiated a campaign of violence, hoping to foment a race war in the United States that would lead to the creation of an Aryan homeland. Among other actions, the Order engaged in bank and armored car robberies and murdered an outspoken Jewish talk-radio host. Their campaign ended in December 1994.

December 2, 1983   The Basque ETA bombed eight American facilities in Spain to protest U.S. policy in Central America.

December 16, 1983   The Provisional Irish Republican Army bombed Harrods Department Store in London.

May 8, 1985   Thirty-eight people were killed and more than 200 injured at a soccer riot in Brussels, Belgium. The riot was started by racist skinheads from France, Denmark, Britain, and Belgium. Most of the victims were racial minorities.

June 1985   Hijackers belonging to Lebanon's Hezbollah hijacked TWA Flight 847, taking it on a high-profile and media-intensive odyssey around the Mediterranean.

October 1985   Israeli jets attacked the Palestine Liberation Organization headquarters near Tunis, Tunisia. The attack sent a symbolic message of Israeli determination, but the incident did nothing to dissuade the PLO from using terrorist methods.

December 27, 1985   The Abu Nidal Organization carried out simultaneous attacks at the Rome and Vienna airports. In Rome, grenades and automatic rifle fire at the El Al counter killed 15 and wounded 70. In Vienna, two were killed and 46 wounded.

January 24, 1987   Four Americans were kidnapped in Beirut, the largest single kidnapping of Americans in Lebanon.

April 1987   Ethnic Tamil rebels in Sri Lanka hijacked several busses. They separated out ethnic Sinhalese passengers, who were mostly soldiers and their families. They then killed 127 of them, including women and children.

November 1987   Operatives from North Korea bombed a Korean Air Lines flight, killing more than 100 people.

November 25, 1987   Two Palestinians flew motorized hang gliders into Israel from Lebanon. One landed inside an Israeli army facility and killed five soldiers before being killed himself.

February 1988   U.S. Marine Lt. Colonel William Higgins was kidnapped by terrorists in Beirut, Lebanon. He was later executed by his captors (most likely in July 1988), who released a videotape of his hanged body to the media.

February 1989   The Ayatollah Ruhollah Khomeini, spiritual leader of Iran, issued a *fatwa,* or religious order, to assassinate author Salman Rushdie. Rushdie had authored a book entitled The Satanic Verses, which many Muslims considered to be blasphemous. A $2.5 million bounty was placed for Rushdie's death.

June 1989   Units of the Chinese People's Liberation Army put down a large and protracted demonstration in Tiananmen Square in Beijing. Several thousand demonstrators were killed or wounded. Demonstrators had demanded greater liberty and political rights. They erected a statue that they called the Goddess of Democracy, which was crushed by a PLA tank.

August 1989   Islamic Jihad bombed a French UTA airliner in Chad, killing 171 people.

1990s   The collapse of communism and the Soviet-led Eastern Bloc severely affected the violent left. When their chief ideological patron—the Soviet Union—dissolved, state sponsorship dried up, and Europe-based training facilities and safe houses were closed.

1992-1994   Thousands of suspected terrorists and supporters were prosecuted before special antiterrorist courts in Algeria. Most were convicted, and many were sentenced to death.

Mid-1990s   Terrorist groups and their supporters began to routinely acquire and use new information and communications technologies.

1992-1998   Approximately 75,000 Algerians were killed during fighting between Islamic extremists and the government. Terrorism was commonly used by the extremists. During the conflict, about 20,000 Algerians went missing.

February 29, 1992   Bosnia-Herzegovina declared independence from Yugoslavia. Bosnian Serbs, backed by the Yugoslav army, refused to accept Bosnian independence. The subsequent fighting precipitated many acts of terrorism, including genocidal "ethnic cleansing."

1993   The Peruvian government convinced Shining Path leader Abimail Guzmán to renounce violence and offered an amnesty to members of the movement. Approximately 5,500 members eventually surrendered, thus ending the worst period of the insurgency.

February 16, 1993   Two car bombs were detonated in Bogotá, the capital of Colombia. Four people were killed and more than 120 injured in the explosions. Government officials said the attacks were the work of cocaine *narcotraficantes*.

June 1993   The United States fired cruise missiles against Iraqi intelligence facilities in Baghdad. The attack was in reprisal for a failed Iraqi plot to assassinate former president George Bush during a visit to Kuwait in April.

October 1993   During an operation to capture top commanders of Somali warlord Mohammed Farah Aideed's militia, U.S. Army Rangers became involved in intense urban combat. The world's press broadcast graphic images of the bodies of American military personnel being dragged through the streets of Mogadishu, Somalia.

1994   Marauding Hutu and Tutsi militias in Rwanda committed genocide against civilians of these ethnic groups, leaving over 500,000 dead.

April 6, 1994   Rwandan President Juvenal Habyarimana died when his plane was hit by two rockets as he returned to Rwanda from Tanzania. Hutu soldiers and militias used the assassination as a pretext to begin the Rwandan genocide, claiming that Tutsi rebels had killed the president. Responsibility for the assassination was never clearly established.

March 1995   The Japanese religious cult Aum Shinrikyō released sarin nerve gas into the Tokyo subway system. Twelve people died, and thousands were injured.

April 1995   In the immediate aftermath of the bombing of the Alfred P. Murrah Federal Building in Oklahoma City, Oklahoma, many media reports stated that the incident was almost certainly of Middle Eastern origin, when in reality it was the work of rightist extremists from the United States.

September 1995   The *Washington Post* published the 35,000-word manifesto of Theodore Kaczynski, also known as the Unabomber. Kaczynski had communicated to the *Post* and the *New York Times* that he would end his 17-year bombing campaign if they published his indictment of technological society.

January 1996   Yehiya Ayyash, Hamas's expert bomb maker, better known as the Engineer, was assassinated when his cell phone exploded next to his ear as he was using it.

January and May 1996   The Jammu and Kashmir Islamic Front (JKIF) claimed responsibility for car bombings in New Delhi, India, and a bus bombing in Rajasthan, where about 40 people died. The JKIF was based in Pakistan, which considers them to be freedom fighters.

April 1996   Targeting the Egyptian tourism industry, Islamic terrorists shot and threw hand grenades at a group of Western tourists outside a Cairo hotel. Eighteen tourists were killed.

July 6, 1996   The Grey Wolves, a Turkish nationalist extremist group, was implicated in the assassination of a Turkish Cypriot journalist. The journalist, Kutlu Adali, had criticized Turkish policy in Cyprus.

September 14, 1996   A Mexican law enforcement commander and two agents were assassinated in Mexico City by *narcotraficantes,* most likely members of the Arellano-Felix drug enterprise based in Tijuana, Mexico.

December 1996   Members of Peru's Tupac Amaru Revolutionary Movement—not affiliated with Uruguay's Tupamaros—took over the Japanese ambassador's residence in the capital of Lima. Hundreds of hostages were taken. Peruvian security forces stormed the residence and ended the crisis in April 1997.

January 1997   A bomb was detonated in Atlanta, Georgia, at a family health clinic that provided abortion services. A second bomb was detonated soon thereafter; it had been timed to explode after emergency response teams arrived on the scene.

January 16, 1997   Two bombs exploded at an abortion clinic in Sandy Springs, Georgia. The Army of God, which had claimed responsibility for prior anti-abortion attacks, was suspected.

February 23, 1997   A lone Palestinian gunman opened fire on tourists atop the Empire State Building in New York City. One Danish national was killed. The nationalities of wounded tourists included people from the United States, Argentina, Switzerland, and France.

April 28, 1998   Bishop Juan José Gerardi was killed in Guatemala, most likely at the hands of a right-wing death squad. He was beaten to death with a cinder block days after releasing the results of a Catholic Church study into human rights abuses during the Guatemalan civil war. The Church study, entitled "Guatemala: Never Again," estimated that the government was responsible for three quarters of the 150,000 people killed and 50,000 disappearances.

June 1997   Mir Aimal Kansi, a Pakistani wanted for the 1993 shootings at the head-quarters of the Central Intelligence Agency in northern Virginia, was arrested in Pakistan by a FBI team. His arrest was the culmination of a fugitive manhunt that had offered a $2 million bounty for his capture.

May 1998   Voters in Ireland and Northern Ireland overwhelmingly approved the Good Friday Agreement of 4/10/1998. It was a milestone in the peace process. The agreement established a process for creating an assembly and disarming the warring paramilitaries.

August 7, 1998   Two car bombs exploded at the U.S. embassies in Nairobi, Kenya, and Dar es Salaam, Tanzania. More than 250 people were killed, and about 5,000 were wounded. Islamic extremists with ties to the Qaeda network were responsible for the attacks.

December 24, 1999   Hijackers seized an Indian airliner and took it on an odyssey from Nepal to Pakistan, India, the United Arab Emirates, and Afghanistan. The hijackers initially demanded $200 million in ransom, the release of 35 Kashmiri nationalists from Indian custody, and the body of a Kashmiri nationalist.

March 2000   An FBI operation to monitor the e-mail of a criminal suspect went awry when its Carnivore surveillance system inadvertently tapped into and read the e-mail of innocent people. This caused an internal row within the Department of Justice. It later exacerbated political controversy about use of the technology.

2001-2002   The use of suicidal "human bombs" intensified during the Palestinian *intifadeh* against Israel. Palestinian secular nationalists and radical Muslims both used the tactic.

January 2001   Biometric technology was used at the American Super Bowl game when cameras scanned fans as they entered the stadium and matched their digital images with those of criminal fugitives and suspected terrorists.

9/11/2001 Terrorists hijacked four airliners. Two of the planes were crashed into the twin towers of the World Trade Center in New York City, causing them to collapse. One plane was crashed into the Army section of the Pentagon building. The final plane crashed into rural Pennsylvania after passengers struggled to regain control of the aircraft.

September 2001 A global "war on terrorism" was declared in the aftermath of the September 11 attacks on the United States.

Late 2001 Letters containing anthrax were sent through the U.S. postal system in the New York and Washington, D.C., areas. Several people were infected, some fatally. This was the first significant attack using a biological agent.

November 2001 Al Qaeda leader Osama bin Laden spoke before a group of followers about the attacks of September 11, 2001. The meeting was videotaped and released to the media. It was one of several videotapes that were produced and released by bin Laden and his followers.

December 11, 2001 The chairman of the Jewish Defense League and another JDL member were arrested on charges of conspiring to bomb an Islamic mosque and the offices of a U.S. Congressman in Los Angeles. The chairman had previously said that Arabs "need a wakeup call."

December 13, 2001 As a bus carrying about 45 Jewish civilians traveled in the West Bank, gunmen detonated two bombs and raked the bus and another vehicle with gunfire and grenades. Hamas claimed responsibility for the attack, which killed about 10 people and wounded more than 30. Hamas carried out this and many other attacks to end Israeli occupation of the West Bank and Gaza.

Early 2002 Intelligence agencies from Morocco and the United States collaborated on sharing information and interrogations of Al Qaeda suspects. At least one terrorist conspiracy was foiled, and important suspects were arrested.

January 2002 Al Qaeda prisoners began to arrive in military custody at the U.S. base in Guantanamo Bay, Cuba. They hailed from dozens of countries, and hundreds were eventually held for interrogation.

January 2002 *Wall Street Journal* journalist Daniel Pearl was kidnapped by terrorists in Pakistan. Photographs of Pearl in captivity were sent to the media. The terrorists later videotaped his execution and released the tape to the press.

February 2002 Religious fighting broke out in India between Hindu and Muslim mobs. It began when Muslim extremists killed scores of Hindu activists aboard a train, and Hindu mobs retaliated by killing hundreds of Muslims.

May 8, 2002 An American citizen who joined and was trained by the Qaeda network was arrested at Chicago's O'Hare International Airport. He was suspected of planning to build and detonate a radiological bomb in the United States.

May 8, 2002 A suicide bomber, possibly affiliated with al Qaeda, detonated a car bomb next to a shuttle bus at a hotel in downtown Karachi, Pakistan. Fourteen people were killed, 11 of them French civilian workers.

June 2002 After a significant political row involving the handling of counterterrorism intelligence by the FBI and CIA, President George W. Bush began a major reorganization of the U.S. homeland security establishment.

June 2002   Israel began construction on a fence system to seal off the West Bank from Israel. The purpose of the fence was to block terrorist infiltration routes.

June 18, 2002   A 22-year-old Hamas terrorist detonated a suicide bomb in a bus in Jerusalem, killing 19 people and wounding at least 55. Many of the victims were high school children. It was the 69th suicide bombing in 21 months. During that period, 547 Israelis and 1,712 Palestinians were killed. The terrorist's family proudly referred to him as a "martyr."

Appendix C

Recommended Web Sites

CHAPTER 1

The following Web sites provide general information about terrorism.

Anti-Defamation League: www.adl.org

RAND: www.rand.org

Southern Poverty Law Center: www.splcenter.org

Terrorism Research Center: www.terrorism.com

U.S. Department of State: www.state.gov/www/global/terrorism

CHAPTER 2

The following Web sites illustrate the classical ideological continuum and the nature of extremism.

British National Party: http://www.bnp.org.uk/links.html

Council of Conservative Citizens: http://www.cofcc.org

Earth First! Radical Environmental Journal: http://www.earthfirstjournal.org

Front National (France): http://www.front-national.com

Socialist Party USA: http://www.sp-usa.org

CHAPTER 3

The following Web sites provide links to examples of the reasons given for political agitation, as explained by activist organizations and movements.

European Federation of Green Parties: http://www.europeangreens.org

National Alliance (U.S.): http://www.natvan.com

New Kach Movement: http://www.newkach.org

Pan Africanist Congress of Azania: http://www.paca.org.za

Puerto Rican Independence Party: http://www.pip.org.pr

CHAPTER 4

The following Web sites are links to international organizations that provide information about countries and human rights conditions.

Amnesty International: http://www.amnesty.org

CIA World Factbook: http://www.odci.gov/cia/publications/factbook

Human Rights Watch: http://www.hrw.org

Iraq Foundation: http://www.iraqfoundation.org

State Department: State-Sponsored Terrorism 2000: http://www.usis.usemb.se/terror/rpt2000/ overviewstate.html

CHAPTER 5

The following Web sites provide links to dissident revolutionary organizations, movements, and information.

Al-Fatah: http://www.fateh.net

Foreign Terrorist Organizations: http://www.state.gov/www/global/terrorism/terror_org.html

Irish Northern Aid (Noraid): http://inac.org

Liberation Tigers of Tamil Eelam: http://www.eelam.com

Terrorist Profiles: http://web.nps.navy.mil/~library/tgp/tgpmain.htm

CHAPTER 6

The following Web sites provide information about leftist organizations, movements, and goals.

Earth Liberation Front: http://www.earthliberationfront.com/main.shtml

Popular Front for the Liberation of Palestine: http://members.tripod.com/~freepalestine

Revolutionary Armed Forces of Colombia: http://www.farc-ep.org

Sinn Féin: http://sinnfein.ie

Socialist International: http://www.socialistinternational.org

Zapatista National Liberation Front: http://www.ezln.org

CHAPTER 7

The following Web sites provide information about rightist organizations, movements, and goals.

Afrikaner Resistance Movement: http://www.lantic.co.za/~awb

Institute for Historical Review: http://ihr.org

Pro-Ulster Volunteer Force: http://members.tripod.co.uk/trueblue

Resistance Records: http://www.resistance.com

Stormfront: http://www.stormfront.org

CHAPTER 8

The following Web sites provide links to discussions of religious and criminal terrorism and extremism:

Army of God: http://www.armyofgod.com

Drug Enforcement Administration: http://www.usdoj.gov/dea

Islamic Propagation Organization: http://www.al-islam.org/short/jihad

Muslim Brotherhood Movement: http://www.ummah.net/ikhwan

Office of National Drug Control Policy: http://www.whitehousedrugpolicy.gov

CHAPTER 9

The following Web sites provide links to organizations that report research on, or discuss, international terrorism.

Global Development Center: http://www.globaldisaster.org

International Policy Institute for Counter-Terrorism: http://www.ict.org.il

Naval Postgraduate School: http://web.nps.navy.mil/~library/terrorism.htm

South Asia Terrorism Portal: http://www.satp.org

Terrorism Research Center: http://www.terrorism.com/index.shtml

CHAPTER 10

The following Web sites provide links to discussions and data about terrorist objectives, methods, and targets.

Al Qaeda "Training Manual": http://www.usdoj.gov/ag/trainingmanual.htm

Anarchist's Cookbook, The: Search engine, enter: Anarchist's Cookbook

Center for Defense Information: http://www.cdi.org

Jaffe Center for Strategic Studies (Tel Aviv): http://www.tau.ac.il/jcss/lmas.html#Terror

Patterns of Global Terrorism (State Department): http://www.state.gov/s/ct/rls

Terrorist's Handbook, The: Search engine, enter: Terrorist's Handbook

CHAPTER 11

The following Web sites are links to the online addresses of major media resources that regularly report news about terrorism:

Al-Jazeera (Qatar): http://www.aljazeera.net

BBC (Britain): http://www.bbc.co.uk

CNN (USA): http://www.cnn.com

Dawn (Pakistan): http://www.dawn.com

New York Times: http://www.nytimes.com

CHAPTER 12

The following Web sites provide information about extremist movements, terrorist ideologies, and "watchdog" agencies in the United States.

Anti-Defamation League Militia Watchdog: http://www.militia-watchdog.org

Hate Directory: http://www.bcpl.net/~rfrankli/hatedir.htm

Prairie Fire Organizing Committee: http://www.prairie-fire.org

U.S. Department of Homeland Security: http://www.whitehouse.gov/homeland

White Aryan Resistance: http://www.resist.com

CHAPTER 13

The following Web sites provide information and data about counterterrorist policies and options.

Coordinator for Counterterrorism, Department of State: http://www.state.gov/www/global/terrorism

Diplomatic Security Service, Rewards for Justice: http://www.rewardsforjustice.net

International Rescue Committee: http://www.intrescom.org

U.N. International Court of Justice: http://www.icj-cij.org

War Criminal Watch: http://www.igc.org/wcw

APPENDIX D

DOCUMENTARIES AND DRAMATIC FILMS

The following documentaries and films depict dissident and state terrorism, or politically violent environments, in their content. Some were released as documentaries, and others were released as political dramas.

DOCUMENTARIES

20th Century With Mike Wallace: Terrorism Against Americans. Prod. The History Channel. Videocassette. CBS, Inc. and A&E Television Networks, 1996.

100 Years of Terror. Prod. The History Channel. Videocassette Series. A&E Home Video, 2000.

Ku Klux Klan: A Secret History. Prod. The History Channel. Videocassette. A&E Television Networks, 1998.

New Bomb Makers, The. Prod. Broadcast News Networks, Inc. Videocassette. A&E Television Networks, 1996.

New Face of Terrorism. Prod. A&E Television Networks. Videocassette. A&E Television Networks, 1996.

New Skinheads, The. Prod. Broadcast News Networks, Inc. Videocassette. Broadcast News Networks, Inc. and A&E Television Networks, 1995.

Terrorism: A World in Shadows. Prod. Liberty International Entertainment, Inc. Documentary Series. Liberty International Entertainment, Inc., 2000.

Terrorists Among Us: Jihad in America. Prod. SAE Productions, Inc. Videocassette. SAE Productions, Inc., 2001.

War at Home, The. Prod. Glenn Silber and Barry Alexander Brown. Videocassette. 1979.

World Trade Center: Anatomy of the Collapse. Prod. Darlow Smithson Film & Television. Videocassette. Discovery Communications, Inc., 2001.

DRAMATIC FILMS

American History X. Dir. Tony Kaye. Perf. Edward Norton, Edward Furlong, Avery Brooks. New Line Cinema, 1998.

Arlington Road. Dir. Mark Pellington. Perf. Jeff Bridges, Tim Rollins, Joan Cusack. Sony Pictures, 1999.

Battle of Algiers, The. Dir. Giolo Pontecorvo. Perf. Jean Martin, Yacef Saadi, Brahim Haggiag. Magna Film Igor Film—Cabash Films, 1966.

Betrayed. Dir. Constantin Costa-Gavras. Perf. Debra Winger, Tom Berenger. United Artists, 1988.

Boxer, The. Dir. Jim Sheridan. Perf. Daniel Day-Lewis, Emily Watson. Universal Studios, 1998.

Clear and Present Danger. Dir. Phillip Noyce. Perf. Harrison Ford, Willem Dafoe, Anne Archer. Paramount Pictures, 1994.

Cry Freedom. Dir. Richard Attenborough. Perf. Kevin Kline, Penelope Wilton, Denzel Washington. Universal Pictures, 1987.

Cry, the Beloved Country. Dir. Zoltan Korda. Perf. Canada Lee, Charles Carson, Sidney Poitier. United Artists, 1951.

Devil's Own, The. Dir. David Cronenberg. Perf. Harrison Ford, Brad Pitt. Sony Pictures, 1997.

In the Name of the Father. Dir. Jim Sheridan. Perf. Daniel Day-Lewis, Pete Postlethwaite, Emma Thompson. Universal Studios, 1993.

Little Drummer Girl, The. Dir. George Roy Hill. Perf. Diane Keaton, Klaus Kinski, Sami Frey. Warner Brothers, 1984.

Men With Guns. Dir. John Sayles. Perf. Federico Luppi, Damian Delgado, Tania Cruz. Clear Blue Sky, Lexington Road, Sony Pictures Classics, 1997.

Missing. Dir. Constantin Costa-Gavras. Perf. Jack Lemmon, Sissy Spacek. Universal Studios, 1982.

One Day in the Life of Ivan Denisovich. Dir. Caspar Wrede. Perf. Tom Courtenay, Espen Skjønberg, James Maxwell. Group B Films—Leontes—Norsk Films, 1971.

Salvador. Dir. Oliver Stone. Perf. James Woods, James Belushi. Hemdale, 1986.

Siege, The. Dir. Edward Zwick. Perf. Denzel Washington, Annette Bening, Bruce Willis, Frank Shalhoub. 20th Century Fox, 1998.

Sum of All Fears, The. Dir. Phil Alden Robinson. Perf. Ben Affleck, Morgan Freeman, James Cromwell, Liev Shreiber. Paramount Pictures, 2002.

Terrorist, The. Dir. Santosh Sivan. Perf. Ayesha Dharker, Vishnu Vardhan. Bhanu Prakash. Phaedra Cinema, 1998.

Year of the Gun. Dir. John Frankenheimer. Perf. Andrew McCarthy, Valeria Golino, Sharon Stone. Columbia Pictures, 1991.

Z. Dir. Constantin Costa-Gavras. Perf. Yves Montand, Irene Papas. Wellspring (DVD edition), 1969.

GLOSSARY

The glossary summarizes terms that were used in this textbook. Students should refer to the glossary to refresh their knowledge of discussions and case studies explored in chapters, tables, and chapter perspectives.

1st Navy Parachute Infantry Regiment. An elite French unit that is similar to the British Special Air Service and the American Delta Force. It deploys small intelligence and special operations squads that are trained to operate in desert, urban, and tropical environments. They are part of the core of French counterterrorist special operations forces.

11th Parachute Division (Paras). An elite French army unit that can deploy as a quick-reaction force to deal with terrorist threats.

25:6. The symbol of the racial supremacist Phineas Priesthood in the United States. It refers to chapter 25, verse 6 of the Book of Numbers in the Bible.

75th Ranger Regiment. An elite combat unit of the U.S. Army that can deploy large formations for counterterrorist missions.

Abbas, Abu. The leader of the Palestine Liberation Front.

Absolute deprivation. A sociological term that indicates the lack of basic human needs for survival.

Abu Nidal Organization (ANO). The designation given to Abu Nidal's movement.

Abu Sayyaf. A Muslim insurgency on the island of Basilan in the Philippines; the group has ideological and other links to Al Qaeda. Founded by Abdurajak Janjalani, who was killed by Filipino police in 1998.

Achille Lauro. A cruise ship that was hijacked by members of the Palestine Liberation Front. During the incident, the terrorists murdered a wheelchair-bound Jewish American.

Act of political will. The notion that one can force change by an absolute commitment to a cause. All that is required is complete and uncompromising dedication to achieving one's goals.

Afghan Arabs. A term given to foreign volunteers, mostly Arabs, who fought as mujahideen during the war against the occupation of Afghanistan by the Soviet Army.

African National Congress (ANC). The principal anti-apartheid movement in predemocracy South Africa.

Afrikaner Resistance Movement. A rightist ethno-nationalist movement in South Africa that promoted the interests of Afrikaners.

Air France Flight 8969. An airliner hijacked in December 1994 by the Algerian Armed Islamic Group. After the hijackers killed three passengers, the plane was permitted to depart the Algerian airfield and made a refueling stop in Marseilles. Intending to fly to Paris, the hijackers demanded three times the amount of fuel needed to make the journey. The reason for this demand was that they planned to blow up the aircraft over Paris or possibly crash it into the Eiffel Tower. French commandos disguised as caterers stormed the plane in Marseilles, thus bringing the incident to an end.

AK-47. A durable assault rifle designed by Mikhail Kalashnikov in the Soviet Union in 1947. It became a common weapon among conventional and irregular forces around the world.

Al Aqsa Martyr Brigades. A Palestinian nationalist movement affiliated with the Palestine Liberation Organization. Noted for its use of suicide bombers, it has committed terrorist violence against Israelis.

Al Jazeera. An independent news service based in the Persian Gulf state of Qatar.

Al Qaeda. An international network of Islamic mujahideen organized by Osama bin Laden in the aftermath of the anti-Soviet jihad in

Afghanistan. Responsible for many acts of international and domestic terrorism.

Albigensian Crusade. A Christian Crusade in southern France during the 13th century. Legend holds that concerns were raised about loyal and innocent Catholics who were being killed along with members of the enemy Cathar sect. The pope's representative, Arnaud Amaury, allegedly replied, "Kill them all, God will know his own."

al-Megrahi, Abdel Basset. An alleged agent of Libya's security service who was convicted and sentenced to life imprisonment by a Scottish court sitting near the Hague, Netherlands, for his participation in the bombing of Pan Am Flight 103 over Lockerbie, Scotland.

al-Sabbah, Hasan ibn. The founder and leader of the Assassin movement during the 11th century.

Amal. A pro-Syrian Lebanese Shi'ite paramilitary movement.

American Knights of the Ku Klux Klan (AK-KKK). An activist faction of the Ku Klux Klan that was prominent during the 1990s.

Amir, Yigal. A Jewish extremist who assassinated Israeli Prime Minister Yitzhak Rabin on November 4, 1995.

Ammonium Nitrate and Fuel Oil Explosives (ANFO). A powerful explosive compound made from ingredients easily obtained from fertilizers and common gasoline.

Amnesty International. An international watchdog organization that monitors human rights issues around the world, focusing on the status of political prisoners.

Anarchism. A political ideology developed during the 19th century that championed the working class and opposed central control by governments.

Anfal Campaign. A genocidal campaign waged by the Iraqi army in 1988 against its Kurdish population. Mustard gas and nerve agents were used against civilians.

Anglo-Israelism. A mystical ideology developed by Richard Brothers during the 18th century. It posited that the Lost Ten Tribes of ancient Israel migrated through Europe and settled in the British Isles. Thus, the British were God's chosen people. The theory was adapted to the American context as the Christian Identity cult.

Animal Liberation Front. An American-based single-issue movement that protests animal abuse. Responsible for committing acts of violence such as arson and vandalism.

Ansar Allah. A group that claimed credit in July 1994 for the bombing at the Argentine-Israeli Mutual Association in Buenos Aires, Argentina, where about 100 were killed and 200 were injured.

Anthrax. A disease afflicting farm animals that can also be contracted by humans. A possible ingredient for biological weapons.

Antistate terrorism. Dissident terrorism directed against a particular government or group of governments.

Antiterrorism. Official measures that seek to deter or prevent terrorist attacks. These measures include target hardening and enhanced security.

Anti-Terrorism and Effective Death Penalty Act. An act passed by the U.S. Congress in 1996, this was the first comprehensive American counterterrorism law. The purpose of the Anti-Terrorism Act was to regulate activity that can be used to mount a terrorist attack, provide resources for counterterrorist programs, and punish terrorism.

Apartheid. The former policy of racial separation and White supremacy in South Africa.

Arafat, Yasir. The founder and leader of the Palestine Liberation Organization.

Arellano-Felix Cartel. A drug-smuggling cartel based in Tijuana, Mexico. Responsible for terrorist violence against government officials.

Argentine Anticommunist Alliance (Triple-A). An Argentine death squad active in the early 1970s. It was responsible for numerous acts of violence against leftists, human rights organizers, students, and others. Some of its clandestine operatives were members of the Argentine security apparatus. After the 1976 coup, Triple-A was integrated into the Argentine state terrorist apparatus.

Armed Forces for National Liberation (Fuerzas Armadas de Liberación Nacional, or FALN). A Puerto Rican *independencista* terrorist group active during the 1970s and 1980s. Responsible for more bombings than any other single terrorist group in American history.

Armed Forces of Popular Resistance. A Puerto Rican *independencista* terrorist organization.

Armed Islamic Group (GIA). An Algerian Islamic resistance movement responsible for terrorist violence in Algeria and France.

Armed Islamic Movement (MIA). An Algerian Islamic resistance movement responsible for terrorist violence in Algeria and France.

Armed propaganda. The use of symbolic violence to spread propaganda about an extremist movement.

Armed Resistance Unit. A cover name used by the leftist May 19 Communist Organization in the United States.

Armed Revolutionary Nuclei. An Italian neofascist terrorist group. Its most notorious act was the bombing of the main train station in Bologna, which killed 85 and injured 180.

Armenian Revolutionary Army. One of several Armenian terrorist groups active in the postwar era that targeted Turkish interests to avenge the Turkish genocide of Armenians.

Armenian Secret Army for the Liberation of Armenia (ASALA). One of several Armenian terrorist groups active in the postwar era that targeted Turkish interests to avenge the Turkish genocide of Armenians.

Army of God. A shadowy and violent Christian fundamentalist movement in the United States that has attacked moralistic targets, such as abortion providers.

Arocena, Eduardo. The founder of the anti-Castro Cuban terrorist group Omega 7.

Aryan Nations. A racial supremacist hate group founded in the mid-1970s by Richard Butler. Originally based in Idaho, the group is organized around Christian Identity mysticism.

Aryan Republican Army (ARA). A neo-Nazi terrorist group that operated in the midwestern United States from 1994 to 1996. Inspired by the example of the Irish Republican Army, the ARA robbed 22 banks in seven states before they were captured. Their purpose had been to finance racial supremacist causes and to hasten the overthrow of the "Zionist Occupation Government." Some members also considered themselves to be Christian Identity fundamentalist Phineas Priests.

Asahara, Shoko. The spiritual leader of the Aum Shinrikō cult.

Ásatrú. A mystical belief in the ancient Norse gods' pantheon. Some Ásatrú believers are racial supremacists.

Askaris. Government-supported death squads in South Africa that assassinated members of the African National Congress and their supporters prior to the end of apartheid.

Assassination. The act of killing a symbolic victim in a sudden and premeditated attack. Many assassinations are politically motivated.

Assault Rifles. Automatic military weapons that use rifle ammunition.

Asymmetrical Warfare. A term used to describe tactics, organizational configurations, and methods of conflict that do not use previously accepted or predictable rules of engagement.

Augustine. A Christian philosopher who developed the concept of the just war.

Aum Shinrikyō. A cult based in Japan and led by Shoko Asahara. Responsible for releasing nerve gas into the Tokyo subway system, injuring 5,000 people.

Ausländer. Literally, "foreigner" in German. It is a derogatory term given by German rightists to unwelcome ethno-national immigrants.

Authoritarian regimes. Governments that practice strict control over public and political institutions and emphasize public order. The media and other public information outlets are regulated and censored by the government. Some authoritarian regimes have democratic institutions.

Avengers of the Martyrs. A government sponsored death squad in Chile during the 1970s that operated under the direction of the security forces.

Ayyash, Yehiya. A Palestinian terrorist bomb maker affiliated with Hamas. He was responsible for scores of Israeli casualties and was eventually assassinated by a remotely controlled explosive device hidden in his cell phone. Also known as the Engineer.

Baader, Andreas. A founder and leader of the Red Army Faction/Baader-Meinhof Gang in West Germany. He committed suicide in prison in October 1977 along with Gudrun Ensslin and Jan-Carl Raspe. The incident became known as Death Night.

Baader-Meinhof Gang. A leftist terrorist movement active in West Germany during the 1970s and 1980s. Also referred to as the Red Army Faction.

Ba'ath Party. A pan-Arab nationalist party.

Bakunin, Mikhail. An early philosophical proponent of anarchism in Russia.

Balkan Route. A drug-smuggling route through the Balkans. Political dissidents are involved with the drug trade, using the profits to fund their activities.

Basque Fatherland and Liberty (Euskadi Ta Azkatasuna, or ETA). Founded in 1959 to promote the independence of the Basque region in northern Spain. Although ETA adopted terrorism as a tactic in reply to the Franco government's violent repression of Basque nationalism, its campaign of violence escalated in the post-Franco era. At least six ETA factions and subfactions have been formed.

Battalion 3-16. A government-sponsored death squad active in Honduras in the 1980s.

Baumhammers, Richard. An American racial supremacist influenced by neo-Nazi ideology who shot to death five people near Pittsburgh, Pennsylvania, in April 2000. A case study in politically motivated lone wolf attacks. Also a case study of a minimal degree of criminal skill.

Begin, Menachem. A leader of the Irgun. Eventually rose to become the prime minister of Israel.

Beka'a Valley. A valley in eastern Lebanon that became a center for political extremism and a safe haven for terrorists.

Berri, Nabih. A leader of the Shi'ite Amal paramilitary, prominent during the Lebanese Civil War during the 1970s and 1980s, as well as during the TWA Flight 847 incident.

Berrigan, Daniel and Philip. Members of the Roman Catholic pacifist left who were leaders of the antiwar and antinuclear movements in the United States during the 1960s and 1970s.

Bhagwan Shree Rajneesh. The leader of a Hindu-oriented cult based in the Pacific Northwest of the United States. The group was responsible for poisoning the salad bars of 10 Oregon restaurants with *Salmonella* bacteria in 1984. More than 700 people fell ill.

Bin Laden, Osama. Founder and leader of the Islamic terrorist Al Qaeda network.

Biological agents. A term used to refer to potential ingredients in biological weapons.

Biometric technology. Digital technologies that allow digital photographs of faces to be matched against wanted suspects. Biometrics was used at American football's 2001 Super Bowl championship, when cameras scanned the faces of sports fans as they entered the stadium and matched their digital images against those of criminal fugitives and terrorists. The game became derisively known as the "Snooperbowl."

Birmingham Six. Six men who were wrongfully convicted of a 1974 bombing of two pubs in Birmingham, England. They were released in 1991 after an appellate court ruled that the police had used fabricated evidence.

Black Hebrew Israelites. An American racial supremacist cult that promotes African racial supremacy. Branches are also known as the Tribe of Judah, Nation of Israel, and Temple of Love. One branch based in Miami and led by Hulon Mitchell (also known as Yahweh Ben Yahweh) was responsible for at least 14 murders during the 1980s.

Black helicopters. Referenced by right-wing conspiracy theorists as evidence of an impending takeover by agents of the New World Order.

Black Hundreds. An anti-Semitic movement in czarist Russia that was responsible for pogroms and other violence against Russian Jews during the late 19th and early 20th centuries.

Black Liberation Army (BLA). An African American terrorist group active during the 1970s. The BLA tended to target police officers and banks.

Black Panther Party for Self-Defense. An African American nationalist organization founded in 1966 in Oakland, California. The Black Panthers eventually became a national movement. It was not a terrorist movement, but some members eventually engaged in terrorist violence.

Black Power. An African American nationalist ideology developed during the 1960s that stressed self-help, political empowerment, cultural chauvinism, and self-defense.

Black Pride. A movement in the United States that emphasized Afrocentric political agendas; experiments in economic development of African American communities; and cultural chauvinism that was expressed in music, art, and dress.

Black September. A campaign waged by the Jordanian army in September 1970 to suppress what was perceived to be a threat to Jordanian sovereignty from Palestinian fighters and leaders based in Jordan.

Blacklisting. A policy of prohibiting political activists from obtaining employment in certain industries.

Blood Libel, The. A medieval European Christian slander that declared that the blood of Christian children was ritualistically used during Jewish holidays. The slander continues to be promulgated in the 21st century.

Bloody Sunday. An incident on January 30, 1972, in Londonderry, Northern Ireland, when British paratroopers fired on demonstrators, killing 13 people.

Blue Division, The. The Spanish fascist volunteer division that fought on behalf of the Germans against the Soviet Union.

Bob Jones University. A religion-based university in the United States that forbids interracial dating.

Boland Amendment. A bill passed by Congress in December 1982 that forbade the expenditure of U.S. funds to overthrow the Sandinista government.

Booth, John Wilkes. A Confederate sympathizer who assassinated President Abraham Lincoln after the conclusion of the American Civil War.

Botulinum toxins (Botulism). A rather common form of food poisoning. It is a bacterium rather than a virus or fungus and can be deadly if inhaled or ingested even in small quantities.

Bourgeoisie. A term frequently used by Marxists to describe the middle class.

Brothers, Richard. The English founder of Anglo-Israelism during the 18th century.

Bubonic Plague. Known as the Black Death in medieval Europe, this disease is spread by bacteria-infected fleas that infect hosts when bitten. The disease is highly infectious and often fatal.

Bureau for the Protection of the Constitution. A government agency in Germany responsible for domestic security and intelligence.

Burke, Edmund. The British "father" of conservatism. An 18th-century intellectual who denounced the excesses of the French Revolution and other challenges to the traditional European order.

Bushido. The Japanese code of self-sacrifice adopted before and during the Second World War. Derived from the ancient code of the samurai.

Butler, Richard. The founder and leader of the Aryan Nations organization. Also a promulgator of Christian Identity mysticism.

Cadre group. Politically indoctrinated and motivated activists. Frequently the core of a revolutionary movement.

Camorra. A Neapolitan secret society that became an organized crime enterprise.

Carlos "The Jackal." The *nom de guerre* for Ilich Ramirez Sanchez, a Venezuelan revolutionary who became an international terrorist. He acted primarily on behalf of the Popular Front for the Liberation of Palestine.

Carmichael, Stokely. A leader of the Student Non-Violent Coordinating Committee in the American South during the 1960s. One of the first advocates of Black Power.

Carnivore. A surveillance technology developed for use by the Federal Bureau of Investigation (FBI) that could reportedly monitor Internet communications. Under law, the FBI could not use Carnivore without a specific court order under specific guidelines, much like other criminal surveillance orders. The FBI eventually redesignated the system DCS-1000.

Castro, Fidel. The leader of the Cuban Revolution.

Caudillo. A term given to a strong leader in Spain. Francisco Franco was the *caudillo* during his regime.

Cell-based terrorist environment. A terrorist environment in which terrorists have organized themselves into small semi-autonomous units rather than in traditionally hierarchical configurations. Difficult to combat because there is no central organization.

Cells. Autonomous groups of terrorists who may be loosely affiliated with a larger movement but who are largely independent of hierarchical control.

Central Intelligence Agency (CIA). The principal intelligence agency in the United States. The theoretical coordinator of American foreign intelligence collection.

Chemical agents. Chemicals that can potentially be converted into weapons. Some chemical agents, such as pesticides, are commercially available. Other chemical agents can be manufactured by terrorists using commonly available instruction guides.

Chesimard, JoAnne. *See* Assata Shakur.

Child soldiers. Children who have been pressed into military service.

Chlorine gas. A chemical agent that destroys the cells that line the respiratory tract.

Christian Identity. The American adaptation of Anglo-Israelism. A racial supremacist mystical belief that holds that Aryans are the chosen people of God, the United States is the Aryan "Promised Land," non-Whites are soulless beasts, and Jews are biologically descended from the devil.

Cinque. *See* DeFreeze, Donald.

Classical ideological continuum. Symbolic political designations derived from the French Revolution. The concepts of *left, center,* and *right* have become part of modern political culture.

Codes of self-sacrifice. Philosophical, ideological, or religious doctrines that create a warrior ethic in followers of the doctrine. Codes of self-sacrifice instill a sense of a "higher calling" that allows for the adoption of a superior morality. Acts of violence carried out in the name of the code are considered by followers to be completely justifiable.

Coercive covert operations. Covert counterterrorist measures that seek to resolve terrorist crises by disrupting and destroying terrorist groups.

Collateral damage. A term used to describe unintended casualties. Usually applied to civilians who have been mistakenly killed.

Collective nonviolence. An activist philosophy of the civil rights movement in the American South that advocated peaceful civil disobedience.

Communal terrorism. Group-against-group terrorism, in which rival demographic groups engage in political violence against each other.

Composite-4 (C-4). A powerful military-grade plastic explosive.

Concessionary options. Conciliatory counter-terrorist measures that seek to resolve terrorist crises by acceding to the terrorists' demands.

Conciliatory responses. Counterterrorist measures that seek to resolve terrorist crises by addressing the underlying conditions that cause extremist violence.

Conservatism. A political ideology that seeks to preserve traditional values.

Contagion effect. "Copycat terrorism" in which terrorists imitate each other's behavior and tactics. This theory is still debated.

Contras. Rightist Nicaraguan counterrevolutionaries trained and supported by the United States during the 1980s.

Counterculture. A youth-centered movement in the United States and other Western countries during the 1960s and 1970s. It questioned status quo social and political values.

Counterterrorism. Proactive policies that specifically seek to eliminate terrorist environments and groups. There are a number of possible categories of counterterrorist response, including counterterrorist laws, which specifically criminalize terrorist behavior and supportive operations.

Covenant, the Sword, and the Arm of the Lord, The (CSA). An American apocalyptic religious and racial supremacist survivalist community in the Ozark Mountains of Arkansas. The group was effectively disbanded in 1985 after prosecutions by federal authorities for, among other charges, possessing a large quantity of poisonous potassium cyanide. CSA had intended to use the toxin to poison water supplies in U.S. cities.

Convention to Prevent and Punish Acts of Terrorism Taking the Form of Crimes Against Persons and Related Extortion That Are of International Significance. A treaty among members of the Organization of American States that defined attacks against internationally protected persons as common crimes. The purpose of the agreement was to establish common ground for recognizing the absolute inviolability of diplomatic missions.

Covert operations. Counterterrorist measures that seek to resolve terrorist crises by secretly disrupting or destroying terrorist groups, movements, and support networks.

Crazy States. States whose behavior is not rational, in which the people live at the whim of the regime or a dominant group. Some crazy states have little or no central authority and are ravaged by warlords or militias. Other crazy states have capricious, impulsive, and violent regimes in power that act out with impunity.

Creativity. A mystical belief practiced by the racial supremacist Church of the Creator in the United States. Creativity is premised on a rejection of the White race's reliance on Christianity, which is held to have been created by the Jews as a conspiracy to enslave Whites. According to Creativity, the White race itself should be worshipped.

Criminal cartels. Cooperative groups of illegal drug enterprises. Involved in the manufacture and smuggling of drugs.

Criminal dissident terrorism. Political violence perpetrated by dissidents who also engage criminal enterprises to fund their movements.

Criminal-political enterprises. Political dissident groups that engage in criminal enterprises, such as smuggling drugs or arms, to fund their movements.

Criminal profiles. Descriptive profiles of criminal suspects developed by law enforcement agencies to assist in the apprehension of the suspects.

Crusades. A series of Christian military campaigns during the Middle Ages instigated by the Pope and Western Christian rulers. Most of these campaigns were invasions of Muslim territories, although the Crusaders also attacked Orthodox Christians, conducted pogroms against Jews, and suppressed "heresies."

Cult of personality. The glorification of a single strong national leader and political regime.

Customer anonymity. A policy adopted in some countries that allows national banks to guarantee customer privacy.

Cyberterrorism. The term given to the use of technology by terrorists to disrupt information systems.

Cyberwar. The targeting of terrorists' electronic activities by counterterrorist agencies. Bank accounts, personal records, and other data stored in digital databases can theoretically be intercepted and compromised.

Days of Rage. Four days of rioting and vandalism committed by the Weathermen in Chicago in October 1969.

DCS-1000. The redesignated name given to Carnivore, the FBI's Internet surveillance technology.

Death night. The term given to an incident that occurred in West Germany on October 18, 1977, when three imprisoned leaders of the Red Army Faction committed suicide with weapons that were smuggled into a high-security prison. Many Germans have never believed the West German government's official explanation for the events of Death Night, and some have suggested that the government was responsible for the deaths.

Death squads. Rightist paramilitaries and groups of people who have committed numerous human rights violations. Many death squads in Latin America and elsewhere have been supported by the government and the upper classes.

Decommissioning. The process of disarmament by the Irish Republican Army that was set as a condition for the Good Friday Agreement peace accords.

Defense Intelligence Agency (DIA). The central agency for military intelligence of the U.S. armed forces.

DeFreeze, Donald. The leader of the Symbionese Liberation Army, a California-based American terrorist group active during the 1970s. DeFreeze adopted the *nom de guerre* Cinque.

Degenerate workers' state. A term used by Trotskyites to describe the Soviet Union.

Delta Force (1st Special Forces Operational Detachment–Delta). A secretive American special operations unit that operates in small covert teams. Its mission is similar to those of the British Special Air Service and French 1st Navy Parachute Infantry Regiment. Delta Force operations probably include abductions, reconnaissance, and punitive operations.

Democratic Front for the Liberation of Palestine (DFLP). A faction of the Palestine Liberation Organization, which split from the Popular Front for the Liberation of Palestine in 1969 and further split into two factions in 1991. It is a Marxist organization that believes in ultimate victory through mass revolution, and it has committed small bombings and assaults against Israel, including border raids.

Department of Homeland Security. A new department of the U.S. government created to coordinate homeland security in the aftermath of the September 11, 2001, homeland attacks.

Dictatorship of the proletariat. The Marxist belief that the communist revolution will result in the establishment of a working class-centered government.

DINA. The Chilean secret service, allegedly responsible for human rights violations and domestic state terrorism during the 1970s and 1980s.

Diplomacy. Conciliatory counterterrorist measures that seek to resolve terrorist crises by negotiating with terrorists or their supporters.

Diplomatic Security Service. A security bureau within the U.S. Department of State that protects diplomats and other officials.

Direct action. A philosophy of direct confrontation adopted by the Students for a Democratic Society and other members of the American New Left movement.

Direct Action (Action Directe). An anti-American and anti-NATO terrorist group in France that was founded in 1979. Direct Action operated mainly in Paris and committed approximately 50 terrorist attacks. It acted in solidarity with Germany's Red Army Faction, Italy's Red Brigades, Belgium's Combatant Communist Cells, and Palestinian extremists.

Directorate for Inter-Services Intelligence (ISI). The chief Pakistani security service.

Dirty War. A term given to a campaign of state-sponsored terror waged in Argentina during the 1970s. Tens of thousands of people were tortured, "disappeared," or killed.

Disinformation. Counterterrorist measures that seek to resolve terrorist crises by disseminating damaging information, thus perhaps causing internal dissension and distrust among the terrorists and their supporters.

Dissident terrorism. "Bottom-up" terrorism perpetrated by individuals, groups, or movements in opposition to an existing political or social order.

Dohrn, Bernardine. A founder and leader of the Weatherman faction of Students for a Democratic Society. She eventually went underground with other Weathermen to form the Weather Underground Organization.

Dynamite. A commercially available high explosive that has nitroglycerin as its principal chemical ingredient.

Earth Liberation Front. A single-issue movement that protests environmental degradation and pollution. A splinter group from the environmentalist group Earthfirst!, the ELF is potentially more radical than the Animal Liberation Front.

East Timor. A former Portuguese colony annexed by Indonesia. Indonesian troops and paramilitaries committed numerous atrocities during a protracted Timorese independence movement.

Echelon. A satellite surveillance network maintained by the U.S. National Security Agency. It is a kind of global "wiretap" that filters through communications using antennae, satellite, and other technologies. Internet transfers, telephone conversations, and data transmissions are the types of communications that can reportedly be intercepted.

Economic sanctions. Counterterrorist measures that seek to influence the behavior of terrorist states by pressuring their national economies.

Einsatzgruppen. Special Nazi SS units that implemented genocidal Nazi policies in Eastern Europe.

Electromagnetic pulse (EMP) technologies. Technologies using an electromagnetic burst from a generator that can disable electronic components such as microchips. If used on a sizable scale, EMP could destroy large quantities of military or financial information.

Electronic trigger. Remotely controlled bombs are commonly employed by terrorists. The trigger is activated by a remote electronic or radio signal.

Emergency Search Team. A paramilitary unit within the U.S. Department of Energy that has counterterrorist capabilities.

End justifies the means, The. A concept wherein the desired goal is so just that the methods used to obtain the goal are acceptable regardless of their immediate consequences.

Engels, Friedrich. Karl Marx's colleague and compatriot during the genesis of what was to become communist ideology.

Engineer, The. The designation given to the Hamas bomb maker Yehiya Ayyash.

Enhanced security. Counterterrorist measures that "harden" targets to deter or otherwise reduce the severity of terrorist attacks.

Ensslin, Gudrun. A founder and leader of the Red Army Faction/Baader-Meinhof Gang in West Germany. She committed suicide in prison in October 1977 along with Andreas Baader and Jan-Carl Raspe. The incident became known as Death Night.

Episode-specific sponsorship. State-sponsored terrorism limited to a single episode or campaign.

ETA (Euskadi Ta Azkatasuna). *See* Basque Fatherland and Liberty.

Ethnic cleansing. A term created by Serb nationalists during the wars following the breakup of Yugoslavia. It described the suppression and removal of non-Serbs from regions claimed for Serb settlement. A euphemism for genocide.

Ethno-nationalist communal terrorism. Violence involving conflict between populations that have distinct histories, customs, ethnic traits, religious traditions, or other cultural idiosyncrasies.

Euphemistic language. Code words used by all participants in a terrorist environment to describe other participants and their behavior.

Executive Order 12333. An executive order by President Ronald Reagan issued in December 1981. It expressly prohibited employees of the United States from assassinating adversaries. The order also forbade U.S. personnel from using anyone hired as an agent to commit assassinations.

Extradition treaties. International agreements to turn over criminal fugitives to the law enforcement agencies of fellow signatories.

Extremism. Political opinions that are intolerant toward opposing interests and divergent opinions. Extremism forms the ideological foundation for political violence. Radical and reactionary extremists often rationalize and justify acts of violence committed on behalf of their cause.

Extremism in defense of liberty is no vice. An uncompromising belief in the absolute righteousness of a cause. A moralistic concept that clearly defines good and evil. The statement was made by Senator Barry Goldwater during the 1964 presidential election in the United States.

Falange. The strongest right-wing party during the Spanish Civil War and during Franco's regime. It represented the Spanish variant of fascism.

Fallout. Dangerous radioactive debris emitted into the atmosphere by a nuclear explosion that descends to earth as toxic material.

Far left. The extremist, but not necessarily violent, left wing. Usually strongly influenced by Marxist ideology. Radical in political orientation.

Far right. The extremist, but not necessarily violent, right wing. Reactionary in political orientation.

Fasces. A symbolic bundle of sticks with an axe in the center, originally symbolizing the power of the Roman Empire. Modern states also use the symbolism of the fasces, and the term *fascist* is derived from the word.

Fascism. An ideology developed during the mid-20th century that emphasized strong state-centered authority, extreme law and order, militarism, and nationalism. Variants of fascism were applied during the 1930s in Italy, Germany, and Spain, as well as in Latin America during the postwar era.

Fatah. The largest and most influential organization within the Palestine Liberation Organization. It formed the political foundation for PLO leader Yasir Arafat.

Federal Bureau of Investigation (FBI). An investigative bureau within the U.S. Department of Justice. It is the largest federal law enforcement agency, and among its duties are domestic counterterrorism and intelligence collection.

Fhima, Lamen Khalifa. An alleged agent of Libya's security service who was acquitted by a Scottish court sitting near the Hague, Netherlands, of charges that he participated in the bombing of Pan Am Flight 103 over Lockerbie, Scotland.

Foquismo.   Ernesto "Che" Guevara's theory of continent-wide revolution in Latin America, in which a revolutionary cadre group would instigate and lead the international revolution.

Force 17.   An elite security unit within Fatah, founded in 1970. It has engaged in paramilitary and terrorist attacks and has served as Yasir Arafat's guard force.

Force 777.   An elite Egyptian counterterrorist unit that has had mixed success in resolving terrorist crises.

Foreign Legion.   A branch of the French armed forces that has historically been composed of foreign nationals. The Legion is able to deploy commando and parachute units to resolve terrorist crises.

Fountain Valley Massacre.   The execution-style slayings of seven Whites and one African American employee at the Fountain Valley Golf Club on the island of St. Croix by Virgin Islands nationalists seeking independence from the United States.

Four Olds, The.   During the Great Proletarian Cultural Revolution in China, Maoists waged an ideological struggle to eliminate what they termed *the Four Olds*: old ideas, old culture, old customs, and old habits.

Fourteen Words.   A rallying slogan for the racial supremacist right wing in the United States. Originally coined by a convicted member of the terrorist group the Order, the Fourteen Words are: "We must secure the existence of our people and a future for White children."

Franco, Francisco.   The leader of the right-wing rebellion in Spain against the leftist republic during the Civil War of the 1930s. He became the dictator of postwar Spain.

Free press.   A media environment wherein few official restrictions are placed on the reporting of the news. The free press relies on ethical and professional standards of behavior to regulate reporting practices.

Freedom Birds.   A term given to female combatants in the Liberation Tigers of Tamil Eelam.

Freedom fighter.   One who fights on behalf of an oppressed group. A very contextual term.

French Navy Special Assault Units.   Elite units of the French Navy that are trained for operations against seaborne targets, coastlines, and harbors. Their mission is similar to those of the British Special Boat Service and the U.S. Navy SEALs.

Fringe left.   The revolutionary left. Often violent.

Fringe right.   The revolutionary right. Often violent.

Fund for the Martyrs.   An Iranian fund established for the benefit of Palestinian victims of the *intifadeh* against Israel.

Furrow, Buford Oneal.   A former member of Aryan Nations who went on a shooting spree in Los Angeles, California, in August 1999. His spree included an attack at a Jewish community center in which five people were wounded, and the murder of an Asian mail carrier.

Fuses.   A very old and low-technology method of explosives detonation that is as simple as lighting a fuse to detonate the explosives. It can be timed by varying the length of the fuse.

Gasoline bomb.   A simple explosive consisting of a gasoline-filled container with a detonator. Perhaps the most common gasoline bomb is the Molotov Cocktail.

Gender communal terrorism.   A conceptual designation describing political violence directed against the women of an ethno-national, religious, or political group.

General deterrence.   The creation of an environment by governments and counterterrorist agencies in which the risks of political violence outweigh the benefits.

Genocidal state terrorism.   State-initiated genocide. The state either involves itself directly in the genocidal campaign or deploys proxies to carry out the genocide.

Genocide.   The suppression of a targeted demographic group with the goal of repressing or eliminating its cultural or physical distinctiveness. The group is usually an ethno-national, religious, or ideological group.

GEO (Grupo Especial de Operaciones).   A counterterrorist and hostage rescue force organized by the Spanish National Police. GEO's training has allowed it to be used in both law enforcement and counterterrorist operations. Most of the latter have been directed against the Basque ETA terrorist movement.

GIGN (Groupe d'Intervention Gendarmerie Nationale).   An elite paramilitary unit recruited from the French *gendarmerie*, or military police. GIGN is a counterterrorist unit with international operational duties.

Goddess of Democracy.   A statue erected by Chinese dissidents during the Tiananmen Square protests against dictatorship. Similar in design to the Statue of Liberty in the United States, it was crushed by a Chinese tank during the government's suppression of the protests.

Golani Brigade. An elite unit within the Israel Defense Force that normally operates in conventionally organized military units. It has been deployed frequently for suppression campaigns against Hezbollah in South Lebanon.

Golden Crescent. The opium- and heroin-producing area of Southwest Asia.

Golden Triangle. The opium- and heroin-producing area of Southeast Asia.

Goldstein, Baruch. A "lone wolf" terrorist who fired on worshippers inside the Ibrahim Mosque at the Cave of the Patriarch's holy site in the city of Hebron, Israel. According to official government estimates, he killed 29 people and wounded another 125. In reprisal for the Hebron massacre, the Palestinian Islamic fundamentalist movement Hamas launched a bombing campaign that included the first wave of human suicide bombers.

Good Friday Agreement. A significant outcome of the Northern Ireland peace process. The agreement was overwhelmingly approved by voters on April 10, 1998, in the Irish Republic and Northern Ireland. It signaled the mutual acceptance of a Northern Ireland assembly and the disarmament, or "decommissioning," of all paramilitaries.

Grail. A designation for the Soviet-made SA-7 surface-to-air missile.

Great Proletarian Cultural Revolution. A period from 1965 to 1969 in China during which the Communist Party instigated a mass movement to mobilize the young postrevolution generation. Its purpose was to eliminate "revisionist" tendencies in society and to create a newly indoctrinated revolutionary generation.

Greater Jihad. In Muslim belief, an individual struggle to do what is right in accordance with God's wishes. All people of faith are required to do what is right and good.

Green Berets (Special Forces Groups). A special operations unit of the U.S. Army. Green Berets usually operate in units called A Teams, comprising specialists whose skills include languages, intelligence, medicine, and demolitions. The traditional mission of the A Team is force multiplication.

Green Police. The popular name for Israel's Police Border Guards.

Grey Wolves. A rightist ultranationalist movement in Turkey that promotes the establishment of a Greater Turkey called Turan, which would unite all Turkish people in a single nation. Responsible for numerous acts of terrorism.

GSG-9 (Grenzschutzgruppe 9). An elite German paramilitary unit that was organized after the disastrous failed attempt to rescue Israeli hostages taken by Black September at the 1972 Munich Olympics. It is a paramilitary force that has been used domestically and internationally as a counterterrorist and hostage rescue unit.

Guerrilla. A term first used during Spanish resistance against French occupation troops during the Napoleonic Wars. It refers to irregular hit-and-run tactics.

Guevara, Ernesto "Che." An Argentine revolutionary and intellectual who was instrumental in the success of the Cuban Revolution. Eventually killed in Bolivia, he developed his own philosophy of a continent-wide revolution in Latin America.

Guildford Four. Four people who were wrongfully convicted of an October 1974 bombing in Guildford, England. They served 15 years in prison before being released in 1989 when their convictions were overturned on appeal.

Hague Convention of 1970. A treaty requiring the extradition or prosecution of hijackers.

Hague Conventions. A series of international agreements that tried to establish rules for conflict.

Hamas (Islamic Resistance Movement). A Palestinian Islamic movement that waged a protracted terrorist campaign against Israel.

Harkat-ul-Ansar. A Pakistan-supported movement in Kashmir that has engaged in terrorism.

Hate crimes. Crimes motivated by hatred against protected groups of people. They are prosecuted as aggravated offenses rather than as acts of terrorism.

Hawala. An ancient transnational trust-based system used to transfer money via brokers.

Heinzen, Karl. A 19th-century revolutionary theorist in Germany who advocated revolutionary terrorism and the use of explosives. Heinzen supported the acquisition of new weapons technologies to utterly destroy the enemies of the people. According to Heinzen, these weapons should include poison gas and new high-yield explosives.

Hezbollah. A Lebanese Shi'ite movement that promotes Islamic revolution. It was prominent in the resistance against the Israeli presence in South Lebanon and frequently engaged in terrorism.

Hitler, Adolf. The leader of the National Socialist German Workers, or Nazi, Party in Germany during the 1930s and 1940s.

Ho Chi Minh. The communist leader of Vietnam in the resistance against the French colonial presence. He later became the ruler of North Vietnam and continued his war by fighting the

South Vietnamese government and the American military presence in the South.

Holy Spirit Mobile Force. A cultic insurgency in Uganda inspired and led by Alice Lakwena. In late 1987, she led thousands of her followers against the Ugandan army. To protect themselves from death, the fighters anointed themselves with holy oil, which they believed would ward off bullets. Thousands of Lakwena's followers were slaughtered in 1987 in the face of automatic weapons and artillery fire.

Hostage Rescue Team (HRT). A paramilitary group organized under the authority of the U.S. Federal Bureau of Investigation. The HRT is typical of American paramilitary units in that it operates under the administrative supervision of federal agencies that perform traditional law enforcement work.

House Un-American Activities Committee. A congressional committee created in the aftermath of a Red Scare during the 1930s to investigate threats to American security.

Hukbalahaps (Huks). A communist insurgency in the Philippines that began during the Second World War as an anti-Japanese resistance movement. After the war, they overtly declared themselves to be communist guerrillas who sought to create a communist state. The government succeeded in crushing them by the mid-1950s. The Huks reappeared in the late 1960s but were again suppressed in 1970.

Human intelligence. Intelligence that has been collected by human operatives rather than through technological resources. Also referred to as HUMINT.

Human Rights Watch. An international watchdog organization that monitors human rights issues around the world.

Hussein, Saddam. The ruler of Iraq who became a prominent figure in state sponsorship of international terrorism and the development of weapons of mass destruction during the 1980s and 1990s. He also attempted to annex Kuwait during the early 1990s, causing the Gulf War.

Ideological communal terrorism. Communal violence in the postwar era that usually reflected the global ideological rivalry between the United States and the Soviet Union.

Ideologies. Systems of political belief.

Imperialism. A term used to describe the doctrine of national expansion and exploitation.

Information is power. A political and popular concept that the control of the dissemination of information, especially through media outlets, enhances the power of the controlling interest.

Inkatha Freedom Party. A Zulu-based movement in South Africa.

Intelligence. The collection of data for the purpose of creating an informational database about terrorist movements and predicting their behavior.

Intelligence community. The greater network of intelligence agencies. In the United States, the Central Intelligence Agency is the theoretical coordinator of intelligence collection.

International Court of Justice. The principal judicial arm of the United Nations. Its 15 judges are elected from among member states, and each sits for a nine-year term. The court hears disputes between nations and gives advisory opinions to recognized international organizations.

International Criminal Court (ICC). A court established to prosecute crimes against humanity, such as genocide. Its motivating principle is to promote human rights and justice. In practice, this has meant that the ICC has issued arrest warrants for the prosecution of war criminals.

International Criminal Court for Rwanda. A tribunal that has investigated allegations of war crimes and genocide resulting from the breakdown of order in Rwanda during the 1990s. The indictments against suspected war criminals detail what can only be described as genocide on a massive scale.

International Criminal Police Organization (INTERPOL). An international network of law enforcement that cooperates in the investigation of crimes. It is based in Ste. Cloud, France.

International Criminal Tribunal for the Former Yugoslavia. A tribunal that has investigated allegations of war crimes and genocide arising out of the wars that broke out after the fragmentation of Yugoslavia during the 1990s. Several alleged war criminals, including former Yugoslavian president Slobodan Milosevic, have been brought before the court. Others remain at large but under indictment.

International law. Multinational laws agreed to by governments and enforceable under international agreements.

International Mujahideen. Islamic revolutionaries who have adopted a pan-Islamic ideology.

International terrorism. Terrorism that is directed against targets symbolizing international interests. These attacks can occur against domestic targets that have international symbolism or against targets in the international arena.

Intifadeh. The protracted Palestinian uprising against Israel. Literally, "shaking off."

Irgun. A Jewish terrorist group active in Palestine prior to the formation of the state of Israel. Its most infamous attack was the 1946 bombing of the King David Hotel.

Irish National Liberation Army (INLA). The INLA grew out of the split in the IRA during the 1970s. The group adopted Marxist theory as its guiding ideology and fought to reunite Northern Ireland with Ireland. The INLA considered itself to be fighting in unity with other terrorist groups that championed oppressed groups around the world. Its heyday was during the 1970s and mid-1980s.

Islamic Jihad. A label adopted by some Islamic terrorists seeking to establish an Islamic state. Groups known as Islamic Jihad exist in Lebanon, Palestine, and Egypt.

It became necessary to destroy the town to save it. An extremist goal to destroy an existing order without developing a clear vision for the aftermath. A moralistic concept to justify terrorist behavior. The statement was allegedly made by an American officer during the war in Vietnam.

Izzedine al-Qassam Brigade. A militant movement within the overarching Hamas movement of Palestinian Islamic revolutionaries.

Jabotinsky, Vladimir. A leader of the Jewish terrorist group Irgun. He was killed in 1940.

Jamahiriya Security Organization. The Libyan state security agency during the reign of Muammar el-Qaddafi. Apparently responsible for promoting Libya's policy of state-sponsored terrorism.

Jammu and Kashmir Islamic Front. A revolutionary proxy supported by Pakistan's Directorate for Inter-Services Intelligence.

Jammu Kashmir Liberation Front. An ethnonational and Islamic dissident movement in Kashmir. The movement has waged an irregular war against Indian occupation of part of Kashmir.

Janjalani, Abdurajak. Founder of the Abu Sayyaf group in the Philippines.

Jewish Defense League. A militant Jewish organization founded in the United States by Rabbi Meir Kahane.

Jihad. A central tenet in Islam that literally means a sacred "struggle" or "effort." Although Islamic extremists have interpreted jihad to mean waging holy war, it is not synonymous with the Christian concept of a crusade.

Jihadi. One who wages jihad.

Joint operations. State-sponsored terrorism in which state personnel participate in the terrorist enterprise.

Jones, Jim. Founder and leader of the American apocalyptic cult People's Temple of the Disciples of Christ. Founded in California, the group relocated to Guyana in the late 1970s. More than 900 followers committed suicide in November 1978 by drinking flavored sugar water laced with poison.

Journalistic self-regulation. The theoretical practice of ethical reporting among members of the press.

June 2nd Movement (Bevegung 2. Juni). Founded in West Berlin in 1971, the June 2nd Movement was anarchistic in its ideology. It was known for bombing property targets in West Berlin. The June 2nd Movement's most famous action was the 1975 kidnapping of Peter Lorenz, a Berlin mayoral candidate. He was released in one day after four June 2nd comrades were released and flown to Yemen. After disbanding in the 1980s, many members joined the Red Army Faction.

Jus ad bellum. Correct conditions for waging war. An element of the Just War Doctrine.

Jus in bello. One's correct behavior while waging war. An element of the Just War Doctrine.

Just War Doctrine. A moral and ethical doctrine that raises the questions of whether one can ethically attack an opponent, how one can justifiably defend oneself, and what types of force are morally acceptable in either context. The doctrine also addresses who can morally be defined as an enemy and what kinds of targets may be morally attacked.

Justice Commandos of the Armenian Genocide. One of several Armenian terrorist groups active in the postwar era that targeted Turkish interests to avenge the Turkish genocide of Armenians.

Kach (Kahane Chai). Militant movements in Israel that carried on after Rabbi Meir Kahane was assassinated. They advocate the expulsion of Arabs from territories claimed as historically Jewish land. *Kach* means "only thus." *Kahane Chai* means "Kahane lives."

Kaczynski, Theodore "Ted." The Unabomber in the United States, who sent bombs hidden in letters and packages to protest technological society. A case study in politically motivated lone-wolf attacks. Also a case study of a medium degree of criminal skill.

Kahane, Rabbi Meir. Founder and leader of the Jewish Defense League.

Kalashnikov, Mikhail. The inventor of the famous AK-47 assault rifle.

Kamikaze. Literally, "divine wind" in Japanese. During the Second World War, the Japanese military sent suicide planes against American warships. These were called kamikazes.

Kansi, Mir Amal. A terrorist who used an AK-47 assault rifle against employees of the Central Intelligence Agency who were waiting in their cars to enter the CIA's headquarters in Langley, Virginia. Two people were killed, and three were wounded. He was later captured in Pakistan, was sent to the United States for prosecution, and was convicted of murder.

Kerner Commission. A term given to the presidential-appointed National Advisory Commission on Civil Disorders, which released a report in 1968 on civil disturbances in the United States.

Khaled, Leila. A Palestinian nationalist who successfully hijacked one airliner and failed in an attempt to hijack another. She acted on behalf of the Popular Front for the Liberation of Palestine.

Khmer Rouge. A Cambodian Marxist insurgency that seized power in 1975. During their reign, between 1 and 2 million Cambodians died, many of them in the infamous Killing Fields.

Khomeini, Ayatollah Ruhollah. An Iranian religious leader who led the Iranian Revolution, which eventually ousted the Shah Mohammad Reza Pahlavi.

Kidnapping/hostage-taking. A method of propaganda by the deed in which symbolic individuals or small groups are taken captive as a way to publicize the terrorists' cause.

Kill one, terrorize a thousand. A paraphrasing of a quotation by the Chinese military philosopher Wu Ch'i. Variously ascribed to the Chinese military philosopher Sun Tzu and Chinese communist leader Mao Zedong.

King David Hotel Bombing. The bombing of a hotel in Jerusalem that housed the headquarters of the British military and the government secretariat before the founding of the state of Israel. On July 22, 1946, the Irgun bombed the hotel, killing 91 persons and wounding 45 others.

Klassen, Ben. The founder of the racial supremacist Church of the Creator in the United States.

Kneecapping. A signature method of violence used by combatants in Northern Ireland and by Italy's Red Brigades. The technique involved shooting a victim in the back of the knee joint, thus shooting off the kneecap.

Komiteh. Revolutionary tribunals established after the Islamic revolution in Iran.

Kony, Josef. Founder and leader of Uganda's cultic Lord's Resistance Army.

Korean Airlines Flight 858. An airliner that exploded over Myanmar (Burma) in November 1987, apparently after sabotage by North Korean operatives.

Kosovo. A region in southern Yugoslavia that many Serbs consider to be their spiritual homeland. It became an international flash point when ethnic Albanian Kosovars sought to secede from Yugoslavia.

Kosovo Liberation Army (KLA). An ethnic Albanian dissident movement seeking independence for the Kosovo region of the former Yugoslavia. The group has used terrorism against Serb civilians and security forces.

Kropotkin, Petr. An early philosophical proponent of anarchism in Russia.

Ku Klux Klan (KKK). A racial supremacist organization founded in 1866 in Pulaski, Tennessee. During its five eras, the KKK was responsible for thousands of acts of terrorism.

Kuclos. A symbol adopted by the Ku Klux Klan consisting of a cross and a teardrop-like symbol enclosed by a circle. Literally, Greek for "circle."

Kurdistan. The regional homeland of the Kurdish people. It is divided between Iran, Iraq, Syria, and Turkey.

Kurds. An ethno-national group in the Middle East. Several nationalist movements fought protracted wars on behalf of Kurdish independence.

La Cosa Nostra. The American version of the Italian Mafia. Traditionally organized into family networks. Literally, "this thing of ours."

Labeling. The attaching of euphemistic terms to the participants in a terrorist environment.

Lakwena, Alice. Leader of the cultic Holy Spirit Mobile Force in Uganda. She claimed to be inspired by the Christian Holy Spirit and preached that her movement would defeat government forces and purge Uganda of witchcraft and superstition. Her followers were annihilated, and she fled the country.

Lashkar e Tayyba. A Kashmiri Pakistani proxy based in Pakistan.

Laskar Jihad (Militia of the Holy War). An armed Islamic group organized in April 2000 in Indonesia. Under the leadership of Ja'afar Umar Thalib, the group waged a communal holy war in Indonesia, primarily against Christians on Indonesia's Molucca Islands.

Law enforcement. The use of law enforcement agencies and criminal investigative techniques in the prosecution of suspected terrorists.

Leaderless resistance. A cell-based strategy of the Patriot and neo-Nazi movements in the United States requiring the formation of "phantom cells" to wage war against the government and enemy interests. Dedicated Patriots and neo-Nazis believe that this strategy will prevent infiltration from federal agencies.

Lebensraum. The Nazi concept that Aryans should colonize Eastern Europe at the expense of indigenous Slavs and other supposedly inferior ethno-national groups.

Left, center, right. Designations on the classical ideological continuum. The left tends to promote social change. The center tends to favor incremental change and the status quo. The right tends to favor traditional values.

Legalistic responses. Counterterrorist measures that use the law to criminalize specific acts as terrorist behaviors and that use law enforcement agencies to investigate, arrest, and prosecute suspected terrorists.

Lemkin, Dr. Raphael. The creator of the word *genocide,* which first appeared in print in his influential book *Axis Rule in Occupied Europe,* published in 1944.

Lenin, Vladimir Ilich. The Russian revolutionary leader and theorist who was the principal leader of the Russian Revolution of 1917. He became the first leader of the Soviet Union and was also the author of several books that were very influential in the international communist movement throughout the 20th century.

Les evenéments. Literally, "the Events" during May and June 1968 in France. Centered in Paris and sparked by massive student protests, *les évenéments* nearly toppled the government of Charles de Gaulle.

Lesser Jihad. The defense of Islam against threats to the faith. This includes military defense and is undertaken when the Muslim community is under attack.

Liberalism. A political ideology that seeks incremental and democratic change.

Liberation Tigers of Tamil Eelam (LTTE). A nationalist group in Sri Lanka that champions the independence of the Tamil people. Responsible for many acts of terrorism.

Liquid metal embrittlement. The process of using chemicals to weaken metals. Such chemicals can *embrittle,* or make rigid, various metals.

Logistically supportive sponsorship. State-sponsored terrorism in which the state provides a great deal of logistical support to the terrorists but stops short of directly participating in the terrorist incident or campaign.

Lone wolf model (lone wolves). A designation describing political violence committed by individuals who are motivated by an ideology but who have no membership in a terrorist organization.

Long hot summer. A term used during the 1960s to describe urban racial tensions that sometimes led to rioting.

Long live death! A slogan of the Spanish Falange.

Lord's Resistance Army. Josef Kony reorganized Uganda's cultic Holy Spirit Mobile Force into the Lord's Resistance Army. He blended together Christianity, Islam, and witchcraft into a bizarre mystical foundation for his movement. The group was exceptionally brutal and waged near-genocidal terrorist campaigns—largely against the Acholi people that it claimed to champion.

Loyalist Volunteer Force (LVF). A Protestant paramilitary in Northern Ireland that was responsible for numerous acts of terrorism.

Luddites. A movement of English workers during the early 1800s; the Luddites objected to the social and economic transformations of the Industrial Revolution. They targeted the machinery of the new textile factories, and textile mills and weaving machinery were disrupted and sabotaged. After 17 Luddites were executed in 1813, the movement gradually died out.

Lumpenproletariat. Karl Marx's designation of the nonproletarian lower classes. Considered by him to be incapable of leading the revolution against capitalism.

Lumumba, Patrice. A Congolese nationalist who became a martyred national hero. The first prime minister of Congo, he was executed by a rebel faction when he fled a military coup in 1961 that was instigated by Mobutu Sese Seko. He was declared a national hero in 1966 and became a nationalist hero in the pan-Africanist movement.

Lynch mobs. Lynch mobs were groups of White American vigilantes who murdered their victims by hanging, burning, or shooting them to death. Most victims of lynching were African Americans. Lynchings were sometimes carried out in a festive atmosphere.

M-16. The standard assault rifle for the U.S. military; first introduced in the mid-1960s.

MacDonald, Andrew. *See* William Pierce.

Macheteros. A Puerto Rican *independencista* terrorist group active during the 1970s and 1980s.

Mala in se. An act designated as a crime that is fundamentally evil, such as murder and rape.

Mala prohibita. An act designated as a crime that is not fundamentally evil, such as prostitution and gambling.

Manifesto of the Communist Party. The seminal document of communism, written by Karl Marx and Friedrich Engels.

Manipulation of the media. The attempt by state and substate participants in a terrorist environment to control or otherwise affect the reporting of news by the media.

Mao zedong. The leader of the Chinese Revolution. His tactical and strategic doctrine of People's War was practiced by a number of insurgencies in the developing world. Mao's interpretation of Marxism was also very influential among communist revolutionaries.

Marighella, Carlos. A Brazilian Marxist revolutionary and theorist who developed an influential theory for waging dissident terrorist warfare in urban environments.

Martyr nation. A theoretical construct arguing that an entire ethno-national people is willing to endure any sacrifice to promote its liberation.

Martyrdom. Martyrdom is achieved by dying on behalf of a religious faith or for some other greater cause. A common concept among religious movements.

Marx, Karl. A mid-19th-century philosopher who, along with Friedrich Engels, developed the ideology of class struggle.

Marxism. An ideology that believes in the historical inevitability of class conflict, culminating in the final conflict that will establish the dictatorship of the proletariat.

Mass communications. The technological ability to convey information to a large number of people. It includes technologies that allow considerable amounts of information to be communicated through printed material, audio broadcasts, video broadcasts, and expanding technologies such as the Internet.

Mathews, Robert Jay. The founder and leader of the American neo-Nazi terrorist group the Order, which was founded in 1983.

May 19 Communist Organization (M19CO). An American Marxist terrorist group that was active in the late 1970s and early 1980s. It was composed of remnants of the Republic of New Africa (described elsewhere in Glossary), the Black Liberation Army, the Weather Under-ground, and the Black Panthers. M19CO derived its name from the birthdays of Malcolm X and Vietnamese leader Ho Chi Minh.

McCarthy, Senator Joseph. A Wisconsin senator who initiated a purge of suspected communists in the United States during the early 1950s.

McVeigh, Timothy. A member of the Patriot movement in the United States and probably a racial supremacist. Responsible for the constructing and detonating an ANFO bomb that destroyed the Alfred P. Murrah Federal Building in Oklahoma City, Oklahoma, on April 19, 1995. One hundred sixty-eight people were killed.

Means of production. A Marxist concept describing the primary source of economic production and activity during the stages of human social evolution.

Media as a weapon. For terrorists and other extremists, information can be wielded as a weapon of war. Because symbolism is at the center of most terrorist incidents, the media are explicitly identified by terrorists as potential supplements to their arsenal.

Media gatekeeping. Similar to journalistic self-regulation. The theoretical practice of ethical self-regulation by members of the free press.

Media scoops. The obtaining and reporting of exclusive news by a media outlet. An outcome of the race to be the first to report breaking news.

Media spin. The media's inclusion of subjective and opinionated interpretations when reporting the facts.

Media-oriented terrorism. Acts of terrorism carried out for the purpose of attracting and manipulating media coverage.

Meinhof, Ulrike. A founder and leader of the Red Army Faction/Baader-Meinhof Gang in West Germany. Meinhof hanged herself in prison on May 9, 1976.

Meredith, James. An American civil rights activist who was ambushed, shot, and wounded in June 1966 as he walked through Mississippi to demonstrate that African Americans could safely go to polling places to register to vote.

MI-5. An intelligence agency in Great Britain responsible for domestic intelligence collection.

MI-6. An intelligence agency in Great Britain responsible for international intelligence collection.

Military Intelligence Service. A government agency in Germany responsible for international intelligence collection.

Military repressive options. Counterterrorist measures that seek to resolve terrorist crises by using national armed forces to attack terrorist bases or other centers of operations.

Military-industrial complex. A term first used by President Dwight Eisenhower to describe the potential threat of economic and political dominance by corporate interests.

Militias. Organized groups of armed citizens who commonly exhibit antigovernment tendencies and subscribe to conspiracy theories. The armed manifestation of the Patriot movement.

Mines. Military-grade explosives that are buried in the soil or rigged to be detonated as booby traps. Antipersonnel mines are designed to kill people, and antitank mines are designed to destroy vehicles. Many millions of mines have been manufactured and are available on the international market.

Mini-Manual of the Urban Guerrilla. An influential essay written by Carlos Marighella that outlined his theory of urban dissident terrorist warfare.

Mitchell, Hulon, Jr. Also known as Yahweh Ben Yahweh (God, Son of God). Founder and leader of a Miami branch of the Black Hebrew Israelites. He taught that Whites are descendants of the devil and worthy of death. Followers who did not practice complete obedience were dealt with harshly, and some were beaten or beheaded. Mitchell and some of his followers were imprisoned. Mitchell's group was implicated in 14 murders during the 1980s.

Moderate center. The central stabilizing political grouping in democracies.

Molotov Cocktail. A simple gasoline bomb consisting of a gasoline-filled bottle with a rag inserted as a wick.

Molotov, Vyacheslav. The Soviet foreign minister during the Second World War, for whom the Molotov Cocktail is named.

Monolithic terrorist environment. A terrorist environment in which a single national sponsor supports and directs international terrorism. Combating this environment is relatively uncomplicated, because attention can theoretically be directed against a single adversary.

Montoneros. A terrorist movement in Argentina during the 1970s. They espoused radical Catholic principles of justice, Peronist populism, and leftist nationalism. The Montoneros became skillful kidnappers and extorted an estimated $60 million in ransom payments. Shootings, bombings, and assassinations were also pervasive. When the military seized control in March 1976, all political opposition was crushed, including the terrorist campaign.

Montreal Convention of 1971. A treaty that extended international law to terrorist attacks on airports and grounded aircraft.

More, Sir Thomas. Author of the book *Utopia.*

Mossad. An Israeli agency charged with carrying out intelligence collection and covert operations.

Moussaoui, Zacarias. A suspected member of the cell that carried out the September 11, 2001, attacks. He was being held in custody on other charges at the time of the attacks and was later prosecuted in federal court.

Movomiento Nacional. Francisco Franco's movement, which consolidated his power and established the model for Spanish fascism.

Mud People. A derogatory term given to non-Aryans by followers of the Christian Identity movement. Mud People are considered to be nonhuman, soulless beasts who dwelt outside the Garden of Eden.

Mujahideen. Individuals who wage war in defense of Islam. Literally, "holy warriors."

Multinational corporations. Large corporations that conduct business on a global scale. They are usually centered in several countries.

Muslim Brotherhood. A transnational Sunni Islamic fundamentalist movement that is very active in several North African and Middle Eastern countries. It has been implicated in terrorist violence committed in Egypt, Syria, and elsewhere.

Mussolini, Benito. The Italian dictator who led the first successful fascist seizure of power during the 1920s.

Mustard gas. A chemical agent that is a mist rather than a gas. It is a blistering agent that blisters skin, eyes, and the nose, and it can severely damage the lungs if inhaled.

N'drangheta. A secret society in Calabria, Italy, that became a criminal society.

Narco-terrorism. Political violence committed by dissident drug traffickers who are primarily concerned with protecting their criminal enterprise.

Narcotraficantes. Latin American drug traffickers.

Narodnaya Volya (People's Will). A 19th-century terrorist group in Russia.

National Alliance. An overtly Nazi organization based in West Virginia that was founded in 1970 by William Pierce, a former member of the American Nazi Party.

National Liberation Army (Ejercito de Liberacion Nacional, or ELN). A Marxist insurgency founded in the 1960s that has operated primarily in the countryside of Colombia. Its ideological icons are Fidel Castro and Ernesto "Che" Guevara. The ELN has engaged in bombings, extortion, and kidnappings. Targets have included foreign businesses and oil pipelines. The ELN has also participated in the drug trade.

National Movement Party (MHP). An ultra-nationalist political movement in Turkey that wishes to unite all Turkic people and to create Turan, or the Great Turkish Empire. MHP has links to the clandestine paramilitary known as the Grey Wolves.

National Security Agency (NSA). An American intelligence agency charged with signal intelligence collection, code making, and code breaking.

Nationalist dissident terrorism. Political violence committed by members of ethno-national groups who seek greater political rights or autonomy.

Nativism. American cultural nationalism. A cornerstone of Ku Klux Klan ideology.

Nazi Holocaust. The genocide waged against European Jews by Germany before and during the Second World War. The first significant anti-Semitic racial decree promulgated by the Nazis was the Law for the Protection of German Blood and German Honor, passed in September 1935. In the end, approximately 6 million Jews were murdered.

Nechayev, Sergei. An early philosophical proponent of anarchism in Russia. Author of *Revolutionary Catechism.*

Neocolonialism. A postwar Marxist concept describing Western economic exploitation of the developing world.

Nerve gas. A chemical agent, such as sarin, tabun, and VX, that blocks (or "short-circuits") nerve messages in the body. A single drop of a nerve agent, whether inhaled or absorbed through the skin, can shut down the body's neurotransmitters.

New African Freedom Fighters. The self-defined "military wing" of an African American nationalist organization called the Republic of New Africa. Composed of former members of the Black Liberation Army and Black Panthers, the group operated in collaboration with other members of the revolutionary underground. It was eventually broken up in 1985 after members were arrested for conspiring to free an imprisoned comrade, bomb the courthouse, and commit other acts of political violence.

New Left. A movement of young leftists during the 1960s who rejected orthodox Marxism and took on the revolutionary theories of Frantz Fanon, Herbert Marcuse, Carlos Marighella, and other new theorists.

New Media. The use of existing technologies and alternative broadcasting formats to analyze and disseminate information. These formats include talk-show models, tabloid styles, celebrity status for hosts, and blatant entertainment spins. Strong and opinionated political or social commentary also makes up a significant portion of New Media content.

New Order. An Italian neofascist terrorist group. The group carried out several attacks in the late 1960s and early 1970s, including a bombing on December 12, 1969, of the famous Piazza Fontana in Milan, causing 16 deaths and 90 injuries.

New Order, The. An American neo-Nazi group that was broken up by federal agents in March 1998 in East St. Louis, Illinois. They had modeled themselves after the Order and were charged with planning to bomb the Anti-Defamation League's New York Headquarters; the headquarters of the Southern Poverty Law Center in Birmingham, Alabama; and the Simon Wiesenthal Center in Los Angeles.

New People's Army. A Filipino Marxist guerrilla group founded in 1969. Its ideology is Maoist, and it engages in urban terrorism such as bombings, shootings, extortion, and assassinations.

New Terrorism. A typology of terrorism characterized by a loose cell-based organizational structure, asymmetrical tactics, the threatened use of weapons of mass destruction, potentially high casualty rates, and usually a religious or mystical motivation.

New World Liberation Front. The name of an American terrorist group active during the mid-1970s. Organized as a "reborn" manifestation of the Symbionese Liberation Army by former SLA members and new recruits.

New World Order. A conspiracy theory common among American neo-Nazis and members of the Patriot movement. It holds that non-American interests are threatening to take over—or have already taken over—key governmental centers of authority. This take over is part of an international plot to create a one-world government.

News Triage. The decision-making process within the media, which decides what news to report and how to report it.

Nidal, Abu. A Palestinian nationalist responsible for numerous acts of terrorism. Frequently an agent of state-sponsored terrorism.

Nihilism. A 19th-century Russian philosophical movement of young dissenters who believed that only scientific truth could end ignorance. Nihilists had no vision for a future society; they asserted only that the existing society was intolerable. Modern nihilist dissidents exhibit a similar disdain for the existing social order but offer no clear alternative for after its destruction.

Nihilist dissidents. Antistate dissidents whose goal is to destroy the existing social order with little consideration given for the aftermath of the revolution. They practice "revolution for revolution's sake."

Nihilist dissident terrorism. The practice of political violence with the goal of destroying an existing order, committed with little or no regard for the aftermath of the revolution.

Nonmilitary repressive responses. Counterterrorist measures that seek to resolve terrorist crises by using nonmilitary assets to disrupt and destroy terrorist groups and movements.

Northern Ireland Act. A law passed in Northern Ireland in 1993 that created conditions of quasi-martial law. The Act suspended several civil liberties and empowered the British military to engage in warrantless searches of civilian homes, temporarily detain people without charge, and question suspects. The military could also intern suspected terrorists and turn over for prosecution those for whom enough evidence had been seized.

Nosair, El-Sayyid. An Egyptian radical Islamic revolutionary who assassinated Rabbi Meir Kahane, the founder of the Jewish Defense League, in New York City in 1990.

Nuclear weapons. High-explosive military weapons using weapons-grade plutonium and uranium. Nuclear explosions devastate the area within their blast zone, irradiate an area outside the blast zone, and are capable of sending dangerous radioactive debris into the atmosphere that descends to earth as toxic fallout.

Off the grid. A tactic used by hard-core members of the Patriot movement who believe in the New World Order conspiracy theory. Believers typically refuse to use credit cards, drivers' licenses, and Social Security, as a way to lower their visibility from the government, banks, and other potential agents of the New World Order.

Office of Homeland Security. An American agency established immediately after the September 11, 2001, attacks. Its ostensible purpose was to coordinate domestic security. Because the Office lacked the authority to set policy for other federal agencies, it was replaced by the Department of Homeland Security.

Official Irish Republican Army. The predominant organization of the IRA until the late 1960s, when the Provisional Irish Republican Army split to independently wage an armed struggle.

Official Secrets Act. An act in Great Britain that permitted the prosecution of individuals for the reporting of information that was deemed to endanger the security of the British government.

Official state terrorism. State terrorism that is undertaken as a matter of official government policy.

Okhrana. The secret police of czarist Russia. Responsible for writing the anti-Semitic *Protocols of the Learned Elders of Zion.*

Omega 7. An anti-Communist Cuban American terrorist group that targeted Cuban interests.

One-Dimensional Man. French existentialist writer Herbert Marcuse's book that influenced the ideological orientation of the New Left.

One man willing to throw away his life is enough to terrorize a thousand. The symbolic power of a precise application of force by an individual who is willing to sacrifice himself can terrorize many other people. A moralistic concept that illustrates how a weak adversary can influence a strong adversary. The statement was made by the Chinese military philosopher Wu Ch'i.

One person's terrorist is another person's freedom fighter. The importance of perspective in the use of violence to achieve political goals. Championed groups view violent rebels as freedom fighters, whereas their adversaries consider them to be terrorists.

One-Seedline Christian Identity. A Christian Identity mystical belief that argues that all humans, regardless of race, are descended from Adam. However, only Aryans (defined as northern Europeans) are the true elect of God. They are the Chosen People whom God has favored and who are destined to rule over the rest of humanity. In the modern era, those who call themselves the Jews are actually descended from a minor Black Sea ethnic group and therefore have no claim to Israel.

Operation Eagle Claw. An operation in April 1980 launched by the United States to rescue Americans held hostage by Iran at the U.S. embassy in Tehran. The operation failed on the ground in Iran when a helicopter flew into an airplane, and both exploded. Eight soldiers were killed, and the mission was aborted.

Operation El Dorado Canyon. On April 14, 1986, the United States bombed targets in Libya using Air Force bombers based in Great Britain and Navy carrier-borne aircraft based in the Mediterranean. The strike was in retaliation for terrorist attacks against American personnel in Europe.

Operation Enduring Freedom. The designation given to the counterterrorist war waged in the aftermath of the September 11, 2001, homeland attacks.

Operation Infinite Justice. The original designation given to the counterterrorist war waged in the aftermath of the September 11, 2001, attacks.

Operation Peace for Galilee. An invasion of Lebanon by the Israeli army in June 1982, with the goal of rooting out PLO bases of operation. It was launched in reply to ongoing PLO attacks from its Lebanese bases.

ORDEN. A right-wing Salvadoran paramilitary that engaged in death squad activity.

Order of Assassins. A religious movement established in the Middle East during the 11th century. It sought to purge the Islamic faith and resist the Crusader invasions. The Assassins were noted for using stealth to kill their opponents.

Order, The. An American neo-Nazi terrorist group founded by Robert Jay Mathews in 1983. Centered in the Pacific Northwest, the Order's methods for fighting its war against what it termed the Zionist Occupation Government were counterfeiting, bank robberies, armored car robberies, and murder. The Order had been suppressed by December 1985.

Organization of the Oppressed. An adopted alias of Lebanon's Hezbollah.

Organization of Volunteers for the Puerto Rican Revolution. A Puerto Rican *independencista* terrorist organization.

Osawatomie. An underground periodical published by the Weather Underground Organization during the 1970s.

Padilla, Jose. An American convert to Islam who was arrested at Chicago's O'Hare International Airport in May 2002. He was suspected of participating in a plan to construct and detonate a radiological weapon in the United States.

Pahlavi, Shah Mohammad Reza. The last Shah of Iran, who was ousted in an Islamic revolution led by the Ayatollah Ruhollah Khomeini.

Palestine Islamic Jihad (PIJ). The PIJ is not a single organization but a loose affiliation of factions. It is an Islamic fundamentalist revolutionary movement that seeks to promote jihad, or holy war, and to form a Palestinian state; it is responsible for assassinations and suicide bombings.

Palestine Liberation Front (PLF). The PLF split from the Popular Front for the Liberation of Palestine–General Command in the mid-1970s and further split into pro-PLO, pro-Syrian, and pro-Libyan factions. The pro-PLO faction was led by Abu Abbas, who committed a number of attacks against Israel.

Palestine Liberation Organization (PLO). An umbrella Palestinian nationalist organization. It comprises numerous activist factions, many of which engage in political violence.

Palmer Raids. A series of raids in the United States during the administration of American President Woodrow Wilson, targeting communist and other leftist radical groups.

Palmer, R. Mitchell. The attorney general who served during the administration of President Woodrow Wilson.

Pan Am Flight 103. An airliner that exploded over Lockerbie, Scotland, on December 21, 1988. In the explosion, 270 people were killed, including all 259 passengers and crew and 11 persons on the ground. Libya was implicated in the incident.

Pan-Africanism. An intellectual movement among Africans and descendents of Africans in the Western Hemisphere that sought to develop political, intellectual, and cultural ties among all African people.

Pan-Arabism. An international Arab nationalist movement that held momentum after the Second World War.

Parachute *Sayaret*. An elite reconnaissance unit within the Israel Defense Force. It has been deployed in small and large units, relying on high mobility to penetrate deep into hostile territory. They participated in the Entebbe rescue and were used against Hezbollah in South Lebanon.

Paradigm. A logically developed model or framework that represents a concept.

Paramilitaries. A term used to describe rightist irregular units and groups that are frequently supported by governments or progovernment interests. Many paramilitaries have been responsible for human rights violations.

Paramilitary repressive options. Counterterrorist measures that seek to resolve terrorist crises by deploying armed nonmilitary personnel. These personnel can include covert operatives, localized militia units, or large armed units.

Participants in a terrorist environment. People who participate in, or are affected by, terrorist incidents, and who are likely to have very different interpretations of the incident. These include the roles of terrorist, supporter, victim, target, onlooker, and analyst.

Party of God. Lebanon's Hezbollah.

Patrice Lumumba Peoples Friendship University. A Soviet-sponsored university in Moscow that attracted students from around the world, particularly the developing world.

Peace Process. An ongoing process of negotiations between warring parties with the goal of addressing their underlying grievances and ending armed conflict.

People Against Gangsterism and Drugs. A moralistic Islamic terrorist group in South Africa.

People Persecuted by Pablo Escobar (Pepes). A Colombian paramilitary that waged a terrorist campaign against the Medellin cartel and its leader, Pablo Escobar. Pepes assassinated at least 50 cartel members and targeted Escobar's family for assassination. It was apparently a death squad made up of former Medellin operatives and backers with a history of supporting paramilitaries.

People's Liberation Army. The Chinese communist national army, founded by Mao Zedong.

People's Temple of the Disciples of Christ. A cult founded and led by Jim Jones. After relocating to Guyana, the hundreds of members of the group committed ritual suicide when followers shot and killed Congressman Leo Ryan and several others; 914 people died, including 200 children.

People's war. A concept in irregular warfare in which the guerrilla fighters and the populace are theoretically indistinguishable.

Permanent Revolution, The. One side of a debate within the international communist movement after the founding of the Soviet Union. It posited that the proletarian revolution should be waged internationally, rather than consolidated in only one country. The theoretical counterpart to Socialism in One Country.

Phalangists. A Lebanese Christian paramilitary movement.

Phansi. A rope used by the Thuggees of India to ritualistically strangle their victims.

Phantom cells. An organizational concept articulated by former Klansman Louis Beam in the early 1990s. Rightist dissidents were encouraged to organize themselves into autonomous subversive cells that would be undetectable by the enemy U.S. government or agents of the New World Order.

Phineas Actions. Acts of violence committed by individuals who are "called" to become Phineas Priests. Adherents believe that Phineas Actions will hasten the ascendancy of the Aryan race.

Phineas Priesthood. A shadowy movement of Christian Identity fundamentalists in the United States who believe that they are called by God to purify their race and Christianity.

They are opposed to abortion, homosexuality, interracial mixing, and Whites who "degrade" White racial supremacy. It is a calling for men only, so no women can become Phineas Priests. The name is taken from the Bible at chapter 25, verse 6 of the Book of Numbers, which tells the story of a Hebrew man named Phineas who killed an Israelite man and his Midianite wife in the temple.

Phoenix Program. A three-year campaign conducted during the Vietnam War to disrupt and eliminate the administrative effectiveness of the communist Viet Cong.

Phosgene gas. A chemical agent that causes the lungs to fill with water, choking the victim.

Pierce, William. The founder and leader of the neo-Nazi National Alliance in the United States. Also author of *The Turner Diaries,* under the *nom de plume* of Andrew MacDonald.

Pipe bombs. Devices constructed from common pipes that are filled with explosives (usually gunpowder) and then capped on both ends. Nuts, bolts, screws, nails, and other shrapnel are usually taped or otherwise attached to these devices.

Plan Victoria 82. A government-sponsored campaign in Guatemala during the early 1980s that was responsible for thousands of deaths.

Plastic explosives. A malleable explosive compound commonly used by terrorists.

Pogroms. Anti-Semitic massacres in Europe that occurred periodically from the time of the First Crusade through the Nazi Holocaust. Usually centered in Central and Eastern Europe.

Pol Pot. The principle leader of Cambodia's Khmer Rouge during its insurgency and consolidation of power.

Police Border Guards. An elite Israeli paramilitary force that is frequently deployed as a counterterrorist force. Known as the Green Police, it operates in two subgroups: YAMAS is a covert group that has been used extensively during the Palestinian *intifadeh,* and YAMAM was specifically created to engage in counterterrorist and hostage rescue operations.

Polisario. An insurgent group that resisted the Moroccan occupation of Western Sahara.

Politically sympathetic sponsorship. State-sponsored terrorism that does not progress beyond ideological and moral support.

Pope Urban II. The Roman Catholic pope who commissioned the first Christian Crusade with the goal of seizing Jerusalem and other territories from Muslim control.

Popular Front for the Liberation of Palestine (PFLP). The PFLP was founded in 1967 by

George Habash. It is a Marxist organization that advocates a multinational Arab revolution, and it has been responsible for dramatic international terrorist attacks. Its hijacking campaign in 1969 and 1970, its collaboration with West European terrorists, and its mentorship of Carlos the Jackal arguably established the model for modern international terrorism.

Popular Front for the Liberation of Palestine–General Command (PFLP-GC). Ahmid Jibril formed the PFLP-GC in 1968 when he split from the Popular Front for the Liberation of Palestine (PFLP) because he considered the PFLP to be too involved in politics and not sufficiently committed to the armed struggle against Israel. The PFLP-GC was probably directed by Syria and has been responsible for many cross-border attacks against Israel.

Port Huron Statement. A document crafted in the United States in 1962 by members of Students for a Democratic Society. It harshly criticized mainstream American values and called for the establishment of a "new left" movement in the United States.

Potassium cyanide. A poisonous chemical agent.

Prairie Fire. An underground manifesto published by the Weather Underground Organization during the 1970s.

Prairie Fire Organizing Committee. An aboveground network of supporters for the Weather Underground Organization, organized into collectives.

Precision guided munitions (PGM). Technologically advanced weapons that can be remotely guided to targets. Some PGMs are referred to as "smart bombs."

Preemptive strikes. Counterterrorist measures that proactively seek out and attack terrorist centers prior to a terrorist incident.

Pressure trigger. Weapons such as mines are detonated when physical pressure is applied to a trigger. A variation on physical pressure triggers are trip-wire booby traps. More sophisticated pressure triggers react to atmospheric (barometric) pressure, such as changes in pressure when an airliner ascends or descends.

Print media. Media outlets that publish newspapers, magazines, and other products that are intended to be read by customers.

Progressive Labor Party. A Maoist faction of the Students for a Democratic Society in the United States. Active during the late 1960s and 1970s.

Proletariat. A Marxist term for the working class.

Propaganda. The manipulation of information for political advantage. It includes the skillful reporting and spinning of the truth, half-truths, and lies.

Propaganda by the deed. The notion that revolutionaries must violently act upon their beliefs to promote the ideals of the revolution. Originally promoted by the anarchists.

Property is theft. The anarchist philosopher Pierre-Joseph Proudhon's belief that systems based on the acquisition of private property are inherently exploitative.

Protocols of the Learned Elders of Zion. A forgery written under the direction of the czarist secret police in the late 19th century. It purports to be the proceedings of a secret international society of Jewish elders who are plotting to rule the world.

Proudhon, Pierre-Joseph. Nineteenth-century philosopher and father of anarchism.

Provisional Irish Republican Army (Provos). A terrorist organization in Northern Ireland that champions the rights of Northern Irish Catholics. The PIRA was formed with the goal of uniting Northern Ireland with the Irish Republic. Also known as the Provos.

Provos. The popular name given to the Provisional Irish Republican Army.

Publicize the cause. The practice by terrorists of disseminating information about their grievances and championed groups. This can be done through symbolic violence and the manipulation of the media.

Punitive strikes. Counterterrorist measures that seek out and attack terrorist centers to damage the terrorist organization. Frequently conducted as retribution for a terrorist incident.

Qaddafi, Muammar el. The ruler of Libya who became a prominent figure in state sponsorship of international terrorism during the 1980s.

Racial Holy War (Rahowa). A term given by racial supremacists to a future race war that they believe will inevitably occur in the United States.

Racial profiling. Similar to criminal profiling, but it uses race or ethnicity as the overriding descriptor to assist in the apprehension of suspects. Race is a legitimate element for criminal profiling, but it cannot be the principal element. Unfortunately, incidents of racial profiling have been documented for some time in the United States.

Radical. A term used to describe members of the far left and fringe left.

Radiological agents. Materials that emit radiation that can harm living organisms when inhaled or otherwise ingested. Nonweapons-grade radiological agents could theoretically be used to construct a toxic "dirty bomb."

Rajneeshees. Followers of the cult leader Bhagwan Shree Rajneesh. In September 1984, the group poisoned the salad bars of 10 Oregon restaurants with *Salmonella* bacteria. More than 700 people fell ill.

Raziel, David. A leader of the Irgun, killed in 1941.

RDX. The central component of most plastic explosives.

Reactionary. A term given to far-right and fringe-right political tendencies.

Red Army Faction (RAF). A leftist terrorist movement active in West Germany during the 1970s and 1980s. Also referred to as the Baader-Meinhof Gang.

Red Brigades. A leftist terrorist movement active in Italy during the 1970s and 1980s.

Red Guards. Groups of young Communist radicals who sought to purge Chinese society during the Great Proletarian Cultural Revolution.

Resistance. A cover name used by the leftist May 19 Communist Organization in the United States.

Red Scares. Periodic anticommunist security crises in the United States, when national leaders reacted to the perceived threat of communist subversion.

Red Zora (Rote Zora). The women's "auxiliary" of the West German terrorist group Revolutionary Cells. Red Zora eventually became independent of Revolutionary Cells.

Regicide. The killing of kings.

Reign of Terror (Régime de la Terreur). A period during the French Revolution when the new republic violently purged those who were thought to be a threat to the prevailing ideals of the revolution. "Terrorism" was considered to be a necessary and progressive revolutionary tactic.

Relative deprivation theory. A sociological term that indicates the lack of human needs vis-à-vis other members of a particular society.

Religious communal terrorism. Conflict between religious groups involving terrorist violence.

Repentance laws. An offer of qualified amnesty by the Italian government to Red Brigades members, requiring them to demonstrate repentance for their crimes. Repentance was established by cooperating within a sliding scale of collaboration. A significant number of imprisoned Red Brigades terrorists accepted repentance reductions in their sentences.

Repressive responses. Counterterrorist measures that seek to resolve terrorist crises by disrupting or destroying terrorist groups and movements. These responses include military and non-military options.

Republic of New Africa (RNA). An African American nationalist organization. The objective of the RNA was to form a separate African American nation from portions of several southern states. Some members opted to engage in political violence under the name of the New African Freedom Fighters.

Resistance Records. A record label that promotes racist skinhead music.

Ressem, Ahmed. An Algerian who was arrested as he tried to cross the Canadian border into the United States with bomb-making components. He and others planned to detonate a bomb at Los Angeles International Airport around the time of the 2000 millennial celebrations.

Revolutionary Armed Forces of Colombia (Fuerzas Armados Revolucionarios de Colombia, or FARC). An enduring Marxist insurgent movement in Colombia that has engaged in guerrilla warfare and terrorism since its inception during the 1960s.

Revolutionary Catechism. A revolutionary manifesto written by the Russian anarchist Sergei Nechayev.

Revolutionary Cells (Revolutionär Zelles). A shadowy Marxist organization that was founded in Frankfurt, West Germany, probably in 1972 or 1973. They adopted an underground cell-based strategy and disappeared into the middle class by holding jobs, owning homes, and raising families. Their terrorist activity included bombings and other criminal activity.

Revolutionary dissident terrorism. The practice of political violence with the goal of destroying an existing order, committed with a plan for the aftermath of the revolution.

Revolutionary Fighting Group. A cover name used by the leftist May 19 Communist Organization in the United States.

Revolutionary Guards Corps. Iranian Islamic revolutionaries who have been deployed abroad, mainly to Lebanon, to promote Islamic revolution.

Revolutionary Justice Organization. An adopted alias of Lebanon's Hezbollah.

Revolutionary Organization November 17. A Greek Marxist terrorist movement.

Revolutionary Tribunal. The revolutionary court established during the French Revolution.

Revolutionary Youth Movement II (RYM-II). A faction of Students for a Democratic Society in the United States. RYM II adapted their ideological motivations to the political and social context of the 1960s by tailoring the ideologies of orthodox Marxism to the political environment of the 1960s.

Rewards for Justice Program. An international bounty program managed by the U.S. Diplomatic Security Service. The program offered cash rewards for information leading to the arrest of wanted terrorists.

Rocket-propelled grenades (RPGs). Handheld military weapons that use a propellant to fire a rocket-like explosive.

Royal Marine Commandos. British rapid-reaction troops that deploy in larger numbers than the Special Air Service and Special Boat Service. They are organized around units called commandos that are roughly equivalent to a conventional battalion.

RPG-7. A rocket-propelled grenade weapon manufactured in large quantities by the Soviet Bloc.

Ruby Ridge. An August 1992 incident in Idaho when racial supremacist Randy Weaver and his family were besieged by federal agents for failure to reply to an illegal weapons charge. Weaver's wife and son were killed during the incident, as was a U.S. Marshal. Members of the Patriot movement and other right-wing extremists cite Ruby Ridge as evidence of a broad government conspiracy to deprive freedom-loving "true" Americans of their right to bear arms and other liberties.

Rudolph, Eric Robert. An apparent affiliate of the Army of God in the United States who became a fugitive after he was named as a suspect in bombings in Birmingham, Alabama, and Atlanta, Georgia. Rudolph was also suspected of involvement in the July 1996 bombing at Centennial Olympic Park in Atlanta during the Summer Olympic Games. He was linked to a militia group in North Carolina.

Rushdie, Salman. The author of *The Satanic Verses*. He was forced into hiding after the publication of the book because of calls for his assassination by Iranian clerics.

Russian Mafia. A term given to the criminal gangs that proliferated in Russia after the collapse of the Soviet Union.

SA-7. An infrared-targeted Soviet-made surface-to-air missile, also known as the Grail.

Sam Melville–Jonathan Jackson Unit. A group that took credit for bombing the Boston State House in Boston, Massachusetts, in 1975. It was a term used by the leftist United Freedom Front.

Samurai. A member of the medieval Japanese warrior class.

Sandinistas. A Marxist movement in Nicaragua that seized power after a successful insurgency against the regime of Anastasio Somoza Debayle. The Sandinista regime became the object of an American-supported insurgency.

Sarin nerve gas. A potent nerve gas. The Aum Supreme Truth cult released sarin gas into the Tokyo subway system in March 1995, killing 12 and injuring thousands.

Satanic Verses, The. A book published by Salman Rushdie that was denounced by many Muslims, which led to a bounty being placed by Iranian clerics for Rushdie's assassination.

SAVAK. The secret police during the regime of Shah Mohammad Reza Pahlavi. Notorious for its brutal suppression of dissent.

Sayaret. Elite Israeli reconnaissance units that engage in counterterrorist operations. Sayaret have been attached to General Headquarters (Sayaret Matkal) and the Golani Brigade. There is also a Parachute Sayaret.

Sayaret Matkal. An elite reconnaissance unit within the Israel Defense Force, attached to the IDF General Headquarters. It is a highly secretive formation that operates in small units and is regularly used for counterterrorist operations.

Scapegoating. A process of political blaming to rally a championed group against a scapegoated group. Usually directed against an ethno-national, religious, or ideological group.

Schutzstaffel. The Nazi SS. Traditionally composed of racially pure Aryans, although the SS also became a kind of German foreign legion toward the end of the Second World War.

Sea Air Land Forces (SEALs). Similar to the British Special Boat Service and French Navy special assault units, the U.S. Navy SEALs' primary mission is to conduct seaborne, riverine, and harbor operations. They have also been used extensively on land.

Sectarian violence. Religious communal violence.

Semtex. A high-grade and high-yield plastic explosive originally manufactured in Czechoslovakia when it was a member of the Soviet Bloc.

Shadow wars. Covert campaigns to suppress terrorism.

Shakur, Assata. The symbolic leader of the Black Liberation Army (BLA) in the United States, formerly known as JoAnne Chesimard. A former Black Panther, she was described by admirers as the "heart and soul" of the BLA.

Shining Path (Sendero Luminoso). A Marxist insurgent movement in Peru. Founded and led by former philosophy professor Abimael Guzmán, the group regularly engaged in terrorism.

Sicarii. The Zealot rebels who opposed Roman rule. Named for the curved dagger, or *sica,* that was a preferred weapon.

Sicilian Mafia. A traditional criminal society in Sicily.

Signal intelligence. Intelligence that has been collected by technological resources. Also referred to as SIGINT.

Signature method. Methods that become closely affiliated with the operational activities of specific extremist groups.

Single-issue terrorism. Terrorism that is motivated by a single grievance.

Sinn Féin. An aboveground political party in Northern Ireland that champions Catholic rights and union with the Irish Republic.

Skinheads. A countercultural youth movement that began in England in the late 1960s. An international racist skinhead movement eventually developed in Europe and the United States. The term *skinhead* refers to the members' practice of shaving their heads.

Skinheads Against Racial Prejudice (SHARPS). An antiracist tendency within the skinhead youth movement.

Skinzines. Publications directed to the skinhead movement. Frequently racist literature.

Sky marshals. Armed law enforcement officers stationed aboard aircraft.

Sleeper cells. A tactic used by international terrorist movements in which operatives theoretically establish residence in another country to await a time when they will be activated by orders to carry out a terrorist attack.

Smallpox. A formerly epidemic disease that has been eradicated in nature, but that has been preserved in research laboratories. A possible ingredient for biological weapons.

Smith, Gerald L. K. An early evangelist for the racial supremacist Christian Identity cult in the United States.

Social cleansing. The practice of eliminating defined undesirables from society. These undesirables can include those who practice defined morals crimes or who engage in denounced political and social behaviors.

Social reform. Conciliatory counterterrorist measures that seek to resolve terrorist crises by resolving political and social problems that are the focus of the terrorists' grievances.

Social Revolutionary Party. A Russian revolutionary movement during the late 19th and early 20th centuries. The group adopted terrorism as a revolutionary method.

Socialism in one country. One side of a debate within the international communist movement after the founding of the Soviet Union. It posited that the proletarian revolution could be consolidated in the Soviet Union prior to waging an international struggle. The theoretical counterpart to the Permanent Revolution.

Sodium cyanide. A poisonous chemical agent.

Soft targets. Civilian and other undefended targets that are easily victimized by terrorists.

Solntsevskaya Gang. A prominent Russian Mafia gang.

Somoza Debayle, Anastasio. The United States-supported Nicaraguan dictator overthrown by the Sandinista-led insurgency.

Special Air Service (SAS). A secretive organization in the British Army that has been used repeatedly in counterterrorist operations. Organized at a regimental level, but operating in very small teams, the SAS is similar to the French 1st Navy Parachute Infantry Regiment and the American Delta Force.

Special Boat Service (SBS). A special unit under the command of the British Royal Navy. The SBS specializes in operations against seaborne targets and along coastlines and harbors. They are similar to the French Navy's special assault units and the American SEALs.

Special Operations Command. The general headquarters for U.S. Special Operations Forces.

Special Operations Forces. Elite military and paramilitary units deployed by many armed forces. They are highly trained and are capable of operating in large or small formations, both overtly and covertly.

Specific deterrence. The creation of an environment by governments and counterterrorist agencies against a specific adversary that communicates the high risks of further acts of political violence.

Spillover effect. Terrorist violence that occurs beyond the borders of the countries that are the target of such violence.

Stalinists. Followers of Soviet dictator Joseph Stalin. They advocated socialism in one country and practiced totalitarianism. Stalinists also brutally consolidated central power in a single leader of the party. The movement counterpoint to the Trotskyites.

State assistance for terrorism. Tacit state participation in and encouragement of extremist behavior. Its basic characteristic is that the state, through sympathetic proxies and agents, implicitly takes part in repression, violence, and terrorism.

State patronage for terrorism. Active state participation in and encouragement of extremist behavior. Its basic characteristic is that the state, through its agencies and personnel, actively takes part in repression, violence, and terrorism.

Stateless revolutionaries. International terrorists who are not sponsored by, or based in, a particular country.

State-Regulated Press. State-regulated media exist in environments where the state routinely intervenes in the reporting of information by the press. This can occur in societies that otherwise have a measure of democratic freedoms, as well as in totalitarian societies.

Stern Gang. A Jewish terrorist group active prior to the independence of Israel.

Stinger. A technologically advanced handheld anti-aircraft missile manufactured by the United States.

Stockholm syndrome. A psychological condition in which hostages begin to identify and sympathize with their captors.

Strong multipolar terrorist environment. A terrorist environment that presumes that state sponsorship guides terrorist behavior but that several governments support their favored groups. It also presumes that there are few truly autonomous international terrorist movements; they all have a link to a state sponsor.

Structural theory. A theory used in many disciplines to identify social conditions ("structures") that affect group access to services, equal rights, civil protections, freedom, or other quality-of-life measures.

Struggle meetings. Revolutionary rallies held during the Chinese Revolution. Denunciations were often made against those thought to be a threat to the revolution.

Student Soviet, The. The section of Paris temporarily ceded to students during the 1968 uprising centered at the Sorbonne.

Students for a Democratic Society (SDS). A leftist student movement founded in 1962 in the United States. It rose to become the preeminent activist organization on American campuses throughout the 1960s. Its factions—the Progressive Labor Party, Revolutionary Youth Movement II, and the Weathermen—were highly active during the 1960s and early 1970s.

Submachine guns. Light automatic weapons that fire pistol ammunition.

Suicide bombers. Terrorists trained to detonate explosives that have been strapped to their bodies.

Sun Tzu. Chinese military philosopher whose book *The Art of War* has been a significant influence on military theory.

Supergrass. A policy in Northern Ireland during the 1980s of convincing Provos and members of the Irish National Liberation Army to defect from their movements and inform on their former comrades.

Suppression campaigns. Counterterrorist measures that seek to resolve terrorist crises by waging an ongoing campaign to destroy the terrorists' capacity to strike.

Survivalism. A philosophy of complete self-sufficiency. Sometimes adopted by those who practice the tactic of going "off the grid."

Swift, Wesley. A Methodist minister in Southern California who reinvigorated the Englishman Richard Brothers's 18th-century mystical doctrine of Anglo-Israelism. Swift was a kind of "prophet" for Christian Identity because of his adaptation of Anglo-Israelism to the American context.

Symbolism, role of. The symbolic value represented by a victim is a fundamental consideration in the selection of targets by terrorists.

Terminal institutions. Institutions under the jurisdiction of criminal justice and military justice systems that provide final resolution to individual terrorists' careers after they have been captured, prosecuted, convicted, and imprisoned.

Terrorism. Elements from the American definitional model define terrorism as a premeditated and unlawful act in which groups or agents of some principal engage in a threatened or actual use of force or violence against human or property targets. These groups or agents engage in this behavior intending the purposeful intimidation of governments or people to affect policy or behavior with an underlying political objective. There are more than 100 definitions of terrorism.

Terrorist. One who practices terrorism. Often a highly contextual term.

Terrorist profiles. Descriptive profiles of terrorist suspects developed by law enforcement agencies to assist in the apprehension of terrorist suspects. Similar to criminal profiling.

Third World. A postwar term created to describe the developing world.

Thody, Walter Eliyah. A self-proclaimed Phineas Priest who was arrested in 1991 in Oklahoma after a shootout and chase. Thody stated that fellow believers would also commit acts of violence against Jews and others.

Thuggees. A mystical movement that existed for centuries in India. They ritualistically murdered travelers to honor the goddess Kali.

TNT. A commercially available explosive.

Tokyo Convention on Offences and Certain Other Acts Committed on Board Aircraft. A treaty enacted in 1963 as the first airline crimes' treaty.

Total war. The unrestrained use of force against a broad selection of targets to utterly defeat an enemy.

Totalitarian regimes. Governments that practice total control over public and political institutions. The media and other public information outlets are completely controlled.

Traditional criminal enterprises. Criminal enterprises that are interested in maximizing their profits. They tend to become politically active only to protect their criminal interests.

Transnational organized crime. Globalized organized crime in which criminal trades (such as drugs) have developed into multinational enterprises.

Trotskyites. Followers of Bolshevik leader Leon Trotsky. They advocated the permanent revolution and argued that the working class must develop an international revolutionary consciousness. The movement counterpoint to the Stalinists.

Troubles, The. The term given to sectarian violence between Catholics and Protestants in Northern Ireland.

Tupac Amaru Revolutionary Movement (Movimento Revolucionario Tupac Amaru, or MRTA). A Marxist terrorist movement in Peru, primarily active during the 1980s and early 1990s.

Tupamaros. A Marxist urban terrorist movement active during the early 1970s in Uruguay. After a number of dramatic attacks, the Tupamaros were eventually annihilated when the Uruguayan military used authoritarian methods, and the general Uruguayan population rejected the movement.

Turan. A mythical pan-Turkish nation, the establishment of which is a goal for many Turkish ultranationalists.

Turner Diaries, The. A short novel written by National Alliance founder William Pierce under the pseudonym Andrew MacDonald. It depicts an Aryan revolution in the United States and is considered by many neo-Nazis to be a blueprint for the eventual racial holy war.

TWA Flight 847. In June 1985, hijackers belonging to Lebanon's Hezbollah hijacked a TWA airliner, taking it on a high-profile and media-intensive odyssey around the Mediterranean.

Two-Seedline Christian Identity. A Christian Identity mystical belief that rejects the notion that all humans are descended from Adam (see One-Seedline Christian Identity). According to this belief, Eve bore Abel as Adam's son but bore Cain as the son of the Serpent. Outside of the Garden of Eden lived non-White, soulless beasts who were a separate species from humans. When Cain slew Abel, he was cast out of the Garden to live among the soulless beasts. Those who became the descendants of Cain are the modern Jews. They are biologically descended from the devil and are a demonic people worthy of extermination.

Ulster Volunteer Force (UVF). A Protestant paramilitary in Northern Ireland. Responsible for numerous acts of terrorism.

UNABOM. The FBI's case designation for their investigation into bombings perpetrated by Theodore Kaczynski. "Un" was short for university, and "a" referred to airlines.

Unabomber. The popular nickname applied to Theodore Kaczynski.

United Freedom Front (UFF). A leftist terrorist group in the United States that was active from the mid-1970s through the mid-1980s.

United Jewish Underground. A shadowy group in the United States that was responsible for several acts of terrorism. These attacks were primarily directed against Soviet targets, such as the offices of the Soviet national airline Aeroflot. These attacks were conducted to protest that government's treatment of Soviet Jews.

United Self-Defense Forces of Colombia. A large rightist paramilitary in Colombia. Unofficially supported by the government and officially supported by progovernment members of the upper classes. It was responsible for numerous human rights violations.

USS Cole. An American destroyer that was severely damaged on October 12, 2000, while berthed in the port of Aden, Yemen. Two suicide bombers detonated a boat bomb next to the Cole, killing themselves and 17 crew members and wounding 39 other Navy personnel.

Utopia. An ideal society.

Vanguard of the proletariat. In Marxist theory, a well-indoctrinated and motivated elite that would lead the working-class revolution. In practice, this referred to the Communist Party.

Vanguard strategy. In Marxist and non-Marxist theory, the strategy of using a well-indoctrinated and motivated elite to lead the working-class revolution. In practice, this strategy was adopted in the postwar era by terrorist organizations and extremist movements.

Vehicular bombs. Ground vehicles that have been wired with explosives. Car bombs and truck bombs are common vehicular bombs.

Viet Cong. The name given by the United States and its noncommunist South Vietnamese allies to South Vietnamese communist insurgents.

Viet Minh (Viet Nam Doc Lap Dong Minh Hoi). An organization founded by the Vietnamese leader Ho Chi Minh. The Vietnam Independence Brotherhood League began fighting first against the Japanese conquerors of French Indochina and then against the French colonial forces.

Vigilante state terrorism. Unofficial state terrorism in which state personnel engage in non-sanctioned political violence. It can include the use of death squads.

Waco. An April 1993 incident in which federal agents besieged the Branch Davidian cult's compound after a failed attempt in February to serve a search warrant for illegal firearms had ended in the deaths of four federal agents and several cult members. During an assault on April 19, 1993, led by the FBI, about 80 Branch Davidians—including more than 20 children—died in a blaze that leveled the compound. Patriots and other rightists consider this tragedy to be evidence of government power run amuck.

Waffen SS. The "armed SS" of Nazi Germany. Elite military units of the SS, composed of racially selected Germans and fascist recruits from occupied territories.

Warfare. The making of war against an enemy. In the modern era, it usually refers to conventional and guerrilla conflicts.

Wars of national liberation. A series of wars fought in the developing world in the postwar era. These conflicts frequently pitted indigenous guerrilla fighters against European colonial powers or governments perceived to be pro-Western. Insurgents were frequently supported by the Soviet Bloc or China.

Weak multipolar terrorist environment. A terrorist environment that presupposes that state sponsorship exists, but that the terrorist groups are more autonomous. Under this scenario, several governments support their favored groups, but many of these groups are relatively independent international terrorist movements.

Weapons of mass destruction. High-yield weapons that can potentially cause a large number of casualties when used by terrorists. Examples of these weapons include chemical, biological, radiological, and nuclear weapons. They can also be constructed from less exotic compounds, such as ANFO.

Weather Bureau. The designation adopted by the leaders of the Weatherman faction of Students for a Democratic Society.

Weather Collectives. Groups of supporters of the Weather Underground Organization.

Weather Underground Organization (WUO). The adopted name of the Weathermen after they moved underground.

Weathermen. A militant faction of Students for a Democratic Society that advocated, and engaged in, violent confrontation with the authorities. Some Weathermen engaged in terrorist violence.

Weinrich, Johannes. A former West German terrorist who was "purchased" by the German government from the government of Yemen. He stood trial in Germany for the 1983 bombing of a French cultural center in Berlin, in which one person was killed and 23 others were wounded. Weinrich had also been a very close associate of Carlos the Jackal.

White Aryan Resistance. A California-based racial supremacist hate group founded by former Klansman Tom Metzger in the early 1980s.

World Church of the Creator. An organization founded in the United States by Ben Klassen in 1973; it practices racial supremacist mysticism called Creativity.

Wrath of God. A counterterrorist unit created by the Israelis to eliminate Palestinian operatives who had participated in the massacre of Israeli athletes at the 1972 Munich Olympics. Also called Mivtzan Elohim.

Wretched of the Earth, The. Frantz Fanon's influential book that championed and sought to justify revolutionary violence in the developing world.

Wu Ch'i. Chinese military philosopher who is usually associated with Sun Tzu.

Xenophobia. The fear of foreigners, frequently exhibited by ultranationalists.

YAMAM. One of two operational subgroups deployed by Israel's Police Border Guards (the other subgroup is YAMAS). It engages in counterterrorist and hostage rescue operations.

YAMAS. One of two operational subgroups deployed by Israel's Police Border Guards (the other subgroup is YAMAM). It is a covert unit that has been used to neutralize terrorist cells in conjunction with covert Israel Defense Force operatives.

Year Zero. The ideological designation given by the Khmer Rouge to the beginning of their genocidal consolidation of power.

Years of Lead. The politically violent years of the 1970s and 1980s in Italy, during which the Red Brigades were exceptionally active. They waged a campaign of violence that included shootings, bombings, kidnappings, and other criminal acts.

Yellow Press. A term popular during the latter part of the 19th and early 20th centuries to describe the biased and sensational character of contemporary media outlets.

Yousef, Ramzi. The mastermind behind the 1993 bombing of the World Trade Center. Also a case study of a high degree of criminal skill.

Zapatista National Liberation Front. Leftist rebels that were originally centered in Chiapas, Mexico. During the late 1990s, they engaged in guerrilla fighting that ended when they were integrated into the Mexican political process.

Zealots. Hebrew rebels who uncompromisingly opposed Roman rule in ancient Palestine.

Zines. A term used for skinzines.

Zionism. An intellectual movement within the Jewish community describing the conditions for the settlement of Jews in Israel.

INDEX